The Crisis of the
Early Italian Renaissance

The Crisis of the
Early Italian Renaissance

*Civic Humanism and Republican Liberty
in an Age of Classicism and Tyranny*

By HANS BARON

REVISED
ONE-VOLUME
EDITION
WITH AN EPILOGUE

PRINCETON, NEW JERSEY
PRINCETON UNIVERSITY PRESS
PUBLISHED IN COOPERATION WITH THE
NEWBERRY LIBRARY
1966

To the Memory of

Garrett Mattingly

Preface to the Revised Edition

ON its first publication, ten years ago, this book was composed of two volumes, the second containing eight *Appendices* and a great number of *Notes: Documentary, Chronological, Critical.* As the preface explained, the historical analysis in Volume One was "intended to be self-contained and intelligible without the extensive appendices and notes of the second volume," but the inclusion of a volume with critical investigations of the humanistic literature of the period seemed indispensable: "Although the fresh element in our approach is the attention paid to the response of early Renaissance thought to the challenge of a political crisis, most of the documents with which we are to work are humanistic writings which have usually been investigated only by students of Italian or neo-Latin literature. As soon as we begin in earnest to search for the political situations which gave rise to these literary products, or influenced their composition, we experience a veritable upheaval of the accepted opinions on the nature and genesis of many of our sources of information. There is, indeed, hardly one major work in Florentine literature around 1400 whose date and occasion have been stated correctly. The changes at which we shall arrive will affect in turn the chronology of a number of later Florentine works and even of some non-Florentine writings. . . . Perhaps this need for combining methods of different branches of scholarship has a wider significance. Reluctance among political historians to follow the lessons to be learned from literary studies and, on the other hand, too little interest on the part of literary scholars in the impact of socio-political developments, still prevent us, at only too many points of Renaissance history, from visualizing the mutual dependence of politics and culture with the same clarity that classical scholarship has since long achieved for kindred situations in the ancient city-states."

In the second edition of this book, there is no longer any need to encumber the historical analysis with studies of the chronology of the writings of contemporaneous humanists, now that the results are accessible and have been accepted by most scholars. It seems preferable to omit the appendices and drastically cut most of the critical notes while leaving their numbering unchanged, thus giving an interested reader the opportunity to use the present text along with the original annotation.* At many points he will find specific cross references to critical digressions in the notes or appendices of the companion volume of the first edition, cited as *Crisis: Appendices.* In other words, the companion volume is now treated as if it had been a separate work and is referred to in the same way as we refer to another volume of preparatory investigations, the author's *Humanistic and Political Literature in Florence and Venice at the Beginning of the Quattrocento: Studies in Criticism and Chronology* (Cambridge, Mass., 1955), cited as *Humanistic and Political Literature.* References to *Crisis: Appendices* are also found when, as frequently occurs, the present notes omit or compress extensive extracts from consulted sources or do not repeat abundant bibliographical information.

After having freed the historical analysis from lengthy critical and textual investigations, I tried to improve the narrative. In the two chapters on Leonardo Bruni's *Dialogi,* the contemporary work the understanding of whose genesis offers perhaps the greatest challenge, investigations of the chronology had in the first edition spilled

---

* Wherever insertions have been made that include additional notes, we have added to the superior number of the preceding note the letter (a), numbering the subsequent, inserted notes (b), (c), etc. (e.g., 3a, 3b, 3c).

from the two auxiliary volumes into the body of the book.
About a score of these more technical pages have now been
excluded from the text and replaced with brief summaries
and references to *Humanistic and Political Literature* and
Crisis: Appendices. On the other hand, the two sections on
the political background of the Florentine crisis (Chapters
2 and 16), which had appeared in the *American Historical
Review* as early as 1952-53 (under the title "A Struggle
for Liberty in the Renaissance: Florence, Venice, and
Milan in the Early Quattrocento") and which were only
partially utilized in the first edition, have now been reproduced at full length. These and several other chapters
have been further integrated through insertion of all those
pages from *Crisis: Appendices* that should be part of the
full historical picture. Finally, new findings from archival
or manuscript sources, as well as the continuing debate of
aspects of the early Renaissance basic to this book, have
made it desirable to strengthen many points with sharpened arguments and additional examples or episodes. Mis-
takes and inaccuracies of meaning and expression have been
rectified, wherever I have become aware of them.

In making these various changes, I have kept in mind
that the addition of more and more detail may overburden
the historical narrative. It is hoped that this danger has.
been minimized by placing at the foot of the respective
pages all insertions, marked with an asterisk, which comment upon rather than supplement the original text.
Polemical discussion has been relegated to the notes at the
end of the volume.

The sections more substantially revised or enlarged
include Chapters 2 and 16, on the political background of
the changes in culture and thought; the sketch of the still-
medieval features of Salutati's Humanism in Chapter 5;
some parts, in Chapters 3 and 7, of the discussion of the
"New View of History" in the Florentine Republic and

of the vexing problems posed by Salutati's *De Tyranno;* considerable portions of Chapters 14 and 15 dealing with "The Dangers of Humanist Classicism" and "Humanism and the Volgare," two areas in which much new research and thinking has recently been done; and finally, at the end of Chapter 18, the outline of the impact of civic Humanism on the ideal of a citizen-army. As mentioned, the two chapters on Bruni's *Dialogi* have been relieved of their too-heavy technical detail. An "Epilogue" attempts to review the major findings of the book from a broadened historical perspective.

Although these sections form merely the smaller part of the story, it is my hope that the effect will be a better balance of the work as a whole, and a more persuasive presentation of the forces which changed the life and thought of Renaissance Italy about and after 1400.

H. B.

The Newberry Library
December 1964

Acknowledgments

This book would not have been published in its present form without the untiring interest of Lawrence W. Towner, Director of the Newberry Library. Aside from the many ways in which he, the Trustees and the Staff of the Newberry have put exceptional facilities at my disposal for all my work, it was Bill Towner's frank criticism of the original version which convinced me that it would be worth trying to draw the various threads of my analysis together in a synthetic epilogue.

In the first edition, the English form owed much to the selfless cooperation of my friend, Fred Wieck. Whereas this text still forms the body of the book, a similar labor of love has been devoted to the many changes, insertions and new pages of the second edition by Marcel and Renate Franciscono.

I am dedicating the book in its changed form to the memory of a great student and writer of history to whom I am particularly grateful. It was Garrett Mattingly who, more than anyone else, strengthened my confidence in the correctness of the ideas and approaches here proposed by his firm belief in their validity and value at a time when others were skeptical. Now that the same picture is being re-drawn in what I hope is a more rounded presentation, I wish the reader to remember the man whom I felt thankfully to be one of my closest friends in spirit until his much too early death.

H. B.

CONTENTS

PREFACE   vii

ACKNOWLEDGMENTS   xi

INTRODUCTION   XXV

PART ONE

CHANGES IN POLITICS AND HISTORICAL THOUGHT

1. THE ELEMENTS OF THE CRISIS: CLASSICISM AND THE POLITICAL TRANSFORMATION   3

> Rise of Classicism around 1400 (3). New role of the Florentine Republic in the history of Humanism (4). North and central Italy at the crossroads: subjugation by the strongest tyrant-state, or a system of regional states? (8).

2. A FLORENTINE WAR FOR INDEPENDENCE   12

The Florentine Republic and the Visconti Tyranny of Milan   14

> Diversity of the Italian regions and the expansion of the Visconti State (14). Medieval, Church-centered Guelphism in the fourteenth century (15). Florentine "Guelphism" comes to mean championship of civic freedom and city-state independence (20). A Florentine policy of federation among the Tuscan city-republics (21). The Florentine encounter with the Visconti (24). Origins of the idea of an Italian equilibrium (25).

A Struggle for Civic Liberty, 1390-1402. Giangaleazzo Visconti and the Challenge of the Year 1402   28

> Florence in an unequal fight (28). Her calls for the defense of liberty fail to rouse the Republic of Venice (35). Milanese propaganda for an Italian peace through unification under one ruler (37). Florence alone to resist Giangaleazzo until his death in 1402 (38).

3. A NEW VIEW OF ROMAN HISTORY AND OF THE FLORENTINE PAST   47

Republicanism Versus Dante's Glorification of Caesar   48

> Leonardo Bruni's reinterpretation, at the beginning of the Quattrocento, of Dante's treatment of Caesar

and his assassins (48). Bruni's views remain a strand
in the Florentine attitude toward Dante (50).
Cristoforo Landino (50). Niccolò Machiavelli
(51). Donato Giannotti (52).

A Vindication of the Roman Republic in Leo-
nardo Bruni's Earliest Works   54
    A forerunner of Bruni's republican interpretation
    of Roman history in medieval Tuscany: Ptolemy of
    Lucca (55). Petrarch (55). Limitations of the his-
    torical appraisal of the *Respublica Romana* during
    the Trecento (57). Bruni's criticism of the role
    of the Roman emperors; his debt to the rediscovery
    of Tacitus' *Historiae* (58).

The Thesis of the Foundation of Florence by
Republican Rome   61
    Bruni's *Laudatio* (61). Dissolution, during the late
    Trecento, of the medieval legend of Florence's
    foundation by Caesar (62).

Prelude to the Historical Philosophy of the Florentine Renaissance   64
    From Bruni's *Laudatio* to his *History of the Flor-
    entine People* (64). Mid-Quattrocento controver-
    sies on Roman Monarchy and Roman Republic:
    Guarino and P. C. Decembrio, at tyrant courts,
    versus Bruni and Poggio in Florence and Pietro del
    Monte in Venice (66). Machiavelli (70). Late-
    Renaissance views of Florence as heir to the
    Respublica Romana (71). Harbingers in the *Lau-
    datio* of Renaissance historical thought (73).

Reflections of the New Ideas in Salutati, Cino
Rinuccini, and Gregorio Dati   75

PART TWO

PROMISE AND TRADITION IN POLITICO-HISTORICAL
LITERATURE ABOUT 1400

4. THE INTERPLAY OF IDEAS AND EVENTS   81

    Deceptive Theories and Sources   81
        Traditional datings of Giovanni da Prato's novel,
        Paradiso degli Alberti (81), of Loschi's, Salutati's,
        and Rinuccini's pamphlets during the Florentine-
        Milanese struggle (83), and of Bruni's *Laudatio*
        and *Dialogi* (83). Paucity and apparent contradic-

tions of our sources on the transition from the
Trecento to the Quattrocento (84).

Political Events and the Chronology of the Works
of the Publicists   88
Actual dates and motivations of the *Paradiso* (89),
and of Loschi's, Salutati's, and Rinuccini's pamphlets (90; cf. 485). Political experience as the
decisive stimulus (92).

5. A CITIZEN'S VIEW AND A HUMANIST'S VIEW OF
FLORENTINE HISTORY AND CULTURE: CINO
RINUCCINI AND SALUTATI   94
The Republican Reading of History, and the
Guelph Tradition   94
Rinuccini's contribution to the nascent historical
outlook of the Florentine Quattrocento (94). Salu-
tati carrying on the medieval-traditional Guelph
idea (96). Salutati's defense of monarchy in support of Dante's verdict on Caesar and the Empire
(99). Vindications of Caesar and the Empire in
Petrarch's late works (102). The climate of the
latter part of the Trecento (103).
Salutati's Civic Humanism and its Limitations   104
From the *De Vita Associativa et Operativa* to the
De Seculo et Religione (106). Salutati's recognition of the "vita activa et civilis" (110). His mis-
givings regarding the "virtus Romana" and the role
of the Roman Republic (112). The impact of the
medieval idea of Empire on Salutati as well as
Petrarch (118).

6. REPUBLIC AND MONARCHY IN LATE TRECENTO
THOUGHT   121
The Rediscovery of Cicero the Citizen and De-
fender of the Republic: Salutati and Vergerio,
1392-1394   121
Petrarch's indignation at Cicero's opposition to
Caesar (121). Salutati as Cicero's vindicator (123).
Role of Padua in the development of early Hu-
manism (126). An advocate of Cicero in Padua:
P. P. Vergerio (127).
Vergerio's Return to Monarchy in Princely Padua   129
Signory and patronage of the Carrara in Padua

(130). Vergerio's advocacy of monarchy under
Carrara influence (132).

Paduan Ideas on Tyranny About 1400: Giovanni
Conversino's *Dragmalogia* on the Preferable
Way of Life"   134
Renaissance tyranny versus "government by discussion" (135). Florence's cultural role seen as inferior
by an admirer of Giangaleazzo (140). A monarchical interpretation of Roman history and medieval ideas of Universal Monarchy in the *Dragmalogia* (143).

7. THE PLACE OF SALUTATI's *De Tyranno*   146
Salutati's Reversal: A Vindication of Caesar's
Monarchy Against Cicero   146
Pre-Renaissance "Realism": A Parallel in His-
toriography to Late-Trecento Art   151
The belief in a divinely ordained Empire resists
the political realism of the Trecento (152; cf.
498). Petrarch (152). Benvenuto Rambaldi da
Imola (153). Salutati (155). The function of
realism in late-Trecento historiography and art
(156). Nature of Salutati's politico-historical realism (158).
Salutati's Dilemma: Dante's Caesarism and Florentine Liberty   160
The puzzle of the *De Tyranno:* the Florentine
Chancellor, during a war for republican liberty,
defends the historical role of Tyranny (160). Political quietism, not scientific objectivity, the nerve
of Salutati's treatise (163). A cleavage in Trecento
humanists between their lives as *literati* and as citizens (166).

8. GREGORIO DATI's *"Istoria* OF FLORENCE 1380-
1406" AND THE BEGINNINGS OF QUATTROCENTO
HISTORIOGRAPHY   167
A Volgare Writer on the Road to Pragmatic History   168
From the epic profusion of the Trecento chroniclers
to a purposeful selection and analysis of causes
(169; cf. 501). Dati's and Bruni's pictures of the
Giangaleazzo period (171).

Harbingers of the Political Art of the Quattro-
cento   172
    Nascent awareness of an inter-regional balance of
    power (175). Rationality in politics and tech-
    nological planning (176).
Dati's Account of the Florentine Wars for Lib-
erty   181
    "Ragione," and the objective appraisal of the en-
    emy's resources, as supports of Florentine resistance
    (183). Florence as the savior of liberty in Italy
    (184).

PART THREE

THE RISE OF LEONARDO BRUNI'S CIVIC HUMANISM

9. PROMISE AND TRADITION IN BRUNI'S *Laudatio*
OF THE CITY OF FLORENCE"   191
    Originality and Literary Imitation   191
        Aelius Aristides' *Panathenaicus* as a model (192).
        Creative features of Bruni's humanistic panegyric
        (193). A leap beyond medieval city-eulogies
        (196).
    The First Literary Portrait of Florence's Political
    Constitution and Scenic Position   199
        Florence's geographic position and scenery as seen
        in the *Laudatio* and by fifteenth century artists
        (199). The geometric spirit in the *Laudatio* (200).
        A new ideal of "greatness" (204). Interest in
        Florence's institutions and their harmonious func-
        tioning as "a work of art" (205). Dati and Bruni
        (205). Bruni and Giannotti (208). Uses of the
        Laudatio, during the fifteenth century, outside
        Florence and Italy (209).

10. THE GENESIS OF THE *Laudatio*   212
    The Thesis that the *Laudatio* Was Written in
    1400   212
    The Post-1402 Origin of the *Laudatio*, and the
    Political Experience of the Giangaleazzo Period   216
        A manifestation of Florentine republicanism after
        the triumph over Giangaleazzo (220).

11. THE GENESIS OF BRUNI'S *Dialogi*   225

> Consequences of the redating of the *Laudatio* for
> Bruni's biography and the chronology of the
> *Dialogi* (226).

The Literary Structure of the *Dialogi*   226

> Contradictions in the two dialogues (227). Dis-
> similarities in their relationship to contemporary
> life and to literary models (228).

The *Dialogus I* of 1401 and the Post-1402 Origin of *Dialogus II*   232

> *Dialogus I*: Bruni between Trecento Humanism
> and classicistic skepticism regarding the attainments
> of the Moderns; *Dialogus II*, a later phase of
> Bruni's development: synthesis of awe of antiquity
> with respect for Florence's past and her native cul-
> ture (241; cf. 512, 514).

12. *Dialogus II* AND THE FLORENTINE ENVIRON-
MENT   245

> Florentine Sentiment in Bruni's Early Curial
> Period   245

> Patriotism, alienation, and a clerical career at the
> Curia (246). A debate on Themistocles and his
> Athenian *patria* (250).

The Petrarch Controversy of 1405-1406   254

Dialogus II and the Early History of the Appraisal of Petrarch   257

> Petrarch's supposed superiority over the Ancients
> as a Christian philosopher (258). The motif of his
> unique "universality" (259). From a view of
> Petrarch's work as a rebirth of Roman poetry to
> the idea of Petrarch as the restorer of the "studia
> humanitatis" (260). Boccaccio (261). Vergerio
> (263). Poggio (265). Bruni (267).

PART FOUR

CLASSICISM AND THE TRECENTO
TRADITION

13. THE CLASSICISTS AS SEEN BY VOLGARE WRITERS   273

> The Volgare School in the Transition Crisis   273

> Results suggested by Parts One to Three: reconcilia-
> tion, after 1402, of Florentine Humanism with

the political and cultural legacy of the medieval
Commune (274). Assumptions current in modern
scholarship: fifteenth-century Humanism the natural ally of Tyranny, alien to the civic and Volgare
traditions (275).

Domenico da Prato's Invective Against Niccoli
and Bruni—a Deceptive Source   279
An apparent testimony against the thesis of
Bruni's reconciliation with the Florentine traditions
(279). Deceptiveness of Domenico's evidence
(282). Bruni's way from the Ancients to the Moderns (282).

Cino Rinuccini's "*Invettiva* Against Certain Slanderers of Dante, Petrarch, and Boccaccio"   286
Rinuccini's demands and Bruni's performance
(287). The *Invettiva* as a source of information
on militant Classicism around 1400 (289).

14. THE DANGERS OF EARLY HUMANIST CLASSICISM   291
Intellectual Change About 1400 According to
Rinuccini's *Invettiva*   291
His picture of philological Humanism (292). Al-
leged traces of paganism (294).

Classicism and Ancient Religion. The Testimony
of Salutati and of Francesco da Fiano   295
Salutati on the necessity of anthropomorphic meta-
phors in every religion (296). Petrarch and Boccaccio on the secret "monotheism" of the ancient
poets (297). The growth of Salutati's defense of
the ancient poets (297). The poets in the light of
Francesco da Fiano's classicism in Rome (300).
Francesco on the sameness of human nature and
the ubiquity of the belief in one supreme divinity
(302). Against the doctrine of the damnation of
all pagans (305). The ancient gods and the Christian saints (307). Salutati on Socrates and Christianity (310). Militant Classicism and the Church
in Francesco's humanistic circle in Rome (312).

The Crisis of Civic Conduct and Outlook   315
Rinuccini's denunciations, and the decay of the
civic spirit among late-Trecento *literati* (315).
Petrarch (316). Boccaccio (317). Giovanni da
Prato (317). Filippo Villani (318). Roberto de'
Rossi and Antonio Corbinelli (320, 324). Niccoli

and the climax of the anti-civic trend (322, 326). Classicism, divorced from the reality of life, in Bruni's literary beginnings (329). The change of attitude in civic Humanism between the late Trecento and the early Quattrocento; Dante seen as a symbol of the *vita civile* (330; cf. 531).

15. FLORENTINE HUMANISM AND THE VOLGARE IN THE QUATTROCENTO 332

The "*Paradiso* of the Alberti" and the Cult of the Volgare 332

The *Paradiso* as a source for the mid-1420's (333). Championship of the Volgare and the resumption of the Florentine-Milanese struggle (335). Espousal of the Volgare by Bruni and his school during his later years (337).

Civic Humanism and the Florentine Volgare to the Time of Lorenzo de' Medici 338

Prejudices in the historical appraisal of the relationship of civic Humanism to the Volgare (338; cf. 533). Bruni on the value and origin of the Volgare; his opposition to the classicism of Flavio Biondo (339).

Toward recognition of the equality of the Florentine vernacular with Latin and Greek (344). From Boccaccio to Bruni (344). Palmieri and Manetti (339, 346). Benedetto Accolti (347). L. B. Alberti (348). Lorenzo de' Medici (351). Cristoforo Landino (352). From militant Classicism about 1400 to ripe Renaissance Classicism about 1475 (353; cf. 539).

PART FIVE

THE AFTERMATH OF THE CRISIS

16. CITY-STATE LIBERTY VERSUS UNIFYING TYRANNY 357

The Experience of the Giangaleazzo Period—a Recurrent Pattern 357

The 1410's: King Ladislaus of Naples in the Role of Giangaleazzo Visconti 359

The lacuna left by the dissolution of the Visconti State after Giangaleazzo's death; Neapolitan aspirations (360). A Florentine-Sienese alliance, resuming the late-Trecento policy of Tuscan collaboration (361). Prosperity after victory (364). A renewed contest between faith in city-state freedom, and longing for the peace of Italy under one lord (365). The failure of Naples' expansion as background of Bruni's *History of the Florentine People* (370).

The 1420's: Filippo Maria Visconti and the Renewal of the Milanese Challenge   370
Return of the determined spirit of the Giangaleazzo period (373). An antithesis prominent in Florentine thought and propaganda: the violence of tyrant-states versus the need of republics for peace (377). Florentine conduct in danger and defeat (380).

Populi Liberi: Florence and Venice Against the Visconti from the 1420's to the 1440's   387
The ideas of political equilibrium and "libertas Italiae" adopted by Venetian statesmen and humanists; the part of economic considerations (387). An anti-Viscontean league among the surviving city-republics: Florence, Venice, Genoa, Siena, Lucca (392). Extinction of the Visconti and emergence of a *Respublica Ambrosiana* at Milan in 1447 (396).
Francesco Barbaro on the choices facing Venice (397). Rise of the Sforza dynasty in Milan; a Florentine alliance with Francesco Sforza under Cosimo de' Medici's leadership (399). The end of republican cooperation (400). Cosimo's program of an anti-Venetian balance-of-power accepted as the logical outcome of Florence's equilibrium policy (401).

17. NICCOLI, POGGIO, BRUNI, AND THE CIVIC OUTLOOK   404
Niccoli and Poggio in the 1420's and 1430's   404
Phases of Bruni's Humanism to the Time of Filippo Maria   409

18. IDEAS BORN OF THE FLORENTINE CRISIS: BRUNI'S *Oratio Funebris* OF 1428   412
The *"Oratio Funebris* on Nanni degli Strozzi"— a Florentine Counterpart of Pericles' *Funeral Oration*   412

Florence and Her Cultural Mission   414
Etruscan and Roman strains in Florence's inheritance according to Bruni; from the *Laudatio* to
the *Oratio Funebris* (414). The Florentine *principatus* in *litterae studiaque* and in Volgare literature, according to the *Laudatio* and the *Oratio
Funebris* (416). Key-role of city-state freedom
in this cultural rise, according to Bruni's *Vita di
Petrarca* (417).

Freedom and the Florentine Constitution   418
From the *Laudatio* to the *Oratio Funebris* (418).
Equality of access to public offices a key to Florence's vigor, in Bruni's eyes (419). The civic ideal
in Buonaccorso da Montemagno's *Disputatio de
Nobilitate*; its dissemination in Burgundy, England and Germany (420; cf. 557). Florentine faith
in free competition among citizens as well as states
(422). A Milanese opposite: Uberto Decembrio's
utopia of enforced training of the best talents by
the prince (425). A sociological analysis of the
Florentine constitution by Bruni in his later years
(427). Active citizenship from Bruni to Machiavelli and Giannotti (428).

The Ideal of a Citizen-Army   430
The ideal of the citizen bearing arms and the
critique of the mercenary system in the Florentine
Renaissance (430; cf. 560). To Bruni's *Oratio
Funebris* (431). Propagation in Bruni's circle:
Palmieri (433), Porcari (434). Echoes during the
1460's and 70's: Accolti, Patrizi, Platina (435).
Impact on Florentine life at the time of Savonarola
and Machiavelli (438).

EPILOGUE   441
THE NATURE AND SIGNIFICANCE OF THE CRISIS
The anatomy of the transition from 1400 to 1450,
as observed in this book (444). The place of Florentine civic Humanism in Renaissance History
(452, 458).

NOTES   463

INDEX   565

ILLUSTRATIONS (Between pages 180 and 181)

Florence as Seen by an Artist of the Trecento (from a mural in the Loggia del Bigallo, 1352)

Florence as Seen by an Artist of the Quattrocento (woodcut copy of a Florentine engraving of about 1480)

Florence as Seen by a German Artist in 1493 (from Hartmann Schedel's *Liber chronicarum*)

INTRODUCTION

THE method of interpreting great turning-points in the history of thought against their social or political background has not yet rendered its full service in the study of the Italian Renaissance. To be sure, the long accepted view that the emergence of Renaissance culture stood in close relationship to the rise of a new civic, or bourgeois, society has proved fruitful in many fields of Renaissance research; and equally useful has been the knowledge that the late Renaissance was molded by a new courtly society, first in the Italy of the signories and principates, and later in the great European monarchies of the sixteenth century. But neither viewpoint helps to explain the fact that one of the greatest forward-strides occurred about the year 1400. By then, the civic society of the Italian city-states had been in existence for many generations and was perhaps already past its prime; and the hour when the Italian courts would transform Renaissance culture to their likeness still lay in the future. The places which held cultural predominance in the first decades of the Quattrocento were not as yet the seats of the tyrants, later to become famous, but rather the remaining city-state republics led by Florence. Yet at that very moment, with comparative suddenness, a change in Humanism as well as in the arts took place which ever since has been considered to have given birth to the mature pattern of the Renaissance. The medieval elements which had survived through the Trecento were then either destroyed or transformed. Antiquity became the model, and the measure of life, in a first era of classicism.

May we assume that so profound a transformation of all ideas of man and life came about without the stimuli of a new and significant experience in the politico-social sphere?

Or that the classicist acceptance of standards antagonistic
to native traditions should then not have produced the
signs of crisis in culture and society that are so well known
from later phases of the Renaissance, inside and outside
of Italy?

In studying the background of the early Italian Renaissance we encounter one remarkable fact: The generation
which was young about the year 1400 witnessed events on
the Peninsula that were decisive for the survival of civic
freedom and for the emergence of a system of independent
states. Although the time had passed when large parts
of Italy were crowded with free cities, and although
Tyranny was marching toward the period when monarchical absolutism would reign supreme, yet, at the turn
from the fourteenth to the fifteenth century, some of the
surviving city-states and local powers led by the Florentine Republic were waging a protracted fight which succeeded in limiting the triumphant progress of Tyranny in
Renaissance Italy. The upshot of the contest was the failure of absolutism to build up one centralized north and
central-Italian monarchy comparable to the political and
cultural structure of sixteenth-century France and Spain;
and the republican freedom of the city-state remained a
vital element in the Italian Renaissance.

Was awareness of the historic significance of this struggle a source of stimulation for the thought and culture
of the Renaissance when Humanism and the arts, in their
first great flowering, had their focus in Florence? The
present book is meant to give an answer to this crucial
question.

It is not our intention to claim that this experience was
the only factor which may have acted upon the transition
around 1400; or that the findings set forth on the following pages establish in themselves a final estimate of the
balance between Tyranny and civic freedom in the Italian

Renaissance. Our study seeks merely to suggest the crudity of the view that by the end of the fourteenth century the time for civic liberty was over and Tyranny was the only possible road into the future. As soon as we no longer take for granted this cliché, we quickly become aware of a forgotten world of actions and ideas in a group of citizens and civic humanists who were not ready to accept the apparent trend of the times as a decision of fate. When their lives and their ideas are reconstructed, the whole period around 1400 begins to shift its accents. Sources published but neglected and sources still unpublished reveal a wealth of new data, and an unexpected pattern emerges. Memoirs and the minutes of city councils tell of civic conduct and convictions such as are usually thought to have disappeared with the medieval Commune. Many historical works of the period, far from being informed by the spirit of rising Tyranny, show the beginnings of an approach to history which was to flourish in the Florentine Republic of the later Renaissance. When we see further that in the creation of the new politico-historical ideas the Florentine humanists cooperated with non-humanist civic writers, we also become aware of facts suggesting that between Humanism and the native Volgare element there existed a relationship very different from the time-honored identification of the Volgare tradition with the medieval Commune, and of Humanism with the Tyranny of the Renaissance. So strong, indeed, became the interpenetration of Florentine Humanism and the civic element in some circles, that early Quattrocento Florence saw the first phase of the *querelle* of the ancients and the moderns: classicism questioned by loyalty to native traditions.

After this transformation of the general picture of the period, the images of some well known humanists of early Renaissance Florence begin to change; we learn to distinguish between mere literary men—the representatives of the new classicism—and humanists nurtured on the political and social experiences of their day. The civic Humanism of the latter reveals its close affinity to the outlook and sentiment of the citizens of the Greek *polis*. Finally, having thus redrawn a formerly dim spot on the map of the early Renaissance, we also see more distinctly the contours of the better known areas: even the characteristic qualities of the literature produced at tyrant courts and of the group of writings echoing the classicism of the *literati* appear more sharply defined; the motives of their antagonism to the contemporary civic forces become more plainly recognizable.

It should be emphasized that an estimate of the bearing of these findings on our total view of the Italian Renaissance is not the burden of the following pages. The author hopes, however, that his readers will pose this wider problem to themselves. In one way or another, the fact that the actions, insights, and guiding values described here existed and had a vital meaning at the moment when the full pattern of the Renaissance emerged, must cause us to look upon all phases of the Renaissance from a changed vantage-point.

Part One

CHANGES IN POLITICS AND
HISTORICAL THOUGHT

CHAPTER 1

THE ELEMENTS OF THE CRISIS:
CLASSICISM AND THE
POLITICAL TRANSFORMATION

EVER since the humanists' own days, the transition from the fourteenth to the fifteenth century has been recognized as a time of big and decisive changes. In the realm of art, the break between the late Trecento schools, still half medieval, and the first Quattrocento generation of Brunelleschi, Donatello, and Masaccio is more radical than that between any other two generations in the course of the Renaissance. In the development of Renaissance thought, it is by humanists roughly coeval with Brunelleschi and Donatello—Niccoli, Bruni, and Poggio in Florence, and such men as Vergerio and Guarino in northern Italy—that Petrarch's Humanism and the mind of the Trecento were profoundly transformed; so profoundly indeed that, in the history of Humanism no less than in the history of art, the beginning of the new century coincides with the emergence of the full pattern of the Renaissance.

Students of the Renaissance, if asked to indicate the most conspicuous factor in the change, will point without hesitation to the new relationship of artists as well as humanists to antiquity. A new, almost dithyrambic worship of all things ancient pervaded the cultural atmosphere. Brunelleschi expended his small patrimony to pass some time studying, drawing, and measuring among the Roman ruins so that his art might become rooted in the world of the ancients. Niccoli, scion of a well-to-do Florentine merchant family, spent most of his fortune on ancient manuscripts and relics of classic art, until in the end he had to depend on Cosimo de' Medici's financial support. Only ancient authors were to be read and imitated—ancient authors in their genuine texts, unadulterated by the hands of medieval copyists; there was to be a break with the traditions founded by Dante and Petrarch in the Trecento. The time had come for the emergence of a brand of classicism characterized by a single-minded, even militant dedication to antiquity such as had been unknown to earlier centuries.

But classicism, however essential its part in the transformation, was not the only factor. No student of Renaissance art today will stress only the progress of classical imitation. We are accustomed to point out that the art of the Renaissance, in spite of its boundless enthusiasm for antiquity, became something vastly different from a mere return to classical forms and that many elements combined to produce a result which was as different from antiquity as it was from the Middle Ages. In reconstructing the development of culture and thought, it is also not enough to say that the revival of classical studies was merely a ferment in a much broader change. We must clearly define the other elements which acted in their own right, partly seconding and partly counteracting and reshaping the influence of antiquity until the results came to be much more than a crude preference for all things ancient.

Among those other elements, the most important was a new position assumed by the Florentine city-state republic.

During the greater part of the Trecento, Humanism had not been grounded in civic society, nor had it been closely associated with any particular one of the Italian

communes. It is true that around 1300, in the days of
Albertino Mussato of Padua, a beginning had been made
toward a union of pre-Petrarchian Humanism with the
civic world. At that time, a new type of civic culture inspired by ancient literature had been growing in the old
city-republics of northern Italy, such as Padua, Vicenza,
Verona, and Milan. But these beginnings had not gone
very far when the independent life of the city-republics
in northern Italy gave way to tyranny. In the advanced
stages of its fourteenth-century development, Humanism
was a literary movement some of whose exponents lacked
all identification with any specific group of Italian society,
while others began to be attached to tyranny. Humanism
at that time was carried on chiefly by grammar-school
teachers and the chancery officials of a multitude of secular and ecclesiastical princes, particularly in northern Italy,
in Papal Avignon, and in the central-Italian territories of
the Church. Petrarch, though Florentine by descent, had
begun the essential training of his mind in Avignon. In
the 1340's, he became spiritually an ally of Cola di
Rienzo's republican revolt in Rome, and took part in it
through political letters and manifestoes. In his later
years, he was associated with several of the tyrant courts
in northern Italy. There was in his native Florence, it is
true, a circle of his admirers, led by Boccaccio, who slowly
prepared the ground for the reception of Petrarch's aspirations among Florentine *literati* and clerics; but it
was not to Florentine culture and politics that Humanism
in Florence during and shortly after Petrarch's generation owed its direction of studies and its guiding values.
Not until the last few decades of the Trecento, when
Coluccio Salutati was the head of the Florentine chancery, and Filippo Villani, last of the three famous members of the family of Florentine chroniclers, wrote his
book *On the Origin of the City of Florence and on Her*

Renowned Citizens, did a gradual process of fusion begin between the humanistic and the civic outlook—whatever fusion there could be between the outlook of citizens who were required to conduct themselves as the members of a city-state republic, and the ideas of a movement still bearing the marks of scholarly aloofness and of the life at north-Italian tyrant courts.

Only a generation later, in the very first years of the Quattrocento, the cultural atmosphere had been transformed. From then on, through thirty years or more, Humanism and the development of Florentine culture were so closely united that for all practical purposes the history of Quattrocento Humanism begins in Florence. Not only did humanistic scholars all over Italy look to the new Athens on the Arno; the most significant effect for the future was that from Florence ideas and interests, such as could develop only in the society of a free city, spread through all Italy. This influence changed most of the ideas held by the humanists of the Trecento. There arose a new historical outlook, a new ethical attitude that opposed the scholars' withdrawal from social obligations, and a new literature, in Volgare as well as Latin, dealing with the family and civic life. Indeed, the more historical scholarship has explored the sociological setting of the early Renaissance, the more clearly has the significance of this Florentine civic component been recognized.

The histories of the Florentine Commonwealth from Leonardo Bruni onward, for instance, served as models of historiography outside Florence not only in so far as they introduced significant innovations of literary form and historical criticism; they also taught a new dynamic concept of history which had grown out of the Florentine experience of civic liberty and the independence of city-states. Within Florence itself, the historical ideas created by Florentine humanists survived to reach maturity in the days of Machiavelli, Guicciardini, and Giannotti—although by then Volgare had become the accepted language and the humanistic technique of presentation was considered obsolete. The link connecting the great Florentine historians of the early sixteenth century with the Florentine humanists of the early fifteenth was their common approach to history from the political experience of Florence.[1]

Again, a civic hue, originally found in the Florentine group, characterizes the voluminous Quattrocento literature of humanistic dialogues and treatises on the *philosophia moralis*. It is not simply that in this literature secularism has gained the ascendency over asceticism; nor is it sufficient to say that classical models have been revived. The heart of the change since the early Quattrocento is that a revolt had taken place against the earlier philosophy of humanistic scholars who, compounding medieval ascetic ideals with stoic precepts, believed that the true sage ought to keep aloof from society and public duties. From the end of the Trecento onward, the ever-recurring themes in the humanistic philosophy of life were the superiority of the *vita activa* over "selfish" withdrawal into scholarship and contemplation, the praise of the family as the foundation of a sound society, and the argument that the perfect life is not that of the "sage" but that of the citizen who, in addition to his studies, consummates his *humanitas* by shouldering man's social duties and by serving his fellow-citizens in public office.[2]

Once we are familiar with these early Quattrocento traits and the change in the role of Florence, we can no longer doubt that the cultural transformation from the end of the Trecento onward must have been accompanied by changes in the external setting. Like other cultural revolutions, this crisis must have included more than the

unfolding of the intellectual and artistic elements prepared by preceding generations. There came a moment
when new standards and new values arose and demanded
their place—a place which the political and social framework of the Trecento had not allowed.

The period of transition about 1400, therefore, must
have been marked not only by the rise of classicism, but
also by a modification of the material frame in which the
ideas of the Trecento had developed. This modification
need not mean that the crisis had socio-economic causes.
Although even in the economic field there may have been
greater differences between the Trecento and the Quattrocento than are usually assumed, it is quite clear that since
the late Trecento social and economic change was slow in
the Italian Renaissance. Nothing in our sources suggests
that the rapid transformation about 1400 was primarily
rooted in this sector of life. No revolt with either social
or economic overtones occurred in Florence between the
1370's and the Savonarolian revolution of the 1490's; and
the unsuccessful rising in 1378 of the "Ciompi," the workers of the Florentine woolen industry, had left no traces
that might have shaped the outlook and culture of the
citizenry about 1400.

If fresh experience in the citizen's life was responsible
for the rapidity and depth of cultural change in Florence,
it must have been in the political arena—experience gained
in the defense of civic freedom and the independence of
the Florentine Republic. And, indeed, around 1400 great
dislocations in the political interrelations of the Italian
states came to a head and produced a violent upheaval
that had long been in the making.

The Italy of the medieval communes had differed sig-
nificantly from medieval Europe north of the Alps. It
had not produced genuine feudalism. The hierarchy of
feudal lords which began to develop in the early Middle

Ages had been nipped in the bud, and the seigneurs of large landed estates had been forcibly transformed into city-dwellers and members of town society. But communal Italy had no more escaped local dismemberment than had the rest of medieval Europe. The many communes, each ruling over the neighboring countryside, were semi-autonomous and only affiliated with each other by the special bonds binding some of them to the Ghibelline group of princes and towns, others to the opposing camp of the Guelphs. Allegiance beyond the local sphere, therefore, was given only to the universal institutions of the Empire or the Church; in Italy no less than elsewhere, political and historical thought was either Ghibelline or Guelph and found its directives in the never-ceasing contests of Emperors and Popes for the leadership of the Christian world. In many parts of early fourteenth-century Italy, it is true, communal localism was gradually giving way to somewhat larger states under the rule of *signori*. But as long as these new political creations had neither reached stability nor established traditions, and as long as the radius of consolidation was as a rule still small, the longing of the age for pacification through the Emperor or Pope only increased. Although many new developments which were eventually to merge in a new political order of the Peninsula had already started, the impact of the new beginnings could not be strongly felt until some spectacular catastrophe broke the continuity of the inherited conditions.

In contrast to the still medieval atmosphere in the Trecento, Italy in the Quattrocento, as is well known, presents the first example of modern inter-state conditions: a system of sovereign region-states each of which had absorbed an abundance of local autonomies, created new loyalties, and replaced the allegiance to the Empire or the Church. One of these new political organisms was a north-

Tuscan region-state under the rule of the Florentine Republic; and it was precisely in the years around 1400 that the final transition to a system of regional states took place during struggles which shook all of north and central Italy to the core.

There can be no doubt about the depth of the impression made by the wars that decided the political structure which the Peninsula was to have in the Renaissance. The issue was an alternative between two diametrically opposed ways into the future. One possible outcome would be a system of equal states including princedoms and republics —an equilibrium of forces making Renaissance Italy in some respects akin to the Greek pattern of independent city-states and, in other respects, a miniature prototype of the modern western family of nations. The other conceivable development was the emergence out of the competition of the surviving Italian states of a national monarchy comparable to those of England, France, and Spain, but unparalleled as a threat of despotic power since north and central Italy knew neither parliaments nor estates general nor any other of the counterpoises to unfettered absolutism that feudalism elsewhere in Europe had left as its legacy to the modern nation-states.[3] Confronted with this tremendous decision, the same pioneering generation of the early Quattrocento that saw the triumph of classicism in all fields of culture experienced on the political plane a contest which, in significance and sweep, was not matched until the end of the Quattrocento when the transalpine European powers invaded the Peninsula.

In many regards, this political struggle was bound to counteract the direction in which the rise of classicism was drawing the intellectual life of Florence and Italy. While humanistic classicists among the Florentine citizens began to turn away contemptuously from the medieval and Trecento traditions of Florentine culture and to discard the old standards of the civic way of life, Florence was thrown into a fight for her existence which put these native traditions and civic ideals to the decisive test.

Did the concurrence of a political trial with the intellectual revolution produce the rich ferment of the years around 1400? Whatever our final verdict will be, a history of the transitional crisis of the early Renaissance must start with an analysis of the tremendous dislocations which brought the Florentine Commonwealth into mortal danger and finally put her into the forefront of a political struggle that redrew the map of Italy for the Quattrocento.

CHAPTER 2

A FLORENTINE WAR FOR INDEPENDENCE

THE political evolution of Italy during the early Italian Renaissance is usually considered as a period of sweeping growth of signory or tyranny, a development supposed to have been accompanied by a fading away of the traditions of the preceding age: civic freedom and a popular culture based upon the Volgare (the Italian vernacular). That this widely held conception oversimplifies the situation is shown by a glance at the five major members of the fifteenth-century Italian states-system, for two of them were states controlled by city-republics. On closer view, the balance proves to be even more favorable to the republican members. Among the five leading powers of Renaissance Italy, only three had risen in the geographic area of the medieval Communes, the original substratum of Renaissance culture. Of these three, one was a tyranny, Milan; two were republics: Florence and Venice.

The Kingdom of Naples and the Pontifical State lay outside the urbanized central and northern parts of the Peninsula. The Italian South, built on Byzantine, Arab and Norman foundations, had formed a centralized monarchy from the times of the Hohenstaufen, resembling in many respects West-European monarchies like France and Aragon. A fully integrated, large state like Naples-Sicily was, however, different from the medieval West. In Southern Italy feudalism was oddly mixed with elements of an advanced bureaucratic administration of oriental origin. But while distinct from the feudal world north of the Alps, this unified state differed even more from the areas in central and northern Italy whose dominating social unit was the city-state under republican or tyrannical rule.

The character of the Papal State had been shaped in part by the world-wide relations of the Papal Curia and in part by the influence of the great feudal families which resided on the baronial latifundia in the district of Rome. Only in the North did the papal dominions reach out into the old urbanized area; there they included half-independent city-republics and local signories, especially Perugia, the foremost city in papal Umbria, Bologna, leading city of Romagna-Emilia, and a number of semi-autonomous provincial towns in the March of Ancona. Except for this urbanized northern belt of the Papal State and for a few adjoining minor principalities, the provinces which gave birth to the Renaissance about 1400 were under the dominion of one typical Renaissance Tyranny on a regional scale, Milan, and of the two region-states under republican hegemony, Florence and Venice.

Among these three neighbors and rivals, the Milanese Dukes had been the first to conquer and organize a regional state and, consequently, were the first cause of the growth of the Renaissance states-system. But if the rise of the Milanese state preceded this challenge, and the formation of the neighbor states under Florence and Venice developed in answer to it, the ultimate decision that there was to be a system of sovereign states in Renaissance Italy depended on the events and moral energies that made this answer effective and preserved the independence of Florence and Venice. The resistance to Milan was due particularly to Florence, since Venice, protected by her lagoon and with her overseas empire, was for a long time merely a half-hearted member-state of the Peninsula. In the last analysis, the historical significance of the early upsurge of Milan did not lie only in her appearance on the Italian scene as an integrated state with a modern administration. It lay just as much in the stimulus she gave to Florence and Venice to adopt her new methods and new spirit within a frame that preserved the legacy of city-state freedom.

The Florentine Republic and the Visconti Tyranny of Milan

The heart of the challenge presented to the neighbor-regions by the emergence of the Duchy of Milan was that tyranny was by its nature a dynamic, expansionist, and potentially unifying factor in inter-state relations. Ever since the emergence of the first tyrannies during the thirteenth century, the despot's independence of historical tradition and democratic procedure had given him a better chance than the republics had to crush rival neighbors and unite victor and vanquished in a provincial state where the citizens of former city-states became subjects under a bureaucratic administration. This process became most intensified in the region in which the advantages of unification were greatest for geographic and economic reasons: in the flat valley of the Po, and especially in its central province, Lombardy.

After territorial integration on a broader basis had been achieved in some parts of northern Italy, tyranny had not stopped on its road of expansion. It had called forth an ever more intense struggle for survival among the aggrandized states, and once the supremacy of one of the remaining despots—eventually the Milanese lord of Lombardy—had been established, there was no limit to the further expansion of his state until the natural boundaries of northern Italy were reached. After concentration of power in his hands had become vast enough, the tide would roll on to the south, to the papal provinces of Romagna-Emilia and Umbria, or to Tuscany.

This had already happened when the first consistent bid for tyrannical integration, early in the fourteenth century, had succeeded in the Northeast—with the state of the Scaligeri of Verona. The Apennines had proved to be no barrier toward the south, and in the 1330's, for the first time, the Florentines had seen neighboring Tuscan cities —especially Lucca—drawn into the orbit of foreign tyranny and bowing to the rule of the *signore* of distant Verona.[1] Soon afterwards, from the 1350's on, the Visconti of Milan became the final contenders for a north-Italian state which attempted to engulf central Italy. During the lifetime of the great archbishop Giovanni Visconti, friend and patron of Petrarch, Florence underwent a period in which her foreign policy had to be concentrated on warding off this danger. When the same threat reappeared toward the end of the Trecento, the hour had come for the decision whether any of the imperiled minor powers, or any coalition of them, would finally stem the course of an already well-established trend. Failing successful counteraction, the northern and central provinces of Italy seemed destined to develop into one vast and powerful tyrant-state incorporating the entire urbanized area south as well as north of the Apennines. In that case, an absolute monarchy of the North would have taken its place alongside the Papal State (probably shorn of some of its urbanized provinces) and the Kingdom of Southern Italy. With the possible exception of half-Eastern Venice, there would have been no continuation of the medieval traditions of civic freedom into the age of the Renaissance.

In the middle of the Trecento, it still seemed impossible for the Florentines to fathom the true nature of the ensuing struggle. Alignments and divisions of the local

powers on the Peninsula had been looked upon during the
Middle Ages as part of the contention between the Emperor and the Pope and their followers, the Ghibellines
and the Guelphs. Thus the emerging alternative between
the building of one absolute, empire-like monarchy on the
one hand, and regional independence with preservation of
civic liberty on the other, still appeared in the guise of the
centuries-old ideology of the fight between Ghibellines
and Guelphs. Like the Scaligeri, the Visconti had risen as
appointed vicars of the Emperors; they were the leaders
of the Ghibelline party on the Peninsula. In the opposing
camp it was the Papacy, then in Avignon, which designed
and organized the resistance against the potential danger
of an expansionist monarchy with its center in Milan. In
the 1350's, the situation appeared to be basically what it
had been in the thirteenth century when the Popes had
thwarted the efforts of the Hohenstaufen to erect an Italian Monarchy on the foundation of the south-Italian kingdom. Since leadership clearly lay in Avignon, the war
against the rising power of the Visconti was waged with
the medieval slogans aimed at rebels against the authority
of the Church, and with the old weapon of ecclesiastical
excommunication.[2]

Florence, in that climate, felt herself to be but one of
the many Guelph city-states that were following and defending the cause of the Church. Modern students have
noticed with surprise how greatly the Florentine diplomats
and chroniclers of the 1350's distorted the causes of the
Florentine participation in the fight against Giovanni
Visconti.[3] In 1349-50, even while the Florentine Republic
was fully aware that Milanese occupation of Bologna
would deprive Florence of an indispensable ally and was
trembling at the thought of Viscontean expansion across
the Apennines, her justification for supporting Bologna
remained her obligation toward the Church, which was

Bologna's suzerain and was to be defended by every member of the Guelph-Papal party.[4a]

This is not to say that Guelph ideology was still determining actual policy as uncontestedly as during the struggle of the Popes with the Hohenstaufen emperors a century before.[4b] Year by year it became more evident that the interests of the Florentine city-state were not simply identical with those of the Church. The Popes were far away in Avignon, while Ghibelline Milan was Florence's close neighbor. If the immense power of the Visconti fell upon Florence in the event of an open Guelph-Ghibelline war, would the Republic on the Arno find herself part of a camp whose members stood up for each other, or would she become a victim to be sacrificed by others for their own salvation? Faced with these doubts, many Florentines did not wish the Republic to suit her political actions to her Guelph creed. When, after Bologna's temporary surrender to the Visconti in 1350, Milanese troops invaded Florentine territory and neither the Papacy nor any other Guelph state gave assistance to the Republic,[4c] a growing neutralist attitude spread among the citizens, culminating in the demand that any future alliance or league be avoided. The more fully the Popes succeeded in gradually reconquering the Papal State, the stronger became the suspicion that, like Milan from the north, the Papal State in its own expansion from the south would not respect the borders of Tuscany. The Florentine Republic did not again become an active member of the Papal-Guelph league during the 1350's. When, in 1359-60, Bologna was once more in danger of being seized by Milanese troops, Florence made no move and left it to the rebuilder of the Papal State, Cardinal Albornoz, to prevent Bologna from falling to the Milanese empire.[4d]

The dangers inherent in mere inactivity soon became obvious, however. Secret assistance from the Visconti was going to all of Florence's enemies south of the Apennines. A German emperor, Charles IV—potential friend of Ghibelline Milan—was to appear before long on the Peninsula. By 1366, therefore, in spite of all former hesitations, a Florentine-Papal league for military protection was again formed, and once this bond had been restored, all the traditional Guelph ideas and slogans were revived and even began to dominate the politics of the Republic. In the city councils it was once more argued that the irrevocable duty of a Guelph city like Florence was to follow the directives of the Church in obedience to the Pope. When the Florentine ambassador to the Curia, Lapo da Castiglionchio, made a famous speech in Avignon pleading for a speedy return of the Pope to Italy, his oration was, in the words of a recent historian, "a florid and grandiose summary of the Guelph creed." "The Guelph argument had not changed in nearly a century." [4e] Yet, though the ideology was medieval, it was now appealed to in a vastly changed world. If the revitalized Guelph league should lead its members into a decisive war against Ghibelline Milan, victory might mean nothing else than the destruction of one of the two rivals for power over central Italy, leaving sole dominance to the ruler of the State of the Church, a neighbor no less dangerous to Tuscany than Milan. The revival of Guelph sentiment which had swept Florence on the conclusion of the Papal league was, therefore, quickly followed by another retreat into neutrality and inaction. From 1368 onward, the Florentine Republic would again refrain for years from taking sides in the struggles which were to decide the future of the Peninsula. [4f]

The position of Florence in the mid-Trecento elicits two comments. One is that Florentine foreign policy at that time was in a state of kaleidoscopic change bound to produce a feeling of frustration and lack of direction. Recent studies of Florentine history have shown [4g] that these continuous shifts were in part dependent upon the frequent alternation in power of various social groups which held vastly divergent views of Florence's foreign policies. Supporting each of the rival programs was a hard core of partisans who, because their views were socially motivated, were never prepared to forsake their party convictions. Whereas the leading families of the patriciate, as bankers of the Popes and competitors for the highest church positions in Tuscany, depended upon close relations with the Curia, the masses of the "new citizens" who had recently immigrated from the countryside felt little allegiance to the city's Guelph past, developed a growing hostility toward the countless privileges enjoyed by the Church within the city-state and, consequently, were loath to shoulder any risks and expenses by entering into Guelph or Papal alliances. Even apart, therefore, from the tangled international scene which prevented the formation of a stable Florentine policy, there were elements in the internal structure of the city's life which made Florence in the mid-Trecento a weak and undecided partner in inter-state relations.

Our second observation concerns the still unbroken dominance of traditional Guelphism during this phase of Florentine history: no new political outlook had yet arisen to replace medieval thought. The only alternative to the Guelph ideas that had been explored—inactive neutrality—offered no defense against the dangers of the growing power conflicts, nor any fresh perspective on the contemporary Italian struggles within the framework of Florence's history or future.[4h] To the still inexperienced *novi cives* it seemed safest for Florence, placed geographically between two integrating regional states, to distrust both and remain aloof from all entanglements. Such an estimate of the situation, obviously, overlooked that the Visconti empire, quite unlike the loosely knit territories of the

Church, was inherently the most dynamic and expansionist state of the Peninsula. From the beginning of Viscontean expansion to the south, therefore, some kind of anti-Viscontean coalition had perforce to be built and rebuilt after short intervals, and since papal leadership continued, and Florence merely joined these coalitions temporarily, they did not cease to appear as revivals of the medieval "Party of the Church."

It was not only in diplomatic propaganda and in the debates of city councils that, under the still unbroken spell of the traditional views of the Church and Empire, the real world of politics seemed to lose its identity. In the following definition of "Guelphism" by a contemporary Florentine historian, Matteo Villani, chief chronicler of the events of the 1350's and 1360's, one is astonished to find no clear reflection of the simultaneous fight between the monarchism of Ghibelline Milan and the civic freedom of Guelph Florence. The Guelphs, Matteo wrote, are those "that follow the Holy Church in the affairs of the world," [5] whereas the Ghibellines are those "that follow the Empire whether it is on the side of the true believers or not." [6] Only as a matter of practical experience he added: since the emperors were Germans and stayed in Italy merely on brief expeditions, they usually left vicars behind—in most cases Ghibellines, of course—who, after the death of the emperor who had appointed them, remained in power and became tyrants. This is why free cities would no longer admit emperors into their walls, and why the Guelph adversaries of the German rulers had developed into "a foundation and firm and stable base of liberty in Italy and inimical to all tyrannies." [7]

When the meaning of the Florentine *Parte Guelfa* was officially redefined by Leonardo Bruni on the occasion of a revision of the Statute of the *Parte* in 1420, the stand for civic freedom had become a part of the Guelph creed itself. The Guelphs still were said to be the party of the Church, but only as far as religion was concerned; on the secular plane they were the party of republican liberty: "If you consider the community of the Guelphs from the religious point of view, you will find it connected with the Roman Church, if from the human point of view, with Liberty—Liberty without which no republic can exist, and without which, the wisest men have held, one should not live." [8] Between the time of Matteo Villani and this rephrasing in the year 1420 there had occurred the revolutionary change in the inter-state structure of the Peninsula as a result of which Florence, after having been for centuries one of the communes in the Guelph-Papal fold, turned into the champion of civic freedom and the chief opponent of Tyranny. [9]

The earliest developments preparing for this change can be traced to the gradual transformation of the neighborly ties that bound the Tuscan city-states to each other. Twice in the past the Florentine Republic had attempted to subjugate the major Tuscan cities and build a Florentine dominion in Tuscany, as Milan had built a provincial dominion in the upper valley of the Po. The first of these attempts had been made from 1250 to 1260 when Guelph Florence after the fall of the Hohenstaufen found herself the strongest power in Tuscany; the second followed in the 1330's when Pisa and Lucca threatened to become spring-boards for native tyranny and for southward expansion of the north-Italian empire of the Scaligeri of Verona. Both times the outcome had been ruin to Florence. The imperialistic policy of the 1250's had ended with the long-remembered military catastrophe of Montaperti on the Arbia; the strain of the continual wars of the 1330's had in 1342-43 caused the dictatorship—also never forgotten—of a Florentine tyrant elected for life, the Duke of Athens. After only one year of the tyrant's rule, the quarreling groups of citizens cooperated to break the spell, and the previously subjected Tuscan cities, which had transferred their allegiance from the Florentine Commune to the new Lord, returned to independence. The proud structure of a Florentine dominion over large parts of Tuscany had disappeared.

By this experience Florence's relationship to Tuscany was changed for a long time to come.[10a] The Florentine territory after 1343 was rebuilt on a narrower basis than it had had for several generations; of the more important cities, only Pistoia in the immediate neighborhood, and, somewhat later, Volterra and Arezzo were again incorporated. Instead, the foremost cities in Tuscany and in the adjacent provinces were joined to Florence by defense-leagues frequently renewed. In the foundation charter of one of the first of these regional confederations—that concluded with south-Tuscan Siena and Umbrian Perugia in 1347—we read that the objective was the common defense against "any prince who would encroach upon Italy from across the Alps, and against any non-Tuscan tyrant."[10b] Gradually, leadership in an anti-imperial and anti-tyrannical confederation with free neighbor city-states became an accepted part of Florence's foreign policy. By the year 1370 even Florence's age-long opponents in the west, Pisa and Lucca, were reconciled and attracted to this alliance system. During the 1370's and 1380's the city-leagues of Florence usually included Pisa, Lucca, and Siena in Tuscany, Perugia in Umbria, and, north of the Apennines, Bologna in Emilia which was the key to the major passes to Tuscany. As metropolis of a free city-state region, Florence staved off the threat of the Visconti for another generation.[11a] In 1374, Coluccio Salutati, Florentine chancellor and humanist, told Lucca, the Tuscan city-state first hit by the Milanese southward drive, that the Florentine people, who had come to detest tyranny at

home, were ready to defend with deeds the liberty of the
other cities. For in doing so, Salutati said, Florence was
following her enlightened self-interest. "The liberty of
this city appears to be all the more secure, the broader
the belt of free peoples surrounding her. Therefore, everyone ought to be convinced readily that the Florentine
people are the defenders of the liberty of all peoples [in
Tuscany], since in defending them they also make the
defense of their own freedom less difficult." [11b]

It is against this background that we must view the
Florentine reactions to the Papacy in the period when
the long and fervent desire of the Italians for the return
of the Popes to Italy approached fulfillment and it became
clear that this change involved the reemergence of the
Papacy as one of the nascent region-states of the Peninsula.
Already the first attempt of the Popes to return to Italy
at the end of the 1360's had produced a threatening
scheme, unexpectedly seconded by the Emperor Charles
IV, to limit the autonomy of the central-Italian cities by
incorporating them in an enlarged Papal State, and it was
only Florentine intercession for the independence of all
Tuscan city-states that eventually assured the freedom of
the republics of Pisa and Lucca.[12a] The climax of the clash
with the Papacy came in the 1370's when central Italy was
shaken by the violent upheaval known as the "War of the
Eight Saints." Papal legates, sent ahead before the Pope
moved finally to Rome in 1377, crushed local autonomies
and began to build up a better integrated state in the
almost lawless region around Rome and in the former
Papal possessions in Umbria and Romagna-Emilia, and
even in parts of Tuscany. In these efforts, they showed
the same systematic ruthlessness which the Italian tyrants
had practiced in consolidating their states. In the mid-
1370's, Florence found herself at the head of a central-
Italian league defending the independence of Tuscany

against the dangers from the Papal State. For a while, all the old allegiances were exchanged; as an ally of the Lord of Milan, Florence, with all resources united in the hands of a new central agency for the war—her "Eight Saints"— was caught in a violent struggle against the Papal armies. After this interlude of emotional upheaval, even for those patricians who from the 1380's onward caused Florence once more to become a "Guelph" city, the political role of the Papacy would never again be the one which every good Florentine Guelph had conceded to the Pope before the "War of the Eight Saints." [12b] The outcome of the war was for Florence an immense strengthening of the tendency to look upon herself as the leader of the free city-states.

By the beginning of the 1380's, northern and central Italy had grown different from each other in political structure and attitude to a degree that had been unknown in medieval Italy. Without over-simplifying a complex situation, we may say that while tyrannical integration and the destruction of the republican freedom of local city-states had reached their consummation in Lombardy, Tuscany had become the home of a provincial coalition of city-republics which included former Ghibelline as well as Guelph members. While "Ghibelline" Milan had arrived at the point on the road to modern centralizing absolutism where the Lord of Milan and Lombardy, in the eyes of war-weary Italy, could take the place once attributed by Dante to a pacifying universal Emperor, "Guelphism" in Tuscany was shedding its medieval hull and emerging as a political program of civic freedom and independence of the central-Italian city-republics. In this changed environment, when almost immediately after the settlement of the Tuscan conflict with the Papal State the old antithesis between the Tuscan metropolis and the expanding tyrannical North reemerged, a larger burden of responsible leadership than ever before fell on Florentine shoulders. Since the Popes, after their return to Rome, were farther removed from direct contacts with the dynamic forces in the Po valley, they were now more inclined to stay in the background and let Florence bear the brunt of the battle. And at that very moment, in the year 1385, the shrewdest and most far-sighted of the many great and ruthless statesmen of the Visconti family took the helm of the Milanese State: Giangaleazzo Visconti.[13]

In 1386 and the following year, in a classic example of *divide et impera* policy, the new Milanese Lord, as an ally of the Carrara of Padua, destroyed the State of the Scaligeri in Verona and Vicenza, only to overrun the Carrara immediately afterwards and to unite the dominions of nearly the entire north-Italian plain in 1388. The paralyzing effect of these events [14] was further intensified by the attitude of the Venetian Republic. It ought to have been the role of Venice, Padua's neighbor, to frustrate Giangaleazzo's design, and since the Milanese conquest of Verona, Florentine diplomacy had worked frantically on a scheme under which Venice should guarantee Padua's independence after obtaining, by amicable settlement, the eastern dependencies of the Carrara State which she considered necessary for her own security. But Florence found both parties unwilling and blind to the Milanese danger. Venice in the end preferred to enter into an understanding with Giangaleazzo in return for receiving as her share of the spoils the Carrara territories around Treviso. The minutes of Florentine council meetings held about the time of the Milanese conquest of Padua allow us to observe that there had been discussion in Florence of vast aid to the Carrara and even of direct intervention in the war against Giangaleazzo. But all such plans were given

up, because the members of these *Consulte* feared that
Florence's active intervention might provoke an armed
clash with Venice.[15a]

We learn from the same minutes that another result of
the Florentine reaction to events in northern Italy was a
plan for friendly adjustment of any quarrels existing between the Commune of Florence and "all the free Tuscans." [15b] Central to the deliberations of one *Consulta* was
the project to make voluntary concessions in Florence's
territorial disputes, especially with Siena, in order to pave
the way for a more solid reconstruction of the Tuscan city-
league which had been weakened since the early 1380's. In
its effort to win Siena back, the Florentine government expressed its motives with the statement that "not only local
neighborhood, but identity of the form of government and
devoted attachment to freedom" made the Florentines and
the Sienese "similar and [even] essentially alike." [15c]
Bologna and Perugia were also called upon to once more
join the alliance. The *libertas* of Bologna, in particular,
appeared to many members of the *Consulte* as inseparable
from the *libertas* of Florence herself; speaker after speaker
dwelt upon the necessity of defending the independence of
both cities together.

Before long, the Florentine government made a second
attempt to change Venice's attitude. In 1389, Florentine
envoys warned the Doge of the danger of the situation.
They were charged to explain that Giangaleazzo was endeavoring to obtain the rule of the whole of Italy by
"taking possession of the Florentine State, and then of the
States of the Venetians and the Genoese; for the others
are of no account, once he has subjugated these." To this
exposition of peninsular interdependence among the Italian
republics, the Venetian government simply replied that
they could see no reason for alarm.[16] So it became definitely clear that the city of the lagoon, secure, or at least

believing herself secure, on her islands, would not throw her weight into the decisive encounter between unifying monarchy and the tradition of independence inherited from the age of the communes.[17]

No less disappointing was the course of events in Tuscany. Here, too, the conventional attitudes and diplomatic methods proved inadequate in the face of a power strong enough to penetrate and dissolve the customary order of every region of the Peninsula north of Rome. Siena and Pisa were soon seen in secret contacts with the Visconti, trying to find in the rising colossus of the North a safeguard for their own immediate security and at the same time a counterpoise to Florence's supremacy in the provincial Tuscan balance of power. Thus the very beginning of the war-filled era, which was not to end until Giangaleazzo's death, was marked by the collapse of all Florentine hopes for a united front of the free city-states on a regional, or an even broader, basis.

The one thing Florentine politics could try to do in this situation, and indeed undertook with vigor as soon as the shock of the Paduan debacle had worn off, was to bring about cooperation with the most directly endangered local powers on the northeastern slopes of the Apennines—Bologna as well as such minor signories as Ravenna, Faenza, and Imola. But these efforts proved insufficient without the active participation of a major north-Italian power—and only Venice could have given the necessary help. If the tide was to be stemmed, the Florentine Republic had to stop the breach with more effective means before the flood could cross the Apennines.

The first objective of Florentine diplomacy was to establish peace by agreeing on a line of demarcation. If Giangaleazzo was willing to respect the Secchia, a southern tributary of the Po passing not far west of Bologna, Florence and Bologna in return would refrain from interfering in Lombardy, northwest of the river. But Florentine attempts to reach such an agreement with Milan remained fruitless.[18] Giangaleazzo's intentions became obvious. Armed intervention was inevitable.

A Struggle for Civic Liberty, 1390-1402.
Giangaleazzo Visconti
and the Challenge of the Year 1402

In the year 1390, the Florentine Republic definitely assumed her place in the resistance against the Visconti on a peninsular scope. She waged the first open war against Giangaleazzo, which lasted from 1390 to 1392. The dangers implied in the rise of the Visconti Monarchy had by then become so evident that Florence could enter the struggle with manifestoes from the pen of her humanist-chancellor, Salutati, proclaiming that the goal of the "Tyrant of Lombardy" could now be discerned: he wanted to become "King." Giangaleazzo had been telling Italy that he was the champion of peace at the very time when he was destroying Verona's and Padua's independence. "These are the labors for peace by which, as he contends, he has striven for the *Pax Italiae*." While preparing for war by every means at his command, he had lured Florence into disarming, only to arm himself; he had armed Florence's former friends, thus making them her enemies. Florence was taking up arms for the defense of her own liberty and for the liberty of the peoples under the yoke of the Visconti. According to another Florentine proclamation: "Ours is a commonwealth not of noblemen (*popularis civitas*), one totally dedicated to trade, but *free*—the most hateful and abominable thing to the Duke; a commonwealth accustomed not only to respect liberty at home, but also to maintain it beyond our borders. It is, therefore, a long-established need for us to strive for peace, for in peace alone can we enjoy our liberty." [19]

In spite of this gradual growth of a new ideology and determined propaganda, the Florentine performance in the war was neither spectacular nor militarily impressive. True, Florence's intervention did infuse into the group of still-independent cities and *signori* in the Northeast the vitality and coherence that ought to have come to the region from Venice; in this respect the war was a success. Moreover, at the eastern flank of the Visconti empire the Paduan State came back into existence, even though impoverished and (because of Venice's occupation of Treviso) reduced in size. Finally, out of the war a larger bloc of northeastern states arose which included the Padua of the Carrara, the Ferrara of the Este, the Mantua of the Gonzaga, the City of Bologna, and the smaller autonomous dominions of the region—all united with Florence in the "League of Bologna." But these successes produced merely a temporary stopgap; the war had not revealed any new energies in the Florentine citizenry that promised lasting resistance to the aims of the Visconti. The League of Bologna was no more than an instrument of balance-of-power diplomacy with the lesser north-Italian tyrants playing the vital role. Even if all members of this coalition stood for independence, few stood for civic liberty. The most significant military success in the war had not been won by any of the city-republics, but was due to the loyalty of the inhabitants of the Paduan territory to their native lord. When the Carrara reappeared in his land, the population responded to his call, and it was with these troops, "nearly all unwarlike peasants, not accustomed to the exercise of arms," that he forced the Milanese garrison to surrender in the face of a general upheaval of the Paduan people.[20] And in addition to the north-Italian *signori*, Florence's war allies had been the King of France and the Duke of Bavaria. Florence, indeed, had gone so far as to agree to French occupation of the entire western Po valley after victory,[21] and when Giangaleazzo had crushed the French he could boast of having defeated foreign invaders with an army "composed exclusively of Italian soldiers." [22] In spite of the call to liberty in the Florentine manifestoes, the hour when Florence could rightly claim to be the savior of the *libertas Italiae* was yet to come.

The emergence of the League of Bologna did not bring any real pause to the smoldering conflict; while the arms rested, the struggle on the diplomatic front continued with undiminished force. Henceforth Giangaleazzo behaved like someone who, in an attempt to pull down a well-cemented barrier, hits every single stone successively, hoping that one will at last give way, or that a multitude of tiny dislocations will in the end break down the edifice. Within Tuscany, Siena (as we know) had been making overtures to Giangaleazzo, and from 1389 on it had admitted Milanese troops. In 1392, after a coup d'état against the Florentinophile government, Pisa accepted a similar arrangement —a success for the Visconti cause which snatched the vital ports on the mouth of the Arno away from Florentine control. In its long-range effects this event led to a fatal weakening of the League of Bologna. Florence, deprived of a reliable connection with the western sea, was forced thereafter to look for another outlet to the world, seeking it across the Apennines in the territories of her northeastern allies, along a road leading eventually to Ravenna or some neighboring port on the eastern coast. But the first Florentine effort to lease a military base on the northeastern slope of the Apennines in order to secure control over the needed highways called forth such violent local suspicions that the alliance began to show serious cracks.[23]

While the League was thus being weakened, confidence and influence rose steadily in the Visconti camp. In 1392-

93, immediately after the war with Florence, Giangaleazzo's Italian plans entered into one of their boldest
phases: the northern parts of the dominion of the Church
were to be transformed into a secular state—a *Regnum
Adriae*—to be ruled by Louis of Orléans, a member of
the royal house of France who had been married to
Giangaleazzo's daughter and could be relied upon to be
a docile ally in central Italy while, at the same time, establishing a link between Milan and France. When this ambitious scheme proved futile, Giangaleazzo turned for help
to another non-Italian power. In 1394-95 the German
king Wenceslaus was beginning to plan for the customary
Italian expedition to obtain the imperial crown in Rome;
before starting out, he looked for allies in the parts of Italy
through which his army was to pass. While Florence and
the League of Bologna declined, true to the old Guelph
distrust of association with the Empire, Giangaleazzo
made clever use of the opportunity. Wenceslaus, in need
of financial resources for the Italian adventure, sold to
the Visconti the title of Duke of Milan and Prince of the
Empire. In the political conditions of northern Italy,
where many of the smaller lords were trying to obtain
or had already obtained some lesser legal titles from the
Empire, this meant a considerable increase of authority for
the Milanese *signori* in their work of consolidating the
newly won possessions.

These were the auspices under which the Florentine-
Milanese struggle approached its climax when hostilities
were resumed in the so-called "Mantuan war" of the years
1397 and 1398. Florence was by now fully aware of the
significance of the situation and, in fact, held her own,
militarily, in the new phase. Milanese raids into the Florentine territory, and almost to the walls of the city, were
endured without detriment to Florentine morale, while
Florence's financial resources and technical inventiveness

were concentrated on foiling Giangaleazzo's efforts to destroy the vital bridge over the Po at Mantua and to
eliminate the strategic northwestern bastion of the League.
But the military successes of the allies were not enough to
offset the fact that the political balance had steadily been
inclining toward the Visconti side; and thus the war,
dragging along, did not prevent the crumbling of the dike
which Florence had maintained so laboriously during the
past half-score years.

Among the most serious odds that Florence had to face
was Venice's continued refusal to take her place in the shifting balance of power on the Peninsula. While Florence,
taught in the hard school of disappointments and immediate perils, was beginning to think in terms of mutual
interdependence and cooperation among the Italian states,
Venice continued to rely on her insular protection and her
ability to keep the furies of the mainland wars from her
doorstep by the short-range means of shrewd diplomatic
gambles. Toward the Florence-founded League of Bologna, Venice had always shown a friendly attitude, but for
as long as possible this friendship stopped short of active
participation. Only when, in spite of the early military
successes, the League's survival appeared more and more
in doubt, did Venice at last join her neighbor-states (early
in 1398) to repair the resilience of the weakened organism.
But after only a few months it became clear that, far from
changing the pattern of Venice's isolationist policy, the
purpose of her intercession was nothing but a calculated
maneuver. By throwing her friends into the lion's path
at the first favorable occasion, Venice hoped to lure the
danger away from her own house. Once her appearance on
the scene had proved to the Lord of Milan that any continued advance in the Northeast would force Venice to
intervene, the Venetian government proposed a compromise. Venice was to withdraw from the League on condi-

tion that Milan would allow the members of the League to live on as more or less independent buffer-states between the Milanese and the Venetian dominions. But the accord failed to provide any guarantee for the future safety of Tuscany, although Venice had been commissioned to negotiate in Florence's name; it stipulated only that Tuscan conquests made by both parties were to be relinquished. On this basis the Truce of Pavia was concluded in May 1398—a feat of Venetian diplomacy to which Florence had to agree unless she was ready to see the Milanese troops, now freed from any counter-weight in the East, continue the war in Tuscany with unrestricted resources.[24a]

What Venice had obtained was a revision both of the timetable and the direction of Milanese expansion. While the small states of the Northeast, saved from immediate incorporation in the Visconti State, were making the best of the situation by concluding special treaties with the victor, Giangaleazzo was at liberty to proceed with building up outright signories south of the Apennines in every place that did not formally belong to the Florentine territorial state. Within less than two years, the entire picture of the Italian inter-state situation was changed, even though the Florentine territory as such was not touched by force of arms. Within the area covered by the former League we find Gonzaga, Este, and Carrara breaking away, sooner or later, from the association with Bologna and Florence, and accepting the friendly hand extended by the Milanese Lord. Their example was quickly followed by the multitude of lesser independent potentates and towns along the Romagna slope of the Apennines. France, which in the past war had been associated with Florence, withdrew her help since the idea of a two-front war in alliance with Florence against Milan was now hopeless. In 1399, the representatives of the city-state of Pisa officially accepted Giangaleazzo as their lord; the separation of Florence from the sea, for which three generations of the Visconti had striven, seemed at last to be final. When in the summer of the same year Siena openly recognized Giangaleazzo's signory, a landslide started among the rest of the greater and lesser lords and communities in Tuscany. Lucca broke the obligations of her still existing league with Florence. Even Perugia in Umbria, finding herself too weak without the helping hand of a strong lord to cope with her desperate economic plight and with never-ending attacks from exiles and mercenaries, allowed herself to be lured by Milanese agents in spite of all Florentine efforts to bring help. A letter was sent to the former friend and ally on the Arno stating that the old, free Commune of Perugia, after so many tribulations, needed rest (*"ut hec civitas tam diu lacessita quiesceret"*), that putting one's liberty under a protector was not identical with falling into serfdom, that Giangaleazzo was Italy's savior from oppression and misery, and that if Florence really considered what was best for Tuscany and Italy, she, too, would voluntarily yield rather than wait until she was forced by "necessity." In a general assembly early in 1400, the citizens of Perugia recognized Giangaleazzo as *signore*.[24b]

By that time all of the important central-Italian inland places, including Cortona and Chiusi, Spoleto and Assisi, were in Viscontean hands; so was the entire coastal district in Florence's Southwest, with Massa and Grosseto its foremost bastions. The Florentine and Bolognese territories alone were left, like a larger and a smaller island surrounded by the Milanese flood. Barring a miracle, northern and central Italy seemed destined to form one monarchy in the century ahead.

Florentine statesmen were entirely aware that the struggle for Florence's independence, and the political crisis of Italy, had entered their eleventh hour. Early in 1400, when the catastrophic change of the map of Italy was an accomplished fact (although the Truce of Pavia had not yet been permanently legalized by a formal peace), a Florentine delegation was sent to Venice for a last attempt to recreate, through a coalition, a semblance of balance between the powers. According to their commission, the Florentine envoys were to declare before the Venetian government that only solidarity among the few remaining republics could save the Peninsula from universal tyranny. They should make a stand, their commission read, against the argument that the enemy of liberty would not live forever. The truth was, the envoys were to insist, that those who once lost their independence would hardly regain it, and that without continued co-operation even the survivors of today would not be able to live on to tomorrow. "To us it seems that all those in Italy who are anxious to live in freedom must band together, and must be interested in, and take care of, their mutual preservation. . . . For it is a mistake to believe that, if one of us should fail to survive, the other could defend his possessions." In the last analysis "the defense of Florence was also that of Venice." [25]

But by that time Venice, still entrusted with negotiating a peace with the victor in the name of both republics, had initiated a final accord on the basis of the existing conditions—the "Peace of Venice" which was signed by all parties in March of 1400.[26] From then on the Florentine Republic, protected no longer by membership in any league except for her alliance with Bologna, and enjoying that protection only so long as Bologna could avoid surrender, was left alone to confront one of those challenges of history in which a nation, facing eclipse or regeneration, has to prove its worth in a fight for survival.

Even in the spring of 1400, however, the moment of the final test had not yet come. The Florentine envoys to Venice had warned that if Venice was not ready to throw

her weight into the Italian balance, "this would mean
casting the Florentine people into despair; they would
feel wholly abandoned and left a prey to the Tyrant." [27a]
In the next one or two years the Florentines, indeed, might
justly have felt more lost, dejected, and alienated from
their precious heritage than in any other period of Florentine history. Abandoned by all her friends, the former
leader of the Guelph city-states, who in 1395 still had
scorned to extend a hand to King Wenceslaus, in 1401
found herself forced to look for the only possible aid in
the person of another German pretender to the Imperial
throne—the newly elected rival of Wenceslaus, Rupert of
the Palatinate. In trying to persuade him to come to Italy,
Guelph Florence learned to speak the language of the
Ghibellines, calling for the defeat of Giangaleazzo as a
"rebel against the Empire." [27b] When Rupert's army of
German knights crossed the Alps and appeared at the outlet of the valley of the Adige into the north-Italian plain,
everyone knew that the impending expedition through the
Peninsula had been prepared largely with Florentine
money. The Florentine Republic stood before the judgment seat of Italian opinion as the party guilty of having
called hated foreign men of arms from beyond the Alps.[28]
The victory of Giangaleazzo's Italian mercenaries over
these invaders—at Brescia, in October 1401, before they
could enter the Italian plain—was bound therefore to appear as a national triumph of Italian arms. It was proclaimed as such by Viscontean propaganda throughout
Italy. Not only was Florence's last hope gone for a new
battle line in the rear of the Visconti empire, but even in
the war of ideas which had accompanied the contest of
diplomacy and of arms, everything Florence had stood for
in her history was on the brink of destruction.[29]

The never-ceasing expansion of the Milanese empire
had been justified from the first by Italy's need for na-

tional strength and peace through unification by the power of one ruler. If one after another of the old city-states of northern and central Italy gave themselves up to the Visconti as Lord—even before the appearance of Milanese troops made this last step inevitable—the cause was not merely and not always expediency. In every Italian province and town there had been a pro-Viscontean group, inspired by Viscontean propaganda as well as Viscontean money.[30] Whereas in all preceding and later centuries the spirit of autonomy in Italian towns, and their pride in the glorious past of civic liberty, were loath to die, we hear of almost no protests in the name of liberty against the triumph of tyranny in the hectic decades of Giangaleazzo's advance—except in Florence. From all the occupied towns there was a steady accretion to the Milanese camp of writers and humanists who were ready to celebrate the Viscontean conquests as the long over-due and hoped-for defeat of particularism and unending strife.[31]

As early as the end of the 1380's, when the cities in the dominions of the Scaligeri and Carrara became Milanese, Antonio Loschi came from conquered Vicenza to voice the hope that Giangaleazzo's generals would join the dismembered parts of Italy together, and that henceforth the Milanese Lord "would rule Italy in peace."[32] From Padua came Francesco di Vannozzo, who in a symbolic *corona* of sonnets represented all the cities of Italy—including Padua and Venice, Bologna and Florence—as dreaming of an Italian kingdom with Rome as its capital and hailing Giangaleazzo as "the Messiah who has arrived" for Italy.[33] When finally, in 1401/02, Giangaleazzo seemed on the point of marching across the Apennines into the heart of central Italy, Saviozzo da Siena came from this old and proud Tuscan city-republic with sonnets that compared the Duke to Caesar encamped on the Rubicon before his march to Rome, and prayed for the success of

Giangaleazzo's enterprise "in the name of every true Italian" while deprecating "the detestable seed, enemy of quietude and peacefulness, which they call liberty." [34] From Giangaleazzo's entourage in Lombardy, Loschi (now in the ducal chancery) continued with manifestoes and poetry to drive home to the Italian public the Milanese claim that all the misery of war engendered by Giangaleazzo's expansion was the result of Florence's intrigues in resisting unification and peace; [35] while Giovanni de' Mussi, chronicler in nearby Piacenza, in passages which still rang in the ears of patriotic Italian historians of the nineteenth century, talked of the need for Lombardy and Tuscany to be under one "natural Lord," who also would annihilate the numberless local dynasts in the neighboring Papal State.[36] When the fortunes of Florence were at their lowest ebb, the Milanese humanist Uberto Decembrio advised the Florentines to recognize that waiting for help from others was vain. The only hope for the future, he said, for Florence no less than for the rest of the Peninsula, was under the rule of the Duke of Milan to rebuild "the State of Italy [*statum italicum*]" which once had been the lord of the world.[37]

In the decisive year 1402, this propaganda, which was effectively shaping Italian opinion, joined forces with the armed power of the Visconti which, freed from the last checks in the North, was ready to roll down to the South, across the Apennines, through the Florentine dominions, and possibly on to Rome. Under the impact of this avalanche the oldest and now only ally of Florence, Bologna, already torn by internal tyranny and strife, gave way. Even here, just as it had been with most other conquered cities, no military force was required to finish the job. After the defeat of the Florentine forces standing near Bologna, groups of the citizenry opposed to the government made a successful plot backed up by Milanese diplomatic help and Milanese money. In June 1402, Milanese troops were admitted into the town, and in July the elected representatives of the citizenry officially transferred the "dominium" of Bologna to the Visconti.

The passes across the Apennines, and practically the entire Florentine territory outside the capital, now lay without adequate means of defense before the Milanese armies. The Florentines expected any day to see the enemy before the gates. Italy, during the next few months, was full of rumors that Milanese troops had crossed the Florentine frontiers, and that the final act of the drama had begun. Yet Giangaleazzo did not give the signal for the attack. The precious weeks and months of the summer, which had to be used if the campaign was to be brought to its conclusion in 1402, passed in inaction. We have no documents that give the causes of Giangaleazzo's hesitation, but the reasons suggest themselves readily to anyone who weighs all the factors of the situation.[38] In Giangaleazzo's long political career, there had been few cases in which great cities had been attacked and taken by outright force. His method, of which he was a past master, had always been to throw over his victim a net woven of superior might and poignant propaganda, and then to wait until the certainty of doom, causing treachery and defection in the adversary's ranks, made minds and fortifications yield voluntarily to the new lord. After a long period of patient waiting, this method had just borne fruit in Bologna. It is readily understandable that Giangaleazzo clung to his tested policies when meeting his last and most dangerous foe; he did not wish to close with him before the ground was materially and morally prepared for a safe and quick success. Even if Florence should not in the end open her doors, as Bologna and Pisa, Siena and Perugia, Verona and Vicenza had done, she was in chains that were bound to chafe and in time to break her. Cut off, as she was, from the two seas, she was frustrated in her vital commercial exchange, surrounded on all sides by a circle of Milanese territories, distrusted and disliked by many of her former friends, who had been swayed by the peninsula-wide campaign for unification and contempt for city-state freedom.*

One cannot trace the history of this explosive stage in the genesis of the states-system of the Renaissance without being struck by its resemblance to events in modern history when unifying conquest loomed over Europe. In a like fashion, Napoleon and Hitler, poised on the coast of the English channel and made confident by their victories over every relevant power but one, waited for the propitious time for their final leap—until the historic moment had passed and unforeseen developments had upset the apparently inevitable course of fate. This is the only perspective from which one can adequately reconstruct the crisis of the summer of 1402 and grasp its material and psychological significance for the political history of the Renaissance, and in particular for the growth of the Florentine civic spirit.

The unforeseen event which in the autumn of the year 1402 changed everything on the Italian scene was epidemic and death. The plague, a constant threat in the age of the Renaissance, especially during long wars, began to ravage northern Italy in the hot summer of that year. In spite of all efforts of the Milanese government to conceal the grim news, it became more and more widely known in the

---

* Even Milanese official proclamations eventually threw off the mask of caution by clamoring for a monarchy with boundaries transcending northern Italy. In 1401, Giangaleazzo himself publicly avowed "that Tuscany and Lombardy should be joined into a single whole" ("*quod Tuscia cum Lombardia fiet unum et idem*"); and in May of 1402, his loyal city of Pavia declared that he was held to be "full worthy to wear the crown of all Italy" ("*totius Italie Diadematis non immerito digno*").[89]

course of September that the halt which the Viscontean army had made at the Florentine frontier had been a permanent halt: on September 3, Giangaleazzo himself had been carried off by the epidemic.

His death was the signal for the resurgence of all his subdued and frightened enemies. For the next fifteen or twenty years the State of the Visconti would once more be confined to the Lombard province around Milan—long enough to allow north and central Italy to lay the foundations for an equilibrium among the independent region-states quickened and hastened in their rise by the shock of the Giangaleazzo crisis.[40]

It is only natural that many Florentines of that period— the decades when civic Humanism came finally into its own—credited their almost miraculous salvation more to the brave stand which they alone had made than to the sudden removal of the tyrant from the scene. The objective historian may wonder as historians since Leonardo Bruni [41] have done, whether, if Giangaleazzo had lived, even Florence's firm will to resist would not have been in vain, and whether the Florentine war for independence might not have ended in something similar to the doom of the other Italian states. But for the climate of life, and for political opinion in Florence, the fact that the Republic had met the challenge bravely meant the difference between victory and defeat. In the middle of the fourteenth century, when tyranny had emerged as an internal threat in most of the Tuscan towns, Florence had had her tyrant in the person of the Duke of Athens; but she had quickly expelled him by a sudden outburst of the Florentine urge for liberty in a series of events to which it would be difficult to find a parallel in other Italian cities. When, about 1400, tyranny threatened civic freedom from the outside and all the other city-states succumbed, Florence again was unique in actively defending and maintaining her freedom.

Throughout the early Renaissance, Florentine character and thought were shaped by the memory of these two historic episodes.

But to return from the effects to the causes of the Florentine perseverance in the war: what ought we to think prompted Florence to hold out so determinedly at a time when no one could foresee that sudden death would undo the lifework of Giangaleazzo Visconti? One answer is that the experienced merchant-statesmen on the Arno must have discerned certain elements of hope beyond the seeming certainty of doom apparent to the average observer. In the first place, even if Florence was at that moment as helpless and comparatively easy a prey as never before in her history, conditions in the camp of the victor, too, were perilously overstrained. All documents which have come to light from the Milanese archives prove the truth of the conviction then held by leading Florentines that the Visconti State was approaching economic exhaustion through the ruinous over-taxation needed to keep large Milanese armies in the field through years and years of aggressive wars.[42] Also, the longer the final catastrophe was delayed, the greater was the chance that the remaining neutral powers, Venice and the Pope, would recover from their shock and eventually help to restore some sort of balance.

But once this has been noted it must also be said that any such reasoning and hope could not spring from cool diplomatic calculations alone, but required a measure of calm self-confidence and faith in native liberty and independence found nowhere else on the Peninsula in the summer of 1402. Whereas a wave of defeatism and treachery swept the ruling groups of the other Italian towns, a story of heroic defiance comes from Florence in the days when the news arrived of the destruction of the small Florentine force near Bologna (at Casalecchio, on

June 26th), indicating that Bologna was as good as lost, and that the Florentine territory lay open before the Viscontean army. True, among the masses of the Florentine city-population and even more among the peasants in the territory, there was no lack of discontent, as the chroniclers tell us.[43] But the reaction of the statesmen in the city-councils was different, and we can speak of it with assurance since the official minutes of a meeting on the day after Casalecchio are available.[44] The question then was whether to try to come to terms with the victor in some way, as all other Italian states had done, or to go on stubbornly with the few possible measures of defense: grant all-out military and financial authority to the officers in charge, provide for local defense by sending citizens as surveyors to the fortifications in the countryside, insure harmony and unity within the ruling group, and step up the efforts to obtain outside help, especially from Venice. These measures, in fact, and no thought of surrender, were advocated by two of the leaders, Filippo de' Corsini and Maso degli Albizzi, and supported generally by the council; there was a feeling in the air of the decisive historic import of the hour. "In adversity *virtus* is put to the test; therefore, we should show audacity and strength, although things at Bologna have gone against us," runs Filippo de' Corsini's comment. "Even though the troops which we had at Bologna are destroyed, we must courageously go on," is Maso degli Albizzi's advice.[45] And similarly all others in the group: "We should not fear, but resist with courage"; "let our minds not be subdued, but roused." There is no chance for compromise, says one of the counselors; "we have long been at war with the lords of Milan, and there will never be peace until one side is destroyed; therefore, we must react bravely and without despondency." [46]

These calls for courage and audacity were not intended to belittle the ultimate gravity of the situation. If it was argued that the Milanese threat could not go on indefinitely for economic reasons, it was also true that Florence, too, was facing economic catastrophe, entirely cut off as she was from the outside world, her industry and trade paralyzed for many years.[47] The only question was which of the two opponents would be the first to suffer economic collapse, and the decision depended partly on the extent to which the Florentine merchants were ready to go on sacrificing their resources in this duel. Strong will and faith were needed also in their efforts to persuade Venice and the Pope to intervene, in spite of the unbroken chain of disappointments in the preceding years. There were signs, it is true, that these two remaining neutrals were beginning to grow genuinely alarmed after the fall of Bologna. But when Florence in the late summer sent envoys to Rome, they made the dismaying discovery that Giangaleazzo was once more trying to buy off a neutral's intervention with a *divide-et-impera* deal. There were rumors of a Papal-Milanese understanding, based on a proposed return of Perugia to the Papal State and on Papal recognition of the Milanese occupation of Bologna.[48] Venice, on the other hand, now offered an alliance to Florence. But this ray of hope, too, quickly disappeared upon closer contact between the two powers. Venice demanded that she was to have a free hand in negotiating with Milan in Florence's name, and consequently the situation that had led to the calamities of the Truce of Pavia in 1398 and of the Peace of Venice in 1400 would have been repeated. Florence declined the help offered with this condition.[49]

From whatever side we approach Florentine conduct in 1402 we are thus led to the conclusion that, in the hour of crisis, moral and ideological forces were at work to help the Florentines to pursue a course different from that of the rest of Italy. In all the other old Italian city-republics, readiness to obey a unifying "new Caesar" made citizens and publicists forget their pride in a past of independence and civic freedom. In Florence, in the summer of 1402, this pride became more vigorous than ever at a unique moment unparalleled in her history: one city-republic face to face with one despotic monarchy, in one of those rare historic situations when all compromises are swept away in the concentration of every political and intellectual resource on a single goal. When the crisis had passed, the real issue of the Florentine-Milanese contest stood revealed: out of the struggle had come the decision that the road was to remain open to the civic freedom and the system of independent states which became a part of the culture of the Italian Renaissance. Five and a half perilous years had gone by since that spring of 1397 when Milanese troops had invaded and ravaged the Florentine countryside. There had been moments when everything seemed lost, when Florentine policy seemed to have broken faith with its own precepts; but the final year of the war, and the outcome of the contest, had fulfilled every hope and justified every claim Florence had held and made since 1390.[50]

One should expect that Humanism, imported to the city on the Arno one or two generations earlier, would become fused with the civic world in the crucible of these great events. Yet little, if anything at all, has been told in modern narratives of the effects of this experience on the humanistic attitude. The reason why this interplay is difficult to grasp, and remains partly concealed from us at the present state of our knowledge, will become apparent as our analysis unfolds; only gradually shall we be able to bring into focus the varied elements needed for an adequate reconstruction.

Even at this point, however, one of these elements can be recognized. The same twelve years in which the Florentine Republic fought her struggle for independence against Giangaleazzo also saw the rise of some of the basic tenets of the historical outlook of the Florentine Renaissance. At that time the role of city-state independence and civic liberty, in the past as well as the present, emerged in a new light.

CHAPTER 3

A NEW VIEW OF ROMAN HISTORY
AND OF THE FLORENTINE PAST

WHENEVER the genesis of humanistic classicism at the turn of the Trecento is analyzed,
the *Dialogi ad Petrum Paulum Histrum* by
Leonardo Bruni is looked upon as the birth-certificate of a
new period.*

On the first day of the conversations depicted in Bruni's
book as held in the house of old Coluccio Salutati and

* Both possible forms of Bruni's first name—"Leonardo"
and (dialectical) "Lionardo"—were used during the fifteenth
century. Now that modern historiography has begun to remember most humanists under their civil, vernacular names instead
of their Neo-Latin pen-names, we need a stable name-form.
The survival, among Bruni students, of both forms points to
the fact that in most contemporaneous and later sources—literary as well as documentary—he was called neither "Leonardo
Bruni" nor "Lionardo Bruni" but "Leonardus Aretinus."
This suggests the wiser choice: a writer known over the centuries as "Leonardus Aretinus" and sometimes even "Leonardus Brunus" will be named "Leonardo Bruni" more fittingly
than "Lionardo Bruni." Other considerations concur with this
decision. In the case of Leonardo da Vinci, modern scholars
have gradually decided in favor of "Leonardo." There is little
sense in talking of "Lionardo Bruni" while saying "Leonardo
da Vinci." This lead has been already followed in Italian scholarship. No one in Italy, to my knowledge, has recently used
any other name than "Leonardo Bruni." This is the form that
also appears in virtually all encyclopedias outside Italy, including
the *Britannica*. Since choose we must, there seems to be no
question what the choice should be.

conducted in the young author's presence, Niccolò Niccoli proclaims the program which initiated the ascendency of the critical-philological spirit of the Quattrocento. How, Niccoli queries, could Scholasticism have succeeded in its attempt to create a valid philosophy based on the authority of the ancients, and in particular of Aristotle, when the works of these professed guides were known imperfectly, and distorted to absurdity by barbaric translations? Until the ancient sources flow clear again, all efforts must be directed with single-mindedness to the task of recovering the classical languages and the genuine readings of the ancient works.

But the same *Dialogi* do not only usher in the new humanistic philology; together with Bruni's *Laudatio Florentinae Urbis* they also record the birth of a new civic sentiment and a new attitude toward the past.[1]

Republicanism versus Dante's Glorification of Caesar

If a full acquaintance with ancient literature and command of the Ciceronian language are accepted as the measure of genuine culture, dark shadows are bound to fall on Dante and his work. And since, furthermore, his political and historical views had been shaped by the medieval idea of universal monarchy, which in Florence's struggle for liberty was beginning to look obsolete, Dante, too, had to be included in the indictment against the centuries soon to be called the Middle Ages.

Yet, Dante had long been the greatest pride of Florence. His poem had captured the imagination of every Florentine citizen; he was the founder of the Florentine language, which was just starting out on its triumphal conquest of Italy. Even though his classical scholarship was faulty in the eyes of the new century, and even though in the *Inferno* he had shown himself a bad judge of history by placing Rome's deliverers from Caesar in the maw of Lucifer, side by side with Judas Iscariot (these are the charges made by Niccoli in the *Dialogi*),[2] still any depreciation of Dante by the classical humanists would have meant an irreparable loss to the continuity of the Florentine tradition.

On the second day of the conversations, therefore, the *Dialogi* make an attempt to show why it is that the cleavage, which has opened up between the world of Dante and the new outlook, did not have to entail a disavowal of the poet who had founded Florentine tradition. As to Dante's greatest offense, his treatment of the Roman republicans, the solution is proposed that Dante had availed himself of historical figures only to serve the ends of his poetical imagination, without actually taking sides with Caesar's tyranny against the last defenders of civic freedom. For is it not true, Niccoli is made to argue in the second dialogue, that Virgil transformed Dido, purest of women, into a love-crazed creature who throws her life away because of passion? Just so we must understand, and forgive, the liberties Dante has taken with the historical figures of Brutus and Cassius. "Or are we to believe that Dante, the most learned man of his age, did not know in what manner Caesar achieved dominion—that he did not know of the rape of liberty, the abject fear of the people when Marc Anthony placed the crown on Caesar's head? Do you believe he did not know what *virtus* Brutus possessed in the judgment of all historical tradition? . . . Dante knew it well, he knew it precisely—but he presented to us, in the image of Caesar, the legitimate prince and most just monarch of the world, and, in the image of Brutus, the rebellious, troublesome villain who criminally murdered this prince. Not because Brutus was such a man; had he been such a one, how could he have been praised

by the Senate as the restorer of liberty? But the poet took
this material as the subject of his poem because Caesar, in
whatever manner, had wielded royal power, and because
Brutus, together with more than sixty of the noblest citizens, had slain him." [3] This interpretation achieved two
purposes at once: no reproach needed to be cast upon Dante
because of the political convictions he had held, and yet a
new set of values could triumph over the Empire conception of the *Divine Comedy*.

Now this solution is not just an oddity characteristic of
Bruni's private views. Like the program of learning and
classicism set forth by the *Dialogi*, this new view of Dante
introduced what was to be a typical reaction in Florence
for many years to come. When Cristoforo Landino in the
1470's composed the basic Dante commentary of the Florentine Renaissance, he, too, declared that it was entirely in
order for Dante to punish Brutus and Cassius, the traitors
of the *"imperadore et monarca humano,"* like Judas, the
traitor of the *"imperadore divino,"* but that a special word
of explanation was needed "lest anybody should make the
mistake to think that Dante wanted to condemn Brutus." [4]
With Bruni, Landino insisted that Dante's Caesar did not
represent the historical Caesar but symbolized the Empire
of the world, and that his Brutus and Cassius were not
the historical Romans but assassins of the true universal
ruler. It was no use, Landino said, to try to avoid this
interpretation by arguing that Dante, while passing his
verdict, had been favorably inclined toward the historical
Caesar because he remembered Caesar's personal greatness
and his victorious campaigns waged for Rome through half
of Europe. The historical Caesar was killed, not because
anyone begrudged him his victories, but because "with the
utmost nefariousness he deprived the *patria* of her liberty." [5] "And surely, it would have been extraordinary
cruelty, and one entirely foreign to the wisdom and sense

of equity of Dante, the great poet, to inflict eternal punishment of such severity upon those who had gone to meet
death out of a most fervent devotion, in order to deliver
their country from the yoke of servitude by a deed for
which, had they been Christians, they would have won
the most honored seats in the highest heaven. . . . Let us
consult the laws of any well-constituted republic, and we
shall find them to decree no greater reward to anyone
than to the man who kills the tyrant." [6] And so, half seriously and half in jest, Landino concludes with this parallel: Of Emperor Trajan it has been told that "his justice
moved Pope Gregory to such compassion that Gregory
with prayers, foreseen by God, caused the emperor to be
raised from damnation to the highest bliss. I find no difficulty in believing that someone else whose prayers were
acceptable to God may have done the same for Brutus." [7a]

In these remarkable passages of Landino's Commentary, which were read by practically every literate Florentine of the later Renaissance, the one element different
from Bruni's arguments is a greater openness of mind
toward the Christian medieval aspect of the Empire concept, an aspect of which the pioneer generation of the early
Quattrocento had lost sight so completely that Dante's
treatment of Caesar had seemed to Bruni nothing but an
arbitrary product of a poet's fancy. But the vigor with
which the citizen's faith in freedom refuses to accept literally Dante's monarchical creed is as strong in Landino
as it had been in Bruni.

To the very end of Florentine liberty, the controversy
stirred by Bruni's *Dialogi* continued to reverberate among
Florentine citizens. A generation after Landino, Niccolò
Machiavelli, when composing his republican-spirited *Discourses*, felt even more embittered at the thought of the
injustice done to Brutus. To Machiavelli, the scene with
Brutus in the maw of Lucifer appeared to be one of the

products of Dante's reckless political passions "that blinded him so much as to make him lose all prudence, learning, and good judgment, and become an entirely different sort of person." [7b]

Thirty years later, in 1546, after the fall of the Republic, two of the most famous Florentines who had participated in the last fight for Florence's liberty met in Rome during their exile—Michelangelo Buonarroti, who during the war had supervised Florence's fortification system, and Donato Giannotti, once the secretary of the *Ten* who had directed the defense of the city. Their talk, one day, produced a striking conclusion to the development that had had its beginning in Salutati's and Bruni's circle one hundred and fifty years earlier. We have a small book of *Dialoghi* from Giannotti's pen which, it would seem, reflects the gist of an actual conversation between Giannotti and Michelangelo on one of their walks over the hills of Rome.[8] According to these dialogues, Michelangelo on that occasion tried to defend his beloved poet, Dante, against Giannotti's strictures. Almost a century and a half after Bruni, Michelangelo was still satisfied to adhere to the view that Dante had used Caesar and his enemies as symbols of the Empire and its traitors without wishing to condemn the historical Brutus; but he found it difficult to argue the case against Giannotti's republican feelings which were still raw from the past struggle. I will not doubt, Giannotti says to Michelangelo, that Dante in deciding upon the punishment in Lucifer's maw thought of the violators of the imperial dignity and not of historical Brutus and Cassius. But why did Dante invent his meeting with Caesar, distinguished by his "piercing look," in Limbo? Did this Caesar, described in such personal detail, also mean the *"majestas imperii"* and not the historical Caesar of flesh and blood? [9]

Landino, we have seen, had given expression to the

lingering tension behind the attempted reconciliation, by saying half-jokingly that he wished someone had done for Brutus what St. Gregory's prayer had done for Trajan in delivering him from Hell. Now, at the end of Florentine freedom, the same sally was turned against Caesar himself by a generation which hated tyranny more fiercely than Landino, the friend of Lorenzo de' Medici, had. For Giannotti ends by saying with a sigh that, however much might be conceded to poetic symbolism, it hurt too grievously to see Caesar in Limbo, while Brutus and Cassius were suffering in Lucifer's maw; the crime of suppressing the freedom of one's country deserved the deepest pit of Hell, and he, Giannotti, wished he could put Caesar in that place, "if he is not already there." [10]

The half-forgotten page from the history of the Renaissance controversy over Dante that we have thus restored * sheds unexpected light on the relationship of Bruni's *Dialogi* to the subsequent course of civic thought in Flor-

* As in the case of many political and historical themes of the Florentines, this page might be concluded with a Venetian epilogue. A glimpse of the Italian literary scene during the Cinquecento shows that the most widely read mid-sixteenth-century commentator on Dante, Alessandro Vellutello of Lucca, whose commentary was published in 1544, had returned to the defense of Dante's verdict on Brutus with a fervid eulogy of Caesar. But Trifone Gabriele, Venetian citizen and well-known writer of the early sixteenth century, who was connected with the Florentine school through his friendship with Giannotti, still adhered to the old Florentine criticism of Dante, if without the patriotic respect of the fifteenth-century Florentines for their great compatriot. "Dante was greatly wrong," Gabriele commented in his *Annotazioni*, "in placing Brutus and Cassius in the *Inferno* . . . because of Caesar's murder. For in truth, as Landino says, on this account they should have been put on the highest seats in paradise. But Dante was too much a partisan of the Empire, and too intent on flattering that party." [11]

ence. Without a knowledge of the later comments on the Dante interpretation proposed in Bruni's second dialogue, one might be doubtful about the significance, or even the seriousness, of Bruni's proposition. Against the background just established, however, it is obvious that Bruni's youthful work made the first attempt to reconsider Dante's politico-historical philosophy through Quattrocento eyes and with a citizen's attitude. It suddenly created an approach unknown to the Trecento, but so congenial to the feeling of the Renaissance that the republican modification of Dante's verdict on Caesar and his assassins remained a lasting strand of Florentine thought down to the Cinquecento.

A Vindication of the Roman Republic in Leonardo Bruni's Earliest Works

The Dante episode in the *Dialogi* is only the most conspicuous expression of a new view of the past and of a fervent partisanship for civic freedom that are both characteristic of Bruni at the time of the Florentine struggle with Giangaleazzo. True, the debates depicted in the *Dialogi* are principally concerned with a new program of culture and scholarship and offer few opportunities for the discussion of historical and political themes. But in the opening scene of the second day great emphasis is placed on the fact that Bruni's *Laudatio*, not much earlier, had established a new historical view of Florence's Guelph heritage. In the *Laudatio*, so the speakers of the *Dialogi* agree, the medieval Guelph-Ghibelline struggle had rightly been looked upon as a revival of the antagonism between the defenders of the free Roman Republic and the Caesars, and this reinterpretation, they concur, had been borne out by Bruni's vigorous criticism of Caesar and the tyrannical rule of his successors.[12] In the *Laudatio*, Bruni

had indeed drawn the first elaborate historical picture of
the destruction of the *virtus Romana* by imperial autocracy
after the end of republican freedom.

This is not to say that there had never before been an
interpretation of Roman history with the emphasis on the
Republic rather than on the Empire. The civic sentiment
in the Tuscan city-states had made itself felt as early as the
thirteenth century. At that time Ptolemy of Lucca, the
author of *Gesta Tuscorum* (Tuscan annals drawn from
Florentine and Lucchese sources),[13] had continued the unfinished *De Regimine Principum* of his teacher Aquinas,
and the parts he added showed an astonishing openness of
mind toward the role played by free city-republics in the
ancient world. Ptolemy, at that early date, had formed the
clear-cut judgment that the power of Rome had been
built up under the consuls and free councils of the Republic, when "no one among the Roman leaders wore a
crown or was adorned with the purple, for his personal
glorification." [14]

Subsequently, about the middle of the Trecento, Petrarch in his *Africa* had ventured a condemnation of the
Roman emperors; in this case the censure sprang from a
combination of humanistic motives with the impassioned
Italian sentiment that developed under the impress of the
decay of the German Empire and the advance of Italian
culture. The name "Africa" alone suggests that the historical interest was turning in a new direction. The subject
of Petrarch's epic is the struggle between Scipio Africanus
Maior and Hannibal, and the final victory of Rome over
Carthage at Zama. Whereas the Middle Ages had seen
the climax of Roman history either in the time of Augustus, under whose reign Christ was born, or of Caesar,
the founder of the Empire to whom the founding also
of countless local states and cities was traced, the imagination of the humanist found a new focus in the Romans of

republican times. To the Petrarch of the *Africa* these times appear as the *"meliora tempora"* that followed the period of the Roman kings. With the assassination of the last king by the elder Brutus "the freedom of our era begins"—the freedom of Scipio's days. The "flowering times of men powerful in battle" emerge with the Republic.[15]

Closely related in spirit to this central theme of Petrarch's epic is a survey of the later course of Roman history which is fitted into the poetic narrative of the *Africa* by the device of a dream-vision looking into the future.[16] The highlight of this excursus falls on Pompey, champion of the Senate against Caesar. Of Caesar, the short, hard statement is made that he, greatest of conquerors, would have been the happiest of mortals if he had known how to limit his passion for power. But "the wretched man could not"; "how shamefully vain ambition tramples on everything!" "He turned his ever-victorious hands against the flesh and blood of his own commonwealth, and stained his triumphs over foreign enemies with the blood of citizens." [17] The *Imperium* that Caesar founded emerges in the *Africa* almost exclusively in its darker aspects. Its throne—so runs the dream prophecy—would be occupied in the name of Rome by foreigners from all lands, and with the intrusion of foreign blood Roman morality and Roman *virtus* will perish apace. "The sceptre and the dignity of the Empire, won by us with so much sweat—foreigners will steal it, men of Spanish or African origin. Who can bear this rise of the scum of the world to the highest dignity—of people who were spared by the sword for ignominious survival? . . . The Empire will always be called *Romanum Imperium;* but the Roman will not always hold the reins. . . . In the end, the power will fall to the North"—to the Frankish and German kings.[18]

These few illustrations of an early emphasis on the *Respublica Romana* (there are not many other examples that could be added to Ptolemy and Petrarch) show that the occasional deviations from the medieval view during the Trecento had not yet come close to any coherent historical critique of the institution of the Empire. However clearly the republican and constitutional ideals of the Tuscan communes had been expressed by Ptolemy, a new appreciation, or rather depreciation, of the *Imperium Romanum* is lacking in his *De Regimine Principum*. And the well-informed arguments against the Empire, which in many ancient authors were waiting to be revived by the humanists, had not yet been adopted by Petrarch. The motive which prompted Petrarch to object in his *Africa* to Caesar's founding of imperial monarchy is Italian nationalism—of a rather narrow sort, a kind of racial nationalism—and not yet a comparison of the contrasting effects that *Respublica* and *Imperium* may have had on Roman *virtus* and Roman culture. Consequently, neither Ptolemy's communal republicanism nor Petrarch's poetical reevocation of the age of Scipio contributed much to a weakening of the centuries-old faith in the necessity of God-willed universal monarchy or the mythical splendor of its founder, Caesar. Immediately after Ptolemy, Dante offered a new defense of Empire and Monarchy; and Petrarch in his later years, and certainly after conceiving the *Africa*, wrote a *History of Caesar (De Gestis Cesaris)*—his most mature historical work—in which hardly a trace of his former censure of the Empire is visible. We shall learn in later chapters that even during the last decades of the Trecento every attempt to make a new approach to the memories of pre-imperial Rome was followed by similar reversals. Broadly speaking, we may even say that there was a recrudescence of the tendency to maintain the ideal of a pacifying universal Empire, because the need

for a superior judge and overlord seemed to be proved
by the unrest of a century in which the lesser Italian states
were waging an ever more hopeless battle for survival
while the tyranny of the Renaissance began to show the
advantages of large-scale monarchy over city-state freedom.

Bruni's criticism of imperial monarchy reveals itself in
all its historical significance and originality when it is seen
in contrast to these features of the preceding century. His
critical approach to the institution of the Empire was bound
to change the climate of Florentine historical thinking immediately; it was by no means simply a more resolute
resumption of the ideas of Ptolemy, or Petrarch, or of any
other medieval opponent to the Empire.[19] In the *Laudatio,*
the criterion for judging the Roman Republic and the
Roman Empire is the presumed effect of the rule of the
emperors on the *virtus Romana*—the psychological impact of the Empire on the energies of the Roman people.
The Republic, Bruni suggests, had seen eminent talents
in every field of endeavor, but "after the republic had been
subjected to the power of one man, those brilliant minds
vanished, as Cornelius [Tacitus] says." [20]

This judgment was something new—and something
which until Bruni's day had been unimaginable—not only
as an expression of humanistic and civic sentiment, but also
because it rested on a new source of information. The statement of Tacitus to which Bruni referred had only recently
become accessible. It is found in the *Historiae,* in the introductory chapter which had not been known to the
Middle Ages. The famous Tacitus manuscript of the first
half of the eleventh century, which includes the first books
of the *Historiae* and the second half of the *Annales* and
is our basic text to this date, had come to light one generation earlier in the old library of Montecassino and had
been brought to Florence where Boccaccio was the first to

study it.[21] In the second half of the fourteenth century, these texts, which were to influence all historical studies during the Renaissance, came to be known to a small number of scholars. Before the century had ended, Benvenuto Rambaldi da Imola in Bologna had a copy available for consultation; in Florence, the original Montecassino manuscript was studied by Salutati's friend Domenico Bandini d'Arezzo, and it finally came into the possession of Bruni's closest friend, Niccoli.[22] Thus it is not surprising that Bruni was familiar with Tacitus at an early date, and from the beginning could base his approach to Roman history on this source of which even Petrarch had still been ignorant.

But Tacitus' appraisal of imperial Rome could be read with very different eyes. It is well known that his acceptance of the imperial monarchy as an historical necessity and his penetrating psychology of autocratic rulers became a guide for monarchical publicists in the period of sixteenth and seventeenth century absolutism. Bruni, in picking the quoted reference from the *Historiae*, selected one possible facet of Tacitus' views, one which in Tacitus' eyes reflected only a secondary effect of the coming monarchy. On this basis Bruni generalized; he gave a wide historical meaning to observations that had been of less significance in Tacitus' own interpretation. The introductory phrase of the *Historiae*, "after the battle of Actium, when the interests of peace required that all power be concentrated in the hands of one man, those great minds disappeared," [23] referred exclusively to the course of Roman historiography, in which Tacitus wished to determine his own place. Historiography, Tacitus wanted to point out, had been stunted in its growth ever since freedom of opinion had disappeared, and so the task of giving an unvarnished account of the post-republican era was still to be performed. To Bruni, the "vanishing of brilliant minds" [24] became a general historical verdict on the effects of the imperial government; it left an indelible impression on him.* When, in 1415, Bruni returned to the analysis of Roman history in the first book of his *Historiae Florentini Populi,* one of his chief concerns, as at the time of his early contacts with Tacitus, was still to establish the causes for the exhaustion and degeneration of Rome under the Empire.[25b]

In this wider historical context, the appraisal of Caesar played a major part.

Dante in his *Commedia,* and Petrarch in the Caesar biography written in his later years, had provided an important epilogue to the medieval admiration for the founder of the Empire by discovering from ancient sources Caesar's personal greatness.[26] In Bruni's own time, not long before the composition of the *Laudatio,* Coluccio Salutati in his treatise *De Tyranno* had enlarged upon a further feature, also first worked out by Petrarch: the attempt to prove, by a political analysis of the condition of Rome toward the end of the Republic, that in Caesar's day Rome had become ripe for the rule of one man.[27]

In opposition to these trends among Trecento writers, Bruni's *Laudatio* prefers to point to the later fate of the Empire. In spite of their personal greatness and virtues, Bruni argues, Caesar and Augustus instituted the tyrant-

---

* It did so also on Poggio and influenced Pier Candido Decembrio, as will be seen presently. According to an apposite statement made by Jürgen von Stackelberg within the framework of a comprehensive history of Tacitus' influence: in view of the thus reconstructed facts, "the history of the reception of Tacitus can no longer be described as a simple curve from a period of monarchical interpretations of Tacitus to a later period of anti-monarchical interpretations. We must rather divide this history into three phases." During the first, in Florence about 1400—brief and initial though it was—"the voice of Tacitus," as can now be seen, "was already thought to be one of freedom—a republican voice in the political debate." [25a]

rule which was eventually to transform the character of the Roman people. Even if their own tyrannical deeds were matched by their achievements and, in a personal account, might be forgiven, still "we cannot forget that you have cleared the way for such evils and crimes as your successors . . . committed." [28]

The Thesis of the Foundation of Florence by Republican Rome

It is a dark picture of imperial crime and violence in Rome which is painted in the *Laudatio*. The hate of monarchy, thus aroused, is then exploited for Bruni's second thesis: that the foundation of the city of Florence by the Romans took place before the baneful effects of despotic rule had debased the character of the Roman people. The fact that Florence had been founded earlier than the "vanishing of brilliant minds" noted by Tacitus, will "make it understood," Bruni argues, "that this colony was conducted hither when the city of Rome saw her power, liberty, gifted minds, and the fame of her citizens in their greatest flower." It was the time when the Republic had proved itself superior to Carthage, Numantia, and Corinth. "Inviolate, unshaken, and still thriving was the freedom of which Rome was deprived by the most wicked thieves not long after this colony had been established here. The result, I think, has been the situation which we have seen developing most perfectly in this city, in the past as well as at present; namely the fact that the Florentine people rejoice in every kind of liberty and stoutly show themselves the enemies of tyrants." [29]

Like the criticism of Caesar and his successors, the claim of the pre-imperial origin of Florence could not have been made much before the time of the *Laudatio*. During the Middle Ages Florence, like so many places in Italy and

Europe, had gloried in tracing her origin to Caesar, founder
of the Empire. Indeed, the medieval *Storie di Cesare* and
Fatti di Cesare had nowhere found a more receptive soil
than in Tuscany and especially in Florence.[30] Caesar, those
medieval legends ran, had pursued Catilina and the remnants of his rebel army to Fiesole in the hills north of
Florence, had conquered the old town, and had founded
Florence on the Arno as a counterpoise to the rebellious
mountain fastness; afterwards, Caesar received valuable aid
from the new colony.[31] We still meet this story, though
with changes in detail, in Giovanni Villani's chronicle,[32]
and even during the second half of the Trecento it was
upheld tenaciously because the glory of Florence seemed to
hinge on the descent from Caesar. In 1381/82, Filippo
Villani, in the first version of his *On the Origin of the City
of Florence*, once again repeated the story in detail; so
firmly was he convinced of its truth that in the chapter devoted to the biography of Dante (*De Vita et Moribus
Dantis*) he traced the poet's family to the noble Roman
colonists who had settled "when the city of Florence was
founded by Caesar." [33]

By the time of Filippo Villani, it is true, humanistic criticism had already begun the task of dissolving the traditional stories of the Middle Ages by rational argument,
armed with the new knowledge of the original sources.
But when we examine the treatment of the saga of Florence
in the most important work representing this phase of late
Trecento thought, Benvenuto Rambaldi da Imola's Commentary on the *Divina Commedia* written around 1380,[34]
we quickly realize that the growing refusal to accept the
popular medieval legends was still something very different
from the subsequent positive thesis that Florence had been
founded when the *Respublica Romana* was in its flower. In
commenting on Dante's adherence to the opinion that Florence hailed from no lesser founder than Caesar, Benvenuto

compares the traditional story of Florence with the traditional stories of Ravenna, Genoa, Venice, and Naples, all of which include alleged foundation of a similar kind. One wonders with amusement, says Benvenuto, "how Caesar should have had time for founding the most famous cities during the pernicious conspiracy [of Catilina] while he was himself under the imputation of having taken part in it" and, according to Q. Cicero, had difficulty in justifying his personal conduct. "And why would the Romans have needed so much time to take the city of Fiesole" in an era when they conquered half the world? "Further, how could the Florentines be among Caesar's allies when Florence was only just beginning to exist?" [35] The outcome of these critical arguments was scepticism. "Thus who founded Florence is unknown to me." It might be that Pliny is correct in his indication of Fiesole as the origin of Florence; "but when, how, by whom [the foundation took place], I confess I know not." [36]

Only two decades later, Florentine citizens, in their keen desire to reconstruct the history of their native city, had solved the problem to which Benvenuto Rambaldi knew no answer. About the time when Bruni in his *Laudatio* was jubilant that Florence was the offspring of the Roman Republic and not of a period when Rome began to obey emperors, Florentine humanists, studying the ancient sources, established in a fashion convincing to their contemporaries the exact historical conditions under which the colony on the Arno had come into being: it was the victorious Roman army under Sulla whose veterans had been settled in the area of Florence not long after the beginning of the first century B.C.

The humanist to whom this work of historical reconstruction was chiefly due was Salutati, the chancellor, who arrived at the theory that Florence was founded by veterans of Sulla, by searching carefully in all classical sources for the early conditions of the Arno valley, in particular the information in the *Bellum Catilinae* of Sallust and in Cicero's second oration against Catilina.[37a] As will emerge from later observations, the result—one of the first mature attainments of the historical scholarship of Humanism—did not become complete until a few years after 1400.[37b]

We may, then, note: both the republican interpretation of Roman history and the view of Florence as the physical descendant, and heir to the political mission, of the *Respublica Romana* were novel elements in the historical thought of the Renaissance at the time when the *Laudatio* and the *Dialogi* were written.

Prelude to the Historical Philosophy of the Florentine Renaissance

The two historical discoveries thus summarized were elements of promise and permanence—they had produced ideas which, along with the reinterpretation of Dante's verdict on Caesar, Brutus, and Cassius, were to remain integral parts of the outlook of the Renaissance. When we compare the historical sketch drawn in Bruni's *Laudatio* with the picture of Roman and medieval history in the first book of his *History of the Florentine People* (written in 1415), we find that the basic pattern of his thought had remained unchanged. It still was woven of two strands of interest: to establish the center of the history of the ancient world in the rise and fall of civic freedom and energy; and to understand the freedom of the Florentine city-republic as a resumption of the work accomplished in ancient city-states.

This is not to say that every fiber of the final texture had been prepared in the *Laudatio*. By the time Bruni wrote the introductory book of his *History*, a basic new factor, still absent from the *Laudatio*, had been added by the discovery of the part the Etruscan city-states played in pre-Roman times. A realization that Italy, and in particular ancient Etruria, had been covered with independent city-states, and that much of this flowering life was subdued by Rome's ascendancy but rose again after the destruction of the *Imperium Romanum*—this wider vista was needed before a ripe dynamic concept of history could emerge, and before the idea of a God-willed universal Empire, transcending history, could be overthrown by a realistic vision of historical growth and decay. But an indispensable factor in this displacement of the dogma of *Roma Aeterna* was the criticism of the effects the imperial monarchy had had on the vital energies of the Roman people. As far as this criticism is concerned, the pioneering ideas of the *Laudatio* remained an integral part of Bruni's outlook as it was set forth definitely in his *History of the Florentine People*.

Bruni's ascription to Florence of the role of heir to the city-state freedom of the ancient world developed in the same two stages. Here, too, his views did not reach maturity until, in his *History*, he had discovered the significance of urban Etruria. The recognition that Tuscany had originally been a country of civic freedom and had reassumed this character after the end of the Roman Empire, explained to him why Florence and Tuscany at the present time formed the region of the greatest city-state independence and the strongest love of liberty. But the approach from this angle alone could not account for the emergence of Florence as the metropolis of modern Tuscany despite the fact that she was the youngest of the Tuscan city-states. Again the Etruscan theory remained in need of supplementation by the ideas first aired in the *Laudatio*: namely, that, in addition to their Etruscan ancestry, the Florentines had coursing through their veins the blood of free Roman citizens which helped to shape their history of freedom; and that Guelphism, in which Florence had assumed leadership, was continuing the fight for the cause for which the Roman republicans had stood.[38]

All these seminal ideas of the *Laudatio* not only were preserved in Bruni's own later work, but they remained characteristic of Florentine thought to the late Renaissance.

The fact of the lasting influence of these ideas needs no detailed illustration with regard to the republican interpretation of Roman history and the bitter criticism of the Roman emperors. During the early Renaissance, Florentine writers are clearly distinguished by these tenets from non-Florentine writers; and where the new historical outlook is found later on outside of Florence as well, it can usually be traced to Florentine sources.[39] The most familiar episode of this kind in mid-Quattrocento humanistic history is the controversy on Caesar and the *Respublica Romana* between Poggio the Florentine and Guarino the courtier humanist in the Ferrara of the Este.[40] The direct connection between these discussions, begun in 1435, and the *Laudatio* is obvious, because the pivot on which the controversy ultimately turned was again the idea—first developed by Bruni in the *Laudatio* under the inspiration of Tacitus—that "the brilliant minds," and with them the cultural energy of Rome, had vanished before the absolutism of the emperors. Cicero and even more Seneca— so Poggio resumes and sharpens the reasoning of the *Laudatio*—already sensed the decay of Roman culture in their day; but Tacitus' authoritative verdict is bound to silence once and for all the admirers of Caesar and of Roman monarchy. As Poggio sums up his observations: "From the words of Seneca in which he states that brilliant minds had been born in the age of Cicero, but later had declined and deteriorated; and from the testimony of Tacitus who asserts that those brilliant minds disappeared

after power had been concentrated in one hand; it is quite
obvious how great a damage Roman letters suffered by the
loss of liberty." [41] Guarino, it is true, had asked Poggio
whether the very flowering of Roman literature under
Caesar and Augustus did not bear evidence that the crea-
tiveness of Roman culture was far from fading with the
rise of monarchical rule. But Poggio counters, maintaining
the position of the Florentine school,[42] that this flowering
after the destruction of freedom by Caesar had been due
to a generation raised under the Republic. "Virgil, Horace,
Livy, and Seneca were born and bred while the Republic
was in its vigor; for Livy was in his sixteenth year when
Caesar was slain, Seneca (as he states himself) could still
hear Cicero's speeches, Virgil was twenty-four when the
battle of Pharsalus between Caesar and Pompey was
waged; Horace was seventeen. Thus all the learned and
eloquent men who lived later either were born in the days
of liberty and nursed on that earlier eloquence, or they
were born soon afterwards, while some seeds of that earlier
eloquence still survived." [43a]

The great historical significance of this controversy, although often denied,[43b] will be still better understood
when one includes a sequel which clearly brings out the
fact that civic-minded humanists in Venice were drawn
into a common front with the Florentine humanists against
the cult of Caesar flourishing at the tyrant courts. In 1440,
a Venetian humanist and jurist in the Papal service, Pietro
del Monte, then nuncio of the Curia in England and later
Bishop of Venetian Brescia,[43c] composed a letter of pamphlet length, addressed to Poggio, in order to strengthen
Poggio's position against Guarino.[43d] This letter, which
Poggio took pains to make known in Italy,[43e] discredited
Guarino's glowing appraisal of Caesar by bringing together
all the statements from antiquity unfavorable to Caesar and

demonstrating in minute detail that Caesar had been a bad citizen and a tyrant.

Here we have rare evidence of the part played by the new Florentine historical outlook in loosening the tongues of republican citizens elsewhere in Italy. Pietro del Monte had received his humanistic education from Guarino during the period when Guarino was teaching in Venice.[43f] As Pietro reports at the opening of his letter, Guarino had even then used his lectures to sing the praises of Caesar at the expense of the *Respublica Romana*. Previously, Guarino had been a student at Padua of Giovanni Conversino, who, as will be seen later, during his Paduan days, around 1400, was an early literary champion of north-Italian Tyranny and a precursor of the controversy of the 1430's through his defense of the Monarchy of the Emperors against the *Respublica Romana*.[43g] Thus, Guarino's classroom in Venice introduced a slice of the intellectual life of the princely courts of Giangaleazzo Visconti's time into the education of young Venetian citizens. Pietro del Monte, as he tells us in his letter, had been revolted even in those early years by his teacher's advocacy of "the enemy of his *patria* and destroyer of sweet liberty." But it was Poggio who finally introduced him to the arguments refuting Guarino, and in his letter Pietro congratulates himself "that I have found in you [Poggio] so good, so strong and so eloquent an advocate and defender of my long-held views and opinions."[43h]

Thus enlightened and confirmed in his original reaction, Pietro ventures upon a frank discussion of the roots of his attitude. The verdict that Caesar's "conspiracy and plot against the *patria*" has effaced the merit of his military achievements sounds natural and convincing, says Pietro, to the ears of a person born in a commonwealth which has remained to the present day an "inviolate temple of liberty." Venice, he says, knows only too well that "passionate desire to extinguish liberty" found in Caesar; for the same desire has incited many emperors and princes to conspire against the liberty of the Republic of Venice. But the Venetians have overcome these aggressors following the maxim "that if liberty ends, let life end also"; [431] and they have learned to pursue a policy with the aim "that, if possible, all Italy, which has been crushed under so many disasters caused by tyrants, may at some time achieve peace, tranquillity, quiet, repose, and the sweetest and most coveted of all human things, liberty. Why, then, should it seem strange to anyone if I, who was born, nursed and brought up in the strongest fortress of liberty and who have never felt the heavy and harsh yoke of tyranny (for all of which I am in the debt of the immortal gods)—if I emphatically and frankly express detestation for Caesar, the infamous patricide, destroyer of Roman liberty, and bitter enemy of his *patria*? For even if there were no other reasons, Nature, mother of all things, compels me to say what I have said." [43J] This statement by a Venetian humanist strikingly demonstrates the relationship of the Quattrocento controversy over Caesar to the deep-rooted differences between the convictions of civic humanists and the outlook of humanists at the princely courts. [43k]

In the 1430's, Guarino of Ferrara was not the only humanist in the orbit of north-Italian tyranny who assailed the republican interpretation of Roman history. A like attack occurred almost simultaneously at the court of Filippo Maria Visconti in Milan, by Pier Candido Decembrio. In this case it was directed expressly against Bruni's *Laudatio*, which at that time began once more to be effective in the exchange of political propaganda between Milan and Florence. In 1436, Decembrio composed a panegyric on Milan (*De Laudibus Mediolanensium Urbis Panegyricus*), meant to counter the theses of Bruni's *Laudatio* by matching them one after the other with similar claims for Milan. [431] Again the debate focuses on the quest for the fate of creative energies under the Empire. Bruni in his *Laudatio,* his Milanese critic says, would have us believe that only under the Republic did Rome have eminent minds in every field of activity; but he forgets that *"divina ingenia"* such as Cicero, Livius, and Virgil flourished "in the days of Caesar and Augustus." How, then, could we accept Tacitus' dictum "that those brilliant minds vanished?" [44] We know from Poggio that the Florentines knew how to answer this challenge. Decembrio's Milanese counterpart to Bruni's *Laudatio* shows in other places how trenchant a weapon of the spirit the politico-historical outlook of Bruni's youthful work still was. To Bruni's praise of Florence as the heir to the *virtus* of the *Respublica Romana,* for instance, Decembrio has no other reply but that Milan was the only city besides Rome where Roman emperors used to be crowned, and therefore the only city which could claim to be a second imperial city.[45] Again, in the face of the pervasive faith of the *Laudatio* in republican liberty, Decembrio can only argue that, since aristocracy, ideally the best form of government, is rarely possible, the seizure of power by one man, like Giangaleazzo Visconti, intent on the advantage and the military greatness of the *patria,* produces in practice the most desirable government.[46]

As to the continuity of the republican interpretation of Roman history among the Florentines themselves, it will be sufficient to mention that the criticism of Caesar and the imperial monarchy, after it had been a favorite theme of Florentine humanists, continued to play an essential role with Machiavelli.[47a] For Machiavelli carried on and developed Bruni's conception that a wealth of human energies was stifled by Rome's universal Empire, but came to the fore again with the rise of free city-republics and other independent states in the post-Roman period. He also repeated the early Quattrocento censure of Caesar, charging that the temporary need for the strong hand of a dictator did not justify Caesar's destruction of the Republic and, thereby, of the health and energy of the Roman people.

Not until the triumph of monarchic absolutism in the latter part of the sixteenth century was the republican interpretation of Roman history in Florence challenged. When in 1599 Giovanni Battista Guarini, who had spent his life at Renaissance courts, wrote in the service of the Grand Duke of Tuscany a *Trattato della politica libertà*, which was to demonstrate that true liberty could exist only under a prince, the opinion reappeared that the history of the Roman Republic, like that of all other free states, had been nothing but one of ruinous internal strife until Rome found rest under the strong hands of the emperors. As Guarini put it, Rome was never "as free as at the time when she had lost her liberty" (*"Roma non fu mai . . . tanto libera, quanto allora ch'era men libera"*).[47b]

Even the theory of Florence's foundation under the Roman Republic remained for a long time an accepted and essential part of the Florentine historical outlook, once Bruni—who had not yet named Sulla in the *Laudatio*—had presented Sulla's veterans as the founding fathers of Florence in the very first lines of his *History of the Florentine People*.[48] Before long, this thesis also carried conviction with Quattrocento humanists outside of Florence. Whereas in medieval Florence everyone who had talked about the Florentine past had also exalted Caesar, during the Quattrocento he would extol the *Respublica Romana* as the mother of the *Respublica Florentina* and tell how veterans of the army of Sulla had settled Florence as a Roman colony. Perhaps this theory was the strongest single factor in bringing about the sweeping change in the general attitude toward Caesar and the Empire.

To point to a few examples illustrating the spread of the theory: When, after Bruni's death, the anonymous author

of an obituary prefaced his eulogy of the deceased humanist-chancellor with a word on the glory of Florence,
his first reference was to the city's origin from the men of
Sulla in 88 B.C. Poggio, who carried on Bruni's work in
Florentine historiography, referred in the very first words
of his continuation of Bruni's *History* to the *"civium
colonia*," founded by Sulla; and so, repeatedly, did Cristoforo Landino, who continued many of the convictions of
the Florentine civic humanists in the time of Lorenzo de'
Medici.[49] Other revealing evidence comes from the Florentine biographers of Dante. Whereas Filippo Villani in
his Trecento life of the poet had taken it for granted that
"the city of Florence was founded by Caesar," [50] Giannozzo Manetti in his Quattrocento biography talks of
"Florence, the city founded by Sulla's soldiers" as a fact
in no need of comment.[51] That disinterested scholarly conviction then concurred with the claim of the Florentine
citizens is proved by Flavio Biondo's inclusion of the Sulla
thesis in his *Italia Illustrata*. Lorenzo Valla, on the other
hand, who wished to refute the Florentine pretensions,
could only sneer that Florence's founder, Sulla, had after
all been "Rome's first tyrant." [52] Substantially this counter-
blast, and not a denial of the Florentine claim, is found
in Pier Candido Decembrio's Milanese *Panegyricus*.[53]

It has seemed advisable to assemble these details from
a variety of sources because the role of the Sulla thesis for
Quattrocento historiography and political thought is too
easily forgotten in consequence of its sudden abandonment not long before the century had ended. At that time
a late classical source became known, the *Liber coloniarum*
or *Liber regionum*, wrongly attributed to Frontinus, which
asserted plainly that Florence had been founded by the
"triumviri." To the writers of the last phases of the
Renaissance—Poliziano, who discovered the *Liber coloniarum* in the library of the Medici, as well as Vespasiano

da Bisticci; Machiavelli as well as Guicciardini; Benedetto Varchi as well as Vincenzo Borghini—the historical reconstruction of the origin of Florence, therefore, became merely a problem in learned criticism of contradictory sources. Usually it was solved by reliance on the *Liber*, and, therefore, contrary to the Sulla theory of the early Renaissance. Sometimes the controversy turned to the question whether the *"triumviri"* to which the *Liber* referred were those of the year 59—Caesar, Pompey, and Crassus—or those of the year 43—Antony, Augustus, and Lepidus; sometimes the judgment of scholars was that the entire problem was still *sub judice*. In any event the outcome could no longer provide the basis for a politically inspiring conviction.[54] But by then the Sulla theory had long fulfilled this function for Renaissance Florence. Among serious Florentine writers, the earlier evaluation reappears, for what is perhaps the last time, in Ugolino Verino's *De Illustratione Urbis Florentiae*, published in 1483, during the period of Lorenzo de' Medici. Here Florence is still celebrated as the "foster-son of Sulla" (*Syllanus alumnus*) who, by offering resistance, alone in Italy, to the tyrant Giangaleazzo Visconti, had proved worthy of the legacy of Roman civic liberty.[55]

The growth of all these basic tenets of Florentine Renaissance historiography, we have seen, can be traced back beyond their first elaborate expression in Bruni's *Historiae Florentini Populi* to the two small works of his youth written on the threshold of the century: the *Dialogi* and the *Laudatio*. The reader of these early writings, it is true, may often feel himself still far removed from the serene maturity of Bruni's major work. The gossip gathered from a wealth of ancient sources and the almost boyish indignation, which serve as background to the verdict of the *Laudatio* on the Roman emperors, show on the surface little similarity with the accurate analysis of the physical

extinction and psychological suppression of civic energies
under the Empire which Bruni's *Historiae* was to set forth;
and there is a world of difference between the naive efforts
of the *Laudatio* to justify Florence's wars on the ground
that any disputed territory had once been a possession of
Florence's mother, Rome, and the later historical appraisal
of Florence's mission to carry on the civic liberty of ancient
Etruria and to continue the fight of the Roman republicans
against tyranny. But however immature the presentation,
the point which matters for an understanding of the years
in which the *Dialogi* and the *Laudatio* were written is that
Bruni, in the bold new approach of his youth to the phenomenon of the Roman Empire, was already inspired by
the same motives which in due time led to the perspective
of Roman history characteristic of the Florentine historiography of the Renaissance.

Furthermore, already in the *Laudatio* we find that the
shift of historical emphasis from the *Imperium Romanum*
to the *Respublica Romana* is inextricably fused with a new
concept of Florence's history as a history of civic freedom.
In the scene of the *Dialogi* in which the significance of the
Laudatio is appraised by the author himself, we read that
for the argument of the *Laudatio* "it had been necessary
to inveigh to some extent against the emperors, in order
to extol the case of Florence." [56] And in the *Laudatio*, the
question is asked and answered *in extenso:* what purpose
is served in a book on Florence by a reappraisal of Roman
history and a criticism of the Roman emperors? "In the
first place, to show that this city has not without right thus
taken sides in the struggle of the parties [i.e. for the
Guelph protection of republican liberty, and against the
emperors and their Ghibelline party]; and, secondly, to
make it understood that this colony was conducted hither
at the good time when the city of Rome saw her power,
liberty, gifted minds, and the fame of her citizens in their

greatest flower. . . . For it makes an immense difference whether this colony was founded at that time, or only later when all *virtus* and *nobilitas* of the city of Rome had already been extirpated to such an extent that her emigrants could no longer produce anything magnificent or outstanding." [57]

Reflections of the New Ideas in Salutati, Cino Rinuccini, and Gregorio Dati

The many new historical discoveries and reinterpretations made about 1400, then, were not matters merely of concern to scholars. The fresh republican view of ancient Rome; the theory of the founding of Florence by Romans of the republican period; the vindication of Dante the Florentine poet; the civic reinterpretation of Dante's Caesarism—all these are facets of one homogeneous frame of thought. They all have a kindred political ring, pointing to a common source of experience and emotion: the struggle for Florence's liberty in the time of Giangaleazzo Visconti.

In many crises in history we find a subtle but unmistakable relationship between the growth of patriotic sentiment and that of historical thought. "True patriotism," Fustel de Coulanges once said, "is not the love of the soil, it is the love of the past, it is the respect for the generations that have preceded us." [58] This "love of the past," this "respect for the generations that have preceded us" is clearly the new factor which found expression in the *Laudatio* and *Dialogi* and created a new climate in Florentine Humanism at the very moment when rising classicism, the other element stirring at the end of the Trecento, was turning the eyes of humanists away from native values and traditions.

That sentiments like those we observed in Bruni's works

were widely current among Florentine writers and humanists during the wars with Giangaleazzo is indicated by the
appearance of the same historical themes, with like political
motivations, in several other Florentine works of the
period. In 1403 Coluccio Salutati, writing as the chancellor
of Florence, published a political pamphlet, his *Invective
Against Antonio Loschi,* which was to justify Florence's
conduct in the wars that had just come to an end.[59] The
charges of the Milanese chancery-humanist, Antonio
Loschi, which Salutati attempted to refute, had been
leveled not only against the current politics of Florence,
but also against her claim to be the heir of the *Respublica
Romana* in Italy. Salutati's answer was the thesis of the
foundation of Florence by veterans of Sulla, supported by
an extensive discussion of all the available source-evidence
—a critical performance which has no parallel in Bruni's
Laudatio.[60]

At some time during the war, in addition to Salutati,
a private citizen, Cino Rinuccini, had replied to Loschi in
a *Response to the Invective of Antonio Loschi.*[61] There we
encounter anew the republican interpretation of Roman
history with unmistakable allusions to the political part this
interpretation played in the conflict with the Milanese
tyrant. The argument of Cino Rinuccini runs as follows:
in order to learn the true worth of monarchical rule, so
highly praised by the Viscontean propagandists, one should
weigh "how Rome grew but little under the kings, acquired the empire over the world within a short time under
the senate, and was again reduced to nothing under the
emperors." [62] We also meet the critique of Caesar, Augustus, and the Universal Empire: Caesar, driven by his
ambition for a power greater than any other Roman
possessed, overthrew the order of all things human and
divine, and eventually caused Rome to lose her ruling
position. "For one ruler in the affairs of mankind [*uno*

nelle cose umane] cannot be perfect"; even though Augustus was a capable leader, a Nero would follow. Had Rome preserved her senatorial constitution, she would have lived on to the present time in the glory won under the Republic. "You should, therefore, understand, you slave," Cino calls out to the Milanese propagandist, "how great the fruits of happy liberty may be; of liberty, for which Cato the Younger did not hesitate to die, that choice mind, whom Lucanus rightly places on a level with the Gods by saying 'the conquering cause was pleasing to the Gods, but the conquered one to Cato.' " [63]

About a decade later, the Florentine citizen Gregorio Dati composed the first historical account of the recent Florentine-Milanese wars, his *History of Florence from 1380 to 1406*.[64] Here, in an historical analysis written in the Volgare, we encounter Bruni's theme of the descent of both Guelphism and the Florentine spirit of liberty from the *Respublica Romana*. In Dati's version, the republican interpretation of the history of Guelph Florence reads: Because the noble families who had been at the helm of the Florentine Republic in the early centuries had followed the cause of the Empire and of signory, and thus had become Ghibellines, "the multitude of the citizens hated them out of a suspicion that the city might fall under the power of a tyrant, as happened to Rome under Caesar." As a consequence, the Florentine people always trimmed the power of the great lords, as a gardener trims the branches of a tree that spread too far; the citizens of Florence remembered that they were descended from those Romans who "under a government of *libertà*" built up their world-wide state and, "if they were to return to the world today, would be the enemies of Caesar and of anyone who impaired that popular constitution and government and reduced it to tyrannical rule. And, therefore, these Florentines, descendants from those free Romans, and following their nature, are always suspicious of those who might infringe upon and take away the liberty of their common popular government, and for this reason they are unfriendly and opposed in their minds to anyone who tries to encroach upon liberty by tyrannical and arrogant conduct. . . ." [65]

No one who familiarizes himself with this much-neglected group of Florentine writings will fail to gain the impression that the Milanese wars had a great and unmistakable impact on the Florentine mind. In the realm of politico-historical ideas, the experience of the Florentine struggle was beyond doubt a potent factor. In other respects as well, we may expect it to have been the mold in which seminal ideas of the Florentine Renaissance took shape.

So much at least we have observed: the war-filled first years of the Quattrocento must have experienced a profound revival of public spirit among many Florentine writers and humanists. Pride in the *patria* and love of freedom are keynotes in all the literary works from which we have drawn our conclusions. And in Leonardo Bruni we have met one of the leading minds of early Quattrocento Florence who in that very period formed a cast of mind as far removed from the outlook of medieval and Trecento writers as from the classicists' contempt for modernity, then in the ascendency in humanistic circles.

Part Two

PROMISE AND TRADITION
IN POLITICO-HISTORICAL LITERATURE
ABOUT 1400

CHAPTER 4

THE INTERPLAY OF IDEAS AND EVENTS

Deceptive Theories and Sources

IN the preceding chapters we have had a bird's-eye
view of the landscape of the late fourteenth and the
early fifteenth centuries. From that vantage-point we
have seen two things in conjunction: while the ideas of
the Florentine Quattrocento were in their seminal phase,
Florence, on the political plane, met one of the severest
tests in her history. A fight for the liberty of the *Respublica Florentina,* and, at about the same time, a discovery
of the historic role of the *Respublica Romana;* a regeneration of political morale in the crucible of the crisis of the
Florentine Commonwealth, and, at about the same time,
a revival of the memory of Roman citizenship among
Florentine humanists—these are elements so closely related to each other that it is hard to believe that they were
not connected as cause to effect, correlated in time as well
as spirit.

Yet this impression is flatly contradicted by the close-
range picture usually drawn of the Florentine literature of
the transition years. In fact, the nearer we come to the
concrete literary documents as they are known and interpreted today, the better we understand why past historians
have failed to reconstruct the interaction between political
and cultural factors. Parts of Giovanni Gherardi da Prato's
Paradise-Garden of the Alberti (Paradiso degli Alberti),[1]
a novel clearly built around some core of historical truth,

seem to indicate that the leitmotifs of the new historical outlook—the republican interpretation of Roman history, and the story of Sulla's founding of Florence through soldiers of the Roman Republic—had emerged much earlier. For if we follow the account of Giovanni da Prato, the conversations held in Salutati's circle after 1400, and reflected in Bruni's *Dialogi*, had had a kind of prelude as early as 1389 in a country-house of the Alberti family called the "Paradiso." There, according to Giovanni da Prato's novel, many educated men of the generation to which Salutati, the humanist-chancellor, and the Augustinian monk Luigi Marsili, theologian and semi-humanist, belonged, met in their younger years as members of a society whose life in many respects still seems to reflect that of the mid-Trecento nobility, known from Boccaccio's *Decamerone*, with its naive gaiety and its pleasure in the telling of stories and anecdotes. In the *Paradiso* group, story telling of the *Decamerone* type alternates with the discussion of philosophical, political, and historical matters, and among these latter we find those two politico-historical topics of crucial interest to the Florentines of the Renaissance, discussed in the novel by Luigi Marsili.

Now if it should really be possible to trace some integral parts of the Quattrocento outlook as far back as the 1380's (since they are said to have served as society talk in 1389, their origin must have been even earlier than that year), it would be difficult to insist on an intimate connection between this outlook and the struggle of the Florentine Republic with Giangaleazzo Visconti. In the late 1380's, Florence and Milan had not yet clashed in open war; at most, a vital antagonism between the Florentine Republic and the Visconti Tyranny could then be foreseen. It might be argued that even if the roots of the new ideas were older than the cataclysmic events of the Giangaleazzo era, still the moment when Florence alone defended the traditions of city-state liberty against monarchical absolutism may have supplied the political experience that allowed these ideas to attain maturity. But even this modified hypothesis will not stand the test if the accepted opinion is indeed correct, that Bruni's *Laudatio* and *Dialogi* were composed in 1400 and 1401. For in that case Bruni's historical outlook would have been formed precisely during the period when Florence, in a glaring breach with her Guelph tradition, was pinning her hopes for survival on the success of the arms of a German pretender to the imperial throne, before the final hour of trial in the duel of the Florentine Republic with the Milanese Tyrant had come.

According to the prevailing chronological assumptions, the only two literary works that could have been conceived under the immediate impact of Florence's fight are the invectives by Salutati and by Rinuccini, presumed to have been written when the war and danger had passed, during 1402/03, in the exultant mood following the triumph.[2] But these two works alone would form too narrow a basis to support the general statement that the ascendence of the new thought followed the new experience in Florence's struggle. And the basis becomes still narrower by another observation. Compared with the *Laudatio*, the two invectives seem to contain little that is not merely a coarser and less mature replica of Bruni's thought. Accordingly, even if Salutati and Rinuccini wrote their invectives in 1402/03 —an assumption never definitely established by detailed evidence—some of their key-ideas, and particularly the historical concepts with which they work, would appear to have originated at an earlier time, independent of the impact of the war. For, if the accepted reading of the sources is correct, these concepts had been formed partly in the pre-war period (that is, prior to the *Paradiso* conversations), and partly during the weary interval between the second war and the last climax (that is, the period to which the *Laudatio* has been ascribed).

The picture which results, then, leaves little room for the assumption that Florence's new politico-historical outlook was in its origin bound up with the experience and the conduct in the wars with Giangaleazzo. This implication could be avoided only if the accepted chronology of our sources were incorrect throughout: if Florentine citizens did not discuss some of the new ideas as early as 1389; if Bruni did not write his panegyric in the lean period of the war, about 1400; and if the two pamphleteers, Salutati and Rinuccini, did not in 1402/03 repeat ideas that had originated before the real weight of the struggle had made itself felt. This means that we should have to challenge the correctness of practically every accepted date of every major work composed in Florence in the decade around 1400.

At first sight this seems to be an outrageous hypothesis. But we have reason to approach our source material and the resulting picture of the time about 1400 with greater caution than is needed for any other phase of the Renaissance. The culture and thought of the early Quattrocento are in so many ways akin to the modern pattern that one is continually tempted to assume the presence also of another parallel to modern history: the variety and richness of sources that allow us to answer many a freshly posed problem without continually revising a meager group of testimonies, and reconstructing unattested phases of sentiment and thought. Yet we must not forget that the transition to the modern abundance of literary sources occurred only gradually, in the course of the Quattrocento, largely as an effect of the spread of humanistic education and, eventually, of the rise of printing. This is one of the reasons why the boundary-line between medieval and modern fields of study is usually drawn about 1500 when the change in the availability of source material begins to allow a change in historiographical method.

Our information concerning the crisis a hundred years earlier not only shows a pre-modern meagerness but is unusually limited even by fourteenth- and fifteenth-century standards. Of Niccolò Niccoli, who in every modern narrative is credited with being the herald of the new philology in the first Quattrocento generation, we have no original work [3] nor any competent contemporaneous biography which would allow us easily to understand the spirit motivating his acid criticism and defiance of the medieval tradition. Likewise, there is no source clearly illuminating the relationship between *literati* of Niccoli's stamp and more civic-minded humanists of his generation. Bruni's sentiment and thought can be readily grasped only when his humanistic production begins to furnish a more abundant source; for the first thirty or more years of his life almost no testimony from his pen has survived, and no contemporary has left a straightforward account of the intellectual climate of Bruni's youth. From one member of Bruni's generation, Pier Paolo Vergerio, we have a rich epistolary collection spanning the time from the late 1380's to about 1415. But this source does not inform us about the particular milieu of Florence; the information comes from Bologna and Padua, and after 1404 from the circle of humanist secretaries at the Curia. The letters of the other major members of the early Quattrocento generation— Poggio's, Traversari's, Guarino's, Francesco Barbaro's, and Bruni's own—do not become plentiful, if they start at all, until this group of humanists has established its place and social position (after 1405, or even after 1410); at the turn of the fourteenth century, a few letters must serve for the reconstruction of whole years. True, there is the inexhaustible correspondence of Coluccio Salutati, which runs to his death in 1406, but it expresses the mind of an old man, of one who had been a leader in the half-century between Petrarch and the pioneering generation of the early Quattrocento, and who can tell us little about the nature of the forces which then revolted and cast a shadow over Salutati's last years.

The result of all these conditions is that our sources on the crisis of the early Quattrocento are perhaps scantier than those on any other crucial event in the history of the Renaissance. For fourteenth-century Humanism we have the treasure of Petrarch's works and letters; and while his exceptional genius may sometimes lead us into a wrong estimate of the average ideas of his age, still the testimony of so brilliant an observer allows us without difficulty to find exact answers even to subtle questions about the origin and development of the Trecento attitude toward past and present, toward Republic and Tyranny, or toward the citizen's world of action and the scholar's "contemplation." With regard to the Quattrocento, on the other hand, we begin to feel firm ground underfoot from the time when the letters and publications of the generation born around 1370-1380 start to become plentiful. But with regard to the intervening period—the end of the fourteenth and the beginning of the fifteenth century—all the minutiae of chronology, personal data, and mutual influences are little known and difficult to establish. It is no exaggeration to say that, among the score of Florentine works and letters written around 1400 on which the history of the transition crisis must be built, almost none has come down to us without some open question concerning its chronology, or some delicate problem concerning its background and origin— embarrassments caused by the scarcity of complementary sources.

These are strong warnings, and they merely introduce the even more incisive observation that the accepted sequence of our sources cannot be reconciled with any intelligible order in the development of Florentine thought about 1400. For, in the first place, if the discovery that Florence was founded in pre-imperial times was made in all details as early as 1389, why then should Salutati in his *Invectiva*, many years later, have taken the trouble to repeat almost literally this theory and all the testimonies from the ancient authors? Again, if the elaborate criticism of the Roman Emperors, contained in Bruni's *Laudatio*, was actually published in 1400, how did it happen that Cino Rinuccini three years later set forth an evidently much less mature phase of this criticism, which in thought and expression is remarkably close to some paragraphs of the *Paradiso*? And why was Salutati's account of the descent of the Florentines from Sulla's veterans so strikingly akin to the corresponding discussion in the *Paradiso*, although nearly fifteen years are supposed to have elapsed since the conversations depicted by Giovanni da Prato?

Still worse contradictions crop up in the chronology of the two major pieces of this group of writings: the *Laudatio* and the *Dialogi*. For while there can be no doubt that the first is referred to in the latter (the accepted dating, 1400 and 1401 respectively, is based on this reference), it remains difficult to deny that the *Laudatio* praises the Florentine triumph over Giangaleazzo in a manner that seems to presuppose the events of 1402. Also, the dating of the *Laudatio* in 1400 and the *Dialogi* in 1401 has puzzling implications for the history of Bruni's development as a humanistic scholar. For we know from other documents that Bruni left the school of Chrysoloras, his Greek master, in May 1400, with little more than two years of study completed, and at that point made his first attempts at translation from the Greek; we also know from indisputable evidence that after finishing the *Laudatio*, whenever that may have been, he immediately launched into translating and critically appraising Plato's

Phaedon—one of the harder tasks of the new Greek scholarship, as he himself declared. Consequently, if the *Laudatio* was written in 1400, we should have to accept that Bruni, within a few months in the summer of that year, progressed from his earliest efforts at translating to the mastery required for the translation and criticism of Plato.[4]

The fact that so many perplexing improbabilities and contradictory assumptions have not aroused the suspicion of students of humanistic literature, or, at any rate, have not provoked criticism penetrating enough to prevent the acceptance of so inconclusive a chronology, brings us to the last and decisive point. Insufficient though some of the accepted views have always been felt to be, they yet could all be fused into a picture which in general came up to expectation and, consequently, lessened interest in the remaining discrepancies. This expectation was that a gradual progress took place from the thought of the Trecento to the thought of the Quattrocento: an evolution from naive story-telling in the society of the *Decamerone*, to a mixture of Trecento fondness for narrating with the beginnings of the new erudition in the *Paradiso*, and on to the learned debates of Quattrocento humanists in Salutati's house, depicted in Bruni's *Dialogi*. Because this continuity and gradual evolution were in the students' minds, the date and conditions presupposed by the *Paradiso* novel were readily accepted as historical truth, and little attention was paid to dissenting sources of information.[5]

Political Events and the Chronology of the Works of the Publicists

Once we realize that the customary interpretation of many sources for the study of the 1400 transition rests on shaky ground and has been accepted largely because it seems to confirm a preconceived theory of Renaissance development, the apparent veto of these sources against the assumption of an interdependence between the ideas and events of the period begins to look less embarrassing. It is entirely imaginable that the same sources seen from a different angle will tell a different story.

In fact, as soon as we undertake systematically to coordinate the works written around 1400 with the events that left their mark on them, the only convincing sequence among them appears to be one that differs radically from the long accepted chronology. Although a detailed examination of every individual text would be needed to lay open the complicated reasons for former misinterpretations,[6] the course of the contemporary political events with which each single work must be coordinated can be so easily traced that a few paragraphs suffice to point out the criteria necessary for reconstructing the chronology of the literature of the period.

As to the *"Paradiso" of the Alberti,* presumed testimony to the emergence of some of the basic elements of Florentine Quattrocento historiography in the 1380's, there can be no doubt that the conversations of the novel reveal familiarity with ideas which can be shown to have been formed in the heat of the subsequent wars with Giangaleazzo Visconti. The *Paradiso* knows of the founding of Florence by veterans of Sulla, a theory still absent from the 1395/96 version of Filippo Villani's *On the Origin of the City of Florence,* and unknown also to Salutati in 1398. The *Paradiso* in fact refers to all the minutiae and conclusions of the critical discussion by which Salutati, as late as between 1398 and 1402, elaborated that theory, until it was made known to the public by inclusion in his *Invectiva* against Antonio Loschi. By the same token we may conclude that the republican interpretation of Roman history, found in the *Paradiso* discussions, echoes some pages of

Cino Rinuccini's *Risponsiva* to Loschi, and, consequently, likewise reflects ideas which actually were not formed before the Florentine experience in the struggle with Giangaleazzo. If we add that Giovanni da Prato wrote his account of the alleged happenings of the year 1389 in his old age, long after the Giangaleazzo period, and that he correctly reproduced from memory the names of the visitors to the Paradiso gardens in 1389, but failed entirely in his attempt to recall the political situation toward the end of the 1380's, profoundly changing the outlook, age, and character of the major partners in the conversations, there can be only one conclusion: the *Paradiso* must be struck from the list of documents expected to throw light on the roots of the thought of the Quattrocento—at least as far as politico-historical ideas are concerned.

It is, then, in the pamphlets of publicists which accompanied the Florentine-Milanese struggle that we must search for the origins of the new outlook. Apart from Leonardo Bruni's *"Laudatio" of the City of Florence*, which is a work of literature rather than a casual political pamphlet and will require a separate discussion in the context of Bruni's early humanistic production,[7] there are the works of three publicists from whose controversy the search for the first stirrings of the Quattrocento ideas must start: the *Invectiva* against the Florentines of Antonio Loschi, the *Risponsiva* ("response") of Cino Rinuccini, and the *Invectiva* (counter-invective) of Coluccio Salutati.[8]

The sequence and exact chronology of these three writings can safely be inferred from the manner in which they mirror the changing events and passions in the Florentine contest with Giangaleazzo. As our preceding study of the history of the Florentine-Milanese wars has brought out, Florence, at the beginning of the decisive clash in 1397, was the leader and moving spirit of a broad coalition fighting the Visconti threat; but this league was gradually dissolved during the next few years, until the Florentine citizens remained the only opponents to Giangaleazzo's empire. For a while they carried on in a dejected mood, under a cloud of general censure for having instigated a German invasion of the Peninsula; but eventually they recaptured their stature in the eyes of Italy by their lone heroic stand. When this course of the fortunes of Florence is used to determine the time of origin of each of the three pamphlets, we recognize the fallacy of the argument placing the controversy of the publicists into the late period when Florence found herself almost alone on the scene, or even when war and danger had passed. The basic feature of the political situation presupposed by all three authors is the unimpaired anti-Viscontean alliance system led by Florence. Since this system split up at the time of the Truce of Pavia in May 1398, the three pamphlets must have originated before the spring of 1398. Once this is established, each author's knowledge or ignorance of certain early events of the war gives us the possibility of determining the precise moment of his writing: Loschi composed his pamphlet very shortly after the outbreak of the war in March 1397; Rinuccini's answer was given not much later, in the late spring or early summer of the same year; and Salutati produced the groundwork of his invective not more than six months after that. Of these results the most surprising is that even Salutati's pamphlet, in its plan and many essential traits, is a product of the time of the first clash of arms—even though it can be established in detail that Salutati's work was not completed at that time, but was resumed, enlarged, and brought up to date in the crucial summer of 1402, and finished and released for publication by the end of 1403.[9]

These chronological revisions inevitably change the

picture of the rise of politico-historical ideas in Quattrocento Florence in two fundamental respects.

In the first place, it is now clear that the beginnings of
the new outlook followed in time the most agitated moments of the Florentine-Milanese struggle. So long as
authenticity was ascribed to the discussions pictured in
Giovanni da Prato's novel, and as it was assumed that the
ideas expounded in the *Paradiso* conversations were abroad
in cultured circles before the war between Florence and
Giangaleazzo had broken out; so long as Loschi was
thought to have published his pamphlet at some irrelevant
moment in the course of the war, and Salutati as well as
Rinuccini seemed to have done their work as publicists after
the war was over—so long the facts seemed indeed to
foreclose any high estimate of the role of the Florentine
fight; there was no place to refute the one-sided emphasis
on the slow and gradual growth of Quattrocento thought
out of the Trecento, and to give due weight to the quicken-
ing and redirecting influence of the experience of the great
contemporary events. Now, however, after the removal
of the *Paradiso*, Loschi's attack and Rinuccini's and Salutati's answers are found to reflect the moment when hostilities had opened and the issues at stake first became discernible. On the other hand, the changes in Salutati's work
are the reflection of the final, dramatic climax of the
struggle. In the winter of 1397-98, when arms were beginning to decide the future of Renaissance Italy, Salutati,
well aware of the significance of the fight ahead, had
parried Loschi's challenge with the question: "Who does
not see that this Florentine city is the defender of the
common cause of liberty in Italy? Who would not admit
that if the Florentine people were defeated, freedom
could not survive, but all Italy would be in helpless serfdom?" And when the citizens of Florence in the summer
of 1402 were feeling what it meant to be left the sole

defenders of the *"libertas Italiae"* against the Visconti, the past five years of Florentine resistance reflected themselves in the proud words, then inserted in Salutati's pamphlet: "We alone, indeed, are the barricade and obstacle which prevents that despotic regime, which has forced so many cities and towns . . . into wretched subjugation, from completing its work through the whole of Italy. That was the sort of peace which your Lord desired. . . . To such a peace, however, I admit, the Florentines have always been adverse and a stumblingblock." [10]

The second and no less significant consequence of our revised chronology is the emergence of a new figure among the pioneering writers at the end of the Trecento. The composition in the spring or summer of 1397 of a pamphlet in defense of Florence and her politics makes the citizen Cino Rinuccini—half-way in age between the humanists Salutati and Bruni, scion of an old family of wool merchants and himself a member of the *Lana* Guild—the first among the publicists to inaugurate the new politico-historical ideas. [11]

CHAPTER 5

A CITIZEN'S VIEW AND A HUMANIST'S VIEW
OF FLORENTINE HISTORY AND CULTURE:
CINO RINUCCINI AND SALUTATI

The Republican Reading of History,
and the Guelph Tradition

IN the literary history of the Renaissance, Cino Rinuccini [1] is known better by his Volgare poetry which
continued the manner of Dante and Petrarch into the
early Quattrocento, than by his Latin studies and prose
writings.[2] His now established priority among the publicists
of the period does not make him an influential writer. But
from the perspective of the growth of Florentine thought
a fact of great significance can be discerned: his humble
work provides documentary evidence that the new interpretation of the history of ancient Rome and of the
Florentine Republic grew out of the experience of Florentine citizens in the clash between civic freedom and
tyranny during the war with Giangaleazzo. Looking from
the year 1397 back into the past, Cino, besides placing new
stress on the Roman Republic, felt that history had long
prepared the city on the Arno for leadership in the cause
of freedom and independence. As early as the first half
of the Trecento, when Tuscany was invaded by a north-
Italian Tyrant, Mastino della Scala of Verona, the Florentines, said Cino, "had saved liberty in Italy"; Mastino
already had become aware that, if by subjecting Florence
"he had cut off the head of liberty, he would have found

the rest to be a dead body, and all Italy would easily have been subjugated." Afterwards, when Florence quickly crushed the tyranny that threatened to arise at home out of those years of external danger, the Florentine citizens in Cino's eyes showed by expelling the Duke of Athens after an eleven-month dictatorship that they had once and for all been taught to love and defend their freedom. In resisting the early Visconti (Giovanni in Petrarch's time, and later Bernabò), they acted in conformity with this lesson, and they would so act in the perils now ahead.[3]

To these reflections on Florentine history, the second half of Cino's *Risponsiva* adds an honor-roll and short biographies of some of Florence's "famous men" (*uomini illustri*) in all walks of civic and cultural life, particularly those of the last hundred years.[4] This was not an entirely original scheme, for a similar collection of even more extensive lives of famous Florentines had been presented in the second part of Filippo Villani's *On the Origin of the City of Florence and on Her Renowned Citizens*, the first version of which was written in 1381/82.[5] Cino most probably knew of his recent predecessor, and some day it may be found that he used *On the Origin* as his model. Yet the pamphlet of the non-humanist, Rinuccini, has a tone of its own. It lists not only the Florentine masters in literature, art, and military performance, as Filippo Villani does, but also merchants, "because not only arms but also trade enlarge the commonwealth."[6] This civic frame of mind makes Cino Rinuccini's pamphlet a direct harbinger of the procession of great Florentines in Cristoforo Landino's *Commentary* on the *Divina Commedia* which, like other well-known books of the mature Florentine Renaissance, has room for outstanding figures of Florence's economic life, justifying their inclusion with the statement "that trade, provided it is exercised with dignity, has always been in high esteem in every commonwealth."[7] It is this vivid picture of Florentine life and history which Rinuccini opposes to the Milanese cry for extinction of city-state independence with the proud boast that no other city than Florence, "not only among those of Italy, but among those of the world," had produced in such a short time so many outstanding men in all fields of literature, of art, and of civic life.[8]

In view of this effective formulation of the new political and historical outlook, it is the citizen Cino Rinuccini who in some respects deserves to be placed side by side with Salutati in the transition of the late Trecento, rather than the monk Luigi Marsili to whom that place has traditionally been accorded.[9]

In a later chapter we shall learn that these are not yet all of Rinuccini's contributions to the coming of civic Humanism. At this point, however, we already know enough to compare the reactions to the Giangaleazzo wars of Cino Rinuccini the citizen, who was active in literary pursuits outside of the circle of the humanistic *literati*, and of Coluccio Salutati the chancellor-humanist.

What strikes us immediately in the light of our present knowledge is that Rinuccini's fresh approach to the part played by civic freedom in Roman and Florentine history has no counterpart in Salutati's *Invectiva*. Salutati, too, places the practical defense of Florence's recent diplomatic moves in an historical frame; but this frame is the traditional medieval Guelph idea with its particular emphasis on the Italian mission of the royal house of France.[10]

To gain a perspective of Salutati's position, we must pay close attention to the nature of the Guelph idea in fourteenth- and fifteenth-century Florence. Since the days when the Papacy aided by the Anjou, side-branch of the house of France, had triumphed over the Hohenstaufen in southern Italy, Guelphism, besides meaning the Party of the Church, had also meant partisanship for the French

Monarchy. What faith in the German Empire had been to the medieval Ghibellines, the idea of a French protectorate over the opponents to the Empire had been to the medieval Guelphs; especially in Florence, the upshot was a sentimental leaning toward France. Throughout the Renaissance this Florentine sentiment showed its vitality whenever France was in need of an ally on the Peninsula. When in the days of Savonarola Charles VIII invaded Italy, the French troops were amazed at the ease with which the Florentines were ready to surrender their strongest fortresses to the approaching army since, conditioned by their old friendly relations and by their sentiments as "members of the Party of the Guelphs," "they were reluctant to take a stand against the house of France." [11] Still later, from the mouth of a Venetian ambassador, we hear the quip that "in the heart of every Florentine, if it could be cut open, there would be found in the very center a lily of gold," the armorial sign of France.[12]

This ever-present inclination of the Florentines was prone to react upon their outlook on history. From the chroniclers of the Trecento onward there was an over-emphasis on the alliance of the Florentine Guelph knights with Charles of Anjou, against the last Hohenstaufen. The Carolingian Franks, conquerors of the Lombards in Italy, were looked upon as French. The legend that Charlemagne had rebuilt the city of Florence after her alleged destruction by Totila placed the chief emphasis on the fact that the royal helper had been a king of France. In fact, the idea that Florence owed her second founding to the "French" emperor and patron saint of the Guelphs appealed so greatly to the Florentine citizens that their adherence to the legend of Charlemagne also saved their faith in the tales about Totila. Whereas Leonardo Bruni's *Historiae* succeeded in destroying the story of the original founding of Florence by Caesar, the story of Florence's destruction by Totila, like that of her second founding by Charlemagne, retained wide currency in the Quattrocento in spite of Bruni's penetrating criticism.[13]

These views of the history of Florence and Italy were among the cruder products of the Guelph attitude; beside them, as we have seen, there was another development, stemming from the same Guelph root: the interpretation of Guelphism as the cause of civic freedom as well as of the independence of states delivered from subordination to the Empire [14]—views which prepared the way for the historical philosophy that came to full maturity with Bruni's *Historiae* and culminated in Machiavelli's *Discorsi*. In this line of the Guelph idea the citizen Rinuccini, under the impress of the Florentine war for independence, became a pioneer. Salutati, on the other hand, at the same time and on the same occasion merely restated the older tenets, from the legends of Totila and Charlemagne to the praise of the French Anjou, enriching them by a fresh laudatory picture of ancient Gaul based on his humanistic reading of the classical authors.[15] One generation earlier, Guelphism with a Francophile slant had had its best literary advocate in Boccaccio.[16] Compared with this predecessor there is little new in the attitude embodied in the *Invectiva*; in the history of the politico-historical outlook of the Florentine Renaissance, the only function of Salutati's pamphlet was that it reemphasized some features of the medieval Guelph idea which, in the light of the thought and the political reality of the nascent Renaissance, were already outdated.

One could, it is true, try to argue that Salutati showed more realism and insight than Rinuccini in looking at the past with the contemporaneous grouping of powers in mind; for on the political horizon of the year 1397-98 the Florentine-French alliance loomed as the dominant factor, as is shown also by the tenor of Loschi's fears and hopes. One might suggest that, at a time when Florence and Bologna were members in a coalition composed mostly of small *signori* and the French King,[17] Salutati's emphasis on France was more appropriate than Rinuccini's enthusiastic praise of Florence's stand for civic liberty. But Rinuccini's reinterpretation was more prophetic than Salutati's pedestrian "realism." The French alliance proved ephemeral; the north-Italian *signori* made their peace with the irresistible conqueror. Eventually the struggle with the Visconti did develop into a war for the existence of Florentine civic liberty. The historical perspective advanced by Cino Rinuccini proved to be both a valuable weapon of the mind in this fight and a correct prognosis of the subsequent course of events. The student of Florentine thought must note, therefore, that the first step toward the historical philosophy of the Florentine Renaissance was made not by the learned humanistic chancellor, but by a citizen lacking humanistic sophistication, who sensed the portentous meaning of the events of his time.

Comparison with Rinuccini reveals still more of Salutati's attitude. Salutati's sentiments during the war must be sought not only in his *Invectiva*. As has been pointed out,[18] Salutati did the major work on his pamphlet in two separate stages, at the beginning and at the end of the war, in 1397-98 and in 1402-03. What was the cause for the long intervening slackening of his interest?

The explanation may lie partly in the embarrassment of an author who, after a first impetuous rush to answer the Milanese propaganda, ran into difficulties as a scholar. A problem that needed time for its solution sprang from Loschi's scepticism towards Florence's claim to be one of the foremost Roman colonies. The time-honored attribution of Florence's origin to Caesar had just been undermined by Benvenuto Rambaldi da Imola;[19] and Salutati in 1398 began to send out inquiries to learned friends in order to determine sources that could provide a better basis —efforts from which emerged the thesis of Florence's founding by Sulla's veterans which was eventually incorporated in the *Invectiva*.[20] But if this difficulty was the cause of the interruption of Salutati's work, it can hardly explain why the interval became a period of about four years. Personal reasons may have played a part. The answer to Loschi was to be a typical humanistic "invective," that is, a personal attack full of vituperation. Previously, Salutati had refrained from indulging in this humanistic malpractice, and from later statements we can see that he disliked this aspect of the *Invectiva*.[21] But this aversion, too, cannot have been the chief factor in his long *désintéressement* in a literary defense which he had first held to be his duty as a chancellor. A glance at his other literary pursuits between the years 1399 and 1401 puts this conclusion beyond doubt. In that period he wrote and published his treatise *De Tyranno* [22]—a work which was to prove that at certain stages of republican life tyranny becomes a necessity; that such had been the situation in Rome at the time of Caesar; and that, consequently, Dante was justified in condemning Caesar's assassins. It is well understandable that Salutati, at a time when he was engaged in an investigation that took so favorable a view of the juridical and historical aspects of monarchy, found it impossible to continue and complete a political pamphlet which deals continuously with the defense of *libertas Florentina,* and with the superiority of republican freedom over monarchy as praised by Loschi.

The composition of a book so monarchical in tenor as the *De Tyranno,* by the chancellor of Florence, in the midst of the Florentine-Milanese struggle, is an astounding phenomenon. Given our observation that substantial portions of the *Invectiva,* including a fervid defense of Florentine civic freedom, were written in 1397-98, prior to *De Tyranno,* it could appear as though the Florentine chancellor set out on a defense of liberty in those years but reconciled himself with monarchy soon afterwards under the impact of the increasingly probable triumph of tyranny in Italy, and returned to his republican convictions when the Florentine Commonwealth proved its vitality in the summer of 1402, and after Giangaleazzo's death. But no one who knows Salutati's personality will believe this possible. He may have been too alien to political passion to maintain the necessary inner tension when the war dragged on, and when the patent antithesis between republic and tyranny was in time beclouded by the alliance of Guelph Florence with the Emperor. Also, old age may have had a share in reducing the vigor of his interest in the ideological struggles that accompanied the war. But this Florentine patriot and imperturbable Stoic— as he always appeared to his contemporaries—was not a political weather-cock.

How, then, should we explain that a Florentine chancellor, in the midst of a war for the survival of civic liberty, in an interval of his work as a publicist for the *Respublica Florentina,* wrote the treatise on the Tyrant? Apparently, the only possible explanation is that in Salutati's own eyes the difference in outlook between the *Invectiva* and the *De Tyranno* did not go so far that he felt the one to defend republican liberty and the other to favor monarchy on a practical level. The difference was marked enough to make work on the two manuscripts at one and the same time difficult for him; yet he would certainly have maintained that they did not conflict with each other. He had engaged in writing the *Invectiva* for purposes of political propaganda, to serve the *patria Florentina* with his pen.

But the *De Tyranno* was intended to defend Dante's views on Universal Monarchy; it was a book by Salutati the humanist, not by the head of the Florentine chancery.

This modification, however, merely shifts the problem we have encountered to another field. Why, one must ask, did the old leader of Florentine Trecento Humanism fall so completely under the spell of the medieval Universal Empire and its inherent monarchism as soon as he was no longer under the immediate impression of the Florentine struggle? And how did it happen, when the war dragged on and he returned to his literary studies, that the feeling for the dangers and needs of the hour could so surprisingly fade from his mind?

An essentially comparable development, we recall, was observed in Petrarch.[23] In his youth, under the stir of Cola di Rienzo's revolution and Rienzo's plans to rebuild a Roman republic, Petrarch had pioneered in passing from the medieval views to a humanistic love for the ancient *Respublica Romana*. Already earlier, he had discovered for himself the age of Scipio and Hannibal and composed the first draft of his *Africa*. When the political expectations roused by Rienzo's adventure had broken down and Petrarch pinned his hopes on the Emperor Charles IV, his early inclination to admire the republican attitude, and to emphasize the *Respublica Romana*, quickly disappeared; the old arguments of medieval monarchism came again to the fore. In Salutati's development, too, we encounter clear foreshadowings of the republicanism of Renaissance Florence during his younger years; until the early 1390's he endorsed substantially the very same views on the Roman Republic that he denounced so violently later on in the treatise on the Tyrant.[24] To a point, the uncompromising harshness of Salutati's reasoning in *De Tyranno* finds its explanation in the fact that a renegade was trying to rub out what he had come to look upon as an error and a blot on his past. We may, then, say that every attempt of the historical writers of the Trecento to cross the line between the historical sympathy for the *Imperium Romanum* and the sympathy for the *Respublica Romana*, had ended with a come-back of the imperial universalism of the Middle Ages. When Salutati with his *De Tyranno* opposed the rise of a new historical outlook on Roman history among the younger generation, it was, therefore, merely the last and most dramatic of many kindred Trecento episodes. It was the most dramatic because now, at the most critical moment of Florentine history, the inherent bent of the Trecento spirit proved its strength in the conduct of the man who was still recognized as the leading representative of the Florentine humanistic group.

In a large measure, therefore, our historical estimate of the impact the political crisis had on the growth of Renaissance thought depends on our knowledge of the strength of surviving political medievalism in the world of the Trecento; of the conflicts which gradually developed in Petrarch's and Salutati's generations; and of the vitality of the medieval thought still preserved on the threshold of the new century.

But an understanding of this intellectual struggle in the background of the crisis of transition requires a more precise delineation of the general character of Salutati's Humanism.*

* In the last analysis it would even require a consideration of the character of the Trecento in general; for the repeated restrengthening of strongly marked medieval convictions and sentiments during the two generations which preceded the Quattrocento is a phenomenon that is not limited to political thought nor to the slowly growing world of Humanism. The observation that after the 1340's there was a reversal of many a step toward a new outlook on life that had been made in the early Trecento applies likewise to art and Volgare literature and to the attitude of men in all social groups to the values of the

Salutati's Civic Humanism and Its Limitations

Salutati's conduct during the last years of his life—he died in 1406 at the age of almost seventy-five—must not, to be sure, obliterate the picture of Salutati the pioneer of civic Humanism. Leonardo Bruni always revered Salutati as his spiritual father; many of the pages which follow will bring fresh evidence that Bruni felt himself indebted not only to Salutati the humanist scholar, but even more to Salutati the humanist chancellor who had stood for a

---

earthly life. To mention merely the major causes, one may perhaps say that during the crucial period of the 1340's the beginning departure from medievalism in various fields of culture had been arrested by the simultaneous operation of three agonizing experiences: the political disappointment following the collapse of Cola di Rienzo's attempt at a federal reconstruction of Italy under the leadership of the city of Rome; the financial breakdown of the Italian banking houses throughout Europe, which ruined nearly all the great fortunes and the middle-class wealth of the time of Dante; and the destruction of countless human hopes by the Black Death. In many ways the psychological consequences of these catastrophes continued to be felt until, toward the end of the century, their memory was dwarfed by the new challenges discussed in the present book. To understand how novel the responses to these challenges were, one must consider the retarding forces which had characterized the period from the 1350's to the 1390's. Even in painting and literature—in the choice of iconographic themes as well as in artistic expression—the spiritual climate of the time of Giotto had been transformed in a fashion sometimes approaching the attitude toward man found in medieval phases prior to the Trecento. This has been demonstrated, particularly for the time from 1350 to 1375, in Millard Meiss' *Painting in Florence and Siena After the Black Death* (Princeton, 1951), a work which through its consistent emphasis on the deflection of many Renaissance-bound tendencies during the latter part of the Trecento gives welcome support to the interpretation of the period that we propose in the chapters which follow.

fusion of the legacy of Petrarch with the civic world of Florence.

But it is equally true that our historical evaluation of Salutati will remain incomplete if we fail to stress the fact that his Humanism, in spite of his pioneering position, remained in some basic respects far from that philosophy of life, and especially that historical and political outlook, which characterized the citizen-humanists of the Quattrocento. Before true Quattrocento Humanism could arise, other and very essential contributions had to be made by citizens who stood outside of the humanistic tradition (such citizens as Cino Rinuccini), and by a younger generation whose thinking had been shaped in the political crisis during Giangaleazzo's last years. Therefore, if we wish to see the intellectual revolt of the time around 1400 in historical perspective, we must select not only those elements of Salutati's Humanism which made the aging chancellor Bruni's forerunner and teacher, but we must also learn to see Salutati as a child of his own generation, still strongly medieval, still groping—as the younger humanists saw him, and as Bruni sketched him in his early writings: an ally in spirit, to be sure, but just as much a representative of a past that had to be overcome if Quattrocento Humanism was to come into its own.

Humanists of the later Quattrocento and of the Cinquecento showed little inclination to count Salutati among the leading spirits of the humanistic movement. The recent revival of historical interest in his correspondence and scholarly works will not entirely reverse their appraisal. What prevented Salutati from enjoying any lasting fame in the humanistic era is that as a writer he was second-rate; his Latin does not belong in the mainstream of language that leads from Petrarch to the great humanistic writers of the Quattrocento, but represents a mixture of humanistic and scholastic elements. In the history of hu-

manistic thought, he occupies a similar position. While
he brought Petrarch's Humanism closer to the political,
moral, and religious world of the lay citizenry, he also
brought back many a medieval element. Here, too, his
thought did not go exactly in the direction which was to
lead to the Quattrocento.

The same appraisal even holds true of Salutati's greatest contribution to Humanism from the layman's world:
his part in the vindication of the *vita activa-civilis*.[25] In his
early years, he had planned a treatise *De Vita Associabili
et Operativa*. He had begun work on it in 1372.[26] To judge
by its title, the work must have been intended to be a
counterpart to Petrarch's *De Vita Solitaria*, and to be written from the point of view of a citizen. If Salutati's work
had been completed, it would have occupied the place in
the history of civic Humanism which was to be filled, two
generations later, by the *Della Vita Civile* of Matteo
Palmieri, a disciple of Bruni. But Salutati's further literary
career proves that the civic mind of the late Trecento did
not yet possess the self-assurance which would have enabled it to remold Petrarchean Humanism; a recurrent
distrust of the values of this world and the recognition,
from the viewpoint of religion, of the superiority of contemplation did not yet allow an unwavering stand in defense of the active life. We hear no more about Salutati's
work on the proposed book about the *vita operativa;*
instead, in 1381, came a treatise *De Seculo et Religione*,
which presented the life of the monastery as the highest
moral ideal—an ideal not applicable to all only because
few men can attain to it. Filippo Villani called this work
"useful to acquire a loathing of the busy life" and compared it in its effect with Plato's *De Immortalitate Animarum* whose study, as Filippo thought, had caused many
readers to take their own lives. There was no doubt, said
Filippo, that every reader of Salutati's book "would leave

the *saeculi vanitas* behind and retire into a solitary and religious life, burning with love for it." [27] We may believe, then, that Salutati's treatise had its share in leading Filippo Villani and other Florentine humanists of the late Trecento from the *vita negotiosa* to the *vita contemplativa*. Their flight from an engaged civic life was a factor to which we shall have to give more attention when exploring the crisis of civic thought and conduct about 1400.[28a]

In the case of Salutati himself, the difference in outlook between the *De Seculo et Religione* and many letters which show his civic-mindedness or worldly disposition is striking; indeed, it creates a challenge for the student of Salutati.

In a sense, the intentions of the *De Vita Associabili et Operativa* and of the *De Seculo et Religione* neither conflicted nor overlapped. The *De Seculo* was composed as a guide for a friend who had entered a monastic order, and the ideas and ideals developed in this vademecum for a monk do not in themselves indicate that Salutati had come to consider them as valid for a layman like himself. It has been argued that his aim in writing the book was to put his skilled and eloquent pen in the service of his friend, just as he was wont, as Florentine chancellor, to write for his Commune persuasive diplomatic letters which cannot always be thought to express his personal convictions. This comment, although literally correct, does not, however, come to grips with the real problem. The problem does not lie in the fact that Salutati, on occasion, lent his humanistic pen to eloquent praise of monastic life as a goal for those who had entered a monastery; the same thing could and would be done by fifteenth- and sixteenth-century humanists. The puzzle lies in the manner in which Salutati carried out his task: his subsequent failure to complete the partly written treatise on the *vita associabilis et operativa*, the logical place for any argument against the *vita monas-*

tica, and his utter pessimism and contempt of the world pervading every line he writes *"de saeculo,"* i.e., on human life outside the haven of the monastery. Only one generation later, a representative of Renaissance Humanism would no longer have felt compelled to make this world appear as repulsive and sinful as possible in order to create a black contrast to the joys of the monastic life. Something of humanistic serenity and the citizen's pride in his own world of action would have been reflected in a fifteenth-century writer's picture of the *"saeculum."* The chapter titles of Salutati's *De Seculo* amount to one of the fullest lists imaginable of medieval vituperation against every aspect of human life. "What else is this world, in which we take so much pleasure, but a *campus diaboli, temptationum palestra, officina malorum, et fabrica vitiorum?"* "The world, indeed, is the disgusting filth of our disgraceful actions" (*immundissima sentina turpitudinum*), "false joy, vain exultation, land of tribulations, sea of misery, shipwreck of virtue, mirror of vanity . . . and meeting-place of everything transitory." [28b] This is not merely seen from the perspective of the monk; Salutati leaves no doubt that in his eyes this scale of values has validity for the layman as well, including himself personally, even though he remains—and feels that he wishes to remain—in the prison of this miserable existence, "which, fool that I am, I have myself failed to keep clear of." As his book is to demonstrate, men are able to escape from their shackles; yet, "to their shame," the majority do not leave behind *"terrenam hanc et corruptibilem patriam"*—even though "I and the other followers of the world" (*ego et reliqui sectatores mundi*) know well enough "what we love and how miserably we are entangled by it." [28c]

Two observations may help to place Salutati's treatise in its proper perspective. One is that there had been an evident change in his outlook between about 1370 when he planned the *De Vita Associabili*, and the years after 1380 when the *De Seculo* was written. For, until the later 1370's, his correspondence had been marked by a strong secularism which had also characterized his views of antiquity, as will presently be seen. About 1380, after misfortune had overtaken so many Florentine families during and after the upheavals of the Ciompi in 1379, he fell into a more somber mood and talked with stronger reservations about the values of this world. The impact of this experience on the gloom pervading the *De Seculo* is clearly indicated in a page of the work itself, where the author turns from his general despair of life to the specific destruction and decay which his own eyes had seen in his beautiful and noble *patria*, Florence. The grand structure of the *Palazzo Vecchio* (we read) had fallen into neglect and, before long, would lie in ruins; so would the Cathedral which, together with its beautiful Campanile, had seemed destined to become one of Florence's greatest prides. "How many and magnificent houses of citizens and how many palaces have been destroyed by the internal discord of our citizens! How many have been annihilated by fires sometimes set deliberately, sometimes caused by chance!" If this is what we see around us, "what ought we to think of those things which, as all agree, are even more perishable?" [28d]

During all the subsequent decades of Salutati's life—this is our second observation—the unquestioning secularism of his youth never returned, but was replaced by tensions and frequent alternations between opposing attitudes. He did not arrive at any reconciliation, as we will find in striking detail when studying the treatise *De Tyranno*. Although on various occasions he advocated the *vita activa*, he insisted that he did not wish to question "the superiority and greater perfection" of the contemplative life, because separation from the world opened the most direct

access to the love of God. Contemplation was "more sub-
lime in view of its high level of thought, more pleasant in
view of the sweetness of tranquillity and meditation, more
self-sufficient in view of its need of fewer things." It was
only through a loophole in his reasoning, namely that the
true best is not the best in every given situation, that
Salutati came to the rescue of the *vita activa*. "The contemplative life is better, I admit; but it is not *always*
preferable, and not for *all*. The active life is inferior, but
ought to be chosen many times." [28e] The outcome was a
perplexing oscillation—not unparalleled in other writers
of the late Trecento—between the various strands of Salutati's thought. Of this vexing phenomenon we will become
repeatedly aware.

The civic contribution which Salutati did make was twofold. He led the life of a citizen: not only did he have a
family, but he served his commonwealth as a political
servant and with his pen. Moreover, he defended this
mode of life in many practical instances of his own conduct and that of his humanist friends, even though he was
not able to justify it as a matter of principle, in a systematic
way. This defense is in particular found in his letters,
where Salutati the citizen revolts against tenets of the humanistic philosophy of the Trecento long before any of
the more academic humanists. To give an example: Salutati, who married young, had originally not seen how he
could justify this betrayal of the studious life, except by
admitting that now he was experiencing the truth of the
saying that man cannot serve both woman and philosophy
—but, in time, he would return and recapture his soul. [29]
By the early 1390's he had the courage to recommend
marriage to men of letters, thus openly disregarding the
advice of Petrarch, his master. [30] On other occasions he
warned friends not to give up the active life rashly because
of the false idea that the peace of the cloister offered a

safer and more direct way out of the misery of this earth. Though monastic seclusion may have served some holy men to escape from the woes of the world, many others had found greater support in their quest of a worthy life in the *"negociosa et associabilis vita."* "To devote oneself honestly to honest activities may be holy, and holier than laziness in solitude. For holiness in a [quiet] country life is useful only to itself, as St. Jerome says. But holiness in a busy life raises the lives of many." [31] About 1400 and in the years immediately following, we find Salutati defending similar convictions against the attacks of well known clerics. In 1401, he addressed himself to a Camaldolite monk, Giovanni da San Miniato, member of an order which emphasized contemplation rather than active work. While you serve only yourself and a few fellow brothers— so we may epitomize this letter—I try to serve all of my many co-citizens. Withdrawing from the world may be the safer thing to do since the human spirit out in the world easily feels itself to be farther from God. But God is close to man also in the midst of secular activities and studies. Just as we derive advantages from the work of past generations, we feel the urge to be of some use to others. The work of students should be like that of peasants who plant trees intended to grow for their grandchildren. [32]

At times, this layman's reaction included bold excursions into more distant fields. For instance, when Salutati, in carrying on Petrarch's disparagement of natural science as a knowledge that does not improve man's moral being, wished to defend the thesis, characteristic of many early humanists, of the preeminence of the study of law over that of medicine, [33] he finally admitted the citizen's high estimate of the *vita activa* into one of his treatises. In his *On the Nobility of the Laws and of Medicine*, he buttressed his opinion with the pointed assertion that the ultimate goal of human life is the use of man's knowledge

in the discharge of his social obligations, such as is implicit
in the jurist's activities; but the ultimate goal can not be
the search for knowledge for its own sake, such as is the
nature of the scientist's pursuits, of which the doctor's profession seemed to Salutati merely a branch.[34] To reinforce
his preference for studies bringing man into contact with
active life, he seized upon the doctrine, familiar to religious
philosophers since Augustine, of the superiority of the will
over the intellect; [35] he thus became the harbinger of a
philosophical motif which grew important in Renaissance
thought two generations afterwards, in the days of Florentine Neo-Platonism. Another instance will attract our attention in a later chapter. There we shall see that Salutati's
readiness to acknowledge truth outside of the sphere of
tradition led him beyond the typical attitude of the Trecento to a more sympathetic reevaluation of the religion of
the pagan poets.[36]

Yet, this is not the whole story. Whether or not the
Humanism of the Trecento would finally be transformed
by the layman's spirit depended in the last analysis largely
on what influence the positive attitude toward the *vita
activa et politica* would have on the evaluation of the
ancient way of life. The crucial experience was the discovery of the features of antiquity that were different from
the half-monastic *vita solitaria* ideals of the Trecento humanists. Without love for the *humanitas* of the ancients,
and without the readiness to be educated by it, there can
be no Humanism; and without minds opened in sympathy
to the values and ideals of the *vita activa et politica* of
Greek and Roman citizens, civic Humanism could not
come into being.

Now at this decisive point Salutati no longer seems
merely a pioneer blazing the trail into the future. Not that
he always failed to look upon antiquity with the eyes of
a citizen; on several occasions (we shall discuss the most

outstanding one, the rediscovery of Cicero as a Roman citizen, in the next chapter) he was the first to observe what was different in the Roman way of life from the ideals of Trecento humanists, and at times he supported and defended what he had discovered. But when he realized that his sympathy with the *vita politica* of the ancients demanded a profound shift in the humanist's relationship to antiquity and a reinterpretation of the history of Rome and the Empire, he retreated just as he had abandoned his plan to write a book *De Vita Associabili et Operativa,* but had written *De Seculo et Religione.* In the case of his recognition of Roman civic life his retreat was not even modified by casual justifications in his correspondence, but eventually issued in an unequivocal recantation.

One of the causes of this recantation was that Salutati did not have both feet on humanistic ground. While his life among the citizens of Florence kept him in touch with civic traditions from which humanistic *literati* of Petrarch's stamp were cut off, it also held him to medieval trends of thought that Petrarch had already largely left behind. Just as Salutati continued to cling to the medieval, prehumanistic aspects of Dante's thought, so he eventually drew near to Augustine's condemnation of the paganism implicit in the *virtus Romana.*[37] This is a change which has been insufficiently emphasized, and even denied outright, by some students of Salutati; yet it is one of the keys to the enigma of the abundant contradictions in Salutati's writings.[38a] Not that in later life he berated the *virtus* of the ancients in the crude tones found in some medieval writers. But suspicion of the political heroes of antiquity, totally absent from the writings of his youth, colored his every approach to the ancient *exempla* especially during the last decade of his life, from 1396 to 1406.

The young notary-humanist, in looking ahead ambitiously to his life's career, had started out quite unashamed of his "*gloriae cupiditas*," according to the testimony of his early letters.[38b] Moreover, as a chancery-humanist he used his pen in the struggles of the Tuscan city-states as if there was nothing higher than the success of one's *patria*. Especially after 1375, as chancellor of Florence during the "War of the Eight Saints," he did not hesitate to repeat what the ancients had said in praise of a citizen's life and the need of his self-sacrifice for the commonwealth. In 1366, when writing to a noble citizen of the small Commune of Buggiano who had been banished, he admonished the exile to remain helpful to his *respublica*, however grievously he had been hurt by his fellow citizens. "There is no love comparable to the love for one's *patria*." Those great ancients had tried to work and fight for their country, even in exile.[39a] In commending a late member of the family of the Counts of Orsini, who had been an eager student of Roman history, Salutati remarked that the example of the great citizens of the *Respublica Romana* "excites in us, as it were, a desire for virtuous deeds and the daring to act as they did." [39b] Among those selected for respectful admiration was the elder Brutus. Who would not praise him "when reading how Brutus . . . put the salvation of his *patria* before the salvation of his own two sons." At that time, Salutati did not hesitate to commend Brutus. Again, in 1374, when trying to convince Francesco Guinigi, new leader of Lucca, of the need for rekindling the old friendship between Lucca and Florence, "*Romane libertatis auctor, Brutus*," together with Manlius Torquatus and Camillus, appeared among the models for the Lucchese "*liberator*" to follow. "For Brutus may claim to have expelled a king and beheaded his two sons when they appeared to want to bring back to Rome the tyranny to which he had put an end." Like Brutus, Guinigi should yearn for liberty and be ready for supreme sacrifices.[39c]

One finds in Salutati's early correspondence no trace of

the Augustinian fears of the earthly thirst for glory, the soul's absorption in political pursuits, and the pagan lack of true justice.[39d] In those years, he acclaimed Brutus the prototype of the just man: "Are you looking for a model of justice (*vis justicie formulam*)? You will find it in Brutus the Elder and Torquatus, who used their public authority over life and death without mercy against their own sons in order to save their *patria* and uphold military discipline." [39e] Quite similar was Salutati's reaction to the tale of Lucretia, the Roman matron, and her self-destruction after she was raped by the son of King Tarquinius Superbus—the famous suicide interpreted and branded by Augustine as an example of pagan vainglory. In a rhetorical *Declamatio,* which Salutati must have composed in his younger years,[40a] the pros and cons of the act are weighed objectively and without deference to the verdict of St. Augustine, in order that every reader might clearly understand Lucretia's motives as based on Roman ideals.

All these statements on Roman *virtus* say nothing, to be sure, that is not found in many later humanistic writers, but this is just the point which one must make to put Salutati's work into historical perspective: initially, Salutati had had an open mind for the civic virtue of Rome and had moved in the direction of the emancipation from medieval reservations and defamations that was to become typical of Quattrocento Humanism. No later work of Salutati's, indeed, shared the popularity of the *Declamatio* on Lucretia, which was copied and recopied in fifteenth-century Florence during the days of civic Humanism.[40b] In clear contrast, we find in many of Salutati's later writings that the vainglory and worldliness of the ancients have become for him an ever present concern. Although as late as the beginning of the 1390's he had been among the first to defend Cicero as a Roman citizen and statesman, by the time of the political and cultural crisis around 1400 the tone of his utterances was changed; in many respects, Augustine as seen through the eyes of medieval writers had reasserted himself. In 1396 we find Salutati defying his own previous claim that Brutus had been impelled to suppress his fatherly feelings by a genuine and exemplary sense of justice. "Do you really believe that Brutus . . . at the moment when he gave the order to have his sons beheaded for their plot to restore the monarchy, simply obeyed rigid justice enthusiastically, but did not rather remember, along with the salvation of his country, the glory which comes from praise in this world?" Surely, Virgil had been correct in writing the famous verse on Brutus' motives (*Aeneid*, VI 823) *"Vincit amor patriae laudumque immensa cupido."* [40c]

Salutati, then, saw something pejorative in the ascription of Brutus' motives to *amor patriae* and *gloriae cupiditas*, and one cannot fail to remember that the same Virgilian words had been the motto of the young Petrarch on the day of his coronation as a poet on the Roman Capitol: he, like Virgil, Petrarch had on that occasion confessed with pride, had been driven by *"amor patrie laudumque immensa cupido,"* because without these goads he would never have written the epic, *Africa*, the picture of Roman greatness for which he was about to be crowned. In the mouth of Salutati in the year 1396, the same words of Virgil serve to expose the evil inherent in the mentality of the ancients. "Has not every group of pagans," Salutati's letter goes on, "burned so ardently with the desire for glory that they directed all their living efforts and their vain deaths to this one end?" [40d]

From that time onward the thought of Brutus and the other Roman heroes seems to have come to Salutati only as a warning against the ambiguity and worldliness of the pagan world. In returning to Virgil's words on Brutus a few years later, he acknowledged that they were meant to celebrate Brutus' deed, together with the heroism of the Greek Ephialtes, as one of the highest examples of *virtus*. Still it is wrong to think, he maintains, that in the hearts of these men there was nothing but virtuous desire; they also harbored loves and passions which slowed their willing response to duty. "Believe me, either would have acted with greater virtue (*virtuosius*) or, at least, without doubt more cheerfully and willingly, if in saving or obeying their *patria* they had passed sentence upon a foreigner or enemy," and not, like Brutus, chafing against his fate, upon his own offspring.[40e] When Salutati, in the last year of his life, entered into a heated controversy with young Poggio (about which more will be said later) that involved the relationship of the moderns to the paganism of antiquity, the probing into Brutus' less overt and praiseworthy motives led Salutati once again to gravely doubt the inherent paganism of Brutus' motivation. "Whoever directs a virtuous action toward anything else but the true and ultimate goal, is sure not to perform an act of virtue, even though we may have to commend him in every other respect." As Virgil had seen so well, Brutus had been a "*glorie captator non minus quam patrie conservator et vindex.*" And even as far as his deed was a sacrifice for his country, the *patria* cannot serve us as the ultimate goal. "For if the *patria* were our true and ultimate goal, we could not adulterate our actions for her by misusing them for praise, lucre, power or honor. . . . The true goal, then, is God himself." [41a] Granted that some ancient sages and leaders did despise death with seemingly stout hearts, in the last analysis, as may be learned from Augustine, they chose death out of fear, or because of a pusillanimity which made it seem too difficult for them to face life. "And they were driven, more than by anything else, by glory." "For our corrupted nature, forgetful of its origin, directs itself toward other ends than God." [41b]

Salutati's last literary work, the *De Laboribus Herculis*, is interspersed with similar accusations. We look in vain (we read there) for the ideal poet in ancient Greece and Rome because impiety, the effect of paganism, and the direction of all labors toward worldly glory "did not allow antiquity to attain the kind of perfection that mortals in their mortal life are well able to reach." [41c] "*Ceca gentilitas*" which "*nichil sibi pro fine [proponebat] nisi gloriam atque famam!*" [41d]

A humanist who in this manner showed himself increasingly open to doubts arising from the spirit of the Augustinian Middle Ages, was also destined to grow increasingly restive under that other departure from medieval ideas which followed of necessity from an admiration for the great citizens of the *Respublica Romana*—the shift of sympathies from imperial to republican Rome. To distrust the sincerity of the Roman citizens who knew nothing higher than their *Respublica* implied a deadly criticism of men like Cicero, Cato, Brutus the younger, and Cassius. In addition to the patriotic sentiment which made Salutati recoil from leveling criticism at the great Florentine poet Dante, there was, then, a medieval strain in Salutati's thought which rendered it difficult for him to conceive that Dante's judgment of Caesar and Caesar's assassins was anything but the unalterable truth. Accordingly, Salutati's change from early praise of the *virtus Romana* to calling it into question was paralleled by a change from early admiration for the citizens of the *Respublica Romana* to a revival of the medieval belief in the religious and political superiority of the Empire. The final step was a recrudescence of the monarchical interpretation of Roman history.

It is important to emphasize that such inconsistency and retraction are indicative not only of Salutati's personality, but of the general character of pre-Quattrocento Humanism. A discord between recent experience and traditional conviction, producing inner unrest and intellectual struggles, and followed by submission to or a compromise with the powers of the past: this is a pattern often repeated in the Trecento.

Even Petrarch was by no means immune to the repressive impact of medieval tradition. He had left the spirit of the Augustinian Middle Ages far behind—his admiration for the Roman character was no longer dampened by condemnation of the Roman "thirst for glory." And yet, in the second half of his life he, too, profoundly changed his attitude toward the last champions of the *Respublica Romana*. In his younger years, during his passionate partisanship for Rienzo, he could say that every epoch of tyranny in Rome had produced its Brutus—the Brutus who drove out the last King, the Brutus who killed Caesar, and the "third Brutus" Rienzo who at this moment was reviving the Roman republic.[42] In later life, Petrarch was unable to see any valid reason for Cato's resistance against Caesar, and condemned Cato's suicide almost as violently as Augustine had done [43]—though he was then thinking more in terms of the political necessity of Caesar's work than of the divine hand guiding it. As with Salutati, the accents of Petrarch's approach to the history of Rome had thus in the course of his life become completely reversed. In the years when he had first conceived his *Africa*, and had been associated with Rienzo, he had given enthusiastic praise to the *Respublica Romana*, at the expense of the emperors. In his old age, profound admiration for Caesar reigned once more supreme. Although the humanistic portrait of Caesar that Petrarch then drew in his Caesar biography was as dissimilar as possible to the customary medieval picture of the founder of the divinely instituted universal state, it remains a fact that in his later life Petrarch, too, turned to the old reverence for the Universal Empire of the emperors.[44]

In the case of Petrarch, no doubt, one basic cause for the reemergence of the faith in the imperial monarchy was that the father of Humanism had little contact with the experience which shaped life and conduct in the Italian city-republics. His interest in the *Respublica Romana* dwindled just as soon as Cola di Rienzo's Roman revolt turned out to be no more than a short-lived venture. If Petrarch called again on the medieval faith in the *Imperium Romanum* for aid, he did so because he, like Dante before him, had come to pin his hopes for a pacification of Italy on a German Emperor, Charles IV. Moreover, his growing interest in Caesar—whom in his youth he had considered the destroyer of Roman liberty—sprang largely from his conviction that Caesar was the prototype of those enlightened tyrants at whose courts Petrarch spent the second half of his life. His *Mirror for Princes*, addressed to Francesco da Carrara, appealed to the authority of Caesar just as his letters to Cola di Rienzo had appealed to the authority of the *Respublica Romana*.[45]

One would think that no other humanist of Petrarch's school was better placed than Salutati, chancellor of Florence, to bring the seminal ideas of Petrarch's earlier years to fruition; and for a while, Salutati was indeed touched by the spirit of Roman citizenship more deeply than Petrarch had ever been. But little by little, the combined pressure of medievalism and of a century in which tyrannical monarchism engulfed an ever larger part of the Peninsula, closed in even on the Florentine humanist. In the *De Tyranno*, written in Salutati's old age, the long and weary process of retreat from the new positions was to reach its climax.

CHAPTER 6

REPUBLIC AND MONARCHY IN LATE TRECENTO THOUGHT

*The Rediscovery of Cicero
the Citizen and Defender of the Republic:
Salutati and Vergerio 1392-1394*

THE humanists' quest in Petrarch's and Salutati's generations for the *Respublica Romana* came to a focus in a passionate debate on Cicero as a Roman citizen and thinker. Of the objectives and sentiments of Caesar and Brutus only indirect evidence by ancient authors was available. But in the works of Cicero the voice of one of the last champions of the Roman Republic had been recorded, and thanks to the discovery of Cicero's letters by the humanists it was heard again clearly from the mid-Trecento on. Thus the discussion of Cicero in the second half of the Trecento became a prelude to the rediscovery of the *Respublica Romana* in the early Quattrocento.[1]

To the Middle Ages, Cicero the author of the *Tusculan Disputations* had been a stoic sage, a model of aloofness and suppression of those passions that govern public life. For a thousand years, there had been no room for Cicero's civic doctrine that man is meant to play an active part in his community and in the state, and not to pursue mere solitary contemplation. Petrarch, through his discovery of Cicero's intimate *Letters to Atticus* in the Cathedral Library of Verona in 1345, was the first to meet the historical

Cicero face to face. He saw a Roman citizen who relinquished his offices in the state only under compulsion, in consequence of Caesar's victory; who from his rural retreat followed political events with feverish attention; and who after Caesar's assassination went back to the confusion of the civil war, and so to his ruin. Petrarch, humanist of the Trecento that he was, shrank back in horror from this discovery. He wrote his famous letter of accusation to the shade of Cicero in Hades: "Why did you involve yourself in so many contentions and useless quarrels," he reproached his fallen idol, "and forsake the calm so becoming to your age, your position and the vicissitudes of your life? What vain splendor of fame drove you . . . into a death unworthy of a sage? . . . Oh how much more fitting it would have been had you, philosopher that you were, grown old in rural surroundings, . . . meditating upon eternal life, . . . and not aspiring to consular *fasces* and military triumphs . . . !" [2]

However much Petrarch admired Cicero's eloquence, his precepts for a cultured life, and his freedom from dogmatism, superstition, and the errors of polytheism—Cicero's civic spirit was to Petrarch nothing but an offense against all the traditions of the Middle Ages. In his humanistic works, written in the solitude of the Vaucluse, Petrarch endeavored to stress the contrast between Cicero's vain and restless political career, and the fruitful solitude of his old age. In the *Rerum Memorandarum Libri* and even more in *De Vita Solitaria*, Cicero is presented as the historic example of a citizen who against his own will bore testimony to the superiority of a solitary life. All of Cicero's literary works, Petrarch insists, were written in the "*solitudo gloriosa*" of his old age. "It was solitude that caused this man's mind to open—and what is more, and this is the strange and wonderful thing: it was a solitude which he abhorred. What, we may ask ourselves, would that mind have accomplished if he had desired his solitude!" [3] But Cicero could not bring himself to forget the Republic which, Petrarch cries, "had gone to pieces from the ground up, as you admitted yourself." "What I find lacking in your life is perseverance, a striving for quietude such as is becoming to a philosopher's profession, and withdrawal from the civil wars once liberty had been extinguished, and the Republic buried and bewailed." The times did not call for freedom but for Caesar's proved and praised clemency. Cicero, Cato, and Labienus should have been content to accept that clemency. [4] In all the works of Petrarch's later life, in his *De Gestis Cesaris* as well as in his *De Remediis*, there is this recourse to the "clemency" of Caesar. [5]

The great historical interest of Petrarch's relationship to Cicero lies in the fact that it allows us to see so clearly the unconscious connection between the way of life of the humanist *literati*, and the monarchical interpretation of Roman history. Petrarch the "Stoic," in whose eyes the striving for quiet and solitude is "becoming to a philosopher's profession," found most congenial those among the many contradictory Roman appraisals of Caesar which insisted that with Caesar's era the days of the tumultuous freedom of the Republic had ended, and that the hour had come for quiet literary pursuits under the protection of a monarch. Petrarch, who was himself to follow this way of life at tyrants' courts, thought the transition to monarchy in Rome an historical necessity.

What would be the effect of Cicero's correspondence, and how would Petrarch's interpretation fare, when Humanism came to be adopted by citizens living in the freedom of the Florentine city-state? In 1392, Coluccio Salutati found himself confronted with an almost exact duplication of the events of 1345. Whereas Petrarch first viewed Cicero's real life and political conduct through his discovery of the *Epistolae ad Atticum*, a still more in-

timate picture of this life and its setting was suddenly revealed to Salutati when he discovered Cicero's *Epistolae
Familiares*.[6] By 1392, Salutati had begun to set forth in
his correspondence casual justifications for the way of
life of a citizen; he was accustomed to talk of Caesar's
"criminal attack on the Republic," and to call the emperors
"tyrants." [7a] Florence, at that moment, was just emerging
from her first war with Giangaleazzo (1390-92) in which
Salutati had so eloquently defended the *libertas* of the
Florentine Republic against the rising Monarchy of the
Visconti.[7b] This was the situation in which Salutati was to
appraise Cicero's participation in the political struggles of
Rome.

Like Petrarch, Salutati was jubilant that Cicero at last
stood before him in flesh and blood, Cicero who thereto-
fore, he said, had been to him no more than an author of
books and theories. But whereas Petrarch's joy had soon
turned to bitter disappointment, the Florentine chancellor
honored and admired the very characteristics that to
Petrarch had seemed unworthy of the life and maxims
of a true philosopher. He did not overlook the weaknesses
in Cicero's character which had repelled Petrarch, and
which no reader of this most ruthless of self-exposures has
been able to ignore since then: Cicero's despair in misfortune, his faint-heartedness in danger, his vanity, and
his improvidence when all went well. But for Salutati, the
positive net result of his study of these letters remained
his new insight into the great final struggle of the *Respublica Romana* that supplied the setting for the life of Cicero
the politician; this positive result was "the observation of
the basis of the civil wars," of "the causes which cast the
metropolis of the world from popular freedom down into
the servitude of monarchy." [8]

When a humanistic friend, the Bolognese chancellor

Pellegrino Zambeccari, reminded Salutati shortly afterward in the true spirit of Petrarch that so unruly and impassioned a life as that of Cicero was unbecoming to a philosopher,[9] Salutati replied that it was the duty of every *"civis et vir bonus"* to rise to the defense of his commonwealth against subversion and tyranny. Solon, according to the *Noctes Atticae* of Gellius, had decreed that a citizen who in times of civic unrest continued to lead his private life was to be considered faithless to his city, and to be expelled. Lucanus was of the same mind when, in his *Pharsalia,* he had Cato ask: "Shall I alone live in leisure" (*otia solus agam*) when the whole world is afire? Cicero had acted as a true philosopher, and as a Roman like Brutus and Cato, neither of whom thought it permissible for a Roman citizen to retire into solitude. And as to the reproach that Cicero had entered upon his political career not without "ambition," we may learn from history "that all Romans desired offices and positions of honor, all coveted praise and glory; this striving was bred into them so deeply by habit, custom and nature that in their writings and in their speech they did not refrain even from self-praise." [10]

Salutati himself may not have gone beyond these statements of fact; he simply noted what his experience of the life around him suggested for the interpretation of Roman conditions. Yet there were implications which, if allowed to develop, were bound to destroy the foundations of the Trecento outlook. If it is the duty of the *"vir bonus"* to defend his commonwealth against subversion and violence, what then of the "stoic" precepts of aloofness and the solitude of the sage? If Brutus and Cassius merely obeyed a civic duty, why Dante's condemnation of them, and what about the appraisal of an Empire built on the subversion of the *Respublica Romana?* If the "ambition" of the Romans, and their "thirst for glory," were accepted as psychological facts, what then was the humanist to think of St. Augustine's reservations?

Some of these implications were promptly brought to the fore by Pier Paolo Vergerio.

Vergerio, Salutati's most gifted disciple in the early 1390's, in those years lived in Padua from where he maintained contacts with the Florentine humanistic circle. During a later stay in Florence, at the end of the 1390's, he was to become Bruni's fellow in the Greek studies under Chrysoloras, and the intimate friend to whom Bruni's *Dialogi* is dedicated. Like Bruni, Vergerio (born in Capo d'Istria) was not of Florentine origin, and, in contrast to Bruni, he never became a Florentine. Yet in trying to place Vergerio geographically, his Latin pen name *Hister* (from Istria) is as misleading as Bruni's cognomen *Aretinus*. Sentimentally Vergerio remained connected with his Istrian home town, as Bruni remained with Arezzo; but for nearly fifteen years (1390-1405), the very years of the crisis of Humanism at the turn of the Trecento, Vergerio found in Padua what Bruni found in Florence: a new *patria* and the stage for a life in which *studia* could unfold side by side and in mutual fructification with political interests.[11]

Padua, as we noted previously, had been an exponent of civic liberty and civic culture in the earliest phases of Humanism. As a political and cultural center in northeastern Italy it was, to be sure, second to Venice; but Venice was aristocratically exclusive—slow to encourage contacts between political citizenship and the Humanism of the intellectual middle class; and it was strongly under the influence of the Orient. At the beginning of the fourteenth century, in the time of Albertino Mussato, Padua had preceded Florence in producing the first example of a civic culture fused with classicism. But when the city-state of Padua began to be crushed between the expansion of the

Visconti and the superior might of Venice, little survived of that early civic liberty and ebullience. The constant danger threatening from abroad was instrumental in bringing into power the native signory of the Carrara, and since the time of Petrarch, who passed the last years of his life as a guest of Francesco the Elder of Carrara, Padua no longer contributed actively to the growth of civic Humanism. Still, she had retained enough of the old atmosphere of a city-state to remain a fertile ground which could receive and develop the ideas that now began to be disseminated from Florence.

This was the situation when the young Vergerio found a refuge and a new *patria* in Padua, and at the same time established close personal contact with Salutati. Vergerio had met Salutati in Florence as early as 1386/87, and again about 1394; from the early 1390's on they were exchanging ideas by correspondence.[12] From the very first, the influence of Florence and of Salutati's personality were powerful factors in shaping Vergerio's mind. As early as 1391 we hear him acknowledge that in Salutati he had found the guide and master of his life.[13] This attachment to Salutati included the adoption of the advocacy of the *vita activa civilis*.

Indeed, no clearer and more resolute formulations of Salutati's civic ideas can be found than those contained in Vergerio's letters in the 1390's—clearer and more resolute even than Salutati's own. Among these postscripts to Salutati's philosophy, there is a remarkable sequel to the defense of Cicero the Roman citizen against the stoic and monarchical objections of Petrarch.

In 1394, doubtless in connection with Salutati's vindication of Cicero of 1392, Vergerio in Cicero's name wrote a reply to Petrarch's letter addressed to Cicero in Hades.[14] As Petrarch had examined the political situation at the end of the Roman civil wars through the eyes of the partisans of Caesar, so Vergerio revived Cicero's and Brutus' faith in the continued vitality of republican liberty—their firm conviction that the Roman civic spirit had not been destroyed for good by the corruption of the moment. Never during the period of Cicero's participation in the civil wars, Salutati's disciple asserts, had Roman freedom "fallen so low that it was beyond the possibility of revival through wisdom and through force." [15] This judgment of Vergerio was based on what we may call the first genuine historical understanding of the spirit of the *Respublica Romana* and its last defenders. To Petrarch's reproaches Vergerio offers an answer which a Roman himself might have given: that Cicero had of necessity spent an active life in the service of the Roman Commonwealth because his philosophy had always aimed not at stoic peace of mind but at the kind of wisdom "which is at home in the cities and turns away from solitude"; in many of his works, Cicero had most highly prized the life of the man who "troubles himself with work for the state, and shoulders the labors one must share in the interest of the *salus omnium*." [16]

Together with the revival of the Roman ethos, the political standards of Cicero and Caesar's assassins become visible again in Vergerio's interpretation. The final verdict, Vergerio makes Cicero say, cannot depend on whether Caesar showed magnanimity and "clemency" toward his enemies; Caesar's crime was that he helped to bring about an era in which "clemency" was needed, whereas "the laws and the Senate" ought to have ruled the state. "For just as the name of cruelty is hateful in a free commonwealth, so is the name of clemency—because we would not get accustomed to calling a man 'full of clemency' if he could not also be cruel with impunity." [17] Our fight, Vergerio's Cicero explains, was against Caesar's monarchical position, not against his person. We would have fought in the same way against any other usurper, be it even Pompey or whoever. We later had to fight just so against Augustus when he, who had at first intended to guide the state in the name of the Senate and the people, "destroyed liberty in order to become a tyrant— he who could have been the first citizen of a flowering commonwealth." As little as Cicero had been able to content himself with Caesar's clemency, just as little could he now be satisfied with "the friendship of a lord" in the place of "the justice becoming to a citizen." [18]

Why did this clear and definite vision of the Roman civic spirit fail to bring about the final historical vindication of the *Respublica Romana?* Why did it not have the strength to shift the emphasis in historical outlook away from the medieval notion of the overriding worth of universal imperial monarchy?

Vergerio's Return to Monarchy in Princely Padua

Our first consideration must be given to Vergerio's personal development.

Even a cursory glance at Vergerio's later writings shows that he did not maintain, let alone enlarge, the views he had formed in the years of contact with his Florentine friends. But the external conditions of the second half of his life were so exceptional that we must know them before drawing any general conclusion from the fact that our search for sequels to the bold ideas of his youth remains in vain. [19]

Vergerio's personal fortunes were closely linked to the fortunes of Padua's independence. The first moves in Giangaleazzo Visconti's drive for expansion had turned Padua, Vergerio's second *patria,* into a weak buffer-state between the large territories of Milan and Venice—and so Francesco Novello da Carrara's return after the catastrophe of 1389 could not mean more than a concluding chapter in the history of Paduan independence. When, after the breakdown of Giangaleazzo's empire, Venice began to consolidate her Italian possessions, the signory of the Carrara and the last vestiges of Paduan independence disappeared: from 1405 onward Padua was a provincial town in the Venetian *terra-ferma* state.

The catastrophe of 1405 ruined Vergerio's career as a humanist and destroyed the continuity of the studies for which he had laid so promising a foundation. Before long, one of the best minds of the pioneering generation of the early Quattrocento was lost to the humanistic cause. For the next ten years he found a refuge in the chancery of the Papal Curia; but this was no congenial soil for his talents. The former champion of the *vita civilis politica* eventually took the lower orders. As a writer of Latin he could not compare with brilliant stylists such as Bruni and Poggio, his colleagues in the Curia. When the Curia had moved to Constance for the Church Council, Vergerio took advantage of the opportunity and about 1417 transferred to the chancery of Emperor Sigismund which was then also in Constance. Later he went to Hungary in the service of Sigismund, and there he spent the last decades of his long life. After he had left Italy, his literary production ceased; he had long been forgotten at home when he died at Budapest in 1444.

One might be tempted to conclude that, if Vergerio's life had remained more stable, his work would have continued its early course. But the literary documents left from his youth show clearly enough that even during the one and a half decades of his connection with Padua (from 1390 to 1405) his intellectual equipment had included elements that were unrelated to, if not irreconcilable with, his discovery and recognition of Cicero the Roman. Even if Padua had not lost her autonomy in the relentless fight for power between Milan and Venice, even if Vergerio had remained a member of the group of Paduan humanists all his life, still, under the conditions of the Paduan environment, his youthful vision of the Roman civic spirit would hardly have grown into a lasting vindication of the *Respublica Romana.*

Paduan literature, to be sure, continued in many respects to cherish the memory of the civic freedom of the by-gone communal period. It did so particularly during the years when the citizens of Padua were struggling desperately against Milan and Venice to defend their independence, while looking to the signory of the Carrara for native leadership in the fight against the external enemy. But these patriotic motives in the recognition of the Carrara dynasty did not alter the fact that Padua during the Trecento had gradually become a typical north-Italian Renaissance Tyranny—a process which by the 1390's had long been completed. In this world, scholars and *literati,* unless they were absorbed by their teaching within the old Paduan University, led the life usual for humanists at north-Italian tyrant-courts: they did not form their minds in the give and take among the citizenry, but held positions either in the princely chancery, or at the court where they educated princes and young courtiers. Vergerio, during his Paduan period, was both a chancery official and a teacher of princes; his most important work, the *De Ingenuis Moribus et Liberalibus Studiis Adolescentiae,* composed soon after the time he had spent in Florence for the study of Greek under Chrysoloras, is dedicated to the Carrara prince whom he tutored.[20]

All this does not mean that the shades of an unusual and splendid past ever ceased to hover over the city and to make its intellectual atmosphere different from that of other tyrannies. These memories lingered even after Padua had become a quiet provincial town within the *terra-ferma* state of Venice. Long after Vergerio's Paduan years, the

humanist Sicco Polentone, a citizen of Padua and from
the 1410's to the 1430's an official in the city's chancery,
clearly showed their mark in his pioneering work on the
history of Roman literature, the *Scriptorum Illustrium
Latinae Linguae Libri XVIII*. The Florentine ideas of
Cicero the Roman citizen and the *Respublica Romana,*
which had been fully hammered out by that time, found
understanding and sympathy in the work of this Paduan
humanist at an earlier time than they were echoed elsewhere in the humanistic literature outside of Florence.[21]
Again, as late as the 1440's we encounter a Paduan specimen of the literary genre to which Bruni's patriotic
Laudatio of Florence had belonged—a panegyric on
Padua, the *De Laudibus Patavii* by Michele Savonarola.[22]
But these late fruits of the Paduan civic spirit throve in
the quiet which followed after the end of Padua's independence. During the era in which the city had still
strained every nerve to preserve its autonomy, and had
found the support necessary for its defense in the vitaliza-
tion of its forces through the Carrara dynasty, it was rather
the interest in the merits of monarchy which was in the
foreground of Paduan literature. Petrarch, during his stay
in Padua, had set a humanistic standard with his mirror-
for-princes for Francesco the Elder of Carrara in 1373;
and Vergerio, in spite of his so warmly acknowledged debt
to Salutati and to Florence, remained in most of his work
done in Padua an heir to this Carrarese tradition. While
Salutati's Florentine disciple Bruni came to compose the
Laudatio Florentinae Urbis and finally the *Historiae
Florentini Populi,* Vergerio wrote not a history of the
Paduan people, but the *Vitae Principum Carrarensium,*
a work imbued with admiration for the ruthless power-
politics by which the Carrara of the early Trecento had
imposed their tyranny. Modern historians have classed
these *Lives* among the early forerunners of Machiavelli's

Prince. In such a book there was no room for the memory of Cicero nor for the legacy which the city-state of antiquity had left to the civic commonwealth of the Renaissance. Instead, it harked back to Caesar as the founder of the Roman Monarchy. Vergerio repeated the tradition that Caesar had assumed power with the words of Euripides "if right must be violated, let it be violated for the sake of power." Thus the luster of the greatest historical model was borrowed for those who had built tyranny in Padua.[23]

It might be said that one should not attempt to make this work of Vergerio's carry too heavy a burden in the argument, because the extent of the identity of Vergerio's own views with the maxims of the heroes of his history has become somewhat doubtful by the recent discovery that substantial parts of the text were adopted from earlier Paduan biographies of the Carrara despots.[24] But we find the same attitude also in an original composition from Vergerio's pen, a fragment called *De Monarchia,* which we can prove originated in the latter part of the Paduan phase of his life—after the years when he had been under the influence of Salutati and Florence.[25] In this short treatise, government by more than one ruler is judged as necessarily producing injustice and abuse of the weaker members of the society. Whether the men in power are many or few, the participation of several minds is bound to produce civil strife, and must, therefore, be considered as a transitional phase leading to monarchy, which will emerge eventually to enforce order and respect for the law.[26] Starting from this assumption, the treatise returns to many aspects of the political and historical thought characteristic of the Trecento. The metaphysical and theological argument reappears that monarchy is the best of all forms of government because it reflects the principle of unity in nature and universe, and the rule of the single

God.[27] Classical antiquity is called on in this context to supply examples of good and bad princes—a purpose for which the personalities of the Roman emperors have to be quoted instead of the citizens of the *Respublica Romana*.

In the 1390's, at the time when he shared with Salutati the experience of the rediscovery of the citizen Cicero, Vergerio had been among the first to read *in extenso* Petrarch's *Africa*, of which only fragments had become known in Petrarch's lifetime. The manuscript of the epic had remained in Padua after Petrarch's death and was then posthumously edited by Vergerio.[28] But the republicanism of Petrarch's poem eventually prevailed over the influence of Vergerio's Paduan surroundings as little as did the memory of Salutati's civic philosophy.[29]

Paduan Ideas on Tyranny About 1400: Giovanni Conversino's "Dragmalogia On the Preferable Way of Life"

The impact of the Paduan milieu on political thought and historical outlook can be reconstructed most vividly with the help of the *Discussion on the Preferable Way of Life* (*Dragmalogia De Eligibili Vitae Genere*) of Giovanni Conversino da Ravenna, who along with Vergerio was the most eminent humanist of Carrara Padua between 1390 and 1405. Giovanni Conversino had been the teacher of most of the ranking north-Italian humanists of the first Quattrocento generation: Vergerio himself, Sicco Polentone, Guarino da Verona, Vittorino da Feltre, Leonardo Giustiniani, and Francesco Barbaro, to mention only the best-known names. If Vergerio's connection with Padua may be looked upon as a relationship comparable to that of Bruni with Florence, Conversino was in age and significance the Salutati of Padua.[30]

When we place Conversino's *Dragmalogia* side by side

with the politico-historical works of Vergerio and treat these writings as representative of one humanistic group, we do not do so arbitrarily. For Vergerio himself must have sensed a kindred spirit in Conversino, since he advised him in a personal letter to send a copy of the *Dragmalogia* to the Pope, or even dedicate the book to him.[31] This work of Conversino's, under a title which seems to promise no more than a contribution to the problems of moral philosophy, had been composed as an essentially political work. It is a dialogue between a native of Padua and a native of Venice, in whose mouths the choice between an existence devoted only to studies and an existence also embracing the *vita activa-politica* is identical with the choice between life under a princely patron and life in a city-state like Venice. Thus the core of the book becomes a comparison between Renaissance Tyranny and Renaissance Republic.

In weighing the source value of Conversino's comparative estimate, it is important to note that his work is not a eulogy *ad majorem gloriam* of the Paduan Lord, although the tenor is that of a consistent praise of Tyranny. The dialogue was written in 1404—at the height of the struggle which doomed the Padua of the Carrara—when Francesco Novello da Carrara had thought it necessary to stop payment of all salaries to his scholars in order to employ all his resources for military defense. Just like Vergerio not much later, Conversino was forced to leave Padua, after twelve years of teaching and of service to the court of the Carrara. He was entirely unconvinced of the need for such drastic measures, and considered them a betrayal of the spirit for the sake of narrow material advantages. His work, composed when, after his departure from Padua, he had found a refuge in Venice, thus turned out to be in some parts an invective against his former Paduan patron rather than a eulogy; nevertheless, it became an unqualified vindication of the superiority of Tyranny, including the past reign of the Carrara in Padua, and an unqualified condemnation of life in a civic society.[32]

It is this absence of a possible desire to flatter a patron which gives unusual value to the *Dragmalogia* as a source. Conversino wanted to set forth the views on Tyranny and Republic which he had formed in the course of a long life. The restless career of an itinerant humanist had caused him to live in many cities of northeastern Italy until, in Padua, he was placed in the storm center of the Milanese-Venetian struggle. His varied and extensive experience, therefore, may be considered in many respects as typical of that of north-Italian humanists in general at the time when Tyranny was molding the political life of the Po valley. In a sense, the *Dragmalogia* tells us about the mind of north-Italian humanists and about their social and political setting in the same way in which most of the other works discussed in this study tell us about the mind and background of Florentine Humanism.

In Conversino's discussion, even more than in Loschi's purposeful propaganda, we are, then, given an opportunity to fathom the political sentiment of the region where Giangaleazzo made his conquests of minds as well as lands. In every town in the path of his advance, Giangaleazzo was hailed by humanists and writers as the prince who would bring unification to all Italy. In the *Dragmalogia* we can observe the blend of experience and selfish interest from which this welcome sprang. Conversino, looking over the political scene of his days, was not thinking of liberty; he was thinking of security, prosperity, and efficient government. Wherever the people themselves have assumed power, he says, peace and progress have been destroyed. This is what had happened in Padua. The ambition and the mutual hatred of the Paduan citizens had brought about invasions of foreign tyrants until the Carrara had put an end to the excesses of both *plebs* and *nobilitas,* and "the city under Tyranny breathed freely once more." [33] This is what had happened in Bologna. In the mid-Trecento, as long as it was a part of the state of Giovanni Visconti, that city had been a flourishing center of architecture and scholarly pursuits. But after the recovery of its autonomy in the loose framework of the Papal State, it had fallen on times of discord and civil strife, until the renewal of monarchical rule, under Giovanni Bentivoglio and under Giangaleazzo Visconti, brought about "regeneration." [34]

On the strength of such observations, Conversino sets forth the following argument: Since partisan passions and private interests direct the opinions of every individual, it happens rarely or never that all the opinions of the citizens of a state meet in harmony and allow effective common action. Acts of public clemency or liberality, which are the bases of peace and prosperity in any community, can therefore not be accomplished in a republic. But in a tyranny, the general interest and the interest of the ruling prince coincide; thus even a "mediocre" prince is better than any republic. Events past and present teach us "that more happiness has been achieved during the lifetime of a single ruler than during a century of people's rule." [35] This greater effectiveness of the prince is the experience which dominates Conversino's life. In his own lifetime, Conversino says, Lewis the Great of Hungary (1342-82), within the span of a single generation, had raised a people from barbarism to the height of civilization.[36] But the examples closest to his heart are the two tyrants who, during the second half of the Trecento, established order and prosperity in the region where Conversino lived most of his life: Niccolò II d'Este of Ferrara, and Francesco II (il Vecchio) da Carrara of Padua—both now dead. Conversino's description of their accomplishments is a revealing commentary on the political ideas of north-Italian humanists in the age of Giangaleazzo. These are the highlights:

To Niccolò d'Este, Ferrara owed its transformation from a mire-bound and evil-smelling place into one of the cleanest, healthiest, most populous, and sightliest of cities. Niccolò paved the streets and laid sidewalks, replaced tile structures with stone houses, raised forts and towers, and fortified the suburbs.[37] His neighbor Francesco da Carrara had no sooner taken the reins than he put Padua's fortifications in good condition, covered the empty spaces in town with stately buildings, stimulated the arts and crafts, introduced the woollen industry, increased the prosperity of the citizens, and bestowed incomparable patronage and care upon the humanistic studies (*studia litterarum*). At the same time he built bridges and aqueducts, moved river beds, transformed exhausted valleys into fertile lands, covered bare hills with imported vines, and, all in all, accomplished so much "that someone unfamiliar with the truth would conclude that these works were the achievement not of one man's lifetime but of many generations." Beyond all this, Francesco had done more for the beauty and cultivation of the Euganean Hills—the pleasant hilly region where Petrarch had spent his last years—than a republic could have accomplished in a century. These achievements of tyrants are seen in proper perspective when one turns to neighboring Venice. There one encounters public buildings that could not be completed within a lustrum and are standing about unfinished; or one sees dams that have not been completed in the course of several lustra. "So slowly do republics work. For the thoughts of their leaders are absorbed by the cares of the moment and too burdened to turn toward the future." Conversino adds: such things occur even in Venice, although the strict oligarchy of that city comes closest to the efficiency of a monarchy.[38]

What applies to political order and economic progress, the argument goes on, also applies to the patronage of the humanistic studies. Princes, who from their childhood on are accustomed to greatness, magnificence, and the desire for glory, and have not labored to acquire their wealth, are the only sort of rulers sufficiently prepared to meet the expenses of patronage.[39] It was the great princes of the leading tyrant families who became the promoters of the new studies: first King Robert of Naples, and then men such as Jacopo da Carrara, Niccolò d'Este and, more than any other tyrant, Giangaleazzo Visconti.[40] No wonder that the patronage given by republican governments does not stand comparison. Where the private life of the ruling men is taken up with "mercenary" commercial pursuits, no interest can be expected in poetry, rhetoric, philosophy, history, or any works of the mind; public councils will not show the liberality needed to provide the funds for such studies.[41] "Where the multitude rules, there is no respect for any accomplishment that does not yield a profit; accomplishments that make money are accepted, those of leisure are rejected. For when everybody is either engaged in piling up money, or is indifferent to a name beyond the city walls, everybody has as much contempt of the poets as he is ignorant of them, and will rather keep dogs than maintain scholars or teachers." The basis for this judgment is, as Conversino tells us, his experience during frequent sojourns at Venice. The bent of mind encountered among Venetian citizens, he says, is entirely commercial, calculating, and averse to all studies. Here is a city whose colonial history competes with that of Rome; yet she has not produced any adequate historiography, but allows the great deeds of her past to fall into oblivion. If the works of her native chroniclers, written in Volgare, were to be endowed with the majesty and conviction of great historical writing, they would have to be

couched in the only language read beyond the local sphere
—Latin; and that would make it necessary to attract by
patronage the services of the best minds from abroad. "For
just as it is unbecoming to sing one's own praises, just so
one cannot exalt the glory of one's own people without becoming suspect of falsehood or guilty of boastfulness; this
is why Rome derived her highest fame from foreign historical writers whose leisure was favored and sustained by
the emperor, because of his good judgment, or perhaps
through good luck; for eloquence is a rare and divine
gift—not the gift of business and want, but of quiet and
plenty." [42]

These are comments of extraordinary interest, because it
rarely happens that our sources allow us so directly to
seize upon the reaction of late Trecento humanists to their
political and social milieu. Even Conversino's observations
on the relations of Humanism to the city-republics of his
day deserve to be considered with care, although he obviously speaks as a partisan of tyrannical rule, who had
spent most of his life in the surroundings of tyrant states.
The fact that the debate between the Venetian and the
Paduan citizen in Conversino's dialogue gives no more
than a bare mention to Florence,[43] must not make us overlook that the analysis is concerned with the nature of Republic and Tyranny in general. Certain remarks in the
introductory pages show that Conversino at the time of
his writing was not too well disposed toward Florence. Admirer of Giangaleazzo Visconti that he was, he echoed the
sentiments of Italian nationalism and indignation against
Florence which had been aroused by Giangaleazzo's propaganda when Florence had called the German army of
King Rupert to invade northern Italy.[44] But Conversino's
dislike of Florence does not blot out the significance of
the fact that around 1400 an informed observer could
comment on the relationship between city-republics and

Humanism in the terms we have related, without fear that he would be given the lie by what was known of Florentine Humanism. Nor is there any reason to suspect that Conversino's version of the relative merits of Republic and Tyranny was due to a lack of acquaintance with the Florentine conditions. In his boyhood, during the 1350's, he had been in personal contact with Boccaccio, and had visited Florence. In the years 1368-69 he had even lived there for some time, as a notary and a teacher at the university. As late as 1400 he had revisited Florence on his way to Rome, and subsequently he had been exchanging letters on scholarly subjects with Salutati.[45]

Only one generation later, no serious writer would have dared repeat Conversino's verdict so far as Florence was concerned; even the Milanese humanists were agreed by then that Humanism on the Peninsula had its focus in the Florentine Republic.[46] Conversino's opinion, then, has a claim to our attention insofar as it reflects the contemporary scene as seen by a critic whose eyes were sharpened by aversion. It helps to drive home the truth of an observation we have made several times before: the almost complete identification, in the first quarter of the Quattrocento, of Humanism with the Florentine Commonwealth was due to forces that were of recent origin. As late as the end of the Trecento, when Conversino gathered the material for his comments, one could still think of the growth of Humanism and the ascendency of tyranny as a single process in which the city-republics played only a minor role. It was the years around 1400 which brought about the decision that the civic element, leading in culture and politics in the age of the Communes but on the decline during the Trecento, was again to come into its own, and that the Florentine Republic was to assume the foremost place.

Among the developments that were still unknown to

Conversino, or were greatly misjudged by him, was the new humanistic historiography. He was well aware that historiography was the field in which the city-republics could make the greatest contribution; but to him they had failed even here, and had been doomed to failure, because success was impossible without the kind of patronage which would attract the best talent from abroad—and only tyranny could offer that kind of patronage. Now obviously the importation of humanistic historians from abroad was not the way in which Florence, during the next few decades, became the cradle of the new humanistic historiography—even though the merchants of Florence began to provide the kind of patronage which Conversino had seen given only by princes. Neither in historiography nor in any other literary field did Florence owe her importance chiefly to the presence of foreign *literati* gathered to enjoy patronage. From Bruni to the great historians of the early Cinquecento, Florentine historiography remained the work of native citizens and humanists.[47] What would Conversino have felt, one wonders, if he had known that by 1429 the Florentine Republic would produce a historiography which caused all Italy to read history with Florentine eyes, while the Milan of the Visconti was trying in vain to attract from abroad humanistic historians of equal caliber? [48] The error that made Conversino misjudge the forces which in his day were revolutionizing the relations among Humanism, tyranny, and the city-republic, sprang from his failure to grasp the significance of the fact that beside the full-fledged humanists there were at work in Florence citizens of the type of Cino Rinuccini. In Florence, citizens were becoming humanists in mind, and soon Florentine humanists would be citizens in mind.

Finally, *Dragmalogia*, which throws so much light on the political convictions and experiences of the humanists in northern Italy, also illuminates the interrelations that existed between the political experience of humanists of Conversino's stamp and the monarchical interpretation of Roman history.

In Conversino's eyes security, progress, and patronage are not found anywhere but under tyranny, and thus the final answer in the quest for the "preferable way of life" amounts to this: No true freedom can be found in this world, excepting the freedom of the man who, inspired by religious faith, renounces all things of this world, honors, possessions, and family. The only other way to what men may call "freedom" is a carefree country life in the midst of nature, dedicated to study and literary work, and this under the protection of a prince who sees to it that all men, assured of the stability of the public order, can follow their own pursuits, and that private, conflicting ambitions do not result in constant strife.[49] The lesson to be learned from history is that only where this protection exists can there be individual freedom and real public efficiency. In ancient Rome, it was the reign of Augustus which made it possible for Virgil, Horace, Ovid, and many others now unknown, to find intellectual freedom and the means of leisure. It was Augustus who turned Rome from a city of tile into a city of marble. It was the reign of Justinian which ordered the civil law.[50] "The Roman empire was founded, and gained its strength, through its kings. Afterwards, when haughty citizens disdained to obey a haughty king, the state came to be ruled by the people (*populariter*), but, God knows, under how many disturbances and revolutions: first tribunes of the people, then generals, and finally *decemviri* full of arrogance harassed the people and the commonwealth. True, we cannot deny that the Roman people accomplished great things under its consuls, although it was then often looked down upon and scorned. But how trifling is this greatness compared with the greatness of the empire and the dignity to which, we read, the Roman people was raised and exalted under the emperors!" [51]

The same lesson is taught by the development of all other nations. In ancient Asia, even female monarchs like Semiramis, Thameris, and Marsepia pacified and enlarged their realms. The Greek *respublicae* of Athens and Sparta, so often praised, were actually exhausted by constant wars and torn by civil strife "and recovered only under kings." To return to Rome: "History teaches that, more glory accrued to the majesty of Rome under the reign of Augustus than during many preceding centuries." [52]

While Florentine citizens and humanists were engaged in working out a new conception of Roman history which eventually was to break down the medieval view of the Roman Empire, the leading humanist of northern Italy thus used the rich store of observations he had laid up during a long life among the north-Italian tyrannies, to buttress the waning historical concepts of the Trecento. The emphasis on the *Respublica Romana* had implications that were explosive; the emphasis on Augustus and the Roman Monarchy fitted in with all the arguments of the medieval and Trecento traditions. The chapter in Conversino's dialogue which sets forth the monarchical vista of Roman history begins in the time-honored fashion, without any change of perspective: "The more similar the creature's condition is to that of its creator, the more beautiful, orderly, and perfect the creature is in its life. Consequently, since the creator and ruler of all things is one, government by one man is in my opinion preferable because of its greater conformity with the universe than any other form of government." [53] Family, Church, Empire: each of them is ruled by one head; consequently, past and present experience of the greater efficiency of tyranny only confirms what has to be expected. [54]

Despite the realism, therefore, which Conversino had

learned through his intimacy with the north-Italian tyrant-states, he had retained unchanged the fundamental traditional conceptions. In Florence, simple citizens, who could not compare with the great north-Italian educator in intellectual brilliance or classical scholarship, had something new to say about the historical past and about the nature of their state; in the world of the north-Italian tyrant courts, even the author of a work as illuminating in respect of the political thinking of northern Italy as the *Dragmalogia* shows himself incapable of drawing from the experience of the Giangaleazzo period the vital new ideas which were soon to destroy the medieval outlook.

In that world of the north-Italian tyrant courts, where medieval monarchism easily fused with the new monarchical experience of Renaissance tyranny, there was practically no chance that Salutati's and Vergerio's discovery of Cicero the Roman citizen and of the *Respublica Romana* could survive, much less that it should develop into a new stimulus for the relationship of the cultured citizen to civic society, and into a new view of the parts played in history by empire, monarchy, and republican freedom.

But was Salutati, then, with all his advantages over Vergerio, well enough equipped to keep his and the young Vergerio's flag aloft in a Tuscan city which in the 1390's still looked comparatively insignificant on the cultural and political map?

CHAPTER 7

THE PLACE OF SALUTATI'S *DE TYRANNO*

Salutati's Reversal: A Vindication of Caesar's Monarchy Against Cicero

WE know from various earlier observations that even Salutati in later life surrendered some basic positions to which he had advanced in his younger years. Would he be capable of fighting a persistent up-hill battle against the combined authority of medieval traditions and the doctrines emanating from the ever-growing tyrannical sector of the Italy of his day? We may assume that all of Salutati's friends and correspondents outside of Florence, most of them chancery officials in north-Italian signories, shared Conversino's opinions; and he could not conceal from himself the fact that the tenor of these opinions, even apart from the confirmation they received from Dante, was in perfect accord with many of Petrarch's ideas. But even in view of all these restraining counterforces, we should hardly suspect how far Salutati eventually was driven back if we did not have the unique evidence of his treatise *De Tyranno*.[1]

We do not know whether Salutati ever read Vergerio's answer to Petrarch, written in the name of Cicero in 1394,[2a] and so we have no way of telling when it was that Salutati came to understand that his defense of Cicero would lead to a clash with the traditional views on Caesar and the Empire. In any case, the preface of *De Tyranno* shows that the controversies which Vergerio had originated in

Padua eventually reached Salutati in the form of an inquiry from a Paduan student: The Florentine chancellor was requested to decide whether the motives and the action of Caesar's assassins had or had not been justified. We know from Bruni's *Dialogi* that this same problem also stirred the younger generation in Florence at about the time of Salutati's writing; for in his first dialogue Bruni, in opposition to Salutati, has his character Niccoli reproach Dante among other things for the injustice of the cruel punishment to which the defenders of Roman liberty are condemned in the *Inferno*, and it is Salutati who is depicted as Dante's partisan. In the second dialogue, he is made to admit that a citizen's models ought to be the Roman heroes of republican times, but repeats his profound respect for Caesar and defends the treatment accorded to Caesar in the treatise *De Tyranno*.[2b] In support of the genuineness of this picture of the old master, we may point to some Latin epigrams of Salutati himself. They were composed probably about the time of the *De Tyranno*, to serve as inscriptions for a portrait cycle of Famous Men in the *Palazzo della Signoria*. Among these short poems we find epigrams on Caesar the conqueror, on Augustus, and on Constantine the Great.[2c] Needless to say, in the eyes of Bruni's generation the admiration ought to have been saved for the great citizen-leaders of republican days, and Salutati himself would in his younger years hardly have sung the praises of Caesar and his successors. In a later chapter we will observe how different a portrait cycle of famous Romans was to look from the changed perspective of the younger generation.[2d]

The preface of *De Tyranno* states in plain words that the long, systematic elaboration of the book's argument is to lead up to the demonstration that "the divine Dante, my fellow-citizen and countryman, was not in error when he consigned Caesar's assassins to the lowest pit of Hell." [3]

When we reach the climax of the work, it becomes evident that this conclusion is tantamount to a passionate reversal of Salutati's former approval of Cicero as a Roman statesman and citizen. As Petrarch once had taken Cicero to task and told him that in his conduct toward Caesar he had failed as a stoic sage, so now Salutati addresses Cicero to tell him that he had failed also in the light of true political philosophy.

This true political philosophy is hardly different from that proclaimed by Conversino, and since the latter visited Florence early in 1400 and had conversations with Salutati on literary subjects,[4] it is quite probable that some of the ideas which we encountered in Conversino's writings were at that time discussed between Salutati, already occupied with his *De Tyranno* (written during the second half of 1400), and his north-Italian visitor who was to compose his *Dragmalogia* only four years later. "Is it impossible, then, for a commonwealth to exist under a monarchy?" the chancellor of Florence, once the writer of republican manifestoes in the 1370's, now asks in his *De Tyranno*. "Did Rome not have a commonwealth while it was ruled by kings? Was she again to have no commonwealth after Caesar, not even under the rule of a most venerable prince?"[5] Salutati reminds Cicero of those teachings of Aristotle's *Politics* which the Middle Ages had always singled out before all others: that monarchy is theoretically the highest form of government, and that it must be considered the best in practice when a ruler is found who is an "*optimus princeps,*" that is, "a good man devoted to wisdom" (*vir bonus et studiosus sapientiae*). "Why do you, Cicero, recoil from what you have learned from Aristotle?" In the end, just as with Conversino, there comes as crowning proposition the medieval argument: that form of human government is best which most closely corresponds to the rule of the world by the one

Divine Lord.[6] And side by side with the reasoning of medieval politics appears the medieval concept of history: The hand of God (*divinitatis vestigium*) can be seen in Caesar and in Caesar's victory.[7] "When Dante, the wise and Christian author, recognized in the outcome of events (which is the truest witness of the Divine will) God's resolve to bring human affairs under one single Roman Monarchy—did he not then have to consider those who dared oppose this disposition as enemies of the Divine will, as men who belonged among the condemned and the rejected?" [8]

The judge, then, of the tribunal before which Cicero was summoned for another time, was once again medieval tradition—and, indeed a narrower medieval outlook than that of Petrarch around the middle of the century. Yet Salutati, even though resolved to defend Dante's views, was himself a humanist. Humanism, then, took part in the debate—but to condemn Cicero, not to absolve him. The new accurate knowledge of the political conditions and of other authors of Cicero's time proved Cicero wrong, Salutati argued. "Answer me, Cicero, please," the long indictment begins, "what port it was that you saw beckoning to the storm-tossed vessel, if it was not the subjection of the state to the will of one victor? . . . Tell me, did you not think of the five years of Sulla's dictatorship which, though stained with blood and fatal to so many of the vanquished, gave yet a certain stability to the state?" And how much more beneficial was Caesar's dictatorship which justly reduced both victors and vanquished to their proper stations and allowed men of all groups to enjoy their lives and positions. Was not this precisely Cicero's own judgment of Caesar, during Caesar's lifetime, in his oration *Pro Marcello?* [9] Any hope for the state, Salutati's analysis continues, was indeed empty and vain unless it was based on the "clemency and equity of the victor" (*victoris cle-*

mentia et equitas). Senate, *ordo equester,* and plebeians
had long been sapped by mutual discord, and were incapable of action. Caesar alone could have cured the state,
he alone could have brought about unity. His assassination
made the remedy, monarchy, impossible for a long time to
come, and kindled anew the civil war.[10]

This, then, was the historical score on which Cicero's
conduct was to be judged: the relentless strife initiated by
Sulla could teach the generation of Cicero "that to bring
such disorders to an end required a monarch who would
provide the standard by which the body politic could be
aligned in the proper order. For that polity (*politia*), or,
rather aristocracy, which was the object of your love,
Cicero, could not provide the cure for the evil because of
the discord among the minds of men. . . ." The result
proved the point: When Caesar's murder had "broken
the harmony of monarchical rule," it became unmistakably
clear "that it was not only expedient but necessary that
the rule be assumed by one ruler" who could bring together the discordant spirits. "If this had not come about
in the person of Augustus, the passions in Rome would
never have been stilled." Otherwise, Augustus would not
have renounced his favorite dream, the restoration of the
Republic, to which he had given so much thought.[11] And
as to Cicero's letters, whose discovery had started the humanistic quest of *Imperium* and *Respublica,* they now
seemed to prove to Salutati, as they had to Petrarch, that
their author could not conceal from himself the fact that
Pompey and Caesar, the two opponents, both had the same
goal, and that both desired supremacy in the state. But
then there could no longer be a question of fighting for
some ideal, or for some party: what mattered was to prevent a new civil war at any cost whatever. The object of
the fight could not be "that nobody at all assumed power
and leadership, but only which of the two would do so

and become the ruler." Both sides were equals in resources and "equals in forgetfulness of duty, in passion
and ambition, and in their readiness to suppress their
fellow citizens, to suspend the laws, and to consider just
whatever pleased or profited the victor. That struggle was
a fight not for the protection but for the subjugation of
the state. Which one took up arms with greater justice, to
quote Lucan, is beyond knowing." [12]

Pre-Renaissance "Realism":
A Parallel in Historiography to Late Trecento Art

What is the place of this piece of keen political analysis
in the development of Renaissance thought?

The shrewd realism, stripped of all illusions, with which
Salutati sets forth the conditions of ancient Rome, has been
considered a great pioneering achievement,[13a] and it would
indeed be impossible to name any forerunner or contemporary of equal accomplishment. A source of inspiration
for Salutati's realistic estimate of the guilt existing on both
sides was, to be sure, Petrarch's *De Gestis Cesaris*,[13b] and
the failure of most students to weigh Petrarch's role as
predecessor has tended to over-magnify the originality of
the *De Tyranno*. But Salutati, in taking Petrarch as his
model, was not a slavish imitator; helped by Petrarch's
understanding of the character and personality of each
of the Roman statesmen involved in the civil wars, he
succeeded in giving a coherent political analysis of the
situation of Rome, an historical task not yet exhaustively
carried out in Petrarch's biography of Caesar. The *De
Tyranno*, therefore, as early as the end of the Trecento,
gives us a glimpse of a significant trend in humanistic
thought, the cool-headed, matter-of-fact acceptance of apparent necessities, destined to become one of the characteristics of Machiavelli's and Guicciardini's objective analysis

of political conditions—a feature which since Burckhardt
has been brought into such sharp relief by students of the
Renaissance.

Yet, once this has been emphasized, we must go on to
say: Salutati's *De Tyranno* is also the very source which
demonstrates that the growth of political realism was not
the only, and not even the decisive, factor in creating the
politico-historical outlook which caused the Renaissance
to find a way of its own and break away from the basic
medieval convictions. The lesson taught by Salutati's treatise is that advanced realism in political details was well
able to exist side by side with the medieval idea of a static
universal empire willed by divine ordination and kept aloof
from natural historical change.[14]

We have already encountered several examples from
the late Trecento that exhibit a similar combination of
keen realism in the analysis of certain sections of life with
a continued adherence to guiding principles of medieval
thought. We have found substantially the same blend in
some later phases of Petrarch's work and thought.[15] In his
De Gestis Cesaris, the mythical figure of the founder of
the Empire was transformed into a rounded human being,
an individual portrayed as the prototype of a Renaissance
tyrant, and, with the help of the information found in
ancient authors, the triumph of the *Imperium* over the
Respublica was for the first time reconstructed as an historical process arising from the inherent weaknesses of
the late Republic. Yet all these epoch-making historical
discoveries helped rather than hindered Petrarch in re-
adopting, during the latter part of his life, the medieval
concept of Universal Monarchy which in earlier years he
had come close to rejecting. We encountered a similar
stage in the development of Renaissance thought when we
observed that Conversino's interest in the progress of political efficiency—a new element expressed in a manner

hardly found before—remained reconcilable with adherence to basic tenets of medieval thought, such as the argument from the monarchy of God to the monarchy of man.[16] And there exists an even closer parallel to the method and central problem of *De Tyranno*. The question of the right or wrong of Caesar and his assassins, and of Dante's verdict, had been touched upon also by most of the Trecento commentators of the *Divine Comedy;* one of the last among them had been Benvenuto Rambaldi da Imola, the great scholar at the University of Bologna, who had dealt with the problem in great detail. His work is of particular interest to us because on its completion in 1383 it was sent to Salutati.[17]

We already know the mental make-up of Benvenuto Rambaldi from his dealings with the medieval legends about the origin of Florence.[18] His exceptional astuteness allowed him to recognize the self-defeating consequences of the assumption that Caesar had founded Florence and many other Italian cities; but Rambaldi was unable to substitute an historical alternative. The new philological methods of the humanists, which he was the first among the commentators on Dante to put to full use, did indeed lead him to deride the gullibility and wishful thinking of the medieval chroniclers—but only to arrive at an *ignorabimus.* In precisely the same way, the new methods led him to a keenly realistic, but also entirely sceptical and negative attitude in his appraisal of Caesar and the last champions of the *Respublica Romana.* For, on the one hand, his reading of the ancient authors, and even more his familiarity with Petrarch's biography of Caesar, gave him a wide knowledge of Caesar's achievements, the personal motives of the assassins which contributed to the deed, the failure of the Roman people to follow the call to freedom, and the miserable end of the murderers; these observations moved him to the conclusion that Caesar had died "a most undeserved death which seemed to have displeased God and men." [19] Seeing, on the other hand, the historical events also through Lucan's eyes and in the light of Cicero's *Philippics*, he also felt compelled to judge "that Caesar seemed greatly deserving of such a death; for the man who had bespattered the whole earth with the blood of citizens, had to repay by flooding the whole *curia* with his own blood." [20] "A wise man must take no sides" was Rambaldi's maxim, as he put it on another occasion.[21] With regard to the struggle between Caesar and the last Roman republicans this meant that he rested satisfied with the conclusion that none of the contestant parties was completely in the right; "both strove for power, both were ungrateful to their *patria*." [22] Was Dante, then, misguided if, in dealing with a situation in which there was wrong on both sides, he declared himself so passionately for one of them? Nothing is more revealing of the nature of late Trecento scholarship than to observe Rambaldi's reaction when he reaches this crucial point of the controversy.

In discussing the passage in *Paradiso* vi that deals with Caesar and the imperial eagle, Rambaldi is keenly aware that (as he says) Dante's standard is the conviction that "the Roman Empire has received the universal rule of the world from God." "And let it be noted here that the Monarchy of the Roman Empire was established under Caesar, extended under Augustus, restored under Trajan, found its justification under Constantine, was set in order under Justinian, consolidated under Theodosius, and strengthened anew under Charlemagne." [23] This is the medieval notion of the God-willed Universal Roman Empire, and Rambaldi leaves no doubt that he is ready to rest his own opinion on this train of thought; for in support of Dante's view he comments from his knowledge of classical literature that, according to Flavius Josephus,

the building of a world-wide empire succeeded only because God willed it, and that, according to Plato, a many-
headed animal is an impossibility—hence, the world needs
"unum caput" and *"unum monarcham."* [24] And to the
verses of the *Paradiso* VI 55-57, "Then, nigh the time
when all heaven willed to bring the world to its own
serene mood, Caesar, at Rome's behest, laid hold of it,"
he adds that these words must be understood to mean
"that, as in the high heaven one is the ruler on whom all
depend . . . , so one ruler is needed on earth." [25] But
what then of the realistic awareness that good and evil
were intermingled in the character of every one of the
actors in the great drama, and that right and wrong were
not all on one side? Evidently, this relativistic objectivity
has made Rambaldi only the more willing to hold that
one must anchor one's final judgment of *Imperium* and
Respublica Romana, and of Caesar and his assassins, in
medieval-religious considerations—in a sphere transcending the scepticism and lack of new standards at which
Trecento realism had arrived.

The attitude displayed by the foremost commentator on
Dante in the late Trecento provides a striking counterpart
to the argument of *De Tyranno.* Although Salutati's
analysis of the political conditions in Caesar's time is
infinitely more searching and penetrating than Rambaldi's,
his motivation and the way he uses his results are clearly
a product of the same phase of late medieval thought:
Realism and criticism are employed to prove the futility
of the standards which in the course of the Trecento have
gradually emerged from the increased knowledge of the
ancient authors, and from the broadened study of Roman
history; once this refutation is performed to the author's
satisfaction, the outcome is interpreted to mean that the
medieval standards and arguments may continue to be
what they had been in the day of Dante. Since vital po-

litical ideals had ceased to be at stake in the civil wars, so we may summarize Salutati's argument, and since in Pompey's and Caesar's Rome the contesting parties had about equal shares of right and wrong, the outcome of the contest must have been determined by something more than merely natural and historical causes: "By divine dispensation it came to pass that Caesar remained victor." [26a]

We can learn from a second source as well that the belief in a providential origin of Universal Monarchy was, indeed, a characteristic element of Salutati's thought at the time when the *De Tyranno* was being written. In his *De Fato et Fortuna*, published in 1399, he had another opportunity to defend Dante, this time against the accusation that his poem had ascribed too much to Destiny and left too little to man's free choice. Whenever, Salutati replied, apparently fortuitous events are actually part of a divine design, man's will is powerless. Of this fact the end of Brutus gives evidence. Although an accidental mistake seems to have snatched success away from him at Philippi, he was doomed because Providence was going to give victory to Octavian in order to establish the unity and peaceful order of the world under which Christ was to be born.[26b] Again the road to Dante's theology of history has been kept open.

In the field of art history, it is common knowledge today that in the late Trecento realism developed along many avenues without transforming the substance of the art which Giotto had created in the time of Dante; just as we know today that even earlier in the Middle Ages Gothic art had given free reign to realism in the treatment of certain facets of life while subordinating this partial realism to the expression of transcendent spirituality. On the other hand, the factor which produced a sudden and incisive change in the art of the first two or three decades of the Quattrocento was the emergence of a new ideal of man, together with the discovery of the laws of anatomy, optics, and perspective, knowledge of which was needed to express that new ideal and could largely be gained in the school of antiquity. Where these new tendencies became dominant, there would be no return to the style of the Middle Ages; hence the full break with the fundamentals of Trecento art.

It is too rarely remembered that these distinctions in the patterns of art also furnish us with a key to the phases of political and historical thought at the turn of the Trecento.[27] The event which had rendered possible Salutati's and Vergerio's historical discoveries in the early 1390's had been the ascendency of new ideals of human conduct: the ideals of the *vita activa civilis* for which there had been no adequate place in the thought of Trecento Humanism. Once this door had been opened, humanists could realize that the life of the citizen of the *Respublica Romana* had found its fulfilment in an active participation in his commonwealth; that the revolt against Caesar had been caused by the danger he had presented to such a citizenship; and that this danger was the situation that held the key to Cicero's philosophy and conduct. The gist of the transformation was that the ideals of the Renaissance citizen began to cast a new light on a neglected facet of the past. When these ideals reached maturity in the literary production of the younger Florentine generation after 1400, the promises of the early 1390's were redeemed.

Once the change is understood in this manner, it becomes clear why the civic sentiment of the Florentines, regenerated by the political crisis of their war for independence, could act as a leaven in the historical thought of the Renaissance; and why writers among the citizens touched only superficially by Humanism, like Cino Rinuccini and Gregorio Dati, or beginners in humanistic work like Bruni, became the pioneers of a new outlook. The break with many of the modes of thought of the Trecento, which is common to all these authors, was caused not so much by the gradual advance of scholarship or of realistic knowledge, but rather by the vigor with which civic sentiments aided the discovery of their ancient counterparts, thereby creating a broader vision of the past that could now be opposed to the traditional views of the Middle Ages and the Trecento. It was the very closeness of all these writers to the experiences and emotions of their own day which provided the stimulus for their historical discoveries.

Once the lingering notions of the medieval theology of history had thus finally been removed, while the lessons taught by the revolutionary events of the Giangaleazzo era were being absorbed into the political outlook, the causal and pragmatic thought, prepared during the Trecento, developed with astounding rapidity. We shall see presently that it is the little remembered *Istoria* of the Giangaleazzo wars by the Florentine citizen Gregorio Dati which in this basic respect represents a greater advance than *De Tyranno*.

In *De Tyranno*, the heart of the argument—the exoneration of Dante's judgment on Caesar and his assassins —was obsolete the moment it appeared. In the name of the younger generation Bruni, in his *Dialogi*, gave the answer at once: Dante's monarchism was to be modified in the light of the convictions held in the Florentine Republic, instead of being used as a weapon against them and as a means to depreciate the ideals of civic freedom represented by Cicero. To the end of the Renaissance, Bruni's reinterpretation, as we have seen,[28] remained the common Florentine reaction to Dante's verdict on Caesar.

At this point we should anticipate a possible objection. Our right to judge Salutati's views by the opinions expressed in *De Tyranno* might be questioned if the approach of this work to the past were basically different from that of Salutati's other piece of political writing in those years: the *Invectiva* against Antonio Loschi. But Salutati's refusal to allow his political realism to influence the bases of his historical outlook in *De Tyranno* is paralleled by his refusal to allow any such influence upon the results of his philological criticism in the *Invectiva*.

We have seen earlier that Salutati in the original version of the *Invectiva*, written almost simultaneously with Cino Rinuccini's *Risponsiva*, clung to the medieval notions of Guelphism, while Rinuccini began to reinterpret Roman and Florentine history from a city-state perspective.[29] In view of Salutati's subsequent discovery of the fact that Florence had been founded by veterans of Sulla,[30] the final version of the *Invectiva*, completed in 1403, ought to have brought out the vital idea that the Florentine Republic was an offspring of the *Respublica Romana*. But no fresh historical picture emerged from Salutati's philological study of the ancient authors. His source material, prepared with such expert criticism that humanists during the greater part of the Quattrocento had little to add to it, is presented in the *Invectiva* without the slightest hint that the settling of Florence by Sulla's soldiers implied the descent of the city from pre-imperial Rome and thereby refuted the city's connection with the founder of the Empire—the pride of medieval Florence. Salutati was satisfied to have his findings prove that the Florentines could claim a Roman origin for their city.[31] We may assume this restraint to have been intentional. For Salutati was in the closest personal contact with Bruni in those years, and thus he must have been aware of what conclusions his discovery allowed him to draw regarding Florence's relationship to the *Respublica Romana*.

Yet Salutati left it to Bruni to elaborate the results of his critical scholarship for historical thought.[32a]

*Salutati's Dilemma: Dante's Caesarism
and Florentine Liberty*

One striking aspect of the *De Tyranno* is its combination of an advanced realism in method and details with
genuine elements of medieval thought. Another striking
aspect is the preoccupation of the author, chancellor of
Florence, with the defense of monarchy and a violent attack on the champions of Roman civic freedom, at the
moment when the Florentine Commonwealth and all
republican life in independent city-states were threatened
with being swept away by the triumph of monarchy on the
Peninsula.

We may assume that Salutati in his younger years—
admiring reader of Petrarch that he was—had not been
unaffected by the criticism of Caesar found in the *Africa*
and other early writings of Petrarch. As late as the mid-
1370's, Salutati entertained no doubt that Caesar "had
committed a crime in attacking the *Respublica*"—even
though he commended Caesar as an example for his
"clementia" after victory.[32b] Dante's medieval view, however, that Universal Monarchy was needed for the sake
of religion, eventually proved stronger than any sympathy
with the *Respublica,* and, consequently, Salutati felt
called upon to come to the rescue of the traditional convictions when he saw them endangered by the new, republican ideas. We have noted that in his later years he
returned in more than one respect from the espousal of
new experiences to the medieval standpoint, and that there
had been parallels to this retraction in the development
of Petrarch. But these observations alone are not sufficient
to explain why Salutati considered it opportune, or even
permissible, to defend his point of view by writing an
unqualified apology for monarchy in the midst of a Florentine war for liberty, and at almost the same time when,

in his *Invectiva,* he publicly defended republican life against monarchy. Nor can the explanation be sought in the theory that Salutati's judgment on the origin and necessity of monarchy in Rome seemed to him unrelated to his verdict on the tyranny of his own age. For if he had not seen any relation whatever between these two phenomena, he would not have found it necessary to introduce his historical justification of Caesar's "Tyranny" by pointing out that by 1400 the term "tyrant" had come to mean two different things: not only a bad and cruel prince, but also a ruler, whether good or bad, who had secured his monarchical position by illegitimate means. Indeed, the first part of Salutati's treatise enlarges on a juridical distinction which had already been set forth in all its essentials half a century earlier by the famed jurist Bartolo da Sassoferrato, who wished to give legal sanction to the emerging institution of signory: the distinction between the despotic ruler who had become a tyrant "by the practice of his rule" (*tyrannus ex parte exercitii*), and the self-appointed ruler who had come to be called a tyrant simply "for lack of a title to his position" (*tyrannus ex defectu tituli*).[33]

Thus it was no accident that Salutati chose for his work the title "De Tyranno" rather than the more obvious "De Caesare" or "De Monarchia." The work was to demonstrate that a tyranny, in the sense in which it was understood in Trecento jurisprudence and Trecento life, had been needed at times in history to replace a rotten liberty, and that for this reason Caesar had been justified in destroying the republican institutions of Rome: not only because he built the God-willed universal empire which was destined to become the abode of medieval Christianity, but also because he established order and efficiency in the Rome of the civil wars, much as did the Trecento tyrants in their cities.

Some of the scholars who have recently drawn attention to Salutati's long-neglected work have seen its special merit in just this impartiality in dealing with the tyranny of the Renaissance; they have looked upon it as the beginning of that sceptical relativism with regard to the forms of government which is often ascribed to Quattrocento humanists in general. Indeed, *De Tyranno* has been praised as a forerunner of the modern, scientifically objective attitude which analyzes its material without being swayed by any personal preferences. This is the main reason why the treatise, ineffective as it was in its own time, has of late become the most frequently edited, translated, and quoted work of the time around 1400.[34]

According to all we have found in our analysis of *De Tyranno*, it would be a crude anachronism to see a display of aloof objectivity in Salutati's rejection of the republican criticism of Caesar and of Dante. Such an interpretation would read into a book of the Trecento points of view characteristic of modern scholarship. Salutati had no intention of writing a carefully balanced comparison of the merits of republic and tyranny. The juridico-political introduction is the least original part of the book; the recapitulation there of a current legal theory serves only to supply Salutati with a point of departure for his real task: in the face of disturbing new historical interpretations, to carry the debate on Caesar and his republican opponents, with the aid of new arguments, back to the uncompromising monarchism of Dante.

An historical work in its ultimate intention, the treatise *De Tyranno* is no exception to the rule that the breadth of an historian's insight into the past depends on the breadth and the originality of the ideas of man and of politics on which he draws. Salutati's historical estimate of Cicero's period is not "objective" in an abstract sense, but inseparably fused with his judgment on the merits or demerits of the ideals in whose name Cicero, Cato, and the assassins of Caesar had fought. "There is no greater liberty," says Salutati, "than to obey an *optimus princeps* who gives just commands." [35] His appraisal of Caesar's opponents leaves them with no motives but presumption (*superbia*), ambition (*ambitio*), and thirst for glory.[36] He justifies his opinion, that the civil war waged by Cato and Pompey's partisans was unnecessary and therefore nefarious by quoting a remark ascribed to Augustus on the occasion of a visit to Cato's house: that the exemplary citizen and man of honor is he who is found free of the desire to disturb the established order of the state. "For so many misfortunes, so much injustice will as a rule follow upon a change in the order of the state," Salutati comments, "that it is better to endure anything whatever rather than to court the danger involved in a change." No political program can ever be so "wise" or so "divine" as to be able to reshape reality according to its original design—the end is always discord, human depravity, and bloodshed. "Because these things threaten, it ought to have been preferable to endure not only the life of Caesar who, we read, exercised extreme clemency, but even the lives of a Sulla and a Marius who could not get their fill of the citizens' blood." [37]

The attitude underlying *De Tyranno* is not an anticipation of modern scientific objectivity but an astounding political quietism. This quietism is so marked that some modern readers, in their attempts to explain the emotional background of the work, have ventured that the tenor of the work bespeaks the twilight of the faith in the Florentine Republic, and the beginning of an adaptation to the tyranny of the Medici which was to come, or to the general trend toward an Italian Tyranny in the days of Giangaleazzo.[38] These interpretations may sound fantastic to those who are familiar with Salutati's personality and with the conduct of the Florentines in the year 1402;

especially fantastic, because in the twenty years preceding 1400, and for at least ten years afterwards, no member of the Medici family played any role on the political scene of Florence, either in the leading circle or in any opposition group. But the astounding quietistic tenor of phrases like those we have cited remains a fact that cries for an historical explanation—all the more since we are sure that no explanation can be given by any facile reference to the ascendency of the Medici. And the knowledge that the only figure that was then generally called the Tyrant, and that hovered threateningly over the Florentine horizon, was Giangaleazzo Visconti—this knowledge only makes the quest for the meaning of *De Tyranno* more difficult.

Although the features of the treatise to which we have referred cannot be symptoms of a declining faith in the *Respublica Florentina*, let alone signs of secret disloyalty on the part of the humanistic chancellor, the work casts a very strange light indeed upon the relationship of Salutati the humanistic writer to the political world in which he lived and took an active part. One thing is certain: at the very moment when Salutati the chancellor of Florence trembled for the survival of the *libertas Florentina*, when he was bound to see the political situation around him as a crucial contest between the Florentine commonwealth and a tyranny threatening from abroad—at that same moment Salutati the humanist, intent on keeping the intellectual traditions of the Trecento unharmed, engaged in upholding the faith in monarchy, and in defending the destruction of Roman civic freedom.

To be sure, the cause of this contradiction was not that, in Salutati's intention and under the program of Humanism which he championed, the citizen's interests and duties were to be given second place, after the interests and duties of the literary man. To make this assumption would be to mistake Salutati completely. For his significance as an

example for the civic humanists in Bruni's generation con-
sisted precisely in that he impressed on the younger men
the necessity that in Florentine society a humanist's way
of life, and the objects of his studies, had to be in harmony
with his duties as a citizen.[39] The treatise *De Tyranno* was
written with the purpose of rendering a patriotic service
to Florence by saving the city's most precious cultural
heritage, the tradition derived from the greatest monument
of Florentine language and literature: the *Divina Commedia*. But the surprising fact is this: Salutati the humanistic writer, who tried to labor for the benefit of the *patria
Florentina*, drew on a thousand literary sources, but treated
the political experience with which he was in touch as
chancellor and citizen as if it did not even exist. What
makes *De Tyranno* a problematical book, and has caused
modern scholars to advance the most contradictory appraisals of it, is the astounding lack of a normal and natural
osmosis between its intellectual intention and the political
exigencies of the moment in which it was composed.

A partial explanation of this anomaly may be that the
years 1400 and 1401 were the very period in which Florentine foreign politics had swerved farthest from its normal course and Guelph traditions by an alliance with a
German pretender to the imperial throne after almost all
Italian allies had been lost.[40] To an extent, therefore, the
consistency with which *De Tyranno* shuns all contact with
the burning questions of the day may be attributable to
an escapist attitude. But this is far from explaining the
general tenor of the book: the fact that a humanistic chancellor of the Florentine Republic could in a literary work
espouse monarchism and the non-resistance principles of
political quietism. Behind this conduct of Salutati on the
eve of the final Florentine-Milanese encounter there
seems to be hidden another fact: that the fusion between
Humanism and the citizen's world was not completely

achieved until the last and final challenge to Florentine liberty in 1402 reshaped the relationship both of citizens and of humanists to their *patria Florentina*. The most important suggestion which emerges from the study of *De Tyranno* as an historical source is that the separation of humanistic literary pursuits from the realities of political life, characteristic of the treatise, reveals all at once a more general trait of Florentine Trecento Humanism—a trait not always found on the surface. When we reach the final part of our study we shall have learned that more evidence can be found to confirm the prevalence of this separation in the late Trecento—that at this point we have touched upon one of the most important contributing causes of the Florentine crisis.

On the other hand, it has also become clear that in *De Tyranno* we have a literary document that reveals no more than a very limited part of the impact of the transition crisis on the Florentine mind. The sources from which we must determine what the turn of the century promised for the future are the works which made determined use of the new developments: the political pamphlets and historical analyses, whether in Latin or in the Volgare, whether literary masterpieces or not, that were produced by men of more flexible mind than Salutati.

Among these writers, there is the author of a work to which we have not yet drawn attention because it was not composed until several years after the decisive events: the history of the Giangaleazzo wars by Gregorio Dati. The vigor with which this work draws on the political transformations of its time makes it the perfect counterpart to the often over-rated *De Tyranno*. Like Cino Rinuccini's *Responsiva* to Loschi, which had initiated this group of Florentine writings, it comes from the pen of an active citizen whose education had not been humanistic in the full sense of the word.

CHAPTER 8

GREGORIO DATI'S
"*ISTORIA* OF FLORENCE 1380-1406"
AND THE BEGINNINGS OF
QUATTROCENTO HISTORIOGRAPHY

G REGORIO DATI'S account of the years 1380-
1406, presumably written soon after 1406,[1] forms
an integral part of the literature that reflects the
Florentine mind during the wars with Giangaleazzo.[2]
At the beginning of our investigation, when we surveyed
the historical outlook growing out of the war, we found
that after Cino Rinuccini, Bruni, and in certain respects
Salutati, Dati was the first writer who embodied in his
work some of the new historical conceptions.[3] Like the
other authors of this group, Dati had been an eye-witness
to the events around 1400. Born in 1362, and a member of
the "Arte di Por San Maria" (later the Silk Guild) from
his early years, he was in his prime when the wars against
Giangaleazzo were fought. Although his service in the
highest offices of the Republic came much later, his standing and position in his guild during Giangaleazzo's last
years were already such that in the crucial September of
1402, when Giangaleazzo died, he was for the first time
Consul of the guild.[4] Being a prominent merchant and
representative of an outstanding guild, he must have been
in close contact with leading citizens; and since his own
political career began in 1404, he soon became associated
with the men who had held public offices during the years
of the crisis.[5] Under these circumstances Dati had a better
chance than any of the writers discussed so far to grow

familiar with the problems, facts, and sentiments that had
determined Florence's politics during the wars with Giangaleazzo.

Dati's narrative, entitled *A History of the long and
most important Italian war which took place in our day
between the Tyrant of Lombardy and the magnificent
Commune of Florence*,[6] is essentially a book of personal
memoirs; yet it is more than that. The reason why it was
not written until after 1406 was Dati's intention to compose an account which evaluated, and explained causally,
the entire Giangaleazzo period. Such an account could not
be given until, in the wake of the dissolution of Giangaleazzo's empire, Pisa with its ports had been conquered
and incorporated in the Florentine region-state in 1406,
and until the economic consequences of the triumphs over
Giangaleazzo and Pisa could be assessed. It is the combination of openness of mind toward the economic aspects
with an eager interest in political and military matters that
gives to the work of this merchant-statesman its particular
strength and makes it a unique expression of the Florentine spirit in his generation.

Furthermore, Dati's history demands attention as a literary link between the events of the Giangaleazzo period
and Bruni's widely known presentation of them in the last
three books of his *Historiae Florentini Populi*. In many
respects, Bruni's celebrated description of the struggle between the Republic and the Tyrant developed and capped
the train of thought which had first come to the fore in
Dati's comments.[7]

A Volgare Writer on the Road
to Pragmatic History

In spite of these qualities, Dati is rarely read and appreciated as an historical writer; as a rule, his work is

used only as a convenient source of detailed factual information.[8] The reason is undoubtedly the immaturity, often naïveté, of his literary art in comparison with the subsequent historiography of the Renaissance. Like so many other products of the period of transition, Dati's *Istoria* was a work bristling with new ideas, and in many ways it anticipated the faculties of political reasoning in the later Renaissance; yet the lack of an adequate politico-historical terminology and of literary elaboration in the humanistic style made this book, too, outdated—though in another sense than the *De Tyranno*—almost as soon as it appeared.

Compared with the chroniclers of the Trecento, Dati's work shows obvious gains as well as losses. There is an unmistakable withering of the epic ease and profusion which constituted the charm of the Villani and other chroniclers of that age. Delight in broad details is replaced by a sustained purposeful selection of facts to answer specific, clearly formulated questions, posed frequently to determine the political, economic, or psychological causes. For this new task Dati invented an unusual form of presentation—a dialogue in which one of the partners successively asks questions such as why certain political decisions were made, why certain consequences followed, what the difference was between the foreign policies of republics and tyrannies, whether economic factors cooperated, and how the wars reacted on prosperity. In answer to these questions the respondent has a chance to range over the whole course of the war and choose his examples freely, without losing the thread of the argument in a vast number of isolated facts such as an annalistic narrative would have to report.

The only Trecento forerunner to political reasoning of this kind in an historical work might be found in the well known prefaces with which Matteo Villani had introduced most of the eleven books of his chronicle—each preface dealing with one selected problem. Matteo Villani's prefatory reflections, however, had been in the nature of general maxims suggested by the events narrated in the chronicle, and not discussions of the material in the light of specific questions; they often were moral or religious rather than political, and they were not followed by any attempt to apply the suggested patterns to the narrative. Once again, therefore, we observe that one of the representative aspects of the thought of the Renaissance—the ascendency of politico-historical reasoning—received a decisive stimulus from the experiences of the Giangaleazzo period.

In Dati's hands the new direction of interest produced a kind of hybrid, half-way between an historical narrative and a political discussion. In the course of the Quattrocento, these two elements were to break apart. Historiography from Bruni's humanism to Machiavelli's realism would learn to reduce epic abundance into a planned, selective order and yet retain a chronological narrative; simultaneously there would emerge the Renaissance genre of the political *discorso,* which was to find its most mature expression in Guicciardini. Nevertheless the hybrid form characteristic of Dati would not entirely die out; occasionally it was tried again in the later phases of the Renaissance. During the 1520's, Bartolomeo Cerretani's *Storia in dialogo della mutatione di Firenze* was cast in this form of presentation; and a later sixteenth-century Florentine example is encountered in the well-known dialogue-history of Jacopo Pitti's *Apologia de' Cappucci.* But even Machiavelli's *Discorsi Sopra la Prima Deca di Tito Livio* and the subsequent countless theorizing *discorsi* on Tacitus' historical works may, in the last analysis, all be thought to have sprouted forth from that cross-fertilization between historical and political interests whose first striking example we find in the *Istoria* of Gregorio Dati.

Aside from the immaturity of Dati's *Istoria* as a literary work, there is another reason, not difficult to discern, which accounts for its limited, or merely indirect, influence on later readers. The description of the Giangaleazzo period given in Bruni's *History of the Florentine People* was soon to eclipse interest in Dati's account. And indeed, a reader who comes to Dati's work from the critical objectivity and the purposeful selection of essentials which are found in Bruni, must feel disturbed by the shortcomings of the transitional stage of which Dati is the representative: the picture often drawn in unalloyed black and white; the full-blown Florentine partisanship; the contrast between the new aspirations and the remaining imperfections—between reasoned penetration and still continued accumulation of irrelevant detail, between the exploration of causality and the naive certitude with which the hand of God is discovered in both success and failure, or the image of Fortune's turning wheel is made to take the place of a genuine explanation. But a closer study reveals that these flaws are mostly on the surface of Dati's work; they do not prevent him from carrying through his analysis of the political, moral, and economic factors in the crucial events of the Florentine-Milanese duel with a penetration that leaves everything previously achieved far behind. His reader should also bear in mind that the continued acceptance of *Fortuna* as a force in history did not prevent a Machiavelli much later from making his accomplished observations of the laws under which historical life proceeds.[9]

A fact which must never be forgotten in the appraisal of Dati is the early date of his analysis. Since it was written about 1407/08 one is inclined to feel that it did not by much precede Bruni's *Historiae* whose first book belongs in the year 1415. But the portions of Bruni's *Historiae* that describe the changes of the Italian scene in the Viscontean wars were not written until almost a generation later: book IX, taking the narrative up to the year 1389, dates from shortly before 1439, while books X to XII, dealing with the war from 1390 to the death of Giangaleazzo, were written early in the 1440's.[10] Thus, the picture of the political events around 1400 to which posterity has grown accustomed through the concluding and crowning portions of Bruni's humanistic description, is in its evaluations a product of hindsight—a review, written after the rise of Cosimo de' Medici, of a period which had taken on a different appearance in the light of subsequent events.

This is not to say that the last parts of Bruni's *Historiae* are entirely removed from the spirit which once had been the keynote of the *Laudatio Florentinae Urbis* and the magnificent first book of the *Historiae*. In fact, the charm of Bruni's appraisal of the Giangaleazzo period depends on the combination of the author's personal detachment, gained in the passing of half a lifetime, with vivid recollections from his youth. But for the source value of Bruni's narrative, the late origin means that his analysis cannot without examination be accepted as a spotless mirror that faithfully reflects the reactions of the Florentines at the time of the Giangaleazzo wars. To test the correctness of the views we have formed of the emotional and intellectual effects of the Florentine struggle, we must turn to Dati who made his comments within a few years of the events, after sharing actively in the plans and decisions, the fears and hopes of his compatriots.

Harbingers of the Political Art of the Quattrocento

Dati's *Istoria* is introduced by a sketch showing the rise of the tyranny of the Visconti and telling how the citizens of Milan, once free men, were transformed into "subjects, all of them born in subjection, which has become their second nature." [11]

The account of the Giangaleazzo period which then follows opens with the observation that the kind of foreign policy which Dati is to describe as characteristic of his time—indeed, it is one of the recurring motives running through his discussions—had not existed prior to 1387-88. In those years, when the Visconti fell upon the dominions of the Scaligeri of Verona and of the Carrara of Padua, Florence had been in close and friendly relations with Padua. How, then, was it possible, Dati asks at the beginning of his analysis, that Florence failed to oppose Giangaleazzo at the outset of his career, when timely intervention could have avoided most of the subsequent dangers and sacrifices?

The core of Dati's answer is that Florence had to go through the school of the fateful events of 1387-88 before she learned to understand the expansionist nature of Visconti imperialism, and the need for a defensive policy extending beyond the borders of Tuscany. The whirlpool of events of 1387-88, Dati notes, found Florence mentally unprepared. "That war," he says, "was a stroke of lightning so sudden" that the Florentine statesmen "were hardly able in so short a time to decide what to do in such a difficult case." [12] Giangaleazzo understood how to support his complaints against the Scaligeri and the Carrara with such shrewd reasons that an intervention on the part of Florence, beyond attempts at mediation, seemed hardly justifiable. The Venetians, neighbors of Verona and Padua, "made no move to undertake a defense which concerned them much more than it did the Florentines" who were so much farther from the scene. Under these circumstances it is quite understandable, Dati concludes, that the most experienced among Florence's statesmen shied away from the enormous expenses and risks of a war, "since they could not conceive that the intentions of the Visconti went even further"—even beyond the great successes already won in northern Italy.[13]

But the consequences of the freedom of action thus obtained by the Visconti quickly taught Florence a lesson. Before long, Giangaleazzo made himself the protector and ally of Siena, and Milanese troops were stationed in the Sienese territory in the heart of Tuscany. All at once the tyrant's "insatiable mind" was recognized; [14] from that moment on Florence became determined at all costs "to act against him in the same manner in which he had acted against us, and to do everything that was necessary to drive him from Tuscany; if he should prove unwilling to comply, one would have to work for his destruction as an enemy." [15] The realization of this necessity changed the political climate of Florence. "Now the Commune of Florence begins to tackle great enterprises"; from now on Florence's politics will show "fine order, and plans far-reaching and magnificent in operation." [16]

The element of greatness and farsightedness, believed by Dati to have directed Florentine politics after 1387-88, is the extension of the radius of Florence's watchfulness and political action beyond parochial pursuits in her native province. Not that Dati was thinking of conquests outside Tuscany. Among the key-ideas of his work is the conviction that Florence neither did nor should covet an inch of ground north of the Apennines. Florence, Dati insists, kept aloof from expansion in the north even at the time of the dissolution of the Visconti State after Giangaleazzo's death, when it would have been "extremely easy" to occupy Milanese possessions.[17] The new element in Florentine diplomacy, so much admired by Dati, is the consistent progress of the system of Florence's alliances through the whole of central and northern Italy. Clearly aware of the fact that Florence's fortunes had become dependent on diplomatic and military changes in far-away lands, Dati rejoices in the energy and long-range vision with which Florentine statesmanship was living up to the requirements of the enlarged political stage. He tries to work out a scheme of analysis that makes the reader sense the constant impact of the dislocations in northern Italy on the relations among the Tuscan states. As a consequence, he is incessantly intent on discovering connections of more than merely provincial extent behind every local event; he tries to lay bare the relations which exist between the happenings in regions geographically far removed from one another. In this new interest we are confronted with the ultimate cause for Dati's bold attempt to break away from the disconnected annalistic enumeration of near and distant, weighty and trifling events that had been the fashion of the chroniclers of the Trecento.

The burden of the task Dati sets himself is to demonstrate how Florence, beginning with the war of 1390-92, learned to shake off parochialism and to adopt the methods of interregional power politics which the aggressor had introduced; how she made up by economic industry, energy of diplomacy, and love of freedom what she lacked in military strength. Facts are selected and appraised from the point of view that, during Giangaleazzo's lifetime, Florence had to beat her enemy at his own game by making his new superior strategy her own: encirclement of the adversary by creating a network of alliances in his rear, and quick invasion of the heart of his dominions and home territory in case of war. Here it is remarkable to note that a citizen like Dati who is only superficially touched by Humanism and writes his history as a by-product of a life spent in economic and political activities, finds the key to the new situation in a parallel from Roman history. The sudden advance of the Viscontean troops, from their Tuscan strongholds nearly to the walls of Florence, in the first months of the war, causes Dati to remember the appearance of Hannibal *"ante portas,"* and also the antidote Rome found against the danger within her own confines: Scipio's expedition to Africa, into the heart of the Carthaginian State, with the result that "Hannibal was recalled from Italy for the defense of his own country." [18] It is a parallel situation and the same type of politics, Dati argues, which from 1389 onward caused Florence to include northern Italy in her field of political and military action, and to open a second theater of the war inside the Visconti State in the expectation that "so much at least would result that Giangaleazzo would be forced to recall his troops from Tuscany." [19] With this model in mind, Dati succeeds in lending unity and coherence to the kaleidoscopic to and fro of the diplomacy of the next ten years. The high points become the successes and failures of the new bold Florentine policy to decide through intervention in northern Italy the contest with an adversary who has too wide a margin of power in Tuscany itself.

As Dati's picture of the ensuing struggle shows, the parallel of Scipio's military policy acts merely as a lever, but the analysis of the events and Florence's diplomacy is no lame imitation of any historical example; it may be called the first rounded portrait of an instance of Renaissance balance-of-power politics, although the term "equilibrium" has not yet entered Dati's vocabulary or argument. The greatest advantage in politics, Dati points out, lies with those who are so intimately familiar with all parts of the world "that, because of their alertness and industry, they can form an idea of the conduct, the condition, and the resources of the opposite party." Now this is the situation of the Florentines who, because of their commercial activities, "know all the doors of entrance and exit in the world," [20] or, as Dati puts it on another occasion, "have spread their wings over the world and have news and information from all its corners." [21] Thus Florence need not helplessly look on and watch how Tuscany is undermined from within after the catastrophes of 1387-88. Dati describes how the Florentines, with the aid of their wide information, far-flung connections, and financial resources succeed in raising an international coalition whose armies are able to invade northern Italy from all directions—the Duke of Bavaria sending German troops from the north, the Count of Armagnac with French soldiers entering Lombardy from the west, while the Florentine forces invade the Visconti State from the east and southeast.[22] There follows a description of the concerted action of these armies, their efforts to join in the center of the Milanese territory, and their initial successes which are said to have gone far enough to make Giangaleazzo fear the worst, but which were lost again because of the conduct of the French Count, who in battle behaved emotionally like a knight, thus destroying the execution of the well planned scheme that depended on the neat performance by every member of his special part.[23]

Now it may be that this analysis of the 1390-92 war exaggerates the logical coherence of the Florentine strategy, the closeness of the lost triumph, and the Milanese concern about the initial successes of the enemy league. But these flaws are precisely those that betray Dati's appraisal as the product of a new attitude of mind. Matteo Villani, in his chronicle about the middle of the Trecento, had been unconsciously exaggerating the role of the Church, and of the community of Guelph states led by the Pope. In spite of Matteo Villani's native patriotism, his description of the part of Florence in the resistance against the Visconti had been strongly under the spell of the medieval universal agencies, the Empire and the Church; Florentine politics still seemed to lack the full spontaneity and scope that are natural to a modern state, and to fall short of them by a wider margin than was quite justified in the mid-Trecento.[24] Dati's overstatements, on the other hand, spring from an ideal of political action prophetic of the state-individualism and the rational mind of the Renaissance: the neighbors of an aggressor, who potentially threatens all of them, banding together in a coalition and attacking from every side in accordance with a carefully prepared plan, until they meet in the heart of the opponent's lands.

As the history of the Florentine-Milanese duel unfolds, we feel more and more distinctly the touch of an author who has outgrown the intellectual habits of the chroniclers of the Trecento. The year 1392 saw an end of the hostilities, but, as we know, this peace was so laden with the seed of subsequent conflicts that the modern student always wonders whether to talk of several Florentine wars with Giangaleazzo, or of one contest fought in three successive stages. No chronicler of the Trecento would have been interested in, or capable of, tracing the continuance of the causes of the conflict through the period as a whole while on the surface, legally, war and peace were alternating. To Dati it is one of the most intriguing problems how to understand the gradual emergence of the second war out of the aftermath of the first. He gives us a remarkable description of the sequence of events in the tense days that followed the inconclusive peace of 1392: the continued presence of Viscontean mercenaries in Siena and Pisa; the confederation of Florence, Bologna, and some middle-sized northeastern powers in the League of Bologna, as an answer to this threat; and, as a consequence of these developments, the constantly growing, nerve-racking suspicion on both sides. For a while, suspicion and nervousness are restrained because "each [side] waited, in order not to be the one that openly made the beginning." But gradually the smoldering ashes burst again into flames, as if of their own accord, so that "eventually it would perhaps be difficult to find proof of who first broke the peace." [25]

After this early example of a realistic analysis of the dynamic forces working beneath the semblance of peace, another high point comes with the description of the military strategy in the Mantuan War of 1396–98. Again, in trying to emphasize the political verve which Florence has developed, Dati becomes guilty of overstating the consequence of the events he narrates; but here, too, the interesting aspect is the direction in which the distortion occurs. Just as in Dati's description of the first war, it is again the rational element in planning and action which assumes exaggerated proportions. Even in war, he states, numerical strength is not all; in that respect the power of the Visconti surpassed Florence by a great margin. But the Florentines, in defending Mantua, "continuously foresaw what actually happened, and they did not meet any situation unprepared." Consequently, they achieved victory, since "it is the usual way of battles that *reason* (*ragione*) wins the day." [26] The appearance in Dati's argument of the word *ragione*, which was to become a keyword in the politics of the later Renaissance, is particularly interesting because we find it with the same new meaning in the diplomatic documents on the Mantuan War. When Venice was about to put an end to the hostilities in northern Italy with the Truce of Pavia, and Florence began to fear that this settlement would pave the way for future Milanese expansion in Tuscany, the Florentine government expressed its apprehensions with the words that the Venetians, in their past diplomatic maneuvers, unfortunately had often shown themselves insensitive to "the subtlety of reason" (*suttilità della ragione*).[27] So it was under the impact of the experiences of the Giangaleazzo era that the Florentines began to refer to *ragione* as a standard of political conduct.

For Dati, in his description of the second war, adherence to *ragione* means in the first place that military strategy has to adapt itself to political strategy by advancing from a defensive conducted in Tuscany, to an offensive carried into the territory of the enemy; and, secondly, that the distinction of the Florentine deeds in this offensive must not be appraised in terms of knightly valor on the battle-field, but in terms of maneuvering for strategic positions and of military technology.

At the center of the military action stands a feat of Florentine engineering, a triumph of "skill and ingenuity" (*arte e ingegno*): the construction of a mighty bridge across the Po, in the territory of allied Mantua, providing a causeway for the Florentine troops into the heart of the Visconti state. This was the Florentine counter-measure to Milan's occupation of Siena and Pisa. Dati's efforts to understand the interrelation of events in northern and central Italy hinge on showing clearly how the fate of both Lombardy and Tuscany depended on the outcome of the struggle for this one key-position. "The Florentines calculated that if, by breaking Giangaleazzo's resistance, they made their possession of the bridge secure, they would always be free to invade his territories—and there, they thought, they would easily find supporters since the inhabitants were discontented with their lord whom they saw bent on war and, as a consequence, destroying them through taxes and the interruption of their commercial activities. Giangaleazzo, on the other hand, calculated that if by using his entire force he conquered the bridge, he would be able to take Mantua as well as the adjoining bastion and, afterward, to send his armies back into Tuscany, without having to fear further for his territories. Each party figured to itself that this encounter was the

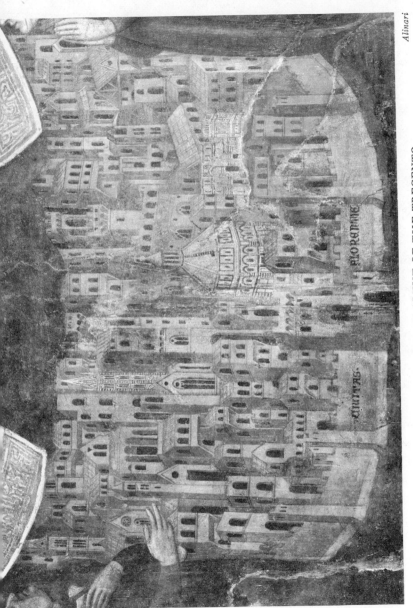

Alinari

FLORENCE AS SEEN BY AN ARTIST OF THE TRECENTO

From a mural in the Loggia del Bigallo (1352)

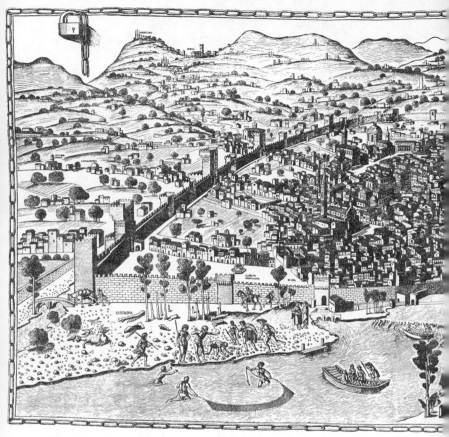

FLORENCE AS SEEN BY AN ARTIST OF THE QUATTROCENTO
Woodcut copy of a Florentine engraving of about 1480

FIORENZA

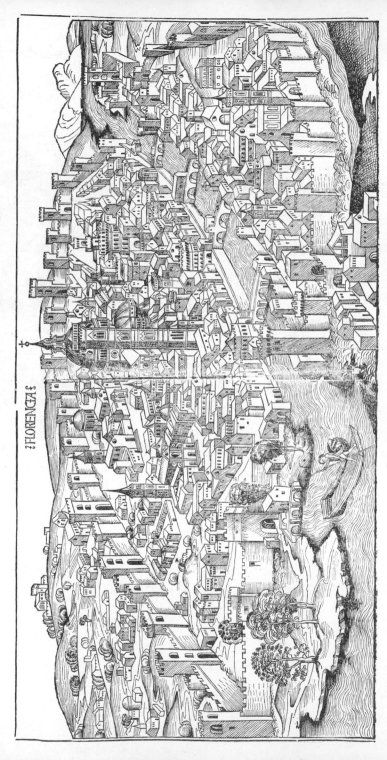

FLORENCE AS SEEN BY A GERMAN ARTIST IN 1493

From Hartmann Schedel's *Liber chronicarum*

one that could decide triumph or defeat in the war." Accordingly, both parties employed every means at their command without counting the cost.[28]

Passages like these give Dati occasion to speak of the "great feats" (*grandi fatti*) performed by the Florentine Republic in her struggle with the Tyrant of Milan. He delights in describing what energies, both of thought and of material wealth, were released by the great clash: the enormous sum—allegedly one hundred thousand florins—spent for bridging the mighty river; the procurement of varied artillery, such as Giangaleazzo had already used in his Tuscan campaigns, for the defense of the bridge; on the other hand, the construction by Giangaleazzo of entire fleets of ships equipped with rams and incendiary machines, which sailed down the stream to shake the supports of the bridge or set them afire; and the various measures of the defenders to protect the pillars, extinguish the fire-sticks carried by the ships drifting past under the bridge, and crush the ships' crews from above.[29]

Besides the expansion of Florentine diplomacy over all Italy and even across the Alps, there was in this military planning and technology something that made Dati sense a fresh, invigorating breeze stirring in his time, and he enjoyed it and rejoiced in the leading role of his native city.

Dati's Account of the Florentine Wars for Liberty

In spite of the military successes, the second Florentine-Milanese war ended in a draw, acknowledged in the Truce of Pavia, because (as Dati believes) there was some hesitation among the Florentine allies lest a too thorough weakening of the Visconti would overly enhance the position of Florence.[30] Thus the decision was again postponed until the struggle came to a head in the third and crucial war at the turn of the century.

At the height of this third war (so Dati describes the situation), Florence, stripped of her allies, and awaiting the moment when the victorious Milanese armies will march on the Arno valley, has remained the last free island in the flood which has engulfed all of northern and central Italy. The narrowed scene on which Florence now must make her stand permits her to attend only to the immediate necessities, and no longer leaves room for the shrewd planning and the far-reaching energy that Dati had admired heretofore in the Florentine politics of his time. But it is precisely this situation which gives him an opportunity to show how the reliance of the Florentine statesmen on the soundness of their political calculations allows them to survive the blows and fears of a catastrophe that on the surface seems to lead inevitably to disaster. Dati's account of this period is all the more valuable because he tells us not just what he himself felt, but also what the state of mind of the "most influential citizens" (the *maggiori cittadini*) was during the months of decision.[31]

If we had to rely only on our other sources of information, we should not become aware that Florence, in the summer of 1402, was still full of hopes based on considered political expectations. According to Leonardo Bruni's impressive and oft-repeated formulation, it was owing to the accident of Giangaleazzo's death "that those who had been left with hardly any hope of salvation felt completely secure, while those who had already thought themselves the victors lost all hope that they would be able to defend themselves." [32] And Buonaccorso Pitti in his much-read memoirs expressed the opinion that, after Giangaleazzo's conquest of all Northern and Central Italy with the exception of Venice and Florence, it would have

been "in the order of things had Giangaleazzo conquered
us"; and "within a short time he would surely have made
himself the lord of Italy." [33] But Bruni who, like most
of the humanists of the early Renaissance, paid little attention to economic factors, and had not, as Dati had, directly observed the conduct of the leading citizens in 1402,
is here no doubt a less valuable witness than Dati. Again,
Pitti, famous as an early example of the adventurer and
gambler in the manner of Benvenuto Cellini, may have
looked upon the bold Florentine decisions of the summer
of 1402 more in the light of a big gamble than did the
sober and shrewdly calculating men at the helm of the
state. Last but not least, both Bruni and Pitti wrote thirty
to forty years after the events.

Dati's account proves the insufficiency of later interpretations. Men of Dati's practical experience, who knew the
impregnability of the major cities of their day,[34] and were
aware that Milan would have to maintain a lengthy siege
with large forces, were convinced that Giangaleazzo was
reaching for something that in spite of all his previous successes was impossible to accomplish. His state would collapse under the excessive strain before he had reached his
goal. As Dati reports, it was known in Florence that Giangaleazzo's revenue, imposing as it was, did not suffice to
pay for the enormous armament, especially when during
the time of war the income from taxes and custom-duties
was cut in half; the Florentines were familiar with the
fact that the Duke was overburdening his subjects and
embittering them to a degree that many of them "wished
for his destruction almost as much as did the Florentines."
In the hour of decision, many citizens of Florence "had
reasoned with pen in hand, and talked as if this was a certainty: it can last only so long. . . ."[35]

Whether these citizens of Florence were actually right
is a question which can be answered as little as any question

about the probable conclusion of historical developments prematurely interrupted. This much, however, is attested by Dati's report: the coolly objective reliance on *ragione*, which had begun to mark Florentine politics, continued, unruffled by the depressing events of the catastrophe of 1402, to have a share in the stamina which distinguished Florence from the rest of Italy at the height of Giangaleazzo's successes. Writing only about five years after the events, Gregorio Dati was convinced that Giangaleazzo had been on the road to self-destruction "even though he did not see his destruction because he died before it happened." [36] As to the Florentine policy during the last years of Giangaleazzo's life, Dati asserts (and he offers examples) that the expectation of Milan's impending economic collapse explains many of Florence's actions. Deliberately she kept no more troops than she could afford to pay in the long run; she hoped to maintain herself on the defensive until the financial breakdown of her opponent. "And the Florentines had made this decision with the intention to carry on the war for a long time, for they were resolved not again to make peace with the Duke. Twice they had been deceived and betrayed, and they did not wish to see it happen for the third time; but they hoped that if they held out in the war they would see him consume himself. . . . And the Florentines saw and understood that he was bound to break down under the burden." [37]

In spite of all his delight in the methods of Florence's policy, however, Dati is the last person to see calculation and cool objectivity as the only or basic causes of Florence's perseverance in the war. His conception of Florence's conduct in her life-and-death crisis has two focal points of equal importance: besides the rise of a new *ragione* in the diplomatic game, there is the birth of a new public spirit. If the wide scope that Florentine politics had gained by the collapse of most local autonomies is one aspect of the period as he sees it, another is the constantly growing isolation of Florence and her need for reliance on her individual energies in the general collapse of her former alliances and disappearance of her peers. The second major theme of Dati's analysis, therefore, is the growth of Florence's awareness of this situation, and her response in the hour of decision: acceptance of her lone stand as a challenge of history to save a chance for liberty in all Italy by securing the survival of the Florentine Republic.

When the discussion reaches the point where Florence's allies and potential friends begin to drop away, Dati enters into a searching and ever more arresting inquiry into the causes of the divergent conduct of the various Italian powers. Why was it that the Tuscan neighbors of Florence threw themselves into the arms of the Visconti with a servility growing apace with the growth of Milan's power, forgetful of all considerations except the desire to see Florence humbled? Several factors cooperated, Dati suggests. One was the hatred which is bound to arise among neighbors one of whom rises above the others by greater commercial activity, as Florence, spurred by the comparative barrenness of her territory, had risen above the rest of Tuscany. And there was also the attraction which the strong and triumphant exercise upon the weak. "Many are the friends of Fortune, and they took the side of the party which, they thought, was bound to win." [38]

But why was Florence not supported by Venice? In 1387–88, Florence had found Venice blind to the dangers lurking in the Milanese occupation of Verona and Padua; [39] and later the conviction was formed in Florence (says Dati) that the Venetian government was trying to see to it that the forces of the Visconti and the forces of Florence "just sufficed for mutual equality, so that the war might not end quickly, but last long enough to weaken both parties to the point where Venice would remain stronger than either of them." [40] To effect this apparently shrewd but actually short-sighted policy, Venice approached Milan with offers of peace whenever the scales tipped in favor of Florence; and when the unintended result, a sweeping victory for Milan, came about, the Venetians, just as the Genoese, stood by thunderstruck, "as if bewitched by the Visconti." [41]

How was this myopic egotism possible at a time when in Florence the interdependence of the fortunes of the Italian states was already well understood? Why did Venice not behave in the crisis as Florence did? Either, argues Dati, because Venice, like Genoa, is ruled by an oligarchy headed by a Doge, and the few could be swayed by the Visconti with offers of personal advantages more easily than was possible where many participated in the government, such as in Florence; or because Venice and Genoa lie on the edges of the Italian mainland, and, therefore, would not believe that the Visconti should find it necessary to turn against them.[42] The Pope, on the other hand, showed himself improvident of the future until Bologna, and with it the northern part of the Papal State, were in Giangaleazzo's hand; besides, many cardinals were receiving pensions from the Visconti. Finally, the King of Naples thought himself too far away geographically, and had his hands full with internal opposition in his kingdom; "and perhaps he relied greatly on the Florentines because they are in the center [of the Peninsula], and so he was not alarmed." As a consequence, Florence as the central state "was the one which bore the entire burden for its neighbors." [43]

And why did Florence not in the end give up the unequal contest, as the other central Italian cities had done? However convincing the Florentine expectation of Milan's collapse under the financial strain may seem to Dati, he does not see in it the chief explanation of Florence's final stand. Strong passions, he finds, were eventually involved on both sides. One of his dialogue-questions runs: how was it possible that the shrewd statesmen of Milan estimated their own resources with less precision than did the observers on the Arno who had to depend on second-hand information? The Duke, so he answers, was driven on by the wrath of a man who sees an obstacle between himself and the goal of his desire—an obstacle which time will not remove and which he, therefore, hoping against hope, thinks to overcome by a sudden assault. For all his thoughts were centered on "becoming lord and king of Italy"; and, but for the opposition of Florence, he felt that he had at his command the means to carry out his scheme. In Dati's formulation, Florence was the "hedge" that stopped Giangaleazzo's advance; "surely, if the Florentines had not held out, he would have found no resistance in Italy; he would have become lord of everything, and would have been without an equal in all Christendom. In consequence, he believed that the Florentines were robbing him of that which they prevented him from acquiring and which he already considered his due; and so he knew no restraint toward them." [44]

Whether or not this is a just interpretation of Giangaleazzo's mind, it is clear that Dati believed the great political decision of his day to have depended on forces of emotion and will more elemental than political calculations or considerations of expediency. If Dati, under the influence of this belief, has read more passion into Giangaleazzo's policies than was actually there, he is fully trustworthy where he gives testimony of things he saw himself, the passionate convictions which, in the troubled summer months of 1402, gave will-power and confidence to the Florentine citizens. The morale of the populace,

Dati reports, was raised by the prophecy of a certain hermit foretelling Giangaleazzo's death precisely for the year 1402. But the educated men of the leading circle put little faith in that prophecy. They were guided and supported by the conviction which had grown strong under the challenges of the last decade: that Florence was destined to maintain aloft the banner of freedom in Italy— even if she had to do it alone; or, as our guide through the Giangaleazzo period expresses himself in words which carry the spirit of the Florence of 1402 more clearly than any paraphrase:

"To be conquered and become subjects, this never seemed to the Florentines to be a possibility; for their minds are so alien and adverse to such an idea that they could not bring themselves to accept it in any of their thoughts. Each time they imagined themselves to have many remedies; and certainly, a heart that is free and sure of itself never fails to bring it about that some way and remedy is found. Always they comforted themselves with the hope, which in their eyes was a certainty on which they could count, that a Commonwealth (*il Comune*) cannot die, while the Duke was a single, mortal man, whose end would mean the end of his empire. . . . Yet the Florentines never rested; when one remedy had worn thin or failed, they immediately resorted to some other." "And one may say that all the freedom of Italy lay in the hands of the Florentines alone, that every other power had deserted them." [45]

Part Three

THE RISE OF LEONARDO BRUNI'S
CIVIC HUMANISM

CHAPTER 9

PROMISE AND TRADITION IN BRUNI'S "*LAUDATIO* OF THE CITY OF FLORENCE"

Originality and Literary Imitation

IN our discussion of the Florentine publicists and historians whose minds were shaped by the experience of the Giangaleazzo era, we have lost sight of the early works of Leonardo Bruni. His *Dialogi*, it is true, do not contribute to the discussion of the new politico-historical themes, except by introducing into the appraisal of Dante a critical note of Florentine republicanism, and summarizing the historical views already set forth in the *Laudatio*. But the *Laudatio* itself is the most vigorous and most complete expression of the new complex of politico-historical ideas that arose during the struggle against Giangaleazzo. Wherever we explore the trends of the historical philosophy of the Renaissance which in the first part of this book have guided us in tracing the new approach of Quattrocento Humanism, we find the *Laudatio* to be the pioneer to which must be traced the development that leads through Bruni's *History of the Florentine People* to Machiavelli and the other great Florentine historians of the late Renaissance.

The attribution to the *Laudatio* of so conspicuous a place has not been usual in works on the Renaissance, but is of fundamental importance for the reconstruction of the genesis of Quattrocento thought. Now that our eyes are sharpened by the study of other Florentine works composed around the turn of the century, we are able to discern that even more of the trends and motives appearing at that time have left their impact on the pages of the *Laudatio*. Our knowledge of the general character of the body of literature to which the *Laudatio* belongs will also help us better to appraise the causes of the underestimation which has been the fate of the *Laudatio* since soon after Bruni's time. The very youthfulness of the new ideas, and their literary presentation which, measured by the standards of the later Renaissance, was still immature, foredoomed all the works produced on the threshold of the Quattrocento shortly to sink into oblivion; yet it is the youthful pioneering quality of those writings on which their historical significance rests. For closer study shows that each of them contains surprising intimations of the motives and forms of thought in which the mature Renaissance was to express itself. In no work of the group is this seminal nature more evident than in the *Laudatio*.

What has particularly confused modern students in their appraisal of Bruni's panegyric is its close imitation of a model from antiquity—a product of the late school of Greek rhetoric: the *Panathenaicus* of the orator Aelius Aristides. A classicistic imitation of a second-rank model— such, accordingly, has been the usual verdict on the *Laudatio*.[1]

It should give us pause that Bruni himself originally held a particularly high opinion of this work, though in later life he thought of it as the product of a period when he was still a beginner.[2] While the *Dialogi* are never mentioned in Bruni's early correspondence, his letters contain repeated reference to the *Laudatio* at the time of its composition; and the author's pride in this homage to his adoptive *patria* expresses itself vividly not only in the praise of the work that is attributed to his friends in the *Dialogi*, but whenever the *Laudatio* occurs in his cor-

respondence.[3] The *Dialogi* were a literary work-of-art
tossed off without effort, in which the hand of a great
writer revealed itself for the first time, and whose fresh-
ness and immediacy have kept it alive to this day. But the
Laudatio—with its ambition to draw a rounded portrait
of a city-state with all its scenic and historical, institutional
and cultural traits—was Bruni's first effort in a genre that
was not only likewise new, but also particularly exacting.
Especially his attempt at an impressive description of the
unique esthetic effect that Florence and her scenery have
on the beholder, and his endeavor briefly to define the
the functions of the Florentine offices and city-councils and
their balanced interplay—the two main themes of the
Laudatio besides its new approach to history and politics [4]
—would not have been possible if the author had not been
able to lean upon a model; and this could be found only
in classical literature. Thus Bruni adopted as his guide
Aristides' panegyric on Athens.[5]

If we compare Aristides' and Bruni's works in detail
we realize at once that imitation of the rhetorical form was
merely one of the ways—and not the most important one—
in which Bruni used his model. To be sure, large sections
of Aristides' speech are a mere rhetorical catalogue of
human virtues, each and every one of which is ascribed to
the Athenians, and Bruni, following this example, devotes
a long and tedious section of his oration to ascribing these
virtues in turn to the object of his eulogy.[6] Still, that is
but one chapter in the *Laudatio*. A greater debt which
Bruni owes to his Greek model is the conceptual structure
of his analysis—the pattern and sequence of his questions
which clearly follow the precedent set by Aristides' description of the State and history of Athens. In this respect,
there existed a real and striking parallel between the portrait of Athens painted by Aristides, and the portrait a
humanist would wish to paint of Florence in the early

Quattrocento. Athens had been the savior of the Greek
city-states against the all-engulfing expansion of the Persian monarchy, and by the energies generated in this
struggle she had become the cultural metropolis of Greece.
In the first decades of the Quattrocento a similar historic
opportunity seemed to open up before that Italian city-
state which had led the fight against the Visconti and was
becoming the fountainhead of Humanism and of a new
Italian literature in the Volgare. For all the aspects of
Athenian history significant in these respects, Aristides had
found a place in his oration—and in addition for highly
illuminating sidelights on the geographical position and
historical descent, and on the constitution, of Athens.

It is difficult to see where else Bruni could have found
an equally convenient synopsis of the Athenian parallels
to Florence. What Thucydides had presented in the funeral speech of Pericles, intended to fit one specific
occasion, was not, in spite of all its superior intellectual
and literary power, a possible model for a full-size pamphlet. The *Panegyricus* of Isocrates, the closest other
parallel, expounded a political program of Greek national
unification under Athens—a program radically different
from the demands of the situation in which Florence and
Italy found themselves around 1400. If Aristides was
more pedantic and more prolix than his famous predecessors, he was thereby best qualified to supply the elementary
assistance of which Humanism, groping for a point of departure, stood in need; as an epitome of the ideas of the
earlier Greek authors from Thucydides to Isocrates, the
work of Aristides was most suitable to bring out the
Athenian counterpart to Florentine conditions.

Since the days when Einhard, for his *Life of Charlemagne,* had adopted the scheme of literary presentation
used in Suetonius' biographies of Roman emperors, classical models had time and again performed just such a

service to the literature of the Middle Ages. The new factors at the dawn of the Quattrocento were, first, that this support was now employed not only for the purposes of biography but also in the portrait of a city-state and a city-state nation. New, also, was the degree to which the model was used not merely as a pattern for formal imitation but also as a stimulus to engage in fresh and original observations. Indeed, the standard by which the *Laudatio* must be judged lies in the measure of independence it shows in transcending its model.

When Bruni comes to the analysis of his first major theme, the geographical position of the eulogized city as one of the causes of her greatness, Aristides' somewhat abstract praise of Athens on the grounds that she held the golden mean between the disadvantages of plain and mountain-steepness, and between the extremes of climate, serves the *Laudatio* as an inspiration for a keen analysis of Florence's position in the Arno plain between the Apennine mountain slope and the smiling hills of Tuscany. Similarly, as Aristides develops the idea that the Athenians were different from the other Greek tribes because in the beginning of Greek history they had been the only true "autochthones," so Bruni discovers the descent of the Florentines from the early Romans of the *Respublica Romana*. Aristides' praise of Athens the savior of Greece in the Persian wars teaches Bruni how and where to stress Florence's role in the wars against Giangaleazzo. The claim of the Greek orator that the constitution of Athens was a perfect blend of the three forms of government is matched by the Florentine writer with an effort to show the harmonious balance in the working of the various Florentine offices and councils. And Aristides' recollection of Athens' cultural principate in Greece helps Bruni to delineate Florence's leading place in both the growth of the *"studia humanitatis"* and the literature in Volgare.

If all these approaches to aspects of Florentine life went much beyond mere imitation of the Greek model, the result also left far behind the attainments of pre-humanistic literature in the Italian city-states. To be sure, patriotic *"laudes"* of a writer's native Commune had been a well known literary genre in medieval Italy, and modern scholars who appreciate the solid substance of factual information contained in them have often been inclined to esteem these medieval eulogies more highly than the work of their humanistic successors.[7] Yet no one before the author of the *Laudatio Florentinae Urbis* had tried to reproduce the total view of a city from both a geographical and historical perspective. No one had endeavored to explain present institutions and politics through a reinterpretation of Italian history in the ancient and medieval past; no one had analyzed the workings of a city-state constitution as the organic interplay of its agencies. And no one had attempted to define either the specific character of an Italian city-state, or its historic mission in Italian politics, or its part in the growth of literature and culture.

The best that Bruni's panegyric had to say about Florence was not borrowed from any ancient or medieval precedent. It stemmed from the experiences and trends of his own day.*

* How far from these attainments of Renaissance Humanism the medieval *Laudes* of cities had remained is seen by a comparison of Bruni's work with one of the most interesting and elaborate of the medieval city-state eulogies, Bonvesino della Riva's *De Magnalibus Urbis Mediolani* of 1288.[8] In the general arrangement of the subject matter, we find strong similarities. In both cases, the eulogy begins with the geographical situation and external appearance of the city, proceeds to the character and the history of the inhabitants, and ends with the proof that the eulogized city deserves a preeminent position in Italy. But the medieval work makes hardly any effort to come to grips with individual traits; it is satisfied to ascribe to the

object of its praise the greatest quantity or largest number of what it considers good or honorable for a city-state. In chapters I and II, after attributing to Milan the most favorable climate, the best rivers and fountains, and the most fertile fields, Bonvesino gives an account of how many castles, city-gates, churches, convents, houses, etc., are found in Milan. The only passage in his description of the *"situs"* of Milan which goes beyond enumeration is the assertion (a classical reminiscence, no doubt) that "the city itself is orbicular in the manner of a circle whose admirable roundness is the sign of its perfection" ("civitas ipsa orbicularis est ad circulli modum, cuius mirabillis rotonditas perfectionis eius est signum"; II 4). But this claim is not made good by the presentation of any concrete evidence; it derives from an abstract, stereotyped ideal, not from a fresh ability to view and analyze the panorama of Milan.

Chapters III and IV, intended to point out the excellent qualities and the wealth of the inhabitants, are also given to statistics only—priceless statistics for the modern scholar, to be sure, from the quantity of the produce and of the grain consumed by men and animals in Milan, to the number of citizens engaged in every industry and profession, providing a survey even more detailed than the famous one for Florence included in Giovanni Villani's chronicle. But the fact remains that what is given is merely a list of figures; no effort is made to correlate causes and effects, or even to tabulate relations between the industrial output and the changing number of firms, as was done in the chronicle of Villani. Chapter V, on the virtue of the citizens, contains a summary of the military deeds of the Milanese— their struggles with neighbor cities, their resistance to German emperors, and their resilience after every defeat. But the individual scenes, realistically told, are not set in a historical framework; there is no appraisal of the historical role of the Empire, nor of the origin, rise, and mission of the Italian city republics. Nor is there any mention of Milan's contribution to the growth of literature and culture. Instead, the long narrative of military deeds, in the casual manner of late medieval popular chronicles, closes with the account of two Milanese *"mirabilia"*: the entertaining episode of a Milanese citizen who was physically stronger than any other known man and, in proportion to his strength, an incomparably voracious eater; and the history of another citizen who, thanks to his "natural wisdom," surpassed everybody else in prudence although he had received no education. The last part of Bonvesino's book depicts the higher values for which Milan stood in Italy: According to chapter VI, her enduring loyalties had always been to the Papal Church, and to the memory of her local martyrs who exceeded in number and fame those of any other city; the greatest calamity in Milan's long history, therefore, had been the loss of the bones of the three Magi of the East, which were sent to Cologne after the destruction of the city by Barbarossa, and never returned. In accord with these loyalties, chapter VII defines the *libertas* of Milan as independence won in the service of the Church, and by faithfulness to the tradition whose basis had been laid by those martyrs. There is no word, either in this or in any other chapter, on the institutions and laws which had made possible, or caused, civic liberty. According to the final (VIIIth) chapter, the principal reasons for Milan's incomparable excellence are: In antiquity, Milan had held the position of a second capital of the Roman emperors; in the medieval Empire, the Archbishop of Milan had had the privilege of presenting the Kings of Italy to the Pope for imperial coronation. Given the fact, furthermore, that the Church of Milan, like that of Rome, had been founded by an apostle, Barnabas, and that Milan had enjoyed the special concession of a liturgy of her own (the "ritus Ambrosianus"), this city was not only superior in dignity to her ancient rival in northern Italy, Ravenna, seat of the Byzantine Exarch, but worthy of becoming, in place of Rome, the home of the Papacy.

Intellectually, then, a work like Bonvesino's *De Magnalibus* falls into the pattern, so often found in late medieval thought, of a keen realistic attitude in matters of local and practical concern, combined with a firm adherence to the medieval political and spiritual standards. This is the *locus* from which we must approach the humanistic eulogies. If we attempt with Novati, Bonvesino's editor, to look upon Bonvesino's love of enumeration as the only valid sign of growing realism and to minimize the significance of the discovery of causes, rules, and structures of political and cultural conditions, we merely mistake our technical interest in rich statistical informaton for a genuinely historical approach to the gains and losses which the mind of the Quattrocento was to achieve.

*The First Literary Portrait of Florence's Political
Constitution and Scenic Position*

Concerning one major achievement of the *Laudatio*, its
contribution to historiography, we have already observed
that, once the rhetorical guise is removed, ideas of great
originality and promise come to light.[9] Although the paragraphs that reinterpreted the relationship of Florence to
Roman history were disfigured by the naive boast that
Florence as the legitimate heir of the *Respublica Romana*
was in the right in all her quarrels with other Italian
states, and although the grotesquely exaggerated accusations against the Roman emperors, scraped together from
every available source, were not meant to be the full historical truth, yet under this dubious husk were concealed
the precious seeds of new historical conceptions of the
origin of Florence, and of the historic role of the Roman
Republic.[10]

The student who takes pains to penetrate beneath the
rhetorical covering discerns equal originality and promise
in the treatment of the other two major topics of the
Laudatio: Florence's geographical position and her constitution.

In Bruni's description of Florence's geography and scenic
beauty, the rhetorical flaw, easily discovered, is the long-
drawn-out sophism that location on the sea, denied to
Florence, is chiefly a source of danger to the integrity and
safety of a city.[11] Although this argument must have
sounded less specious in an age familiar with the anti-
maritime and anti-commercial reasonings in Plato's *Republic* and in Aquinas' *De Regimine Principum*, the modern commentators of the *Laudatio* are right in charging
this portion of the work with sophistry and apologetics in
favor of inland Florence.[12] But the substance of the paragraph lies deeper. Not only are the benefits of an inland

site defended with the fresh and, in the case of Florence, sound observation of the advantage of places which are situated half-way between the two coasts of a peninsula and which, by virtue of this location, can become the focus of a region reaching from sea to sea,[13] but the major task of the *Laudatio* at this point is to praise Florence's cleanliness and incomparable scenic position. Only the first of these two themes has been sufficiently remembered by Bruni students.[14] But even more revealing of the growing spirit of the Renaissance is Bruni's endeavor to recreate and explain the unique impression of scenic beauty that the city makes on the visitor—in a literary description which to this day has not lost its power.

In the *Laudatio,* we may say, the first attempt is made to discover the secret laws of optics and perspective that make the Florentine landscape appear as one great scenic structure.[15a] The site of the city, so Bruni points out, is almost the geometric center of four concentric circles. The city itself is dominated by the *Palazzo Vecchio*, visible embodiment of central power, in which, as Bruni's characterization runs, the whole scene centers as in a "mighty castle." Seen in a wider perspective, this stronghold reveals itself as the center of a central zone—as "the castle of a castle"; for the entire city in her ring of walls looks from the distance like a castle towering over a larger Florence.[15b] If one leaves the walls of the city proper, one enters this larger city of country houses and splendid mansions dotting the surrounding hills, their white masonry recalling Homer's description of the snow shimmering on the hills and mountains. "The city herself stands in the center, like a guardian and master; towns surround her on the periphery [of the picture], each in its place. A poet might well speak of the moon surrounded by the stars; and the whole is very beautiful to behold. Just as on a round buckler, where one ring is laid around the other, the innermost ring loses itself in the central knob which is the middle of the entire buckler: Just so we here see the regions like rings surrounding and enclosing one another. Among them, the city is the first, like to the central knob, the center of the whole orbit. The city herself is ringed by walls and suburbs. Around the suburbs, in turn, lies a belt of rural mansions and estates, and around them the circle of towns; and this whole outermost region is enclosed in a still larger orbit and circle. Between the towns there are castles, and towers reaching into the sky. . . ." [16]

The lucid symmetry of this picture reminds the reader of such chapters in Gregorio Dati's *Istoria* as the description of the concentric attack on Lombardy by the allied armies in the war of 1390-92, or of the struggle for the bridge of Mantua, a graphic epitome of the entire war of the years 1397-98.[17] In Bruni as in Dati, we sense the same style, the same approach to the visual world, that are so well known from the great contemporaneous masters of architecture and the plastic arts—Brunelleschi and Donatello. In every field—the visual arts, literature, and historiography—the Florence of the first years of the Quattrocento shows the same turning away from an indiscriminate interest in an abundance of insignificant details—the same effort to seize upon the large structural traits—the same delight in what is rational, symmetrical, and open to mathematical calculation. Just as the technological emphasis in Dati's description of the battle for the bridge at Mantua foreshadows the spirit of the wars of the later Renaissance with their applied science of fortifications and war machines, and just as Dati's insight into the interrelationship of north and central Italian politics reveals the attitude of mind from which sprang the ideas of equilibrium and balance-of-power—just so, the picture of the *urbs florentina* as the geometric center of the surrounding countryside is a striking anticipation of the ideal of the "perfect city," and of what has been called the "geometric spirit" of the Renaissance.*

Moreover, the heightened consciousness of "greatness" and vigor that inspires Bruni's work as well as Dati's, is largely an effect of the experience that Florence in the

* This position of the *Laudatio* in the development of the Quattrocento spirit is seen in full perspective when we compare Bruni's description of Florence with the earliest known panoramic view of the city by a Renaissance artist. This is a Florentine engraving of the 1470's or 1480's which was copied and recopied by many of the painters and engravers who pictured Florence in the later Renaissance. In spite of this exceptional success, which demonstrates its appeal to the taste of the period, it has come down to us, except for one fragment, only in a faithful woodcut copy of the early sixteenth century. (Center spread between pp. 180 and 181.) [18] Because of the completion of Brunelleschi's dome, the focus of the picture has shifted from the *Palazzo Vecchio* to the Cathedral, but otherwise the panorama of the late Quattrocento provides a perfect illustration of what the *Laudatio* had envisaged more than two generations before: there is the same convergence of the whole picture in a towering central "castle," the same successive "rings" of city fortifications, suburbs, hill-towns, castles, and higher mountains surrounding this center. In the course of our discussions, we have come to realize again and again that vital elements found in an analysis of Florentine thought on the threshold of the Quattrocento remained essentially the same throughout the Renaissance. The fact that we encounter the panoramic vision of the *Laudatio* in an artist's view of Florence in the time of Lorenzo de' Medici is a reminder that our observations on Florence's literature may serve also as a commentary on the art of the Florentine Renaissance.

By the same token, the dissimilarity established between the literary works of the Trecento and those of the Quattrocento has a close parallel in the contrasts encountered when we pass from Trecento to Quattrocento art. In a Trecento painting of the *"Civitas Florentie,"* preserved as part of a mural executed 1352 in the *Loggia del Bigallo* (see the illustration facing

struggle against Giangaleazzo had outgrown provincial
narrowness and attained the position of a great power, and
at the same time had become a cultural rival of Athens and
Rome. Bruni himself expressly testifies to this relationship
in the *Laudatio;* his picture of the mighty city, and of the
magnificence of her landscape, is used to answer the puzzle
confronting his generation: how this one city in all Italy
had defied the superior power of the Visconti. Many have
been amazed, he says, how Florence all by herself could
have mustered the planning skill, the resources, and the
"magnitudo animarum" that such resistance called for.

---

p. 180), we find the buildings of Florence still clustered in the
medieval manner around an invisible center. The *Palazzo
Vecchio,* instead of being magnified in its significance, as in
Bruni's description of Florence, lacks any distinction, in spite
of its mighty bulk: all buildings, while realistically showing some
characteristic features, are alike in importance and size. The
laws of perspective do not provide a yard-stick for a gradation
of detail; nor is the surrounding landscape admitted into the
picture to serve as a reference-point for perspective and proportion. There is the same difference between the mural of the
Trecento and the engraving of the 1470/80's that we have
found between the chronicles of the Villani and Bruni's
Laudatio and *Historiae*—the difference between the late
medieval pleasure in details without accents and distinctive
order, and the interest of the Renaissance in mathematical rule
and the natural order of things.

The nature of this difference can be still further clarified by
a comparison of the two Quattrocento creations which we have
singled out—the literary work from the beginning of the century and the artistic from its latter part—with the first panoramic view of Florence come to us from north of the Alps: a
somewhat crude south-German woodcut, evidently an adaptation of the Florentine engraving, in Hartmann Schedel's well
known world chronicle published in Nuremberg in 1493. (See
the illustration facing p. 181.) There we again find strong
realistic elements, but they bear unmistakably a late-medieval
stamp. Florence is seen stretched out along the Arno river,
focused in Brunelleschi's dome, and slowly rising on both

But "this amazement lasts only so long as people have not looked upon this most beautiful city, and have not seen her magnificence. For as soon as they have set eyes on her, all such amazement fades and disappears. Indeed, we see that this is evident to all, and no one has ever come to Florence who would not admit to this experience." [19] Those who from a neighboring hill see spread below them the panorama of this city blending with her countryside, and afterwards experience the impression of the city herself, "are instantly so changed in their opinions and sentiments that they are no longer amazed at the mightiest and most sweeping exploits performed by this metropolis." [20a] It

---

banks. However, the more distant mountains of the Italian panorama have disappeared; and the neighboring hills have been flattened and equalized, so that little is left of the impression of Florence's scenic situation. In place of being framed by that wide scenery, the city-walls have grown into a high protective barrier, massive enough to dwarf the city-buildings as well as the hills of the neighboring countryside. Instead of seeing the architectural beauty of a city forming part of a majestic natural setting, we have that feeling of shielding refuge and protective seclusion from the outside world which is evoked by so many picturesque medieval towns whose small buildings lie in the shadow of the churches of their patron saint, separated from the land outside by the high rim of their walls. Yet Florence, Bruni had said—and the engraving of Lorenzo de' Medici's period followed him—in a wide Tuscan landscape "stands in the center, like a guardian and master. . . . Around the suburbs lies a belt of rural mansions and estates"; and "towns surround her on the periphery, each in its place"; "and this whole outermost region is enclosed in a still larger orbit and circle. Between the towns there are castles, and towers reaching into the sky. . . ." Thus the *Laudatio* had conveyed that vision of a larger and integrated geographic whole which, certainly not by chance, had developed in Italy at the time when the parochialism of medieval towns was left behind and there grew up regional states and inter-regional policies of an ever-widening scope.

was, then, in order to make his readers understand what forces had halted the giant of Milan, that Bruni reproduced the profound impression of scenic grandeur, strength, beauty, neatness, and rationality.

It is another and more difficult question to decide to what extent the impression of the victorious resistance to the Milanese colossus also played a part in the burgeoning of youthful vigor in Florentine art. Those who recall Donatello's St. George of 1415-16 [20b]—the first book of Bruni's *Historiae Florentini Populi* was also written in 1415—will be certain that even the arts did not remain untouched by the climate of the time of the Florentine-Milanese struggle.[20c]

It is in chapters like the description of Florence's geographical position that we become aware of the extent of the contribution humanists around 1400 were able to make where they allied themselves with the civic interests and were inspired by the patriotic élan of the period. In a similar way, the *Laudatio* made a significant forward stride in a field which was to play a great and well-known role by the sixteenth century, but is rarely remembered in the history of early Humanism: the study and analysis of the Florentine constitution.

Here, too, the new trend within Humanism indubitably reflected interests which at that time were current in the Florentine citizenry at large, outside the humanistic circles. The realization that the free institutions of the Florentine Republic had passed the test of the struggle with the Milanese Tyranny also caused, only a few years later, a Volgare writer, Gregorio Dati, to include a synopsis of the Florentine constitution in his work. The analyses of Florence's institutions both in the *Istoria* and in the *Laudatio* were something new of their kind in Florentine literature; yet each was profoundly different from the other. Dati in a special book appended to his history, listed

and described the various offices in all branches of administration, the city-councils, and the vast number of
officials appointed year by year for the territory. While
this description, based on abundant statistical material, was
the first survey of a systematic character, Bruni the humanist was the first to strive for careful selection of those
aspects that showed organic interaction and a purposeful
unity of the Florentine institutions. The ultimate task he
had set himself was to show that the web of offices and
councils in Florence had to be understood as a system of
measures to prevent, by mutual control, each of the agencies from arrogating tyrannical powers. By shrewdly as-
signing functions and setting limitations to each agency,
Florence had taken care "that there be liberty, without
which the Florentine people thought there could never
be a life for them." [21] It is the preservation of this liberty,
together with equality before the law, "toward which
all the institutions and ordinances of this republic are
tending, as toward an ensign or a port." [22] At the end of
our history of the Florentine crisis, when we survey the
ideas which, born from the crisis, were to remain alive
throughout the Renaissance, we shall observe that this
concept of Florence's constitutional life, like the historiographical discoveries of the *Laudatio*, was maintained and
developed by Bruni in his later years, until it came to pave
the way for the discussions of the Florentine constitution
in the late Renaissance. [23]

Once again we must insist on the profundity of Bruni's
departure from medieval ways. There had been earlier descriptions of the offices and city-councils of Italian city-
states; for Florence we have a surprisingly accurate, though
brief and not yet well-proportioned specimen of such a
factual report from as early a time as the 1330's. [24] We do
not know whether Bruni was acquainted with those medieval beginnings of institutional analysis. At any rate, they

would not have provided him with a model for the task at hand. He wished, so he stated in an introductory remark, to bring out the "inner order, neatness, and workman-like construction" (*ordo rerum,* . . . *elegantia,* . . . *concinnitas*) of the Florentine institutions. "For just as harpstrings are attuned to each other so that, when they are twanged, a single harmony arises from all the different tones, . . . just so this farsighted city has so adapted all her parts to each other that from there results a harmony of the total structure of the republic (*summa quaedam rei publicae sibi ipsa consentanea*). . . . Nothing in this state is ill-proportioned, nothing improper, nothing incongruous, nothing left vague; everything occupies its proper place which is not only clearly defined but also in the right relation to all others." [25a] The intellectual distance, from the mere listing of offices in medieval *"laudes"* of cities to this interest in relatedness and integration, is as great as that between the listing of *"mirabilia"* of nature and art in some medieval works and Bruni's description of the position of Florence in her countryside, or that between the epic profusion of facts and episodes in the Villani chronicle and Dati's picture of the interaction of all political affairs in north and central Italy.

In an analysis of the Florentine constitution made by Bruni in 1413 at the request of Emperor Sigismund—a counterpart from the next decade of Bruni's life to his examination of Florence's institutions in the *Laudatio*—we find the same aversion to a mere collection of accidental facts. It is not sufficient, so Bruni explained on that occasion, to inquire "whether an institution of the state is attested to have been founded by our ancestors. Rather, it is necessary that we understand and explain *why* it was instituted. For it is by knowing the *cause* that we gain knowledge of a thing." [25b]

It should be said that, in light of the later development

of Renaissance thought, even these attainments of Bruni's early writings appear as merely a beginning, still guided by strong dependence on classical examples. The very simile of musical harmony in the *Laudatio* was not drawn from fresh experience; it echoed ancient Pythagorean ideas. By the time the efforts to create an integrated picture of the Florentine institutions had come to maturity—in Machiavelli, Guicciardini, and Giannotti—original minds were to choose their analogies from fields in which Renaissance Florence had achieved her greatest glory: the visual arts. When Giannotti, in the famous study of the *Repubblica de' Veneziani* which was to prepare his analysis of the Florentine constitution, wished to explain why discussion of the *"cose universali"* had to precede more particular observations (*"particularità"*), he gave as his exemplar the sculptor who at the beginning of his work hews from his block rough outlines of all the major parts of a statue, and the painter who, "before depicting an image in its particulars, draws certain lines by which the shape is presented in a general way." [26] And in the introduction to Giannotti's work on the *Repubblica Fiorentina*, the principle that constitutional reforms should be adapted to existing conditions is likewise set in parallel to the practice of the artist—this time the architect. For architects, says Giannotti, when they are asked to build on old foundations, do not alter them unnecessarily, but "design a structure which is in harmony with the qualities of the foundations that are there." [27]

The element which sets these words of one of the great representatives of the later realistic school apart from Bruni's formulations in the *Laudatio*, is the at last uncontested prevalence of observations from the life of the Renaissance over literary borrowings from ancient sources. But this difference must not cause us to overlook the decisive fact: that the step which allowed the Florentine constitution to be examined for its general traits, its "causes," and its inner balance and interplay, and to be interpreted in the manner of the Renaissance as "a work of art," had been taken at the dawn of the Quattrocento —in writings which, under classicistic garb, anticipated the development of the subsequent century.*

˟ The degree to which this early-Quattrocento anticipation of Renaissance thought was still a purely Florentine phenomenon may be measured by the half-hearted reception of the *Laudatio* outside Florence. That Bruni's work was widely circulated there can be no doubt. We have already mentioned the Milanese work produced as a counterpart to Bruni's Florentine eulogy, P. C. Decembrio's *De Laudibus Mediolanensium Urbis Panegyricus* of 1436.[28] But we may wander much farther to the north from Milan without losing track of Bruni's work. In 1438, we see its influence in a description, from the pen of Enea Silvio Piccolomini, of the city of Basel, then the seat of the Church Council.[29] And when in the 1450's or 60's an English writer with humanistic inclinations, Thomas Chaundler, later Chancellor of the University of Oxford, argued the superiority of the episcopal city of Wells over that of Bath, he used as a pattern the description of a city found in Bruni and Decembrio, instead of any medieval precedent.[30]

In the case of a provincial English town like Wells, there was, of course, no opportunity to use Bruni's analysis of the offices and laws of the Florentine Republic. What Chaundler could adopt from him and could add to his story of the deeds of the bishops of Wells was a partly literal transcription of the paragraphs in which Bruni had described the topography of Florence—the merits of her geographical situation, her visual appearance to a visitor, her cleanliness. Even Decembrio and Enea Silvio, however, did not take over from Bruni, in the essential points, much more than the English author had done. To be sure, in the depiction of two major cities like Milan and Basel a larger part of Bruni's sketch of a city profile and urbanized countryside could be reproduced or employed as a guide. In addition, Decembrio could use passage after passage, once coined by Bruni for the description of Florence's wars for "liberty," in order to describe the wars waged by Milan when

building her empire or (as Decembrio maintained) in fighting for Italy's national interest.[31] But there is nothing, either
in Decembrio or in Enea, to rival Bruni's presentation of a living constitution, and this is all the more remarkable, because
these two great mid-fifteenth-century readers of the *Laudatio*
were obviously impressed by this aspect of Florence's republican vitality; yet they had nothing of relevance to offer on their
part. Decembrio understood so well the superiority of Bruni's
constitutional analysis over the naive delight in external glamor
found in the medieval *"Laudes,"* that he described his planned
procedure—not far from Bruni's attitude—as being akin to
that of a portrait-painter who, having first formed a total
"idea" of the person to be portrayed, starts his work by de-
lineating the head. To the depictor of a city, Decembrio said,
the "head" with which to begin was the *"rerum publicarum
administratio,"* while the description of imposing and decorous
buildings, "which the multitude so highly esteems," must be
likened to the addition of apparel and ornament to the image
of the painted person. Just as in the presentation of an individual features like *"ratio"* and the *"dignitas persone"* must be
considered first of all, so, in the picture of a city, *"reipublice
cura"* and *"civium dignitas equitasque vivendi"* must be given
first place—which means the city's *"leges et instituta . . . a
maioribus tradita."* [32]

But in spite of this blueprint, which so forcefully reflects the
mind of Bruni's generation, Decembrio finds it impossible,
under the conditions of Milanese absolutism, to follow up his
own program. For after mentioning Plato's preference for the
"timocracy" of the Laconians and Cretans, he maintains that
sometimes one man can rule the state without doing violence
to any citizen and that Milan had found such a ruler in
Giangaleazzo Visconti. After this bow to his Prince and a brief
tribute to the glorious wars by which Giangaleazzo had built
up his state, Decembrio does not say a word about the *"leges
et instituta"* of Milan. They have lost their significance after
the rise of the perfect ruler whose will has become the law.[33]
In Enea Silvio's description of the city-republic of Basel, on the
other hand, there is a neat enumeration of the highest offices—
the two city-councils, the mayor, the guild-master, and the
highest judge.[34] But of the real novelty of Bruni's method—
the discovery of the needs which had given birth to each office,

and of the cooperation and mutual balance of the various agencies—little has been learned, even though Enea's work may be on a par with that of Bruni on some other counts, as, for instance, in the shrewd attention paid to the juridical procedure in the Basel courts.[35]

For our appraisal of the historical place of the *Laudatio Florentinae Urbis,* these glimpses of the history of its influence are of considerable value. For, this history confirms that, although Bruni's work, at least from the 1430's onward, was widely circulated, admired, and imitated as a product of humanistic rhetoric, it remained for a long time far ahead of any example of the same literary genre outside Florence, especially through its pioneering grasp of political reality.

CHAPTER 10

THE GENESIS OF THE *LAUDATIO*

The Thesis that the "Laudatio" Was Written in 1400

W E know enough by now of the character of the *Laudatio* to be sure of its intellectual as well as emotional relatedness to the group of Florentine writings with which we have become familiar in the second part of this book. In spite of its Latin garb and its superiority as a literary work of art, it was intended to meet the same political and patriotic challenge out of which arose the humbler pre-humanistic works of Cino Rinuccini and Gregorio Dati; like them, the *Laudatio* states clearly that that challenge was the struggle of the Florentine Republic against the Tyrant of Milan.[1]

With regard to the writings of publicists that accompanied the Florentine-Milanese struggle, we have been able to observe that those pamphlets were all conceived under the immediate impact of the fears and exultations which accompanied the beginning and the climactic conclusion of the war. For Rinuccini's *Responsiva* and the first draft of Salutati's *Invectiva*, once they are examined against the background of the war events, are found to be, quite contrary to the traditional view, the opening flourishes of the struggle which began in 1397. We also have established that it was the crisis of 1402 which produced a second favorable moment for latent ideas to develop and react on the Florentine mind. We know some-

thing about this effect of the year 1402 from Salutati's resumption of work on his *Invectiva;* and Gregorio Dati's
eye-witness report assures us that the breathtaking tension of the summer of 1402, and the subsequent triumph,
did act as a mighty stimulus to civic sentiment and historical thought.

In contrast to these twŏ high-points, 1397 and 1402, the
middle years of the war from the Truce of Pavia in May
of 1398 to the beginning of Giangaleazzo's final southward
thrust toward the end of 1401 were, as we have seen, a
period in which the appalling loss of Florentine prestige,
the unchecked Viscontean expansion into Tuscany and
Umbria, and the embarrassment caused by the Florentine
alliance with a German pretender to the imperial crown
conspired to smother fresh political ideas or historical reinterpretations of the role of city-state freedom.[2] Could it
be that Leonardo Bruni—who, though not yet a Florentine
citizen, was as much under the immediate influence of the
Florentine atmosphere as were the writers we have discussed—remained immune to these successive impacts of
the contemporary world when he composed his *Laudatio*
and reaffirmed some of its main ideas in the *Dialogi?* If
it were true that these works fall into the chronological
places to which they have usually been assigned—the
Laudatio in the year 1400, the *Dialogi* in the early part
of 1401—then Bruni would have developed into the
patriotic, Florentine-minded author of the *Laudatio* in the
very years which saw the morale of the citizenry at its
lowest ebb, and which still lacked the inspiration that
sprang from the events of 1402.

Before resigning ourselves to this paradox, we should
remember that all past discussions of the chronology of
Bruni's literary first-fruits were carried on in a phase of
scholarship which was not yet wont to examine systematically the possible interrelationship of thought and po-

litical experience. Nor must we forget our observation that the chronology of Bruni's early writings, as accepted for many years, was incapable of producing an intelligible account of the beginnings of his career as a student and translator of Greek.[3] Since better methods for correlating ideas and actuality have effectively reversed the traditional dates of practically all related contemporary works, these methods may also give us a key to the chronology of Bruni's youthful writings.[4]

It is not without reason, to be sure, that Renaissance students, since the days when Georg Voigt wrote his basic work on Humanism and Alessandro Wesselofsky rediscovered the forgotten products of the Florentine Volgare school, have again and again looked to the years 1400 and 1401 for the dates of Bruni's earliest works. For although all references to the *Laudatio* in Bruni's and Salutati's letters fall into the years after 1402,[5] and although the *Laudatio* does mention the fact that Giangaleazzo "eventually had occupied Bologna" [6]—an event which did not take place until the June of 1402—yet in a source equal in authority to the *Laudatio* and Bruni's and Salutati's letters we are confronted with apparently conclusive evidence that the *Laudatio* was in existence as early as 1401. For Bruni, in his *Dialogi,* on the second day refers to the "oration in which I have assembled the glories of the Florentines" not only in a passing note (which might conceivably be an interpolation), but in a lengthy review of its contents that forms an essential portion of the conversation; the panegyric, as we know, is praised by the participants as a particularly commendable patriotic achievement of the young author.[7] That the *Dialogi* was written in 1401 seems at first sight indisputable because there appears to exist a veto against any hypothesis of their later origin. According to the introductory words, the conversations took place on an Easter Day, and further on one reads that Luigi

Marsili "died seven years ago." Since we know with certainty that this fourteenth-century theologian and semi-humanist died in August 1394, the implication is that the discussions retold in Bruni's booklet took place on Easter 1401; and careful study of the dedication to Vergerio and of the group described in the *Dialogi* confirms that the work cannot have been conceived much later. For after 1402, Vergerio's connection with Florence was a matter of the past and Poggio, who is missing among the partners in the *Dialogi* conversations, had taken Vergerio's place in the circle of Salutati.[8]

Of course, there might be an escape from this embarrassment by the same way which allows us to resolve the puzzle of Salutati's *Invectiva*. One could conjecture that Bruni's *Laudatio*, like Salutati's pamphlet, was drafted before 1401, but resumed and completed after the crisis of 1402. However, precisely this conjecture, advanced as early as 1889, was soon shown to be improbable and unworkable; and a reexamination of every aspect of the tempting hypothesis proves that the theory of a gradual genesis of the *Laudatio* is an illusion to which there can be no return in whatever formulation.[9]

Ever since this sole imaginable escape from the puzzles of the *Laudatio* has proved closed, the solution of the problem has been sought in the assumption that the passages which seem to refer to Giangaleazzo's last years, or even to the time after his death, are actually directed to earlier events of the war; and that the oldest reference to the completion of the *Laudatio*, in Bruni's *Epistola I 8*, apparently belonging to the years 1403 or 1404, was really written in 1400. These were the theses which F. P. Luiso believed to have proven in 1901,[10] and even so competent a critic in the field as R. Sabbadini came to call the ascription to 1400 "la data definitiva." [11]

If this chronology were really the last word, it would

render meaningless all our observations on the curve of the political experience in the Giangaleazzo wars, and on the impact of the crisis of 1402. But the theory does not stand the test of our findings on the fluctuations of Florentine political experience and sentiment around the year 1400.

*The Post-1402 Origin of the
"Laudatio," and the Political Experience
of the Giangaleazzo Period*

The core of any attempt to prove that the *Laudatio* originated before the last and crucial phase of the Florentine-Milanese struggle, would have to be the demonstration that it was written by an author who did not know the course of the war beyond the first few months of the year 1400. For this purpose, Luiso, the father of the 1400 theory, examined the somewhat vague references in the panegyric to a number of political events and endeavored to establish their identity with actual happenings of the time. In the pursuit of these efforts he made a startling discovery: he found that Bruni's description of the war may be considered in many details to fit the crisis of 1401-1402 less well than it fits the late 1390's. For all the facts which form the climax of Bruni's narrative— grave defeats of Giangaleazzo, his offer of peace, his surrender of part of his conquests in northeastern Italy— correspond to occurrences in the period between the successful Florentine defense of Mantua in the year 1397 and the peace effected by Venetian intervention in March 1400. There is indeed, Luiso argued, only one single reference which would seem to compel identification with an event of 1402: Giangaleazzo's occupation of Bologna.[12] Now it is very strange, Luiso goes on to reason, that only one occurrence of the year 1402 should be included in the

pamphlet while even the ending of the war through Giangaleazzo's sudden death is not mentioned. A single reference which is out of character with the context is suspect.
The four words *"tandem etiam Bononiam occuparat"*
might be interpolated; or they might represent a hyper-
bolical distortion of a minor incident in the time of Bologna's perils and vacillations around 1400, especially during the year 1399 when, as Bruni himself later related in
his *Historiae*, the Florentines suspected Giangaleazzo to
have succeeded in establishing secret bonds with Bologna.[13]

There is, doubtless, something alluring in this line of
reasoning. The observation that the references of the
Laudatio are focused on events prior to 1400, instead of on
the situation at Giangaleazzo's death, calls to our attention a fact that needs explanation. And since a very striking
trait of Bruni's pamphlet is thus disclosed, one easily un-
derstands why Luiso's conclusions have impressed many a
student as a light shining at the exit of a labyrinthine
maze. But is the observation that nearly all the political
and military events referred to in the *Laudatio* fall into
the span of time ending with the peace of March 1400 sufficient proof of the author's ignorance of later political developments? Is it not possible that Bruni omitted certain
happenings as less suitable for his purposes? This assumption would allow a simple explanation for the fact that we
find a reference to one specific incident that to all appear-
ances belongs in the year 1402. For the defection of
Bologna to Giangaleazzo is an event which tends to increase admiration for Florence's triumph, by accentuating
the impression of her lone perseverance in the war.

Bruni himself in later years admitted the subjective nature of the selection and presentation of facts in the
Laudatio. In defending his work against criticism, he distinguished the literary genre of "panegyric," which he had
followed, from "historiography," which is pledged to ob-

jectivity.[14] The former, he said, was to inspire the reader by effective oratory, even at the expense of exactitude in details.[15] Now the account in the *Laudatio* of the political and military vicissitudes preceding the peace of March 1400 is a genuine model of what arbitrary rhetorical emphasis can achieve while still avoiding outright falsification. By narrating first the recognition of Giangaleazzo as Lord of Pisa, Lucca, Perugia, and Assisi—all happenings of the years 1399 and 1400—and only afterwards the Florentine military successes in the defense of Mantua in 1397-98, Bruni succeeds in engendering the historically misleading impression that the Florentine resistance led in the end to a victory on the field of battle and the frightened retreat of the tyrant into his capital. It is thanks to this skillful disguise of the true sequence of events that Bruni, in the excursus on the Giangaleazzo war contained in the chapter on Florence's scenic beauty, can tell his readers that the city eventually "not only repulsed the invader and checked the course of his victories, but even overthrew him after a long war." [16]

Once this stratagem of the *Laudatio* is discerned, there remains no difficulty in understanding that Bruni could not, without detriment to his plan, wind up his historical survey with Giangaleazzo's sudden death. The whole rhetorical scheme of the tyrant's defeat and enforced suit for peace would have been destroyed. It is, in fact, difficult to see what Bruni could have done, in order to attain his ends, about the two decisive events of 1402—the fall of Bologna and the death of the enemy—except what we actually find in his work. On the one hand, the account of Giangaleazzo's recognition as Lord of Bologna had to be appended to the narrative of the extension of his rule to Pisa, Lucca, Perugia, and Assisi in 1399-1400; in this way the fall of Bologna in 1402 lost the appearance of being a catastrophe for Florence, which it actually was. On the other hand, nothing definite was to be said about the reasons for the subsequent collapse of Giangaleazzo's state and the survival of the Florentine Republic; the reader was to forget that the eventual triumph of Florence was due not only to the *virtus* of the Florentines, but also to the whim of *fortuna*.[17]

After discovering this underlying structure of the panegyric, we understand that Bruni's neglect of the final war events does not necessarily prove his ignorance of them nor, consequently, the composition of his work at an early date. So much at least we may state with confidence: An intentional omission of the neglected facts is equally possible.[18] The ultimate criterion in judging Bruni's knowledge or ignorance of contemporary events cannot be found in the information which he himself wished to impress on his readers. It must be sought in such of his statements as show him off guard; in passages which convey his general estimate of past, present, and future, and consequently disclose his experiences, fears, and hopes.

Here we must recall the changes in the climate of political opinion during the span of time in which the *Laudatio* must have been composed.[19] There was a world of difference between the political constellation after the peace forced upon Florence by Venetian arbitration in March 1400, and that after Giangaleazzo's death. In the spring of 1400 the concessions made by the Duke of Milan in northern Italy were compensated by his gaining a free hand south of the Apennines. With regard to Florence, nothing was agreed upon but a mutual surrender of the conquests made by either party during the past war—a settlement which left Giangaleazzo in undisputed possession of the central-Italian empire with which he had surrounded Florence in a gradually tightening stranglehold. The immediate Florentine reaction to this *pax Venetiana* was a feeling of utter dismay, a general outcry that the peace treaty, so far as Tuscany was concerned, did not put an end to the struggle but merely improved Giangaleazzo's chances to prepare for his decisive attack. "A peace dictated to us by our adversary," a treaty "which may rather mean [a new] war," and an evasion of the real problems: thus the settlement was described in official Florentine documents.[20] To find an escape from this predicament, Florence from the autumn of 1400 to the autumn of 1401 made her desperate attempt to encircle Milan by an alliance with King Rupert of Germany—a union which, as has been pointed out, was an embarrassing incident in the long history of Guelph anti-imperial traditions, a break with the Florentine past.[21]

One must compare these conditions with the state of Italian affairs in the autumn of 1402, the end of a challenging and critical year in which Florence, abandoned by all her allies, had fought on alone until she finally remained as the triumphant survivor. It was then that Tuscany became free of Milanese troops for the first time in more than a decade; the Florentines, as we shall later learn from Gregorio Dati and others among his contemporaries,[22] were so firmly convinced of the finality of the Viscontean collapse that they once more left northern Italy to itself, as they had done before the rise of Giangaleazzo's empire. Not until fifteen or twenty years later, when Giangaleazzo's son, Filippo Maria, again raised the Visconti power to nearly its former extent, did Florence realize that her feeling of permanent security and triumph over "tyranny" had been a blunder.

By the comparison of these two phases of the international situation we can see clearly in what respect a Florentine author writing in 1400 was bound to differ from one writing in 1403 or later. The despairing mood of the Florentines in the summer of 1400 was exactly the opposite of their later confidence that the drive of the

Visconti toward one large monarchy in northern and central Italy had been permanently foiled; in that summer, the Florentine citizenry was far from filled with pride at having triumphantly withstood an ultimate trial. At the end of 1402, on the other hand, when the Florentines looked back upon their stubborn resistance, it could readily appear as a victorious fight of the Florentine Republic not only for herself but for the deliverance of Italy from the yoke of the tyrant.

In the light of these changes in the political climate let us now read the final estimate with which the *Laudatio* concludes the account of the Giangaleazzo wars:

"With such a mind this commonwealth was endowed, with such a measure of *virtus* did she meet in strife the most powerful and resourceful enemy, that she compelled him who shortly before had menaced all Italy and believed that nobody could withstand him, to wish for peace, to tremble within the walls of Milan, and in the end not only to abandon the cities of Tuscany and the Flaminia, but even to lose the largest part of northern Italy. . . . What greater thing could this commonwealth accomplish, or in what better way prove that the *virtus* of her forebears was still alive, than by her own efforts and resources to liberate the whole of Italy from the threat of servitude? In consequence of which feat she receives congratulations, praises, and thanks from all nations every day." [23]

Against the background of the preceding political analysis, this statement conveys unquestionable allusions to post-1400 events. We may concede that the phrase, that Giangaleazzo lost "the largest part of northern Italy" (*Galliae maximam partem*), is too indefinite to indicate with certainty whether the dissolution of the Visconti State after 1402, or only Milan's surrender of the Paduan and Mantuan territories in 1400, was in the author's mind; though one may hazard the opinion that even a writer

intent on rhetorical effects would hardly have called
"Galliae maximam partem" that fraction of northern Italy
around Padua and Mantua which Giangaleazzo had returned. There is no doubt, however, about what Bruni
had in mind when he stated that Giangaleazzo was compelled "in the end to abandon the cities of Tuscany and
the Flaminia." For this phrase is not merely in contradiction to the state of affairs in March 1400—at that time it
could not even be imagined as a rhetorical over-statement.
Else we should have to assume that a Florentine author
dared to boast of the abandonment of "the cities of Tuscany" by the Milanese troops at the very moment when
the streets of Florence were echoing with indignation at
the "treachery" of Venice in stipulating the Milanese
evacuation of northeastern Italy while allowing the occupation of "the cities of Tuscany" to continue unimpeded.
With this explicit phrase, we may definitely say, Bruni can
have alluded only to the happenings after Giangaleazzo's
death.

And what about the designation of Giangaleazzo as the
powerful and resourceful enemy "who shortly before had
menaced all Italy," and Bruni's assertion that Florence "by
her own efforts and resources liberated the whole of Italy
from the threat of servitude"? These sentences imply that
such a threat no longer existed by the time the paragraph
was written. Moreover, we need not be afraid that these
expressions may be among those rhetorical hyperboles
which are not to be taken at face value. For the same
sentiment of a happy and glorious escape from a past crisis
appears as the keynote wherever the *Laudatio* touches
upon the war with Giangaleazzo.

In the chapter on Florence's military exploits (the *"res
foris gestae"*), the section whose concluding passages we
have just been interpreting had opened the praise of the
Florentine deeds in the war with Giangaleazzo with the

question: Could anyone deny that "all Italy would have fallen into the power of the Ligurian enemy [i.e. Giangaleazzo as Lord of the western part of northern Italy], had not this one commonwealth withstood his might with her energy and wisdom? For who in all Italy was then comparable to that enemy in power and relentless energy? Or who would have endured to the end the onset of a foe whose very name brought terror to every mortal man?" The Milanese Duke, Bruni goes on to say, could have been a happy and eminently able prince, had he repressed his vicious desire to sow discord among the states of Italy in order to rule over the divided. But Florence remained mindful of her traditional mission to preserve the freedom of Italy; she resisted, and saved all.[24]

It is exactly from the same retrospective point of view that the Milanese struggle is seen in the first part of the *Laudatio,* in the chapter on Florence's scenic beauty. "This Duke," Bruni says there, "a prince who, on account of his resources and power, was a source of fear to transalpine nations as well as to all Italy, puffed up in his hopes, vainglorious in victory, racing along like a tempest, occupying everything with amazing success, found himself confronted with this one commonwealth, which did not only repulse the invader and check the course of his victories, but even overthrew him after a long war, . . . a war the magnitude and length of which was admired by all people, so that everybody was wondering whence such immense energies, resources, and monies needed for the war had become available to one single city." [25]

Though it is literally correct to say with Luiso that in all these passages there are no references to specific events of the years 1401 and 1402, we must be on our guard lest by clinging to apparent tangible "facts" we forfeit the spirit for the letter. Fitting the *Laudatio* in its historical place, we may state with confidence that none of the paragraphs which we have analyzed could have been phrased before the threat of Giangaleazzo's empire had ceased to exist and Florence again felt secure in her final victory. Indeed, there could be no more genuine testimony to Florence's proud and lonely stand in 1402 than the quoted passages of Bruni's panegyric.[26]

CHAPTER 11

THE GENESIS OF BRUNI'S *DIALOGI*

OUR proof that the *Laudatio* dates after 1402 * not only reverses the chronology accepted for the *Laudatio* itself, it also points the direction in which the ultimate solution of the problem of the first molding factors of Bruni's Humanism must be sought.

* More exactly, the *Laudatio* must have been composed either in the summer of 1403 or in the summer of 1404. For the proof that the work originated after 1402 makes it certain that the earliest September 5th on which Bruni's *Epistola I 8* can have been written and, consequently, the *Laudatio* can have been completed (the letter establishes this connection)[1a] was September 5th, 1403. Since the death of Giangaleazzo occurred on September 3rd of the year 1402,[1b] the panegyric cannot as yet have existed on September 5th, 1402. For a *terminus ad quem*, on the other hand, we must consider that Bruni's translation of Plato's *Phaedon*, which had been in progress when *Ep. I 8* was written, was dedicated to Pope Innocent VII some time between December, 1404, and the middle of March, 1405.[1c] Consequently, the latest possible date for *Ep. I 8* and the completion of the *Laudatio* was the September of the year 1404. Whether written in 1403 or in 1404, the *Laudatio*, just as the final version of Salutati's *Invectiva*, originated not long after the experiences of 1402.

When the *Laudatio* and the *Invectiva* are carefully compared, it seems that the completion of Bruni's panegyric preceded the long delayed publication of Salutati's *Invectiva*.[1d] Since the latter was released to the public toward the end of 1403,[1e] it is more probable that the *Laudatio* was published in September 1403 than in September 1404. In either case, the *Laudatio* may be regarded as a quickly matured fruit of the preceding political crisis.

One of the consequences of the changed chronology is that we escape from the necessity of assuming that Bruni, after only two years of Greek instruction in Chrysoloras' school, emerged as the mature translator of Platonic dialogues. For since the same letter of Bruni (*Epistola I 8*) which refers to the publication of the *Laudatio* also tells of the start of work on the *Phaedon*, of other far-reaching plans of Plato translations, and of Bruni's mature standards in the appreciation of Plato's style, the transfer of the date of the *Laudatio* from 1400 to after 1402 restores to Bruni's biographer an opportunity to reconstruct his development as a philologist and critic in the form of an organic process covering a reasonable span of time.[1f]

Still more important prove the consequences for understanding the factors that created the civic strand in Bruni's Humanism. Once we accept that the *Laudatio* cannot have been composed prior to the Florentine ordeal of 1402—neither in a first draft supplemented after 1402, nor in its final version—the only remaining way to explain the discussion of the *Laudatio* in the *Dialogi ad Petrum Paulum Histrum,* i.e. in a work dedicated to Pier Paolo Vergerio in 1401,[2] is to assume that the existing text of the *Dialogi* is not identical with that which was sent to Vergerio in 1401. Thus, as the outcome of all previous observations, the probability emerges that the contradictions in our sources which obscure the origins of Bruni's civic Humanism are indeed caused by the composition of one of his early works in two phases: however, not of the *Laudatio,* but of the *Dialogi.*

The Literary Structure of the "Dialogi"

Even in examining the external form of Bruni's *Dialogi,* one feels at several points impelled to conjecture that the two dialogues were composed at different times.[3]

To begin with, a small group of manuscripts exists [4]—some of them of a very early date—that contain only the *first* dialogue, preceded by a *Prooemium* which clearly indicates that it originated during Easter of 1401 when it was sent to Pier Paolo Vergerio.[5] On the other hand, all references to the *Laudatio* found in the *Dialogi* and, consequently, all those passages that must have been written after 1402, occur without exception in the *second* dialogue.[6] Another cause for suspicion is that the author seems to have given no formal title to his work, for there are endless variations in the older manuscripts,[7] and the traditional name of *Dialogorum Libri Duo,* familiar from Bruni's earliest biographies written about the middle of the fifteenth century, can be shown to have appeared only about the time of his death.[8] In the *Prooemium* we find that Bruni, who is most conscientious in comparable statements in all his prefaces,[9] characterizes this work as *"disputatio illa"* related *"in hoc libro,"* not—as the complete manuscripts present the work—as *two "dialogi"* related in *"libri duo."* [10]

Furthermore, Bruni maintains in the *Prooemium* that the disputation he recounts was held "in Salutati's house" [11] —an assertion which, though true of the scene in the first dialogue, is entirely untrue of the second because the participants in the debate meet on the second day in a country house owned by Roberto de' Rossi.[12] It is no less astonishing that the reader, on reaching the end of the first dialogue, is never told, nor made to realize, that a second dialogue will follow,[13] and that one sees the members of the previous discussion group reassemble at the opening of the second dialogue [14] without the slightest explanation in either dialogue of why the same group that on the first day had met by chance also convenes on the second.[15] Needless to say, none of these obvious incongruities would any longer be puzzling if we were to assume that *Dialogus*

II had not yet been conceived at the time when the *Pro-oemium* and the first dialogue were written and dispatched to Vergerio.

Similar vexations plague us, and the same solution for our perplexities suggests itself, when we turn to the literary fabric of the two dialogues and their relationship to the facts known about the men who converse in Bruni's work.

In the *Prooemium,* we are given a preview of the participants in the conversation and are told that Salutati and Niccoli will be depicted in their true character. "We have made every effort," Bruni assures Vergerio, "to preserve the manner of each of them most faithfully. How far we have succeeded in this endeavour you will have to judge." Niccoli's role especially is accurately outlined in this preview. "Niccoli, who made himself the opponent of Coluccio, is both fluent as a speaker and most passionate in goading others." [16] Is this a possible characterization of Niccoli's character and behavior in either dialogue? And can the promise "to preserve the manner of each of them most faithfully" refer to the conversation on the second as well as the preceding day?

As far as *Dialogus I* is concerned, the characterization of Niccoli is excellent and to the point. There he is in fact the eloquent and reckless assailant of everything dear to Salutati. In the clash of his sarcastic temper delighting in paradoxical provocations, with Salutati's natural dignity expressed in balanced judgment, the author reproduces true to life the hue of Niccoli's intellect and temperament which we could reconstruct from other sources on Niccoli even if we did not have the first dialogue. In *Dialogus II,* however, Niccoli's temper and conduct are changed; they now appear quite different from those of the ironist "who made himself the opponent of Salutati and is . . . most passionate in goading others." For the Niccoli of the sec-

ond dialogue retracts, or disavows, what he had advanced
the day before. "Do not believe that I stand for those
accusations myself," he now owns, "but what I had heard
others say I reported yesterday to you, you know for what
reason"; namely, to provoke Salutati into putting forth his
own opinion.[17] Niccoli's task has now become the discovery
of a middle ground, where the younger men and the old
master can meet and where a determined classicism can be
reconciled with Florentine traditions. The expressions of
personal esteem for, and half-agreement with, Dante and
Petrarch which Niccoli now uses stand out in marked contrast to his "most passionate" and "goading" speech in the
first dialogue and also to what we know about the historical
Niccoli from other sources. Even many years later, the real
Niccoli could still occasionally be blamed, by Bruni as well
as other humanists, for defamatory remarks about the
three great Florentines of the Trecento uttered in a tone
closely reminiscent of the remarks attributed to him in
Dialogus I.[18]

The impression that the Niccoli and the general situation depicted in the second dialogue are no longer those
reproductions of real life which Bruni had in mind when
writing his preface, is borne out by certain differences in
the relationship of the two dialogues to the classical model
—Cicero's *De oratore*—which guided Bruni in his choice
of dialogue form.[19] While the irreverent attacks by the
Niccoli of the first dialogue are couched in a language shot
through with remarkable individuality for which it would
be difficult to find a model in classical literature, the words
introducing and explaining Niccoli's recantation in the second dialogue are practically a replica of passages from the
second book of *De oratore*. There [20] Bruni found a situation somewhat similar to what he wanted to present in his
second dialogue: a group of friends, mostly younger men,
beseeching the true hero of the conversations, who is

reluctant to give the necessary lengthy exposition of his opinions, to refute some bold over-statements set forth on the preceding day by a member of the group. To be sure, Bruni did not take his real plot or leading ideas from this model. In the Ciceronian scene, Crassus after some evasions politely yields to the insistent requests of his friends, while Bruni's idea of letting the burden of the correction fall on the shoulders of the insolent aggressor himself is a delightful invention. But even so, there were in the *mise-en-scène* employed in *De oratore II* several elements coinciding exactly with Bruni's needs, most of all the manner in which Antonius, Crassus' opponent, retracts his statements of the day before by confessing that his former arguments had been advanced only in order to challenge Crassus, but had not been his true mind.

As far as literary expression and the stage-setting of the conversations are concerned, we can indeed find a Ciceronian precedent for almost every aspect of the recantation episode in *Dialogus II*. For instance, Niccoli in retracting his provocations contends that his assertions of the day before had not been his own convictions, "but what I heard others say I reported yesterday to you," [21] and this with the intention of provoking Salutati to enter into the debate; but now he, Niccoli, would speak his true mind. Exactly the same motif reappears in *De oratore II*, if not with a precisely identical meaning or context, yet clothed in the same words; there can be no doubt about Bruni's borrowing. Antonius in *De oratore* maintains that Crassus on the preceding day "by no means indicated what he felt himself, but what was said by others," [22] while he, Antonius, "had intended by refuting you [Crassus] to entice these disciples away from you; but now it seems that I must not so much fight with you as say what I feel myself." [23] And whereas Bruni's Niccoli, after finishing his recantation, is accepted again into the circle by Roberto de'

Rossi with the words "This night, Niccolò, has given you back to us; for yesterday, statements were made by you which clearly were out of harmony with our circle," [24] Crassus in *De oratore* turns to Antonius saying "The night, Antonius, has calmed you and returned you to us a human being; for in your speech of yesterday you had described to us an orator without humanity." [25]

Judging from these observations, we may put down as a fact that there exists a difference of intent and texture between Bruni's two dialogues. The charm of *Dialogus I* lies in the faithfully realistic reproduction of the clash between two Florentine generations about 1400. The author's obvious aim here is to make this exciting experience come alive by presenting not only the struggle of ideas, but also the marked personalities who gave vitality to the clash of opinions. Even the picture drawn as a background for the discussion—a casual meeting of the friends on a holiday stroll through the streets of Florence and their visit to the old chancellor at his Florentine home—is clearly taken from Bruni's own experience and has the local touches of the Florentine atmosphere. It is quite different both from the Greek scene in Plato's works, and from the refuge of Roman statesmen in their country villas in Tusculum depicted in *De oratore*.

In *Dialogus II* the relationship between reality and imagination has changed. Though Bruni's great literary ability succeeds in creating a scene no less lifelike than that of the first dialogue, comparison with his model makes it certain that the scene is now fictitious: an artistic design brought to life with the help of many Ciceronian details and no longer a sublimation of actual happenings in the Florentine environment. Behind the "addition" on the second morning of a new member, the young Florentine Pietro di ser Mino, to the debating group, it is not difficult to sense the appearance in the first chapters of *De oratore II* of two new participants in the debate (Catulus and Caesar); and the resumption of the conversations under a "colonnade" (*porticus*) on Rossi's estate doubtless echoes the *"porticus haec ipsa"* of *De oratore II 19*.[26] Accordingly, we will also have no doubt that the attempt in this imaginary scene, to find a middle ground between the two fighting lines of the first dialogue, is not a solution that had been found in a real discussion of Bruni's friends; it is a new program which Bruni personally had developed, although it is attributed to an allegedly transformed and recanting Niccoli. Having reached a solution of his own, Bruni, quite naturally, can no longer be satisfied with giving a reproduction—even though heightened by art—of the ideas and personalities of his environment.[27]

The "Dialogus I" of 1401 and the Post-1402 Origin of "Dialogus II"

The obvious dissonance in thought and sentiment between *Dialogus I* and *Dialogus II* has long been a source of embarrassment to Bruni scholars. It has, indeed, proved to be so confusing that no *consensus* could ever be reached on the author's intentions in writing his work, and on the source-value of his changing representations of Salutati and Niccoli.[28a]

The contrast in climate between the two dialogues can best be measured by the fact that a reader who stops at the end of the first is bound to see in Bruni's work the very opposite of what he would see if he were to read to the end of the second. In the first case the discussion, instead of serving as a vindication of the three great Florentines of the Trecento, would seem to be nothing but a diatribe against the spirit of the pre-classicist Trecento; and until the late nineteenth century it was the bad fortune of the *Dialogi* to be circulated in print only in the version which includes no more than the *Prooemium* and *Dialogus I*.[28b] When eventually, as late as 1889, the second dialogue became available in print,[29] the critical investigation of the work gave rise to two interpretations [30] which agreed on one point only: that, given the essential inconsistencies in the ideas of the two parts, the personal conviction of the author had to be sought in one or the other. One group of scholars (in fact, the majority) pointed to the local color of the first dialogue, and to the conformity of the ideas of the first-dialogue Niccoli with the information from other sources about the historical Niccoli. This group discarded the retractions in the second dialogue either as "rhetorical" exercises in the art of disputation in accordance with Salutati's introductory request, or as a hypocritical or ironical concession to the conservatism of the reading public made by an author satisfied with having presented the revolutionary views of Niccoli and his friends as a phase of the debate. Other scholars accepted the assurance of Niccoli on the second day that his previous sneers were aimed only at provoking Salutati to speak his mind. Consequently they regarded Niccoli's recantation either as a reflection of the attitude of the historical Niccoli, or as the revelation of Bruni's own views— an interpretation supported by the similarity of the ideas of the second-day Niccoli with Bruni's opinions in his *Vite di Dante e di Petrarca* and in other later works. In this light the attacks of the first-day Niccoli appeared as rhetorical exercises in the manner of the "disputations" recommended by Salutati at the beginning of the debate.

Not until recently, in fact, was the first attempt made to solve the enigma of the *Dialogi* by doing justice to both parts. Vittorio Rossi, not long ago, explained the existence of the ideas of the first and the second Niccoli side by side in the mind of one author with the theory that it was the reflection of a dissonance inherent in the humanistic atti-

tude toward Dante.[31] Humanists of the Quattrocento,
Rossi argued, could not escape from the dilemma of being
offended by the pre-humanistic medievalism of Dante's
political and historical outlook and by his inadequacy in
philological criticism, while being aware at the same time
of Dante's significance as a poet and harbinger of many
aspects of the Renaissance attitude towards man and life.
This, at first sight, seems to be a most appealing appraisal
of the double-faced work; it has become the most widely
accepted interpretation, especially among Italian scholars.
Rossi himself has confidently called it the final solution of
the long controversy about the "meaning" of the *Dialogi*.[32]
Yet if our observations on the successive composition of
the two dialogues at different stages of Bruni's life are
correct, a completely different explanation of the dishar-
monies is called for, indicating not a split, but a progressive
change of Bruni's outlook. Is Rossi's celebrated theory,
then, no more than an ingenious but delusive specu-
lation? [33]

The crucial point in all past debates has been the unmistakable mutation separating the first-dialogue Niccoli and
the Niccoli of the second day. This change has attracted
our attention before. It may be well to bring together
here what we have gathered at various places.

In *Dialogus I,* we find Salutati complaining of the
neglect of the art of "disputation" by the younger members of his circle; this gives the young men an opportunity to express their latent enmity against the medieval
aspects of Trecento culture. Niccoli, on this occasion, reveals himself as both a harbinger of the innovations coming with the Quattrocento, and an impatient radical whose
boundless admiration for antiquity is responsible for a
wholly negative attitude toward his own age. Scholastics,
he argues, have looked upon ancient philosophers and
especially Aristotle as their safe and final authority; yet

those ancients would not have recognized as their own the writings attributed to them, preserved as they are in corrupt texts and translated without taste and sense. While the literary legacy of antiquity is in such a pitiful state, no real culture is possible, and any disputation is necessarily built on shaky ground. By developing this thesis with passionate force, the Niccoli of the first dialogue implicitly points out the tasks which a new humanistic philology was soon to tackle. When it did, with Bruni one of the leading intellects, it presented an alternative to medieval scholastic culture and produced the feeling that Florence, focal point of the new studies, was on the road to becoming the equal of Athens and Rome.

But to the Niccoli portrayed by Bruni this subsequent development of Humanism is still unknown; to him the new awareness of the inadequacy of the available Latin translations of Plato and Aristotle means merely that his own world and age are incapable of reaching down to the sources of true culture. Out of this sentiment there springs that acid and often scurrilous ridicule against everything not ancient which is the other marked trait of the Niccoli of the first dialogue. This tendency reaches its climax after Salutati's attempt to show the absurdity of the classicists' reversal of all values, by pointing out that in Florence the modern age had, after all, produced a Dante, a Petrarch, and a Boccaccio. This casual comment spurs Niccoli on to assert the utter failure of these three alleged equals of the ancients, in a series of accusations almost too ruthless, depreciatory, and often petty to be taken seriously —attacks made in a half-laughing, half-sneering fashion which has always impressed readers of Bruni's work as reflecting the attitude of the historical Niccoli. And, as we know, these sallies, highly effective in their vivacity despite their exaggeration, are not refuted by Salutati in *Dialogus I*. When they are counteracted in *Dialogus II* by the recognition of Dante's greatness as a poet, and of Petrarch's role as a pioneer in the initial phase of Humanism, the change of viewpoint comes not from Salutati but from Niccoli himself; for Bruni, to whom Salutati had delegated the vindication of the three great Florentines, asks Niccoli to make up for his former ruthlessness by a recantation. Niccoli eventually does so with obvious pleasure, contending that his charges of the day before had not reflected his true opinion. He then discovers for himself a way to praise Dante and Petrarch in spite of the faults he found in them before.

Now, while the transformation of Niccoli's convictions is doubtless the device linking the two dialogues together, it is obvious that precisely for this reason the elaborate portrait of Niccoli offers the least opportunities for the discovery of possible unintended fissures between the outlooks of the two dialogues. According to the story which forms the background of the conversations, it is quite natural that we should find two Niccolis entirely inconsistent with each other in thought and temper, or rather a Niccoli who, due to the *tour de force* of his "recantation," shows himself desultory in his convictions. The fact, then, that Niccoli in the second dialogue appears changed in his attitude towards Florentine patriotism, pride, and traditions, may or may not indicate that Niccoli's transformation had been planned by the author from the first.

But the situation is different with regard to the other participants in the conversations, especially Salutati and Bruni himself. Niccoli's change of mind, whether real or pretended, would not affect the others. On the contrary, they are supposed to remain the same persons to the end when Roberto de' Rossi at last welcomes Niccoli back into their circle, saying that Niccoli's opinions on the first day had been "out of harmony" with this group.[34] There would be no room, therefore, for inconsistencies in the outlook and behavior of the other participants in the conversation had the *Dialogi* been planned as a whole from the start, and executed as a whole before publication. Yet, when we carefully compare the conduct of Salutati and Bruni in the first with that in the second dialogue, we do meet contradictions and changes in their attitude hardly less pronounced than those apparent in Niccoli's opinions.

To begin with the role played by Salutati, it is not difficult to see that his reactions to Niccoli's attacks are of a different nature on the first and on the second day. On the first day he is presumed to be engaged in a personal quarrel: Niccoli versus Salutati, not versus the consensus of the whole circle, is the theme of *Dialogus I*. Nobody but Salutati, therefore, could be expected to plead the cause of the Florentine Trecento triumvirate. Indeed, he does not hesitate to say that he considers himself the butt of Niccoli's attacks, and is ready to reply to him in due course. "But time prevents me," he says at the end, expressly referring to himself, "from undertaking the defense of these men [Dante, Petrarch, and Boccaccio] and protecting them against your abuse. . . . Therefore, I will defer this defense until some other more convenient time." [35] But in the second dialogue, when he is asked by Roberto de' Rossi to make good that promise, he quite unexpectedly tries to distort the former situation and devolve his voluntarily assumed obligation on Bruni. "Did I not express my opinion on those preeminent men sufficiently yesterday?", he now asks.[36]

Technically the author's motive for making Salutati behave in this way is clear: in consequence of Salutati's refusal to be the counter-speaker, the obligation to exonerate the three great Florentines of Niccoli's charges passes eventually to Niccoli himself; and this turn of the conversation is the cause of the dramatic liveliness of the dialogues in the form in which we have them. But Bruni's

great literary art in first creating and then relieving the
tension produced by Salutati's promise and subsequent
change of mind must not make us overlook the fact that
for the attainment of the author's goal it would not have
been necessary to have Salutati make a solemn promise at
the end of the first dialogue, only to break it later arbitrarily and with half-true assertions. As the events are set
forth in the *Dialogi*, Salutati (as one modern critic has it)
hardly plays a creditable role, and it is difficult to see why
Bruni should have presented the old master in so equivo-
cal a position.[37] More precisely, if Bruni, when writing
Dialogus I, had already been planning to make the other
members of the circle compel Niccoli to recant, and to
undertake the defense of the three great Florentines himself, he would have had no intelligible reason for letting
Salutati make his promise and thus create a situation from
which he could not extricate himself without contradicting
his own words. Under these circumstances, there is a strong
suspicion that Bruni, during the composition of *Dialogus I*,
had still been thinking in terms of a duel between Niccoli
and Salutati only, and had not yet envisaged a unanimous
circle of friends before whom Niccoli would have to make
amends for his offense. This suspicion receives added support from Bruni's own changing role as a participant in the
conversations.

In *Dialogus I*, Salutati calls Leonardo Bruni a zealous
partisan of Niccoli. "So fully do I see Leonardo agree with
Niccolò in every opinion," Salutati says after Niccoli's
opening attack on modern culture and scholarship, "that I
believe indeed he would rather go astray with him than
follow the truth with me." And Bruni explicitly confirms
this alliance with Niccoli by answering Salutati he knew
well that what Niccoli had set forth "was a plea in my
cause no less than in his own."[38] At that time, then, the
plot of the second-day debate could hardly have been in

the author's mind. For before the transgressor Niccoli can be imposed upon to recant, Salutati must be in a position to escape his obligation by knowing that he can rely on Bruni. Of the same Bruni of whom he had said the day before that he knew him to be in agreement with Niccoli "in every opinion" and to prefer to go astray with his friend Niccoli, Salutati now relates a different story: that Bruni had long been begging him to put in writing a "panegyric" (*laudes*) of the three great Florentines (which, of course, would have been contrary to the wishes of the Niccoli of the first dialogue); and that Bruni himself was the most suitable member of the group to sing their praises. "For the man who has praised the city as a whole," as Bruni had done in his *Laudatio,* "is the proper person to praise these men as well." [39]

Such contradictory statements cannot stem from the same context and cannot have been put down by the author at one and the same time. Between the writing of the two scenes something must have changed the situation. One does not see how Salutati could be made to say in *Dialogus II* that Bruni was the best arbiter and had long asked for a defense of the three great Florentines, unless Salutati had ceased to consider Bruni a blind follower of Niccoli. And since it is the writing of the *Laudatio* which, by Salutati's statement, qualified Bruni to champion the memory of the great Florentines of the Trecento, the *Laudatio* would seem to have been published between the composition of the two dialogues.

It could be argued, of course, that Salutati's sentiments about Bruni as expressed in the *Dialogi* are after all no authentic source-evidence and may have been put down without too much consideration for historical fact. However, even in a fictitious work a simultaneous composition of such contradictory statements on Bruni would seem to be utterly improbable. For we should then have to assume that Bruni, in the same publication in which he made the other members of his circle praise him for the patriotic service rendered through the *Laudatio,* and in which he was particularly intent on appearing before his readers as a devoted defender of the proud historical tradition of his adoptive *patria,* should have been careless enough to weaken his claims by making Salutati say that he, Bruni, was a partisan of Niccoli's ideas.

Moreover, the inference that the altered relations between the chief partners in the two dialogues reflect an actual change in Bruni—from a time when he was strongly under Niccoli's influence to a time when, in the defense of the Florentine tradition, he was on Salutati's side and against Niccoli—is strengthened by information outside of Bruni's work suggesting the same changes in his personal relations and friendships.

In order to evaluate this outside evidence, we must remember that at least one definite historical fact regarding Bruni's and Salutati's relationship is ascertainable from the *Dialogi:* In 1401, the union of friendship and scholarly cooperation between the two men, intimate though it was,[40] was not yet such as to make Bruni Salutati's perfect ally in the controversy over the legacy of the three great Trecento Florentines. For the remark, that Bruni would rather go astray with Niccoli than be on the right path with Salutati, could not have gone into the dialogue unless there existed at that time a certain feeling of difference and Salutati was complaining that Bruni in some vital matters agreed not with him but with Niccoli.

However, in the winter of 1405-06 (that is, at or shortly after the time when *Dialogus II* originated if written after the *Laudatio*)[41] we find in Salutati's correspondence some utterances intimating that he and Bruni were a team, as were Niccoli and Poggio. In some letters belonging to the first months of 1406, Salutati called Bruni "more than half of my mind, my own self through and through," saying at the same time that Niccoli was Poggio's "second self." [42] Now it is most improbable that Salutati with these expressions meant to indicate a degree of personal friendship. For in the winter of 1405-06 it was Niccoli who lived in closest personal contact with him in Florence, whereas Bruni and Poggio lived in daily exchange and most intimate friendship at the Curia (then in Viterbo), where they had both found positions through mutual advice and efforts. Between Salutati and Bruni, on the other hand, strained personal relations had existed since November 1405, an irritation which was not removed until Salutati's death in May 1406, and which in December 1405 and January 1406 expressed itself in angry letters. As to Salutati's linking Poggio and Niccoli, though they had been living in separate places since 1403, it is an important point that Salutati then was embroiled with Poggio in a violent epistolary controversy about almost the same questions, centering on the appraisal of Petrarch, that several years earlier had brought about the clash between Salutati and Niccoli in the scene portrayed in *Dialogus I*.[43]

When all these data are considered, the alignment in Salutati's group by the beginning of 1406 becomes a matter of considerable interest for the background of the *Dialogi*. The upshot is that the situation then was precisely that presupposed in the second dialogue. Like the documentary data ascertainable from the manuscript transmission, the few available contemporaneous epistolary testimonies thus prove to be in harmony with our basic hypothesis.

The observation that Bruni by the time of the composition of the second dialogue had entered into an alliance of the mind with Salutati, and that this alliance had much to do with the appearance of the *Laudatio*, prepares the ground for the crucial argument in an historical criticism

of the *Dialogi:* the change in Bruni's relationship to Salutati is only an indication of a more general and more incisive change—*Dialogus II* is rife with a conscious Florentine and civic sentiment which, though characteristic of
the *Laudatio,* is entirely absent from *Dialogus I.*

We cannot, of course, expect this sentiment to come to
the fore at many points in the course of a literary and philological debate which is little concerned with Florence's
historical past and her political position. Nevertheless, the
vindication of the three great Florentines of the Trecento
is clearly set forth as part of a transformation of Bruni's
attitude toward Florence. For, as we know, the conversation of the second day, before returning to the quest of
Dante, Petrarch, and Boccaccio, is introduced by an episode
(a new prologue in its literary function) which gives to
the historically-minded patriotism of the *Laudatio* a place
in the discussions of the *Dialogi.*[44]

The aspects of the *Laudatio* emphasized in *Dialogus II*
are the reinterpretation of Roman and Florentine history
from the viewpoint of civic freedom, and the implicit critique of the medieval idea of imperial monarchy. The two
most valuable fruits of the *Laudatio,* so the friends in
Dialogus II agree, are, first, Bruni's disclosure of an historical connection between the love of liberty in Guelph
Florence and the sentiments once animating the Roman
citizens who upheld the legacy of freedom against the
tyranny of the Roman emperors; and, second, the shift of
accent in historical outlook from Imperial Rome to the
Roman Republic.

The climax of this introductory scene of the second dialogue comes when Salutati is made to offer a kind of recantation; he must retract the monarchical leanings of his
De Tyranno before Niccoli himself is called upon to denounce his literary heresies against the Florentine tradition. While Salutati at the opening of the dialogue still

maintains his championship of the cause of Caesar and the Roman emperors as displayed in *De Tyranno,* he finally has to admit that from a Florentine perspective the shift of emphasis to Republican Rome is justified and even needed. Despite the admiration for Caesar which he has learned from Dante, Salutati eventually is made to say that he would concede that a citizen should seek a guiding example not in Caesar, but in the great figures of republican times like Marcellus and Camillus.[45]

It is against the background of this politico-historical preamble that the effort of *Dialogus II* to rehabilitate the memory of the three great Florentines of the Trecento, on the grounds that they form "not the least part of the glory of this our city," [46] reveals itself as an incident in the restrengthening of the civic spirit by the final crisis of the war for Florence's independence. The second dialogue, in contrast to the radical classicism and youthful irreverence of the first, stands side by side with the *Panegyric on the City of Florence.*

From the perspective of previous Bruni scholarship this means: the two opposing schools of thought, which have so long obscured the historical place of the *Dialogi* by their alternate emphasis on one of the two dialogues as the alleged expression of the author's true mind, have not been wholly mistaken in their observations, but have placed an erroneous interpretation on the facts observed. Those half-truths now merge in the realization that two different minds have left their marks on the *Dialogi*. But the emerging broader synthesis is not a picture of Quattrocento Humanism wavering between two possible attitudes toward the Trecento legacy, as Vittorio Rossi has proposed to interpret Bruni's changing relationship to Dante in the first and second dialogue. Rather, it is the picture of two minds characteristic of two successive stages in Bruni's development: one the spirit of the years when Bruni still regarded the views of his older friends as alternatives between which he had not yet made his final choice; the other the spirit of the time when he had come to look upon both sides as half-truths between which he had discovered a new position for himself, meant to absorb, transform, and replace both Salutati's Trecento outlook and the negative radicalism of Niccoli's classicism—the first phase of Bruni's civic Humanism.[47]

CHAPTER 12

DIALOGUS II AND THE FLORENTINE
ENVIRONMENT

WITH the demonstration that the *Laudatio*
and *Dialogus II* originated later than 1402,
we have established the crucial basis for an
historical understanding of Bruni's formative years. Like
the pamphlets of the contemporaneous Florentine publicists, Bruni's two pioneering works were shaped, or deeply
influenced, by the historic events of the Florentine-Milanese struggle.

This is not to say, however, that *Dialogus II* was necessarily written on the morrow of the Florentine triumph,
as was the *Laudatio*, the work of either the first or second
summer after Giangaleazzo's death.[1] But even if *Dialogus
II* did not immediately follow the war—the possibility of
a somewhat later date will be pointed out presently [2]—the
study of the circumstances of its composition and of the
motives of its author sheds light on the effects which the
patriotic impulse of the war left on the cultural life of
the quieter years that followed.

*Florentine Sentiment in Bruni's
Early Curial Period*

With the *Laudatio* and *Dialogus II*, Bruni's civic Humanism was reaching a point from which it might have
developed in harmonious continuity. But in the decade
between 1405 and 1414, a change in the external condi-

tions of his life caused a long interruption of his connection with Florence. As a result, his sentiments toward the city fluctuated intensely during the postwar years.

For a young humanist from the Florentine territory, like Bruni, who did not belong to any of the merchant families of the metropolis where he had to make a living, there existed only one possible position: that of Chancellor—and Salutati, though now very old,[3] was still in vigorous health. To be sure, life in Salutati's circle and work on the *Laudatio* had taught Bruni to feel passionately for Florence, and the experiences of the year 1402 had inspired him with the resolve to become the historian of the Florentine people.[4] Yet he was soon forced to realize that he would have to choose between legal work in Florence (he had studied law in Florence for four years before becoming a full-fledged humanist in Salutati's and Chrysoloras' circles [5a]) and a career in some chancery elsewhere in Italy. Accordingly, after a temporary return to the much-disliked legal studies, Bruni in 1405 decided to accept a position as *secretarius apostolicus* at the Curia, where Poggio had already gone in 1403 as a *scriptor* and *abbreviator*.

However reluctant Bruni was to take this step, once he felt at home at the Curia he began to look back on the days when he had thought himself a Florentine as a dream now past; his sentiments and outlook began to assimilate themselves to those of other humanists at the Curia. By 1407, in addition to his curial office, he had accepted a canonry at the Florentine Cathedral.[5b] Although in the fifteenth century such a prebend was not infrequently held by someone who did not intend to be a clergyman in residence, and even by an occupant who had not taken the (formally required) minor orders, still this clerical appointment took Bruni near the point of final separation from the civic way of life. But time would show that the experience of his youth was to be the stronger element: while Poggio remained in Papal service most of his life and in many respects developed into a typical representative of the humanist *literati* at the Curia, Bruni renounced his canonical position as early as 1409 and, a year later, interrupted his curial secretaryship by a brief tenure of the Florentine chancellor office, even if, at that time, only for a few months. In early 1412, this was followed by his marriage,[5c] though not as yet by the final abandonment of his curial office. In 1415, however, presumably as soon as his financial circumstances permitted, he returned to Florence and henceforth lived there as a citizen and head of a family, making good the promise given in the *Laudatio* to write the history of Florence. From 1427 onward, he permanently served his republic in the office that Salutati had once held.

This uneven course of Bruni's life meant that his outlook as a citizen and as a Florentine patriot, which we have seen growing rapidly under the impact of the crisis of 1402, was, only a few years later, to be overshadowed by other experiences that continued for almost a decade. In other words, the period of his life spent at the Curia gives us a chance to discover a *terminus ad quem* for the composition of the second dialogue. For a work so deeply permeated with love for Florence and civic sentiment as *Dialogus II* cannot have come from Bruni's pen during the time when he had found new ideals and a sphere of action at the Papal Curia.

Yet, though our sources allow us to trace this change in some detail, our net is not yet sufficiently fine-meshed. Since Bruni's patriotic feeling for Florence had been so deeply rooted, it is extremely improbable that his loyalties would have changed overnight on his arrival in Rome. The second dialogue may be a document of the years spent in Florence, but equally well it may be the product of

the time when the author was not yet finally acclimatized
to the Curial atmosphere and was looking back with longing upon his past in the circle of friends gathered around
Salutati. Everything, therefore, hinges upon whether we
can exactly fix the date of so delicate an emotional process
as the temporary fading of Bruni's attachment to Florence after his move to the Curia.

We may procure a touchstone from our previous findings by reexamining the expressions of Bruni's sentiments
before and after the experience of 1402. In *Dialogus I,*
of 1401, we find him still far from thinking of Florence
as his adopted home. While it is a great part of man's
happiness, he writes in his dedication to Vergerio, to
possess "a glorious and noble *patria*" still "we are lacking
this part of happiness because our *patria* has been ruined by
the frequent blows of *Fortuna,* and has been almost reduced to nought." This means that Bruni then was thinking of Arezzo as his "*patria.*" His consolation, he goes on
to say, is that he is permitted to live in that city which is
superior to all others in stamina, beauty of architecture,
and cultivation of "*studia humanitatis.*" [6]

In the *Laudatio* and in *Dialogus II,* this feeling of being
a foreigner among the wonders of the Florentine world
has completely disappeared. In the *Laudatio,* which shows
Bruni deeply engrossed in the history and political problems of Florence, he feels his connection with her to have
become so permanent that he already has formed the intention of using his humanistic abilities at some future time
to write the history of Florence.[7] From *Dialogus II* one
gathers that the service performed by the *Laudatio* to Florence's glory and historiography had in his own mind
earned him the place of a Florentine among Florentines.
All citizens ought to be thankful to the author of the
Laudatio, one of the partners in *Dialogus II* says,[8] and
Salutati is made to declare that Bruni as the writer of the

Florentine eulogy is the right person to undertake the defense of the three great Florentines who in the dialogue are called the pride "of this our commonwealth," and again "our citizens" who have brought glory and laurels "to our city." [9]

With this earlier development of Bruni's feelings for Florence in mind, let us look at the course of events after his departure from the city in March of 1405. On his arrival in Rome he found himself in a trying situation; there was not only the burden of his new office, but a revolt of the Roman populace which repeatedly put him, like other officials of the Curia, in very real danger, until the Curia took refuge in the quiet country town Viterbo, where Bruni arrived on August 8th, 1405, and stayed until March 1406.

From the time of this stay at Viterbo come several of Bruni's letters and literary works showing his love for Florence and feelings of allegiance unimpaired if not augmented by the glamour of the past and his longing to return. In a letter of September 13, 1405, addressed to Salutati, he upbraids himself for having been foolish enough to forsake the city on the Arno and the group of friends around Salutati. He describes the beauty and cleanliness, and the flowering of the new studies once enjoyed in Florence, so glowingly that Salutati replies dryly, Bruni seemed to feel he must repeat his eulogy of Florence whenever occasion offered.[10] In this correspondence of September 1405, Bruni calls Florence *"Florentia nostra."* [11] How deeply he was still imbued with the civic evaluation of life, one also senses in the funeral oration which he wrote at Viterbo for a young Florentine patrician, a *nepote* of Cardinal Acciaiuoli, who had died at the Curia.[12] On that occasion he quoted the word of Themistocles of Athens that without the atmosphere and opportunities of the splendid *"patria"* where he was born of a noble family, he would have had no hope of achieving lasting fame even with all his talents. In Bruni's picture of the city on the Arno as the scene of the brilliant beginnings of the young Florentine patrician, Florence means as much for the growth of his personality as Athens had meant for Themistocles.*

* The passage in the *Laudatio Othonis* runs: "Therefore one must attend to family and *patria;* for even Themistocles, that Athenian of the highest *virtus* and assiduity, believed that without his distinguished *patria* he could never achieve fame." [13a]

Undoubtedly, Bruni here followed a way of reasoning initiated by Salutati. The Themistocles anecdote to which Bruni referred—Themistocles' alleged answer to a native of the island Seriphos who had charged that Themistocles owed his eminence to the greatness of his *patria,* not to his own *virtus*—had always been familiar to readers of the classics by way of Cicero's *De senectute,* 3, 8. But in most medieval manuscripts of *De senectute,* Themistocles' reply had run: "Neither would you have become *nobilis* if you were an Athenian, nor would I be obscure if I were a Seriphos islander" (*"Neque tu, si Atheniensis esses, nobilis extitisses, neque ego, si Seripius essem, ignobilis"*). That is, Themistocles had boasted that he owed everything to himself. It was Salutati who recognized the corruption of this text and established a version of the passage essentially identical with the phrasing today accepted as genuine. In this version, Themistocles exclaims: "By Hercules, neither would I have become *nobilis* if I were a Seriphos islander, nor you famous if you were an Athenian" (*"Nec hercle si ego Seriphius, nobilis; nec tu si Atheniensis esses, unquam clarus fuisses"*). That is, Themistocles had with humility admitted the advantage which the privilege of being an Athenian citizen had given him over the native of an obscure island.

Salutati realized the original meaning of the anecdote in part because he discovered that the phrasing which he selected is handed down in Plato's *Republic* (I, 329 s.), where the same anecdote is told. But he would hardly have paid such thorough attention to the textual problem and solved it, had he not been guided in his interpretation by his civic convictions. This can be gleaned from his own comment in the letter in

We are not surprised, then, to find that when the Florentine chancellorship became vacant by Salutati's death shortly after Bruni had returned to Rome with the Curia, in May 1406, he was among the competitors for the post, though that time without success.[14] It was the summer and autumn of the year 1406, however, which brought about a decisive change of mind in Bruni and opened a new phase of his inner life. When in December 1406 the post of the Florentine chancellor happened to become available again, Bruni's old friends in Florence wished to seize the unexpected chance of winning him back. But meanwhile, Bruni had found in his Curial office what now appeared to him an even greater and more valuable task for his life.

---

which he drew Pier Paolo Vergerio's attention to the version of the anecdote in Plato's *Republic*. As Salutati tells Vergerio, the phrasing of Themistocles' dictum that he preferred "branded the disputatious man from Seriphos with a twofold obscurity, that of his *patria* and that of his person, while acknowledging that all of his own [Themistocles'] *nobilitas* was due to his *patria*. This is the wise reply of a philosopher; this is the modesty and the frank confession of a citizen who has deserved well of his *patria*." [13b]

To this interpretation Vergerio objected "that it is proper neither for the *virtus* nor for the self-reliance of a man like Themistocles" to attribute so much to external conditions, "for we see men of superior *virtus* becoming famous even if they come from the peasantry and the socially lowest place." [13c] Obviously, a humanist who did not belong to the Florentine circle could not bring himself to accept the thought that a man owes so much to his *patria* and has to have a great *patria* in order to make himself *nobilis*. Bruni, on the other hand, saw eye to eye with Salutati. Few other examples show so strikingly the role which life in the Florentine city-state played in the renewed understanding of the values that had guided life in the ancient city-state. The episode also illustrates how deeply Bruni, as a young humanist, was indebted to Salutati for his civic outlook on life.[13d]

The winter in Viterbo, when Bruni lived in recollection of the past more intensely than ever before, had been followed by a series of events that made him alive to the present: the return of the Curia to Rome which was a stronger counterpoise to the Florentine memories than sleepy Viterbo; and, in November, the succession to the Papal See of Gregory XII, whose avowed policy was the settlement of the Schism in the Church, if necessary at the price of his own abdication provided the Pope in Avignon would do the same. For the phrasing of the manifesto setting forth this policy, a document possibly decisive in the history of western Christendom, Gregory requested drafts from various secretaries, and the one proposed by Bruni appeared to the Pope and the Cardinals superior to all others. When Bruni in December replied to his friends in Florence that he no longer wished to apply for the chancellor's post, his letter glowed with satisfaction at this success. He was possessed not only of a humanist's pride, but also of a new hope that it might be granted him by fate to use his now acknowledged literary ability in the service of the settlement of the Schism. He did not allow his friends to place his name among the possible candidates for the Florentine post. "Now that there is good hope that this baleful Schism can be ended," he told them, "I believe that I should live here [at the Curia]." [15]

When one examines Bruni's picture of the scene in the Consistory where his draft was selected, one no longer encounters a trace of feeling that the honor accorded to him was at the same time a triumph for the Florentine school and the circle around Salutati to which he owed his humanistic training. Just as he did when *Dialogus I* was sent to Vergerio, he again feels himself to be not a Florentine, but a son of his native Arezzo. "The city of Arezzo," he adds to the description of his triumph, "which some believe they may look down upon, carried the prize." [16]

In the same letter, rejecting Niccoli's advice to insert a reference to the Florentine conquest of Pisa in the *Laudatio*, he seems to have completely forgotten his intention to some day become the historian of Florence. The recent Florentine victories, he tells Niccoli, should not be added to the *Laudatio*, but deserve depiction in an historical work, and "your co-citizens" (*cives tui*) should commission somebody conversant with the matter to write such a history. "Your co-citizens," from one who had talked of "our Florence" only one year before—and the detached advice to look around for an historian of the Florentine victories, from the man who had considered the writing of the history of Florence the *opus magnum* that he "hoped to attack some day"! Surely, a more complete reversal of sentiment and of plans for a life's work could not be imagined.

We need no further evidence to conclude that a writer of letters like these would no longer have been able to write a work such as *Dialogus II*, laden with fervent Florentine patriotism and pride in the attainments of the *Laudatio* for Florentine historical philosophy.

There has become visible, then, a clear break after which *Dialogus II* could not have been composed. The dividing line, we now see, does not coincide with Bruni's departure from Florence. From the viewpoint of the development of Bruni's Humanism, his stay at Viterbo from August 1405 to March 1406 must still be reckoned part of his early Florentine phase, and must therefore be included in the period in which he felt as a Florentine and *Dialogus II* could have been written. The composition of *Dialogus II*, we may conclude, must have taken place either between the completion of the *Laudatio* and Bruni's departure from Florence, that is, between September 1403 and March

1405; or during the period in which he was looking back with longing to his Florentine years, the time of his stay at Viterbo from August 1405 to March 1406.

The Petrarch Controversy of 1405-1406

There is a second way in which we may hope to define and illuminate this phase of Bruni's life. The Florentine sentiment which characterizes the second dialogue is (as we know) particularly pronounced in Bruni's effort to vindicate the memory of the three great Florentines of the Trecento. We should, therefore, carefully compare this aspect of the dialogue with any events that, during the period which we have just delimited, may have rekindled the controversy of 1401.

At least as far as the views on Petrarch are concerned, the old dispute did break out anew in Salutati's circle at the time of Bruni's stay in Viterbo, during the fall and winter of 1405-06.[17] This revival of a crucial controversy gives us a welcome opportunity for a glance at the history of the Florentine attitude toward Petrarch, after we have said so much about the changes in attitude toward Dante.

The exact details of the Petrarch controversy in the winter of 1405-06 can be reconstructed from Salutati's letters, even though nothing has come down to us but fragments of the documents containing the renewed attacks by members of the younger generation. It was in August 1405 [18] that Poggio, speaking also for an unnamed acquaintance who had long been an admirer of Salutati, addressed to Salutati from the Curia a pamphlet in letter form which attacked a eulogy of Petrarch composed by Salutati in his youth. This eulogy, written in 1379 and since then widely circulated as an introduction to manuscript collections of Petrarch's works,[19] had been conceived in the true spirit of the Trecento: Petrarch was proclaimed superior to all the poets and writers of antiquity. That Salutati was sincere in this assertion is shown by the fact that the same judgment had already been penned by him in 1374, upon the news of Petrarch's death, and again in 1375 when, under the fresh impression of the death of Boccaccio, he looked back upon the past.[20]

No wonder, therefore, that he obstinately defended his convictions when, in the autumn of 1405, he received Poggio's critique which obviously was somewhat scornful and overbearing, as Niccoli's attacks against Petrarch and Dante had been.[21] We have the letter in which on December 17, 1405, Salutati took Poggio violently to task, virtually maintaining the entire line of thought which he had been upholding since the 1370's. Poggio, thereupon, immediately attempted to tone down his attack, mostly, as may be gathered, out of personal consideration for the aged master. Like the Niccoli of *Dialogus II* (one is tempted to say), he produced a recantation in which he himself now praised Petrarch in his own way. This we know from Salutati's next letter, dated March 26, 1406, from which we also learn that Salutati, who knew his Poggio well, refused to accept this sudden change of mind at face value. He suspected that consideration and friendliness were behind it all, and therefore repeated once more a large part of his earlier arguments, going far afield and quite ready for the fray. But this was the last literary effort of the seventy-five-year-old man; he died on the fourth of May.[22]

As for Bruni, he was a close spectator of this quarrel between his two most intimate friends. As a papal secretary he must have been in almost daily contact with Poggio, first in Rome during the late summer of 1405 when Poggio composed his critique,[23] and afterwards in Viterbo during the autumn and winter when Poggio crossed swords with Salutati.[24] Though so close to Poggio, Bruni cannot be suspected, however, of having been the unnamed "admirer" of Salutati at the Curia who, Poggio stated in his letter, had endorsed his attacks. For it was Bruni whom Salutati told in a letter that he would answer Poggio's assault on Petrarch in a way that would serve Poggio right for his abuses and would teach him a lesson.[25] Salutati could take Bruni thus into his confidence only if he was sure that Bruni was not Poggio's anonymous accomplice. From an earlier discussion we know that at that time Salutati felt more closely akin in spirit to Bruni than ever before.[26] In January 1406, he declared repeatedly that Bruni was "half and more of my own self," while two months later he maintained that a similarly close relationship existed between Poggio and Niccoli.

This assurance about Bruni's personal position during the controversy of 1405-06 clears the way for the essential question: whether Bruni, far from being a secret partner in Poggio's attacks, did not rather stand in a relationship to the controversy suggested by the strange duplication of a recanting Niccoli in *Dialogus II* and a recanting Poggio in 1405-06. Could it be that Poggio's moderation in his later letter was due to Bruni's influence, just as the understanding mind of the historian Bruni expresses itself in the moderation of the recanting Niccoli in *Dialogus II?*

Before we can answer this question, we must know whether one of the two attempts at reconciliation may have served the other as a model. This, in turn, is a problem whose solution requires knowledge of the preceding phases of Petrarch's reputation. If it could be shown that Niccoli's and Poggio's "recantations" contain, in their attitude toward Petrarch, closely related ideas that had not existed before, we could be reasonably certain that one of the recantations was written with a knowledge of the other.

"*Dialogus II*" and the Early History of the Appraisal of Petrarch

The successive phases of Petrarch's fame form one of the chapters in the history of historical outlook in the early Renaissance that, though well explored in factual detail, in large areas still lack an historical evaluation. Although the often florid and unprecise wording of fourteenth-century statements on Petrarch demands an inquiry that at times may seem oversubtle, the conclusions which emerge are nevertheless clear-cut.

Let us begin by pointing out that while we have been completely justified in speaking of a "recantation" made by Niccoli in *Dialogus II,* this must not be taken to mean that the second Niccoli is harking back to the ideas of the older generation on either Petrarch or Dante. Niccoli's speech in the second dialogue is a "recantation" inasmuch as he forgoes the half-ironical, sarcastic attitude of the first Niccoli (or rather, tones it down, because even in *Dialogus II,* in Bruni's lifelike presentation, Niccoli retains something of the scoffer he was in real life). The second Niccoli no longer dares to cast Petrarch aside with arguments no better than that Petrarch's *Africa,* after many promises, was never completed, wherefore its author stands convicted of mere bragging; or that his *Bucolica* does not adhere strictly to the rules of pastoral poetry; or that his invective is not always in accord with the best rules of rhetoric.[27] These superficial exaggerations are replaced by a more serious stand. But upon closer inspection this new interpretation is as remote from anything ever expressed by Salutati as the earlier attacks had been.

If one looks at the substance of the ideas behind the dazzling irony of the attack, one may even say in a sense that the arguments of the first Niccoli have more of the

Trecento attitude toward Petrarch than has the verdict which Bruni, speaking through Niccoli, eventually reaches in the second dialogue. The contention of the first Niccoli, that Petrarch had tried in vain to measure up to the ancients, was by no means unprecedented among Trecento humanists. On one occasion, when only the rise and fall of classical Latin and rhetoric (the *"facultas dicendi"*) were in question—some time around the middle of the 1390's— even Salutati had not hesitated to say that Petrarch and Boccaccio had remained far behind the ancients.[28] Salutati's judgment of Petrarch's work as a whole was not, however, determined by such partial criticism, and in his dispute with Poggio in 1405-06 he held fast to his original conviction of Petrarch's "superiority" over all the great figures of antiquity. The reason was that the essence of the new studies, in the eyes of a humanist of the late Trecento like Salutati, was to be sought in that philosophy of Christian Stoicism which had found its most perfect expression in Petrarch's *De Vita Solitaria, De Otio Religiosorum,* and *De Secreto Conflictu Curarum Suarum,* the three works which Salutati once grouped together as the pinnacle of that humanistic philosophy which he admired.[29] It was for this reason that in 1405 Salutati declared Petrarch to be superior not only to Cicero, but to Aristotle and Plato as well.[30] To the end he remained convinced that Petrarch had been able as a Christian to combine classical *"eloquentia"* with a perfection of *"doctrina"* inaccessible to pagan antiquity.

There was no possibility for the humanists of the younger generation to return to such arguments colored by the thinking of the Middle Ages, not even in the conciliatory mood of a "recantation." Poggio, in his reply to Salutati in the winter of 1405-06, expressly rejected them.[31] Nor does the Niccoli of the second dialogue in his rehabilitation of Petrarch mention any arguments of this nature. The juncture, where the recanting Poggio and the recanting Niccoli were to a degree reconciled with tradition, must be sought elsewhere.

This juncture is not reached at a turn of the debate where the younger men could meet the older half-way; at that point no incisive reinterpretation was needed. As far back as the 1350's, the Florentine admirers of Petrarch had been accustomed to see one of the reasons for his superiority over all ancients in his equal mastery of both prose and poetry, while Virgil, according to a dictum of Seneca, had been found wanting in his prose, and Cicero had lost his fluency when attempting to write poetry.[32] Salutati never praised Petrarch without employing this argument; neither his letters of 1374 and 1379 [33] nor those of December 1405 and March 1406 [34] fail to refer to it. To the humanists of the early Quattrocento this way of reasoning had some appeal because Petrarch's ability to write in verse as well as prose, in Latin as well as the vernacular, seemed to suit their ideal of many-sidedness in intellectual pursuits. Even if they were no longer willing to accept this argument as proof of Petrarch's superiority over Cicero and Virgil, they found nevertheless that in his many-sidedness lay one significance of his attainments. But it took time before this Quattrocento view of Petrarch as the most universal writer and poet came to the fore. In fact, the new aspect was not clearly elaborated until Bruni's *Vita di Petrarca* of 1436 and the subsequent Latin *Vita* of Petrarch from the pen of Giannozzo Manetti.[35] What the Niccoli of *Dialogus II* has to contribute to this theme is nothing new as yet. First he remembers from a trip to Padua, where Petrarch had lived during his last years, that in the Paduan circle of humanists much emphasis had been laid on the claim that Petrarch had been greater than the ancients on account of his equal mastery of poetry and prose. Then Niccoli adds that he had heard the same argu-

ment in Florence in his youth; Luigi Marsili had supported it, and rightly so. If "foreigners thought like that,"
how could we Florentines be "colder . . . in the praise
of our fellow citizen"? [36] Evidently, in this whole train
of thought *Dialogus II* does not go substantially beyond
the range of earlier ideas.

In the same breath, however, the second Niccoli sets
forth a further reason for his change of mind. We should
agree to the praise of Petrarch, he says, "particularly because he was the one who restored to life the *studia humanitatis* when they were already extinct, and opened for
us the path (*cum . . . viam aperuerit*) to show in what
manner we could acquire learning." [37] In this passage we
are confronted with what we may call the germ of an appraisal of the founder of Humanism from an historical
perspective—Petrarch seen as the pioneer upon whose
shoulders all those must stand who succeed him in carrying
on the *"studia humanitatis,"* even when they have out-
stripped him in design and methods, as the first dialogue
maintains and the second does not retract. Here, then, it
seems, we at last encounter an element emerging from
the transformation of Humanism about 1400. At that time
the pattern created by Petrarch began to appear as part of
the past, because in the light of puristic classicism and the
new exacting philology it was found insufficient; but for
this very reason it could be appraised historically as the
reopening of the path for all further progress in the
"studia humanitatis."

On reexamining the Trecento views of Petrarch, however, we soon discover that their difference from the formulation in the second dialogue is on the surface not pronounced enough to be noticed unless we study the transformation of every component part. While Salutati, in his
appraisals of Petrarch, had never used an argument similar
to that of the Niccoli of *Dialogus II,* the notion that, after

a thousand years of oblivion, some leading mind had at last reached again the level of the ancient accomplishment, and had made it easier for others to follow—this notion had sprung up almost automatically as soon as the spiritual and artistic powers of the great artists and poets of the Trecento were recognized by their contemporaries. Even before Petrarch's generation and the coming of Humanism, about 1330, one of the earliest commentators on Dante had stated that the great poet-philosophers of antiquity had for a long time fallen into oblivion, but "by this poet the dead poetry was revived; he raised poetic craftsmanship and caused us to recall to our minds the poets of antiquity"; [38] and Boccaccio not only continued the same notion in his *Life of Dante* but, moved by the genius of Giotto, also applied it (in an episode of the *Decamerone*) to the art of painting, which, thanks to Giotto, had returned to the standards of antiquity, after it had lain dead and buried for many centuries.[39] Petrarch himself, in the days of his coronation as a poet on the Roman Capitol, and of Cola di Rienzo's Roman revolt, had adhered to a passionate faith in the "rebirth" (*renasci*) of the classical world of Roman Italy. His hopes at that time had been directed both toward the reestablishment of the political greatness of Rome, and toward the renewal in the realm of poetry of the Latin preeminence once won by Virgil. Although the failure of Rienzo's Roman revolt crushed the hopes for a political rebirth, Petrarch seemed to have achieved the resurrection of Latin poetry in the manner of the ancients.

It was Boccaccio who, toward the end of his own and Petrarch's life, in a letter written in 1372 to Jacopo Pizzinga, used the notion of "resurrection" for the most explicit Trecento comment on Petrarch's work. In Petrarch's coronation on the Capitol, Boccaccio argued, an element of Roman life had been revived that had been slumbering for more than a thousand years, waiting until Petrarch "removed the thornbushes and undergrowth with which man's negligence had encumbered the road, restored with a firm dam the pavingstones that had been half eaten away by the rains, and so *opened the way for himself as well as for those who wished to ascend after him*" (*sibi et post eum ascendere volentibus viam aperuit*).[40] Even if direct literary evidence were not available, we should have to assume that this manner of regarding the author of the *Africa* was included in the mental equipment of Bruni and Niccoli as a legacy from the Trecento; and the use of the identical expression "*viam aperuit*" by both Boccaccio and Bruni, each time in connection with Petrarch's winning the "*laurea*," reveals Bruni's acquaintance with Boccaccio's letter.

What originality, then, remains in Bruni's appraisal of Petrarch as attributed to the Niccoli of *Dialogus II* when we compare it with Boccaccio's letter of 1372? No doubt, there is one basic difference. Boccaccio's letter, in the true Trecento manner, was merely concerned with Petrarch the restorer of the poetry of ancient Rome, but had not yet considered Petrarch the founder of a new discipline of literary studies. The reason for Boccaccio's writing to Pizzinga had been his satisfaction upon learning that such a prominent personage as Pizzinga (he was a high functionary and chancery head, "*magister notarius*," at the Sicilian court) had decided to try his hand at the Latin poetry revived by Petrarch, just as his predecessors had once participated in medieval chivalrous poetry. Under such circumstances Boccaccio's letter was intended to encourage the distinguished novice by pointing out to him that the road of Latin poetry had been "prepared, thrown open, and smoothed" (*paratum, adapertum stratumque*) after Petrarch had made a beginning.[41a] Obviously, this is something essentially different from Bruni's retrospective appreciation of the historic greatness of Petrarch as the man who made the first breach and showed the way for all further progress in the *"studia humanitatis."* *

A twofold transformation of Boccaccio's concept of Humanism and of Petrarch had, in fact, to take place before anyone could conceive the idea attributed to the recanting Niccoli of *Dialogus II:* it had to be realized that Petrarch's *Africa* and Virgil's *Aeneid* were not of equal poetic value, and that the essence and task of Humanism were different from a revival of Roman poetry; and, secondly, there had to emerge the puristic classicism and rigorous philology identified with the name of Niccoli, in the light of which Petrarch's Latin scholarship appeared as a preliminary stage, historically indispensable but on a lower plane than the present.

We can point to an example which illustrates the significance of these two elements. One of Pier Paolo Vergerio's early works gives us an opportunity to observe the transition from the Trecento appraisal of Petrarch to the Quattrocento concept at its mid-point. Vergerio composed a *Vita Francisci Petrarcae* in 1397, before he went to Florence for the long stay which allowed him to become a member of Niccoli's and Bruni's circle.[42] Being one of the first to help lay the foundation for the humanistic course of studies in the Quattrocento, Vergerio was no longer

---

* After the first quarter of the Quattrocento, even average opinion would no longer consider the historic achievement of Petrarch and his followers in terms of Boccaccio's acclamation of a return to Italy of the Muses of Roman poetry. Petrarch's attainments would by then be conceived as restoration of the true *"studia," "litterae,"* and *"eloquentia,"* while by the same token it would be realized that his role had been, in a more profound sense, the rediscovery of the Ciceronian ideal of *"studia humanitatis."* The rise of such a conception of the new studies was to become the distinguishing mark between the Quattrocento view and that held in the Trecento.[41b]

committed to those half-mystical Trecento notions of the *"poeta"* and the resurgence of ancient poetry that had caused Boccaccio to see in Petrarch's solemn coronation on the Capitol the very climax of the movement Petrarch had started. On the other hand, since Vergerio by 1397 had not yet lived through the intellectual revolt of the Florentine humanistic group, he did not yet see Petrarch's work as a phenomenon of the past, and consequently did not hold the notion that Petrarch had stood merely at the beginning of a road that subsequently was to lead on to a maturer phase. To him, Petrarch was not so much the "first" pioneer (*il primo*, as he later was to Bruni in his Petrarch biography), as the "incomparable" (*unicus*) leader of the new studies. Petrarch, so Vergerio recounts, in the course of time "neglected poetry, and was attracted by divine studies, while poetry was relegated to the role of an ornament. . . . In a unique way he devoted himself to the knowledge of antiquity. His eloquence was brilliant and powerful, . . . and, to tell the truth, he alone brought back to our age the *dicendi facultas*, which for so many centuries had been banished and almost become unknown." [43] Vergerio, therefore, while modifying Boccaccio's view of Petrarch as the renovator of Roman poetry, was far from anticipating the wording and meaning of the idea set forth in the *Dialogus II;* and the comparison of his Petrarch appraisal with the latter merely serves to bring out the peculiarity of the formulation used by the Niccoli of the second dialogue.

In the appraisal of Petrarch's work from an historical perspective we have, then, found a thought-motif that could not make its appearance in the humanistic outlook until the classicist revolt in Niccoli's day had directed itself against the accomplishments even of the Trecento. The crucial question is whether this new feeling of historical distance was also present when Poggio sent his apology to Salutati in the winter of 1405-06.

As noted earlier, fragments of Poggio's letters have been preserved through literal quotation in Salutati's replies, and so we know the following passage from Poggio's attempt to reconcile Salutati early in 1406: In spite of his former attacks, Poggio said, he had always esteemed Petrarch's eloquence (*eloquentia*) and erudition (*doctrina*) more highly than anybody else had done. "And my opinion has been that all those who are interested in our studies owe him very much. For he was the first who with his labor, industry, and watchful attention *called back to light* the *studies almost brought to destruction*, and *opened the path* to those others who were eager to follow"—the word "studies," in Poggio's definition, meaning history, poetry, eloquence, and philosophy.[44] This is exactly the concept expressed by the Niccoli of the second dialogue in his statement that Petrarch "*restored* to life the *studia humanitatis* when they *were already extinct*, and *opened* for us *the path* upon which we could cultivate learning." [45] Not only is the general perspective of Petrarch's attainment alike in both passages, but the characterization is made up of almost exactly the same parts: decay of the "*studia*," restoration through Petrarch, and the "opening of the path" for later humanists—all this used as an argument for Petrarch's vindication by members of a generation which felt that Humanism had in essential respects progressed beyond its founder.

We must, of course, reckon with the possibility that Poggio, like Bruni, was acquainted with Boccaccio's portrayal of Petrarch, and that both were drawing upon it as a common source. Indeed, some literal coincidences between Poggio and Boccaccio make it certain that Poggio knew Boccaccio's letter.[46] But the fact that Boccaccio was

Bruni's and Poggio's common source is not sufficient to explain their close affinity. To repeat our previous observations: Boccaccio had not been dealing with Petrarch's contribution to the subsequent humanistic movement (the *"studia humanitatis,"* as Bruni has it, or the new trend of studies in history, poetry, eloquence, and philosophy, as Poggio says), but with the importance of Petrarch's example for the restoration of the ability to write Latin verses in the classical manner; and there had been no hint in Boccaccio's argument that Petrarch was the representative of an initial and therefore still imperfect phase. For to Boccaccio the figurative expression of the "opening of the path" did not mean that Petrarch had been the first to indicate a new direction in which others would continue; to Boccaccio the simile meant that Petrarch had cleared an overgrown, forgotten upward path, and had himself reached the summit to which others now could climb after him.[47] Thus the problem now reads: how did it come about that both Bruni and Poggio, while knowing the older interpretations of Petrarch current in Florence and in particular that proposed by Boccaccio, developed the older views in the same direction, in almost the same words, at about the same time?

No doubt the explanation of such a coincidence can only be that one of the two friends drew upon the work of the other. This means we are confronted with an alternative: either Bruni, when attributing to Niccoli his recantation in *Dialogus II*, was familiar with Poggio's recantation of January/February 1406; or *Dialogus II* was in existence or being prepared when Poggio, in close proximity to Bruni, composed his recantation.

We may hope to solve the problem of intellectual authorship by comparing the attitudes of Bruni and Poggio toward Petrarch in their later years. As to Poggio, there does not seem to be in all his later writings any further concern with the vindication of Petrarch, except an occasional admiring paragraph on Petrarch's retired life which is to be recommended as a model for the true *"vita contemplativa et studiosa."* [48] This silence is significant because it shows how uncharacteristic of Poggio's true interest was the theme he once alluded to in his apology of 1406. In 1444, when Poggio in his biographical sketch of Bruni had to characterize the *Dialogi* along with Bruni's other writings, he did not touch upon the motives for Bruni's reappraisal. He only reported that Bruni, after subjecting the "learning, eloquence, and works" of Dante, Petrarch, and Boccaccio to strong attacks in the first book, made amends in the second by praising their "virtue"; [49] he did not seize the opportunity to explain that in Bruni's eyes Petrarch's *virtus* was laudable because it had been used to open the path for the new studies.

If, on the other hand, we turn to Bruni, we find him in his *Vite di Dante e di Petrarca* of 1436 clinging to and elaborating upon the historical argument which we know from *Dialogus II* and Poggio's letter of 1406. [50] "Petrarch was the first," the verdict of the *Vite* runs, "who called back to light (*rivocò in luce*) the gracefulness of the lost and extinguished ancient manner of writing (*l'antica leggiadria dello stile perduto e spento*). And assuming that [the result of these efforts] was possibly not perfect with him, still it was he who discovered and opened the path to this perfection . . . ; and surely he did enough by merely pointing the way for those who were to follow after him." [51] Here the key words of the second Niccoli are repeated almost literally and have become an integral part of an historical philosophy that gives perspective to the pioneer qualities as well as to the limitations of Humanism in Petrarch's day. For Bruni now explains that the rebirth of classical culture was produced by the gradual revival of the *"popoli italici"* after the breakdown of the

Roman Empire; when "the cities of Tuscany and other cities" were slowly reemerging, they began also "to turn their activities to the studies," slowly and "weakly" at first, but ever more strongly until, with Petrarch, the point was reached where the classical pattern could be resumed, though still "imperfectly." [52]

In the light of these differences between Bruni's and Poggio's views in later years, we can have little doubt about the authorship of the new appraisal of Petrarch. If Poggio had been its intellectual father, a random remark which was so little in keeping with Poggio's accustomed views that it was immediately suspected by Salutati and which in fact was never repeated by Poggio in his later life, would have been taken over by Bruni almost literally, to be developed and finally made the leitmotif of Bruni's Petrarch biography thirty years later; an integral part of Bruni's historical outlook would be a fruit stolen from the garden of a neighbor who had no reason to grow it, and had no use for it except on one occasion.

Obviously, this means that Bruni was the true author, whereas Poggio was the borrower of an idea accepted at a moment when he was looking for a means to placate Salutati. Or we may say that *Dialogus II*, which made so essential a contribution to the attitude of Renaissance Florence toward Dante, also marked the beginning of a new view of Petrarch.*

* This result allows us to complete the dating of *Dialogus II* as follows: either Poggio knew *Dialogus II* in the winter of 1405-06 because Bruni's work was already known to the reading public, in which case it must have been composed before March 1405, since Bruni, as has been pointed out,[53] can hardly have found time and inspiration for this kind of work between his departure from Florence (March 1405) and his arrival at Viterbo (August 1405); or else, the revival in the autumn of 1405 of the same quarrel that had once been carried on between Salutati and Niccoli, this time between Salutati and Poggio,

caused Bruni to compose his second dialogue as a more mature solution of the old problem. In this case the connection between the "recantations" of Niccoli and Poggio would be that Bruni, in 1405-06, conceived Niccoli's speech for the second dialogue while he was witnessing Poggio's quarrel with Salutati, and that Niccoli's speech was put to immediate use by Poggio.[54] In any event, this conclusion rounds out the proof that *Dialogus II* was written either while Bruni, after composition of the *Laudatio*, was still in Florence or during his brief stay in Viterbo—between the autumn of 1403 and the spring of 1406.

Part Four

CLASSICISM AND THE TRECENTO
TRADITION

CHAPTER 13

THE CLASSICISTS AS SEEN BY VOLGARE WRITERS

The Volgare School in the Transition Crisis

OUR recasting of the chronology of Florentine politico-historical literature written at the turn of the Trecento not only makes intelligible the relation of nascent Quattrocento thought to the political crisis; it also reveals the unexpectedly active role that representatives of pre-humanistic and Volgare traditions played in the genesis of the Florentine Quattrocento ideas. The Milanese propaganda attack by Antonio Loschi at the beginning of the decisive clash in 1397 roused defenders of the Florentine cause in all camps in Florence: the citizen Rinuccini, and the humanist Salutati. And it was Rinuccini, and not the humanist-chancellor, who from the vantage-point of the struggle against tyranny succeeded in seizing upon some elements of a new political and historical outlook. In the framework of a typical citizen's miscellany, Rinuccini combined practical political observations with fresh glimpses of the past and with an attempt to assemble a literary hall of fame of all the great men who had enhanced Florence's glory.

The attitude of the humanists at that moment and in the subsequent phase of the struggle did not, our observations show, fully reflect the new experience until the closing years of the war. Around 1400, problems of puristic classicism and literary themes were still absorbing every

interest in humanistic circles, as we know from Bruni's
Dialogus I and especially from the fact that Salutati's defense of Dante, in his *De Tyranno*, remained aloof from
any thought of the values which were at stake for the
Florentine Republic. Reconciliation and fusion between
the humanistic outlook and the civic spirit came only when
Florence stood up to the final crisis. Completed under the
impact of the climactic year 1402, the second version of
Salutati's *Invectiva* is witness to that stage; and an even
more decisive and profound change is shown in Bruni's
development from *Dialogus I* to the *Laudatio* and
Dialogus II. Finally, while some of the innovations found
in Rinuccini were thus continued on a humanistic level and
there reached maturity, the merchant-statesman Gregorio
Dati, writing in Volgare, drew the picture of the Giangaleazzo period in the first politico-historical analysis conducted in a true Quattrocento manner. This work, as yet
little influenced by Humanism, became the forerunner of
Bruni's humanistic account of the Milanese wars in his
Historiae Florentini Populi, as we have seen.

Our result so far, then, is: the impact of the struggle
of the Giangaleazzo era was felt most rapidly not by the
humanistic *literati* and erudites, but by citizens in the
political battle-line; the new experience was turned to
account first of all by writers outside the humanistic circles.
The works of the Florentine humanists were the crest of
the wave; below and before them went polemical pamphlets and chronicle-histories composed in, or quickly
translated into, the Florentine mother-tongue.

Gradually, however, Humanism and the civic tradition came to live in a kind of symbiosis. In order to
clarify this relationship, we first examined the immediate
effects which the experience of the Giangaleazzo period
exerted on the Florentine political and historical outlook,
inside as well as outside the humanistic circle. In the

decades which followed the dawn-of-the-century crisis, other sectors of the outlook of Florentine Humanism were gradually drawn into the same new current, and we must deal with some of them now; for it is only in the light of the continuous growth of Quattrocento thought that we can view in full historical perspective the interaction of learned Humanism with the civic and Volgare trend. In their immediate encounters at the turn of the century, and in the dust and struggle of daily life, there often seemed to be nothing but friction and hostility between the two schools of thought. At many points the defenders of the older forms of civic culture tried to restrain what to them seemed excesses of the new admiration for antiquity and a lack of proper respect for the traditions of their own city and age.

Listening to the violent complaints of members of the traditionalist school we do, indeed, find it easy enough to form the false notion that the relation was all one of enmity; and this has been the customary mistake since Alessandro Wesselofsky, almost a century ago, discovered what he considered a pioneer of the Volgare trend, in the "Paradiso" of the Alberti. In fact, his error in regarding this novel as a genuine historical source arose largely from its supposed role as a testimony to the successful rivalry of the Volgare school with Latin Humanism in the 1380's. Whereas one of the causes for overrating the novel was the desire of Wesselofsky and many of his successors to find evidence of an intermediate stage in the transition from the society of the Decamerone to the humanistic circles of the Quattrocento,[1] another cause was the satisfaction at having discovered a source which seemed to show that substantial advances in the direction of Renaissance thought and criticism had been made in the Volgare school of the Trecento before and without the help of Humanism.

Wesselofsky had come upon the *Paradiso* not by chance, but through a systematic search for the riches of Volgare literature on the eve of the triumph of Humanism. He had been pursuing his researches under the influence of the important mid-nineteenth-century school of Italian scholarship which is known by the name of the *"Nuovi Savonaroliani"* or *"Piagnoni"* (the "tearful," as Savonarola's followers were called); a school of which so great a Renaissance historian as Pasquale Villari was also a member. This group of students—fervidly devoted to the cause of Italy's national unification, the all-important issue after 1850—regarded the ascendency of Renaissance Humanism as a misfortune for Italy's moral and national energies. They all approached the Renaissance from the viewpoint that it was the time when signory superseded the free republic and when the mercenary band of the *condottiere* took the place of the citizens' army of the medieval commune, while among the emerging sovereign region-states that balance-of-power system was formed which prevented Italian unification for centuries to come.[2]

Under the cloud of this predominant conception, all Humanism appeared as a veiled or open ally of court and tyranny and as a natural opponent of Volgare culture and the traditions of the medieval commune. The legacy of the communal period, after receiving a decisive blow from Humanism, was thought to have been doomed in the Renaissance, except for a brief respite during Savonarola's revolt against Renaissance classicism and paganism. The desertion from the ways of the medieval commune was considered to have taken place at one and the same time in both the literary and the political fields; Humanism spelled the doom of Volgare literature, civic spirit, and love of liberty. The loss suffered in the Quattrocento, said Wesselofsky, in the fundamental inquiry with which he introduced his edition of the *Paradiso*, was as significant as the gain; the great age of humanistic culture under the Medici "initiated the political decay, which is inseparable from the literary decay [i.e. of the vernacular literature]. . . . In proportion to the decline of the old liberty, there was the upsurge of the classical culture of the [Medicean] Principate." [3] This "continued gradation of both decay and progress" (Wesselofsky intended to show) [4] had begun in the time of Bruni, and the Niccoli known from the *Dialogi*, with the clash between a Latin speaking *scuola erudita* and a *scuola volgare* still clinging to the legacy of the great leaders of the Florentine Trecento. [5]

Perhaps the chief reason why so biased a picture, which any comprehensive study of Bruni's works ought to have corrected, could remain unopposed was Wesselofsky's discovery, or reappraisal, of several products of the *scuola volgare* which seemed to confirm in plain words that Humanism was the deadly enemy of the earlier and healthier trends. Among the sources in this category, first published by Wesselofsky *in extenso*, were two invectives against alleged excesses of the rising humanistic school—pamphlets which ever since have held a central place in the historical appraisal of the transition about 1400 and of Bruni's youth. [6] One of these pamphlets is entitled "Invective against certain slanderers of Dante, Petrarch, and Boccaccio" (*Invettiva Contro a Cierti Calunniatori di Dante, Petrarca e Boccaccio*) and comes from the pen of the same Cino Rinuccini with whom we have become so familiar through his *Risponsiva* to Loschi. [7] The other pamphlet was written by a certain Domenico da Prato, poet of vernacular sonnets that imitate Dante, Petrarch, and Boccaccio in a rather artificial and superficial fashion and show a strong surviving influence of medieval chivalric poetry. Domenico da Prato belonged to the generation of Bruni and Niccoli, and was one of the many newcomers from the Florentine territory who entered the intellectual middle-class of the metropolis by way of the notarial profession. During the war with Filippo Maria Visconti, in the mid-1420's, he composed a long patriotic poem as his contribution to Florentine political literature.[8] His invective against the circle of the classicists—the "sect" (*setta*) of the *bilingui o trilingui*, as he calls them [9]—was to form a preface to his collected poetry, and, therefore, lacks a proper title.[10] Although neither Rinuccini's nor Domenico's pamphlets reveal the names of the persons attacked, both works were said by Wesselofsky to be directed against Bruni as well as Niccoli; in addition, according to Wesselofsky's never refuted interpretation, Rinuccini's *Invettiva* gives evidence that the estrangement of the humanistic group from the literary ways of medieval Florence was accompanied by a decay of the civic spirit.[11]

After our observations on the deep dissensions within the humanistic camp that divided militant classicists and more traditionally-minded humanists and placed Bruni close to citizens like Cino Rinuccini and Gregorio Dati, we must wonder whether the prejudices that misled the students of the *Paradiso* did not also distort the interpretation of these minor Volgare writings. When they are studied without the anti-humanistic bias of Wesselofsky's day, what do these sources really tell us? How can we reconcile their testimony with the evidence of Bruni's closeness to the older Florentine tradition, and of his gradual separation from militant classicism? Finally, if it can be shown that the *communis opinio* on Rinuccini's and Domenico da Prato's invectives has carried on prejudices inherited from the "*Nuovi Piagnoni*," what is the true picture of the relationship between civic Humanism and the Volgare tradition in the early Quattrocento?

Domenico da Prato's Invective
Against Niccoli and Bruni—A Deceptive Source

It is advisable to examine first the polemical pamphlet of Domenico da Prato in spite, or just because, of its comparatively late origin. For the case of the *Paradiso* has warned us of the danger that a late and inferior source may distort the historical perspective and thereby blind us to better information close at hand.

Now it is true that the late origin of a source need not in every case mean that it is worthless. But since our appraisal of Bruni's early works has clearly indicated conditions wholly different from what Domenico suggests, we must be prepared once more to seek our way past a deceptive guidepost.

Wesselofsky himself, it seems, was not aware of the late origin of Domenico's pamphlet; or if he was, vaguely,[12] it did not prevent him from using the work as a voice from the time about 1400. But as early as 1902, A. Della Torre, in the penetrating study of early Quattrocento sources with which he buttressed his history of the *Accademia Platonica di Firenze*, observed incidentally that Domenico at some points reveals a knowledge of Bruni's *Epistola X 25*, written in May 1418, and of Bruni's translation of Aristotle's *Nicomachean Ethics* which did not become available to the public until 1417.[13] When these clues are used in a systematic analysis of Domenico's composition, it appears that the time of his writing cannot have been very long after the thus established *terminus a quo*. For Domenico tells us that he has "not yet seen any historical, philosophical, or poetical works appear" in Bruni's and Niccoli's circle;[14] this means that he has not yet come to know Bruni's extensive literary production from the early

1420's onward. In other words, Domenico's attack took place around 1420. That it was directed against Bruni as well as Niccoli is evident from the allusions to various works of Bruni.[15]

It was, then, about 1420, nearly twenty years after the events described in *Dialogus I*, that Domenico turned on the humanistic circle to which Bruni and Niccoli belonged and accused its members "for their wrong judgment in condemning Dante, Petrarch, Boccaccio, Salutati, and others."[16] If this contention were to be accepted at face value,[17] it would amount to evidence of Bruni's continued sympathy with Niccoli's disparagement of the three great Florentines of the Trecento, and would cause us considerable embarrassment. For we have concluded that Bruni departed from Niccoli's opinions as early as 1405, or even 1403-04, when writing *Dialogus II;* by 1436, his appreciation of Dante, Petrarch, and Boccaccio was to produce a full-length rehabilitation in their *Vite.* How, then, could it happen that in the years about 1420 Bruni impressed Domenico as being in conformity with Niccoli's "condemnations"?

In preceding chapters where we traced the early history of the reputation of Dante and Petrarch, we found that Bruni's attempts at a reappraisal were far from implying that he had returned to the standards of their pre-humanistic admirers. His vindication of the leaders of the Trecento sprang from an historically-minded attitude toward them, but he did not sacrifice his faith in a new type of Latin and Greek erudition for his own day, or in the program of advancing beyond Dante's pre-humanistic outlook on antiquity and history. In consequence, despite all differences in tone and approach, it was not entirely impossible for Bruni to appear as one with Niccoli to a writer for whom true admiration of Dante seemed to imply contentment with the medieval lore woven into the poetry of the *Divine Comedy*.

There can be no doubt that Domenico's verdict was based on this viewpoint of an old-fashioned conservative, uninitiated in the humanistic intentions. His knowledge is limited; for the only motivation he can find for the reserve of his adversaries toward the Trecento is that they "condemn" the great minds of the past from Dante to Salutati "because of their desire to show off as being more excellent and intelligent." [18] Now the facts adduced to bear out this judgment disclose great differences in the tone and level of the utterances ascribed to the various members of the incriminated group. One of them, we are told, called Dante's poetical imagination wanting because many potentially helpful Latin and Greek authors have been unknown to the Florentine poet. This is precisely the sort of criticism which our other sources attribute to Niccoli. And again we are reminded of the well-known Niccoli manner when, in other passages of Domenico's invective, we read that certain members of the circle punned that, since Dante's Italian poem had been written *"vulgarmente"* (which may mean *vulgarly* as well as *in vulgare*), it would be best to use the leaves of the *Divine Comedy* for fishmongers' paper-bags.[19]

But did these scoffers include Bruni? The one accusation in this context which is directed against ideas found in Bruni's works is of a very different nature. One member of the group, so Domenico complains, had "said and, what is worse, put in writing, that Dante has not understood Virgil with regard to the origin of Mantua." [20] This note of censure is obviously aimed at Bruni's *Ep. X 25*. Bruni's crime in that letter (or, rather, critical treatise in epistolary form) had been the refutation of the fantastic medieval legends about the founding of Mantua that were still

accepted and spread abroad by Dante; for Bruni had
produced conclusive proof of the Etruscan origin of that
city—one of the first published results of his mature
method of historical criticism.

Evidently, then, Domenico lacks an understanding of
the nature of the movement he assaults. This impression is
confirmed when we examine the immediate purpose and
argument of his censure. His accusations against the group
around Niccoli and Bruni were made in an introduction to
his collected poems; they were intended as an attack to
forestall the humanistic criticism that an imitation of the
Trecento manner was outdated. The arrogance of the
young Latin humanists, Domenico contends, is based on a
train of thought that will fatally hamper all future work.
The view that the attainments of the ancients are exemplary and superior to those of the present day, he argues,
is fated to paralyze all creative energy; [21] in fact not a
single historical, philosophical, or poetical work has yet
been seen to emerge from all this ado among the enthu-
siasts for antiquity. This reproach, now, could with an
appearance of justice be applied to Niccoli who throughout his life was sterile as a writer.[22] But was it true of
Bruni? That Bruni was meant to be included in Domenico's critique precisely at this point follows from the fact
that Domenico in the same breath takes exception to
opinions quoted almost literally from Bruni's preface to
his translation of Plutarch's *Vita Sertorii*, published in
1408/09.[23a] In that preface, written a few years after his
move from Florence to the Curia, Bruni had drawn a dark
picture of the inability of the Moderns to rival the
Ancients. About the same time, he had lamented in his
correspondence with Niccoli that "we people of today
are clearly dwarfs (*homunculi*), and even if we were not
dwarfs in spirit, our lives have not the stuff needed for
lasting glory." [23b] This gloom about the world in which

he lived was not, however, to remain Bruni's last word. Already in his first Florentine period, the influence of Niccoli's pessimistic classicism had eventually been outweighed by the patriotic fervor of the Florentine struggle against Giangaleazzo: Bruni had attempted to achieve with his *Laudatio* for Florence what Aristides, the orator, had achieved for Athens. After Bruni's return in 1415 from the Curia to the bracing atmosphere of the Florentine Republic, the feeling of the inadequacy of the past performance of the Moderns, far from leading him to literary unproductiveness, rather increased his determination to do for Florence what the ancient historians had done for Rome. In the preface to his *Historiae Florentini Populi*, written about 1418, he dared to say that Florence's attainments "will not appear inferior in any part (*nulla ex parte inferiores*) to those great deeds and events of Antiquity which we are used to admire whenever we read of them." [23c]

It must be conceded that about 1420 someone with no more than an external knowledge of the literary pursuits in the Niccoli-Bruni circle could not yet know of Bruni's *Historiae;* for though the first three books and more were finished by that time,[24] they were not made known to the reading public until the end of the 1420's.[25] Nor could Domenico surmise that Bruni's preparations had progressed so far that within a few years he would produce publications in many other fields, including the "philosophical" and "poetical." [26] But their appearance totally refuted Domenico's bold inferences about the nature of the type of Humanism he attacked. However interesting Domenico's argument may sound as an early episode in the *querelle des anciens et modernes* which thenceforth remained inseparable from the history of Humanism, as a commentator on Bruni he does not appear to be very trustworthy. Indeed, we could form no more glaring a misconception of Bruni's Humanism than by accepting Domenico's description of it as part of a movement indulging in merely negative criticism, sterile because of its belief in the inferiority of the Moderns.

An equal narrowness and incomprehension are at the bottom of another major argument employed by Domenico in his attack. His adversaries, he says, while not accomplishing anything new, try to cut a figure as productive workers by pretending that their translations from the Greek into the Latin are on a level with the original works.[27] Evidently, the object of this critique is the program outlined in the preface to Bruni's translation of Plutarch's *Vita M. Antonii* (1404/05), where Bruni had given an *exposé* of the creative faculties and the too easily forgotten merits of the good translator.[28] In order to show the fallacy of these claims still more clearly, Domenico adds that the newly proclaimed inclusion of Greek in the requirements of culture is a dangerous mistake. These ambitious innovators, he says naively, do not remember Cicero's statement that the Latin language is not poorer but much richer than the Greek. Why then demand that Greek should be made part of the curriculum? [29]

The facts behind this criticism are that Bruni, showing a much better understanding of Cicero than Domenico did, had stated in his preface to the *Antonius* that the Greek language was "more copious" (*uberior*) and therefore capable of expressing an idea in more varied fashions; but, given the pithiness and precision of Latin, one could attain equal perfection in Latin translations without that abundance. Domenico had read these passages, and also Bruni's introduction to his translation of the *Nicomachean Ethics* where the same comparison with Greek is used for the defense of Latin. To Bruni this comparison supplied a basis for the argument that the great works of the Greeks could and should be recast in a Latin of equal merit.[30] Domenico, however, thought it grist for the mill of his naive reasoning that the new study of Greek under Bruni's leadership was useless affectation.

It is with the awareness of this mixture of distortion and ignorance that we must weigh Domenico's intimation that in the circle of Bruni and Niccoli it was usual to attack and "condemn" the great Florentines of the Trecento, including Salutati. For to Domenico, the ultimate proof of the unsoundness of any preoccupation with Greek was that when the study of that language was put on the humanistic agenda, the great leaders of the Trecento appeared of necessity imperfectly prepared.[31] To a critic like Domenico it was inconceivable that anybody could leave the culture of the Trecento behind, and yet respect the legacy of Dante and Petrarch and esteem the Volgare side by side with Latin and Greek. How, then, could this ignorant informant give valid evidence of Bruni's motives and intentions?

On the other hand, we should commit an equally serious mistake by using so unreliable a source to judge the character of the Volgare movement during the transition crisis. The intellectual struggle on the threshold of the Quattrocento would lose much of its historical significance if one of the chief endeavors of the defenders of Volgare culture and civic tradition had been an effort to turn back the clock with regard to the new study of Greek and the historical criticism of medieval legends. In order to do justice to the part that the civic element played in the resistance to militant classicism, and to form an estimate of the true nature of Bruni's indebtedness to the Florentine world outside the circle of the humanistic *literati*, we must turn to the testimony of another source—the *Invettiva* of Cino Rinuccini.

Cino Rinuccini's "Invettiva Against Certain Slanderers of Dante, Petrarch, and Boccaccio"

Once Domenico da Prato's confusing comment has been disposed of, it is the *"Invettiva" Against Certain Slanderers of Dante, Petrarch, and Boccaccio* by Cino Rinuccini which emerges as our most important source of information. It is, indeed, as revealing for the relations between Humanism and the civic traditions as Cino's *Risponsiva* to Loschi has turned out to be for the background of Quattrocento historiography.

This does not mean that Cino's *Invettiva* can be called an open book to the casual student. In the first place, like almost every literary work of around 1400, it has come down to us undated. There is, of course, an obvious *terminus ad quem:* the death of Cino, which occurred in 1417.[32a] But this date has little significance in view of our discovery that by that time Bruni's humanistic development had already run through several substantially different phases. Also, just as in the pamphlet of Domenico da Prato, the names of the adversaries under attack are not given in the *Invettiva.* Since we have found that Bruni's outlook after 1402 was very different from what it had been in 1401, and that it was at no time entirely identical with Niccoli's, the vague statements of Wesselofsky and his successors that Cino was aiming at the *scuola erudita* and that this "school" was "Bruni's and Niccoli's circle," are of little help. The individuals whom Cino had in mind must be identified, and his assertions must be compared with the appropriate phases of Bruni's development, before the verdicts given in the *Invettiva* can serve to reconstruct the background of the crisis.[32b]

The literary structure of the *Invettiva* offers a unique occasion to determine the positions which some of Cino's contemporaries had reached at the time of his writing. In reproducing the mistaken ideas of his adversaries, Cino often indicates the viewpoints which they ought to adopt but have not made their own. Now wherever these suggestions coincide with opinions actually held by some of Cino's humanistic contemporaries, the works expressing these opinions cannot yet have existed, or at least cannot yet have been known to Cino when he wrote his satire By using this convenient opportunity to identify contemporary works which Cino cannot have had in mind when making his attack, we may reach some definite conclusions on how much, if at all, Cino's critique was aimed at Bruni's early literary production.

We may begin with Cino's assertions on what the classicists whom he was chastising said about Dante and Petrarch, and his reflections on what they ought to have said. "They ridicule," we hear, "the books of Petrarch, the laurelled poet, saying that his work *On Illustrious Men* is a medley, fit to be a text for Lenten sermons; they do not say how universal he was as a poet in Latin as well as Volgare. . . . They say that the famous Dante Alighieri, most glorious of poets, was a poet for cobblers; they do not say that the diction of poetry soars like an eagle above all others. . . . Dante, the illustrious poet, prefers to depict the deeds of men in Volgare in order to be of greater use to his fellow-citizens than he would have been by writing Latin. And those detractors ought not to break out into blatant laughter because . . . Dante with marvellous brevity and grace puts two or three similes into one rhythm in Volgare, such as Virgil does not set forth in twenty hexameters. . . . Therefore, I hold that poetry in Volgare is a thing of much greater difficulty, and demands greater excellency, than poetry in Latin." [33]

On reading the first two of these passages, we are startled to find that from Bruni's *Dialogi* we are familiar not only with the opinions considered shameful by Cino, but also with his counter-arguments. For while the derisive remarks at which Cino takes offense are parallels to the sneers of Niccoli in *Dialogus I*, the standard which Cino recommends is the same as that used in Niccoli's retractions in *Dialogus II*. Just as Cino urges, the Niccoli of the second dialogue finds reasons vindicating Dante and Petrarch in a poet's superiority over scholars and mere *literati* (Dante is not to be judged on a level "with men of letters, but above them," the Niccoli of the second dialogue says),[34] and in the unique versatility of Petrarch (who alone was great in verse as well as prose and in both Latin and Volgare, according to the same Niccoli). Again, in the *Laudatio* Bruni shows himself so far removed from any classicistic prejudice against the Volgare that he bases his claim for Florence's cultural preeminence upon Florentine achievements both in the Volgare language and in the revival of classical studies. All Italy, we read in the concluding paragraph of the *Laudatio*, looks up to Florence as a model of purity and refinement of language; for this one city can point to citizens (that is, of course, to the three great writers of the Trecento) "who in this popular and common tongue have shown all other men to be mere infants." [35]

Bruni, then, from 1403 on fulfilled the demands of Cino's program. And he did so not only in the question of due respect for Dante and Petrarch and the rights of the Volgare: we find a like agreement when we consider what Cino has to say about the other two major themes with which Bruni was concerned in those years—the history of Florence and the new enthusiastic study of Plato.

"As to history," we read in Cino's *Invettiva*, the classicists whom he attacks "discuss with great heat whether or not there existed historical accounts before the time of Ninus, and how many books were composed by Livy, and why they are not all available today, and what the errors of the historians are; and on that score they assert that Valerius Maximus is not detailed enough, [the text of] Livy mutilated, and the [medieval] chronicles too prolix. And they waste so much time in these vain disputes that they are unable to learn any true story or, if they learned it, cannot remember it at the right time and place when it is useful in the interest of the commonwealth." [36] With regard to their admiration for Plato: "They say that Plato is a greater philosopher than Aristotle, and refer to St. Augustine who called Aristotle the first of the philosophers —always excepting Plato. They do not say why this is conceded by St. Augustine: because Plato in his conception of the soul is in greater conformity with the Catholic faith. . . ." [37]

When we compare these reproaches with the *Laudatio,* we see at once that Bruni—by developing a philosophy of history from the standpoint of civic liberty, by giving glowing accounts of the Florentine deeds of the past, and by resolving to write the history of Florence—did "learn" and "remember" Florentine history for the benefit of the commonwealth in the way called for by Cino, and did even more than Cino demanded of the younger generation. Also, when we look at Bruni's preface to his *Phaedon* translation we find that Bruni's arguments in favor of Plato studies were, in 1404/05, precisely those considerations whose absence Cino deplored: Plato's belief in the immortality of the soul, and his conformity with the Christian faith.[38]

In view of so many striking coincidences between Cino's demands and Bruni's fulfillments we may say: if Cino, when he wrote his *Invettiva,* had known the *Laudatio,* the *Dialogus II,* and the introduction to Bruni's *Phaedon* translation, it would mean that he was asking the younger men, whom he was calling to account, to do precisely what the most original mind among them had done already. So there are only these alternatives: either Cino's *Invettiva* was written prior to the publication of that group of Bruni's works; or, if it was written at a later time, then Cino had no knowledge that the attitude of one of the leading members of the censured circle had recently developed along the road he recommended. In either case Cino, when picturing the group of classicists as turning away from Florentine interests and traditions, must have envisaged the kind of classicism which influenced Bruni only in the period that preceded the composition of the *Laudatio* and *Dialogus II*. And, furthermore, since Cino's accusations accord excellently with the scene set forth in *Dialogus I*, we may look upon the *Invettiva*, whether written simultaneously or in retrospect a few years later, as a source that informs us about the same early stage of the classicists' challenge as does *Dialogus I*.

From these findings we may draw a number of more general conclusions. In the first place, if the development of Bruni's attitude was in such close agreement with the views and wishes of a writer as representative of the older civic school as Cino Rinuccini, this is more and welcome support of our view that Bruni's outlook in the *Laudatio* and *Dialogus II* must be regarded as a reconciliation with the civic tradition. Secondly, the fact that Cino's censures refer to the phase of Humanism presented in *Dialogus I* means that in Cino's work we have a further source to draw upon in cases in which the information found in the first dialogue is insufficient or too much obscured by the provocative irony that colors the attacks of the Niccoli of *Dialogus I*. Finally, since *Dialogus I* and Cino's *Invettiva* allow us by their mutual illumination to stake out a small but safe domain of knowledge on the nature of militant classicism during the years around 1400, we may eventually go on and enlarge the boundaries of this domain by comparing other contemporary sources with the information gathered from Bruni's and Cino Rinuccini's portrayals.

CHAPTER 14

THE DANGERS OF EARLY HUMANIST
CLASSICISM

Intellectual Change About 1400
According to Rinuccini's "Invettiva"

THE most important contribution we owe to the *Invettiva* is the minute description of the thought and conduct of the Florentine *literati* about 1400. Here we have the verdict of an observer trained in Latin who could judge classicism in the light of the older Florentine traditions.

We may be sure that Cino, in spite of the cursoriness of his contacts with humanistic culture, was not a narrow-minded reactionary who rejected the humanistic movement from the start. One trace, at least, of his interest in humanistic literature has recently been found: in 1383, he had a copy made for himself of Boccaccio's *Genealogiae Deorum.*[1a] During the latter part of his life, in his *Risponsiva*—which, written in 1397, must have been the earlier of the two pamphlets from his pen—we find him still in cordial sympathy with the group of young humanists whom he afterwards attacked in his *Invettiva.* At the end of the procession of illustrious Florentines inserted in the *Risponsiva* as a testimony to Florence's greatness, Cino told Loschi triumphantly that there was nothing more joyful and encouraging to him than to watch "how during my lifetime in my city a *brigata* of young men of eminent talents is growing up, which would be fit for

Athens, most cultured of all cities." [1b] In the *Invettiva*, the term *"brigata"* reappears,[2] indicating that Cino has the same group of young Florentine intellectuals in mind; but now he is incensed against their ways, and in open conflict with his former friends. Consequently, in the years after 1397 the attitude of the Florentine humanists must have shown changes, or at least a strengthening of former inclinations, at which a citizen of Cino's stamp took offense. These years were the period which, besides Bruni's *Dialogus I*, saw Salutati's *De Tyranno*.

In using Cino Rinuccini as a witness for those years, we must be fully aware that his report has of necessity its defects as well as its virtues. The reason that Cino did not become estranged from the older foundations of civic culture was that his understanding of the nature of the humanistic attainments, in spite of his personal contacts with the classicist humanists and their literary pursuits, remained limited. Many a passage in which he naively states what the censured youth did not believe and say, but in his opinion ought to believe and say, reveals his difficulty in disentangling himself from the outdated medieval lore in which he had been reared. His judgments on the classicism at the turn of the century, therefore, are drawn from his observations of side-issues and implications rather than the conscious aims of the humanists. In many cases, however, it is precisely his knowledge of these collateral effects which adds for us the necessary supplement to the testimony of *Dialogus I* and a very few other humanistic writings.

Cino's first contribution to our understanding of the period has already been noted: he tells us of sneers at the Florentine poet-triumvirate that are closely akin to the utterances attributed to the Niccoli of Bruni's first dialogue.[3] Without this parallel report by an outsider like Cino, we could not be entirely sure that ironical attacks on

Dante, Petrarch, and Boccaccio, such as we read in *Dialogus I*, do not only echo an occasional controversy, but may be regarded as typical of Niccoli in the years around 1400.

In a similar manner, Cino's reproaches fit in excellently with what we know from Bruni about the intellectual fashions that accompanied the rise of critical philology. This does not mean that Cino's account can be taken without the grain of salt which is needed in consulting an invective. According to the prologue of the *Invettiva*, its author had been unable to stand Florence any longer, and therefore had been wandering through the world (a journey from which he alleges to send his invective home to Florence), because he did not want to listen any more to "the vain and foolish disputations of a group of prattlers." [4] These fellows, "in order to appear most erudite to the man in the street, cry out in the public square, arguing how many diphthongs existed in the language of the ancients, and why today only two of them are used; which grammar is the better one, that of the time of Terence the comedy-writer, or the refined one of Virgil the epic poet; and how many metres were used by the ancients in their poetry, and why today the anapest with four short metrical feet is no longer used. And with such fantastic speculations they waste all their time." [5] This is satire, beyond doubt; but the question is whether it keeps close enough to reality to give the final touches to our picture.

In addition to remembering several similar traits of the Niccoli of the first dialogue, we may recall a parallel from one of Bruni's early letters. In 1405, during his stay with the Curia at Viterbo, when Bruni allowed his memories to wander back to the "company that met in Salutati's house," he described the discussions of the circle of which he had been a member by talking of the meetings in which "together with the other friends I eagerly pursued the study of Greek, or . . . where we learned the meaning of *dispongere* (*dispungere*—to punctuate), of *versuram facere* (borrowing to pay a debt), of *boni consulere* (to regard favorably), of *decoquere* (to become bankrupt), of *alucinari* (to wander in mind), of *nauare operam* (to render assistance), of *celeres* (i.e., *equestres,* knights), of *nequitia* (worthlessness and wickedness), and of a thousand other things of this sort." [6] Here we catch the like temper of the dawn of the new philology; the passion for accuracy and the meticulous attention to ancient usage are precisely the same in the humanist's own story. The scenes seen by the stranger in the Florentine market-place and Bruni's recollections join together harmoniously.

But now there are cases in which Cino's assertions cannot so easily be checked and supplemented by reports in contemporaneous Florentine sources. For example, is he equally trustworthy when he charges the classicism of his age with what seems to him a paganizing trend of thought? "As to the philosophy of things divine," we read in the *Invettiva,* "they say that Varro wrote many books on the worship of the pagan gods in a very elegant style, and they praise him most excessively, preferring him in secret to the doctors of our faith. They even dare to say that those gods are truer than this [God of ours]; and they do not remember the miracles of our Saints." [7]

In the case of Cino's story of the sneers against Dante and Petrarch we should hardly dare take Cino's contentions seriously if we did not have the chance to verify them with the help of *Dialogus I.* Shall we believe that his clear and well-substantiated assertion of the emergence of paganizing tendencies in the classical enthusiasm of Niccoli's group rests on mere invention? [8]

The possible effects of classicism in the realm of religious sentiment have not been weighed sufficiently in studies of the early Quattrocento crisis. In the beginnings of modern scholarship the supposed "paganism" of the fifteenth-century Renaissance was for a while emphasized so disproportionately that, in reaction, a strong inclination to depreciate it has developed. But though this depreciation may be correct in a general verdict on the character of the Renaissance, it need not exclude the possibility that in some specific stages the growing awareness of classical religiosity may have acted as a spur to radical and militant trains of thought. Obviously, the appearance of the first wave of uncompromising classicism at the turn of the Trecento must have created particularly favorable conditions for a militant attitude.

Even though Rinuccini's assertion of paganizing tendencies is restricted to the Florentine circle, it may be possible to discover its background by looking beyond the city of Florence and beyond the year 1400.

Classicism and Ancient Religion. The Testimony of Salutati and of Francesco da Fiano

This much at least is attested by the contemporaneous *Dialogus I:* the name of Varro was in the mouth of classicists at the beginning of the Quattrocento. For among the ancient works whose loss, in the opinion of the Niccoli of the first dialogue, has made the attainment of true culture so difficult, the books of Varro are especially mentioned as a source containing "knowledge of things human and divine." [9] And there is more revealing evidence at hand.[10]

During the last decade of his life, Salutati was occupied with an immense scholarly work entitled *De Laboribus Herculis,* a handbook of the mythological allegories used by ancient poets that was intended to supplement Boccaccio's well known *Genealogiae Deorum* and might have become its permanent companion had not death prevented Salutati from adding the finishing touches for publication.[11] One of the most significant traits that distinguish Salutati's work from that of Boccaccio—besides an evident growth of criticism and exactitude—is the advance made toward the rehabilitation of ancient religion as reflected in classical poetry. In the introductory chapters of Salutati's *Hercules* we find a systematic discussion, substantiated in subsequent parts of the work and intended to show that an adequate conception and expression of God's nature is beyond human power in any age of history. Christian and non-Christian religions alike, Salutati concludes, must take refuge in anthropomorphic representations of the effects of the divine being. The biblical manner of saying that God "saw," "talked," grew "angry," the *De Laboribus Herculis* argues, is in the last analysis on one plane with the representation, by the pagan poets, of God in the image of one or the other deity. Occasionally the exchange of words between Jupiter and Juno portrayed by the poets is likened to the biblical conception of God speaking to Christ.[12] In the light of this religious epistemology, ancient polytheism in the strict sense appeared as a product of decay. Primeval man possessed some notion of the true God, but since there was not yet divine revelation as a guide, idolatry crept in as time went on; not however, without one great exception—the poets, the best of whom preserved the knowledge of the one God even while making use of mythology as an indispensable vehicle of poetry.[13]

The source from which this whole group of ideas had been drawn was the religious philosophy of ancient Stoicism. It was accessible to the humanists of the early Italian Renaissance in many quotations from the literature of the stoic school contained in classical and medieval writings; the numerous fragments of Varro cited by Augustine in his *City of God* were the core. Varro, therefore, played a significant role for Salutati too, though largely as a disputed source, since Salutati was intent on snatching away from the stoic philosophers as much as possible of the monotheistic interpretation of mythology, in order to attribute it to the poets.[14] Petrarch and Boccaccio already had made some use of this theory as an apparent key to the minds of the ancient poets,[15a] but it was with Salutati that the idea of the "theology of the poets" (*theologia poetarum*) influenced the interpretation of the relationship between Christianity and classical religion more deeply in consequence of his strong emphasis on the inadequacy of human concepts of the Divine and on the consequent need for anthropomorphic personification. Even Salutati, however, did not definitely move in this direction until the end of the 1390's; for in his earlier comments on classical mythology and religion he had been guided by much stronger reservations about paganism. The vigor of his later tendency to justify some aspects of the ancient religion, therefore, would seem to have been caused by the humanistic temper at the turn of the Trecento. Something distinctly real appears to have caused Rinuccini's accusations.*

* The relative aggressiveness of Salutati's *Hercules* treatise is important for the historical appraisal of the intellectual crisis about 1400. The following sketch of the development of Salutati's attitude toward the religion of the ancient poets will illustrate the assertion that at that time something new was being added which had not existed in Salutati's earlier years.

There had been an earlier phase of Salutati's reflections on the ancient poets—during the years 1378-79. At that time he had exchanged letters with Ser Giuliano Zonarini, chancellor of Bologna,[15b] polemical pamphlets in which he proves to be familiar merely with the standard medieval arguments: enjoyment of ancient poetry is legitimate *despite* the pagan mythology of the poets, because that mythology, after the victory of Christianity, is no longer dangerous; and some of the ancient poets, especially Virgil, in the midst of their errors, give indication of presentiments of Christian doctrines (including the dogma of the Trinity) that are special gifts of divine revela-

But did not Rinuccini overshoot the mark when he intimated that the ancient deities were being compared with
the Saints of Catholicism and that there was even a certain
favoring of polytheism in the camp of the classicists? There
can be no doubt that Salutati was innocent of such interpretations and extreme positions. In his *Hercules* and in his
letters he often points out that his assertion of a secret
monotheism of the poets meant simply that "in the midst
of the darkness of paganism" there was a chance to glimpse
the truth; he wanted to set forth a doctrine strong enough

---

tion. Salutati's active interest in the theme of the *Hercules*
treatise began in precisely the same years: between 1378 and
1383, he wrote a short explanation of the myths surrounding
the figure of Hercules—a work which was as yet no more
than a commentary on Seneca's tragedy, *Hercules Furiens*.[16a]
A reading of this early version of the *Hercules* shows that
Salutati at that time did not as yet ascribe monotheistic beliefs
to the poets, nor evaluate their religion as sympathetically as he
would in later years. The *poetae* were not yet supposed to have
been free of the errors of the *philosophi* concerning the nature
of the soul, but were said to have erred themselves by following
the erroneous teachings of the various schools of philosophy.[16b]
In consequence, Salutati was still apologizing in the medieval
manner for reading the pagan poets in spite of their errors,
instead of justifying them as early seekers after genuine piety
and truth.

This type of justification does not seem to appear in Salutati's
works until the end of the 1390's, and it is highly probable that
an important stimulus to the development of Salutati's thought
came from the well-known rumor, according to which in the
year 1397 the *condottiere* Carlo Malatesta of Rimini had
plunged the famous ancient statue of Virgil in Mantua into the
Mincio river with imprecations against the poets and with the
challenging assertion that only Saints deserved statues. In his
endeavors to make a safe case for the poets, Salutati began to
develop the idea of the equal need of both poetry and religion
to employ figurative speech.[16c] From these still cautious beginnings, he developed after 1400 the idea that any human notion
of the divine, in any religion, was bound to be anthropomorphic;

to defend the humanistic love for classical poetry against
the charge of polytheism.[17] So little indeed had he a parallel in mind between pagan deities and Catholic Saints that
in all his references to the widespread theory of the origin
of religion from the apotheosis of great human beings he
never forgot to stress the inherent danger of idolatry; he
liked to expound the opinion of the Fathers that those
deified heroes who had seduced their contemporaries by
their glamor and power were demons.[18]

---

and by the time of his death in 1406, this idea had grown into
a kind of religious philosophy used as a key for the proper approach to classical mythology. Simultaneously, he had revived
Petrarch's and Boccaccio's theory on the secret monotheism of
the ancient poets. Through the combination of this theory with
the thesis that human notions of the divine were inevitably
anthropomorphic, the explanation of the polytheistic stories of
the poets as shells concealing the kernel of a purer insight appeared more convincing than ever, and produced a spirit of
aggressiveness formerly unknown. Simultaneously with the exposition of his theory in the final version of the *Hercules* treatise
in 1405-06, Salutati presented the new interpretations in various polemical letters of almost book length, especially letters
addressed to, and directed against, the two monks Giovanni da
San Miniato and Giovanni Dominici.[16d] In these letters as in the
treatise, we find not only the argument that theology and poetry
are akin in their common use of figurative speech, but also the
reference to the teachings of Varro, and the opinion that the
poets had come nearer to religious truth than the philosophers
had.[16e] This fact did not escape a student of Salutati, Alfred v.
Martin, who noted [16f] that all of Salutati's earlier statements
"had been guarded when compared with what is said in *De
Hercule*. . . . He, who with advancing age grew constantly
more Christian-minded, grew more and more extreme in his
defense of antiquity" (that is, in the defense of ancient poetry
and the Greek and Latin poets; otherwise, Salutati's increasing
reliance on stricter Christian standards produced an ever
stronger suspicion of the *virtus* and the philosophy of the ancients, as we observed when exploring the limitations of Salutati's civic Humanism, pp. 113ff. above).

Despite this alibi for Salutati, it is easy to imagine that the thin boundary-line was not always carefully respected in the more extreme humanistic wing; indeed, we are able to prove that such was the case. In Rome, among humanists at the Curia, at least, ideas very similar to those hinted at by Cino Rinuccini arose at about the same time. Their author was Francesco da Fiano, a humanistic chancery official at the Curia and also head of the chancery of the Commune of Rome.[19a] During the 1380's and 90's, Francesco had experienced much of the misery that was the lot of so many chancery-humanists in the late Trecento. For a while, fortune had driven him restlessly about the Peninsula, from the northern reaches of central Italy down to Naples. Nonetheless the Curia, which employed him intermittently in various positions in the papal chancery and in the administration of Rome, always remained the spiritual home of this Roman-born scholar (Fiano is a little township in the Roman territory).

In 1406, therefore, when, after the return of the Curia of Innocent VII from Viterbo to Rome, such men as Bruni, Poggio, Vergerio, and Loschi were in the papal chancery simultaneously, Francesco da Fiano could by comparison with these newcomers consider himself a Roman of long standing and play the part of Nestor among the younger humanists. The exchanges which he then had with members of the younger generation—he competed with Loschi in writing Latin verses—are episodes which, like his occasional correspondence with Petrarch in his younger years, have not yet been wholly forgotten in the history of Humanism. We have a description of those Roman years in a Latin poem written in retrospect in 1425 by a humanist of Brescia, Bartolomeo Bayguera, who in the time of Innocent VII's pontificate had been forced by party strife to leave his native city and take refuge at the Curia from about 1405 to 1410. In this poem, the figure of Francesco da Fiano stands out as that of a cicerone who showed the younger humanists around the ruins of ancient Rome and inspired them with enthusiasm for the ancient poets and the remains of classical art. As late as 1416—he died in Rome in 1421 [19b]—Francesco could be asked to compose an invective against the modern *perversores* of the ruins of ancient Rome.

Francesco da Fiano belonged to the age group between Salutati and Bruni and exerted considerable influence on his contemporaries and on many younger humanists. We may some day be able to form an adequate idea of the nature of this influence with the help of Francesco's numerous letters and poems, still scattered unpublished through Italian libraries; but what is known of this material allows us to sense a marked intellectual quality, in spite of a style which falls short of the standards that were rapidly being accepted at the beginning of the Quattrocento. The mediocrity of form goes a long way toward explaining why Francesco, despite the esteem in which he was held by a number of more famous humanists, had little success in his literary and professional career; but it must not cause us to overlook his place in the history of classicist ideas around 1400. Almost every letter and poem from his pen is in some way a document of the aggressive attitude of classicism characteristic of those years.

The strongest expression of this attitude is found in Francesco's one major surviving work, a defense of the ancient poets against modern "revilers" and "detractors." Written no earlier than 1399 and no later than September 1404,[19c] the *Contra Oblocutores et Detractores Poetarum* echoed an actual episode in Roman life. In the presence of the Pope, an orator had delivered an address that drew heavily on pagan poets and this had caused resentment among many members of the Curia.[19d] To refute prejudices and doubts, Francesco da Fiano composed an "invective" which he dedicated to the future Pope Innocent VII, then Cardinal Cosimo Migliorati, the first decided protector of the new humanistic studies on the Papal See. Like Salutati's *De Laboribus Herculis*, the *Contra Oblocutores et Detractores Poetarum* was a systematic treatise based on the two assumptions that a kinship in spirit existed between allegorical language found in the Bible and the allegories of poetry, and that the greatest minds among the classical poets had secretly adhered to monotheism. But, unlike Salutati, Francesco da Fiano had made these ideas more provocative by employing a brand of classicism ready to defend, if certainly not the superiority, yet in some sense the equality of antiquity to the Christian world even in the sphere of religion.[19e]

Francesco's impatience with any undue differentiation between Christian and classical conduct is best illustrated in the concluding paragraphs of his work, where he casts a glance at the poets' natural passion to acquire fame (their "*cupiditas gloriae*"). To be sure, ever since there had been humanists, they had wondered whether they were allowed to give in to this desire and justify it; in particular, Zanobi da Strada and Boccaccio,[19f] following the example of Petrarch in his youth, had concluded that here was the motive-force which had raised man above the animal and superior minds above average people.[20] Up to a point, the humanist could refer for this claim not only to Cicero, but even to St. Augustine, who in his *City of God* had acknowledged the striving after glory as the mainspring of the political greatness of the Romans and as a relatively justifiable incentive to political action, though in the heart of the true Christian believer it was to be replaced by nobler urges. To the mind of a classicist of about 1400 like Francesco da Fiano, this differentiation of human nature in pagan and Christian times was unreal. Without this spring of human energy, he argued, there would have been neither Saint nor secular hero. Just as the great generals of ancient times would not have plucked up their courage to overcome the hardships of campaigns waged across the seas and through forbidding mountains, so Augustine and the other great Fathers of the Church would not have had the patience for their vast literary undertakings, had they not been impelled by the same psychological spur. "Though they were Saints," says Francesco, "they were human beings as well; and since we are all drawn to the desire for glory by our human nature (*"humanitas"*) as if by a hook, I am convinced that they, too, at one time or other were inflamed by an ardent desire for praise and a name among men." If this desire had not cooperated with their religious zeal, they would hardly have sacrificed so many of their nights and given so much care to the literary appearance of their works.[21]

In light of this emphasis on the likeness of human nature in the pagan and the Christian worlds, the older humanistic claim, that the use of allegory was common to both poetry and the Bible and that the best of the ancient poets had been monotheists, took on a new and aggressive tone. The old custom, Francesco argued, of making a distinction between biblical "types" or "tropes" or "figures" (allegorical and yet literally true) and ordinary poetical "allegories" was nothing but sophistry.[22] When four animals were accepted in Christianity as symbols of the four evangelists, this was in substance equivalent to the creation of mythological figures by the ancients; [23] for the ancients, too, even though they depicted individual deities as personifications of the divine, were alive to the truth that there was only one God. "Not only among the peoples who are included in the religion of holy Christianity, but also among all other nations we find the conviction that God created the universe and is the maker of everything." [24] As is seen from passages like this, the older

notion, that monotheism had been the privilege of the
poets in a pagan world otherwise lost in the darkness of
polytheism, is transformed by the new enthusiasm for antiquity into the conviction that antiquity as a whole was
in its essence little different from the Christian world. Nobody will ever persuade me to believe, Francesco protests,
that such eminent minds had adhered to polytheism.[25]
No doubt, of course, the ancients had been unable to foresee the Christian doctrine, for they had lacked guidance
by biblical revelation. But "in my opinion," Francesco
maintains, "it was enough that through some grace granted
them for their merits they came very close to the truth";
so close, he feels, that, after modification of very little,
we find them most of the time in accord with Holy
Scriptures.[26] It would have been beyond human power to
achieve still more, and it was not their fault, but by divine decree that they failed to be enlightened by a fore-
knowledge of the later coming of Christ, such as was
granted to the Prophets.[27]

With this sentiment, Francesco da Fiano finds strong
words against the unfairness of the doctrine of eternal
damnation decreed for all pagans. The passage deserves
particular attention. Some of the opponents of Humanism
insist, so Francesco reports, "that the works of the ancient
poets must not be read for the reason that their souls—
condemned by our religion because they have not been
cleansed by the water of holy baptism nor have shared in
the Christian perfection—are being tormented below with
diverse tortures." [28] As a Catholic Christian, Francesco
says, I shall always believe as the Holy Church believes;
but the demand to shun the poets for those reasons is "as
ridiculous as it is fallacious"; for if those reasons were
valid, then one could neither make use of the pagan masters of Roman Law, nor read Aristotle or Plato. To all
these writers "it was denied from on high, not only to

know the coming of Christ, but even to have an intimation of it. However, in this matter I should like to have an answer from Augustine, and an answer from Origen. If Homer, Hesiod, Pindar and Menander, if Caecilius, Plautus, Terence and Lucillius and many other poets were famed for their eloquence in both languages so long a time before the coming of Christ—how could they have believed in him who was born innumerable years later? How could that light of truth which illumines the whole man shine in their minds so long before the time, if indeed to foreknow the future is not a human but a Divine attribute? . . . If, then, the intervening span of so many years robbed the ancient poets of the knowledge of Christ, I leave it to the finer judgment, and to the more mature sense of justice of Augustine and Origen and other Catholics to decide whether, since in the laws and canons no punishment is fixed for what only in the future will become a transgression, it is justice or injustice that, as they hold, these poets have been cast into the infernal pit for what only in the future was to be a sin." [29]

One might try to minimize the significance of this protest by pointing out that Francesco, absorbed as he was in the study of the Church Fathers most familiar to him, seems to have forgotten that Thomist teaching for more than a century before his own day had been that many righteous pagans were saved because, by divine grace, they possessed not only clear, "explicit" knowledge of God's existence and providence, but also an indistinct, "implicit" faith in a Mediator, and thus fulfilled the condition of salvation. But in noting Francesco's neglect of Aquinas' conciliatory solution of the problem, we must not overlook the more important aspects of the situation in which Francesco wrote. Whether he was ignorant of the Thomist doctrine, or whether he knew and rejected the theory of "implicit" faith by insisting that the ancient poets

could not have had even an intimation of the later coming
of Christ [30]—we are warned not to overestimate the role
of this Thomist doctrine in early Renaissance Italy; we
must be prepared to find that, in the first generation after
Petrarch, when intimacy with the ancient authors had
grown, humanists, here as elsewhere, cut their paths in
their own fashion. Whether known or unknown to Francesco da Fiano, Aquinas' standpoint would have been of
little avail to a humanist of his type. For Francesco knew
enough of the ancient poets to feel certain that before the
age of Augustus there could have been no question of a
foreshadowing of Christian dogma.[31] He deemed worthy
of admiration and love men of the pre-Christian era whom
he considered to have had no prescience of the Christian
doctrine and upon whom he looked as equals and friends
in spirit, not because they had been vaguely Christian believers, but because moderns and ancients alike were
"men," and therefore could vie with each other in "*humanitas.*" The failure to fall back on Aquinas' obliteration of the difference between ancient thought and Christian dogma was to remain a characteristic of humanistic
writers. From Francesco's protest that the ancients could
not be condemned for not having known truths unknown
in their day, there runs a continuous line of development
to the statement of Erasmus, made with Socrates and
Cicero in mind: "Whatever is pious must not be called
profane. . . . Perhaps the spirit of Christ diffuses itself
more widely than we assume in our interpretation. And
there are many in the community of Saints who are not
in our catalogue"; [32] and to the final denial in the early
sixteenth century by many bold minds, quickened by Humanism, of the Augustinian doctrine of the damnation of
the pagans.[33]

On the other hand, just as remarkable as this spiritual
kinship of early and late Humanism is the difference in

tone between Francesco's outburst and the period when
many dared to people the hereafter with the good men
of all ages, and Erasmus taught diffidence of judgment
concerning the mysteries of religious dogma by saying
"where the soul of Cicero now dwells is perhaps not for
human judgment to decide." [34] The early classicist of
Francesco da Fiano's type, at the turn of the Trecento,
was still unable to see his way to a clean rejection of the
old Augustinian teaching. Francesco, full of bitter irony,
merely turned against Augustine and Origen with the outcry that he was leaving it to their sharper and more mature judgment whether it was fair or not to refuse the
ancients the excuse of guiltless ignorance, an excuse accepted by every human law. Even though only an outcry
and not an attempt at the establishment of a new position,
Francesco's sharply pointed question yet implied a challenge to the medieval tradition which reveals a more
aggressive irreverence than could be found among classical
humanists in many generations to come. We are not even
surprised to find in Francesco traces of the attitude which
Cino Rinuccini must have had in mind when he com-
plained that in his time there were humanists who "praise
Varro most excessively and . . . do not remember the
miracles of our Saints." Varro, besides Cicero's *De Natura
Deorum* and some poets influenced by stoic ideas, is a
particularly important source of Francesco's strong convictions. Varro's monotheistic sayings, which Augustine
had collected for Christian criticism, are, in spite of their
pantheistic tinge, reproduced in Francesco's invective with
completeness such as had probably never been achieved by
any earlier humanist.[35] Again, the popular cult of the
Saints and their miracles serves Francesco as evidence
that there exists a counterpart in the Christian world even
to what we are accustomed to term the polytheism of the
ancients. "If, indeed, we are willing to consider the thing

itself, its essence and effect, and not what the words seem to say on the surface, our faith, too, has its Gods. For what the ancients called Gods, we call Saints." [36] If Augustine (Francesco says) exposed the superstitions connected with the pagan gods, he intended to brand ancient abuses, but not to prove that the errors of the ancients were essentially different from our own. "I at least am convinced that Augustine, if he lived in our day, would direct the same irony against certain 'Saints' made such not by proved miracles, not by the Mother Church, but by the inane and ridiculous belief of nameless people. . . ." We moderns, too, he adds, have helpers to whom the populace turns for cures in cases of headache, podagra, cough, or childbed fever. As for the attitude of the ancients, one finds the same ironical condemnation of superstition as in Augustine, the same insight into the dangers of perversion of true religion, in an enlightened pagan priest such as Balbus in the second book of Cicero's *De Natura Deorum,* though he did not know the Christian faith.[37]

Does this mean that Francesco "dares to say that those gods are truer than this [God of ours]"—the accusation Cino Rinuccini raised against the classicists—and that Francesco "prefers Varro in secret to the doctors of our faith"? There can be no doubt that that is not what Francesco da Fiano says or intends to say. Nevertheless, the consequences drawn by him from his own attitude show that, if Rinuccini is at this point guilty of an exaggeration, it is not without basis. For what Francesco does say is that in a certain respect at least the testimony of a pagan such as Varro must be given more weight than that of the Christian Fathers, and for the following reason: "It is no less effective a demonstration of the Christian verities," he says, "if they are set forth by dissenters rather than by consenters. The praise appears to be of greater value and more reliable when Hannibal's excellence is extolled by Scipio, his enemy, than when it is extolled by his father, relatives, or friends . . . Therefore, the argument of our theologians appears to be confirmed by another one no less effective when in addition to the writings of the Saints that have Catholic approval we adduce such works of pagan authors as intimate the priesthood of Christ." Too easily, Francesco goes on to say, do we forget the maxim, found in the *Digest*, that "no one should be considered a fit witness in his own cause." "I for one feel, and this is a general opinion: fighting with home-grown arguments only means exposing one's cause to ridicule and failure." [38] Could not the implications of this standpoint, with a very slight twist of meaning, indeed appear identical with "preferring Varro . . . to the doctors of our faith"?

By availing ourselves of these forgotten annotations of a humanist at the Curia to one of the problems disputed about 1400, we are in a position to include in the picture of the transition on the threshold of the Quattrocento a trait that is anything but negligible and proves that Cino Rinuccini, even where his report seems most suspicious, did not merely give play to his fancy or indulge in slander. We may admit that few parallels to the ideas of Francesco da Fiano appear in the known contemporary Florentine sources. But it is easy to see that offensive comments like some of those quoted can be expected to have been the very last to be confided to paper; and though the writings of Salutati to which we have referred are incomparably tamer in their mode of thought and expression, by probing through the outer shell of what he wrote in the last decade of his life we have seen enough to say that many of the ideas so audaciously put into words by Francesco da Fiano were basically shared by his Florentine colleague. If the tone is different, it is the same melody which is played in the two contemporaneous vindications of the poets against "detractors" of ancient monotheistic piety, and of the figurative speech characteristic of religion as well as poetry.

Where Salutati did not consider his formulations with as much caution as he undoubtedly exercised in a work like the *Hercules* treatise which deals with the delicate themes of pagan mythology, he can quite unexpectedly produce the very tone of Francesco da Fiano's writing. When Cicero's championship of the *Respublica Romana* had been revealed by the rediscovery of his *Epistolae Familiares*, Salutati, in the first burst of elation, had gone further in his repudiation of the medieval respect for Caesar and the Empire than he was ready to maintain when becoming aware of the consequences.[39] Similarly, in his comments on the greatness of ancient men who had not yet known Christianity, there can be found phrases, inspired by a fervent love of antiquity, which he would certainly have denounced had he recognized their implications; but it is precisely these unguarded outbursts of feeling that give us precious clues to the mind of early classicism. Thus in Salutati's *De Fato et Fortuna*, in a section apparently written in 1396, we encounter a remark about Socrates which is particularly valuable since, in all phases of the Renaissance, judgments on Socrates' personality and philosophy can serve as the epitome of the humanistic attitude toward pagan antiquity. If Socrates, worthiest of men, had lived in the days of Christ—so Salutati ponders—and had not only known the pagan ideas of earthly glory, but had also had an intimation of true blessedness, he would no doubt have become the greatest of Christian martyrs. If we recall Socrates' demeanor in prison, and imagine that, instead of the pagan errors, he had come to know the Christian truth and had seen Christ preaching, crucified, triumphant in death, and resurrected

—could we believe that Socrates, after seeing all these signs, "would have become a fugitive from Rome in fear of death, a deserter of the Christian faith and of the cause of the eternal and unalterable truth," as did Peter the Apostle who tried to flee from a martyr's death and had to be moved to return to Rome by an apparition of Christ? [40]

Here, indeed, we are confronted with an expression of the same spirit that we know from Francesco da Fiano's manner of referring to the Fathers of the Church. In reading Salutati's passage, as in reading the many similarly attuned comments by Francesco da Fiano, we sense the distance still separating those voices of the early days of classicism from the Humanism of the time of Erasmus, when the chief lesson to be drawn from Socrates' self-sacrifice was the more or less open recognition that piety and the spiritual autonomy of man are not dependent on belief in the letter of any religious doctrine. The overpowering love of the generation after Petrarch for antiquity had remained more rigidly bound to medieval ways of thought, but at the same time had produced a much fiercer aggressiveness. At the end of the Trecento, the beloved ancients suddenly appeared so surpassing in their human greatness that they dwarfed the great figures of the medieval-Christian tradition, and gave rise among the humanists to the naive and daring question: would not the ancients have proved themselves greater and better men than the familiar champions of Christianity, if fate had cast them in the Christian role?

Now our assumption that, around 1400, ideas appearing among chancery humanists at the Curia in Rome could easily find their way to Florence need not be merely inferred from casual observations which show that tendencies found in the Roman circle are occasionally paralleled by submerged traces in Florentine works. The Curia in Rome was not the chancery of just another Italian region-state, but an inter-Italian meeting-place where Florentines were constantly employed; a frequent epistolary exchange kept alive the connections between the humanists of the two cities. Francesco da Fiano had long been among the correspondents and friends of Salutati; [41] and since we know from other sources that Francesco often served his foreign friends as cicerone through the classical ruins of Rome, and on such occasions gave free vent to his passionate love for the past grandeur of antiquity, [42] little imagination is needed to perceive the ways in which his passion and the love of his Florentine visitors for antiquity inspired one another on these walks through the Forum and the Roman hills, when the friends looked with indignation upon the churches and monasteries that had been installed in the resplendent shells of the ancient buildings. From a letter written later by one who had been Francesco's disciple in Rome we can still catch an echo of the sentiments of those early, exuberant days of classicism. In 1416, Cencio de' Rustici, then one of the humanistic secretaries at the Council of Constance, sent a request to his former teacher to compose an invective against those who had treated with contempt and destroyed the remains of the architecture and art of ancient Rome. To Cencio, the reckless destroyers—devoid of humanity and culture, as he calls them—were all the narrow-minded people who had seen danger to the Christian religion in the admiration of works of art representing ancient gods; but the worst among them were the Roman Popes, in whose trust fate had placed the remains of Rome. On this daring note, Cencio hoped, his old master would compose a new "invective" in defense of the glories of antiquity. "I believe, says Cencio, [43a] that "they [the Bishops of Rome] followed the intention of a certain braggart who, despairing of his ability to make himself a name through *virtus*, set the temple of Diana at Ephesus on fire. In the same way the high-priests of our religion applied themselves to the ruin and destruction of the city of Rome, since they held little admiration for her excellence and beauty and were in no way able to follow her as a model. Let us, therefore, inveigh with our curses against such barbarous and savage folly." *

We do not know whether, among the channels by which these belligerent sentiments of Roman classicists reached the Florentine group in the time of Cino Rinuccini, there was any direct correspondence between Francesco da Fiano and members of Bruni's and Niccoli's circle. From later years we have a document showing Bruni and Francesco in epistolary exchange; [44] and even then the harsh tones familiar from the *Invective Against the Detractors of the Poets* are still heard. Bruni had asked Francesco some questions about the time and causes of Ovid's exile in Tomi, and whether the poet had eventually returned to Rome. The reply he received was introduced by a restatement of the conflict between Francesco's classicism and the realities of his life. Francesco was old now; the time was

* To realize the precursory position as well as the utter recklessness of these expressions of the mind of early Quattrocento classicism, one must compare them with the references to the same subject in the famous letter which, under the inspiration of Raffael, then papal overseer of the antiquities of Rome, was phrased by Baldassare Castiglione and addressed to Pope Leo X in 1518 or 1519: "How many Popes, Holy Father, possessing the same dignity as Your Holiness, but not the same knowledge, ability, and highmindedness, . . . have demolished the ancient temples, statues, triumphal arches, and other magnificent buildings! . . . How many have reduced ancient pillars and marble ornaments to lime! The new Rome, which we now see standing in all its beauty and grandeur, adorned with palaces, churches, and other buildings, is built throughout with the lime obtained in this way from ancient marbles." [43b]

gone, he said, when with exultant pleasure he had fed on the *"dulcissima carmina"* of Ovid and other ancient poets. He was trying to forget "the sacred Muses of the divine and immortal Maro and of the other members of his sacred profession," as well as Cicero's "heaven-sent eloquence." "In order to fulfill my obligations toward the respectability of my profession as a clergyman (a profession which I have joined in order not to be in want of food and clothing), I am forced in the matins to read, and sometimes sing, . . . the homilies of Beda, Origines, Johannes Chrysostomus, and Gregory [the Great]." "If such works," Francesco went on to say, "are compared with the lucid felicity of the wonderful eloquence of the ancient poets and orators, those homilies, even though their authors were Saints, would seem to be dead coals, to use the words of Dante Alighieri, the Florentine poet." [45]

In looking over these scattered traces of sentiments which for obvious reasons were rarely confided to paper, and even less frequently propagated in the open, we glimpse elements of the classicists' revolt that lie deeper than those we can recognize in the authors on whom we must mainly depend in reconstructing the history of the new philology and the attacks against the legacy of the Trecento. But even though essential details of such forgotten undercurrents may never be recovered, this part of the picture must not be entirely overlooked if we want to understand the boldness and vigor of the humanistic mind in the Trecento transition. Suddenly, we see here the dangers inherent in the enthusiasm for antiquity; there was a threat even to Christianity and the Church. The rise of the first unbounded devotion to antiquity in the opening decades of the new century charged every sector of intellectual life with an explosiveness that is too easily underrated.

The Crisis in Civic Conduct and Outlook

In the long run, it is true, these threats did not materialize in the religious field; the Christian tradition was rooted too deeply in the minds of almost all humanists of the Quattrocento. But the situation was different with regard to the growing contempt for the medieval traditions of Florentine civic life, whose hold over the minds, and whose capacity to resist the attacks of the *literati*, could not compare with the latent resources of the Christian Church.

In Cino Rinuccini's *Invettiva* we find that his reproaches against the menace of classicism grow in breadth and number when it comes to the effects of the classicists' attitude on civic sentiment and conduct. His charges that the younger men were drifting away from civic duties are, indeed, so conspicuous that they attracted Wesselofsky's special attention, as we have seen; but Wesselofsky took them for evidence that the civic spirit was dying as a consequence of the coming of Humanism.[46] Now that we know that Rinuccini's arguments were made before Bruni and his school built up a new type of civic Humanism, the testimony of the *Invettiva* is seen to illustrate the conditions of Florence's intellectual life at one particular moment toward the end of the Trecento.

This is the gist of Rinuccini's accusations against the "*brigata*" of the younger classicists:

"Of housekeeping and family they have no high opinion, but with contempt of holy matrimony live an inordinate and dissolute life, and do not care for a father's dignity and the benefit of having children. They are such as to deserve the sentence of the Roman censors, Camillus and Postumius, who ordered the fortunes of two men, who had remained chaste [and would not marry] unto old age, to be confiscated for the community; threatening them with double punishment if they should dare complain in any way of so just a ruling.

"As to politics, they do not know which government is better, monarchy or republic, the rule of many or that of a few elect. They shun hard work [for the common weal], affirming that he who serves the community serves nobody; neither do they give advice to the Republic in the [councillor's] robe, nor do they defend her, arms in hand. Nor do they remember that the more common a good is, the more divine it becomes." [47]

We may exclude the possibility that Cino directed these imputations against Bruni. As a resident alien who did not obtain the rights of a citizen until 1415, Bruni could not be accused of shirking a citizen's duties. And it is also difficult to see how he could have been charged with "contempt of holy matrimony" when he was a student without office or substantial wealth, far from the stage in life where he would have to choose between the citizen's married life and the unfettered existence of the humanistic *literati*. If he had led a licentious life in those years of his unmarried youth (nothing, however, is known on this score), nobody could have called this "contempt of matrimony." [48]

Cino's report, therefore, far from rendering the dubious service of offering information on Bruni that can be gained better from an analysis of Bruni's own works, here as elsewhere depicts general tendencies which came to the fore toward the end of the century. Do we have any other evidence to confirm and illustrate Cino's assertions?

To a point, the attitude which offended the citizen Rinuccini had been ever-present among the literary men of the Trecento. The disciples of Petrarch, like their master, had not adapted themselves to the necessities of "housekeeping and family" in the citizen's life, not even when Humanism was transplanted to Florence. It is a

well-known fact that Boccaccio in his Latin writings faithfully carried on Petrarch's ideal of the aloofness of the
sage and of contempt for married life and civic responsibilities. Boccaccio's humanistic works are indeed filled with
vicious diatribes against matrimony; and in his biography
of Dante—a work most widely read in the late Trecento—
he looks upon the unhappy course of Dante's life as a
kind of punishment falling upon a great mind that allowed
itself to be dragged down into the whirlpool of petty
family worries and cares for the administration of the
commonwealth.[49]

Thus the great leaders of the Trecento whom Cino
Rinuccini so much admired had themselves not established
any final harmony between their ideals and lives as *literati*,
on the one hand, and the needs of the civic world on the
other. A more penetrating critic than Rinuccini, therefore, might have seen that the roots of the disease lay
deeper than in the unsocial attitude of the young classicists.
That men untouched by classicism were not immune to
the contagion is highlighted by the example of Giovanni
Gherardi da Prato. Although Giovanni as a champion of
the Volgare and adherent of the older Dante tradition may
be thought to be, and certainly considered himself Rinuccini's successor among the younger generation, yet in his
attitude toward the civic way of life he did virtually share
the outlook of the humanistic *literati*. According to a self-
characterization which Giovanni gave in later years, he
had throughout his life held in contempt honors, fame,
and the opinion of the multitude, and had left to others
the troubles of matrimony and family cares which poison
man's life; in solitude and poverty, he said, he had pursued the sweet study of wisdom.[50]

But if it is true that a civic attitude had never taken root
and established an accepted pattern of behavior and
thought among Trecento humanists, the dangers inherent

in the rise of classicism were only the greater. These
dangers can be sensed when we compare Filippo Villani,
last of the writers of the Villani chronicle, and author of
the *On the Origin of the City of Florence and on Her
Renowned Citizens*, with the two earlier chroniclers of the
Villani family, Giovanni and Matteo. Whenever Filippo
touches upon the achievements of his uncle and his father,
who were already recognized as the pride of Florence's
medieval historiography, he does not fail to add some su-
perciliously kind words for them, which are disparagement in disguise. Though their chronicles were "nothing
very beautiful," he would say, because they were written
in Volgare, both authors deserved credit for collecting and
preserving material invaluable as a basis for future Latin
works from the pens of "more delicate and superior
talents." *

* A perusal of the complete text of the phrases in question
illuminates the effect of the growing classicistic extremism better
than any comment. In the "Prologus" to his continuation of
the chronicles of Giovanni and Matteo Villani, Filippo remarks
on his father, Matteo: "We can say that he is rightly to be
praised for the extent to which he, in the style accessible to him,
kept the memorable things that happened in the world at the
time when he wrote from becoming lost, thus preparing the
material for more delicate and superior talents who would transform his memoirs into a happier and more exalted style." In
his *De Origine Civitatis Florentiae*, Filippo comments upon
Giovanni and Matteo: "Giovanni, my uncle, and Matteo, my
father, tried to entrust to Volgare literature what memorable
events the times brought with them. To be sure, they did not
accomplish anything very beautiful; they did it, I think, so that
the events would not be lost to those who with better minds
promised to do better, and in order to prepare the material for
a more polished presentation. The reason for their recapitulation was perhaps that they, as far as it was up to them, did not
want to allow the deeds worthy of record in the public annals
which the centuries had performed, to be lost by the negligence
of the pen." [51a]

Already with Filippo Villani—a full generation before the classicists of the Niccoli circle—this disappearance of due respect for the older ways of Florence went hand in hand with the desertion of the citizen's *vita civilis*. Filippo was married and had children, but, in contrast to the earlier chroniclers in his family, he withdrew from his responsibilities in his guild as well as in the commonwealth in proportion as he became more deeply absorbed in his writings and studies. To be sure, his book *On the Origin of the City of Florence* could have been written only by a fervent Florentine patriot, and there are many passages revealing the touch of a citizen who was taking his place among the humanists. In the chapter on Dante's *vita et mores*, which otherwise follows faithfully the biography in which Boccaccio had castigated the poet for leaving the safety of his study to take part in public life, Filippo's characterization shows Dante as a "dutiful citizen" (*officiosus civis*), "fully devoted to the glory and exaltation of his *patria*"; a man who even in exile "tried to the best of his ability to cooperate in the reform of his republic." To a degree, Filippo was already pursuing the course eventually leading to Leonardo Bruni's Quattrocento portrait of Dante as Florence's greatest, exemplary citizen.[51b] It is the more remarkable that this instinctive aversion to Boccaccio's *literati* critique of Dante remained without impact on Filippo's own conduct and ideals. By the time he had begun his *On the Origin*, so he himself says in its introduction, he had long since chosen the *vita solitaria* because he knew full well "that it is the most remote retreats which are wont to nourish the *bona studia*."[52] Among the works of Salutati, therefore, he chose *De Seculo et Religione* for special emphasis, calling this treatise a book "useful to acquire contempt for a life filled with occupations, where we become attached to worldly goods which do not last."[53] The reader of the book on the origin and the renowned citizens of Florence receives the author's advice to look upon the *vita solitaria* as the more valuable way of life, in fact the indispensable condition for the fruitful pursuit of studies.[54a] Such, we may think, was the normal outlook of the older members of the group of educated citizens with whom Leonardo Bruni was connected in the years of his early studies.[54b]

One may look upon Roberto de' Rossi, partner of the conversations in Bruni's dialogues and Bruni's companion in the studies of Greek under Chrysoloras, as another example. To his death he remained celibate, devoted to his books and literary friendships and to the teaching of younger citizens who met in Rossi's house, as Vespasiano da Bisticci described Rossi's life in a charming paragraph of his biography of Cosimo de' Medici, one of the members of Rossi's circle. The feeling of later humanists from Bruni's school that in this way of life there was something at variance with natural civic conduct is attested by Giannozzo Manetti's enumeration, in an appraisal of Rossi, of activities that had no place in Rossi's existence. Writing in the 1450's, Manetti gave this characterization: Rossi, "who had been born in a noble and famous family, deemed everything else inferior—the offices of the commonwealth as well as marriage, family, and a life of external splendor—and devoted his uninterrupted and admirable industry to the study of all the various *litterae* . . ." and to the many disciples who gathered in his house.[55a] In his younger years, to be sure, Rossi had entered upon a rather full career in public office although, as a descendant from a *Magnati* family, he could not serve on the highest boards. Within the short span of time from 1385 to 1393 he had been among the *Ten of Liberty,* in three other significant administrative posts, and three times in the *Council of the Commune.* Among these offices were at least two— *podesterie* in the territory—which could easily have been declined. But after 1393—that is, during the years of his retired studies and the ascendancy of classicism—although his name had been taken off the roster of the *Magnati*, giving him access to the most responsible and esteemed positions, he no longer served in any elective office, despite the fact that on various occasions (in 1403, 1411, 1412 and 1414) he was called upon to appear as a counselor in *consulte* of the government—invitations which prove that he had not fallen from grace but that he withdrew of his own free will. Thus, in the case of Rossi, the archival evidence fully bears out the picture drawn in our literary sources.[55b]

For a further example among Rossi's contemporaries and circle, we may refer to Antonio Corbinelli—like Rossi a respected member of the group of citizens who attracted Chrysoloras to Florence and acquired a knowledge of Greek through his instruction. Corbinelli, who collected one of the best Greek libraries of the early Quattrocento, according to Vespasiano da Bisticci "devoted himself entirely to his studies of Latin and Greek letters." [56] We find that he was known in humanistic circles as an advocate of the philosophy that a true "sage" must avoid matrimony and family life; [57] and he had an illegitimate son by a concubine at the time of Cino Rinuccini's accusations.[58] As for his attitude toward the citizen's political obligations, the documentary evidence does not, perhaps, admit of a final judgment on his motivation.[59a] There is no doubt that up to the time of Rinuccini's writing, Corbinelli had not yet served in any elective office; he did not enter upon his first position, an administrative office in the territory— the *podesteria* of Settimo—until April 1410.[59b] But since at that time he was only in his early thirties (he was born in 1378), it is not easy to disprove the suggestion that the only reason for his failure to occupy any office between 1400 and 1410 may have been his youth. It is odd, however, that even the position of 1410 was not followed by another until five and a half years later when Corbinelli appears among the *Signori;* whereas during the last decade of his life (1416-25), his public positions followed each other year by year, while he was also serving in several high offices of his guild (the *Lana*), in which he had not formerly been active. Since Antonio Corbinelli belonged to a family unusually well represented in the elective offices (all his brothers had full careers from their early years), the most probable explanation of the unequal curve of his own *vita publica* is that Antonio in the first part of his life, like some of his companions in his humanistic circle, had purposely refrained from the discharge of political activities, and that it was because of those long years of absence from public life that his contemporaries formed the impression that this student, who also frowned on married life, was a man "devoted entirely to his studies of Latin and Greek letters," as Vespasiano da Bisticci later said.

But the most memorable exemplar of the life of the self-seeking "sage" ("self-seeking" from the viewpoint of the citizen of the commune), of a life which could indeed give the impression of "contempt of holy matrimony," as Cino Rinuccini's accusation runs, was Niccoli. Our well informed authority is again Giannozzo Manetti, one of Niccoli's and Bruni's closest younger friends. So perfect and concrete a counterpart to Rinuccini's assertions is Manetti's restrospective view of Niccoli's life that it is worthwhile to cite the chief paragraphs in full. "At no time whatever," Manetti says of Niccoli, "did he give himself over to striving after public offices, . . . or to marriage in order to have children, but he preferred to live a happy life with his books, without much property or honors, unmarried, free of worries about transitory things, in leisure, peace, and tranquillity. In this way, abstaining from public occupations, and from almost all private business, he enjoyed the leisure . . . of *literati* and superior minds." Through his whole life, Manetti sums up, Niccoli spent his time "on liberal studies of this kind, without toil, wife and children, not burdened with any private or public business." [60a]

Niccoli's portrait in the obituary written on his death by Poggio confirms this characterization in all relevant points. Although Niccoli's flight from the burdens of public office may not have been stressed quite as strongly by Poggio as it was by so civic-minded a humanist as Manetti, Poggio, too, is emphatic about the fact that Niccoli had lived only for his studies, books and friends, while "*honorum cupiditas*" and political "*ambitio*" had remained foreign to him. Contemptuous of material wealth, "he led a bachelor's life without wife and children." [60b] He lived, as Manetti depicts Niccoli's domestic manners, "content with the attendance of a single maid-servant, in conformity with the example of Socrates the great philosopher, and Ennius the ancient poet, and of so many other erudite men." Whether the scandal to which the concubinage with this maid-servant gave rise in the 1420's had had any prelude at the time of Cino's writing we do not know. [61] There may have been, however, more incidents of this kind in Niccoli's circle, as the case of Corbinelli suggests.

Examples of the type of citizen turned socially irresponsible man of letters, then, were undoubtedly in the public eye, and Cino's report once more draws our attention to a very real and too much neglected trait of Florentine life about 1400. Even Salutati, by Cino's standards, was not above reproach. To be sure, life had led the humanistic chancellor away from the outlook of socially unburdened *literati*. Having published during the early 1380's, in his *De Seculo et Religione*, a guide which inspired Filippo Villani to withdraw from civic life, Salutati had gradually become a literary champion of the *vita activa-politica*, at least in his correspondence with humanistic friends—an exception in Trecento Humanism in and outside of Florence.[62] Yet Cino's other charge—indifference to the struggle between Republic and Tyranny, between Rule of the people and Oligarchy—would have fitted none of the contemporaries more justly than the author of *De Tyranno*, censor of Cicero's fight for his political convictions, and advocate of quietistic yielding to the powers that be.[63]

Of the literary products of Salutati's and Bruni's close associate Roberto de' Rossi, translator of various Greek works, little has come down to us; yet this little again reflects the world of the aloof sage and retiring literary man.[64] Those, Rossi says in the foreword to his translation of Aristotle's *Analytica Posteriora*, who have become aware of how the wicked in this world oppress the noble and the wise, must indeed be foolhardy if they do not flee the hardships and the false allurements of the world. The primary value of literary studies, in his eyes, is that they help to turn the student away from the futilities of this life—a value so great that it alone, Rossi feels, would suffice to justify his labors even if his translations should not have the additional merit of being useful to his fellow-citizens.[65] The finest fruit of the reading of Aristotle's works on logic is that this study, by calling into play man's rational powers, makes him conscious of his divinity and kinship with the angels.[66] How, then, would a humanist, who was moved by these sentiments, react to the stirring political events that fell into the years of Rossi's lifetime?

While Rossi was translating the *Analytica Posteriora*, Florence, in 1405-06, was waging the war which led to the conquest of Pisa and its incorporation in the Florentine dominion. Works like Dati's *Istoria* and Bruni's *Historiae*

Florentini Populi, which took their initial inspiration from the consciousness that Florence by this act had finally made herself a region-state with its own coast and ports, show the important role which this experience played in the growth of a politically-minded civic Humanism with historical interests. Rossi's reaction to the same experiences was an increased feeling of the vanity of all political concerns compared with the lasting significance of intellectual pursuits. He added to his work some verses stating that at the very time when he was endeavoring to give Latin-speaking men access to the ancients' exalted mansions of the mind, his Florentine fellow-citizens were busy constructing fortifications in conquered Pisa and building up their power in every other possible way—erecting towers reaching into the sky to warn and intimidate the pitiful remnants of the Pisan citizenry, "while the stars continue to turn in their unchanging course." [67a] The documents strikingly confirm this bent of mind in Rossi's later years. When in the early 1410's, at the time of the northward thrust of Ladislaus of Naples into central Italy, Rossi was asked for his opinion in a *consulta* of invited citizens, he told the *Signoria* that men of learning had always been opposed to war as a means of settling disputes between states.[67b]

Here we should also note a biographical fact. It is hardly without significance that Niccoli's and Rossi's intellectual interests were first shaped in the school of Luigi Marsili, the Augustinian friar of the Florentine convent of Santo Spirito. Both are classed, in Poggio's obituary on Niccoli, among Marsili's closest disciples. "Our Niccoli," says Poggio, "never left Marsili's company, spent most of his time with him and was instructed by him in the best precepts for life. . . . For it is often found that we imitate the conduct of those in whose company we are educated. Steeped as he was in this way of life, Niccoli plainly scorned two things: wealth and the zeal for public office." He thus embraced as "the best rule for life . . . that one should be free for literary leisure and not be burdened by either wealth or ambition." [67c]

In Niccoli's case, aloofness from the political passions that filled the era of the Viscontean wars produced even farther-reaching effects.[68] In the years of the resistance against Giangaleazzo, Niccoli had mocked the Florentine people as misguided fools and had called the ruling men a gang of tyrants and robbers.[69] A decade later, as we shall see, he was among those who tried to prevent Florence from resisting the attempt of King Ladislaus of Naples to establish in large parts of Italy a monarchy after the example of Giangaleazzo.[70] By these tokens, it is highly probable that in the days of Giangaleazzo Niccoli had been one of those who lent a favorable ear to the Milanese propaganda of peace and unity. During the war with Pisa, at any rate, he asserted that the ruling group had embarked upon this enterprise only in order to ruin the Florentine citizens with expenditures made necessary by the war, and so to throw them all the more helplessly at the mercy of their rulers.[71] With an air of superiority he declared the incorporation of Pisa and other cities into the Florentine territory to be "childish madness" (*puerorum deliramenta*), winning trophies which would only bring disaster to Florence.[72a]

The almost contemporaneous source from which we take these facts—an invective which the citizen and humanist Lorenzo di Marco de' Benvenuti directed against Niccoli—leaves, furthermore, no doubt that the cause of Niccoli's hatred for the men who ruled Florence during the stormy years of the political crisis must be sought elsewhere than in a general pacific attitude of the middle classes, or in their rebellious mood against the ruling oligarchy. The Niccoli were an old and respected family of citizens, with long standing in the *Arte di Lana* to which so many members of the ruling circle belonged. It is true that none of Niccoli's five brothers is ever found in the high offices normally open to a family of such standing, and that we may have reason to wonder about the causes for the apparent lack of customary political ambition in this one family.[72b] But this does not mean that the Niccoli had fallen out with the ruling group, for several of the brothers did serve in certain middle-rank offices for which they seemed particularly equipped. One of them, a prominent lawyer, was no less than ten times consul of his guild, and others served in diplomatic missions in which their personal connections could be especially useful to the state. The reason why Niccolò Niccoli was so bitterly attacked by some contemporaries, was, however, not this general lack of political fervor in his family, but rather two aspects of his personal conduct that made his case quite singular.

In the first place, since he was the eldest of the Niccoli brothers, he had been in his youth quite regularly called upon to sit in the city councils, and it would have been clearly up to him to proceed from this customary springboard [72c] to the usual career of at least a few administrative offices. But after 1404 he no longer appeared even in the city councils, and the only administrative post which he seems ever to have occupied until the upheavals of the year 1434 was (with the exception of a one-year trusteeship of the University of Florence, which was near to his heart) a place, in 1413, on a board appointed to reduce the city's founded debt. Around 1404, therefore, it became evident that Niccoli was disinclined to enter upon the career in office to which he had seemed destined by everything in his background (he may well have declined offices offered to him about that time), and Cino

Rinuccini when writing his invective could easily have felt that Niccoli was evading his obligations as a citizen.

Secondly, from precisely the same period onward Niccoli showed his embittered, sovereign contempt of all the foreign-policy decisions of the Republic, first during the war with Pisa and, subsequently, during the Florentine resistance to King Ladislaus of Naples' expansionist policies. According to Benvenuti, he once exclaimed that "he would submit rather to the command of a tyrant than to the power and rule of a few." [73] In the opinion of our informant, the cause of Niccolò Niccoli's attitude was that he was a bad citizen, who took less interest in civic concerns than was necessary to make even a mediocre citizen.[74] That Niccolò had also become alienated from his own brothers—active merchants, though not men of politics—was likewise caused ultimately by the revolt of the *literatus* against civic conduct. Niccoli, the writer of the invective states, felt nothing but "insolent disrespect" for the life of the industrialists of the *Lana* Guild from whom he was descended; [75] for he used to lament that he had been raised "in a textile workshop, . . . among common hired hands and the lowest human dregs," [76] among illiterate people from whom he could learn nothing but "barking" (*latrare*).

In order to determine Niccoli's place in the struggle between classicism and civic Humanism, one must be aware of the kinship of this passage with Giovanni Conversino's opinion that republics are poor soil for Humanism because their leaders are men absorbed in "mercenary" commercial pursuits,[77] an assertion made even while Cino Rinuccini in his *Risponsiva* included among the *"uomini illustri"* of Florence merchants and men-of-arms, as well as *literati* and artists, "because not only arms but also trade enlarge the commonwealth." [78] That we find the same contempt for the civic way of life in Niccoli as in Conversino, the north-Italian adversary of communal life, has its psychological explanation in Niccoli's estrangement from his family traditions and social environment; and in him, it fused with the classicist's scorn for the times in which he lived.

The earliest product we have from Bruni's pen—a Latin poem, written in 1397/98, *On the Approach of the Emperor* (*De Adventu Imperatoris*)—allows us to observe how far even Bruni had been at the outset of his career from that fusion of Humanism and civic experience that he was to achieve after the events of the Giangaleazzo era.[79] During the years following Giangaleazzo's investment with the ducal title in 1395, King Wenceslaus repeatedly sounded the Italian states about the possibility of his coming to Italy to be crowned emperor—an expedition which, if carried out, could have counted on the support of Giangaleazzo, as well as on the accustomed hostility of the Guelph states and particularly of Florence. While the Florentine Republic was preparing herself for a repetition of the oft-experienced situation in which she, as leader of the Guelph city-states, would close her gates to the German army on its march to the south, Bruni addressed a call to Rome, in the language and tenor of ancient poetry. For although Rome under fourteenth-century conditions of power and political energies was bound to play a minor role beside the flowering north and central Italian states, she assumed first rank in the imagination of a youth brought up in the literary imitation of classical examples. Remembering the Roman resistance to foreign armies invading the Peninsula in antiquity, the young Latinist on the Arno wrote: "Rome, hurry and make thy cohorts strong with mighty soldiers. War is now coming, ye Roman citizens. Lift up the shining ensigns of the bird of victory, fulfill your duty toward the *patria!*" Just as it was in the times of Hannibal and

Pyrrhus, the present day shall again see Romans "who preserve the law and learn to serve even if they must shed every drop of their blood." At last the enemy retreats into his Cimbrian regions.[80]

Here we have a revealing illustration of the dominance of an abstract classicism in the surroundings in which Bruni learned to take his first steps toward becoming a humanist. In one way or another, Florentine Humanism at the end of the Trecento (to repeat a previous formulation) shows everywhere a lack of natural osmosis between the tenets of the *literati* and the realities of life. One generation later, Bruni's disciple Matteo Palmieri, in his dialogue *Della Vita Civile*, was able to give full expression to a Florentine civic attitude, although he was then only of about the same age at which Bruni had still been spellbound by the idea of *Roma Aeterna*. Young Palmieri, in the 1430's, could do so because meanwhile, principally through Bruni's efforts of a lifetime, there had come about that change in the inner structure of Florentine Humanism which may best be described as the transition from a classicism unconnected with the citizen's active life to civic Humanism.[81]

In summing up the precious information in Cino Rinuccini's report and in the related sources which his guidance has allowed us to place in focus, we may say, then, that some of the too much neglected components of the situation at the end of the Trecento were these: a disinclination on the part of the humanistic and semi-humanistic *literati* to accept the burdens and responsibilities of the citizen; an indifference to the fundamental struggle of the period between republican liberty and tyranny; and a lack of interest in the history of the Florentine Commonwealth, which seemed to pale beside the glamor of the revived memories of the ancient world.

The full historical perspective of these conditions is

gained when we confront them with that spirit which only a few years later found expression in Bruni's *Laudatio* and *Dialogus II*, and in Gregorio Dati's *Istoria*, and which eventually caused Bruni, in complete opposition to the outlook of the intellectuals around 1400, to praise marriage and family as the foundations of a sound commonwealth, and to base the verdict on Dante on the observation that he, in contrast to Petrarch and Boccaccio, had led a married life and served his city in public office and the citizen-army. It is this antithesis between the last years of the fourteenth century and the time after 1402 which definitely allows us to recognize the profundity of the change brought about by the political experience which reshaped Florentine Humanism on the threshold of the Quattrocento.[82]

CHAPTER 15

FLORENTINE HUMANISM AND THE VOLGARE IN THE QUATTROCENTO

The "Paradiso of the Alberti" and the Cult of the Volgare

WHEN we began our reconstruction of Florentine thought at the end of the Trecento, we cleared the ground by removing from the list of historical sources the *Paradiso degli Alberti* of Giovanni Gherardi da Prato. To round out the picture, we must return to Giovanni's novel once again. For in refuting anachronistic illusions and ascertaining that in the discussions of the *Paradiso*-society we are confronted with ideas of the post-Giangaleazzo period, we did not only destroy an alleged document for the year 1389—we also restored a potential testimony for the early fifteenth century.

As a Volgare poet, Giovanni da Prato has always been looked upon as a disciple of Cino Rinuccini, and his work as a Quattrocento continuation of Rinuccini's Petrarchian poetry and cult of the three great *corone fiorentine*.[1] Now that the civic traditions kept alive by Cino Rinuccini have proved to play a part in the growth of Florentine Humanism at the beginning of the new century, how will this insight affect the historical appraisal of his partisan and disciple?

In a way, we must now make amends for the unfairness shown to Giovanni da Prato's novel in earlier parts of our study. There, we were so intent upon denying to the

Paradiso an historical value unjustly ascribed to it that we could consider its negative aspects only: its dependence on other sources, its lack of originality, and the backwardness of an author who in the full light of the Quattrocento adapted himself to the achievements of Humanism by superficially imitating them even while he remained deeply attached to the intellectual and emotional world of the Trecento.[2] But in a period so prone to surrender to a classicism hostile to the Florentine traditions, Giovanni's clinging to Florence's Volgare culture, even when bound up with old-fashioned modes of thought, represented a positive element as well. In the surroundings in which civic Humanism developed, Giovanni da Prato, in spite of his lack of originality in all things humanistic, made his own contribution by his unswerving love of the Florentine tongue, and by his zeal to prove that there was still room for vernacular culture in a world changed by Quattrocento classicism; like Cino Rinuccini, he was one of those to whom was due the preservation of a precious heritage. He helped keep alive the flame till the time came when cultivation of the Volgare was at last included in the program of Florentine humanists.

Seen from this angle, Giovanni da Prato's *Paradiso*, though it belongs to a phase of the development other than has long been assumed, remains an important document for the history of Florentine civic Humanism. The conversations of the novel offer a unique opportunity for observations on the surroundings in which the humanistic movement led by Bruni overcame the humanistic prejudice against the vernacular.

To be sure, such an interpretation of the *Paradiso* presupposes that it was written before Bruni's widely read *Vite di Dante e di Petrarca*, composed in 1436, initiated the active interest of the Florentine humanists in the Volgare; and since the study of the *Paradiso* has always centered on what was assumed to be its source-value for the 1380's, scholars have usually paid little attention to the exact date of its composition. But there can be no doubt that the novel was written in the late winter of 1425-26, or not much later. For the author indicates in the opening passages that he wrote his work when his professional activities had come to an end and he was going to spend the "remainder of his life" writing—a situation which occurred early in 1426 when Giovanni, as an effect of the financial emergency produced by the war against Filippo Maria, had been deprived of his Dante lectureship at the Florentine university and also had lost his long-held position as an architect-counselor on the nascent cathedral dome after a violent quarrel with Brunelleschi over technical details.[3a]

As we may learn from this date of the *Paradiso* novel, its author, though far from being a precursor of the literature of Giangaleazzo's day, was by no means a mere straggler who came along after all decisive events, literary and political, had taken place in the era of the Viscontean wars; his work came in time to serve us as a source of information on the later years of Bruni's generation. In respect of the date of its origin as well as of the ideas discussed in its conversations, the *Paradiso* must be classed as a contemporary parallel, outside the humanistic group, to the works produced by Bruni and his circle after his return to Florence in 1415. Attempts to prove that some of the historical themes which determine the direction of interest in the *Paradiso* conversations are already modeled on the first book of Bruni's *Historiae* do not stand up under a critical test. Though without originality, working mostly with ideas he had picked up in his early years from the publicists of the Giangaleazzo period, Giovanni da Prato is nonetheless a valuable witness because his work preceded the phase when all historical discussion in Florence came under the spell of Bruni's *History*.[3b]

It is this chronological position which makes Giovanni a guide to the background of Bruni's work. He shows us how strongly the horizon of the Florentine citizens in the 1420's was dominated by the historical curiosity which the political events at the turn of the century had stimulated—and this before the first books of Bruni's *magnum opus* had been published.[4] He also allows us to see, more clearly than any other writer of the period, that, while the rise of historical criticism had to wait for the work of the humanists, there was in the civic world another development which Florentine Humanism could afterwards use as a basis: a heightened idea of the tasks of the Volgare.

Between the Florentine Volgare literature of the Trecento, and the newer period of Volgare literature beginning with the names of humanists like Bruni, Palmieri, and Alberti in the 1430's and 1440's, there is an interlude in which our sources make it difficult to see beyond the classicism of a narrow group of Latin writers. The *Paradiso* provides an opportunity to observe Volgare culture during that interlude after the Giangaleazzo era. To judge by this source, one aspect of the interests of the early Quattrocento outside of learned humanistic circles would seem to be the survival of considerable scholastic and other Trecento elements, unless this impression must in part be attributed to Giovanni's reminiscences of his distant youth. But new at any rate was the confidence in the ability of the Volgare to serve as an adequate medium not only for poetry and prose fiction, for which it had served in the Trecento, but also for reasoned discussions on originally humanistic subjects. The same soaring of Florentine national sentiment, we may say, which inspired the humanists of Bruni's generation to create a new historical view of antiquity and the Florentine past, anchored minds of the stamp of Giovanni da Prato ever more firmly in their pride and confidence in the capacities of the Florentine vernacular.

In its own sphere, Giovanni's literary production, too, was clearly molded by the experience of the struggle between the Florentine Republic and the Viscontean Tyranny. In his younger years, he had contributed to the propaganda war against Giangaleazzo a Volgare poem in defense of Florence.[5] In the *Paradiso*, written after the renewal of the war with Milan under Filippo Maria Visconti, his heightened Florentine and republican consciousness is noticeable at many points. It appears in the apostrophe to the "fellow-citizens in this illustrious *patria*, . . . who devote all their time and attention to the affairs of our sacred Republic, in order to . . . maintain her in her sweet liberty";[6] continues in the poetical opening vision with its admiring emphasis upon the "zealously guarded, sweet liberty" of the Athenians and the greatness of Rome under the consuls of the Republic;[7] and is finally documented by the leading part played in the novel by politico-historical subjects, all of them appraised from the point of view of republican liberty.[8] But the fresh and original element, molded by these experiences, is, in Giovanni da Prato's own words, "the ardent desire, which spurs me on incessantly: to exalt our mother-tongue as well as I can and know, and to ennoble it in the way it has already been ennobled and exalted by the three crowns of Florence (*da tre corone fiorentine*) more than by anybody else."[9] The program of civic culture which he tries to set forth through the practical example of the conversations in the novel is based on the conviction "that the Florentine idiom is so refined and copious that one can express, argue, and debate in it any abstract and profound thought with the most perfect lucidity."[10]

Although Giovanni's work was neither completed nor

published, and, consequently, exerted no influence on subsequent developments, it allows us to sense the atmosphere of Volgare Florence at a stage when the Volgare movement had not yet affected the literary production of Florentine humanists. This is not to say that Giovanni's trust in the Volgare was then completely unparalleled in the humanistic camp, or that Bruni, leader of the humanistic group, was in his earlier years blind and deaf to so deep-reaching a trend of the Florentine intellectual milieu. On the contrary, Bruni would hardly have responded to the rising interest in the Volgare as he did in his later years, had he not from the first been sensitive to the resurgent pride in the Florentine vernacular among cultured citizens. The concluding paragraph of his *Laudatio* had already celebrated Florence for her preeminence not only in the new humanistic studies but also in Volgare speech. "This city alone in all Italy," the passage runs, "is deemed to use the purest and most cultivated speech. Therefore, all those who wish to speak well and faultlessly take their model from this one metropolis. For this city calls men her own who in this popular and common tongue have shown all others to be mere infants." [11] But from this first boast of Florence's superiority even in the language of Italy it is a far cry to a recognition of the Volgare as a potential equal of the classical languages, or to the active creation of Volgare literature. The latter was not produced by Bruni and his school until the 1430's. At that time, Bruni wrote his *Vite di Dante e di Petrarca* and some Volgare poems, as well as a *Novella* which has a distinguished place in Florentine Volgare writing,[12] while the disciple closest to him in the citizenry, Matteo Palmieri, composed his book *Della Vita Civile*—"On the Civic Life."

That the environment in which civic Humanism grew up favored this ultimate inclusion of vernacular writing in the humanistic program, was due to the pertinacious efforts of such citizens as Giovanni da Prato. From his claim in the 1420's that the Florentine idiom was not only the medium of a great poetical literature, but equal to the demands of any abstract reasoning and logical exposition, it is only a step to Bruni's final verdict in his Dante biography of 1436 that "every language has its own perfection, its own sound, its own refinement and *parlare scientifico*." [13]

Civic Humanism and the Florentine Volgare to the Time of Lorenzo de' Medici

In our conclusion that the *Paradiso degli Alberti*, though it did not introduce the new historical outlook, illustrates the background of civic Humanism by its championship of the Florentine Volgare, we have taken for granted that the reconciliation of classicism with the vernacular trend, characteristic of Bruni and his school during the latter part of his life, was of fundamental and permanent significance for the branch of the humanistic movement which we have called "civic Humanism." This is by no means a matter of general agreement, given the still prevailing effects of the prejudice that the Humanism of the Quattrocento was by its nature the undoing of Volgare culture and of the traditions of the medieval Italian city-state. By casting a glance at the later course of events, we shall be able to discern the direction of the movement which we have watched, and in a fashion conclude the account of its genesis. [14]

When Bruni, in the mid-1430's, made the statement that every language has its own perfection, he introduced into Humanism not only a novel argument, but also a new literary task. For in his *Vite di Dante e di Petrarca* he made a determined attempt to deal in the Florentine vernacular with subjects from the fields of aesthetics, literary criticism, and historical philosophy which heretofore

had been treated only in the long since perfected medium
of Latin and which, as the pioneering author felt forced to
admit himself, "can be expressed only with difficulty in
the Volgare." [15]

How tightly closed the border between Humanism and
the Volgare usually still was at that time is well attested
by the experiences of Matteo Palmieri, who composed his
Della Vita Civile at about the same time. When this young
citizen and disciple of Bruni undertook to rediscuss some
problems, taken from Latin works, in the form of a Volgare dialogue, many of his humanistic friends tried to
dissuade him from publication. Although they approved
the plan and contents of the book, they found fault with
him, Palmieri tells us, because "I had undertaken to compose books in Volgare for publication." His friends warned
him that problems derived from ancient literature and illustrated of necessity with classical examples would only be
derided by the multitude; and their vivid descriptions of
how readers unfamiliar with classical works would brutally
misunderstand and pervert what Palmieri wanted to tell
them in the vernacular tongue so disheartened the young
author that for a while he did not dare to complete and
publish his work.[16] This typical reaction of the humanistic
circle as late as the 1430's well illustrates the necessity of
the humble efforts of such advocates of the Volgare as
Cino Rinuccini and Giovanni da Prato to create an atmosphere in which the school of Bruni could begin to adapt
the Volgare to intellectual tasks formerly looked upon as
the domain of Latin, and eventually to claim that every
language had its "own perfection" (*ciascuna lingua ha sua
perfezione*).

We are in a position to trace how Bruni gradually
reached his new views in the mid-1430's. In 1435, while
the Curia stayed in Florence, there had been a heated discussion among several humanists of the Papal chancery

and Bruni about the nature and historical origin of the
Volgare language. On that occasion Flavio Biondo had
maintained, and finally put into writing in his treatise *On
the Words of Roman Speech,* that the Volgare had
branched off from Latin during the period when Roman
Italy was being transformed by the Germanic invasions.
Under these circumstances the Volgare seemed to Biondo
a bastard born of Latinity and Gothic-Vandal usage—a
bastard, because Biondo, in addition to much critical penetration and superior learning, displayed the typical classicist's disdain of a language alienated from the ancient
standards. After Rome's capture by the barbarians, he
stated in terms of obvious contempt, "all were contam-
inated with and deeply polluted by this barbarous language; and gradually it has come about that, instead of
the Roman Latinity, we have this Volgare, an adulterated
speech mixed with outlandish usage." [17a] To this verdict
Biondo added, after becoming better acquainted with the
history of the Germanic migrations, a still more telling
expression of his standards in an excursus of his *Italia
Illustrata.* Eventually, he now said, the Lombards, "the
most haughty of all the foreign invaders of Italy, attempted to overthrow the respect enjoyed by the *Imperium Romanum* and Italy and even to destroy them
completely." They tried "to found new laws and change
the manner and customs of the people and the appellations
of things (*rerum vocabula*). I, therefore, venture to assert that at the time of the Lombards we find the beginning of the transformation of the Latin language and
Roman speech (*locutionis romanae latinis verbis . . . mu-
tationem*), which had been used not only in Italy but also
by most of the nations subject to the Empire, into what is
now called the Italian Volgare (*volgarem italicam*). This
fact had not yet been known to me at the time when I
addressed the treatise *De locutione romana* to Leonardus

Aretinus. . . .[17b] Even the institutions of public administration and the forms of private life were carefully
changed by those Lombards, and the madness of this
nation went so far that they entirely disregarded the
Roman characters and invented new letter-signs which by
their absurdity indicated the barbarity of that people. Quite
to the contrary, the Ostrogoths, Roman citizens, and people judging with equity, took a delight in Roman script
and did not stain it with any barbarism." *

Biondo's views were opposed by Bruni with the theory,
which has earned him the scornful criticism of most modern students, that the Volgare had been a product of antiquity itself. There had always existed, he argued in an
important letter (*Epistola VI 10*), a popular way of speaking, side by side with the *"literatus sermo"*; and this popular speech was essentially identical with the Volgare even
in the days of Cicero and Terence. It had no similarity to
"the manner of sentence conclusion, inflexion, the precise
use of words, construction, and accentuation" employed in
literary Latin. All this was beyond the range of the common people, and of the nurses and other women from
whom young Romans received the rudiments of their
speech.[18] But then as today, those using the popular manner of expression and transmitting it to the young pro-

* It is important to note that the pejorative estimate of the
"adulteration" of the Latin language, which in all these passages by Biondo is inevitably attached to the theory of a "barbarian" origin of the Volgare, remained harnessed to the establishment of the historical facts wherever this theory spread in
the Renaissance. Poggio Bracciolini, when agreeing to the
theory in 1450, noted that the barbarians *"inquinaverunt linguam latinam,"* and until the sixteenth century there persisted
the general tendency to contrast *"illam veterem integram,
castam et incorruptam linguam"* and *"novam hanc, pollutam
et contaminatam ac vulgarem"*—"polluted" and "contam-
inated" after the Gothic, Vandal, and Lombard invasions.[17c]

vided a necessary preparation for the refinements of Latin elegance; "not because they inflected cases, or varied their choice of words and concluded periods in the literary fashion, but because they spread a speech that was pure, graceful and in no way like that of barbarians." In other words, then as now, there have been "grace and dignity of thought" in popular speech, even without the sophistication of the literary Latin; there has been "a sort of vernacular pleasantness." [19a] "For the Volgare speech, too, has qualities which commend it in its way, as is evident in the poetry of Dante and of others who speak it free of faults."

The difficulty encountered in determining the motives that prompted Bruni's hypothesis of the existence of the Volgare in Roman times has been one of the obstacles to a clear distinction of his civic Humanism from "classicist Humanism." For the most widely shared opinion has long been that Bruni, who held that Latin could not have been spoken by Romans lacking a literary education, betrays the mind of a classicist who thought his beloved Latin too noble for vulgar people and consequently must have disdained the vernacular and the Volgare culture.

On this score, we should not forget that our information about the course and relevance of the controversy regarding the Volgare in 1435 is derived chiefly from Biondo; his description of his quarrel with Bruni as a disagreement concerning historical fact, namely, as to which strata of Roman society had used literary Latin, does not necessarily cover all the reasoning behind Bruni's position. At any rate, Bruni's short extant letter in reply to Biondo culminates in the assertion that the very remoteness of the Volgare from the strict rules of literary Latin gives the Volgare "qualities which commend it in its way." [19b] One wonders whether the pattern of Bruni's thought on the issue of language might not have run parallel with a

somewhat kindred theory on the origin of knighthood
(*militia*) that he had set forth in 1421. In the treatise
De Militia, he had tried to prove that knighthood (*militia*)
was not simply a product of medieval developments, but
had its roots in ancient Rome. Here, where we have fuller
information on Bruni's reasoning, thanks to the treatise
De Militia, we see that his tracing of a medieval development to ancient origins was intended to enhance its prestige. Is it not very probable that Bruni's intention was
the same when in later years he thought he could trace
the Volgare to Roman roots?

So much at least is obvious: fifteenth-century humanists
could use the historical theory that Latin and the Volgare
coexisted in ancient Rome to support the conviction that
the Volgare idiom, in addition to the sophisticated Latin
speech, was playing a valuable and indispensable role in
the education of their own time. It is quite true [19c] that
Leon Battista Alberti and others after him would condemn
Bruni's theory for the very reason that the hypothesis of
the coexistence of two languages in Rome appeared obnoxious to their own efforts to make the Volgare the prevailing language of literature as well as of popular speech.
On the other hand, Biondo's assumption that all Romans
had used a single language did encourage Alberti in his
endeavors to make the Volgare the language of everybody
in his day. But these later uses of Bruni's and Biondo's
theories do not prove that the same implications had been
seen originally, at a moment when no one had as yet
dreamed of proposing a dethronement of the Latin language and when the only question was the extent to which
the Volgare was to be recognized as a minor partner.
Sound historical criticism does not allow us to attribute to
Bruni's understanding of his thesis any overtones that are
not consistent with his comments in the *Epistola VI 10*,[19d]
the one surviving document on the question from his hand.

Bruni's failure to carry out his promise that an amplification of his thesis would follow this letter, may have been caused by the fact that before long he became aware of the futility of the assumption that there had been two languages in ancient Rome; soon, competent scholars were accepting Biondo's reasoning as factually convincing. But Bruni, while no longer insisting on his mistaken interpretation of the conditions of ancient Rome, replaced it in 1436 with an appraisal of the Volgare based on an historical analogy between the languages of Rome and Florence. If Florence's native speech was not a Roman product, it could claim equal status with Latin as a new product of a new age. As Bruni puts it in his *Vita di Dante* with the significant words which must now be reread in their full context: "Whether the writing is in Latin or in Volgare does not matter; the difference is no other than that between writing either in Greek or in Latin. Every language has its own perfection, its own sound, its own refinement and *parlare scientifico*." [20a]

That much had never been claimed for the Volgare during the Trecento, nor had the Volgare ever been seen in so broad an historical perspective. Dante himself, despite all his praise of the Volgare as the "new sun" for those to whom the old sun of the Latin could give no light, had in the medieval manner placed Latin as "*lingua grammaticalis et artificialis*" on an entirely different and higher level than the "*linguae naturales vulgares*." [20b] He had not doubted that "the Latin makes many intellectual conceptions possible which the Volgare cannot formulate . . . ; its efficacy is greater than that of the Volgare." [20c] It is true that Boccaccio in his *Vita di Dante*, in words which on the surface look rather similar to Bruni's expression, had stated that Dante had "shown effectively" that "any lofty matter can be treated in Volgare poetry" (*con essa* [i.e., *la poesia volgare*] *ogni alta materia potersi trattare*) and that Dante consequently had elevated the Volgare and brought it into esteem among Italians just as Homer and Virgil had done with their own languages among the Greeks and Latins." [20d] But the treatment of every *"alta materia,"* of which Boccaccio spoke, referred to Dante's *poetry*, especially in the *Divina Commedia,* and to nothing else; and even here Boccaccio eventually retreated in the manner characteristic of Trecento writers. In his last work, the *Commento* on the *Inferno,* he finally conceded that Dante, "when speaking Latin, has much more skill and majesty than when he uses our [Volgare] mother-tongue." [20e] It was, indeed, not until a few years before the composition of Bruni's *Vita di Dante* that Giovanni da Prato, in the already quoted passage, judged that in the Florentine idiom of his period "one can express, argue, and debate every abstract and profound thought (*ogni astratta e profonda materia*) with the most perfect lucidity." [20f]

Bruni, then, took up a line of reasoning already in the air among his contemporaries, but redefined more sharply the crucial claim that the Volgare was not only a vehicle for great poetry but had "its own refinement and *parlare scientifico*" (*suo parlare limato e scientifico*). And he gave weight to this idea by making for the first time the general statement that these capacities, instead of being peculiar to Latin, were accessible to "every language." He even dared to make the final inference that if the Latin and the Volgare as literary languages are potentially not different, the choice between writing either in Latin or in Volgare was to be viewed in the light of the Roman choice "between writing either in Greek or in Latin." To be sure, all this was proffered only in the form of an aphorism, and one may rightly doubt that Bruni was aware of the full implications which these theses were bound to have for the eventual dethronement of Latin as a privileged language. But his aphorism brought into focus tendencies which had arisen in Florence during the early Quattrocento crisis. *In nuce* it heralded the direction which the *questione della lingua* was to take during the next century. In this sense one can agree with a recent student who has said that Bruni's statement seems to have "a strangely modern flavor." [21]

Once the view of an historical parallelism among three equal languages—the Greek, the Latin, and the Volgare—had emerged, it began to act as a leaven, to the detriment of the classicist bias. After a final vindication of the Volgare had been pronounced by the leading Florentine humanist in a work itself written in Volgare and more widely read among Florentine citizens than any other of his writings, the problem of the dignity and value of the Volgare was to stir Florentine minds until the opinion of the humanist chancellor had become the general opinion.

Presumably in the first half of the 1440's Giannozzo Manetti wrote a new *Vita Dantis* in Latin.[22] In spite of the ever-growing fame of the three great Florentines of the Trecento, Manetti tells us, many of those trained in the humanistic way still felt contempt for them because they were repelled by the fact that Dante and Petrarch in their Latin writings had failed to measure up to the classical standards. And though there was now Bruni's reappraising biography, in addition to Boccaccio's *Vita di Dante*, the most highly cultivated men, says Manetti, would not read Bruni's work because it was written in Volgare. Manetti, therefore, did two things: he clothed the newly formed notion of Dante in a Latin garb, that is, he wrote a Latin *Vita* which incorporated (almost literally in some places) Bruni's revaluation of Dante the Florentine citizen and Volgare writer; [23] and he took pains to meet the classicists' objections by emphasizing the historical parallel that Dante had cultivated and ennobled the Volgare in the same way in which Homer and Virgil had cultivated and ennobled Greek and Latin.[24]

By the middle of the 1460's, when Benedetto Accolti was serving as Bruni's third successor in the chancellor's office, decisive strides had been made toward the recognition of the Volgare as a third literary language raised to this rank by Dante. This is indicated by Accolti in his *Dialogue on the Preeminence of the Men of His Age*,[25] the first systematic defense of the modern age and especially modern Florence against the classicists' overestimation of antiquity. There were by this time "many" in Florence, he tells us, who wondered whether they should think in terms of a single language as a medium for rhetorical expression, or whether there might be two.[26]

Coluccio Salutati, half a century before, had not dared in his most glowing praises of Dante to contend more than that Dante would have been equal or even superior to Homer and Virgil "if he had been able to write poetry in Latin with the same grace as he wrote in his mother-tongue"—a verdict still repeated by Poggio at the Curia in 1440, and even by Palmieri.[27] In the eyes of Benedetto Accolti, Dante and Petrarch could be considered equal with the ancients by their attainments in Volgare. Accolti freely admitted that in their Latin works they had not equalled the classical models, but that did not lessen their stature. In fact, it was a further merit of Volgare writers that they had achieved something creditable, though not perfect, even outside their mother tongue. Accolti's judgment of the eloquence of his own age illustrates how he made use of these changed standards in practice. It does not matter, he says, whether an orator employs Latin or the Volgare; what does matter is whether or not his performance shows beauty and dignity.[28a] Compared with Salutati's views, these words reveal a profound change of climate in humanistic opinion—the change initiated by Bruni's statement in 1436.

Three well-known names in particular—Leon Battista Alberti, Lorenzo de' Medici, and Cristoforo Landino—may stand for the phases through which Bruni's open-minded notion of the equal right of every language developed into a humanistic theory capable of justifying and encouraging the rise of a new Florentine literature in the vernacular.

The first step was taken by Leon Battista Alberti in his *Della Famiglia*. This was a work of the type of Palmieri's *Della Vita Civile*, written roughly at the same time (1433-34), before the author, a descendant of an exiled Florentine family, had ever been in Florence. After his arrival in the city in 1434 for an extensive stay, not only did the language of his work have to be profoundly remolded to conform with the living usage of the Florentine vernacular, but Alberti's outlook became intensely influenced by the currents and cross-currents of Florentine cultural life. We know from other works of Alberti, especially the dedication letter to his treatise *On Painting*, that the creative atmosphere of the life on the Arno now caused his confidence in contemporary Florence to shake his classicistic prejudices. While far from Florence (so he said), he had believed the many people who affirmed that Nature had grown old and tired since the days of the unique achievements of the ancients. In experiencing life in his ancestral city, however, he realized "that talents, sufficient for any worthy task, are still alive in many men" and that in artists like Brunelleschi, Donatello, and Masaccio the contemporary world had "talents that cannot be valued less than those of the famous ancients." [28b]

In regard to the quarrel about the relationship of the Florentine vernacular to the ancient Roman language, one notes that Alberti, after watching the controversy between Bruni and Biondo in 1435-36, prefixed a defense of the Volgare to the third book of the *Della Famiglia*.[28c] He there first stakes out his ground by consenting to Biondo's denial of the existence of two idioms in Rome, and reiterating Biondo's assertion that the Volgare had originated from barbaric contamination of the noble language of Rome in the days of the Gauls, Goths, Vandals, and Lombards.[29] But once he has accepted this much, he quite surprisingly makes a fresh start and, like Bruni in his Dante biography, builds his chief argument on the historical analogy of the Latin and the Volgare as languages entitled to equal rank and function, each in its time. In the interpretation of this Florentine humanist, Biondo's assumptions on the universality of the Latin language in ancient Rome mean that Roman men of letters had written not in the esoteric language of a privileged few, but "in a manner which they intended to be understood as clearly as possible by all their people." Was it not in order that a present-day humanist also wished to write in the language intelligible to all in his time? True, "the ancient Latin language was very rich and most ornate," but this did not mean that "our Tuscan language of today" (*la nostra oggi toscana* [*lingua*]) did not offer a medium potentially as serviceable to distinguished minds as the ancient language, if they would only avail themselves of it. The authority of the Latin idiom had been accepted throughout the world because of its use by many outstanding intellects; "surely our own language will become similar [to the Latin idiom] if only our learned men will make every effort to refine and polish it by their studies and labors." [30] This was Alberti's answer to the charge brought against him and from which his work long had to suffer as did the work of Palmieri: that he had dared to profane treasures reserved for the educated few.[31]

We find a parallel to Alberti's interpretation of Biondo's theory in the opinion of the contemporaneous author of the earliest known Italian grammar, the *Regole della Lingua Fiorentina*. Its preface argues against the assumption that a well organized language like Latin was not spoken by everyone in ancient Rome but, then as now, was intelligible merely to a few scholars. Those who hold this view, the author of the *Regole* suggests, will abandon their error when they realize that today's popular language, the Volgare, lends itself to treatment in grammars of the kind composed in antiquity by the grammarians of Greek and Latin. In other words, for the author of the *Regole*, the Volgare reflected something of the rationality of Latin and, as a result, partook of Latin excellence. Whether or not Alberti himself was the writer of this grammar (an ascription debated ever since and recently shown to be almost certain), the author must have belonged to the Florentine group influenced by Alberti, and thus we find that the first attempt at a systematic study of the Italian vernacular by a humanist takes us again to the civic world of mid-Quattrocento Florence. When Pietro Bembo, in Rome and Venice, during the first quarter of the sixteenth century finally laid down the rules of the Volgare, he accompanied his work with the same claim—that the Volgare should stand as a literary language of equal right beside Latin, just as Latin had stood beside Greek, and that it was capable of equal refinement and discipline. Essentially, this was the climax of the efforts that had started in the days of Alberti and his Florentine friends.[32]

Whereas for Florentine historiography and political philosophy the era of Lorenzo de' Medici, with its restriction of civic liberty and vitality, must be considered a period of decline, the fusion of Humanism with the Volgare tradition proceeded undisturbed during the second half of the Quattrocento in Florence and even reached its consummation in Lorenzo's circle. Next to Poliziano, the statesman-poet Lorenzo enhanced the growing confidence in the Florentine idiom by his own example and defended it not only as a poet, but with arguments that supported the parallel between Florence and Rome with considerations taken from the political sphere. In the commentary that accompanies Lorenzo's collected sonnets, after 1476,[33] the claim is made that Latin, like any other tongue, had originally been the language of one single city or province. Its rise to the position of a universal language was not due to its superiority (the Greek language had been greater), but because "the expansion of the Roman empire not only made the Roman language known throughout the world, but also made its adoption almost inevitable." [34] Since the beginning of civic Humanism, the Florentine philosophy of history had been intent on interpreting the growth of Rome as a natural phenomenon which could find parallels in the growth of other nations; now the same notion was applied to the relationship between the Roman and the Florentine languages. All the great literary languages, Lorenzo argues, the Hebrew, the Greek, and the Latin, had been "spoken languages and vernaculars" in their first stages.[35] Consequently, a Florentine had a good right to see his own tongue in the same light, and to entertain similar hopes for it. The splendid attainments of the Volgare in the Trecento had been mere beginnings; they had proved that the Florentine vernacular could be adapted to every need. Since then it had reached its "adolescence" and was approaching its "youth and adulthood," which might be aided by the growth of the Florentine regional state (by *"qualche prospero successo ed augmento al fiorentino imperio"*). There was reasonable hope, therefore, that the Florentine language would eventually emerge as a competitor on an equal footing with the ancient languages.[36]

In Cristoforo Landino, Lorenzo's age possessed a humanistic scholar who was to create a synthesis of lasting renown between these Florentine claims and the dominant classicism of the century. In phrases almost identical with those once used by the champions of the older Volgare school in the days of Cino Rinuccini and Giovanni da Prato, Landino pointed out that Dante had demonstrated the aptitude of the Florentine idiom for the expression and discussion of any intellectual subject whatever; and he drew an historical parallel, just as the citizen-humanist Giannozzo Manetti had done, to the effect that Dante had accomplished as much, if not more, for the Volgare as Homer had accomplished for Greek and Virgil for Latin.[37] Landino succeeded in bringing these tenets of the older Florentine school into harmony with the classicistic doctrine. In his lectures at the Florentine university, and in his celebrated commentary on the *Divina Commedia*,[38] he taught that Dante had been equipped for his great work by his study of the ancients. Not until the poet had become intimately familiar with Latin poetry and eloquence and was capable of introducing the achievements of earlier ages into the Florentine language, did he develop into the finished artist of the *Commedia*. Similarly, all later accomplished writers in Volgare, from Petrarch, Boccaccio, and Bruni to Palmieri, Alberti, and Lorenzo de' Medici, were at the same time proficient in Latin studies.[39] There is, therefore, no conflict between the Latin and the vernacular studies: the humanistic cultivation of Latin is needed in the very interest of the Volgare. Just as Latin grew rich by incorporating the attainments of Greek, so the Volgare, by embodying Latin teachings, will grow even richer. The Athens of Demosthenes and the Rome of Cicero will be followed by a third flowering of letters in a free republic where civic eloquence is trained in a native tongue.[40] "Let no one believe that he could express himself eloquently, nay even tolerably, in Volgare without previous genuine and perfect familiarity with Latin letters." [41] The watchword now is: "Whoever wants to be a good Tuscan, must necessarily be a good Latin." [42]

With these ideas of the later Florentine Quattrocento in mind, we can now finally discern the historical significance of the struggle between Humanism and the Volgare school at the dawn of the century. Even in the time of Lorenzo, literary practice and theory were certainly in a phase of classicism; but it was a new type of classicism, essentially different from the extremism which about 1400 had repudiated every interest in Florentine history and Florentine language on the ground that the one thing which counted and was worthy of being remembered was antiquity. The classicism which had gradually emerged by the end of the Quattrocento was a synthesis of originally opposing trends; it was a prototype of the relationship to antiquity known in the sixteenth and seventeenth centuries in many Western countries, until, on a larger scale and with even more momentous consequences for the modern mind, it reached its final phase in France in the age of Louis XIV. In all these various developments we ultimately find a humanistic classicism willing to employ the ancient model as a guide in building a new literature with a new language in a new nation. [43]

Part Five

THE AFTERMATH OF THE CRISIS

CHAPTER 16

CITY-STATE LIBERTY VERSUS
UNIFYING TYRANNY

The Experience of the Giangaleazzo Period—
a Recurrent Pattern

THERE is one aspect of our history of the early Quattrocento crisis which more than any other compels us to cast a glance at the subsequent development. The period when Florence in her struggle with Giangaleazzo Visconti defended civic freedom and finally remained the only antagonist to the threat of despotism, was but a fleeting episode in the development of the Italian Renaissance: no more than five years, or even no more than those few hectic summer months of the decisive year 1402. The reader may often have wondered why an experience cut so short by Giangaleazzo's sudden death should have determined the feelings and thoughts of several subsequent generations.

The answer is that the political situation, in which the genesis of Quattrocento Humanism had taken place during Giangaleazzo's life, was changed only temporarily by his death. Events at the turn of the century had wrought an irrevocable transformation in the inter-state relations of the Peninsula. Even when Giangaleazzo's commanding figure had disappeared from the scene, the deadly threat to the independence of the Italian city-republics and minor tyrannies by the expanding imperialism of the strongest principality arose again and again, with many of the scenes and situations of the Giangaleazzo period repeating themselves even though the players had changed; and the effects were felt from the 1410's and 1420's into the middle of the Quattrocento. The days, indeed, had passed when small states could defend their independence in isolation. Soon Giangaleazzo's place was taken by other powerful princes on the Peninsula: first by the ruler of the south-Italian kingdom, and afterwards by Giangaleazzo's son and successor. The memory of the Giangaleazzo era remained alive because Florence's inescapable involvement in the power-relations of the Peninsula, in the ever-extending interplay which Gregorio Dati was the first to demonstrate in an historical work, had become an experience which was repeated every day.

The cataclysmic events, which, within four or five years, had swiftly wiped out every independent state between Rome and Milan with the exception of Florence, and in 1402 for a while had left the Florentine Republic the only opponent to despotic Monarchy in Italy, did not repeat themselves. But the calmer days that had preceded the stormy time of Giangaleazzo's expansion—the days when each region of Italy was relatively free to attend to its own affairs—were also gone. Again and again Florence found herself called upon to defend the fruits of her past struggle. Now trying to stir up all dormant elements of resistance in Italy, now acting within coalitions, she was for decades to remain the barrier against successive threats of new monarchical expansion.

What was characteristic of the first half of the Quattrocento, therefore, was not yet a definite new order of interstate relations in Italy, but the constant reappearance of a situation of deadly peril to every independent state, and of Florentine leadership in response to this challenge—a response which at first often took the form of a slow reaction after bitter quarrels within a house divided against itself, but ultimately stirred up emotions strong enough to allow the ideas of 1397 and 1402 to reach their full elaboration.

In order to understand fully the scope of the turn-of-the-century crisis, we must be aware of the psychological forces kept alive by such recurrent situations of danger. Too little is usually said in our histories of the early Renaissance about the impact of these challenges on the growth of the humanistic mind. So, in the last part of our investigations, we must return to the political transformations in Florence and Italy which had stirred up so many new energies in the time of the intellectual crisis.[1a]

The 1410's: King Ladislaus of Naples in the Role of Giangaleazzo Visconti

How did it happen that the ambitious program of the Visconti, the outgrowth of a century of north-Italian development, was, soon after Giangaleazzo's death, for a while taken over by a south-Italian prince?

Giangaleazzo had dealt a death-blow to medieval localism in three great sections of north and central Italy which afterwards developed into region-states. When the Visconti empire was dissolved, Venice began to occupy the north-eastern states that were now accustomed to foreign rule—events which will require our attention later. Florence pursued the same policy in parts of Tuscany. In 1405-06 her growing territorial state, in a cruel sequel to the wars with Giangaleazzo, incorporated the city of Pisa, master of the mouth of the Arno. By its partisanship for Giangaleazzo, Pisa had almost sealed Florence's fate in the past struggle [1b] and had again endangered Florence in 1404 when the Pisan *signore*, a bastard son of Giangaleazzo, ceded his rights to the port of Leghorn and the sovereignty over Pisa to France. There were conditions inviting similar developments in the northern parts of the Papal State. Bologna in Emilia, Perugia and Assisi in Umbria, and many towns of local preeminence in both provinces now were republics whose independence had already once been forfeited; they all were easier victims than ever before to a potential centralizing power.

During the second half of the Trecento, in the time of the war of the Eight Saints, the power decreed by fate to accomplish unification among the minor lords and cities under the dominion of the Church had seemed to be the Papal See itself. But after the return of the Popes from Avignon to Rome the Schism had blunted the edge of the Papal might and made the scale of the Papacy sink so low that at a certain point the Papal suzerainty even over the Neapolitan Kingdom, one of the pivots of the political order of Italy since the fall of the Hohenstaufen, was in danger of being replaced by the supremacy of the crown of Naples over the Papal State. If this had happened, the long, patient efforts of the Popes to rebuild their authority in the central-Italian region from Rome to Bologna would only have led the way to an Italian Monarchy ruled by the former Papal vassal in the South.

That hour seemed to have come during the period which followed the disintegration of Giangaleazzo's empire.[2] When King Ladislaus of Naples, in 1408, received the homage of the city of Rome and her territory, the whole dominion of the Church seemed about to fall under his rule. Before the year 1408 came to an end, all Umbria, including Perugia, Assisi, and many places in the other northern Papal provinces were under Neapolitan sway. In the following year, Gregory XII ceded the administration of the Papal State to the King in a formal pact. By the spring of 1409 Cortona, southern outpost of Tuscany, was in Ladislaus' hands; his troops were stationed near Arezzo and Siena. What finally stopped the King in his

advance to the north was a league concluded between
Florence and Siena for the mutual protection of their
territories—a league which included Ladislaus' Papal and
Neapolitan adversaries and was capable of becoming the
center around which resistance to Neapolitan expansion
might rally.[3]

One effect of these rapid and unexpected events was that
Florence once more found herself a member in a Tuscan
alliance standing for republican freedom. In the latter
part of the Trecento, Florence had as a rule been the head
of Tuscan city-leagues, and the prevailing sentiment had
been one of kinship and common pride in the preservation of civic liberty in Tuscany while tyranny was engulfing the remainder of central and northern Italy.[4]
The affiliation of Pisa and Siena with Milan during Giangaleazzo's lifetime, and the destruction of Pisa's independence after his death, had threatened to poison future rela-
tionships between Florence and the surviving Tuscan city-
states. With the Florentine-Sienese pact against the Neapolitan danger the alliance between these two cities, and
thus the friendship between northern and southern Tuscany, was restored.

We have persuasive evidence of how political cooperation between the two republics immediately produced a
new solidarity in political outlook and sentiment. In 1413-
14, the *palazzo pubblico* in Siena was decorated with
frescoes depicting the virtues needed in a commonwealth,
each painting surrounded by portraits of, and Latin epigrams on, ancient Roman "famous men" representing
these virtues. Such fresco series of Roman statesmen and
generals had become fashionable since the Carrara had
set an example in their palace at Padua during the last
years of Petrarch, who helped in the selection and supplied
the Latin inscriptions for the Paduan *"Sala virorum illustrium."* The Sienese plan of 1413, however, was dif-

ferent from all other contemporary designs because the others join portraits of Caesar and some of the emperors to those of the heroes of the *Respublica Romana,* whereas at Siena we are suddenly face to face with the republican view of history that had emerged among the Florentines during the era of Giangaleazzo. In the Siena portrait cycle, just as in Bruni's writings, history teaches that Rome had been great under the freedom of the republic and was ruined when personal ambition was directed toward a throne. Pompey and Caesar appear, but not as symbols of virtue; their figures stand apart from the other portraits, above an epigram which says that when "blind ambition had made these two men take recourse to arms, the end had come for Roman liberty" (*ambitio sed ceca duos ubi traxit ad arma, / Libertas romana perit . . .*). The cycle of heroes runs from Brutus the regicide to Brutus the murderer of Caesar, who stands nearest to the virtue of Fortitude, sharing distinction of place with Cato, "who chose death in order not to live under a lord," and Cicero, who for "sweet liberty" died as *"pater patriae."* Here, then, we see the new views of Florentine Humanism spreading to Florence's allies under the stimulus of a united stand against the king of Naples, as has been argued by the scholar who was the first to disclose this interplay of art and political sentiment. "From now onwards, the use of Roman republican heroes remained a permanent feature of Sienese civic art"; through all the vicissitudes of Siena's constitutional development, down to the sixteenth century, "the spell of the Roman republic survived." [5a]

Neither should we underrate the importance which the return of the principal city of southern Tuscany to the republican camp had for the political climate of Florence. A strong community of outlook between northern and southern Tuscany was to remain an established fact with few interruptions to the end of the Renaissance. Without this *rapprochement* it would have been impossible for Machiavelli, a century afterwards, to rely for his general estimate of the Italian situation on the belief that all Tuscany, in contrast to Lombardy with its need for tyrannical rule, had always been and would always remain a region of civic equality, fit for the republican way of life.*

* The fact that the nearly one hundred and fifty years between the rapprochement of the year 1409 and the end of Siena's independence saw periods of conflict, and even moments of armed clashes, between Siena and Florence, must not distract our attention from this general perspective. In the first half of the Quattrocento, the reestablished friendship of the two Tuscan republics was disturbed only during Florence's attack on Lucca in the early 1430's, when Siena became fearful of her stronger neighbor and aided Lucca; but from 1433 to 1447 Siena was again in alliance with Florence against Filippo Maria Visconti. After 1447, during the period of drastically shifting inter-state relations out of which the equilibrium system of the late Renaissance arose, Siena stood for a while with Venice and Alfonso of Naples against Florence; but when the peace of Lodi in 1454 made reconciliation possible, she joined the *"Santissima Lega"* so quickly that Alfonso was full of indignation with his short-term Sienese ally. Between 1478 and 1480, when after the conspiracy of the Pazzi Florence's Italian position and Lorenzo de' Medici's authority were in jeopardy, there was another outburst of Sienese-Florentine rivalry, and Siena became once more a diplomatic and military ally of Naples. But from 1480 on, both in the periods when Siena enjoyed full republican freedom, and during the decades when she was under the lordship of Pandolfo Petrucci, the relationship between the two major states of Northern and Southern Tuscany was continually one of friendship and mutual cooperation, even though the normal amity was now and then disturbed by dissensions, misunderstandings, and even by secret deals with other Italian states, made for the purpose of exerting pressure. As Machiavelli, after 1515, described the outcome, contrasting Lombardy and Naples, regions accustomed to obeying a despot, with Tuscany which still refused to tolerate anything but a

Another effect of the steadily increasing expansion of the Neapolitan Kingdom was that Florence, as a member of the league against Ladislaus, soon experienced a resurgence of the conviction that the fate of liberty in Italy was a question of active resistance to the growth of the strongest monarchy before it had attained irresistible power. This renewal of the sentiments of the Giangaleazzo period had to be forced upon a reluctant Florence. At first, when the danger from outside had vanished because of Giangaleazzo's death, the recent struggle had not seemed to the Florentines to be the prelude to a new phase in Italian inter-state relations but rather a nightmare that was over and done with, the terrors of which would quickly be compensated for by an era of unparalleled prosperity, especially after the capture of Pisa with its vital ports in 1405-06. The disintegrating state of the Visconti was left to itself; Florence showed no interest in the restoration of independence to the north-Italian states which had been under Giangaleazzo's yoke.

The hopes and longings which then filled the minds of the Florentines are evident in Gregorio Dati's contemporary political analysis of the postwar period. Florence, we are told, was amazed and elated to find that, after decades of wars and great sacrifice which during the long siege of

---

free life: "in the territory of Tuscany, small as it is, one finds that there have long been three republics, Florence, Siena, and Lucca; and that the other cities of this province, though in a way servile, yet are of such a mind and have such a constitution that either they maintain their freedom, or would like to do so" (*Discorsi*, I 17 and 55). During the 1550's, when the hour had come in which the Medici, who had been made Dukes of Florence with the help of Spain, decided also to include Siena in their Grand-duchy of Tuscany, the last Florentine republicans, like Donato Giannotti and Bartolommeo Cavalcanti, looked on the defense of Siena's liberty as their own cause and aided Siena's last fight by their advice and active cooperation.

Pisa in the end had led the city nearly to bankruptcy,[5b] everybody was richer than before. In particular, all real estate values soared; according to Dati's estimate, Florentine wealth was increased by one quarter. Something like an economic philosophy of boom and boundless confidence in a new era of peace developed. As long as the tyrant of Lombardy had lived and Pisa had been an inimical neighbor, Dati wrote before 1410, there had always been a suspicion that the Florentine possessions might be lost through a new war. "Now that he [the Lombard tyrant] is dead, his party ruined for ever, Pisa in Florence's possession, and the Florentines are sure that there cannot be war again, every property is safe and . . . [the Florentines] are going to be wealthier than ever before." Florence was on the threshold of a golden age—provided that the Florentines, now "that there is no longer a danger of war being waged against them, do not embark on war against others." [5c]

With this firm faith in Florence's stake in peace, and tired from the greatest wars the city had ever waged, Florence not only cared little what happened north of the Apennines but was bent on doing everything to come to peaceful terms with the new conqueror from the South. Even after the conclusion of the Florentine-Sienese league in 1409 Florence was only half-heartedly back in the fight and seized the first opportunity to restore peace through compromise. This opportunity came in 1411 when Ladislaus, in order to break up the anti-Neapolitan alliance, offered in return for a sum of money to cede to Florence the most disquieting part of his conquests in Giangaleazzo's former empire, Cortona, the bastion of southern Tuscany.

But it was just these fluctuations and enticements of Neapolitan diplomacy which revived the memory of the Giangaleazzo period. While the members of one faction continued to favor association with Naples to the point where Leonardo Bruni could consider them Neapolitan partisans [6]—among the Florentine *literati* we find such partisanship in Niccoli who showed himself an enthusiastic admirer of the King [7]—in another group of the citizenry suspicion spread that the conqueror was making compromises in order to eliminate Florence's potential allies one by one, and so to pave the way for a Peninsular Monarchy.

That Ladislaus' designs amounted to this ambitious scheme has been doubted by recent scholars.[8] But many of his contemporaries at least had no doubt about the ultimate design of the Neapolitan King. Whether we interpret his actions as offensive or as defensive, he had placed Rome in a position little better than that of a town in his southern kingdom; he had absorbed Perugia and many smaller places in the North, in fact, everything up to the Sienese and Florentine borders; Florence—just as in Giangaleazzo's day, though this time she was associated with the Sienese South of Tuscany—remained the only obstacle to a Monarchy spanning two thirds of the Peninsula. As we learn from the Florentine chroniclers, it was soon the common feeling—a feeling perhaps in part influenced by the memory of the similar sequence of events in the time of Giangaleazzo—that Ladislaus' words deserved no confidence because "his mind was absolutely set on engulfing our liberty." The words *"a Firenze, a Firenze,"* we are told, were the King's war-cry in those years; he promised his soldiers that he would make them rich by the "sack" of Florence; "he wore insignia on which one read: '*o Ciesar, o nichil,*' he desired the Empire." [9] The statement of such a humanist-statesman as Lorenzo de' Benvenuti that Ladislaus was threatening the "freedom of all Italy," and "plotting to bring all Italy into serfdom," assures us that even Florentine officials who must have had a first-hand knowledge of the situation were then convinced of the seriousness of the danger.[10] That the fears of Florence were the hopes of the Neapolitan camp is attested by the fact that two of Giangaleazzo's best known propagandists, who had praised the Milanese Lord as the presumptive unifier of Italy—Antonio Loschi and Saviozzo da Siena—now eulogized the King of Naples as the man of destiny for the unification of Italy.[11]

Many incidents in 1413 and 1414 seemed to duplicate the course of events of Giangaleazzo's last years. In 1413, the King of Naples suddenly resumed his drive from the point where he had paused in 1409 under the impact of the Florentine-Sienese alliance. The last sparks of the autonomy of the city of Rome were finally extinguished; the Papal city was stormed and brutally pillaged by Neapolitan troops. Immediately afterwards the King with his victorious army marched to the north. In the spring of 1414 he had his headquarters in the heart of Umbria, near Perugia, and, though still trying to avoid open conflict with Florence, was poised to cross the Apennines and occupy Bologna. In the wars against Giangaleazzo, Bologna had been the last door whose closing shut Florence off from the outer world. The conquest of Bologna by a potential enemy who was in possession of Umbria, Rome, and Naples, and thereby of the vital roads connecting the northern and southern parts of the Peninsula, would have almost encircled Florence once again, except for her now assured access to the western sea.

At this point the smoldering conflict between those who wished to appease the Neapolitan conqueror and the elements who had been at the helm of the state when Florence was fighting the Milanese tyrant, burst into flames. A strong group within the city-councils still insisted on peace at any price. Their thesis was that war always produces incalculable danger and economic disaster; that republics can bide their time since the power of monarchies comes to an end with the death of their rulers. This attitude shows one of the possible effects of Florence's deliverance by the enemy's death in 1402. But the conviction of the very men to whom Florence's perseverance against Giangaleazzo had been due was (in the words of a judicious and cautious old statesman such as Niccolò da Uzzano) that "for the protection of our liberty we must shoulder anything." Gino Capponi, the soul and leader of the past enterprise against Pisa, then uttered the often quoted words "better would it be to live under the rule of the Ciompi [that is, the laborers of the woolen industry, who had ruled Florence in the revolution of 1378] than under the tyranny of the King." He felt sure of Ladislaus' unreliability; while listening to pretenses of peace, Florence was losing her natural allies. One should strive for peace, but only peace "with security and honesty. . . . Peace is the counsel of all traitors." [12]

What peace with security meant was outlined by one of the citizens who had been in office during the desperate resistance in 1402, Filippo de' Corsini. The only peace acceptable to Florence, he said, would be one which would assure the independence of Bologna and Siena along with that of Florence—an independence to be guaranteed by Venice and the Pope.[13] Thus the two key-ideas of the Giangaleazzo period came back to life: Florence's interest in the survival of other independent city-republics in central Italy, and the awareness of the need for inter-regional cooperation among Tuscany, the Venetian Northeast, and the Papal State, if the rise of an all-inclusive monarchy in the northern parts of the Peninsula was to be avoided.

To what extent the determination of the Giangaleazzo period had reemerged became apparent when this goal was only partially attained. When Agnolo Pandolfini, head of the peace party, returned from a special mission to Naples with the draft of a pact in which Ladislaus promised to give up his recent designs on Bologna and agreed to admit Bologna and Siena as sovereign partners in a friendship treaty, provided Florence recognized his other conquests, the general distrust of any new concession was so deep and genuine that the Council of the Two Hundred refused ratification of the drafted peace no less than twenty-five times; its acceptance was finally more or less enforced by the responsible men in office.[14] Capponi, fearful that in the wake of the proposed concessions Bologna might be lost and the ring around Florence be closed again, intimated that Pandolfini should be impeached for having exceeded his authority.[15]

The wholly unexpected death of the King of Naples only two months later, in August 1414, suddenly made this passionate discussion and revolt seem like much ado about nothing. Death, once again, cut through the knot before the ultimate decision had been reached. But if, for this reason, the events connected with King Ladislaus appear as relatively unimportant in the long-range political development of the Renaissance, we must emphasize their significance for their momentous psychological effect. The hopes and fears and political ideas of the Giangaleazzo period had been rekindled before their memory had faded from the Florentine mind. When Leonardo Bruni in his memoirs, the *Rerum Suo Tempore Gestarum Commentarius*, comes to these events, he gives no indication that the situation which developed in 1413-14 appeared to him essentially different from the Florentine predicament during the perils around 1400; he describes both moments in almost the same terms. The King of Naples was so formidable and so dominated Italy, he says, that "no hope for resistance could be seen." It was merely his premature death which "delivered the Florentines and the other free city-states from their grave suspicions and from the most evident and certain danger; for as long as he lived, there were no ways of escape that did not end in the need to submit." [16]

It was in 1415, immediately after the end of the Ladislaus episode, that Bruni returned from the Curia to settle down in Florence as a citizen and take up the labors on his *History of the Florentine People.* According to the preface, written before the international situation changed again, he had begun work under the impress of Florence's ascendency to the position of an Italian power; a position to which the city had attained, he said, by meeting the twofold threat from Giangaleazzo and from Ladislaus, and by rounding out her territorial state with the occupation of Pisa. To Bruni, the triumphs over Giangaleazzo, Pisa, and Ladislaus were three stages of one continuous development in which Florence had grown from a local city-republic into a consolidated state whose field of action extended "from the Alps to Apulia through the whole length of Italy" and included diplomatic intercourse with the north-Alpine countries. His courage to undertake his bold and novel task sprang from the proud persuasion that Florence "in our time" had reached the point where Rome had stood after her victory over Carthage. [17]

We may say then: The plan of the *Historiae Florentini Populi,* and the historical outlook of its great first book, owed their origin to the experience of the Giangaleazzo period seen through eyes that had been sharpened by the repetition of almost the same cycle of political events in the time of Ladislaus of Naples.

The 1420's: Filippo Maria Visconti and the Renewal of the Milanese Challenge

Thus the new pattern of Italian politics had been rehearsed when, only a few years later, tyrannical expansion once more threatened from the North, the seat of the Visconti.

By the end of the second decade of the Quattrocento, the State of Milan had recovered from the decline into which it had fallen after Giangaleazzo's death; its reconstruction was nearing completion at the hands of the last of the great empire-builders in northern Italy, Filippo Maria Visconti. About 1420, Milan had reached the stage where any further expansion was bound to be a step along the road that once had led Giangaleazzo to supremacy in Italy. Was Florence again to allow the Visconti power to grow beyond control? At this point, to give assurance of his limited intents, Filippo Maria offered the demarcation of the respective spheres of interest in a formal treaty such as Florence had tried in vain to obtain from his father. If Florence would give him a free hand north of the line she had proposed to Giangaleazzo in the 1380's and 1390's (a line which, in the west, ran roughly north of the crest of the Apennines, and in the east left Bologna and the Papal Romagna to the south outside of the Viscontean sphere), the Duke promised to refrain from any interference in the Romagna or in Tuscany.[18]

Was this offer anything more than the device, now well established, of concentrating expansion in one sector, in order to turn upon the rest later with redoubled might? The group of Florentine statesmen who had frowned upon compromising with Giangaleazzo, and who had warned against the pact with Ladislaus, now warned against leaving at the mercy of Filippo Maria the smaller states of northern Italy which were already calling for aid—the potential allies of Florence in case of a new Milanese attack. Gino Capponi seems to have foretold exactly what afterwards happened: that Filippo Maria would use the assurance of a sphere free of Florentine intervention to seize Genoa and Brescia, the two remaining bastions in the

west and east of Lombardy, only to come forward with a
greater demand once he was in possession of them.[19] But
although Capponi was seconded by Niccolò da Uzzano,[20]
the Duke's offer was in the end accepted; too deeply in-
grained was the profound aversion to a new entanglement
which would automatically have put an end to the prosperity that appeared to be the well-earned reward of
Florence's resistance to Giangaleazzo.

Having obtained a free hand in northwestern Italy,
Filippo Maria immediately seized Parma and Brescia and
then threw himself upon the Republic of Genoa. There
were at once protests in Florence insisting that such unrestricted aggression had never been sanctioned by the
Florentine promise of disinterest in the northern parts.
But the government, resolved upon the preservation of
peace, believed that diplomatic skill could beat Milanese
diplomacy at its own game. Surprisingly, in 1421, Florence purchased the port of Leghorn, the one place of
outstanding importance on the Tuscan coast that was
in Genoese possession. This deal was thought to remove
the threat of a Milanese foothold on Florence's seaboard
in case Genoa with her dependencies should be incorporated
in the new Visconti State. At the same time the money paid
in the bargain would strengthen Genoa's power to resist,
while Florence lived up to the letter of her obligations
and did not interfere in the affairs of northwestern Italy.
But before long it turned out that diplomatic feats were
of little avail against an avalanche of military might and
dynamic propaganda. So well prepared was the Milanese
enterprise and so effective was Milanese propaganda in
persuading Genoa she would gain immense material advantages by becoming the port of the Viscontean State,
that the Genoese people forced their Doge, who had been
the soul of the resistance and of the secret arrangements
with Florence, to abdicate his office. Repeating the ex-

ample of so many cities in the time of Giangaleazzo, Genoa with all her dependencies except Leghorn was included in the Visconti State by negotiation.[21]

The annexation of Genoa had been preceded and was followed by the occupation of large parts of the Po valley in a general movement toward the east that soon went beyond the demarcation line. When the *signore* of Forlì, a city of the Romagna lying south of the line and controlling one of the main roads across the Apennines, died in 1423, the Milanese government came forward with the claim that he had asked Filippo Maria to act as tutor for his son. Just as previously in Genoa, a revolt arose among the people in the crucial hour. Milanese troops, stationed in the neighborhood beforehand, restored order, and never left Forlì again.

From this moment on, the sentiments known to us from the end of the Giangaleazzo period begin to tinge every word and every thought in Florence. For a short while the group which had adhered to a strict appeasement policy toward Ladislaus, and which was still led by Agnolo Pandolfini and now seconded by Giovanni de' Medici, made a last desperate attempt to prevail; but it no longer found support among the citizenry. It is well that the voices of the opposition have been preserved; for only against this background can the significance of the rising anti-Viscontean and republican civic temper be fully understood. The Duke, Pandolfini admitted, had broken his word; but if peace was preserved, he argued, the Duke might change his plans, or his expansion might have repercussions in the south-Italian kingdom, the rival power. In any event Forlì did not belong to Florence; there was no reason to go to war because of what was happening in the Papal Romagna. "Even if it is true that the Duke occupied Forlì, he did not take it from us; also, we can defend ourselves in that direction by means of foot-soldiers." [22] On this last point, the majority of the Florentine citizens had begun to judge otherwise. When Giangaleazzo had occupied Bologna and other Romagna towns, Florence had no longer been able to defend herself. To think in terms of peninsular interdependence, to realize that Florence's existence was of necessity bound up with the preservation of independence in other Italian regions— this was the lesson gradually learned by early Quattrocento Italy. The almost unanimous rejection of Pandolfini's arguments [23] is proof that by the early 1420's this lesson had been assimilated by the majority of Florentine citizens.

Machiavelli in his *Discorsi* later judged that Filippo Maria, who had counted on the dissensions in Florence, had lost the fruits of his grand enterprise because, as he learned, war always made the Florentines unite.[24] There is in fact only one mood expressed in the Florentine documents from that moment on: a constant recollection of the experiences of the Giangaleazzo period, and faith in the mission of the Florentine Commonwealth to prevent the final victory of the Visconti. In meetings during May 1423, in which the appointment of *Dieci di Balìa* was proposed (of "Ten of War" with dictatorial powers, whose nomination was equivalent to Florence's mobilization), two leaders of the ruling group, Niccolò da Uzzano and Rinaldo degli Albizzi, took the floor. Up to now, said Rinaldo, public opinion in Italy (*opinio Italicorum*) had been that the Florentine government would never act, whatever the developments might be. "Seeing this disposition of Florence," the Duke of Milan had dared to seize Forlì, transgressing beyond the agreed demarcation line. Now that things had come to such a pass, Florence's reaction must "be readiness to risk all of our resources." [25] Side by side with this call for a reversal of the character of Florentine policy, we find Niccolò da Uzzano's warning that the pattern of Milanese policies should be learned from the events of the Giangaleazzo period: "We have witnessed the procedure of the father and the forefathers of this prince. His father's policy was to acquire sway over Lombardy before moving against us. . . . The people here assembled in free consultation will save our liberty by courageous action. . . . Help has always been found in taking timely precautions"; therefore, Florence was to prepare for defense and nominate the *Dieci*.[26]

When, subsequently, the *Dieci* were elected "*con somma concordia e unità*," [27] and even more so when the next *Dieci* were elected five months later, the decrees of nomination circumscribed their task in neat words as the protection of Florentine liberty against a thrust of tyrannical subjection that had gone on for generations. The Ten Men were elected, the first statement ran, to prepare against "the crafty and vicious actions, full of fraud and cunning" devised by the tyrant of Milan; for his true ultimate aim was to crush the liberty of the Florentine people, "just as it always was the wish of all the ancestors of this hypocrite, who knows how to conceal his mind and intention with contradictory and deceitful words." [28] Five months later, the war-powers of the Board of Ten were renewed with the motivation that "the perfidious tyrant not only endeavours to subject Florence's freedom to his tyranny," but has also carried on unjust oppression elsewhere.[29] While the war preparations were gathering strength, the government sent ambassadors to Milan and to the Pope with instructions to declare that Florence was determined "to preserve that liberty which our fathers had bequeathed to us"; "and, as the evidence of our past history clearly shows, we shall persist in this determination for ever." [30]

Contemporaneous private letters show that this language was more than official rhetoric. In October of the same year, Rinaldo degli Albizzi, who at that time was in the camp of the Florentine troops as a military commissioner, exclaimed in a letter to an intimate friend at home that the Duke of Milan, looking at the inconsistencies of Florence's past policy, must feel that he was dealing with infants. Yet "reason and honesty" were with those whom Pandolfini was still trying to oppose. "And, therefore, you must keep up the firm hope that God will be with you. . . . I wish we were real men and would beat the Duke to the draw; it would be greater glory than the Romans ever gained." [31] "For no great and memorable deed," Rinaldo added *viva voce* in a *consulta* after his return to Florence, a few months later, "is done without danger." [32]

The last remark was made in a speech in which Rinaldo degli Albizzi, at a meeting of citizens invited by the government to give counsel, asked for Florentine military intervention in the Romagna. It was early in 1424, when events had come to a climax through Filippo Maria's seizure of Imola, another Romagna town, not far from Forlì. This time the unexpected occupation took place even while peace negotiations were going on at the Duke's own bidding. Thus Filippo Maria recklessly confirmed by his deeds what Florence had long claimed to be the method of tyrants. Open war against the Duke was preceded by a Florentine manifesto approved in all city-councils with overwhelming majorities. Here the Florentine view of the Italian situation was illuminated from yet another angle.[33] "Making a show of sweetly praising peace," the manifesto proclaimed, the Lord of Milan in 1420 had requested and received a settlement of the existing differences "from the Florentine people, pacific and tranquil by nature." [34] But to him the word of peace was merely a pretext for steady expansion: the occupation of Genoa, and of Forlì, Imola, and other Romagna towns. Florence, putting her case before all Italy, was determined not to allow "the hypocrite, who always calls for peace, under this disguise to prepare for major wars" and "in the name of peace to impose the yoke of servitude." [35] Following the example of her Roman ancestors, defenders of liberty against Pyrrhus, Hannibal, and many powerful kings, Florence had taken up arms, convinced now that only by force "could she procure for her people not the shadow, but the reality of peace"—a peace implying restoration of independence to the suppressed cities of the Romagna, and the reestablishment of the demarcation line of 1420.

"The Florentine people, pacific and tranquil by nature" —this passage in the manifesto throws light on one of the roots of the Florentine sentiment. As early as the time of the first encounter between the expansionist Visconti State and Florence in the mid-Trecento, Matteo Villani had observed in his chronicle that the citizens of a republic depended on prosperity and therefore on peace, while tyranny was a source of military aggression. In the same vein, Salutati in his *Invectiva* fought Loschi's accusation that Florence had been the aggressor in the war with Milan by the argument that those who ruled Florence were not guided by "innate ambition" (*ingenita ambitione*) as noblemen are, but by the "interests of trade" (*bonitate mercatoria*). "And since there can be no greater enemy to merchants than the tumult and confusion of war, and since nothing is more detrimental to commerce and industry, no one can doubt that the merchants and industrial men who have sway over the government of our Republic love peace and shrink from war." [36] When the crisis of the Giangaleazzo period had passed, Gregorio Dati found a key to the past events in this inherent peacefulness of a civic and commercial society. "The Florentines," he reasoned in some remarkable paragraphs of his *Istoria*, "live on peace, and profit by it as the bee profits by the honey of the flowers; they never resolve on war unless to gain

peace." "In Florence no occasion for war appears so just
and unavoidable that the people would not hurriedly turn
toward any argument for peace laid before them; it seems
that their nature is made for peace, and that war is something forced upon them." [37] This, it appeared to Dati,
became evident when the Florentines, who on Giangaleazzo's death were in an easy position to occupy whatever
they wished of the disintegrating Visconti State, left Giangaleazzo's north-Italian possessions untouched. "They
never wanted to acquire territory in Lombardy or [else-
where] beyond the Apennines; for they are content to live
within their boundaries and thus enjoy greater security
and quietude than they could by having possessions farther
away. And they have waged the past war . . . only to
the point where they could be sure that they would not be
attacked or intimidated again. When they saw that this
goal had been attained, they recalled their troops to
Tuscany and let the flames ablaze in Lombardy do their
work by themselves." [38]

These convictions came to the fore when Filippo Maria's
bid for supremacy made Florence painfully aware what
opportunity she had missed after Giangaleazzo's death. In
June 1423, Nanni degli Strozzi, one of the leading minds
in the then forming anti-Viscontean coalition, visited
Florence. Descended from a branch of the Strozzi family
which had been exiled from Florence in the preceding
generation, this scion of a Florentine merchant family had
become a *condottiere* and military leader at the court of
the Este of Ferrara who, since their federation with
Florence against Giangaleazzo's advance after 1388, had
been again and again among Florence's most faithful allies
and, next to Bologna and Florence herself, the heart of
all anti-Viscontean coalitions. When this advocate of a
determined stand against Filippo Maria's penetration into
the Romagna was in Florence, he "demonstrated" during

the negotiations (according to the account of a Florentine eye-witness) "that we ourselves had caused the greatness of the Duke, first by recalling our troops from Milan after the death of the old Duke, instead of taking Milan; and, secondly, by concluding peace with Filippo Maria" (that is, through the demarcation treaty of 1420).[39]

A few months later, these arguments were echoed in the official utterances of the Florentine government. When the last Milanese envoys arrived in November—for the visit during which the Duke suddenly seized Imola, which was the final signal for the outbreak of hostilities—the answer they received from Niccolò da Uzzano in the name of the *Signori* and the *Dieci* mentioned Florence's non-interference in the Lombard affairs after Giangaleazzo's death and the continuation of a policy of *désintéressement* at the time when Filippo Maria was reducing to submission the former victims of his father. "She never listened to [the calls for help from] Cremona, Crema, Brescia, and Parma which, had Florence shown any interest in their favor, would not have been reduced to their present state." [40] The same view of the events leading up to the Florentine-Milanese conflagration was used for practical diplomatic ends when Florence tried to enlist the aid of the Pope in the expulsion of Filippo Maria from the Papal Romagna. In the instructions for the ambassadors to Rome we read: After Giangaleazzo's death, Florence permitted the rule of the Dukes of Milan to continue undisturbed, although at that time "it would have been very easy completely to extirpate and annihilate their house." Despite the many acts of aggression of the preceding Dukes, Florence was content to see them no longer threaten her own liberty; she did not hesitate to pledge her permanent disinterest in northern Italy, therewith depriving the smaller north-Italian states of any hope of resistance. But Filippo Maria, contrary to the spirit and the letter of that understanding,

occupied Forlì and Imola and was now penetrating the
Romagna with his influence, thus threatening the State
of the Church as well as Florence.[41]

But just because there was a good deal of truth in the
contention that republican commercial Florence had been
intent on peace once Giangaleazzo was dead and Pisa conquered, the Florentine Republic was poorly prepared for
war, and the immediate military result of her determined
response was a series of crushing defeats on the battlefield.
In July 1424 the Florentine forces sent to the Romagna
to liberate Forlì were annihilated in the battle of Zagonara;
the foreign *condottiere* in command of the Florentine
troops changed sides and went into the service of the
Duke of Milan. In the next year, when Florence had made
supreme efforts to extricate herself from the grave perils
following this defeat by building up a strong army under
the leadership of the best-known *condottieri* of Italy,
these troops, too, were so completely defeated (at Valdilamone, in February 1425) that of the four *condottieri* who
had led the Florentine mercenaries one remained dead on
the battlefield, while the other three fell into Milanese
captivity. Two years later, more ill luck was added: by the
death of Nanni degli Strozzi in a military action at Ottolengo on the Po, May 1427, the Florentine League lost
the only efficient general who was not a hired mercenary
but a fervent supporter of the resistance against the
Visconti and the soul of the conduct of the war by the
coalition. It was the death on the battlefield of this Flor-
entine-at-heart that inspired Bruni to compose a funeral
speech, the *Laudatio Iohannis Strozzae Equitis Florentini*,
which represents the greatest literary monument to the
spirit of Florence in her struggle against the Tyranny of
the Visconti.[42]

The pride and confidence which dominate this second
panegyric on Florence (for such is the form and meaning

of the speech on the fallen general) were not, therefore, the reflection of an easy, pleasurable period; they were a high flight of the spirit wrenched from the sorrows of defeat and the adversities of life. The struggle for the rebuilding of the Florentine fortunes in the years which followed the catastrophe of the summer of 1424 had molded the passionate faith in the *patria* which permeates Bruni's oration. The situation in which the work of reconstruction had started was one of those crises typical of the life of republics at moments when unexpected defeat suddenly reveals a state of unpreparedness in men's minds as well as in their material resources. As Giovanni Cavalcanti, the coeval historian known for his graphic but also hate-inspired descriptions of the clashes of the various groups of the citizenry, relates: At the news of the disaster at Zagonara, "fear was general, and the citizens showed themselves deeply dismayed"; those excluded from active participation in the public offices (like Cavalcanti himself) began to assert openly that the catastrophe had come about because the men in power had wanted war, and now the Republic was paying the price. "Inside the *cerchio del reggimento* one opposed the other. . . . Women and small girls with childish voices, praying in the churches, called to the immortal God for mercy; because of the sad news the city was shaken with lamentation and sorrow." [43]

Contemporary documents show that these scenes of despair merely mark the transition to a more vigorous phase of Florence's history, even though later historians, ever since Machiavelli, have used the picture drawn by Cavalcanti as proof of the decay of unity and public spirit among the Florentine citizens. [44] The ultimate cause of the divergences of opinion in the year 1424 was that Florence, in clinging to peace for the preservation of economic prosperity, had allowed the balance of power on the Peninsula to tip once more in favor of Milan and was now being crudely awakened to reality. If the balance was to be redressed, immense economic sacrifices were needed. Would the industrialists and merchants who were to bear the brunt of the economic battle be willing to bring these sacrifices?

A few doggerel verses in Volgare allow us to sense something of the tense, excited mood which had seized the citizenry after the arrival of the catastrophic news from the battlefield, and before the reluctant councils had begun to face the appalling financial situation. Apparently right after the Zagonara defeat, there was a poetical exchange between messer Antonio di Matteo di Meglio, *cavaliere*, who only recently had assumed the office of *Araldo della Signoria*, and the notary, Ser Domenico da Prato, whose somewhat naive and ill-informed attacks on Niccoli and Bruni we met when tracing the school of advocates of the Volgare of the preceding decade.[45] Antonio di Meglio may well have been charged to write his verses by that group of leading citizens who had urged undaunted resistance to Giangaleazzo, Ladislaus, and Filippo Maria, and who would soon be ready for the sake of military preparedness to support the needed reform of the Florentine system of taxation. The poem then composed by the "herald" of the *Signori* is an apostrophe to Florence, the common mother. How did it come about, Antonio laments, that the heel of the Tyrant crushes thy limbs, and that "thy reputation, once first in all Italy, is now submerged"? Has all the foresight with which the Florentines of the past managed to set bounds to aggressive power passed out of existence? Are Avarice and Envy to conceal the Florentine resources in the hour of need?[46] Where discord springs from the unwillingness of the citizens to make the necessary material sacrifices, no doctor of Paris or Bologna will by his art save liberty. "You want to be the leaders . . . of Italy? It would be nearer to truth to call you usurers and traitors." [47] Do not attempt to delude yourselves! From the beginning the tyrant-house of the Visconti has been Florence's fierce and mortal enemy. "Still we are Florentines, free Tuscans, Italy's image and light. Let there rise again that rightful scorn which always in the past emerged among us when the time was ripe; do not wait any longer! For in procrastination lies the real danger. . . . To repent when the time has passed will be of no help." [48]

Domenico da Prato in his answering poem makes Florence, the despairing mother, reply to these exhortations that her deepest sorrow was caused not by the enemy without, but by the poison in the hearts of her own sons. No new Brutus will arise among a people that only knows the maxim: "Let us make money and we shall have honor" [49] —no new Horace Cocles will strive to gain imperishable glory by self-sacrifice among a people which, for fear of losing its usurious lucre, chooses abject surrender to the enemy.[50] I can no longer bear it, Florence the mother cries out, to see my triumph-laden Senate so humiliated that a mere breeze may lay it low. These are the sights that have aged and weakened me—now I, like Joshua, have nothing left but to hope in the Lord.

To what extent were these plaints justified by an actual decline of the public spirit? We may take for granted that Domenico da Prato's indignation mirrors sorrows and suspicions which had affected many among the middle and lower strata of the citizenry. But Domenico's bitter pessimism, here as in his appraisal of Bruni's Humanism, is far from being a true estimate of the developments that were actually in the making. The minutes of the councils of the Republic prove that inside the *Palazzo della Signoria* there was the same stiffening of patriotic feeling. The mutual accusations within the ruling group, reproachfully mentioned in Cavalcanti's account, were rapidly replaced by a new agreement and a straightforward trend in Florence's foreign policy. There is no trace in the public documents of any substantial faction still advocating acquiescence in the *fait accompli* created by Filippo Maria in the Romagna. The Florentine merchants and industrialists began to grow reconciled to the need for unusual expenses; every advice and vote in the councils was for holding out, while plans were being put forward which were to give rise to the institution of the *catasto* in 1427, a more modern and more equalized system of taxation of movable as well as landed wealth than had ever before existed anywhere in medieval Europe. It is true that this system disappointed the great hopes originally placed in it, that in the course of the next few decades it developed into an oppressive instrument of arbitrary confiscation, and that the financial provisions for the new war proved in the long run to be a crushing burden that undermined unity in the ruling circle and indirectly helped to pave the way for the rise of the Medicean principate. But these were later developments, which to a large extent were caused by the general decay characteristic of the finances of most Italian states in the course of the unceasing wars from the mid-1420's to the mid-1450's; [51] they must not make us misjudge the immediate response of the Florentine citizens to the renewed political crisis.

On the arrival of the news of the rout at Zagonara a new *consulta* was called, a meeting of citizens invited from among the supporters of the régime, former incumbents of the leading positions, and representatives of the various branches of government. The very features which reduced the political effectiveness of such a gathering—its legal inability to make decisions, to take a vote, or even to combine the endless list of individual suggestions into a joint proposal [52]—serve to make its proceedings a uniquely informative source for the study of public opinion in its various shades. At the beginning of the gathering [53] the chord which was to sound throughout the session was struck by one of the leading statesmen of the Giangaleazzo period, Rinaldo de' Gianfigliazzi, now aged and seconded in his counsel by a son: "Liberty is more useful than anything else, there is nothing that must not be risked for its salvation"; "the Dukes of Milan have always been enemies, and always tried to reduce us to submission"; "we must not be frightened by the set-back." [54] From then on, each successive speaker offered variations on the theme that a commonwealth, just as an individual, proves its worth in adversity and must not swerve from its appointed goal: "We must strive for our freedom with a stout heart, and not forsake ourselves; . . . *virtus* stands firm under adversity and so reveals itself." "It is in adversity that men who want to lead a free life are put to the test; in times of good fortune everybody can behave properly." "*Virtus* is achieved in adversity; freedom is not for sale for all the gold in the world." Thus ran the opinions of the next three speakers (two of them of the Strozzi family), who were all asking for increased efforts after the initial defeat.[55] An even fuller, paternal warning that the citizens must not be found weak in the hour of trial, came from Niccolò da Uzzano: "*Virtus* reveals itself in adversity; when things go smoothly, anybody can carry himself well. . . . The greater the danger, the greater must be the provision for it. And liberty is to be valued higher than life. . . . The spirit cannot be broken unless one wills it so." [56]

Within this great uniformity of feeling there was room for individual shades of opinion. Since the Machiavelli family, soon afterwards, had a member (Girolamo) who under Cosimo de' Medici became a martyr for his republican convictions, we may perhaps think of family tradition when in 1424 we find Francesco Machiavelli dwelling upon some of the ideas that were to become the favorites of Niccolò three generations later: the condemnation of tyranny as destructive of civic virtue, and the exaltation of the citizen who serves with his own person in the defense of the commonwealth. As the Machiavelli of the time of Filippo Maria Visconti argues: "The enjoyment of freedom makes cities and citizens great; this is well-known. But places under tyranny become deserted by their citizens. For tyrants fear the *virtus* of good citizens and engage in their extermination." While many more mercenary troops are needed, Francesco Machiavelli goes on to say, there is also need for "raising citizens who are qualified to take their place in the *castella*" in the Florentine territory.[57]

Some of the counselors find their inspiration in the example of ancient Rome; from the warmth of their references to the past one feels what the example means for their conduct. One of these citizens is a magister Galileo Galilei. To him "among the other great and laudable things recorded of the Roman people two are unforgotten: their refusal either to lose courage in adversity or to be flushed with success. The greatness of the Roman mind showed itself more in misfortune than in good fortune. The wood of the tree is an image of hope: wounded, it bursts into leaf and is covered again." [58] Another speaker points to Florence's Roman ancestors. A monument to the Roman mind, he says, is in the verse of Virgil "Yield not to ills, but face them more boldly thou, Even as thy fortune suffers thee." [59] "We who descend from the Romans must take heart and carry ourselves like men." Due to her Roman origin, Florentine history had followed the example of Rome, especially in the time of Giangaleazzo. When Giangaleazzo took Bologna, Florence behaved in a manner worthy of her Roman forefathers by standing fast in supreme danger; as a consequence, Giangaleazzo ultimately lost Bologna and all of his other conquests.[60a]

There is something rhetorical in many of these protestations on the public platform; but that does not mean they have an air of unreality. For our taste, a touch of ostentation pervades everything bred in the atmosphere of the humanistic Renaissance, and this trait of the Quattrocento comes doubly to the fore in the democratic enjoyment of oration in Florence. But after this has been said, a deep impression remains of the vigor of the public spirit in Florence on the eve of the second period of her wars against the Visconti, and of the kinship of the Florentine attitude at that time with the state of the Florentine mind in the days when Giangaleazzo had seemed to be irresistible.

"Populi liberi": Florence and Venice Against the Visconti from the 1420's to the 1440's

We cannot here discuss the later course of the Florentine-Milanese struggle. On the surface, the difference between those years and the time of Giangaleazzo is considerable. That Florence, after the defeats of 1424 and 1425, was not overrun by the Milanese armies was due to the intervention of Venice. This intervention, however, was not a chance event. It was the crowning success of the policy Florence had pursued from the 1390's onward: the program designed to build an alliance among the *populi liberi* on the Peninsula. The psychological situation, therefore, remained essentially unchanged. Though Florence was no longer the protagonist of 1402 but merely a member of a coalition, still the antagonism between "liberty" and "tyranny" continued to determine the political climate.

Venice's long unwillingness to be drawn into the war against Milan had been caused partly by economic considerations. Even in the days of Giangaleazzo, a guiding objective of Venice's Italian policy had been to maintain control of the roads and Alpine passes on which Venetian commerce moved to Germany, Austria, and Hungary.[60b] Once Venice had found that this immediate economic interest was being respected by Milan, she had held it permissible to leave a free hand to Viscontean expansion, provided Milan's accessions were made in a southerly direction across the Apennines—the purport, as we know, of the Truce of Pavia (in 1398) and the Peace of Venice (in 1400). When, as a consequence, Florence was almost submerged by the Viscontean tide, Venice hardly moved.

After the dissolution of the Visconti empire following Giangaleazzo's death, the ultimate aim of Venice's policy of isolation remained unchanged, although it was now pursued in combination with a policy of building up a *terra ferma* state in the Venetian region. The immediate task of Venice was to forestall the dangers from the power-vacuum left by Giangaleazzo's death—dangers looming largest from the buffer-state of the Carrara in Padua. Restored in 1390, and in 1404 made to incorporate conquered Verona, this state might easily have developed into a new tyrannical threat on Venice's doorstep. The Republic of St. Mark, therefore, conquered between 1405 and 1421 all the neighboring territories and fused them into a solid region-state—including to the west Padua, Vicenza, Verona and the roads leading to the Brenner, and to the northeast the disintegrating old German March of Friuli with the Alpine passes leading to Austria and Hungary. Once this strong barricade against all mainland dangers had been raised, the statesmen of the old Venetian school were ready to allow Filippo Maria to renew the policy whose crowning success had been denied by fate to Giangaleazzo.

Seen from a regional and solely economic angle, the possible triumph of the Visconti even seemed to promise some advantages which would not issue from a Florentine victory. We are in a position to reconstruct Venetian reasoning on this point, thanks to the preservation of two speeches delivered in the years 1422 and 1423 by the Doge Tommaso Mocenigo, one of the leaders in the creation of the Venetian *terra-ferma* state.[61] The gist of Mocenigo's argument, when it is freed of the many furiously anti-Florentine insertions made by a later forger, appears as a well-pondered program of purely economic expediency. A vital part of the Venetian trade, he said, was carried on with the Visconti State; the Milanese territories in turn furnished most of the agricultural produce needed for Venice's sustenance, and were among the indispensable buyers of Venetian goods. To allow this "fine garden for Venice" to be devastated by the fury of war, or even to harm it by Venetian arms, was folly. Also, any advance of the western frontier of the Venetian territory from the hilly Veronese region to the flatter western parts would necessitate a larger standing army and, consequently, lead to a permanent drain on Venetian finances. On the other hand, subjection of the Florentine Republic to the Viscontean empire would not be altogether an evil. After the loss of their independence, numerous Florentine merchants, accustomed to the way of life in a republic, might emigrate to Venice and transplant Florence's woolen and silk manufacture there, just as a number of Lucchese merchants had done on a similar occasion. Venice was now master of the gold in the Christian world, respected and feared everywhere. Her future prosperity depended on remaining at peace. If she should enter into war with Milan, every fortune would be reduced to a fragment of its value. "You will risk our gold and silver, our honor and authority, and from being lords of the world you will become the servants of your army captains." [62]

Burckhardt, in his analysis of the State of the Renaissance,[63] referred to the reasoning in Mocenigo's speeches as proof of how exclusively Venetian policy of the Renaissance was guided in its objectives by economic considerations. But this is only one of the many points where Burckhardt's categories of approach fail to do full justice to the spirit of the early Quattrocento. In the case of the ideas that guided Venice's politics, just as in other cases of early Quattrocento thought we have observed,[64] the down-to-earth realism representative of the last Trecento generation, that of Mocenigo, was not the all-determining trait of the incipient Quattrocento, nor the element that led the way into the future; this brand of realism which in a time of change refused to reconsider the accepted standards from new vantage-points no longer dominated the minds of the younger men who had lived through the experience of the Visconti wars during their formative years. The exclusive significance accorded by Mocenigo to economic considerations rested on his aloofness from the ideals which were to act as a determining force in interstate relations in Italy immediately after him. He had not brought himself to recognize that the upheavals of the Giangaleazzo period had forever changed the political situation in northern and central Italy; he refused to accept those new ideas of peninsular equilibrium and solidarity against a common threat which in his own lifetime had sprung up in Florence. "Florence is not the port of Venice, neither for overland nor for water traffic," he argued before the Venetian Senate in 1422; "our roads of transit are in the Veronese territory. It is the Duke of Milan who has common borders with us, and it is he with whom we must maintain good relations. . . . Genoa could harm us, for she is powerful on the seas and is controlled by the Duke. These are the powers with which we must be on a friendly footing." [65] But Mocenigo knew that among the younger generation of Venetian statesmen a group had already emerged which advocated a complete reversal of the policy pursued during the last thirty or forty years. Their thesis was that if Florence should lose her independence, Venice would find herself deprived of a vital ally. Mocenigo pointed to "the young *Procuratore di San Marco,*" Francesco Foscari, as the leader of this new interventionist faction; the speech of the old Doge was a passionate warning against the new trend. Foscari, Mocenigo tells us, was urging that the Venetians ought to come to the rescue of the Florentines "because their weal is also our weal, and, by the same token, harm to them is harm to us." [66]

There is more behind this intonation and outlook than a mere shift in the estimate of political and economic expediency. The cause of the departure of the younger men from the maxims of their elders was the triumph in Venice of the same ideal of *libertas Italiae* which had first been hammered out in Florence under the impact of the struggle with Giangaleazzo.

Recent scholarship, with its strong belief in the prevalence of economic factors, has been inclined to reinterpret this basic conflict in purely economic terms. Not only Mocenigo's (so it has been argued) but also Foscari's policy was determined by economic considerations and ultimately by a shift in the investment needs for Venetian wealth after the *terra-ferma* state had been established. Since (so the reasoning goes) the Turkish threat had discouraged further trading ventures in the East, men of the younger generation "preferred to build up securely anchored fortunes by the acquisition of large landed estates in the *terra-ferma* state." In order to protect these new investments, they endeavored "to drag the republic toward the west" into an alliance with Florence, and finally into the war against Milan.[67] There might be some ground for such inferences if the older generation had been lukewarm in the annexation of the *terra-ferma* state; in fact, however, Mocenigo and his predecessor had been its major architects. The question on which the two generations parted company was not whether Venice's new dominion was for any reason worth protecting, but whether its defense demanded preservation of Florentine independence as a prerequisite. What Mocenigo failed to believe was that the fate of the one republic was bound up with that of the other.

In 1423, only one year after Mocenigo's attempt to restrain the younger men, Francesco Foscari became Mocenigo's elected successor in the office of Doge. From then on, a fraternal feeling and a kindred political program developed in the two leading Italian republics. When toward the end of 1425 a Florentine envoy, Lorenzo de' Ridolfi, arrived in Venice on the mission which was to result in a formal league, he immediately reported home (quoting almost literally the words to which Mocenigo had objected in Foscari's program a few years earlier) that the interviews with the leading Venetian statesmen had convinced him that "they have, and will have, the same regard for the preservation of your sovereignty as for that of their own." [68] Everywhere in Venice it was now recognized, Ridolfi reported, that future peace in Italy was bound up with the survival of the *libertà* of Florence.[69] The pact concluded with the envoys was itself different in design from the many *pro tempore* combinations which had given a kaleidoscopic character to the Venetian diplomacy of the preceding decades. The new alliance was to last ten years even if peace with Milan should be reached sooner; otherwise it was to continue until the Milanese threat had disappeared.[70]

With the emergence of this confederation the Quattrocento stage was definitely set in accordance with the pattern envisioned by Florentine citizens in the days of Giangaleazzo Visconti. Almost immediately humanistic imagination began to play upon that historic scene when the envoy from one of the two great Italian republics appeared before the august senate of the other with the solemn charge that tyranny after destroying freedom at home is bound to destroy the freedom of its neighbors, a charge echoed in the reply of the Doge that there exists an eternal conflict between tyrannies and free peoples, and that Venice must not allow Florence, "the other leader [*caput*] of freedom in Italy," to perish. The most striking feature of this symbolic interpretation of the event of 1425 is that it is first found in the work of a contemporary humanistic chronicler of Milan, Andrea de' Biglia. Even a man like Biglia, son of a noble Milanese family, would, being a humanist, see the conflict as a contest between republican liberty and tyranny; all he was able to do in defense of the Milanese cause was to weaken the impressiveness of that antithesis by adding another imaginary speech by a Milanese envoy, pointing out that the Florentine Commonwealth had not always kept exemplary relations with its neighbors, whereas the Roman Republic had found it possible to live on friendly terms with foreign princes.[71] Even two generations later, at the end of the Quattrocento, this scene from early Renaissance history—the speech of the Florentine ambassador, "the envoy of a free commonwealth, come to request aid and help for liberty from a free people"; the counter-speech of the Milanese envoy; and the plea for the protection of Florentine liberty by the Doge—was still alive, and was included in the official humanistic history of the Republic of St. Mark commissioned by the Venetian Senate: Sabellico's *Rerum Venetarum Decades*.[72]

We have sufficient evidence to state that by the middle of the 1420's the hope for permanent cooperation between the "free peoples" of Italy became an inspiring political ideal among Venetian as well as Florentine humanists. In Venice, the chief proponent of this program was Francesco Barbaro, one of the ranking statesmen and the chief promoter of Venetian civic Humanism during the 1420's, 1430's, and 1440's. To Barbaro the term *libertas Italiae*, which in those decades became an ever-present political watch-word, had a twofold meaning: preservation of a system of independent states on the Peninsula, and confederation of the surviving republics for the sake of civic freedom.[73] In 1426, when the Florentine-Venetian league had at last become a reality, Barbaro told Lorenzo de' Medici, Cosimo's brother, that this alliance had laid "a foundation for the protection of *libertas*" and had checked Filippo Maria's design to make himself lord of Italy.[74] About the same time, another well-known humanist-statesman in Barbaro's circle, Andrea Giuliano, declared that war with Milan had become inevitable since all efforts to convince Filippo Maria of the necessity to keep peace with Florence had failed; Venice had had no choice but to enter into the struggle to preserve her *terra-ferma* state and—so it was now said in the same breath—to fight "for the liberty of the Commonwealth of Florence, for her own liberty, and for the liberty of all Italy." [75] In the ensuing military clash, Francesco Barbaro's leadership and personal courage were put to the test in a difficult defense of Brescia against the assault of a superior Milanese army. When Barbaro later looked back on his achievement, he prided himself that by his military performance he had deserved well not only of Venice, his "*patria*," but of all "*liberi Italiae populi*." [76a]

After Genoa had broken away from Milanese dominance in the winter of 1435-36, the idea that a decisive encounter was taking place between the city-state republics on the one side and the reemerging empire of the Visconti on the other gained in circulation. Barbaro called for a "common plan," to enable the city of Genoa "to unite with the Venetian republic and the *populus florentinus* for Italy's liberation from fear and danger." [76b] The instructions for the Florentine ambassador to the reestablished republic of Genoa read that a choice had to be made between a league of the republics, and a truce with the Tyrant conceding the failure of the cause of liberty.[76c] Even in the official language of Venetian diplomacy, "*tota Italia* would rejoice if the city of Genoa could be kept free." [76d] When the alliance between the three republics of Venice, Florence and Genoa was finally concluded in May 1436, the reason given in the formal document was the defense of liberty against tyranny.[76e]

A common line on the basic questions of inter-state policies now existed among four surviving republics: Florence, Venice, Genoa, and Siena—a growing republican confederation which was still further augmented when, in 1438, a truce put an end to the quarrels separating Florence and Lucca. Three years later, this understanding was followed by the conclusion of a Florentine-Lucchese league that lasted undisturbed until the French invasion in 1494. Barbaro, in the late 1430's, began to talk in his letters of "the free peoples federated in equality." In 1440, Pietro del Monte, who may be looked upon as a younger member of Barbaro's and Giuliano's circle, claimed Venice had made it her program "that, if possible, all Italy, which has been crushed under so many disasters caused by tyrants (*universa Ytalia, . . . tantis cladibus tyrannorum oppressa*), may at some time achieve . . . the sweetest and most coveted of all human things: liberty." [77]

A Florentine parallel to the attitude of these Venetian statesmen and humanists is found in Giannozzo Manetti, who, after Genoa's deliverance from Filippo Maria, in the period of the Florentine-Venetian-Genoese league, composed two humanistic *Laudationes* on Genoa in which the

Genoese were presented as modern Romans, their victories as triumphs in the interest of *libertas* in Italy, and a confederation between the three republics as the natural road into the future.[78] It was in the political atmosphere of these decades of political cooperation that Poggio, the Florentine (in 1435) and Pietro del Monte, the Venetian (in 1440) with so much verve and unanimity defended the *Respublica Romana* against Caesar, thus bringing cherished ideas of the Giangaleazzo period to a head in literary battles already known to us.[79a] Even as late as about 1460 the Florentine chancellor, Benedetto Accolti, defending the "Moderns" in his *Dialogue on the Preeminence of the Men of His Age* against the classicists' scorn, listed among the reasons for modern Italy's equal claims with antiquity the emergence of city-republics that were the peers of ancient Athens, Sparta, and Rome—and especially the fact that Florence, Venice, and Siena had preserved their independence to the present day. In Benedetto Accolti's eyes, the statesman of recent times who had most closely approached the greatness of the ancient political leaders was Francesco Foscari, the protagonist of the alliance of the republican city-states.[79b]

The high point of this republican sentiment was reached in the late 1440's when Milan, after Filippo Maria had died without issue in 1447, made an attempt to revive her pre-Viscontean past by proclaiming a *Respublica Ambrosiana*. At the news of the revolution in Milan, the Venetian government hastened to send an envoy to declare that Venice, unyielding though she had been in the struggle against the dead destroyer of liberty, was ready to enter into friendship and alliance with a Milanese republic.[80] This was the height, but also the turning of the tide that had begun when the Milanese bid for an Italian Monarchy had first been met by the Florentine bid for the preservation of the heritage of the free Italian

Commune; the long struggle which had opened with the fight for Tuscan independence was to be concluded in northern Italy.

After the breakdown of the Visconti Monarchy, in 1447 as at the end of 1402, the vast complex of territories fused in the Milanese State threatened to fall apart and produce a vacuum in the newly formed system of Italian states—a situation fraught with hardly less danger than the preceding accumulation of Viscontean might. The ultimate decision about the form of the new balance now devolved upon Venice. On receiving the news of Filippo Maria's death and the foundation of a Milanese Republic, Francesco Barbaro sent a solemn warning to a leading member of the Venetian government.[81a] A turning point, he said, had been reached in Venetian politics. The alternative now was "either to enlarge our dominion, or to augment common liberty and save the peace of Italy." Many people in Venice would clamor for expansion beyond the Milanese border. However, the mission of Venice was "to *associate* the energies of northern Italy through our authority on a basis of equity, and not to *dissociate* the country by force of arms. . . . We have undertaken this war not for the sake of domination, but to repel force by force and to provide for peace. . . . We have called the people of Milan, like others, to liberty, and we have talked in these glorious terms not because we expected to subject everything to our power, but to take sides as free men for the freedom of others." [81b]

The present situation was explosive, Barbaro went on. With the death of the last Visconti, the Florentine-Venetian alliance, after having worked for more than twenty years, had reached its goal and, consequently, had come to its logical end. Any annexation of Milanese territory by Venice would increase Venetian power beyond that of Florence and implicitly destroy the possibility of further cooperation. Or again, "if the suspicion should arise that we desire to lay down the law to our allies and neighbors" (for instance in the case of the less powerful people of Genoa), all of them would turn against Venice and resist. There was only one way open to the Venetian Republic: not to violate the possessions of the now free people of Milan and to accept them into the alliance. "We must try to reach a lasting peace instead of a victory that cannot last long. We must prefer the glory of saving common liberty to the danger, now looming large, of civil and other wars. We must get along with our allies, with our enemies, with everybody, showing so much moderation that we will long be able to glory in the championship of Italian liberty, instead of being looked upon, after a short while, as those who, bent on change, were responsible for wars and the rule of violence." [81c]

This was the valedictory word to the period which had saved what in Quattrocento Italy was called the *libertas Italiae*. That it meant the end of a period was due not merely to the failure of the Venetian government to act with the wisdom recognized, as Barbaro's memorandum proves, by those who had lived with an open mind through the experiences, and had shared the ideals, of the generation which had seen the Italian city-republics waging a common fight. The ultimate obstacle to Barbaro's program was that Milan, which had not known freedom for almost a century and a half but had seen success and strength under tyranny, was not the soil in which a new, vigorous republic could take root. In the midst of growing disunity and disorder, some of the subject communes in the Milanese territory broke away; towns in the immediate neighborhood, like Lodi and Piacenza, were ready to put themselves under Venetian rule, preferring the control of the faraway city on the lagoon to that of the nearby provincial metropolis. When Venice yielded to the tempta-

tion of these offers, the brief psychological moment for an
enlarged republican league, with the *Respublica Ambrosiana* as a member, had passed. Confronted with the
prospect that Venice might gain a lasting foothold in the
heart of the Milanese plain, the Ambrosian Republic
preferred to rely on her leading *condottiere*, Francesco
Sforza. When he succeeded in reconquering Piacenza for
Milan and inflicting two crushing defeats on the Venetian
troops, Venice made the most daring gamble of her *divide
et impera* policy by suddenly concluding an alliance with
the victorious general and encouraging him to conquer for
himself a princedom carved out of the Milanese territories. The old Visconti State was in danger of being cut
up into a weak republic and a weak tyranny hostile to each
other and both playing into the hands of Venetian imperialism.

It was this prospect of a *Pax Venetiana* replacing the
dreaded *Pax Mediolanensis* that dissolved the emotional
ties as well as the political cooperation between Florence
and Venice. The shrewd attempt made by Venice to balance the scattered fragments of the former Visconti State
against each other was taken up by Florence on a grander
scale and applied to Italy as a whole. After events had
proven Barbaro correct, Cosimo de' Medici performed
the masterstroke of his diplomatic career. Breaking the
long political tradition of the early Renaissance, he led
Florence to make common cause with Sforza, first by remaining neutral, and later by entering an outright alliance
which enabled the *condottiere* to conquer the city of Milan,
put an end to her new-fangled republican liberty, and
build up an integrated principality in Lombardy as a
counterpoise to the Venetian region-state—a tamer and
less dangerous successor to the tyranny of the Visconti.[81d]

From 1451 on, public peace and the power-balance in
Italy depended on two opposing coalitions: the Florentine

Republic in alliance with the new Milanese Tyranny on the one side, and the Venetian Republic with the Kingdom of Naples on the other. Finally, in 1454 and 1455 both alliances gradually merged in one *"Santissima Lega,"* which included the Papal State as its fifth strong partner, while the remaining smaller states—among them the republics of Siena, Lucca, and Bologna (the last under the principate of a local *signore*), and a number of second-rank principalities, especially the dominions of the Este and the Gonzaga—grouped themselves around these five major powers. This "Holy Alliance" of Renaissance Italy, by preserving the independence of the states which had survived, realized at least a part, and an essential one, of the program of *libertas Italiae* which had emerged from the resistance against Giangaleazzo; and although it did not guarantee absolute peace nor prevent occasional minor wars, it did give the Peninsula a period of consolidation and comparative quiet which lasted until, at the end of the century, the West-European powers invaded Italy.

In Florence, during the late 1440's, all the authority and resourcefulness of Cosimo de' Medici had been needed to convert the citizenry to this policy of separation from their sister-republic Venice.[82] Leonardo Bruni was then already in his grave; but Giannozzo Manetti, who in the 1430's had advocated the idea of a republican alliance among Florence, Venice, and Genoa, became a victim of the changing conditions. He was one of those who could not easily resign themselves to the break-up of what so long had been tradition in Florence's foreign policy. As an ambassador to Venice in 1448, and on later occasions, he tried to work for a *rapprochement* between the two republics, but his efforts were counteracted by Cosimo, and there can be no doubt that his repeated show of sympathy for Venice played a substantial part in his later economic destruction and exile by the ruling party.[83]

The course of events—Sforza's success and the development of Venice into the most aggressive power in Italy— eventually silenced such opposition. As early as 1451-52 we find the Florentines complaining in diplomatic negotiations that Venice had forgotten their "ancient friendship" and "so many years of alliance" and common exertions; that she had decided upon "dividing Italy" between the Venetian Republic and the Kingdom of Naples. Venice is accused of an "inordinate appetite" and the intention "to occupy Lombardy and in due course gain the *imperio d'Italia*." With the roles of the actors changed, it is now the Venetian, instead of the Milanese, government which is said to have found out that Florence was the potential obstacle to expansionist designs in Italy. From that time on, the general opinion in Florence began to be that, if Cosimo had not prevented the Venetians from dominating northern Italy after Filippo Maria's death, "they would subsequently have become rulers over all peoples in Italy." [84] The erection of a dam, by Cosimo, against Venetian imperialism appeared as the logical continuation of Florence's previous resistance to the expansion of the monarchies of northern and southern Italy; the memory of the great struggles of the early Quattrocento began to fuse with the conviction that Cosimo de' Medici had been the founding father of the *libertas Italiae*. After 1470, we read in an historically not quite exact Florentine critique of Venetian politics: when about 1400 Milan possessed "Genoa, Siena, Pisa, Bologna, Lucca, the Romagna, and three quarters of Lombardy, . . . the Duke of Milan would surely have made himself King of the Italians" but for Cosimo's "aid, prudence, and treasure"; when Ladislaus of Naples had subjected Rome, and finally had taken Cortona in Tuscany, he would have been bound to become "King of Italy" but for the fact that Cosimo "became instrumental in ruining him"; and, subsequently, "when the *signoria* of Venice seized the cities of the Milanese territory, she would have made herself Queen of Italy" had Cosimo not reversed the course of Florence's policy. One generation later, the creation of a balance against Venice still appeared as the inevitable culmination of the Florentine road toward *libertas Italiae* to Guicciardini, who in his *Storie Fiorentine* as well as in his *Dialogo del Reggimento di Firenze* maintained that Venice, if she had put herself in possession of the Milanese State after 1447, would quickly have become the ruler of all Italy; and that Cosimo de' Medici, accordingly, had saved "the liberty of Florence and of all Italy." [85a]

When Simonde de Sismondi, in his classical history of the Italian city-states, undertook early in the nineteenth century to give the first modern estimate of the political changes in the mid-Quattrocento,[85b] his verdict was that the Ambrosian Republic, which was ready "to live in peace with all," had been driven under the yoke of the Sforza by a Venetian attack staged "without provocation"; and that this interference was the event which made impossible any lasting confederation among three great Italian republics and caused the weakness of Italy that became apparent during the foreign invasions of the late Renaissance.

What we must add today to qualify Sismondi's estimate is that the Ambrosian Republic did "provoke" Venice's intervention in the sense that she was powerless to keep intact the regional state on whose preservation the equilibrium and the peace of Italy rested. It was not simply the vicious "ambition" of the Venetian doge Foscari (as Sismondi saw it), and even less that of Cosimo de' Medici and Francesco Sforza (as Venetian historians continue to charge to the present day),[85c] nor the crime of any other statesman or state, which prevented the period of Florentine-Venetian cooperation from ushering in an age of ever broader republican confederation. Ultimately responsible for the failure was the fact that republican Milan had committed the "crime" of being unable to muster the strength for self-defense which is required of every major member in a balanced system of closely interrelated states —lest there result a power-vacuum inviting violent dislocations through expansionist moves of the neighbor states.

But before this fateful change of conditions and convictions in Florence and all Italy took place, the Renaissance and the humanistic movement had been growing for half a century in an atmosphere of freedom. However much or little Venice produced during the Quattrocento in the way of an indigenous civic Humanism among her patricians, her contributions belong essentially to the first half of the century. In Florence all the new trends that had appeared since the end of the Trecento then found a climate congenial to their growth and fused all antagonistic elements in a unity of feeling and thought which from the 1420's on made the Florentine school the leading and most fully integrated group within Italian Humanism. By the mid-Quattrocento, the foundation had been laid not only for the states-system of the Renaissance and the Humanism of Florence, but also for the political outlook and historical philosophy which were to grow to maturity in the last period of Florentine republicanism, when the Principate of the Medici was again swept away.

CHAPTER 17

NICCOLI, POGGIO, BRUNI AND
THE CIVIC OUTLOOK

Niccoli and Poggio in the 1420's and 1430's

THE reaction to the reemergence of the Viscontean
challenge after 1420 did not remain limited to
political cooperation among the surviving city-
state republics. We have come to see that the new
danger quickly had its effect on the outlook, ideals and
literary pursuits of the most varied groups of the Florentine citizenry. In the city-councils, speakers frequently recalled the experience of the crisis of 1402, and pointed to
Florence's Roman origin and to parallels in Roman history.[1] The same ideas and historical remembrances reached
citizens ignorant of Latin through the medium of poems
written in Volgare.[2] In Giovanni da Prato's dialogue-
novel, composed at the request of politically active fellow citizens, we found proof that topics discussed in the
days of the Giangaleazzo period—the role of the *Respublica Romana* and the place of liberty in the Florentine
past—were being revived in nonhumanist circles.[3] At the
same time patriotic pride in the native tongue of Florence
reached its height and eventually changed the attitude
toward the Volgare inside the humanistic school from
Matteo Palmieri, in his *Della Vita Civile*, to Leonardo
Bruni, in his *Vite* of the great Florentines of the Trecento.

The new political perils and passions must have been
felt in the quiet of many a humanistic study-room. Even
a life-long copyist of classical manuscripts such as the well-

known scholarly scribe Antonio di Mario then showed that
he was alive to the significance of the hour through which
his native city was passing. At the end of the scholarly
copies which he finished during the critical autumn, winter
and spring of 1425-26, he gave vent to his sorrows and
patriotic feelings in appended notes stating that his patient work (one of the first complete transcriptions of
Gellius' *Noctes Atticae*, and a translation of Eusebius'
Chronicon) had been done at a time "when our Republic
had to withstand the fierceness and hardship of the war
with the Duke of Milan for the defense of liberty" and
when, subsequently, Venice, under its Doge, "had allied
itself with our Florentine Republic in the defense of their
libertas, fighting together manfully and bravely against
the tyranny of the Milanese Duke, who, with iniquity,
had unjustly attacked our Republic during the past
years." [4]

Confronted with so many indications of the impact that
the renewed political crisis had on Florentine literary life,
one wonders in particular about the influence on the three
men who, a quarter of a century earlier, had been the
pioneers of humanistic classicism: Niccoli, Poggio, and
Bruni.

Niccoli, we have had many opportunities to observe, remained throughout his life the militant classicist of the
years about 1400; and in the political struggles of the
time, his disinterest in Florence's liberty, characteristic of the non-citizen-like attitude of his youth,[5] also
never changed. Our information allows us to conclude
with certainty that at the time of the Neapolitan expansion under King Ladislaus, Niccoli was as little impressed
by the dangers to Florentine independence as he had been
in the time of Giangaleazzo; he was even among those
who spread the tenets of Neapolitan propaganda in Florence. The reproaches contained in the invective against

Niccoli written by Lorenzo de' Benvenuti, a few years after Ladislaus' death, are too well substantiated with regard to Niccoli's political conduct to be dismissed lightly. In Benvenuti's list of accusations we read that Niccoli saw in Ladislaus a "new Caesar," as it were, who had "descended from heaven"; that before witnesses he declared his preference for the King over those who held the power in Florence; and that his enthusiasm for Ladislaus' victories and military brilliance was such that after the King's death he thought it advisable for a time to remain in the retreat of his home.[6] There is no information, nor is there any reason to assume, that later on the renewed clash between the Florentine Republic and the Viscontean Tyranny wrought any change in the outlook of this self-sufficient man of letters, or in the direction of his studies and literary interests.

Very different was the intellectual and emotional development of Poggio. In describing the crisis at the threshold of the century, we had to portray him as a young, aggressive classicist, more closely akin to Niccoli than any other member of Salutati's circle. He had been characterized as such by Salutati himself during the bitter controversy about the right of the three Florentine *"corone"* of the Trecento to be counted as worthy rivals to the great men of antiquity. To a degree, as we know,[7a] Salutati's defense had renewed the medieval reasoning that the ancients as pagans must have been surpassed by the Christian writers of Florence's past. But Niccoli and Poggio, so Salutati insisted, had not only forgotten this simple truth, but were wilfully biased against their own period and their own contemporaries. Let us remove from that *"laudatissima antiquitas"* (Salutati had pleaded with Poggio) *"totam hanc auctoritatem, umbram et opinionem"* in which we have enveloped it, all the apparent eminence which we tend to attribute to what is old. If you do this, "you will gladly become aware that these two centuries in which we have got to live [i.e., the fourteenth and fifteenth centuries, for Salutati was writing in 1405] are no mediocre times. . . . But you [Poggio] and your companion [*alter ille,* indubitably Niccoli] have so much maligned *modernitas* that you no longer give preference to one man over another, but to one age [antiquity] over another age [modernity] as if you were judges of the one and the other." [7b]

At that time, then, Poggio had indeed been one of those *literati* who deprecated their own world because antiquity and its memory had absorbed all their interest and determined their scale of values. Yet there can be no doubt that in Poggio's more mature years, after the reappearance of the Milanese threat, the Florentine *patria* and her liberty began to play a new role even in the life of this classicist. Under the impact of the renewed Florentine-Milanese confrontation during the 1420's, Poggio became more of a Florentine and civic-minded humanist engaged in the political issues of his own day than he had ever been before, and this although he had meanwhile spent much of his adult life outside of Florence at the Curia in Rome. After the disaster of Zagonara and the other exasperating Florentine defeats of 1424 and 1425 which marked the beginning of the war against Filippo Maria, there appear in Poggio's letters signs of personal concern over the political events—expressions of the anxiety of a Florentine patriot.[7c] Words such as "we who are born in free communities have been brought up to detest tyrants; and we proclaim before the world that we have undertaken this war for the protection of liberty in Italy," a passage found in a letter of 1427 to Francesco Barbaro, would hardly have come from Poggio's pen in former years.[8] By the mid-1430's, we find Poggio sharing the Florentine views also with regard to the republican interpretation of Roman history. At that time he had the significant controversy with Guarino of Ferrara who defended Caesar against the Florentine reproaches. Poggio, in the vein of the Florentine citizens, praised Scipio, the hero of the *Respublica Romana,* and insisted that the flowering of Roman literature under Augustus was due to writers whose minds had been formed under the freedom of the Republic.[9]

Not much later—in 1438—Poggio even appears among the Florentine publicists in the struggle with Filippo Maria; the force of events pushed him into the fray. During an interval in the fighting, the Milanese humanist Pier Candido Decembrio, in the name of the Duke, had addressed to Florence a curious product of Milanese propaganda—a letter filled with extravagant praise for Florence and accompanied by assurances of the Duke's intention to respect Florentine *libertas.* To this letter Poggio replied by formulating what the Florentines wished the Duke to understand under the name of "liberty." While liberty is dear to every human heart, in Florence a "more solid and truer" kind exists than can be found elsewhere. "For not one or another single man governs here, nor does the arrogance of optimates or noblemen command, but the people are called on the basis of equal right to perform public functions in the commonwealth. As a consequence, highly placed and humble persons, members of noble families and commoners, rich and poor work together with a common zeal for the cause of liberty." [10] This is the explanation, Poggio argues, why Florence has always been ready to sacrifice everything for the preservation of her liberty. If Florence has long been the focus of the *"studia humanitatis"* as well as of civic virtues, "we attribute all that to the effects of liberty alone, the possession of which has long encouraged and spurred our ability to cultivate *virtus.*" [11]

Here the tone of the *Laudatio Florentinae Urbis* reappears in a public letter—with the difference, however,
that the fruits of Florentine liberty are now sought in a
wider field, and that the tenor is noticeably more democratic. This evolution cannot be fully explained by the
impression of the Milanese wars on Poggio himself. The
chief interpreter of the political experiences of the period
for Florentine humanists was still Bruni, just as he had
been during the contest with Giangaleazzo. Poggio, who
had gradually absorbed Bruni's outlook on the *"tre corone
fiorentine"* of the Trecento and on the role of civic liberty
in ancient Rome, was again making himself the herald of
ideas originally coined by Bruni.[12]

And so, just as we have had to consult Bruni as our
chief witness on the crisis of the early Quattrocento, we
must turn to him again for our estimate of the effects of
the renewed Florentine struggle.

Phases of Bruni's Humanism to the Time of Filippo Maria

After his return to Florence in 1415, on the morrow of
King Ladislaus' death, Bruni began to carry out the program which he had set for himself under the impress of
the experiences of 1402.[13] When the precise chronology
of his major works composed in the middle period of his
life is reconstructed, the course of his literary activities
from the time of the Florentine triumph over the Neapolitan danger to the reappearance of the Milanese threat, and
to the new decisive clash with Milan under Filippo Maria,
can be traced as follows.

Within the first five or six years after settling down as
a citizen, Bruni became the historian of Florence, as he
had promised in the *Laudatio*. By 1421 the first four books
of the *Historiae Florentini Populi* had been written,[14] and

the same years had seen the composition of a considerable number of lesser politico-historical works: a brief treatise on the Etruscan origin of Mantua which, as has been mentioned, was a pioneering piece of historical criticism; [15] a history of Rome's struggle with Carthage, essentially an adaptation of Polybius, the *Commentaria Tria De Primo Bello Punico;* [16] a comparative study of the military organizations of Greece, Rome, and Florence, and of the allegedly ancient origin of medieval knighthood, the treatise *De Militia;* [17] and, finally, a contribution to the Quattrocento transformation of the Guelph idea, the preface-introduction to the new Statute of the *Parte Guelfa,* framed in 1419.[18] During the same span of time, Bruni broke ground for what may be called the new civic philosophy of life; he translated into Latin Aristotle's *Ethica ad Nicomachum;* [19] he translated and commented upon the (pseudo-) Aristotelian *Economics;* [20] and he composed a polemical pamphlet, his *Oratio in Hypocritas,* which expressed the layman's attitude toward some aspects of monasticism.[21]

But once Bruni's publications had followed the strains of civic interest in his Humanism that far, the civic tenor began to fade once again from his thought and literary production. While work on the *History of the Florentine People* was interrupted for many years, the Bruni of the earlier 1420's (to be precise, from 1421 to 1427) became the author of most of the works on which rests his fame as one of the great philological scholars and educational writers of the early Quattrocento. It was then that he composed his outline, an attempt at reconciliation, of the leading schools of ancient ethics, the *Isagogicon Moralis Disciplinae,*[22] and that, in his *De Studiis et Litteris,* he produced a masterly guide to the humanistic study of *litterae* from the viewpoint of both form and content.[23] He also continued to translate a wealth of Greek authors—though now he no longer included works with historical and political themes;[24] and, under the stimulus of the rediscovery, made in 1421 in northern Italy, of Cicero's *Orator* and some portions of other rhetorical works of Cicero's (sections unknown to the Middle Ages), he became absorbed in problems of rhetoric and the new methods of philological translation—studies which culminated in his treatise *De Interpretatione Recta*.[25]

In view of this direction of Bruni's studies after 1421 it would indeed be difficult to conjecture what the further course of his Humanism might have been, and whether he would ever have returned to his *History of the Florentine People* and his former politico-historical interests, if the psychological factors molding his outlook on life had not been transformed by the return of a political situation that strongly resembled the perilous condition of the Florentine Republic in his youth. Under the influence of the changed political climate brought about by the renewed expansion of Milan and the conclusion of the Florentine-Venetian League, the half-buried civic strain in Bruni's work reemerged. He entered a third period of civic Humanism, which resumed and broadened the results of the two earlier periods when his thinking had been shaped by the impression of the Florentine struggles with Giangaleazzo[26] and King Ladislaus.[27] This time fortune allowed Bruni closer contact with the political events themselves; as the Florentine contest with Filippo Maria developed he did not remain a mere onlooker. After serving as Florentine ambassador to the Pope in 1426, he was appointed in the late autumn of 1427 to the Florentine chancellorship, an office which he held until his death in 1444.[28]

How much this public activity was to mean for Bruni's intellectual development became evident almost directly after he assumed office.

CHAPTER 18

IDEAS BORN OF THE FLORENTINE CRISIS:
BRUNI'S *ORATIO FUNEBRIS* OF 1428

The "Oratio Funebris on Nanni degli Strozzi"—
a Florentine Counterpart to Pericles' Funeral Oration

IN May of 1427, Nanni degli Strozzi, the Ferrarese general of Florentine descent who had been one of the most active and most highly respected leaders of the anti-Viscontean coalition,[1a] was fatally wounded in an encounter at Ottolengo on the Po; he died early in June. Bruni was asked by friends of Nanni in Ferrara to write a eulogy in honor of the fallen leader. He set to work on it in the autumn. However, since he became Florentine chancellor soon afterwards, he could not fully discharge his obligation until some time later. When he returned to his labor about April of the following year, the speech on Strozzi was the first literary work to which he put his pen during his chancellorship. It now grew into something fundamentally different from the mere obituary which Bruni, according to his correspondence, had planned in the autumn of 1427.[1b]

As the chancellor of Florence, Bruni felt, he was to speak on the scion of an old Florentine family, fallen in the early phase of a perilous war whose outcome lay veiled in the future. This was a situation reminiscent of that in which, according to Thucydides' report, Pericles had given his famous funeral speech for the first Athenian citizens that had been killed in the Peloponnesian war—a speech which, far beyond its immediate scope, had become the greatest monument to the Athenian Republic, *patria* of the fallen men. His thoughts on Pericles' speech, Bruni allowed his eulogy of the dead general to grow into a Florentine counterpart to Pericles' oration—a new "Laudatio" of the Florentine Republic no less than of Nanni degli Strozzi. Thus, twenty-five years after the *Laudatio Florentinae Urbis*, there came from Bruni's pen a second panegyric on Florence, reformulating many of the ideas that had grown out of the war against Giangaleazzo Visconti. A comparison of these two illuminating documents gives us a unique opportunity to observe the gradual unfolding of the ideas of the Giangaleazzo period.[2]

The question may be asked, to be sure, to what extent such humanistic imitations of classical models can be at all considered genuine expressions of Florentine convictions. But already in the work of his youth, the *Laudatio*, Bruni had been far more than a mere imitator of Aristides' eulogy on Athens, the Greek pattern he then followed. Twenty-five years later, he showed himself even less dependent on the model he was now using. What he adopted from Pericles' speech was Thucydides' literary scheme, and the spirit of the Athenian public funeral oration where the praise of the fallen citizen-soldiers was couched in a panegyric upon the city for which they had sacrificed their lives: her origin, her political and cultural preeminence, her civic freedom, and the virtue of her citizens in battle.

That the outcome was something which moved men of the Quattrocento profoundly, and that it was an expression of Florentine views and evaluations comparable in effectiveness to those of the publicists in Giangaleazzo's era, is indicated by the immediate, uneasy reaction in the Visconti circle. Only one year later, the Archbishop of Milan recommended to Filippo Maria's secretaries that they hire the skillful humanistic pen of Antonio Beccadelli Panormita to write the history of Milan, because the interpretation of events by Florentine and Venetian minds was influencing public opinion to Milan's detriment.[3] The writings specifically named by the Archbishop were the two works on which Bruni, under the spur of the new conflagration, had been working during the first year of his chancellorship: the *History of the Florentine People,* of which he then wrote the fifth and sixth books; [4] and the funeral oration for Nanni degli Strozzi, "of which everyone who has read it knows well how greatly it lowers the estimation of the Prince [Filippo Maria] and of our *patria*." [5] This harm to the Milanese cause had not been produced by any accusations or calumnies: it was the political implications and Renaissance ideals inherent in Bruni's concept of Florence's historical mission for liberty and humanistic culture which impressed the readers of Bruni's speech and acted as a weapon against Milan.

Florence and Her Cultural Mission

Pericles, according to Thucydides, had opened his eulogy of the Athenian Commonwealth with the claim that Athens' institutions were an original creation, not copied from her neighbors but rather an example to other city-states; against this background he depicted Athenian civic freedom. At the end he claimed that Athens had also set an example in the field of culture; she was "the school of Greek culture." [6] These were the motifs that echoed in Bruni's mind when he wrote of Florence and her place in Italy. But he conceived the difference of the Florentine constitution from those of her neighbors, and Florence's being the school of culture for the rest of Italy, in the terms of the Renaissance.

In the historically-minded manner of the Quattrocento,

Bruni sought the uniqueness of Florence's institutions and liberty in her inheritance from the past. For the young historian of 1403, her mission in Italy had hung by the thin thread of the assertion that Florence had been founded by Rome a few decades before the rise of Caesar's monarchy; thus Florence was the chosen heir of the *Respublica Romana*. But this had proved in several respects to be an immature solution of the problem. What was claimed here for Florence could be applied just as well to many other cities founded in Rome's republican era (an objection soon raised by non-Florentine humanists); and in the last analysis this mode of reasoning was still within the confines of the medieval habit of tracing everything valuable and noble to *Roma Aeterna*. When Bruni in 1415 wrote the first book of his *History,* after his return to the city on the Arno which by then had shown herself the peer of the Neapolitan Kingdom, the superior of Rome in Ladislaus' days, he found an essential supplement to his former views in the discovery that Italy had been full of independent states before the Roman domination, and that Etruria especially had been the home of an early urban civilization and city-state liberty. The heritage of that pre-Roman urbanism and freedom had survived in Etruria-Tuscany down to Bruni's day.[7]

In the panegyric of 1428, the two views are fused in a sound and lasting formulation: Florence was descended from both the Etruscans and the Romans, politically and culturally the most eminent peoples of the Peninsula— "colony of the Romans, commingled with the old inhabitants of Tuscan origin." [8] And since it was the Etruscans from whom Italy had originally received a great many of her religious and political institutions, Pericles' boast for Athens also fitted Florence: both cities, far from having imitated their neighbors, had from early times served as a model to others.[9]

Even more pregnant with historical significance was Bruni's application of the claim that Athens had been "the school of Greek culture." As late as 1404, we observed in a preceding chapter, it had been possible for a well informed north-Italian humanist like Giovanni Conversino to look upon the role of the Italian city-state republics in the development of Humanism as negligible in comparison with that of tyranny.[10] The Florentine counter-claim, as defined in Bruni's *Laudatio*, had been moderate and incomplete, when measured by what the modern student would ascribe to the Florence of the beginning Quattrocento. Bruni, in 1403, had taken pride in the fact that the Florentine vernacular was recognized throughout the Peninsula as the model of Italian speech; Florence called her own the greatest writers in Volgare. As to the humanistic movement, he briefly stated that the *artes liberales* were flowering in the Florentine city, just as they had flowered "among every leading people." [11]

Twenty-five years later, the attainments of Bruni's generation could be seen with greater clarity. As Athens had done in Greece, thus Bruni argued in 1428, Florence is holding a *principatus* of *litterae studiaque* in Italy thanks to her pioneering role in both Volgare literature and Humanism. After the proud boast that Florence had been the home of all the great poets of Italy, the panegyric of 1428 goes on to ask with a view to Florence's role for the new studies: "Who has called this already wholly lost skill of expression (*hanc peritiam dicendi*) back into light, usage and life, if not our citizens? Who, if not our Commonwealth, has brought to recognition, revived and rescued from ruin the Latin letters, which previously had been abject, prostrate and almost dead?" The *litterae politioresque disciplinae*, it is true, were thriving elsewhere as well, but their roots had been in the Florentine development. "Indeed, even the knowledge of Greek letters, which for more than seven hundred years had fallen into disuse in Italy, has been called forth and brought back by our Commonwealth with the result that we have become able to see face to face, and no longer through the veil of absurd translations, the greatest philosophers and admirable orators and all those other men distinguished by their learning. Finally, the *studia humanitatis* themselves, surely the best and most excellent of studies, those most appropriate for the human race, needed in private as well as public life, and distinguished by a knowledge of letters befitting a free-born man—such *studia* took root in Italy after originating in our city." [12]

With these remarkable passages, the panegyric of 1428 achieves a decisive advance in the Florentine self-awareness of the humanistic Renaissance.[13] In the long history of the Renaissance idea, this is the first clear conception of the vital interrelationship between the humanistic movement and the Florentine city-state.[14] Before long, the implicit new historical view was being fully developed by Bruni himself. In his *Vita di Petrarca*, in 1436, he set forth the theory that already in antiquity, and again in the post-Roman centuries of Italian history, the fortunes of the free city-state had determined the ascent and descent of culture. His effort to perceive the historical background of Petrarch's work led him to conclude that, with regard to antiquity, "one may say that the letters and studies of the Latin language followed a course parallel to the state of the Roman Commonwealth: . . . When the liberty of the Roman people was lost as a consequence of the rule of the Emperors, . . . the healthy condition of the studies and letters also perished." As the Empire was succeeded by the rule of Goths and Langobards, "barbarian and foreign nations," a "gross and coarse" (*grossa e rozza*) era began in the field of studies also. And when the "*popoli italici*" regained liberty after the deluge, "the

Tuscan and other cities began to recover their strength
and spend time and effort on the studies," until, in the
days of Dante and Petrarch, the classical level was gradually regained.[15] Ever since this mature historical reinterpretation by Bruni, the Florentine Renaissance held to
the doctrine of the dependence of literary culture on political freedom, and eventually also used it to explain the
flowering of the visual arts in the Greek republics, in
Rome, and in the Italian communes.[16]

For the appraisal of these later phases of the historical
outlook of the Renaissance it is important to know that it
was in the 1420's and 1430's that the rise of Humanism
began to be viewed as an historical movement intimately
connected with the history of the Florentine city-state, and
not merely as the learned work of isolated scholars.

Freedom and the Florentine Constitution

The best thing Athens had to teach Greece, according
to Thucydides' Pericles, was Athenian freedom. It is the
freedom of the Florentine citizen which forms the center
of the panegyric of 1428. Florence's laws, says Bruni,
"aim, above all, at the liberty and equality of all citizens";
the Florentine constitution, therefore, falls under the
forma popularis of government.[17]

What is the nature of this Florentine liberty and equality? In the *Laudatio*, which had already proclaimed that
"the Florentine people thought there could never be a
life for them without liberty," [18] the answer had still been
given predominantly in terms of constitutional technique.
There was true freedom in Florence, Bruni felt, because
the supreme power in the Republic was prevented from
becoming tyrannical by being vested in a board of nine
peers changing every two months; [19] and because special
legislation directed against the old feudal nobility had re-

duced the influence of the great, and brought about the citizens' equality before the law.[20] In the panegyric of 1428, the repressive legislation against the old nobility, which enabled the bourgeoisie to rise, is nothing more than a secondary circumstance; the heart of Florence's republican freedom now is seen in the free access of every citizen to public offices and honors. In Bruni's own words: "Equal liberty exists for all . . . ; the hope of winning public honors and ascending is the same for all, provided they possess industry and natural gifts and lead a serious-minded and respected way of life; for our commonwealth requires *virtus* and *probitas* in its citizens. Whoever has these qualifications is thought to be of sufficiently noble birth to participate in the government of the republic. . . . This, then, is true liberty, this equality in a commonwealth: not to have to fear violence or wrong-doing from anybody, and to enjoy equality among citizens before the law and in the participation in public office. . . . But now it is marvellous to see how powerful this access to public office, once it is offered to a free people, proves to be in awakening the talents of the citizens. For where men are given the hope of attaining honor in the state, they take courage and raise themselves to a higher plane; where they are deprived of that hope, they grow idle and lose their strength. Therefore, since such hope and opportunity are held out in our commonwealth, we need not be surprised that talent and industry distinguish themselves in the highest degree."[21]

These passages are among the most beautiful expressions of the civic ideal in the period when Florence was locked in struggle with the Visconti. We see here the faith in freedom, generated by the long wars against tyranny, transforming the social outlook of Florentine humanists. And more examples could be found. Simultaneously with, or even before Bruni's speech on the fallen Strozzi, one of the most widely read and long remembered Renaissance treatises on true nobility was produced in Bruni's circle: the *Disputatio de Nobilitate*, presumably written by Buonaccorso da Montemagno the Younger.[22] There a patrician and a plebeian of ancient Rome are depicted vying with each other, in two fictitious speeches, for the hand of a beautiful girl of noble descent. The object of the work is to demonstrate the superior merit of the lowly born plebeian who has risen by his own effort. Like Bruni's oration for Strozzi, the speech of the victor is modeled on a classical example, the anti-aristocratic speech of Marius in the 85th chapter of Sallust's *Jugurthine War;*[23] but the ancient model is again thoroughly transformed. Whereas Sallust's Marius is a plebeian upstart who plays up the crude virtues acquired in a soldier's life against the refined degeneracy of the patrician, and derides letters and the knowledge of Greek as playthings for noble lords, in the Florentine disputation it is culture and learning which have made it possible for the victor to attain true nobility of spirit—but not by erudition alone: the final standard is the confidence that Nature extends the same chance to become noble or ignoble to the high and the lowly born alike, according to the fruitful use they make of their lives. "For such is the mind of mortals: resting on itself, free, and made for both nobility and ignobility. In this most excellent task of humanity nobody can accuse Nature that she has not been generous." "Whoever has not attained distinction should blame himself; he complains unjustly about bad fortune." To the author of the *Disputatio de Nobilitate*, this competition among men must include the pursuits of public-political life, just as Bruni thought. In his youth, so Buonaccorso's plebeian pleads before his judges, he had been started on the path of virtue by the study of the Greek philosophers; but at a certain point "he began to perceive that human spirits grow in excellence when they come into contact with the life of the common-wealth." [24] As a consequence, he had tried to attain nobil-ity by serving the community in public offices and in the perils of the battlefield.*

* The novelty of this outlook is confirmed by the unusual suc-cess of Buonaccorso's disputation not only in Italy, but through-out Europe—a chapter in the history of the dissemination of Florentine early-Renaissance thought which is still to be written in detail, although today the major phases are known. The *Dis-putatio de Nobilitate* was one of the earliest works of the Quat-trocento to be rapidly copied outside Italy and translated into the important vernaculars; its fortunes demonstrate the provocative impression made by the social notions of Florentine civic authors on northern readers.

We do not know the approval or disapproval with which the *Disputatio* was read at the court of Burgundy, focus of late medieval chivalrous culture. However, as early as 1449 a French translation, under the title of *Controversie de noblesse,* was made by Jean Mielot, secretary to Duke Philip the Good. It was copied several times and eventually printed in Bruges—not later than 1478—by Collard Mansion, the collaborator of William Caxton.

We are much better informed about the reception of the work in England. A translation into English was made by one of the earliest travelers to humanistic Italy, John Tiptoft, who during the years 1459-60 lived in Guarino's circle in Padua and Ferrara, and in the following year visited Florence, and probably, therefore, became acquainted with the Latin text. His translation seems to have been checked against the Latin orig-inal, although, presumably, he had been using Mielot's French rendering in the first place. When in 1481 Tiptoft's English version was printed by Caxton under the title *The Declamacion of Noblesse,* an epilogue was added from which we can ob-serve that for the English printer the outcome of the alterca-tion was not the implicit victory of a new cultural and social ideal over the prejudice and conduct of the patrician class. Rather, the work seemed to him to present an intriguing, un-solved problem placed in the cross-light of opposing arguments. For in commenting on the concluding plea of the plebeian to his judges—"which character and conduct is the more noble,

There can be no doubt about the interdependence of these ideas and the vigorous public spirit that had grown out of the fight of the Florentine Republic for her survival as an independent state. Bruni's assertion of the psychological need for free competition among fellow-citizens had been preceded by his picture of the role of free competition and equality among states, presented in the first book of his *Historiae*. We can trace with accuracy the

---

is now left to your decision" (*utra earum nobilior sit, in vestra nunc sententia relinquitur*)—Caxton remarks that a decision, then, had not been reached in the altercation itself, but had been left to the judgment of the reader.

That Caxton's understanding of the problem was shared in other countries north of the Alps, transpires from the prefatory remarks of the translator into German, Niclas von Wyle, who in 1470 included Buonaccorso's work among his *Translationen oder Teutschungen*, the earliest vernacular garner of Italian humanistic writings for the German reader. As Niclas von Wyle put it, the work of Buonaccorso represented "a plea and a counter-plea" on whose respective merits judgment was to be passed by the person to whom the translation was dedicated, "in order that this precious plea and counter-plea may not be found to lack a [final] verdict." This person was Count Eberhard of Württemberg, who seemed to be an ideal judge of true nobility because he was so richly endowed with the three qualities producing "nobility" which Niclas von Wyle enumerated without discrimination: wealth, virtue, and high descent—a definition which in the German translator's hands obtained a strongly aristocratic and at the same time pre-humanistic flavor by the tracing of the Count's fabulous pedigree to Abraham, Aeneas, and Romulus.

The difference between the social views held outside Italy and the civic standards of Florentine humanists emerged most strikingly when Buonaccorso's story of the contest between a Roman patrician and a Roman plebeian was used, largely in a literal imitation, as plot for the earliest English secular drama —*Fulgens and Lucres*—composed by Henry Medwall about 1497. In the framework of a drama, of course, the verdict on the merits of each suitor for the hand of the high-born lady

transition from that phase of his thinking to his understanding of Florentine freedom in 1428. When he phrased
the words in the Strozzi oration that men who can hope
for public honors raise themselves, but that they lose their
strength without that hope, he was not imitating something
he had found in Thucydides. For Pericles, in Thucydides'
account, merely says that in the Athenian democracy,

---

could not be left to the reader's good sense. The lady's decision
had to be shown in the crowning scene; and given the inner
structure of the contest, there was no doubt that the palm must
be won by the plebeian's virtue. But while accepting this outcome, the English author did not conceal that such an ending
was to himself and his audience a thrilling exception to the
rules of social life and by no means the expression of a new
ideal. For when the lady, in his drama, has decided that "in
this case" the plebeian was indeed "the more noble man" and
that she must "condyscend" to him, she quickly deprecates any
thought that her verdict might indicate a change in the social
standards: "And for all that I wyll not dispise / The blode of
cornelius, I pray you thinke not so: / God forbede that ye
sholde note me that wyse, / For truely I shall honoure them
wheresoeuer I go / And all other that be of lyke blode
also, / But vnto the blode I wyll haue lytyl respect / where
tho condycions be synfull and abiect. / I pray you all syrs as
meny as be here / Take not my wordis by a sinistre way."
Excited exclamations by the plebeian's servant emphasize still
further the deviation from the normal course of life: "Yes by
my trouth I shall witness bere . . . / How suche a gentyl-
woman did opynly say / That by a chorles son she wolde set
more / Than she wolde do by a gentylman bore." Moreover
in Medwall's presentation, the plebeian's victory does not impress the reader as a triumph of new values because the author
has cut the nerve of the humanist ideal by omitting the part
in the hero's "nobility" played by his interest in studies and
books and by his inner drive toward freedom of the mind and
philosophic wisdom. In Medwall's play, in short, an upstart
distinguished by unusual ability and moral qualities has taken
the place of the Florentine champion of a new civic virtue and
education.[25]

"while the law secures equal justice to all alike in their private disputes, the claim of excellence is also recognized; and when a citizen is in any way distinguished, he is preferred to the public service, not as a matter of privilege, but as the reward of merit. Neither is poverty a bar, but a man may profit his country whatever be the obscurity of his position."²⁶ Bruni, as has just been pointed out, was also not repeating an idea he had already held when depicting the Florentine constitution in the *Laudatio*. Even as late as 1413, the psychological interpretation of freedom as the spark struck by equality in competition seems still to have been absent from his mental armory. In that year, on a journey with the Curia to northern Italy, he was asked by Emperor Sigismund, as previously mentioned, for a brief written exposition of the Florentine constitution; and a copy of his reply has been preserved in a Florentine library.²⁷ While again asserting that "liberty" was at the root of the organization of the Florentine Republic, and that the substance of "genuine and true liberty" was civic *"paritas et aequalitas,"*²⁸ Bruni still saw the means to achieve this equality in nothing more than legal checks on office-holders and powerful citizens. Precisely as he had judged the causes of Florentine liberty in the *Laudatio*, he said that in Florence any perilous predominance of individual citizens was reduced to *"paritas mediocritasque"* by dividing the supreme power among nine colleagues elected for only two months, and by repressing the power of the nobility through special legislation.²⁹

One year later Bruni returned from the Curia to settle down in Florence as a citizen and begin work on his *History of the Florentine People*. In the first book, describing the withering away of the urban culture that had flourished throughout Italy and especially in Etruria before the Romans, and observing that the ascendency of Rome had put an end to the independence of city-states all

over the Peninsula, he phrased his observations in this
way: Although Rome's domination over Italy had ended
wars and dangers for Etruria, the old Etruscan civilization
began to die from within. "For it is Nature's gift to mortals that, where the path to greatness and honor is open,
men easily raise themselves to a higher plane; where they
are deprived of this hope, they grow idle and lose their
strength. Thus, when at that time domination had been
transferred to the Romans, and men were no longer permitted to try to rise to public honors or spend their time
in matters of great import, the Etruscan *virtus* totally
faded away, weighed down much more by leisure and
inaction than by the sword of the enemy." [30]

It is evident in this historical appraisal that Bruni applied to the interpretation of the past the political experience of a period when every nerve in Florence was being
strained to prevent the reemergence of a universal Italian
state that, like the Empire of Rome, would stifle the individual growth of Florence's state and culture. Bruni's
explanation of Florentine liberty in 1428 [31] was nothing
but an extension of these views from relations among states
to relations among individual citizens—a transference to
the social sphere of an insight gained in the international
arena.[32]

To broaden our perspective of these Florentine ideas,
we should compare a contemporaneous humanistic voice
from the Milanese camp. In the 1420's, Uberto Decembrio, who had been among the first translators of Plato's
Politeia, dedicated to Filippo Maria Visconti four books
of dialogues *De Re Publica,* inspired by Plato and also
influenced deeply by the spirit of the north-Italian Renaissance Tyranny—a work which among other things advised
the Prince how to select the right men for his administration.[33] A true child of the period around 1400, Uberto
Decembrio, like his Florentine contemporaries, was con-

vinced that there was no worthy *nobilitas* unless it was self-acquired and independent of the accident of birth. Every man (so Decembrio had evidently learned from Cicero's *De Officiis*) was intended by Nature not only to become a rational being like all his fellow men, but also to play an individual role by cultivating and employing his particular gifts. Since "no one can resist nature and be happy," human happiness and the welfare of the whole body politic require that every individual find the profession, and the rung on the social ladder, for which Nature has intended him. To see to this is the duty of the prince —not only to render his subjects happy, but in the interest of the stability of his power.[34] "For when a man of a noble and choice mind makes his living in a mean occupation, his disposition will be changed from a beneficial to a false and malicious one." Gifted individuals who have missed their true vocation are prone to degenerate morally and in time become the shrewdest traitors, plotters against the prince, and the perpetrators of crimes well-planned beyond the ingenuity of lesser natures.[35]

The perfect prince, therefore, should enforce the employment of his subjects in accordance with the gifts Nature has given to each of them—and this even against the will of the parents who, as a rule, wish their sons to continue the father's profession. "A prince who pays proper attention to all things is to select some authoritative and experienced men before whom, at an appointed place in the city, the children have to be brought by their fathers at the beginning of their boyhood, so that those men may carefully examine the nature of each boy to determine what his strongest aptitudes are. When this is done, the examiners are to inform each of them and explain to him for what profession he seems most fit; they are to instruct the father to train the child for the profession for which he has been designated; and a heavy fine is to be placed on violators—unless the prince pleases otherwise. By such an order, I believe, the Athenians and the Spartans stabilized their commonwealths." If the parents are unable to meet the cost, the prince will provide funds from the public coffers; if the sons of old families show themselves fitted only for mediocre occupations, he will enforce upon them the decision of the board.[36]

This utopia, which makes enforcement from above a necessary condition for the happiness of the individual citizen and for the security of the state, constitutes, as it were, the Milanese rejoinder to the conviction of the Florentine humanists that, where the honors of the commonwealth are accessible to all citizens in free competition, "men take courage and raise themselves to a higher plane." In political outlook as well as in historical thought, monarchical and republican humanists, by the 1420's, had learned to fathom the different visions of man on which their opposing social ideals rested.

As to the later Florentine development, Bruni's conviction, formed during the struggle of the pre-Medicean Republic with the Visconti, that the Florentine constitution was a specimen of the *forma popularis* of government, and that equality of all citizens was the heart of Florentine constitutional life, was modified by the later 1430's when Cosimo de' Medici had come to power. When Bruni about 1439 was again asked for a brief analysis of the Florentine constitution, his judgment, expressed in a pamphlet written in Greek, *On the Politeia of the Florentines*,[37] was that the Florentine Republic had long since become a mixture between rule of the few and rule of the people. In a masterpiece of early-humanistic sociological reasoning, Bruni then argued that Florence had been a fully democratic republic only as long as all her citizens had fulfilled their civic duty of bearing arms for the republic themselves; when Florence had begun to rely on mercenary soldiers, influence had shifted to aristocrats and to the rich, since educated intelligence and financial resources had become more important than the risking of the citizen's life.[38] From the middle of the Trecento onward, so Bruni saw it now, Florence had been developing into a mixed state where the people merely accept or veto the laws, while preparation and formulation of all decisions lie in the hands of a small ruling group.[39]

We need not ask here whether this change in Bruni's appraisal was justified in the light of the first years of the Medicean Principate (perhaps it was truer than the widely accepted modern interpretation that the coming of Cosimo to power meant simply the strengthening of the popular element); nor can we dwell on the fact that this mature product of Bruni's sociological analysis represented a landmark on the road from early Quattrocento Humanism to the political science of the sixteenth century. What concerns us here is the observation that the youthful proud belief in the democratic liberty of Florentine life, which had arisen in the wars for independence against Giangaleazzo and Filippo Maria, was daunted in the years of the Medicean Principate. In the interpretation of Florence's constitutional liberty as well as of the *libertas Italiae*, sober resignation replaced the élan of the first Quattrocento generation from the 1440's or 1450's onward.

But this resignation was not the last word in the history of the Florentine ideas of civic liberty. In the late Quattrocento, when Medicean predominance over the Republic was swept away, the early Quattrocento conviction of the role civic freedom had played in inter-state relations throughout history and in the internal life of Florence again came to the fore. Machiavelli's philosophy of history was based on the persuasion that political *virtù*, to achieve its full growth, had always needed the active citizenship extant in small free states; like Bruni, Machiavelli saw a

disastrous effect of the rise of the Roman Empire in that
it stifled the vitality of every autonomous commonwealth
and put an end to competition among states. It was in view
of this historic phenomenon that Machiavelli delivered
the dictum that consummated the historical outlook of the
civic humanists from Bruni's school: the teaching of history
was that "where many states exist, there emerge many
efficient men," while "where a great number of states no
longer exist, *virtù* by necessity becomes gradually extinct,
because the cause responsible for *virtù* among men has disappeared."[40] A generation after Machiavelli, Donato
Giannotti, drafting the last great program of democratic
constitutional reform for Florence, was to advocate, in the
true spirit of Florentine civic Humanism, the admission
of all active citizens to the councils and offices on the
ground that only the full satisfaction of man's natural
ambition could assure internal peace and education for
citizenship in a free state.[41]

In returning to Bruni's oration on Nanni degli Strozzi
in the year 1428, we may then emphasize that it was the
pervasive dynamism of the Florentine faith in freedom
that made the Milanese government fear the effects of
both Bruni's *History of the Florentine People* and his
funeral speech on the fallen citizen-general.[42] In that
speech, the practical consequences of the ardent republicanism of Florence are clearly drawn by Bruni himself.
To sense the effectiveness of his plea against Renaissance
Tyranny, we must again listen to his own words. "We do
not tremble before one lord, nor are we servants to the
power of a few," Bruni explains the Florentine sentiment.
The preconditions indispensable for liberty—equality before the law and equal access to the civic rights and offices
—"cannot exist under the rule either of one man or of a
few." The eulogy of monarchy implies ideal qualities in
a ruler, such as are not met among men. "As a conse-

quence, the praise of monarchy has about it something fictitious and shadowy, as it were; it is not straightforward and concrete. To kings, as historians tell us, the good men are more suspect than the bad, and kings are always fearful of the *virtus* of others. The situation is not very different under the rule of a few men. Thus the rule of the people remains as the only legitimate form for the administration of the state; then liberty is genuine, equality before the law exists for all citizens, and the ambitions of *virtus* can thrive without suspicion." [43]

In looking back from these fervent expressions of Florentine republican sentiment voiced by Bruni in the first year of his chancellorship to Salutati's cool and almost pro-monarchical stand in *De Tyranno,* one measures the length of the road civic Humanism had traveled in the struggle for liberty against the Visconti.

The Ideal of a Citizen-Army

The concept of citizenship which sets the tone of Pericles' speech rests on the conviction that in a healthy republic the citizen must serve his commonwealth on the battlefield as well as in public office. In a similar way, the nerve of Bruni's eulogy is the praise of the fallen Strozzi as an exemplar of citizen-soldiership.

When Bruni wrote his oration, the citizen-in-arms in Italy had for two or three generations been replaced by mercenaries. Nevertheless, one could make no greater mistake than to suspect that Bruni was thoughtlessly following his classical model, or playing an idle game of humanistic rhetoric. The truth is that even here the ancient precedent helped to bring fully to the fore ideas that had grown out of the reality of Florentine life and were to reach maturity in the history of the late Florentine Renaissance. [44]

The ideal of reviving the citizen-army of the medieval commune (in the light of the later Florentine development, it was the anticipation of an actual necessity rather than merely a romantic dream) had been with Bruni for years when the impact of the renewed peril from the Visconti, the news of Nanni degli Strozzi's death, and Thucydides' influence fused in the 1428 oration. Here again the new train of thought had its starting point in the days of the struggle with Giangaleazzo. Although that war had been fought on both sides by mercenaries, when in 1397 Milanese armies had invaded Florentine territory, Cino Rinuccini had threatened that the citizens themselves would again take up arms.[45] And Bruni, in 1403, describing in his *Laudatio* the military deeds of medieval Florence, dwelt with unmistakable regret upon the fact that only in earlier generations "the Florentine people themselves went to war and took up arms." [46]

These boasts and historical reminiscences foreshadowed a growing criticism of the prevailing mercenary system. For Bruni the next step came when, in translating Plutarch, he learned more and more to admire the people of antiquity. He then began to look upon the contrast between the efficient soldiership of ancient Greece and Rome and the bloodless disorderly encounters of the modern mercenaries, with the same disgust for his own time that three generations later became characteristic of Machiavelli. The latter may have known Bruni's preface to his translation of Plutarch's *Vita Sertorii*, composed in 1408, where Bruni breaks out into the lament: "May I perish if I am not right in judging that, compared to antiquity, our own performance is childish and theatrical: our lack of order, discipline, and military expertness, our cowardly unwillingness to engage in close fight, and our contentment with skirmishes, flights, and pursuits in the manner of boys." [47]

Eight years later, while translating the *Nicomachean*

Ethics, Bruni found himself confronted with Aristotle's dictum that professional soldiers are ready to face the danger only on the assumption that they are the stronger party, but otherwise "turn cowards" and "are the first to fly, while citizen-forces die at their posts . . . ; for to the latter, flight is disgraceful and death preferable to safety on those terms." [48] No doubt, Bruni was deeply impressed by this view. In his *De Militia* of 1421, he showed himself interested in working out a sort of comparative historical analysis of the organizations of military defense in Greece, Rome, and Florence. In the funeral oration of 1428, all the events leading up to Nanni degli Strozzi's death are arranged so as to give a convincing illustration of Aristotle's passage. After a day of harrowing marches, Bruni relates, Strozzi's exhausted men were busy making camp and preparing their food when suddenly the troops of the Visconti broke from ambush and threw the scattered, unsuspecting soldiers into confusion. A general rout began. But "now it quickly became clear how great the difference is between the sense of honor in a foreign soldier and in a citizen. For the others, prizing nothing higher than their own salvation, gave way instantly; this man, however, holding the love for his *patria* higher than his own salvation, threw himself into the fray immediately, attempted to block the way of the enemies, and, by inciting and admonishing his companions and resisting the enemy with his own body, checked for a while the general onslaught." This self-sacrifice of the citizen at the crucial moment was enough to give the mercenaries time to collect themselves and to prevent a defeat which might have decided the war in favor of the Visconti. Strozzi, however, was carried back to camp with mortal wounds. [49]

This picture of the citizen-soldier, patterned on the model of the ancients, was the consummation of the Florentine experiences accumulated since the struggle with

Giangaleazzo. Thenceforth, while the war with Filippo Maria ran its course, the discussion of the citizen bearing arms did not again disappear from the literature of civic Humanism. In Bruni's *Vita di Dante* of 1436, the performance of the Florentine citizen-army in the battle at Campaldino, and Dante's own valorous part in it, are given so much space that the narrative of the fight comes close to overstraining the framework of the biography.[50] Not much later, in the ninth book of the *Historiae Florentini Populi*, which was written in 1437/38, Bruni discussed the final abolition of military service for Florentine citizens in the year 1351. This action, he judged, "surely meant nothing else but making the native population unfit for war, so that [the Florentines] had to look to others for the defense of their fortunes, unprepared as they were to defend themselves and fight for the *patria*." [51]

In his *Della Vita Civile*, written about 1433, Matteo Palmieri tells us that some people thought it dangerous to put arms into the hands of the citizens. But this fear seemed to him pusillanimous, because "great and memorable things have never been done, and will never be done, without danger." Palmieri, like his master Bruni, saw in the institution of citizens fighting for their homes, whether in the past or the present, a sign of political health. Although arguments may be found in favor of either citizen-soldiers or mercenaries, he said, "the upshot is that in all past centuries no city has ever been found to achieve first rank except by the *virtù* of her citizens and by their own hands." For only the citizens themselves care enough for their own cause; mercenaries are fond of war because they live by it, yet they are unreliable in the face of danger. Only in rare emergencies, therefore, did the ancients use hired soldiers; "and, similarly, in our own city about everything we own was captured by our forefathers' own hands." [52]

It would be wrong to expect the views accepted in Bruni's circle to have produced an immediate, practical effect during a period in which the *condottiere* and his mercenaries, despite the widespread lamentation about the misery produced by the mercenary system, were indispensable in every major battle. But the point is that to all future Florentine debates about the defense of the city the convictions of the civic humanists had added a leaven the subtle impact of which would still be felt when, from the late fifteenth century on, a Florentine militia again became a political factor to be reckoned with.

There is more than one piece of evidence that the remembrance of the ancient citizen fighting for his commonwealth continued to combine with practical considerations. Palmieri's *Della Vita Civile* had affirmed that in the Florence of his time it was "a widely discussed question" (*vulgare quistione*) "which are better, troops composed of mercenary soldiers and hired men, or armies formed by assembling one's own citizens." [53] We glimpse the reality behind these words when we find Stefano Porcari, a Roman who served as Florentine *capitano del popolo* in 1427, dealing with precisely this moot question in a public speech on the *piazza* of Florence. He, too, recounts that "people were given to arguing about (*si suole disputare*) what may be more useful for a republic: to have its citizens go into battle or to have them defend their commonwealth by hiring soldiers with their money." [54] Porcari declared that he personally preferred the mercenary system for his own time, but admitted that there were "many who consider it more useful for the republic to be defended personally by its citizens." [55] In this connection, Porcari distinguished the Carthaginian system of a mercenary army commanded by citizen-officers (this seemed to him substantially identical with the Florentine practice) from Rome's reliance on citizen-soldiers. There is no mistaking

the warmth of the respect for the Roman system shown
by its Florentine adherents. In Porcari's phrasing of their
arguments, only the citizen who fights for his country, his
family, and his possessions has in his heart that "fervent
stimulus" without which there is no readiness for sacrifice. Many nations in history have won surprising victories, thanks to the energy released through the institution of a citizen-army—especially the Romans, who would
have neither built nor preserved their empire had they
not been "*forti e valorosi cittadini*," and "who always
fought with their own hands and would have considered
it shameful if any but their own citizens had been the
cause of the Roman victories." [56]

In the orations delivered during the tenure of his Florentine office, Porcari echoed faithfully the problems and
attitudes he encountered in Florence.[57] He would hardly
have discussed the question had it not been in the air. As
late as the 1450's, it continued to stir the imagination of
the Florentines, as we gather from a poem of 1452 by
Cristoforo Landino. The young citizen-humanist of Bruni's
school called to mind the battle at Campaldino in which
Dante, according to Bruni's *Vita,* had proved himself on
the battlefield to be a true citizen. "Do not wage this war
with hirelings," Landino's poem warns. "Let the example
of the ancestors repeat itself. Have the daring to rely on
your own hands." [58]

From the 1460's onward, republicanism and civic Humanism were waning in Florence, and soon the philosophical and religious trends of Neo-Platonism would take
their place. By using Benedetto Accolti's *Dialogue on the
Preeminence of the Men of His Age* (1459/64) to determine the climate of the times, we learn that the disgust of the citizens with their *condottieri* and mercenaries
had not waned. To judge from Accolti, all the complaints
and accusations known from Bruni's *Sertorius* Preface were

still heard, accompanied by the contention that every-thing had been better in the hardy, disciplined armies of antiquity.[59] But the antithesis of the ancient to the modern was no longer accompanied by the assumption that the political life of the ancients had been superior because it had been built on defense by citizen armies. Antiquity, too, Accolti insists, had its mercenaries and among them unfaithful generals and soldiers, as for instance under the late Empire when Roman armies were a mixed lot of soldiers from all over the world, guilty of every imaginable "*perfidia, avaritia et libido.*" [60] On the other hand, the fact that modern military art is different from that of antiquity does not make it inferior as long as it is in har-mony with the exigencies of our age. To Accolti, there was no doubt about the efficiency, fervid energy and great-ness of many of the contemporary *condottieri*, who in his book appear in a long muster-roll of modern military glory.[61] By the 1460's, therefore, the point was reached where the world of the ancient citizen gradually ceased to serve as a model for Florentine citizens; the very rela-tionship with antiquity which had been the center of the thought of civic Humanism began to wane. Accolti's dia-logue is certainly not identical with the consensus of his Florentine contemporaries. But one cannot overlook that a few years later, from the late 1460's, the age of Lorenzo de' Medici was opening. For many years to come we hear no more of Florentines trying to find help for their own time by learning from the historic examples of the an-cient citizen-armies.

This does not mean, however, that the influence of the ideas of civic Humanism on the problem of mercenaries or self-defense had come to an end. By the 1460's and 1470's, some of those ideas had begun to be reflected in political works written elsewhere in Italy by authors who had some direct relationship to Florence. In this literature we find acceptance of the belief in the moral and even practical superiority of armies recruited from the population of a state. The most effective of these writings, the *De Institutione Reipublicae* by Francesco Patrizi—a treatise written during the 1460's, translated into many languages, and several times reprinted during the sixteenth century— laid down a detailed plan for a militia of robust peasants trained in time of peace. The author was a Sienese humanist who, in his younger years and before he was banished from Siena in 1457,[62] had been an active citizen in his native city. He did not start writing his book until he had, in exile, as his letters relate, come into contact "with a great number of Florentine citizens, who have become my friends."[63] We may assume that personal bonds with Florence had a similar significance for Bartolomeo Platina, who in 1471 dedicated to a Gonzaga prince of Mantua a comprehensive treatise, *De Principe*, considerable portions of which had already been worked out in the form of a dialogue and dedicated to Lorenzo de' Medici, under the title of *De Optimo Cive*, about ten years earlier. When reading Platina's ideas about the need and possibility of trained armies of citizens or subjects of a state, one cannot forget, even though his work was eventually dedicated to a prince, that the author, at the time of its inception, had spent four formative years in Florence, from 1456 to 1461 [64]—during the period in which the debates reflected in Accolti's dialogue took place and Patrizi enjoyed the *"consuetudo plurimorum Florentinorum civium."* Platina had, indeed, established relations in those years with the two principal heirs to the tradition of civic Humanism, Donato Acciaiuoli and Alamanno Rinuccini.[65] Like Patrizi's *De Institutione Reipublicae*, his book was helping to keep alive the ideas which had been handed down by the Florentine humanists of the first half of the Quattrocento.[66]

Not much more than two decades after Platina's work, we reach the time of Savonarola, when republican liberty returned to Florence. That the idea of a reorganization of the civic militia now reasserted itself outside the humanistic circles, can be inferred—and has long been inferred—from an elaborate program set forth in the pamphlet of a follower of Savonarola, Domenico Cecchi, printed in 1496.[67] The old ideals of civic Humanism were to reemerge and join these practical endeavors when, not much later, the idea of a Florentine militia shaped on the example of the Roman armies gained an essential place in the thought of Machiavelli, Guicciardini, and Donato Giannotti. By 1527-30, the time of the last Florentine Republic, the defense of the city had to a large extent returned into the hands of the citizens, and for a while the citizen-militia bravely resisted the superior armed might of Spain. Thus even in the reemergence of a body of citizens fighting their own battles—the factor which lent color and greatness to the last days of the Florentine Republic of the Renaissance—we still discover a vestige of the trends which had begun more than a century before.

In the last analysis we may say that all the elements of Florentine politics and culture had been developing according to a similar pattern, even though there were variations in different fields. The claim that Florentine Volgare literature was to become the equal of Greek and Latin literature, and that every language could have its own perfection, grew undisturbed from the years of the wars against the Visconti to the period of Lorenzo de' Medici, to Machiavelli, and on to the subsequent Cinquecento school of Florentine criticism. In other fields of intellectual life—the evolution of historical thought as well as the growth of the ideals of civic liberty, participation in the *vita politica*, and the defense of the common-wealth—the Principate of the Medici, after the middle of the Quattrocento, caused temporary deviations; but the earlier course of Florentine ideas was not lost. The seeds sown during the transition from the Trecento to the Quattrocento had taken root and grown until the middle of the century. What had been achieved by then would live on or reemerge and remold conduct and thought when in the days of the Republic of Savonarola and Machiavelli the civic freedom of Florence was restored.

EPILOGUE

THE NATURE AND SIGNIFI-
CANCE OF THE CRISIS

WE have traced in this book many aspects of the life of the two generations whose members played a part in the political and cultural transition around 1400. At the end we may well ask in what sense the conjunction of events and ideas which we observed can be said to amount to a "crisis" in the early Renaissance.

The term "crisis," in recent years, has become a rather hackneyed word in the vocabulary of historical writers. It often means no more than a period of danger or suspense, preserving little of its more precise meaning of a turning-point in the growth of an organism, institution, or people threatened by some weakness or disease, but finally regaining health and strength by successful resistance or adaptation to a vital challenge.

Our account has used the concept of "crisis" in the second and more profound sense: we have attempted to conceive the changes found in many areas of Italian life about 1400, especially in Florence, as both the climax and the incipient transformation of imbalances that had successively built up during the Trecento. Or, more exactly, we have noted two such processes and crises, one in the political life of Italy, the other in the genesis of humanistic culture. When both came to a head about 1400, it was the revolutionary shift in Italian politics which deeply influenced the outcome of the cultural crisis. The coincidence of these two developments, we have proposed, was largely responsible for the immense vitality and the quick pace of

Florence's intellectual life during the early Quattrocento.

To grasp the nature of the transition from the Trecento to the Quattrocento, one must be aware of several phases of this passage: how Trecento culture had come to the point where it revealed an innate inflexibility; how, by the turn of the century, unbounded classicist dedication to antiquity was opening new avenues but remained in many respects out of step with basic needs of the time; and how, eventually, civic Humanism in Florence found new answers to new challenges, calling into being ideas on life, history, and politics that were to stay in ascendancy throughout the Renaissance. Unless we assign to each of these phases its proper place, we will understand neither the nature of the crisis nor the subsequent development of the ideas of the Renaissance.

It is the special function of the chapters forming *Part One* of our account to ascertain that we are not deluding ourselves when we assume that the transformation about 1400 was more incisive than the changes experienced by any other single generation during the fourteenth and fifteenth centuries, and that on many counts the innovations at that time caused rapid shifts from "medieval" to "Renaissance." At the center of the transition we find the sudden rise of Florence to a key position, first in Italian politics and, subsequently, in Humanism and in Renaissance art. Never before had there existed a situation like the one in which Florence took her lonely stand in 1401-02. Until the third quarter of the fourteenth century, all political struggles in Italy had been cloaked in the medieval antithesis of Guelphs and Ghibellines. Every concrete interest had seemed to lose its identity by being regarded as a mere incident in the relationship between the Papacy and the Empire; none of the Guelph and Ghibelline cities, and Florence was no exception, had been or appeared to

be an autonomous state. At the climax of the Florentine-
Milanese confrontation, the situation in Italy became for
the first time fully secularized. The State of the Visconti
stood for monarchic integration and centralized power,
the Florentine Republic for the heritage of the free city-
states. Though the opponents still called themselves
Ghibelline and Guelph, medieval political theology and
the universalism of the Papacy and Empire no longer
shrouded the nature of the struggle nor the political values
which were at stake. The passion and will-power with
which the Florentines maintained their independence were
felt to be the moving forces of a struggle for civic liberty,
not, in the manner of the Trecento, of a religious crusade.
The policy of the surviving Italian states—Venice, Naples,
and even the territorial state of the Popes, in addition to
Milan and Florence—led to the first realization that the
various powers were interdependent and that their rela-
tionships were dominated by the forces of *"necessità"* and
"ragione."

It was the double experience of the secularization of
politics and of the rise of a republican city-state to a foremost place in the Italian scene that caused a revolution in
the politico-historical outlook of the Florentines: the history and nature of the Empire was for the first time envisaged without medieval and theological disguises. The
work of the Roman emperors of antiquity was henceforth weighed with an eye to civic liberty, freed from the
assumption that in the history of the Empire one had to
recognize the hand of God. Caesar was to be judged not
as the founder of a God-willed universal order, but by
the consequences of his political ambition for the freedom
and civic energies of the Roman people. Dante appeared
to be wrong in his appraisal of Caesar and his enemies; the
view of the ancient and medieval Empire enshrined in
the *Divina Commedia* became alien to Florentine readers.

By the same token, the medieval legend which credited
the founding of Florence to the divinely appointed architect of the Empire was now exposed as groundless and
prejudiced; humanistic criticism seemed to prove that
Florence was a Roman colony established at the time of
the *Respublica Romana*, and that in Florence, therefore,
the blood and civic-mindedness of free Roman citizens
had lived on to the present. Obviously, some of the key-
stones of the medieval outlook had suddenly crumbled;
questions and answers which were to characterize the
Renaissance had replaced them almost overnight.

Such, our account suggests, is the general nature of the
transition around 1400; but the picture would remain
vague could we not trace the genesis of the new outlook
in detail. This is the burden of *Part Two*. To begin with,
if we are to ascribe to the political experience of the year
1401-02 the function of a catalyst in the emergence of
new ideas, we must be absolutely sure that every mature
expression of the new thought was formed later than 1401-
02. Since most of the Florentine writings of the period are
not dated by their authors, the establishment of the exact
chronology is an indispensable premise for a history of
the Florentine crisis. Fortunately, our investigations give
a neat result: not a single source in which we find the
new politico-historical ideas in a mature form originated
earlier than 1402.

This does not mean, of course, that no vestige of the
new outlook had come to light before the Florentine-
Milanese conflagration reached its climax after 1400.
There had, indeed, been important harbingers and interesting pioneering efforts, such as precede every great historical change, for several decades and even generations.
But these had never lasted; each time they had been followed by some return to medieval ideas. Beginning with
Petrarch himself, this inability to stand firm when new

discoveries of ancient authors or of history or any observations of the contemporary world contradicted old traditions had been the very mark of the Trecento, giving the intellectual history of fourteenth-century Italy its drama, but also its frustrating quality. Like Petrarch, the representatives of the last Trecento generation—including Salutati—are constantly caught in such retreats. After having been the first to discover and vindicate in Cicero the Roman citizen and advocate of a life engaged in action for the state, Salutati—in *De Tyranno*—reverted to the condemnation of Cicero within the framework of a defense of Caesar and of the medieval belief in the divine ordination of universal Monarchy. When sustained criticism of Dante's bias in favor of the founder of the Empire spread among the younger generation, Salutati passionately rejected every step leading beyond Dante's medieval world. Just as he continued to view the final struggle with Milan in the light of the medieval Guelph idea, so he eventually returned in more than one respect to Augustine's dim view of the pagan *virtus* of Rome. Humanists living in the milieu of the north-Italian courts, like Giovanni Conversino and even Pier Paolo Vergerio, revealed a very similar turn of mind. However keen their observations on antiquity and on life in modern tyrant states, they proved incapable of breaking away from the heritage left by the medieval fusion of theology with the defense of Monarchy and the Empire.

As a result of our reexamination of fourteenth- and early fifteenth-century political literature, we have recognized that it was, indeed, Florentine republicanism which around 1400 introduced a perspective of the historical past free from the medieval entanglement with theological concerns. We have also found that Humanism was not the only creative force about 1400: some of the major innovations were first made by citizens who had been but slightly touched by Humanism—men like Cino Rinuccini and Gregorio Dati. Responding faster than the humanists to the practical challenges of the Visconti wars, these writers were quick to stress the element of city freedom, rather than the role of papal universalism, in the Guelph idea. Dati also appears to have been the first historian to argue clearly in terms of the nascent policy of equilibrium. He emphasizes facts from which causes and effects can be inferred; he is convinced that "reason" is superior to the uncontrolled bravery of knighthood in politics and war. Thus, earlier than in any humanistic writing, basic categories of the politico-historical thought of the Renaissance are encountered in the contemporary history of a citizen who, together with Bruni, is also our most eloquent witness to the profound influence which the defense of Florentine independence against Giangaleazzo exerted on the strengthening of Florentine republican sentiment. It is through writers like Cino Rinuccini and Gregorio Dati that we fully realize how superficial our knowledge of the growth of Humanism remains until it is placed in the framework of political writing and thought preceding, and contemporary with, the literary work of the humanists.

On the other hand, it is the life of the greatest Florentine humanist of the period, Leonardo Bruni, to which we must turn in order to appraise the lasting significance of the transformation of 1400. This subject is taken up in *Part Three*. Only in studying a great individual, representative of his time, can we hope to become aware of the profounder motivations in the changes of thought. In Bruni's early writings we not only find the most sensitive response to the problems of the transition period, we also encounter ideas and interests, known from other sources, as part of a personal development within whose framework the general problems become human and understandable. This is true first of all of Bruni's deep involvement in the experience of the Viscontean wars. When his *Laudatio Florentinae Urbis* is placed in its correct chronological niche—the moment of Florence's greatest elation after the test of 1402—it is seen to reflect both Bruni's own youthful aspirations (culminating in his intention to become the historian of Florence) and the mood and expectations of the city on the morrow of the Florentine triumph—this despite the fact that Bruni's small work is in its literary form a piece of rhetoric not yet fully illuminated by the new and original views of nascent civic Humanism. However, enough of the traditional clichés have been transformed to show that in this pamphlet appear the rudiments of virtually all the ideas (unrivaled elsewhere in Europe) that were to characterize Florentine historiography and Florentine discussions of constitutional forms and processes during the next hundred years. The great originality of the *Laudatio*, as we have observed, becomes all the more evident when one recalls the mixture found in medieval city eulogies of historical truth and legend, of secular and religious concerns, and of the significant and the trivial. In comparing this traditional attitude with the geometric spirit of Bruni's description of Florence and her scenic grandeur, with his search for causation and his sensitiveness to proportion, and with the keen analysis which the *Laudatio* applies to the historical perspective of ancient Rome as well as to the picture of the Florentine constitution, one realizes that in this work the threshold between the Medieval and the Renaissance has been crossed. In many of these respects, indeed, the *Laudatio* is a precursive counterpart to early-Quattrocento art.

The *Dialogi*, on the other hand, provide the crucial testimony to Bruni's personal development, especially since we can now distinguish the portions written before the trial of 1402 from what was added subsequently. We learn from

an analysis of the text that between the composition of
the first and second dialogue Bruni's convictions and relations to his friends passed through a brief, critical period—
a struggle which more than any external document makes
us aware of how the rise of a militant classicism and the
impact of Florence's ordeal and victory agitated the minds
of the humanists in Florence's civic circles and set one
against the other. As an attentive reading of the two dialogues reveals, it was the experience of 1402 which alienated Bruni from Niccoli's unbounded veneration of
antiquity and depreciation of the present, and thus preserved his civic Humanism at the time when it had just
taken root. After reflecting, in *Dialogus I*, Niccoli's aggressive contempt of the Florentine traditions of the Trecento in the name of a classicism that valued nothing but
antiquity, Bruni came into his own in *Dialogus II*, conceiving the ways to rehabilitate Dante and Petrarch that
were to remain those of the Florentine humanists throughout the fifteenth century. While Poggio, the third of the
three younger humanists in Salutati's circle, continued
Niccoli's classicism for many more years, Bruni, as early
as the time of *Dialogus II*, entered upon the two roads
along which he was to advance to uncontested leadership
in civic Humanism: on the one hand, that which took him,
as the historian of Florence, from the *Laudatio* to the
Historiae Florentini Populi, and, on the other, his fresh
revaluation of Florence's cultural heritage, beginning with
the reappraisal of the *"tre corone fiorentine"* in *Dialogus
II* and culminating with his *Vite di Dante e di Petrarca*
thirty years later.

Having discovered the key to Bruni's early development in the succession of these two phases—one of unbounded devotion to antiquity and another in which the
Florentine tradition was reaffirmed against the narrow
standards of classicist purism—one quickly recognizes that

Bruni was answering a challenge spread far and wide at the turn of the Trecento. There was, indeed, much to be feared as well as welcomed. The recognition of antiquity as the sole valid standard was apt to bring about not only bold independence from medieval standards, but also an atmosphere of artificiality in which the only thing that counted was imitation of the ancients; Dante and all Volgare writers were scorned, and even Petrarch, as a mere beginner of the classical studies, appeared unacceptable. Cultivated citizens, believing in the all-inclusive superiority of antiquity, came to disdain the age and society in which they lived; they neglected their civic duties. And along with ancient literature, built as it was on classical mythology, even pagan religion might be included among those ancient things instinctively revered. One of the tasks of *Part Four* is to demonstrate that all these dangers were real at the turn of the Trecento; that, simultaneously with the political crisis of Italy, a militant kind of classicism was, indeed, diverting educated men from participation in communal life; and that the coming of civic Humanism must be largely interpreted as a reassertion of the public spirit against such dangers.

Part Four explores still other traits of civic Humanism. In the Florentine city-state, lovers of ancient literature, when reading Aristotle and Cicero, began to perceive that the ideals accepted by the citizens of the ancient city-states could serve as an ethic of social engagement for citizens in their own modern states. Beside the type of humanistic scholar who defended withdrawal on the double ground that it was apt to minimize his contacts with the inferior modern world and could serve him as a bridge to religious contemplation, there was henceforth to be a type of humanist who found the crucial subject for his studies in history and politics and who, following the ancient model, was expected to be not only a man of culture but also a better and more useful citizen. At the same time, Florentine humanists learned still another lesson from antiquity: just as Athenian citizens had built their culture by using their own vernacular, Greek; and just as the Romans, despite their respect for Greek, had become great by using their own vernacular, Latin; so modern Florentines, despite the humanistic study of Latin, ought to hold in esteem their modern vernacular, the language of Dante. From the time of the crisis at the turn of the Trecento, these trends—the civic ethics of the *vita activa-politica*, the new realistic study of history and politics, and the vindication of the Volgare—were gradually and tenaciously built up. When, after the middle of the Quattrocento, the great time for a humanistic engagement in the life of the commonwealth had passed, the defense of the vernacular *lingua fiorentina* as a worthy competitor with Greek and Latin attained, along with the new historical studies, a central position in the intellectual world of the Florentine humanists. During the sixteenth century, all over Europe, most of the ideas connected with the vindication of the modern vernaculars and with the struggle against rigid classicism continued a pattern of thought that had had its earliest precedents among Florentine humanists of the Quattrocento. These precedents have usually not been sufficiently noticed, but the line of Florentine Quattrocento thought on the Volgare traced in the last chapter of *Part Four* should suffice to underscore their importance.

One uncertainty regarding the Florentine crisis in the early Renaissance still remains—a doubt concerning its presumed historic effectiveness. Since we ascribe to the changes around 1400 an influence lasting for decades and, in some respects, for generations, one would expect either that the initial challenge continued for a long time or that the transformations included social and institutional changes that permanently altered the environment. We know, however, that Florence's hour of trial was cut short by Giangaleazzo's sudden death, and this premature elimination of the deadly threat must have diminished the impressiveness of the Florentine triumph. We have also seen that Florence's institutions and economic-social conditions did not undergo any major alterations during the late Trecento and the early Quattrocento. How, then, can the brief period of crisis in Florence's struggle with Milan account for constant changes in the humanistic outlook?

Part Five gives the answer. Although it lasted no more than a few years, and although it was not reinforced by incisive social changes, the clash between the Florentine Republic and Giangaleazzo's empire did initiate a new historical epoch. Until after the middle of the Quattrocento, Giangaleazzo's attempts to conquer large parts of the Peninsula were taken up successively by other aggressive princes, and Florence remained the champion of city-state freedom in Italy during this entire period, withstanding the threats and inroads of Renaissance Tyranny. Hardly had Ladislaus of Naples' efforts during the 1410's to extend the Southern Kingdom toward the north as far as Tuscany come to an end when Giangaleazzo's son took up the southward expansion of Milan. It is true that the dramatic situation of 1402 in which Florence was left the only antagonist to the Visconti did not return during the 1420's-40's, but this does not mean that the antagonism between city-state and tyranny had any less an impact on the political climate. Although the Florentines could no longer claim that the liberty of Italy depended on Florence alone, Florence was now a leading member in a stable alliance of Italy's republican states. In the atmosphere of a common struggle of all the elements standing for "*libertas*" in Italy, the political and historical outlook engendered by the brief period of Florence's lone championship against Giangaleazzo could crystallize into mature ideas widely accepted in Italy. When looking at the Florentine political conduct during the wars with Ladislaus and Filippo Maria, we find among the Florentine statesmen and the members of the citizen councils reactions similar to those of the days of Giangaleazzo Visconti—the same way of reasoning and the same determination in the city's diplomacy. The only major difference is the now congenial response from allies, especially from Venice. Not until the late 1440's, after the final demise of the Visconti regime, was the era of friendly cooperation among the republics to be replaced by the cool atmosphere of the equilibrium diplomacy of the later Renaissance. We have referred to the voices of warning and personal dismay which at that time were heard among both Florentine and Venetian humanists and which give us striking glimpses of the profoundness and inevitability of the change that came about between the first and the second half of the century.

Typical of the intellectual situation which prevailed from the 1420's to the 1440's is the fate of the *Laudatio*. During the 1430's, Bruni's eulogy, which had remained little noticed for almost three decades, began to be read widely. It was bitterly attacked in a Milanese imitation which, without much originality, applied many of Bruni's observations to Milan, while Bruni in Florence was by that time restating in mature form the daring suggestions of the *Laudatio* in his *Historiae Florentini Populi* and in his *Vite di Dante e di Petrarca*. Meanwhile, even a humanist who during the wars with Giangaleazzo had been as little touched by the civic attitude as Poggio Bracciolini, had developed into a champion of the Florentine criticism of Caesar. By the 1430's, Poggio was defending the *Respublica Romana* and the republican *virtus* of ancient Rome against the Caesar cult of the humanists at the north-Italian tyrant-courts—in one of the great politico-historical controversies of the time, in which Venetian

humanists stood shoulder to shoulder with their Florentine allies. But perhaps the most memorable outcome of
the situation prevailing in the 1420's and 1430's was that
the Florentine ideas on civic liberty, which had first come
to the fore in the pamphlets composed in resistance to
Giangaleazzo, were now given their final formulation in
an ever closer relationship with the ancient civic ideals.
Late in the 1420's, Buonaccorso da Montemagno, in interpreting the Florentine ideal of social mobility from the
perspective of the struggle between plebeians and patricians
in ancient Rome, composed the small work that became
a medium through which the Florentine belief in civic
virtus influenced the still chivalric literature in the transalpine countries. At about the same time, during a second
climax of the Florentine-Milanese encounter, the Florentine recognition of a citizen's untrammeled right to rise
socially and to participate actively in the state found its
proudest expression in Leonardo Bruni's creative adaptation of Pericles' *Funeral Oration*. For although, under the
actual conditions of Florence's political life, there was now
less opportunity for the realization of these claims than
there had been two or three generations previously, the
ideal itself still was, and remained, an ever recurrent persuasion among the Florentines down to the time of
Machiavelli.

When all these observations have been given their
proper place, what do we learn for the appraisal of the
Renaissance from the crisis in which the Florentine commonwealth and nascent humanistic culture were challenged
and regenerated about and after 1400? In our Introduction, we have tried to put ourselves on guard against any
rash attempt to establish a balance of liberty and despotism
in Renaissance Italy from the material assembled in this
book. We have tried, to be sure, not to give only the Flor-

entine side of the recounted events, and on occasion we have not failed to consider as well their perspective as seen through the eyes of publicists and humanists hostile to Florence. In fact, we have placed in focus a number of neglected documents from the Milanese side, proceeding from the works of writers and poets in the service of Giangaleazzo, to humanists like Giovanni Conversino, Uberto Decembrio, and Pier Candido Decembrio. But it remains true that a comparative appraisal of the legacies of the opposing camps about 1400 to the thought of the Renaissance would have to start from an approach that is not primarily concerned with the historic consequences of the Florentine contribution.

Even comprehensive accounts of the period, however, will hardly ever succeed in determining the relative significance of the component elements definitively. There is no final gauge for measuring the republican or the tyrannical contribution in quantitative terms. Any comparative historical appraisal is bound to be qualitative; that is, its validity depends on what value we ascribe to the developments which we compare. If we can make one of the groups or movements of the Renaissance better understood and, in consequence, better appreciated, a certain shift of emphasis in our conceptions of Renaissance and Humanism will be in order. This is all we can hope for, and this has been attempted for early Renaissance Florence in the present book. The greater clarity and precision at which we have arrived should, in the future, prove a weight in the balance, whatever the changing estimates of the sum total of the Renaissance may be.

In one respect, the effectiveness of our criteria may be assessed more quantitatively. Historical perspectives differ in usefulness according to whether they bring into focus merely the area for which they were worked out, or whether their pattern, useful at one point, subsequently proves applicable to broader fields. At the end of our analysis, therefore, we should ask to what extent the answers found to the problems of the political and cultural transition about 1400 can serve as keys to more inclusive historical phenomena—other and wider aspects of Florentine history, as well as the later growth of Renaissance Humanism outside Florence and Italy.

Let us, at this point, once more recall the sequence of the developments which we have traced for the time about 1400. We began by observing the impact of the Florentine wars for independence on the republican convictions of the Florentines, initially during Florence's unaided fight against Giangaleazzo and, subsequently, during the long period of association with other Italian republics. Awareness of this impact made us alive to the fact that a restrengthening of the communal spirit became one of the molding forces of the early Florentine Renaissance. Secondly, in trying to keep in view the rise of Classicism in many areas of Renaissance culture around 1400, we discovered a growing alienation from established traditions and a disinclination to take on the indispensable tasks of the day, especially in the Florentine commonwealth—a danger emerging from the area of culture that grew simultaneously with the menace of a triumph of Visconti despotism in politics. We have seen that in both respects a crisis developed which called forth fresh energies and creative adaptations. Third and finally, we found that in Florence the answer to this double challenge was the rise of a humanistic education which endeavored to prepare citizens for engagement in the tasks of their own age and state—civic Humanism.

It can easily be seen that every stage of these developments was paralleled or closely complemented in other areas of fifteenth-century Florentine history. In the present book, we have explored almost exclusively the influence of changes in the inter-state conditions of the Peninsula that plunged Florence into a war of survival and prepared the rise of an equilibrium system and of rational diplomacy, thus creating the background for the political and historical thought of the Renaissance. This, however, cannot have been the whole story of the interaction of ideas and events in the early Quattrocento. The confidence in the *"libertas Florentina"* and the readiness for sacrifice and extraordinary exertions that are found in the city-councils must have had wider reverberations in the constitutional life of the Republic. As for economic conditions, we must make a distinction. We have noted that no major economic changes are discernible that could have caused, or contributed to, the crisis at the turn of the Trecento. On the other hand, it is well known that the Florentine region-state which emerged from the struggle with the Visconti empire soon entered upon one of the boldest economic enterprises in Florentine history—namely, the creation not only of a Florentine navy but also of a state merchant-fleet on the model set by some of the Italian maritime cities. Simultaneously, especially during the 1420's to 40's, Florence tried to rebuild her industry and trade by a mercantilist policy based on the new territorial dominion. Undoubtedly, in both these areas of Florentine life—the institutional development of the last pre-Medici Republic and the endeavors at maritime and industrial expansion—we find developments that can be fully understood only against the background of the responses which Florence had made to the challenge of the inter-state conflagration at the beginning of the century.

Something similar is true of the aftereffects on the history of Florentine Humanism. There have been relatively few opportunities in this study to trace the actual emergence among Florentine humanists of an attitude of active engagement in Florentine political life and, in interrelation with it, of a humanistic philosophy of the *vita activa-politica*. The reason is that these developments largely followed the events at the turn of the century after a number of years had passed, since moral attitudes need time to grow. It was, indeed, not before the second quarter of the Quattrocento—not until about the time of Bruni's "*Oratio Funebris* on Nanni degli Strozzi"—that the ripe fruits of the new civic philosophy appeared. But though there is a time lag when compared with the rapid rise of the new politico-historical outlook, there can be no doubt that the emergence of the *vita activa* philosophy in Florence cannot be seen in its proper framework unless the crisis about 1400 is given its due place. The same framework is needed to elucidate the fact that, during the early Quattrocento, Florence for several decades was the focal point of Italian Humanism, as it was of Italian art. It is this framework which explains that a substantial part of the philosophy of life and the philosophy of history characteristic of the Quattrocento first appeared in Florence, from where the new ideas spread throughout the rest of the Peninsula. The better this unique place of Florence in the early Quattrocento is recognized and established from the sources, the wider will appear the range of the invigorating influence of the preceding crisis.

By engendering a new type of Humanism—*civic Humanism*—the transition about 1400 and in the early Quattrocento even transcended in significance the history of Florence and of Renaissance Italy. Civic Humanism, as it emerged from the challenge of the crisis, exhibited, as our analysis has shown, several diverse facets. There was the new philosophy of political engagement and active life,

developed in opposition to ideals of scholarly withdrawal.
There was the new historical interpretation of Rome and
the *Imperium Romanum* from the vantage-point of contemporary political experience. And, finally, there was the
fresh approach to a vernacular Humanism and a defense of the moderns against the ancients—the still inconsistent, but already unmistakable demand that in the
present-day world, in dealing with one's own state, language, and literature, one should act as the ancients acted
in dealing with *their* states, languages, and literatures.
Obviously, these are not tendencies and attitudes that appeared accidentally at about the same time, within a few
decades after Florence's political crisis. They represent
complementary trends; they form a coherent pattern—
inseparable elements of a type of Humanism not fully
developed before the early Renaissance. What we learn
from Florentine culture after 1400, therefore, is that we
must not think of Humanism as an intellectual movement
already basically complete in the Trecento, and merely
adapting its outlook during the Quattrocento to the needs
of diverse social and regional groups inside and outside
Florence. We come much nearer to the truth when we think
of Humanism as an organism, some vital parts of which
did not develop until the Quattrocento. Humanism, as
molded by the Florentine crisis, produced a pattern of
conduct and thought which was not to remain limited to
Florentine humanists. From that time on there would
exist a kind of Humanism which endeavored to educate
a man as a member of his society and state; a Humanism
which refused to follow the medieval precedent of looking upon the Rome of the emperors as the divinely guided
preparation for a Christian "Holy Empire" and the center
of all interest in the ancient world; a Humanism which
sought to learn from antiquity by looking upon it not
melancholically as a golden age never again to be realized,

but as an exemplary parallel to the present, encouraging the moderns to seek to rival antiquity in their vernacular languages and literatures and in many other fields. Whereas such an approach to the past and to the present had nowhere been found before 1400, it became inseparable from the growth of Humanism during the Renaissance.

This is not to say, of course, that all these characteristics —or, indeed, any—were to appear in every later humanist. We can easily find other types of basic humanistic attainments and approaches to the past and present. But Renaissance Humanism would by no means occupy the place in the growth of the modern world that is rightly attributed to it had those traits ever disappeared again after they had emerged from the early-Quattrocento crisis. They thoroughly shaped the aspirations of the later Italian Renaissance, outside as well as inside Florence, as everyone is aware who remembers the function of the new politico-historical thought and of vernacular Humanism in sixteenth-century Italy. They appeared in the transalpine countries, sometimes encouraged by the influence of Italian—and, especially Florentine—writings, and sometimes freshly re-created among humanists who served the rising western nation-states under conditions not so different from those which, during the early Italian Renaissance, had prevailed among humanists in the Florentine Republic. And although this type of a socially engaged, historically-minded, and increasingly vernacular Humanism far from exhausts the rich variety of the humanistic movements of the Renaissance, in many respects it was the salt in the humanistic contribution to the rise of the modern world.

Whenever we want to visualize this contribution to modernity and its historical growth, we must revive the memory of what happened in Florence and among her citizens and humanists during the early Quattrocento. In this far-reaching impact, not only on Renaissance Italy, but on the entire course of Humanism, lies the ultimate significance of the developments whose history has here been traced.

NOTES

CHAPTER 1

[1] Until the first appearance of the present book, there had been no comprehensive effort to prove the emergence of the major tenets of the historical philosophy of the Renaissance as early as about 1400. Claudio Varese's *Storia e Politica nella Prosa del Quattrocento* (Turin, 1961) has contributed some interesting detail and used a similar approach for a number of Florentine writers of chronicles and memoirs not included in the present account, especially Buonaccorso Pitti, Giovanni Morelli, and Giovanni Cavalcanti. Cesare Vasoli, "Storia e Politica nel Primo Umanesimo Fiorentino," *Itinerarî*, XIII (1955), refines the thesis of the genesis of the historical thought of the Renaissance about 1400 by adding some pertinent comments. For attempts to trace some of the topics from the early to the late Renaissance, cf. the sketches by August Buck, *Das Geschichtsdenken der Renaissance* ("Schriften und Vorträge des Petrarca-Instituts Köln," no. 9, 1957) and H. Baron, "The *Querelle* of the Ancients and the Moderns as a Problem for Renaissance Scholarship," *Journal of the History of Ideas*, XX (1959).

An early outline of the author's ideas on the growth of the Florentine outlook on history from early Humanism to Machiavelli was given in the essay "Das Erwachen des historischen Denkens im Humanismus des Quattrocento," *Historische Zeitschrift*, CXXXXVI (1932). The recognition that Machiavelli, in spite of his acrimonious criticism of his humanistic predecessors in historiography, was in vital respects indebted to Bruni's historical outlook and method may today be considered an established fact. It has been successively revealed by G. Salvemini, *Magnati e Popolani in Firenze dal 1280 al 1295* (Florence, 1899), esp. p. 243; E. Santini, *Leonardo Bruni Aretino e i suoi "Historiarum Florentini Populi Libri XII"* (reprinted from *Annali della R. Scuola Normale Superiore di Pisa*, XXII [1910]), esp. pp. 117-122; P. Joachimsen, *Geschichtsauffassung und Geschichtsschreibung in Deutschland unter dem Einfluss des Humanismus* (Leipzig, 1910), esp. p. 224; and W. K. Ferguson, *The Renaissance in Historical Thought, Five Centuries of Interpretation* (Boston, 1948), p. 15. The close connection between Bruni's civic Humanism and the historical philosophy of early-sixteenth century Florence to which this book will often refer, has been fully recognized by Rudolf von Albertini, *Das florentinische Staatsbewusstsein im Übergang von der Republik zum Prinzipat* (Bern,

1955), for the politico-historical outlook of Machiavelli's Florentine contemporaries; and by Gennaro Sasso, *Niccolò Machiavelli: Storia del suo pensiero politico* (Naples, 1958), for Machiavelli himself.

[2] Some aspects of the transformation of humanistic thought in the civic atmosphere of early-Quattrocento Florence were sketched for the first time in the author's preface to his edition of *Leonardo Bruni Aretino, Humanistisch-Philosophische Schriften* (Leipzig, 1928), where the term "civic Humanism" (*Bürgerhumanismus*) was first used. Subsequent studies which elaborate the picture of this transformation and complement the present book include: "The Historical Background of the Florentine Renaissance," *History*, n.s. XXII (1938), and in an enlarged Italian translation in *La Rinascita*, I (1938); "Cicero and the Roman Civic Spirit in the Middle Ages and the Early Renaissance," *Bulletin of the John Rylands Library*, XXII (1938); "Franciscan Poverty and Civic Wealth as Factors in the Rise of Humanistic Thought," *Speculum*, XIII (1938).

A kindred view of fifteenth-century civic Humanism in Florence is found in Eugenio Garin's fundamental works, especially *Der Italienische Humanismus* (Bern, 1947), in Italian under the title of *L'Umanesimo Italiano: Filosofia e vita civile nel Rinascimento* (Bari, 1952); and *La cultura filosofica del Rinascimento Italiano* (Florence, 1961). For an estimate of the role in recent scholarship of the problems posed in the present book, cf. especially: Denys Hay, *The Italian Renaissance in Its Historical Background* (Cambridge, England, 1961); William J. Bouwsma, *The Interpretation of Renaissance Humanism* (Washington, D.C.: American Historical Association, 1959); G. Radetti, "Le Origini dell'Umanesimo Civile Fiorentino nel Quattrocento," *Giornale Critico della Filosofia Italiana*, XXXVIII (1959); R. Spongano, "L'Umanesimo e le Sue Origini," *Giornale Storico della Letteratura Italiana*, CXXX (1953), reprinted in *Due Saggi* cited p. 541, note 43 below; F. Chabod, "The Concept of the Renaissance," in Chabod's *Machiavelli and the Renaissance* (London, 1958).

[3] On the Italian Peninsula, assemblies of estates or feudal parliaments developed only in Sicily, Naples, Sardinia, the Papal State, and in Friuli in the northeast, and Monferrat and Piedmont in the northwest; the remainder of central and northern Italy did not experience the growth of any of the representative provincial institutions characteristic of the late feudal age. Cf. the survey of *Il Parlamento in Italia nel Medio Evo e nell' Età Moderna* by A. Marongiu, vol. XXV of the "Études Présentées a la Commission Internationale pour l'Histoire des Assemblées d'États" (Milan, 1962).

CHAPTER 2

[1] Cf. F. Schevill, in the chapter, "Florence Encounters the Problem of the Despot (1313-1343)," of his *History of Florence* (New York, 1936).

[2] For the still ecclesiastical and crusade-like hue of this fight see C. Capasso in *Bollettino della Società Pavese di Storia Patria*, VIII (1908), 265-317, 408-436; and G. Romano, *ibid.*, III (1903), 411-432.

[3] F. Baldasseroni, *Studi Storici*, XII (1903), 85-89.

[4a] According to Matteo Villani's account of the years 1361-1362 in his *Cronica*, X, 57.

[4b] We are now well informed about Florence's mid-Trecento foreign policy, its social background and the increasing futility of medieval Guelph ideology through the fundamental studies of Gene A. Brucker; see his *Florentine Politics and Society, 1343-1378* (Princeton, 1962), esp. pp. 140-147, 172-183, 221-243. The rich material in the Florentine archives has here been fully utilized and integrated for the first time. One should not forget, however, that "Guelphism" did not really wither away during the latter part of the fourteenth century, as Brucker, in agreement with many other recent scholars, makes it appear. Rather, there was a transformation of the medieval Guelph ideology into a well-defined "Guelphism" of Renaissance Florence—a development whose basic significance for Florentine politico-historical thought during the Quattrocento will emerge in several pages of the present book. Simultaneously with and independently from Brucker, Marvin B. Becker reached many essentially similar conclusions in a number of important papers, among which the most comprehensive is "Church and State in Florence on the Eve of the Renaissance (1343-1382)," *Speculum*, XXXVII (1962), 509-527.

[4c] Cf. Brucker, *op. cit.*, pp. 141f.

[4d] Cf. *ibid.*, pp. 181ff.

[4e] Cf. *ibid.*, pp. 224ff., 233f.

[4f] Cf. *ibid.*, pp. 235f., 241ff.

[4g] See Brucker, *op. cit.*, pp. 138ff., 182f., 241ff.; Becker, *op. cit.*, pp. 515ff., and Becker's "An Essay on the *Novi Cives* and Politics, 1343-1382," *Mediaeval Studies*, XXIV (1962), 35-82.

[4h] To quote Brucker, *op. cit.*, p. 183: Florence's "refusal to defend Bologna against Bernabò's invasion [in 1359-60] was essentially a negative gesture; it was no substitute for a foreign policy. Opponents of Guelf diplomacy had not yet evolved a coherent plan to meet the serious threats to Florentine security, from the Visconti behemoth to the armed companies."

[5] ". . . che seguita ne' fatti del mondo la Santa Chiesa."

[6] ". . . che seguitano l'imperio, o fedele o infedele."

[7] ". . . fondamento e rocca ferma e stabile della libertà d'Italia e contraria a tutte le tirannie" (Matteo Villani, *Cronica*, IV, 78 and VIII, 24).

[8] "Universitatem Guelforum, si ad divinum respicias, cum Romana Ecclesia, si ad humanum, cum Libertate coniunctam reperies, . . . sine qua nec Respublica constare ulla potest, nec sapientissimi viri existimarunt vivendum." For Bruni's authorship, see note 18 to Chap. 17. In the preceding Statute, phrased in 1335, the "Parte e Università de' Guelfi" had been defined as identical with the "devoti di santa Chiesa." There was as yet no suggestion that Guelphism was connected with "liberty," or that the Ghibellines stood for "tyranny." Cf. the *Prologo* of the Statute of 1335 in *Giornale Storico degli Archivi Toscani*, I (1857), 4.

[9] On the survival and transformation of the Guelph idea in Renaissance Florence cf. the writer's "Die politische Entwicklung der italienischen Renaissance," *Historische Zeitschrift*, CLXXIV (1952), 43f., 48f., and *Crisis: Appendices*, pp. 445f.

[10a] A change which, although basic for the political position of Florence on the eve of the Renaissance, has hitherto been little known. Cf. *Crisis: Appendices*, pp. 446f. Recently, however, it has been more widely recognized, though variously interpreted; see Brucker, *op. cit.*, pp. 140f. On N. Rubinstein's important findings, also basically in accord with the pages that follow—"Florence and the Despots: Some Aspects of Florentine Diplomacy in the Fourteenth Century," *Transactions of the Royal Historical Society*, Ser. v, vol. II (1952)—cf. *Crisis: Appendices*, pp. 446f.

[10b] Against any "signore sceso d'oltremonte, o da qualche tiranno non toscano." See Francesco Briganti, *Città dominanti e comuni minori nel medio evo* (Perugia, 1906), pp. 197ff., where the subsequent leagues of Florence with the Tuscan cities up to 1392 are listed.

[11a] As Brucker, *op. cit.*, p. 268, with a view to the late 1360's, remarks: "A theme frequently articulated in *Pratiche* sessions was that Florentine security depended on the maintenance of free, republican government in the Tuscan towns." "Florence had become the dominant power in Tuscany, her hegemony based not upon military might, but upon a recognition of her value as a protector of Tuscan liberty." Cf. also Brucker, pp. 351f.

[11b] "Tanto tutior huic urbi sua videtur esse libertas, quanto latius se liberi populi circunfundant. Ex quo debet cuique facile persuaderi Florentinum populum libertatis cuiuslibet populi defensorem, in quibus et suam libertatem faciliori cura defendit" (Salutati, *Ep. III*

17, in *Epistolario di Coluccio Salutati* ["Fonti per la storia d'Italia," no. 15-18, Rome, 1891-1905], ed. F. Novati, vol. I, pp. 194f.). See also *Crisis: Appendices,* p. 447.

¹²ᵃ G. Pirchan, *Italien und Kaiser Karl IV in der Zeit seiner zweiten Romfahrt* (Prague, 1930), pp. 208, 222, 380ff., 404ff.

¹²ᵇ For the lasting after-effects of the "War of the Eight Saints" cf. Becker, "Church and State," pp. 523ff.

This historical label was not given to the war by contemporaries but originated a few generations later, probably by mistake, as R. C. Trexler, "Who Were the Eight Saints?", *Renaissance News,* XVI (1963), 89-94, has shrewdly established. The emotional term, *Otto Santi,* was used by contemporaries not for the "Eight with dictatorial power" (*Otto di Balìa*) who were the war leaders, but for another board of eight charged with the sensitive task of taxing the clergy and seizing church property to help finance the war. When, about 1445, the chronicler, Domenico Buoninsegni, assumed that it was the central *Otto di Balìa* that had been nicknamed *Otto Santi,* all later historians of Florence, beginning with Poggio Bracciolini, gave the war this apparently natural and characteristic epithet, and even today no more appropriate term is available.

¹³ See D. M. Bueno De Mesquita's *Giangaleazzo Visconti, Duke of Milan, 1351-1402* (Cambridge, 1941), an indispensable guide through the labyrinth of the diplomacy of the period, which, however, neglects the works of the contemporary publicists and thereby some of the most revealing testimonies for the *meaning* of the Milanese-Florentine struggle. Cf. *Crisis: Appendices,* pp. 386 and 447f.

¹⁴ See the account of the contemporary, Gregorio Dati, p. 173 below.

¹⁵ᵃ See the opinions of the citizens consulted by the government in the *consulte* of November 23-25, 1388, published by G. Collino in *Archivio Storico Lombardo,* XXXVI (1909), pp. 339-349; esp. the opinions, "quod dominus Paduanus non adiuvetur neque palam neque occulte, ne Veneti provocentur et veniatur ad guerram cum ipsis . . ." (p. 343, similarly pp. 343-344), and "non capiatur guerra cum comite propter Venetos" (p. 345). On the *Consulte* records as an historical source, see pp. 384f. and note 52 to Chap. 16 below.

¹⁵ᵇ ". . . quod omnibus Tuscis liberis comune [of Florence] se uniat, pacificet et concordet" (*op. cit.,* p. 347).

¹⁵ᶜ "Nos esse vobis non solum vicinitate situs, sed identitate regiminis, ac studio libertatis, et similes et conformes"; passage in a Florentine letter to Siena of April 11, 1390, quoted from the copy in the Florentine archives by N. Rubinstein, "Florence and

the Despots: Some Aspects of Florentine Diplomacy," *Transactions of the Royal Historical Society*, ser. v, vol. II (1952), p. 32.

[16] De Mesquita, *Giangaleazzo*, p. 107, from archival documents.

[17] On Venice's attitude during this period see G. Bolognini, *Nuovo Archivio Veneto*, IX (1895), 3-110, and R. Cessi, *ibid.*, n.s. XXVIII (1914), 233-307.

[18] De Mesquita, *Giangaleazzo*, pp. 342-345; N. Rubinstein, pp. 43f.

[19] "Nos . . . Tyranno Lombardiae, qui se Regem facere cupit et inung[u]ere, bellum indicimus, et pro libertatis nostre defensione ac libertate populorum, quos tam grave iugum opprimit, arma movemus." "Nos popularis civitas, soli dedita mercature sed, quod ipse tanquam rem inimicissimam detestatur, libera, et non solum domi libertatis cultrix, sed etiam extra nostros terminos conservatrix, ut nobis et necessarium et consuetum sit pacem querere in qua solum possumus libertatis dulcedinem conservare." For these manifestoes cf. *Crisis: Appendices*, pp. 448f., and E. Garin, "I cancellieri umanisti della Repubblica fiorentina," in his *La Cultura Filosofica del Rinascimento Italiano* (Florence, 1961), pp. 14f., where the point is made that Salutati must have been the author.

[20] See the reports in De Mesquita, *Giangaleazzo*, pp. 123 and 346 (". . . cum sint omnes quasi rustici inermes et non assueti in factis armorum").

[21] Shown by L. Mirot, *Revue des Études Historiques*, C (1933), 499f.

[22] ". . . cum totis gentibus . . . italicis." From a communication on the battle of Alessandria sent by Giangaleazzo to the Pope, quoted in N. Valeri, *Vita di Facino Cane* (Turin, 1940), p. 40.

[23] See De Mesquita, *Giangaleazzo*, pp. 193-196.

[24a] De Mesquita, *Giangaleazzo*, pp. 231ff., 238, 244

[24b] The letter from Perugia's chancellery was recently discovered and published by Hermann M. Goldbrunner in *Quellen und Forschungen aus italienischen Archiven und Bibliotheken*, XLII-XLIII (1964), 362-367; see esp. 365ff. The editor, pp. 285ff. ("Die Übergabe Perugias an Giangaleazzo Visconti, 1400"), gives a convincing analysis of Florence's sincere but eventually futile desire to help her ally, as well as of the distress that forced Perugia, like other central-Italian communes, to seek the haven offered by Giangaleazzo.

[25] ". . . la nostra difesa è la loro medesima." See the commission given to the Florentine envoys to Venice, April 7, 1400, published by De Mesquita, *Giangaleazzo*, pp. 365-370.

[26] For the situation created by the Peace of Venice cf. H. Kretschmayr, *Geschichte von Venedig*, vol. II (Gotha, 1920), p. 249.

[27a] In the commission cited above in note 25.

[27b] See N. Rubinstein in *Bulletin of the Institute of Historical Research*, xxx (1957), 127.

[28] The only comparable situation in Florence's past had occurred in 1352 when the Archbishop Giovanni Visconti had been on the brink of invading Tuscany, and Florence had promised the German king Charles IV half of his military expenses as soon as the German horsemen arrived in Italy as allies against Milan. But that deviation from Florence's Guelph tradition had amazed all Italy, as Matteo Villani tells us in his chronicle (III, 6); it was not repeated in the period of Florence's moral and material recovery during the latter part of the Trecento; and negotiations in 1352, unlike 1401-02, had eventually not succeeded in bringing a German army to Italy. For an example of the Italian national sentiment turning against Florence after 1401, see Giovanni Conversino da Ravenna, note 44 to Chap. 6.

[29] For the lasting impression made by Giangaleazzo's propaganda and for the role of the Milanese historian Andrea Biglia cf. *Crisis: Appendices*, pp. 450f.

[30] Cf. *Crisis: Appendices*, p. 451, for Genoa, Bologna, and Prato.

[31] For our knowledge of the range of this pro-Visconti political poetry cf. *Crisis: Appendices*, p. 451.

[32] In 1396, in a poem addressed to Giangaleazzo, he urged him "to think of peace accomplished through war" ("ut pacem cogitet per viam belli"). See *Crisis: Appendices, ibid.*

[33] ". . . che è giunto il Messia." See *Crisis: Appendices, ibid.*

[34] ". . . per parte d'ogni vero Italiano"; ". . . detestabile seme, nimico di quiete e caritate, che dicon libertade" (*ibid.*).

[35] *Ibid.*

[36] *Ibid.*

[37] See N. Valeri, *Vita di Facino Cane* (Turin, 1940), pp. 111f.

[38] Personal ambitions and jealousies among the Milanese *condottieri*, to which De Mesquita prominently refers (*Giangaleazzo*, pp. 288-292), cannot possibly have caused a personality like Giangaleazzo to give up the consummation of his plans and victories for the entire remainder of the decisive year.

[39] Quoted by De Mesquita, *Giangaleazzo*, pp. 305 and 310.

[40] Conditions in Milan after Giangaleazzo's death are described in N. Valeri's *L'Eredità di Giangaleazzo Visconti* (Turin, 1938).

[41] Bruni, in his *Historiarum Florentini Populi Libri XII* (in "Rerum Italicarum Scriptores," nuova ed., tom. XIX, parte III, ed. E. Santini, p. 288), concludes that the Florentines, before Gian-

galeazzo's death changed everything, "had hardly any hope of salvation left" ("vix ullam salutis spem reliquam habebant").

[42] The testimony of the documents is discussed by Valeri, *op. cit.* Contemporary Florentine opinion is known through Gregorio Dati (see pp. 183f. below) and Giovanni di Paolo Morelli, who in his *Ricordi* (ed. V. Branca [Firenze, 1956], pp. 398f.), like Gregorio Dati, expressly ascribes Giangaleazzo's inaction after Bologna's fall to his financial calamity.

[43] Giovanni Morelli, *op. cit.*, pp. 395f. For other testimonies see F. T. Perrens, *Histoire de Florence*, vol. VI (Paris, 1883), p. 94.

[44] Extracts, from the "Liber Consiliorum secretorum Comunis Florentie," are published in the *Commissioni di Rinaldo degli Albizzi per il Comune di Firenze dal 1399 al 1433*, ed. C. Guasti (3 vols., Florence, 1867-73), vol. I, p. 11.

[45] "Quod in adversitatibus virtus probatur: et ideo, licet adversa sint ex parte Bononie, sumenda est tamen audacia atque vigor." "Quod licet profligate sint gentes nostre, que erant Bononie, audendum tamen est."

[46] "Quod nemo expavescat, sed forti animo resistat." "Non submergatur animus, sed elevetur." "Diu habuimus bellum cum Vicecomitibus Mediolani; nec unquam poterit esse concordia, nisi una partium deleatur: et ideo forti et magno animo resistatur."

[47] See R. Piattoli, "Il problema portuale di Firenze . . . 1402-5," *Rivista Storica degli Archivi Toscani*, II (1930), esp. pp. 159-161, where the cutting off of all Florentine roads and ports in Giangaleazzo's last years is shown to have made it possible for him to hope for "the economic and, in consequence, the political break-down of his opponent."

[48] See De Mesquita, *Giangaleazzo*, pp. 370f.

[49] *Ibid.*, p. 285.

[50] For the relationship between the picture of the Florentine-Milanese struggle just proposed and earlier views of the political development of the Renaissance, see "Interpretations of the Political Background of the Early Renaissance," *Crisis: Appendices*, pp. 379ff. In Italy, the first scholar to reconsider the place of Florence and the city-state republic in the resistance against the Visconti and to relate the ideas of the period to the Florentine-Milanese struggle, was Nino Valeri. A summary and appraisal of his fundamental *L'Italia nell' Età dei Principati dal 1343 al 1516*, "Storia d'Italia," vol. V (Milan: Mondadori, 1949), is given in H. Baron, "Die politische Entwicklung der italienischen Renaissance," *Historische Zeitschrift*, CLXXIV (1952). Valeri's own estimate of the general historical importance of political events around 1400 as pictured in

the present book may be found in a chapter, "La 'Tragedia' d'Italia nel Giudizio degli Storici," in *Storia di Milano*, vol. II (Milan: Fondazione Treccani degli Alfieri, 1956), pp. 509-519. Garrett Mattingly, *Renaissance Diplomacy* (Boston, 1955), also offers basic contributions to the understanding of the influence of the political events of the Giangaleazzo period on the emergence of the Renaissance pattern in political thought and practice; cf. esp. pp. 55ff., 69f.

CHAPTER 3

[1] Whenever Bruni's *Dialogi* is cited, page references will be to two editions: *Leonardi Aretini ad Petrum Paulum Istrum Dialogus*, ed. Th. Klette in his *Beiträge zur Geschichte und Litteratur der Italienischen Gelehrtenrenaissance*, vol. II (Greifswald, 1889), pp. 39-83; and the reissue of Klette's text by E. Garin in his *Prosatori Latini del Quattrocento* (vol. 13 of the series "La Letteratura Italiana. Storia e Testi" [Milan, 1952]), pp. 39-99. Garin, besides adding an Italian translation, has revised Klette's punctuation and has occasionally corrected the text on the basis of Florentine manuscripts. We have followed this greatly improved version in our quotations.

The other major work of Bruni's youth, the *Laudatio Florentinae Urbis*, has never been published in extenso. Accessible in print are only some extracts published by Klette in an appendix to his edition of the *Dialogi* (pp. 84-105). Since a complete and reliable text of the *Laudatio* is indispensable, a critical text has been reconstructed by collating cod. Laur. 65 c. 15, of mid-Quattrocento Florentine origin, quoted as *L*, with four other good fifteenth-century manuscripts. For an appraisal of these manuscripts and for more details on the existing printed editions of the *Laudatio* and the *Dialogi*, cf. *Crisis: Appendices*, p. 454, and *Humanistic and Political Literature*, pp. 69ff., 128.

[2] Dante, *Inferno* xxxiv, 31ff. Bruni, *Dialogi*, ed. Klette, pp. 61f.; ed. Garin, pp. 68f.

[3] "An to putas Dantem, virum omnium aetatis suae doctissimum, ignorasse quo pacto Caesar dominium adeptus fuerit? Ignorasse libertatem sublatam et ingemiscente populo Romano diadema a M. Antonio capiti Caesaris impositum? . . . Non ignoravit haec Dantes, non, sed legitimum principem et mundanarum rerum iustissimum monarcham in Caesare finxit; in Bruto autem seditiosum, turbulentum ac nefarium hominem, qui hunc principem per scelus trucidaret; non quod Brutus eiusmodi fuerit; nam si hoc esset, qua ratione a senatu laudatus fuisset tamquam libertatis recuperator? Sed cum Caesar quocumque modo regnasset, Brutus autem [Garin: enim] una cum amplius sexaginta nobilissimis civibus eum inter-

fecisset [Garin: interfecissent], sumpsit poeta ex hoc fingendi materiam" (*Dialogi*, ed. Klette, pp. 76f.; ed. Garin, pp. 88f.).

[4] Landino, *Comento Sopra la Comedia di Danthe Alighieri* (1st edn.: Florence, 1481), fol. s, 5v.

[5] *Ibid.*

[6] *Ibid.*

[7a] Landino's comment is reprinted in *Crisis: Appendices*, pp. 455f.

[7b] Machiavelli in his *Dialogo intorno alla nostra lingua*, written in the autumn of 1515 when he was starting work on the *Discourses*, as I have tried to show in *Bibl. d'Hum. et Renaiss.*, XXIII (1961), 449-476. The passage on Brutus' punishment, *ibid.*, 474.

[8] *Dialoghi de' giorni che Dante consumò nel cercare l'Inferno e 'l Purgatorio*; discovered and first published as late as 1859; critical edition by D. Redig de Campos ("Raccolta di Fonti per la Storia dell' Arte," vol. II, Florence, 1939). On the afterglow of republican pride found in these dialogues see *Crisis: Appendices*, p. 457.

[9] Ed. Redig de Campos, pp. 90f., 95f.

[10] *Ibid.*, p. 96. The original text of the quoted paragraphs of Giannotti's dialogue is reprinted in *Crisis: Appendices*, pp. 457ff. Whatever the historical reliability of Giannotti's alleged discussion with Michelangelo, Michelangelo, under the pressure of Giannotti's impetuous republicanism, in spite of his reverence for Dante, must have been of two minds. He did allow himself to be persuaded by Giannotti to begin work on the famous—never finished—bust of Brutus now in the Bargello, a striking testimony to his participation in the Florentine cult of Brutus, by then more than a century old. Cf. D. F. Gordon's recent article on "Giannotti, Michelangelo and the Cult of Brutus," in *Fritz Saxl, 1890-1948* (London, 1957), pp. 281ff.; for Michelangelo's civic views in general, G. Spini, "Politicità di Michelangelo," *Rivista Storica Italiana*, LXXVI, 1964.

[11] Quoted in M. Barbi's *Della Fortuna di Dante nel secolo XVI* (Pisa, 1890), p. 245, n. 1.

[12] *Dialogi*, ed. Klette, pp. 68f.; ed. Garin, pp. 76f.

[13] For the fact that Ptolemy himself gave his annals the characteristic title of *Gesta Tuscorum*, see B. Schmeidler in his edition of *Tholomei Lucensis Annales*, "Monumenta Germaniae Historica, Scriptores," n.s., tom. VIII (1930), p. 243.

[14] *De Regimine Principum*, III, 6: "Quod inter praesides romanos nemo portabat diadema, nec induebatur purpura, ut magnificaretur in ea . . ."; III, 12: ". . . ipsorum potentia ad omnes mundi plagas videbatur diffusa, sub consulibus tamen: quia superstitibus regibus cum finitimis sollicitabantur regionibus, et modicae adhuc erant virtutis." Cf. ed. by J. Mathis (Turin, 1948), pp. 29, 44, 53.

[15] "Nostri libertas incipit evi"; "florida . . . viris . . . armipo-
tentibus etas" (*Africa*, ed. N. Festa, "Edizione Nazionale delle
Opere di Petrarca," vol. I [1926], lib. III, 774; lib. II, 138).

[16] *Africa*, liber II.

[17] "O felix si forte modum sciat addere ferro!/ Nesciet heu!
noletque miser; sed turbine mentis/ Victrices per cunta manus in
publica vertet/ Viscera . . ./ . . . Quam turpiter omnia calcat/
Ambitus, ut totum imperium sibi vindicet unus" (*Africa*, II, 228-
235).

[18] *Africa*, II, 274-278; 288-293.

[19] This statement needs emphasis because it is in sharp contrast
with the widespread assumption, traceable in particular to F. Ercole's
influential works, that the republican interpretation of Roman history and an historical criticism of Caesar had been solidly established
by early commentators of Dante at least one generation before Bruni.
For the fallacy of this view, which is not based on a single piece of
evidence, see *Crisis: Appendices*, pp. 459f. The only one among
the Dante commentators of the Trecento who seriously raised the
question of the justice of the deed of Brutus and the other slayers
of Caesar was Benvenuto Rambaldi da Imola, who did so because
he was more deeply influenced by early Humanism than any other
Trecento commentator and therefore more familiar with the views
of the ancient authors. But Rambaldi's historical considerations did
not as yet result in anything approaching a vindication of the role
and right of the *Respublica Romana*, as will be seen in due course
(pp. 154f. below).

[20] "Nam posteaquam res publica in unius potestatem deducta est,
preclara illa ingenia (ut inquit Cornelius) abiere" (*L*, fol. 144v;
ed. Klette, pp. 93f.). Bruni's quotation is not precise, Tacitus actually having said "magna illa ingenia" (not "preclara illa ingenia")
"cessere" (not "abiere")—proof that Bruni was quoting from memory. See note 23 below.

[21] Except for Paulinus Venetus, Bishop of Pozzuoli, who, a few
decades before Boccaccio, had drawn upon the manuscript at Montecassino for information on the history of Pozzuoli and neighboring
towns. For Paulinus as well as Boccaccio cf. J. von Stackelberg,
Tacitus in der Romania (see note 25a below), pp. 46f. Boccaccio,
however, cannot himself be charged or credited with "stealing" the
manuscript from Montecassino and taking it to Florence (a long-time
assumption). Rather, this had been done by Zanobi da Strada;
see G. Billanovich, *Romance Philology*, XVII (1964), 696.

[22] R. Sabbadini, *Le Scoperte dei Codici Latini e Greci ne' Secoli
XIV e XV* (two vols., Florence, 1905 and 1914), vol. II, p. 254. On
the rapid spread of familiarity with Tacitus during the first decades

of the Quattrocento see G. Zippel's *Giunte e Correzioni* supplementing G. Voigt's *Il Risorgimento dell' Antichità Classica* (Florence, 1897), pp. 11f., and J. von Stackelberg, *Tacitus in der Romania*, p. 48.

[23] "Postquam bellatum apud Actium atque omnem potentiam ad unum conferri pacis interfuit, magna illa ingenia cessere" (Tacitus *Historiae* i 1).

[24] See notes 20 and 23 above.

[25a] Jürgen von Stackelberg, *Tacitus in der Romania: Studien zur literarischen Rezeption des Tacitus in Italien und Frankreich* (Tübingen, 1960), p. 60.

[25b] Bruni, *Historiae*, pp. 14f.

[26] Dante in the famous passage, *Paradiso*, VI, 55ff.; for Petrarch cf. p. 152 below.

[27] See pp. 149ff. below and note 11 to Chap. 7.

[28] "O Cai [*variant* Gai] Cesar, quam plane tua facinora Romanam urbem evertere! Sed comprimam ipse me. Sunt enim qui Lucanum, doctissimum et sapientissimum hominem, vera de te scripsisse permoleste ferant. Nec fortasse carent ratione. Etsi enim multa ac magna in te vitia erant, multis tamen ac magnis virtutibus obumbrabantur. Quamobrem de te silere tutius erit. Et simul filium tuum eadem illa ratione preteribo. . . . Fuerunt enim in illo, ut in patre quoque fuerant, vestigia quedam virtutum que vitia quoque tolerabiliora faciebant. At hec monstra, quibus imperium tradidistis, nulla virtute redempta erant a vitiis, nisi forte virtus est omni conatu rem publicam delere nec ullo flagitio quantumvis maximo abstinere. Quare etsi cetera vestra obliviscar, illud tamen neque oblivisci neque ut vobis non succenseam adduci possum, quod viam tantis malis tantisque sceleribus [*variant* malis sceleribusque] patefecistis quanta successores vestri omni genere impietatis nequitieque ediderunt" (*L* fol. 144r-144v; ed. Klette, p. 93).

[29] "Sed quorsum hec? . . . ut . . . intelligeretur eo tempore hanc coloniam deductam fuisse quo urbs Romana potentia, libertate, ingeniis, clarissimis civibus maxime florebat. Nam posteaquam res publica in unius potestatem deducta est, preclara illa ingenia (ut inquit Cornelius) abiere" (*L* fol. 144v; ed. Klette, pp. 93f.). "Hec igitur splendidissima Romanorum colonia eo maxime tempore deducta est quo populi Romani imperium maxime florebat, quo potentissimi reges et bellicosissime gentes armis ac virtute domite erant, Carthago, Numantia, Corinthus a stirpe interierant, omnes terre mariaque omnia in potestatem eius populi venerant. Nichil calamitatis populo Romano ab ullis hostibus inflictum erat. Nondum Cesares, Antonii, Tiberii, Nerones, pestes atque exitia rei publice,

libertatem sustulerant. Sed vigebat sancta et inconcussa libertas, que tamen non multo post hanc coloniam deductam a sceleratissimis latronibus sublata est. Ex quo illud evenire arbitror quod in hac civitate egregie preter ceteras et fuisse et esse videmus: ut Florentini homines maxime omnium libertate gaudeant et tyrannorum valde sint inimici. Tantum, ut opinor [*variant* Tantum opinor], odii adversus invasores imperii et rei publice eversores iam ex illo tempore Florentia concepit ut nec hodie quidem videatur oblita, sed si quod illorum vel nomen vel vestigium adhuc superest id hec res publica dedignatur et odit" (*L* fol. 142v-143r; ed. Klette, pp. 91f.).

³⁰ E. G. Parodi in *Studj di filologia romanza*, IV (1889), 496f.; P. Santini, *Quesiti e Ricerche di Storiografia Fiorentina* (Florence, 1903), pp. 61-87.

³¹ On these medieval legends, according to which "Cesare, Augusto, gl'Imperatori sono i fondatori, difensori, restauratori di Firenze," cf. P. Villari, *I Primi Due Secoli della Storia di Firenze* (Florence, 1893), vol. I, pp. 52-60, esp. 59, and A. Del Monte ("La storiografia fiorentina dei secoli XII e XIII," *Bullettino dell' Istituto Storico Italiano*, LXII [1950], 175-282), who, p. 182, defines as the core of the medieval legend that "Florence became the daughter and heir of Rome—established by Caesar, the founder of the Empire, . . . destroyed by the barbarians, and rebuilt by the Romans and by Charlemagne, the restorer of the Empire." Similar comments in N. Rubinstein, "The Beginnings of Political Thought in Florence. A Study in Mediaeval Historiography," *Journal of the Warburg and Courtauld Institutes*, V (1942), esp. pp. 208, 215f., and M. Mariani, "La Favola di Roma nell'ambiente fiorentino dei secoli XIII-XV," *Archivio della Società Romana di Storia Patria*, LXXXI (1958), passim.

³² Giovanni Villani, *Cronica*, I, 38 and 39.

³³ "dum . . . Florentiae civitas per Caesarem conderetur" (*De Origine Civitatis Florentiae et Eiusdem Famosis Civibus*, in the collection, ed. G. C. Galletti, *Philippi Villani Liber de Civitatis Florentiae Famosis Civibus . . . et de Florentinorum litteratura principes fere synchroni scriptores* [Florence, 1847], p. 8. The passage remained unchanged in the revised version of 1395/96 (cf. *Le Vite di Dante, Petrarca e Boccaccio scritte fino al secolo decimosesto*, ed. A. Solerti [Milan, 1904], pp. 82 and 83). For more details, see *Humanistic and Political Literature*, pp. 30f.

³⁴ For this date as well as Benvenuto Rambaldi's familiarity with Florentine conditions and ideas see *Crisis: Appendices*, p. 463.

³⁵ *Comentum super Dantis Aldigherij Comoediam*, ad *Inf.* cant. xv, ed. J. P. Lacaita, vol. I (Florence, 1887), pp. 509-511. The text is reprinted in *Crisis: Appendices*, pp. 463f.

[36] "Quis ergo aedificaverit primo Florentiam, ignoro; nec credo, quod a Florino nobili cive romano fuerit sic denominata, nec a Campo Florido, sicut etiam isti dicunt, cum dicat Plinius, quod Florentia olim habuerit ortum a Faesulis; sed quando, quomodo, vel per quem fateor me nescire" (*ibid.*, pp. 510-511).

[37a] See *Humanistic and Political Literature*, pp. 19ff.

[37b] See pp. 76, 99f., 159 below. We may note that F. Lanzoni's *Genesi, Svolgimento e Tramonto delle Leggende Storiche* ("Studi e Testi," no. 43; Rome, 1925), entirely ignores this Florentine chapter of early Renaissance historical criticism, despite the promise of its title to deal with the "waning" of the medieval legends. It does refer to Renaissance criticism of the legends about the founding of Milan (by Merula and Calchi), but Milanese criticism did not reach that stage until two to three generations after the achievements of the Florentine humanists during the transition from the Trecento to the Quattrocento.

[38] These various aspects of Bruni's mature historical thought are today well known. After E. Fueter's rather disparaging views of humanistic historiography, and especially of Bruni (in his *Geschichte der neueren Historiographie* [Munich, 1911], pp. 16ff.)—followed by still more derisive comments, as late as 1936, in F. Schevill's *History of Florence* (p. XVII)—a marked revaluation of Bruni as an historian has gradually come about through the studies of G. Salvemini, E. Santini, P. Joachimsen, H. Baron, W. K. Ferguson (see note 1 to Chap. 1 above) and a paper by B. L. Ullman on "Leonardo Bruni and Humanistic Historiography," in his *Studies in the Italian Renaissance* (Rome, 1955), pp. 321ff.

[39] For the Florentine authors after Bruni see *Crisis: Appendices*, p. 465.

[40] Cf. *ibid.*

[41] Poggio in his *Defensiuncula Contra Guarinum Veronensem*; in Poggio's *Opera* (Basel, 1538), pp. 365-390. After quoting Cicero, from *De Officiis* ii 1.2, and Seneca, from the preface to *Controversiae* (actually not a work of Seneca the philosopher, but of Seneca the Elder, as Poggio did not yet know) as witnesses to the decay of Roman culture, Poggio continues: "Accipe tertium quoque [after Cicero and Seneca] gravissimum historici doctissimi Cornelij Taciti testimonium, qui vel solus Guarinum deijciat ex arce utputa Minervae." After a full quotation from *Historiae* i 1, Poggio goes on: "Cum ergo et Senecae verbis, quibus illa praeclara ingenia Ciceronis aetate nata esse, deinde in deterius decrevisse affirmat, et Taciti testimonio asserentis [edn. 1538: asserentes] magna illa ingenia post imperium ad unum delatum defecisse apertissime constet quanta iactura sit secuta in literis latinis libertate

amissa, rectissime scripsisse me dico . . . latinam eloquentiam cor-
ruisse" (*Defensiuncula*, pp. 372f.). Poggio's use of the words
"praeclara ingenia" in this passage is definite evidence that he had
Bruni's *Laudatio* in mind; for the expression in the Seneca passage
to which Poggio refers actually runs "omnia ingenia" (as Poggio had
correctly quoted from Seneca previously), while Tacitus speaks of
"magna ingenia." It had been Bruni in his *Laudatio*, as we have
noted (note 20 above), who, inadvertently transforming Tacitus'
statement on the disappearance of talents in historiography into a
general judgment on the disappearance of intellectual brilliance,
also altered Tacitus' "magna ingenia" to "praeclara ingenia."

[42] Poggio states explicitly that his thesis—"Caesar was the par-
ricidal murderer of the Latin language and the literary arts as
much as of his *patria*, because, after the destruction of the republic,
Latin eloquence collapsed"—had been treated by Guarino as
"the very core of the entire dispute" (". . . tanquam robur
fortissimum totius disputationis"; *Defensiuncula*, p. 370. Poggio's
formulation in his preceding letter had been: "Non enim magis
patriae quam latinae linguae et bonarum artium extitit parricida.
Una enim cum libertate corruit latina eloquentia, et studia literarum
quae in ipso flore prius fere quam inciperent extincta sunt. Erat in
culmine eloquentia; erant caeterarum bonarum artium incrementa,
quae statim prostrata re publica defecerunt. Erant complures viri
doctissimi simul eloquentissimi, quos civilis clades absumpsit.
Vigebant studia philosophiae et caeterarum liberalium artium
tempore libertatis; quam nisi delevisset Caesar, crevissent latina
ingenia, neque Graecis ullo doctrinarum genere cessissent. At vero
libertate extincta, subsecuta sunt imperatorum portenta nepharia,
qui et doctos semper ac virtutem oderunt, et adversati sunt literarum
studiis et doctrinae." *Opera*, 1538, p. 365).

[43a] *Defensiuncula*, p. 371. I have made the following emenda-
tions: "Orti et nutriti sint vigente republica," instead of *Opera* 1538
"ingente republica," and therefore "while the republic was in its
vigor"; "Itaque quot docti et eloquentes," instead of *Opera* 1538
"quod," and therefore "Thus all the learned and eloquent." So
strong was the effect of this historical reinterpretation, that the
opinion that Roman literature decayed after the loss of political
liberty was shared (so Poggio tells us in his *Defensiuncula*, p. 372)
even by Niccolò Niccoli, who (see pp. 326ff. below) in his practical
political conduct was the least faithful among the Florentine humanists to the republican ideals. How it happened that Poggio—
who in many respects was a chancery humanist at the Curia in his
intellectual make-up despite his Florentine origin—could by the
1430's become a mouthpiece of Florentine political convictions

and historical ideas, is a question which will become intelligible
when the picture of the Florentine development has been fully
redrawn, and with which we shall deal in the chapter on "Niccoli
and Poggio in the 1420's and 1430's" (Chap. 17).

[43b] Most strongly by F. Gundolf, *Caesar. Geschichte seines Ruhms*
(1st ed. Berlin, 1925), who declares the entire humanistic "praise
for Cato and Brutus and reproof of Caesar" to be "merely rhetorical": "Poggio would have championed the opposite opinion with
equal *brio*." See the criticism of Gundolf's misinterpretation in
Crisis: Appendices, pp. 467f.

[43c] On Pietro del Monte see two papers by A. Zanelli in *Archivio
Storico Lombardo* (1907), and J. Haller's introduction to his *Piero
da Monte. Ein Gelehrter und päpstlicher Beamter des 15. Jahr-
hunderts. Seine Briefsammlung,* "Bibliothek des Preussischen Historischen Instituts in Rom," vol. XIX (Rome, 1941).

[43d] Attention was first drawn to Pietro del Monte's letter to Poggio
by E. Walser in his *Poggius Florentinus, Leben und Werke* (Leipzig, 1914), pp. 172f. Only a few sentences from the letter have
been published in J. Haller's cited edition of Pietro del Monte's
Briefwechsel, pp. 142f. The passages quoted on the following pages
are reproduced from extracts made by this writer many years ago
from the then MS. Lat. Fol. 366 of the Preussische Staatsbibliothek
Berlin, fol. 63v-64r, 66v-67r, and 69v. The version in the Berlin
manuscript is the original form of the text which, according to
Walser, *loc. cit.*, is also preserved in the MS. Bibliothèque de la Sor-
bonne, no. 229. For other manuscripts containing Pietro's letter see
Haller, *op. cit.*, p. 142, and R. Weiss, *Humanism in England during the Fifteenth Century* (2nd ed., Oxford, 1957), p. 24, n. 7.

[43e] Poggio presented the letter to the Pope; Walser, *op. cit.*, p.
173.

[43f] Haller, *op. cit.*, p. 11. Guarino was teaching in Venice during
the years 1414-1419, with interruptions.

[43g] See pp. 143f.

[43h] Already in his youth he had learned to regard Caesar as a
"turbulentus civis" and "patrie hostis eversorque libertatis dulcis-
sime." In later years he had rejoiced ". . . quod te talem tantum-
que ac tam disertum veteris sententie et opinionis mee patronum ac
defensorem . . . nactus sum."

[43i] ". . . ut qui libertatis finis fuerit, idem sit et vite."

[43j] ". . . ut, si fieri posset, universa Ytalia, que tantis cladibus
tyrannorum oppressa est, aliquando pace, tranquillitate, quiete, ocio
ac rerum omnium mortalium dulcissima et optatissima libertate
potiretur. Quid igitur cuiquam mirum videri debet, si in libertatis
arce munitissima natus, nutritus, educatus, gravissimumque ac duris-

simum tyrannidis iugum nusquam expertus, quamobrem diis immortalibus omnia debeo, Cesarem scelestissimum patricidam, eversorem romane libertatis, hostem patrie acerbissimum, pleno ore ac libera voce detestor? Ad id enim, ut dixi, etiam si cetera deessent, me cogit compellitque natura, rerum omnium parens."

[43k] On the political background of Pietro del Monte's ideals of Florentine-Venetian collaboration, cf. below, p. 395, and *Crisis: Appendices*, pp. 393-394.

[43l] Decembrio's *Panegyricus* is published in *Archivio Storico Lombardo*, ser. IV, vol. VIII (1907), 27-45, though in an apparently slightly altered version from Decembrio's last years (around 1473); the version of 1436 seems not to have been preserved in its Latin original.

[44] "Pene oblitus es: Ciceronem, Livium et in primis Maronem, divina ingenia, Cesaris et Augusti temporibus . . . floruisse. Quo igitur illa preclara ingenia, ut Cornelius inquit, abiere?" (*ibid.*, p. 40).

[45] *Ibid.*, p. 41.

[46] *Ibid.*, pp. 32f.

[47a] See *Arte della Guerra*, historical excursus near the end of lib. II, and *Discorsi*, II 2, II 4, II 5, for Machiavelli's views on the pernicious consequences of the subjection of all city-republics and independent states under the empire of Rome; *Discorsi*, I 10, and the discussion in O. Tommasini, *La Vita e le Opere di Machiavelli*, vol. II, part I, pp. 159ff., for Machiavelli's criticism of Caesar.

[47b] Cf. R. V. Albertini, *Das florentinische Staatsbewusstsein . . .*, pp. 294f., who has recently drawn attention to Giovanni Battista Guarini's *Trattato*. Von Albertini comments that this late-sixteenth-century writer, with his changed historical appraisal, "finally parted company with Florentine civic Humanism."

[48] Bruni, *Historiae*, pp. 5f. On the puzzle of the omission of Sulla's name in the *Laudatio*, cf. *Humanistic and Political Literature*, pp. 99-101.

[49] For the Anonymus, Poggio, and Landino cf. *Crisis: Appendices*, pp. 468f.; for Landino, also the poem of 1452 cited in note 58 to Chap. 18 below, where the Florentine citizens are addressed as "*Syllanidae.*"

[50] See note 33 above.

[51] "Florentiam . . . a Sillanis militibus . . . conditam." Manetti, *Vita Dantis*, in *Le Vite di Dante . . .* (see note 33 above), p. 113.

[52] For Biondo and Valla cf. *Crisis: Appendices*, p. 469.

[53] Decembrio, *Panegyricus*, p. 39.

[54] The sources for the history of Renaissance opinion on the founding of Florence are gathered in an excursus in book IX of Benedetto

Varchi's *Storia Fiorentina* (in the edn. Florence 1838-41: vol. II, pp. 52ff.). That it was Poliziano who discovered the *Liber coloniarum* and initiated the renewed ascription of Florence's origin to the Empire, has been demonstrated by N. Rubinstein, "Il Poliziano e la Questione delle Origini di Firenze," in *Il Poliziano e il Suo Tempo: Atti del IV Convegno Internazionale di Studi sul Rinascimento* (Florence, 1957), pp. 104-107. Even today it is still *sub judice* whether the information contained in the *Liber coloniarum* is definitive. According to Schanz-Hosius (*Geschichte der Römischen Literatur*, vol. II, part II [4th edn., 1935], p. 803) it remains "problematical" and the contents of the *Liber* is largely "distorted" in the preserved versions. The sources that might be weighed against the authority of the *Liber* are essentially those once collected by Salutati; see the list of authorities in N. Rubinstein's attempt to save a remnant of the theory of the Sullan foundation in a note on "The Date of the Foundation of Florence" in the *Journal of the Warburg and Courtauld Institutes,* IV (1940-41), pp. 225ff.

[55] For Verino and popular sixteenth-century handbooks cf. *Crisis: Appendices,* p. 470.

[56] Ed. Klette, p. 68; ed. Garin, p. 78.

[57] "Sed quorsum hec? dicet fortasse quispiam. Utriusque videlicet gratia: primum, ut ostenderem non iniuste hanc civitatem eiusmodi partes suscepisse; et simul intelligeretur eo tempore hanc coloniam deductam fuisse quo urbs Romana potentia, libertate, ingeniis, clarissimis civibus maxime florebat . . . : ut plurimum intersit tunc an inferiori tempore colonia hec fuerit deducta, cum ita iam omnis virtus ac nobilitas Romane urbis extirpata erat ut nichil preclarum neque egregium qui ex ea migrabant secum possent efferre" (*L* fol. 144v; ed. Klette, p. 93f.).

[58] Fustel de Coulanges, *Questions historiques* (Paris, 1893), p. 6.

[59] For Salutati's *Invectiva,* and its editions, see below, note 8 to Chap. 4.

[60] See pp. 63f. above, 99f. below, and *Humanistic and Political Literature,* pp. 19ff.

[61] For Rinuccini's *Risponsiva,* and its edition, see note 8 to Chap. 4.

[62] "Hai mai letto, come Roma sotto i Re poco crebbe, sotto il Senato in poco tempo acquistò lo imperio del mondo, sotto gl'Imperadori quasi al nulla è ritornata?" (Rinuccini, *Risponsiva,* p. 220).

[63] "Come Cicerone testimonia, la temerità di Caio Cesare, perchè per oppinione si fisse nell' animo essere più degno che gli altri di principare, le cose umane e le divine rivolse, e di Roma le svelse; perocchè, come di sopra è narrato, uno nelle cose umane non può essere perfetto, e presupposto che uno ne sia assai idoneo, come fu Ottaviano, non poi i susseguenti, come Nerone. . . ." If Rome had

remained "nell' ordine Senatorio costituto, anzi insino al mio tempo sarebbe durato con accrescimento in gloria, come già fe' in quella Repubblica. Intendi adunque, o servo, quanto sia il frutto della bella libertà, per la quale non dubitò morire quello esquisitissimo Cato posteriore, il quale Lucano di raggione agguaglia agli Iddei, dicendo: 'la cagione vincitrice piacque agl' Iddei, ma la vinta a Catone' " (*ibid.*, p. 247f.).

[64] For Dati's *Istoria*, and its editions, see note 2 to Chap. 8.

[65] "Fu . . . che gli antichi Fiorentini che vennono in grandezza, seguitavano la parte imperiale e signorile, e la moltitudine gli ebbe in odio per sospetto di non venire sotto tiranno, come venne Roma sotto Cesare per lasciarlo fare troppo potente; e per detta ragione sempre hanno tirati a terra [*Manni:* drieto] i grandi e i potenti, acciò che e' non trapassassino il modo comune [*Manni:* comune e civile]; hanno fatto come il buono ortolano che pota e ricide i rami degli arbori che si distendono troppo, acciò che durino più e facciano migliore frutto e non dieno uggia e non facciano danno alla terra e all' altre semenze, e a quelli che sono magri mettono dappiè dell' umore che gli conforti, e questa natura ha quel populo per ragione che sono nati e discesi [*Manni:* perocchè sono discesi] di que' romani che, con reggimento di libertà, avevano acquistata la signoria del mondo e posta Roma in pace e riposo e onore [*Manni omits* e onore] più che mai fusse; i quali, se ora tornassono al mondo, sarebbono i nimici di Cesare e d'ognuno che guastò quello stato e reggimento popolare e ridusselo a tirannia. E però questi Fiorentini, nati di que' Romani liberi, seguitando la natura loro, hanno sempre sospetto di chi potesse occupare e tôrre loro la libertà del loro reggimento popolare comune [*Manni:* e civile *instead of* comune] e per questo sono nimici e contrari d'animo [*Manni omits* e contrari d'animo] di chi studia occupare per tirannia e superbia la libertà . . ." (*Istoria*, ed. Pratesi, pp. 120f.; ed. Manni, pp. 112f.).

For Dati's theory that Florence was founded during the republican period of Rome cf. *Crisis: Appendices*, p. 472.

CHAPTER 4

[1] *Il Paradiso degli Alberti. Ritrovi e ragionamenti del 1389. Romanzo di Giovanni da Prato*, ed. A. Wesselofsky (Bologna, 1867) in the series *Scelta di curiosità letterarie*, vols. 86[I]-86[II], containing Wesselofsky's introduction (henceforth quoted as "Wesselofsky, I" and "Wesselofsky, II") and vols. 87-88, containing the text of the *Paradiso* (henceforth quoted as "*Paradiso*, I" and "*Paradiso*, II"). We shall become more familiar with this work, and the various problems it poses, in the second section of this chapter, and in Chapters 13 and 15.

[2] The formerly accepted dating of Bruni's *Laudatio* and *Dialogi* is discussed in Chapters 10 and 11. For the dating of Loschi's, Rinuccini's, and Salutati's invectives, see the discussions in *Humanistic and Political Literature*, pp. 38ff.

[3] Except his brief, casual guide for searchers for old manuscripts in German monasteries, the *Commentarium in peregrinatione Germanie*; best edition in *Classical Philology*, XVI (1921), 251-255.

[4] These embarrassing implications of the accepted chronology are examined in *Humanistic and Political Literature*, pp. 114ff., "Bruni's Development as a Translator from the Greek (1400-1403/04)."

[5] Cf. the survey of the appraisals of the *Paradiso*, from Wesselofsky and Voigt to recent scholars, in *Humanistic and Political Literature*, pp. 14ff.

[6] This examination has been made in *Humanistic and Political Literature*, Chap. I, "Giovanni da Prato's *Paradiso degli Alberti*," and Chap. II, "Publicists During the Florentine Struggle with Giangaleazzo Visconti of Milan (1397-1402)."

[7] See Chapter 10.

[8] *Invectiva Lini Colucci Salutati in Antonium Luschum Vicentinum*, ed. D. Moreni (Florence, 1826). A few sections of the *Invectiva* have been reedited and translated into Italian by E. Garin in the volume, cited in note 1 to Chap. 3, *Prosatori Latini del Quattrocento* (pp. 1-37). Garin has collated the two Florentine manuscripts used by Moreni and found that Moreni's edition had been done with great care. Loschi's work is still available only through its inclusion in Salutati's *Invectiva* where Loschi's entire text is reproduced to serve as the basis for a running commentary against it. But at least two separate manuscripts have recently been discovered by N. Rubinstein and Paul O. Kristeller (according to information from Prof. Kristeller). Cino Rinuccini's *Risponsiva* is preserved only in an unsatisfactory, in several places incomplete, contemporary translation into the Volgare; published by Moreni, *op. cit.*, pp. 199-250 together with Salutati's *Invectiva*.

[9] For all these conclusions cf. the chapters of *Humanistic and Political Literature* cited in note 6 above.

After the results of our historical criticism of Salutati's *Invectiva* had been generally accepted for nearly ten years, Professor B. L. Ullman, in his *Humanism of Coluccio Salutati* (Padua, 1963, esp. pp. 33f.), recently denied the validity of these and other propositions of the present book from the standpoint of "philologians," as he terms his position on p. 48. In Ullman's own words: "I am unable to accept the chronology proposed by Baron (*Crisis*, p. 76, etc.; *Humanistic and Political Literature in Florence and Venice*,

p. 51). He would have Coluccio begin his book in 1397 and finish it in 1402-03 and speaks of 'first draft,' 'final version,' 'two strata,' etc. There is no shred of evidence for this." "Since Salutati was refuting Loschi point by point, it is natural that some of his statements fit 1397 or 1398, when Loschi wrote, rather than 1403."

The truth is that the conclusions drawn from the historical analysis of Salutati's pamphlet make out an unusually strong case. As I showed in *Humanistic and Political Literature*, Salutati reveals ignorance of what was to happen to Florence's alliances after 1398 and to the Visconti State in 1402; he says that things that did happen would never happen. Also, since it can be shown through independent analysis that Cino Rinuccini knew and answered Loschi's attack as early as the late spring or early summer of 1397, it is very difficult to believe that Salutati, the chancellor, remained unfamiliar with Loschi's pamphlet until 1403 while a Florentine citizen whom he must have known well had read and answered it in 1397.

Ullman's reason for dismissing this persuasive evidence and for not even attempting to explain why it can be neglected, is the existence of a letter of Salutati to a friend in Rimini, Pietro Turchi, that accompanied one of the first released manuscripts of Salutati's *Invectiva* (*Ep. XIII 10*, vol. III, pp. 634ff.). From this letter, dated September 11, 1403, we learn that Turchi had sent Salutati a copy of Loschi's *Invectiva* with an expression of hope that Salutati would compose a counter-invective in defense of Florence, and Salutati, after considerable hesitation, was now returning to Turchi the manuscript of Loschi's pamphlet together with his finished reply. About this letter Ullman remarks: "Actually Coluccio's letter to Pietro Turchi, written September 11, 1403, makes clear that Coluccio was nearing his seventy-third birthday (February 16, 1404) when he received Loschi's treatise from Turchi. He says, moreover, that he is returning Loschi's invective and enclosing his reply, written, therefore—all of it—in the summer of 1403." Evidently, Ullman is drawing his conclusions totally from an *argumentum ex silentio*. Since Salutati's letter fails to say that Salutati had known Loschi's work and begun, but left unfinished, a reply to Loschi several years before Turchi's letter arrived, the letter of Salutati is taken as evidence that Salutati had been ignorant of Loschi's work before Turchi's copy arrived. Ullman therefore would argue that no portion of Salutati's *Invectiva* can have been written before 1403.

The correct reasoning is that even an outright statement by Salutati to the effect that he was thankful to Turchi for making him familiar with Loschi's attack would not be all-decisive, but would have to be taken with a grain of salt. For since historical criticism of Salutati's work yields such strong arguments as noted, we would rather have to assume, as long as the results cannot be controverted, that Salutati—out of courtesy or for other, easily imaginable reasons —allowed himself in a letter of thanks a phrase not in strict conformity with the entire truth.

As far as I can judge, however, the letter says nowhere directly or indirectly that Salutati had been unfamiliar with Loschi's work before receiving Turchi's copy. The text of Salutati's letter begins: "You have demanded from me, distinguished sir, . . . that I reply to that most petulant detractor, who has injured the name of Florence with such insolent slander, . . . according to the merits of his madness"; no further information on the circumstances which made Salutati familiar with Loschi's invective is added to these words. Granted, if there were no reason for suspicion, we would be inclined to conclude from the cited phrase, since it answers the receipt of a manuscript which the sender had considered new to Salutati, that Salutati owed the knowledge of Loschi's work to the sender (Turchi). But as long as other sources and methods of investigation clearly suggest that Salutati had been working on a reply to Loschi previously, we cannot overlook the fact that the words of the letter are ambiguous and vague, and therefore open to a different interpretation.

It is astonishing that Ullman did not take this obvious ambiguity into consideration, but, instead, pressed the text for exact information which it does not contain. As he contends, the letter "makes clear that Coluccio was nearing has seventy-third birthday (February 16, 1404) *when he received Loschi's treatise from Turchi*" (the italics are mine), but the letter says nothing of the sort. How could it say any such thing, since it is dated September 11, 1403 and was, of course, written sufficiently long after Turchi's communication to allow Salutati to carefully complete or prepare (he made special studies of relevant ancient authors), compose, and have copied for Turchi the final text of his *Invectiva* before it was mailed to Turchi together with Salutati's letter in September. Since, moreover, we know that a difficult chapter was shown in its finished form to one of Salutati's friends as early as July, the arrival of Turchi's communication must have been much nearer to February 16, 1403 (Salutati's seventy-second birthday) than to February 16, 1404. The phrase in Salutati's September letter—"februarius enim mensis septuagesimum et tertium adducet annum"—cannot mean, therefore, that "Coluccio was nearing his seventy-third birthday *when he received Loschi's treatise from Turchi*." What Salutati really says is that, after receiving Turchi's communication, he had asked himself "quid, Line Coluci, facies? *an septuagenarius*," that is: what are you going to do? do you want to publish poisonous invectives for the first time in your life now that you are a "septuagenarian." It is only after he has made this use of the term "septuagenarian" that he adds as proof that he was, indeed, a septuagenarian the comment that he was nearing his seventy-third birthday (February 16, 1404) when writing his September letter (not when receiving Loschi's treatise from Turchi).

When all our observations are added up, this case of a suspected contradiction between an author's own statement and the facts determined by historical criticism of his work represents one of those problems for which, as proposed in our preface, a fully satisfactory solution can be found provided that we are careful to employ the methods of the historical critic as well as those of the literary scholar.

[10] "Quis non videt hunc nostrum populum tueri communem causam libertatis Italiae, qui non fateatur victo populo Florentino libertatem stare non posse, qui non agnoscat nobis servitute subactis totam Italiam sine remedio . . . servam fore?" (Salutati, *Invectiva*, pp. 88f.). "Nos obex, nos obstaculum soli sumus, ne cursum perficiat per omnem Italiam ille tyrannicus dominatus, qui tot urbes, tot castra, totque oppida miserrima conditione subegit. Hanc pacem dominus tuus optabat. . . . Huius autem pacis . . . , fateor, Florentinos semper hostes et obstaculum extitisse" (*ibid.*, p. 189).

[11] Salutati was born in 1331, Cino not long after 1350 (according to Aiazzi, quoted in *Crisis: Appendices*, p. 476), Bruni in 1370. The recent widely accepted hypothesis that Bruni was born as late as 1374 is not in harmony with several facts known from Bruni's life. In this writer's opinion, G. Calò's scepticism (*La Rinascita*, II [1939], 227f., reprinted in Calò's *Dall' Umanesimo alla Scuola del Lavoro* [Florence, 1940], vol. I, pp. 38f.) regarding the reliability of Bruni's occasional comparison of his age with that of Vergerio—the only substantial reason for doubting that Bruni was born in 1369/70 as is attested otherwise—points in the right direction. For the literature on Cino Rinuccini see the first note to the next chapter.

CHAPTER 5

[1] For the older literature on Cino Rinuccini's life and role as a Volgare poet see *Crisis: Appendices*, p. 476. Basic supplements from the archives have been recently published by Lauro Martines, "Nuovi documenti su Cino Rinuccini . . . ," *Archivio Storico Italiano*, CXIX (1961), 77-90. According to Martines' findings in his *Social World* (see note 54b to Chap. 14 below), esp. p. 66, Cino, despite his championship of an engaged, active citizen life, is not found in any more important offices than occasional membership in city councils. But this is easily explained by the fact that

the Rinuccini family, on account of their role in the revolt of 1378, had during the aristocratic restoration of the 1380's been excluded from nearly all offices.

[2] His Latin writings (*Risponsiva* and *Invettiva*) have in fact come down to us only in Volgare translations. See note 8 to Chap. 4 and note 32b to Chap. 13.

[3] The Florentines had already been the saviors of "la libertà in Italia" when Mastino della Scala, "grandissimo tiranno in Lombardìa, la fiorente Fiorenza in libertà desiderò inghiottire, sottilmente veggendo, che se avesse tagliato il capo della libertà, arebbe veduto il resto del corpo morto, e agevolmente sarebbe tutta Italia soggiogata." Although all Lombardy, "sempre . . . notissima di tiranni," was subservient to Mastino, Florence resisted. (*Risponsiva*, ed. Moreni—see note 8 to Chap. 4—p. 200.) "Siamo adunque di così ottimo et unico bene [i.e., the *libertà*, for which Cato died] non solo conservatori, ma accrescitori." And, indeed, Florence had already stood the decisive test when the Duke of Athens was forced by the citizens to resign his tyranny only after eleven months. "Fu e sarà questo a noi continuo esempio di non solo conoscere, ma onorare, adorare, conservare la libertà" (*ibid.*, pp. 248f.). On Florence's resistance against Giovanni and Bernabò Visconti, see *ibid.*, pp. 203f. For Cino's new emphasis on the Roman Republic, see pp. 76f. above.

[4] *Risponsiva*, pp. 226-247.

[5] See above note 33 to Chap. 3.

[6] ". . . perchè non solo l'arme, ma la mercanzia amplificano la Repubblica . . ." (*Risponsiva*, pp. 245f.). In his political correspondence, Salutati, too, often praised the "mercatura" as the nerve of Florence's liberty and power; see Garin, *La Cultura Filosofica*, p. 14. But this is something different from breaking the classicist prejudice and carving out a niche for merchants in a Florentine hall of fame.

[7] See the "Apologia nella quale si difende Danthe et Florentia da falsi calumniatori," which introduces Landino's *Commentary* on Dante, and includes in its list of great Florentines a group of merchants "perchè sempre fu havuto in prezo in ogni città la mercatura, pure che sia exercitata con degnità" (edn. Florence, 1481, fol. [Vv]).

[8] *Risponsiva*, ed. Moreni, p. 247.

[9] For a criticism of the role ascribed to Marsili see *Humanistic and Political Literature*, pp. 30-32; for the differences between the school of Marsili and civic Humanism, cf. pp. 325f. below. On Marsili's personality and works, U. Mariani, *Il Petrarca e gli Agostiniani* (Rome, 1946), pp. 66-96.

[10] Since there was no longer a Florentine-French alliance after the middle of 1398, all of the long sections of Salutati's *Invectiva* dealing with Florence's relationship to France may be ascribed to the original draft of the winter of 1397-98.

[11] See Comines, *Mémoires*, Book VII, chapter IX, where this observation is made on the occasion of the unexpected delivery of Sarzana, a fortress with which Florence might have held off the French expedition for an indefinite period, as Comines believed. Burckhardt, in this connection, speaks of the "direful naïveté" and the "Guelph superstition of the Florentines"; but his assertion that Comines had said the French were received "comme saints" seems to be a mistake.

[12] Marco Foscari, in his *Relazione* of 1527, in E. Albéri, *Relazioni degli ambasciatori veneti al Senato*, ser. II, vol. I (Florence, 1839), pp. 78f.

[13] Cf. the evidence in *Crisis: Appendices*, p. 478.

[14] See pp. 20f. above.

[15] Salutati, *Invectiva*, pp. 163-174, and passim.

[16] F. Macrì-Leone, "La Politica di Giovanni Boccaccio," *Giornale Storico della Letteratura Italiana*, XV (1890), esp. 98f.

[17] See p. 29 above.

[18] See p. 91 above.

[19] See pp. 62f. above.

[20] See *Humanistic and Political Literature*, pp. 21-23.

[21] *Ep. XIII 10*, September 1403; *Epistolario*, vol. III, p. 637.

[22] For the date and publication of Salutati's *De Tyranno* cf. *Crisis: Appendices*, p. 479.

[23] See pp. 56f. above.

[24] This change in Salutati's views will be pointed out presently in detail. Consider also Salutati's acclaim of Cicero the Roman citizen and Cicero's stand for the *Respublica Romana* in 1392; see pp. 124f. below.

[25] On Salutati's pioneering role in this respect see L. Borghi, "La dottrina morale di Coluccio Salutati," *Annali della R. Scuola Normale Superiore di Pisa*, ser. II, vol. III (1934), esp. 93ff., and E. Garin, "I Trattati Morali di Coluccio Salutati," *Atti dell'Accademia Fiorentina di Scienze Morali 'La Colombaria'* (1943), 53-88. Salutati's twilight position in the transition from Medievalism to the Renaissance had already been observed by the first modern student of Salutati's *Weltanschauung*, Alfred v. Martin. The somewhat odd result was that v. Martin, in a monograph published in 1913 (*Mittelalterliche Welt- und Lebensanschauung im Spiegel der Schriften Coluccio Salutatis*) portrayed Salutati as the representative of a medieval outlook—and three years later (in *Coluccio Salutati und das humanistische Lebensideal* [1916]) discussed him in another

monograph as a spokesman for Humanism. The analysis of Salutati's thought given in various chapters of the present book will be guided by the questions whether the variations of Salutati's thought may not be explained largely as successive phases of his intellectual development, and whether the discord found in his *Weltanschauung* is not characteristic of Trecento humanists and does not merge into the wider problem of the intellectual struggle which produced a crisis of transition on the eve of the Quattrocento.

[26] Salutati, *Ep. III 9*, January 21, 1372, *Epistolario*, vol. I, p. 156.

[27] ". . . utilem ad detestationem negotiosae vitae, qua bonis temporalibus implicamur." "Sane non dubito quin . . . lector . . . in solitariam et religiosam vitam non secedat, et in eius amorem exardescens . . ." (Filippo Villani, *De Origine*, ed. Galletti, p. 19).

[28a] See pp. 316ff. below.

[28b] *De Seculo*, ed. Ullman, p. 4.

[28c] *Ibid.*, pp. 3, 83, 87. Accordingly, it would be entirely inadequate to judge with the editor of the *De Seculo et Religione*, B. C. Ullman, that Salutati's *De Seculo* is a work of rhetoric which "does not reflect its author's mind," and that Salutati, in case of need, could have also argued against the monastic way of life." ("Liber ergo Colucii non est speculum mentis auctoris sed demonstrat eius facultatem disputandi. . . . Si res postulasset, contra vitam monasticam perinde disputare potuisset," *Praefatio*, p. vi).

[28d] *De Seculo*, p. 61.

[28e] "Melior est contemplativa, fateor; non tamen semper nec omnibus eligibilior. Inferior est activa, sed eligendo multotiens preferenda" (Salutati, *Ep. X 16*, 1398, vol. III, p. 305).

[29] Salutati, *Ep. I 12*, June 20, 1366, *Epistolario*, vol. I, p. 32. The device cited, "non posse simul uxori et philosophie servire," came from St. Jerome's *Adversus Iovianum*, and had often been repeated by medieval humanists and writers.

[30] *Ep. VIII 3*, July 23, 1392, *Epistolario*, vol. II, pp. 365-374— a letter attacking many arguments against matrimony, both of the medieval ascetic tradition and by Petrarch.

[31] "Sancta quippe rusticitas solum sibi prodest, ut ille [St. Jerome] ait. Negociosa vero sanctitas multos edificat . . ." *Ep. VIII 18*, July 22, 1393, *Epistolario*, vol. II, p. 453. Similarly *Ep. IX 4*, Oct. 24, 1392-94, vol. III, pp. 50f.: "Crede michi: . . . non produxisset nos natura politicos, hoc est associabiles, si conversatio prorsus non dirigeret ad salutem."

[32] The above is an extract from *Ep. XII 20*, September 21, 1401, *Epistolario*, vol. III, pp. 541-542. The passages referred to are in *Crisis: Appendices*, p. 482.

[33] For this controversy see *Crisis: Appendices*, pp. 482f.

[34] *De Nobilitate Legum et Medicinae*, ed. E. Garin (Florence, 1947); cf. esp. pp. 28, 36-39, and also Borghi's comments, *op. cit.*, p. 94.

[35] Cf. Borghi, *op. cit.*, pp. 100f., and E. Garin, *Der italienische Humanismus* (Bern, 1947), pp. 24ff.

[36] See pp. 295ff. below.

[37] Also circulated through Orosius; but Salutati refers directly to *Civitas Dei* in *Ep. XII 4*, 1401, *Epistolario*, vol. III, p. 472.

[38a] This denial is found especially in Ullman, *op. cit.*, pp. 47-48, though it seems to me to be based on a rather incomplete and not always accurate critique. A number of quotations from Salutati's writings added, in the present second edition, to the paragraph that follows, will enable the reader to form his own opinion. Changes in Salutati's attitude during the course of his life had already been noted by A. von Martin, *Humanistisches Lebensideal*, pp. 126, 263f.

[38b] Some letters of this type are listed in von Martin, *op. cit.*, pp. 119f.

[39a] *Ep. I 7*, 1366, vol. I, p. 21.

[39b] Whoever hears of them, "titillante quasi quodam virtutum pruritu, ad idem audendum . . . animetur" (*Ep. II 18*, 1369, vol. I, p. 105).

[39c] *Ep. III 17*, 1374, vol. I, pp. 191f.

[39d] Cf. also the list of fervent praises of unlimited devotion to the state in von Martin, *op. cit.*, pp. 125f.

[39e] *Ep. VII 11*, 1370's (or at least not later than 1392), vol. II, p. 292.

[40a] See F. Novati in *Epistolario di Salutati*, vol. IV, pp. 253f.

[40b] As any glance at the catalogues of fifteenth-century Florentine manuscripts shows. Novati (see previous note) already was aware of about forty manuscripts, and there must be many more.

[40c] *Ep. IX 13*, 1396, vol. III, p. 116.

[40d] *Ibid.*, p. 117.

[40e] *Ep. XII 24*, 1401, vol. III, p. 562.

[41a] "Qui virtutis actum in aliud quam in finem verum et ultimum dirigit, certum est actum non efficere virtuosum, licet cunctis sit aliis respectibus commendandus." "Nam si patria verus et ultimus finis esset, non possemus que pro patria gerimus, in laudem, lucrum aliquod, potentiam vel dignitatem . . . mutare. . . . Verus enim finis est ipse Deus" (*Ep. XIV 22*, 1406, vol. IV, p. 164).

[41b] "Super omnia trahebantur gloria." "Corrupta quidem natura, principii sui oblita, se dirigit in aliud quam in Deum" (*Ep. XII 4*, 1401, vol. III, p. 471).

[41c] *De Laboribus Herculis*, ed. Ullman, p. 64.

[41d] *Ibid.*, p. 381. For other examples of Salutati's attacks in his later years upon the thirst for glory among the ancients, cf. von Martin, *Mittelalterliche Weltanschauung*, pp. 70f.

[42] Petrarch to Rienzo from Avignon, middle of June 1347. Ed. K. Burdach, *Vom Mittelalter zur Reformation*, vol. II, part III (Berlin, 1912), p. 68. See also the verses on one of the murderers of Caesar, Decimus Iunius Brutus, in *Africa*, II, 150-152: ". . . animosaque pectora Bruti / Ante oculos habeo, stupeoque ubi condere ferrum / Audeat."

[43] *De Remediis*, lib. II, dial. 118: Why try to flee from the rule "viri omnium non tyrannorum modo, sed principum clementissimi atque mitissimi . . . ?" Cato's real motive probably was not flight from Caesar, "quam ut Stoicorum decretis obtemperaret suumque nomen grandi aliquo facinore clarificaret. . . . En tibi alia praeter invidiam causa moriendi vanitas stulta?" In his *De Gestis Cesaris* (*Hist. Caesaris*, ed. Schneider, p. 292) and in *Ep. Var. 33*, Petrarch notes that his criticism of Cato had been stimulated by Augustine's censures.

[44] That is, since Petrarch's enthusiastic epistolary exchanges with Emperor Charles IV during the 1350's. As far as Petrarch himself is concerned, the reappearance of imperial monarchism was not tantamount to a reappearance of the medieval religious arguments in justification of the Empire—the arguments on which Dante's thought had been built. But such an identification was to take place again among Petrarch's pupils and friends, who soon believed to see full harmony between the view of Petrarch in his later years, and Dante's medieval idea of Empire.

[45] Petrarch, *Epistolae Seniles, Ep. XIV 1*, end of 1373; sometimes as a separate pamphlet with the title *Qualis esse debeat, qui rempublicam regit*. The references to Caesar in Fracassetti's edition of the *Ep. Sen.*, vol. II, pp. 342f. The changes in Petrarch's outlook were first firmly established by Guido Martellotti, "Linee di sviluppo dell' umanesimo Petrarchesco," *Studi Petrarcheschi*, II (1949), 51-80, esp. 54ff., and have been further traced in two papers by the present writer in *Bibliothèque d'Humanisme et Renaissance*, XXIV (1962), 7-41 ("The Evolution of Petrarch's Thought"), and XXV (1963), 489-530 (on successive changes of Petrarch's *Secretum*).

CHAPTER 6

[1] The significance of the Cicero controversy in the Trecento for the rise of a civic attitude toward life was pointed out years ago by this writer in his paper "Cicero and the Roman Civic Spirit in the Middle Ages and the Early Renaissance" (*Bulletin of the John*

Rylands Library, XXII [1938], 84-89). But the same controversy also represents an important episode in the humanistic rediscovery of the *Respublica Romana*, and in the Renaissance revolt against the medieval notion of Universal Empire. It is from this viewpoint that we approach the controversy here, scanning a greater wealth of sources.

2 Petrarca, *Epistolae familiares*, *Ep. XXIV 3*, ed. V. Rossi, vol. IV (Firenze, 1942), pp. 226f.

3 *De Vita Solitaria*, II, tr. 8, c. 4 (in the older editions, c. 2), ed. A. Altamura, Naples, 1943, p. 131. Cf. also the polemical passages against Cicero in *De Vita Solitaria*, I, tr. 3, c. 2, and II, tr. 10, c. 7 (in Altamura's ed. c. 6); and in *Rerum Memorandarum Libri*, lib. I, c. 4 and 15, lib. III, c. 43 (ed. G. Billanovich, Firenze, 1943).

4 *Ep. Fam. XXIV 3*, ed. Rossi, p. 226; *Ep. Fam. XXIV 4*, p. 228.

5 *Historia Julii Caesaris*, ed. C. F. Chr. Schneider (Leipzig, 1827), pp. 292f. *De Remediis*, lib. II, dial. 118.

6 Salutati had asked Milanese friends for a manuscript of Cicero's *Ep. ad Atticum*, but received from the treasures of the old Cathedral library at Vercelli a manuscript of the *Epistolae familiares*. See Novati's note in his edition of Salutati's *Epistolario*, vol. II, p. 340.

7a Cf. *Crisis: Appendices*, p. 486.

7b Cf. pp. 28f. above.

8 "Vidi . . . bellorum civilium fundamenta et quid caput illud orbis terrarum de libertate populica in monarchie detruderit servitutem" (*Ep. VIII 7*, 1392, *Epistolario*, vol. II, p. 389).

9 This emerges from Salutati's answers.

10 *Ep. IX 3* and *IX 4*, *Epistolario*, vol. III, pp. 25f., 50.

11 For Vergerio's life see pp. 129f. below.

12 See the *Epistolario di Pier Paolo Vergerio*, ed. L. Smith ("Fonti per la Storia d'Italia," vol. 74, Rome, 1934), introduction pp. xiv f., p. 53, note 2, and the letters nos. xxxi ff.

13 *Ibid.*, *Ep. XXVIII*, p. 55; *Ep. XXXI*, p. 62; *Ep. XXXIII*, p. 66.

14 The first to draw attention to Vergerio's rejoinder seems to have been B. Ziliotto, *La Cultura Letteraria di Trieste e dell' Istria* (Trieste, 1913), pp. 40f., but he saw in it nothing but "un' innocente esercitazione rettorica." The text is now available in an "Appendice" to Vergerio's *Epistolario*, ed. Smith, pp. 436-445; for its fortunes, see *Crisis: Appendices*, p. 496, note 2. The passages referred to in the notes which follow are found in *Crisis: Appendices*, pp. 486f.

15 Vergerio's *Epistolario*, ed. Smith, p. 442.

16 *Ibid.*, pp. 439f., 444.

17 *Ibid.*, p. 441.

[18] *Ibid.*, pp. 441-443.

[19] The dates for Vergerio's later life have been established by L. Smith in *Archivio Veneto-Tridentino*, x (1926), 149-157, and *Archivio Veneto*, ser. v, vol. iv (1928), 92-141.

[20] For the completion of *De Ingenuis Moribus* by June, 1402, see L. Smith in Vergerio's *Epistolario*, p. 254, and G. Calò in *La Rinascita*, ii (1939), 228, 232, reprinted in *Dall' Umanesimo*, pp. 40, 43. That Vergerio was the tutor of Ubertino da Carrara seems highly probable according to Calò, *Rinascita*, pp. 243, 245f., *Dall' Umanesimo*, pp. 56, 58f.

[21] H. Baron, *Bulletin of the John Rylands Library*, xxii (1938), 91.

[22] In 1446 or 1447; see A. Segarizzi, ed., *Rerum Italicarum Scriptores*, n. ser. tom. xxiv, parte xv (1902), p. viii.

[23] For this tendency of the *Vitae Principum Carrariensium* and for the reference to Caesar, see B. Ziliotto, *La Cultura Letteraria*, p. 59.

[24] As established in "Ricerche intorno al *De principibus carrariensibus et gestis eorum liber* attribuito a Pier Paolo Vergerio seniore" (*Università di Padova, Pubblicazioni della Facoltà di Lettere e Filosofia*, vol. xxiii, Padua, 1946) by Carmela Marchente, who also definitely proves Vergerio's authorship.

[25] For the date of Vergerio's *De Monarchia* cf. *Crisis: Appendices*, p. 488.

[26] *Epistolario*, p. 448.

[27] *Ibid.*, p. 447. The passage is quoted in *Crisis: Appendices*, p. 488.

[28] N. Festa, *Saggio sull' "Africa" del Petrarca* (Palermo, 1926), pp. 40-46; G. Billanovich, *Petrarca Letterato*, vol. i (Rome, 1947), pp. 381-384.

[29] For a correction of the accepted information on Vergerio's relations with Florence after 1400, see *Humanistic and Political Literature*, pp. 107ff., "A Letter of Pier Paolo Vergerio (*Epistola* lxxxxvi) and Bruni's *Laudatio*."

[30] Conversino, whom Lehnerdt was the first to distinguish from Malpaghini—both had originally been known under the name of Giovanni da Ravenna—has become for us a living personality through Sabbadini's reconstruction of his life and works in *Giovanni da Ravenna. Insigne Figura d'Umanista (1343-1408)* (Como, 1924). Sabbadini reproduces extracts from most of Conversino's writings, but confines himself to paragraphs that contain data on Conversino's life. An analysis and historical appraisal of Conversino's humanistic ideas, his moral philosophy, and political attitude, are still a desideratum. For the title and textual tradition of the

Dragmalogia—here used in MS IX 11 of the Fondazione Querini-Stampalia, Venice—see *Crisis: Appendices*, pp. 489f.

³¹ This advice is mentioned in a letter of Conversino to Vergerio, written in 1406, and published by Sabbadini, *op. cit.*, p. 229.

³² The cessation of payments to the Paduan scholars, and Conversino's indignation about this action, are described on the introductory pages of the *Dragmalogia*. For the date of the treatise, see Sabbadini, p. 105.

³³ Fol. 18v. An edition of the passages of the *Dragmalogia* used in our analysis may be found in *Crisis: Appendices*, pp. 490-495.

³⁴ Fol. 19r and 20r.

³⁵ Fol. 16b and 18v.

³⁶ Fol. 19r.

³⁷ Fol. 19r.

³⁸ Fol. 18v and 19r.

³⁹ Fol. 17r-17v.

⁴⁰ "Novissime omnium in hac virtutis laudibus Johannes Galeacz liberalitatem supergressus est, non dico poetas et oratores, qui rarissimi comparent, sed medicos eciam iuris consultos qui predicarentur ad eliciendum fruendumque indiscussa erogacione [MS: erragacione] munificus" (fol. 17v). A similar reference to Giangaleazzo's patronage is found in the introduction to the work, fol. 4r.

⁴¹ Fol. 17r.

⁴² Fol. 17v-18r and 29vᴵ-30rᴵᴵ.

⁴³ The Venetian interlocutor and defender of the Venetian Republic introduces the section dealing with the relative merits of Tyranny and Republic with the words: "Tuus iste sermo de gubernatoris officio in hanc me coniecturam divertit, uniusne principis an plurium dominatu *ceu nostra ceu Thuscha* [apparently a reference to Florence] felicius urbs regatur" (fol. 16v). Beyond this, he does not cite Florence in the course of his argument.

⁴⁴ In the introductory words of the work: "Quid enim ignominiosius Cesaree magiestati, quam si mercenarius agnoscitur. Hunc, inquam, elatio florentina stipendio allexit in Latium. . . . Pudor Italice probitatis accire barbaros, quo preda barbaris pateat Italia."

⁴⁵ For the details of this relationship, see *Humanistic and Political Literature*, Chap. v, Excursus "The Date of Salutati's *Epistola XII 10*," esp. notes 8-10.

⁴⁶ Cf. already Loschi's modest denial when, on Salutati's death, he was told he was expected to take Salutati's position in the humanistic movement: "How could I, who was born in the region . . . settled by the Cimbri whom Marius had conquered, how could I ever exclude the Florentines who are born to eloquence from the heritage of their compatriot and master?" (See Loschi's letter to Giovanni Tinti da Fabriano, Oct. 25, 1406, in Salutati's *Epistolario*,

ed. Novati, vol. IV, p. 477). For another example of involuntary admission that the Humanism and historiography of the Florentine school were superior, see the letter of Bartolomeo della Capra discussed on pp. 413f. below and *Crisis: Appendices*, p. 432.

[47] This feature of Florentine historiography, which has not always been sufficiently taken into account, is excellently brought out by Sabbadini in his *Il Metodo degli Umanisti* (Florence, 1920) with the following words: In Venice, Milan, Genoa, and Naples, "the historians were commissioned by the Republic or by the Court, in whose interest and for whose greater glory they had to slant their writings. The only exception are the Florentine historians, who, although they tend to extol their own city, set to work from a personal urge and patriotic feeling" (pp. 84f.).

[48] See the letter of Bartolomeo della Capra mentioned in note 46 above.

[49] Fol. 19v. Consequently (thus fol. 23f. asserts), true liberty can be obtained only in a life of leisure in country surroundings, unencumbered by social and political burdens; and a long section (fol. 31ff.) is meant to prove that the freedom obtainable in a life of scholarship and independence of mind is more genuine than political liberty.

[50] Fol. 17v and 19r.

[51] "Per reges romanum fundatum est et vires cepit imperium. Deinde, ubi regi superbo superbi cives parere contempserunt, populariter res acta est, deus bone quanto fluctu et turbine civitatis, primo tribunis [MS: tribunus] plebis, deinde militaribus, mox insolencia decemvirali populum urbemque vexantibus. Inficiari non possumus romanum populum sub consulibus magna gessisse, licet despectum sepe atque derisum. Sed quantulum est ad eam collata magnitudinem imperii et dignitatis, ad quam sub cesaribus sublimatum exauctumque [MS: exauctam, sublimatam exauctamque] legimus" (fol. 18v).

[52] Fol. 18v and 19r.

[53] ". . . quod omnis creature status, quo similior conditori, hoc pulcrior, ordinacior et perfectior existit; quare cum rerum auctor et rector unus sit, unius gubernacionem [MS: gubernamen], quoniam universi conformius, melius esse iudico" (fol. 16v).

[54] "Conducibilius ac divinius urbes ac regna mecum fateare oportet unius quam multitudinis ducatu componi, quod . . . creator, nempe deus, hominem continuo sub obediencie lege constituit. . . ." "Quoniam dampnabiliter superbiret impenderetque ruine, si moderamen superioris . . . contempnens propria usurparet vivere libertate, omnis prope Theutonis plaga, velut Italia [MS: Italie], Romanum Imperatorem veneratur . . ." (fol. 19r-v).

CHAPTER 7

¹ We have no less than three Latin, one Italian, and one English edition of *De Tyranno*. The Latin text was edited by A. v. Martin, *Coluccio Salutati's Traktat vom Tyrannen* (Berlin, 1913), and by F. Ercole, *Der Tractatus de Tyranno von Coluccio Salutati* (Berlin, 1914); both editions have fundamental introductions; Ercole's text is founded on a more complete manuscript basis. Ercole's introduction has been republished in Italian in his volume *Da Bartolo all' Althusio. Saggi Sulla Storia del Pensiero Pubblicistico del Rinascimento Italiano* (Florence, 1932), pp. 219-389, and the text of his edition—used in the following quotations—is reprinted in *Coluccio Salutati. Il Trattato 'De Tyranno' e Lettere Scelte*, ed. F. Ercole, "Scrittori Politici Italiani," vol. IX (Bologna, 1942), pp. 1-38. The latter volume, on pp. 153-184, also includes an Italian translation. An English translation, with a discussion of the political conditions of the late Trecento interpreted in the light of Salutati's treatise, is found in E. Emerton's *Humanism and Tyranny. Studies in the Italian Trecento* (Cambridge, Mass., 1926), pp. 25-116.

²ᵃ For the fortunes of Vergerio's letter see *Crisis: Appendices*, p. 496.

²ᵇ Cf. pp. 242f. below.

²ᶜ For these three epigrams and their background see N. Rubinstein, in the study cited in note 5a to Chap. 16 below, pp. 194f. and 198.

²ᵈ See pp. 361f. below.

³ Prefatio, § 5.

⁴ See above note 45 to Chap. 6 and the references there given.

⁵ Cap. IV, § 14.

⁶ IV, 15-16.

⁷ V, 4.

⁸ "Verum cum autor iste doctissimus christianus videret ex rerum effectibus, qui divine voluntatis verissimi testes sunt, deum decrevisse res hominum sub una Romanorum redigere monarchia, nonne debuit eos, qui conati sunt huic ordinationi, qua ratione potuerunt, obsistere, velut dispositioni Dei contrarios, inter damnatos et reprobos deputare?" (V, 6).

⁹ IV, 10-11.

¹⁰ IV, 12-13.

¹¹ "Nam in illa, quam diligebas, politia vel aristocratia, malorum remedium vel esse non poterat dissidentibus animis, vel tam difficulter et periculose, quod nichil minus tempori conveniret . . . : ut nedum utile, sed necessarium fuerit ad unum devenire principem, in cuius manibus tot rerum motus et animorum contrarietates iustitia et equitate regnantis simul discerent convenire atque coalescere. Quod si

factum in Octavio non fuisset, numquam romana rabies quievisset . . ." (IV, 17-18).

[12] ". . . quando quidem non omnino ne quisquam, sed uter regeret et rerum summam et moderamen assumeret, certabatur. . . . Utrimque par impietas, par furor et equalis ambitio, par votum opprimendi concives, tollendi leges, et illud equum ducere, quod placeret prodessetque victoribus. Non tuende rei publice, sed opprimende certamen illud fuit. Quis iustius induit arma, scire nefas, ut ille ait" (III, 9).

[13a] Ercole, in the introduction to his edition of De Tyranno, pp. 172f., and in Da Bartolo, pp. 379f.; A. v. Martin, in his edition of De Tyranno, pp. 40f., 59f.

[13b] Particularly those sections of it referred to below (notes 19 and 22).

[14] Both Ercole and v. Martin, encountering these surviving medieval elements in the treatise, judged them to be carry-overs of negligible significance; the relevance of the work was to be sought exclusively in its new realistic method. It is only near the end of the treatise—thus both argued—that the medieval theological arguments appear and Caesar is considered as creator of the imperial dignity; up to that point, Caesar is visualized realistically as if he were one of the *signori* of the Trecento (cf. Ercole, in the introduction to his edition, p. 14; *Da Bartolo*, pp. 228f., 266ff.), and Caesar's assassins are discussed and condemned according to "natural" political standards (cf. v. Martin, p. 42). The weakness of this appraisal is that the late appearance in the treatise of the arguments derived from medieval tradition does not mean that they are of small significance to the author; the section in which they are taken up is the chapter which deals with the verdict on Caesar given by Dante—the climax of the entire discussion, and the logical context for acceptance or rejection of the medieval teaching of Universal Monarchy. What matters is not frequency or place, but the function of the surviving medieval notions in the web of Salutati's argument: the question whether the realism found in the treatise extends to those fields where the medieval tradition could be vitally endangered, or whether the mainsprings of Dante's thought—the medieval ideas of Universal Empire and of the likeness of Monarchy to the divine order of the world—have remained intact.

[15] See pp. 57 and 102f. above.

[16] See p. 144 above.

[17] See note 19 to Chap. 3 and *Crisis: Appendices*, p. 463, note 34.

[18] See p. 63 above.

[19] "Sic adeo mors illa indignissima visa est displicuisse Deo et hominibus" (*Benvenuti de Rambaldis de Imola Comentum super Dantis Aldigherij Comoediam*, ed. P. Lacaita [Florence, 1887],

vol. II, p. 560). Rambaldi's whole description, pp. 560-561, of the hostile reaction of the Roman people against the assassins is nothing but a repetition—a plagiarism, according to modern standards—of what Petrarch had dramatically narrated at the end of his *De Gestis Cesaris* (*Historia Caesaris*, ed. C. F. Chr. Schneider [Leipzig, 1827], pp. 334-335), where the final conclusion had also been: "ut evidenter ostenderetur caedem illam nec Deo nec hominibus placuisse."

[20] *Benvenuti . . . Comentum*, vol. II, p. 561.

[21] "Unde nota, quod pulcerrima pars sapientis est nullius esse partis, sicut scriptum est in Inferno" (comm. on *Par.* canto XVII; vol. V, p. 195).

[22] ". . . sed uterque petebat regnum, uterque ingratus patriae . . ." (IV, p. 447). To be compared with Petrarch, *Historia Caesaris*, ed. Schneider, pp. 217f., ". . . ut utriusque partis merita non usque adeo, ut putantur, imparia et utrumque . . . regnare voluisse . . . constaret."

[23] *Benvenuti . . . Comentum*, IV, pp. 423, 418f.

[24] IV, p. 423.

[25] IV, p. 435.

[26a] "Dei dispositione factum est, ut victor Caesar fuerit" (*De Tyranno*, III, 10).

[26b] See W. Rüegg on Salutati's *De Fato et Fortuna* in *Rinascimento*, V (1954), 38.

[27] Cf. this writer's notes on the problem of "Realism" in the art and intellectual life of the Renaissance in *Journal of the History of Ideas*, IV (1943), 45-48, and XI (1950), 503-505.

[28] Pp. 50f. above.

[29] See pp. 98f. above.

[30] See pp. 76, 89 above.

[31] For the details of Salutati's and Bruni's attitudes toward the Sulla theory, cf. *Humanistic and Political Literature*, pp. 19ff., 100f.

[32a] A parallel is that in the introductory, juridical part of his treatise, Salutati produces a theory which, when compared with the teachings of Bartolo da Sassoferrato's preceding Guelph jurisprudence, enhances the prerogatives of the Empire. Cf. *Crisis: Appendices*, pp. 500f.

[32b] "Nefas rempublicam invasit"; *Ep. III 17*, 1374, ed. Novati, I, p. 197.

[33] See *Crisis: Appendices*, p. 501. It is important to recognize Salutati's dependence on Bartolo, if we are to avoid overmagnifying the originality and significance of the introductory juridical chapter of Salutati's treatise. The purpose of *De Tyranno* was to defend Dante's politico-historical philosophy with intellectual weapons taken from Petrarch's Humanism, and the first chapter merely was

to present some definitions and proper terminology from current legal theories that could aid this purpose. *De Tyranno* cannot be adequately appraised as being an original contribution to the ideas of public law in the Renaissance; its historical place depends on how much or little it contributed to the growth of politico-historical thought.

[34] For a criticism of recent appraisals of Salutati's *De Tyranno* see *Crisis: Appendices*, pp. 502f.

[35] *De Tyranno*, IV, 14.

[36] IV, 19-20. The passage is quoted in *Crisis: Appendices*, p. 503.

[37] IV, 9-10. Cf. *Crisis: Appendices*, p. 503.

[38] See for instance S. Frascino in *Civiltà Moderna*, vol. II (1930), 871, and E. Emerton, *Humanism and Tyranny* (see note 1 above), pp. 56-58, 63. For a criticism of Emerton's small but thoughtful and well-written book, which has served many English-speaking students as a cicerone to the political problems of the early Renaissance, cf. *Crisis: Appendices*, pp. 503f.

[39] Even in the famous humanistic controversy on true *nobilitas* and how it can develop—whether a man must have a great *patria* to reach personal greatness, or needs only individual talent—Salutati was the first to defend the civic point of view against the individualistic pride of the *literati* and influenced Bruni's convictions, as we shall see in the chapter on Bruni's "*Dialogus II* and the Florentine Environment," pp. 250f. below.

[40] See the references on p. 36 above.

CHAPTER 8

[1] In all probability in 1407/08, except that the appended analysis of the Florentine constitution, in the ninth book, may have been added in 1409/10. See *Humanistic and Political Literature*, Chap. III, "The Date of Gregorio Dati's *Istoria di Firenze 1380-1406*."

[2] Gregorio Dati, *L'Istoria di Firenze dal 1380 al 1405*, ed. L. Pratesi (Norcia, 1904). As to the limitations of Pratesi's edition, which make it necessary also to consult the edition published by G. Manni, Florence, 1735, see "The Date of Gregorio Dati's *Istoria*," just quoted, passim. Although Manni's manuscript basis is at many points corrupted or incomplete, Pratesi's text, constructed with the help of late manuscripts, can not be accepted with confidence. Our quotations follow Pratesi's text, but refer also to Manni's version in places where the divergence of the two editions affects the meaning of the text and the genuine reading is not obvious.

[3] See pp. 77f. above.

[4] See F. Flamini's survey (though not complete) of Dati's public

activities, with references to archival documents, in *Giornale Storico della Letteratura Italiana,* XVI (1890), 2f.

⁵ As early as 1404, his name was entered in the list of those entitled to the office of "Gonfalonieri di compagnie," and drew a lot for 1412. In 1405, he was one of the "Ten of Liberty" ("Dieci della libertà") appointed during the war against Pisa. See Dati's *Libro Segreto,* ed. C. Gargiolli, "Scelta di Curiosità Letterarie," vol. 102 (Bologna, 1869), pp. 79, 82.

⁶ "La storia della lunga e grandissima (*Manni* grande) guerra di Italia che fu a questi nostri dì tra il tiranno di Lombardia, duca di Milano, e il magnifico Comune di Firenze." *Istoria,* ed. Pratesi, p. 11; ed. Manni, pp. 1f.

⁷ Given Bruni's custom not to name his sources, but to make free use of them in his narrative, his dependence on Dati's account is difficult to establish; so far it has not been proved in literal details. (Cf. E. Santini in his introduction to the edition of Bruni's *Historiae,* pp. x f.) But the similarity of the politico-historical categories employed by the two authors is striking, and it is hard to believe that Bruni, who is known to have exploited the extant literature of Florentine political memoirs, and who must have been in frequent personal contact with Dati when he himself was chancellor and Dati one of the most active statesmen during the late 1420's and early 1430's, did not know Dati's work at all.

⁸ Two exceptions are Gino Capponi, who in his *Storia della Repubblica di Firenze* (vol. I, p. 533), remarked as early as 1875 that Dati's history deserved the title of "Political Discourses concerning the State of Florence and the City's Way of Life" and characterized Dati "as a thoughtful man who observes and appraises things from the inside, penetrating and practical, and who knows well how to portray the quality and the temper of this Florentine people"; and V. Rossi, who in his *Quattrocento* (3rd edn. [1933], pp. 185f.) notes Dati as a man of "relative maturity of thought" among his contemporaries, distinguished by his "endeavours to recognize psychological causes (*cause umane*) and the logical connection of actions." These hints, however, have never been followed up, and the typical judgment of students of humanistic historiography has remained that in Dati "none of the true critical spirit which is the achievement of the Renaissance" is found. (See E. Santini in *Annali della Scuola Normale Superiore di Pisa,* XXII [1910], pp. 102f.) Now it is quite true that Dati, the citizen writing in Volgare, proves himself alien to the historical criticism which humanists like Salutati and Bruni knew how to apply to traditional legends, and that he, in the manner of earlier chroniclers, does at times find the explanation of the events he describes in the

just victory of piety and faith. However, we have already seen (note 65 to Chap. 3) that these limitations of the non-humanist did not prevent him from viewing the history of the free Commonwealth of Florence and its relationship to the *Respublica Romana* in the manner of later Quattrocento historiography. Moreover, the criticism of sources and the exposure of legends are not the main points of a work that is primarily devoted to the study of the most recent past. The crucial qualifications for such a task are rather an understanding of the nature of political action and of the lasting interests of each state working behind the decision-making of the diplomats. We must determine what role Dati played in the development of these capacities which became as important for the historiography of the Renaissance as did the humanistic criticism of the sources. Along these lines, Claudio Varese, in a chapter—"Una 'Laudatio Florentinae Urbis': La 'Istoria di Firenze' di Goro Dati" —of his *Storia e Politica nella Prosa del Quattrocento* (Turin, 1961) has now made some valuable contributions which elaborate the pages that follow.

[9] On Dati's use and conception of *Fortuna* see *Crisis: Appendices*, pp. 508ff.

[10] More accurately, between 1441 and Bruni's death in February, 1444. The chief evidence for this date lies in the fact that books XI and XII, with slight alterations, include a few passages already found in Bruni's *Rerum Suo Tempore Gestarum Commentarius* written between the second half of 1440 and the first half of 1441.

[11] *Istoria*, ed. Pratesi, p. 14; ed. Manni, p. 5. For the Italian text of our quotations from Dati cf. *Crisis: Appendices*, pp. 510-513.

[12] Ed. Pratesi, p. 27; ed. Manni, p. 19. The documentary reconstruction of Florence's politics in 1388, by G. Collino, *Archivio Storico Lombardo*, XXXVI (1909), 11f., 15f., confirms Dati's points: the deceitfulness of Giangaleazzo's diplomacy, and the inability of the Florentine politicians to grasp its scope immediately.

[13] Ed. Pratesi, p. 26f.; ed. Manni, p. 19.

[14] Ed. Pratesi, pp. 29, 37.

[15] *Ibid.*, pp. 27 and 29f.

[16] "Ora comincia il Comune di Firenze a mettere le mani a' grandi fatti; ora sono chiari i Fiorentini dell' animo insaziabile del tiranno, ora seguitano i belli ordini e i grandi consigli e le magnifiche operazioni" (ed. Pratesi, p. 37; ed. Manni, p. 30).

[17] Ed. Pratesi, pp. 96f.

[18] *Ibid.*, pp. 37, 50.

[19] *Ibid.*, p. 37.

[20] "Gran vantaggio ha colui nelle guerre che per sua sollecitudine e industria può sapere i portamenti e lo stato e la possa

della parte contraria; e però i detti Fiorentini, che sanno tutti i pertugi d'entrare e d'uscire che sono al mondo, a un' otta spiavano ogni dì ciò che faceva il Duca e si provvedevano a' rimedi loro, onde più salutevoli potessino vincere" (ed. Pratesi, p. 61; ed. Manni, pp. 56f.).

[21] ". . . hanno distese le loro ali per tutto il mondo e d'ogni parte sanno novelle e hanno avvisi" (ed. Pratesi, p. 37; ed. Manni, p. 30).

[22] Ed. Pratesi, pp. 37ff.

[23] *Ibid.* See also note 9 above.

[24] See p. 16 above.

[25] "E finalmente sarebbe forse fatica a ritrovare la prova di chi prima rompesse . . ." (*Istoria*, ed. Pratesi, p. 47; ed. Manni, p. 41).

[26] "E questo era antiveduto di provvidenza (*Manni* provveduto) con bastie e isteccati e con la gente de' Fiorentini che aspettavano di continuo quello che avvenne e a niuna cosa furono giunti sprovveduti. . . . E posto che le genti de' Fiorentini fussino assai meno, si come è usanza delle battaglie che la ragione vince, . . . guadagnarono i Fiorentini maravigliosa vittoria" (ed. Pratesi, p. 53; ed. Manni, p. 48).

[27] The document is cited in De Mesquita, *Giangaleazzo*, p. 222.

[28] Ed. Pratesi, p. 52; ed. Manni, pp. 46f.

[29] Ed. Pratesi, pp. 51-53.

[30] Dati, *Istoria*, ed. Pratesi, pp. 53f.

[31] *Ibid.*, p. 74.

[32] This is the concluding sentence of Bruni's *Historiae* (see above note 41 to Chap. 2); almost the same wording occurs in his *Rerum Suo Tempore Gestarum Commentarius*, pp. 432f.

[33] "Ed era innordine di vincierci però ch'egli era signore di Pisa, di Siena, di Perugia . . ." (Buonaccorso Pitti, *Cronica* ["Collezione di Opere Inedite o rare," vol. 91, Bologna, 1905], p. 134).

[34] Cf. *Istoria*, pp. 43f., 49f.

[35] ". . . avevano fatta la ragione con la penna in mano e dicevano come di cosa certa: tanto può durare . . ." (*Istoria*, ed. Pratesi, p. 71; ed. Manni, p. 67).

[36] *Loc. cit.*

[37] *Loc. cit.*

[38] Ed. Pratesi, p. 59; ed. Manni, p. 54.

[39] Ed. Pratesi, p. 27.

[40] Ed. Pratesi, pp. 54f.; ed. Manni, p. 49.

[41] Ed. Pratesi, p. 73; ed. Manni, p. 69.

[42] *Loc. cit.*

[43] *Loc. cit.*

[44] Ed. Pratesi, p. 72; ed. Manni, p. 68.

⁴⁵ "D'essere vinti, cioè sottoposti, [the citizens of Florence] non ebbono mai alcun dubbio perchè gli animi loro sono tanto a lui contrari e avversi che non lo potevano consentire in alcun loro pensiero, e ogni volta pareva loro avere molti rimedi—siccome fa il cuore franco e sicuro che mai non li manca via e rimedio—e sempre si confortavano con una speranza che pareva avere loro la cosa sicura in mano, cioè che il Comune non può morire e il Duca era uno solo uomo mortale, chè finito lui, finito lo stato suo. . . . Ma non si stettono mai i Fiorentini che, consumato o mancato uno rimedio, non ricorressono subitamente (*Manni* sollecitamente) all' altro." "E puossi (*Manni* E però si può) dire che tutta la libertà d'Italia stesse solo nelle mani de' Fiorentini, che (*Manni* perchè) ogni altra potenza li abbandonò" (ed. Pratesi, pp. 74, 73f.; ed. Manni, pp. 70 and 69).

CHAPTER 9

¹ Kirner, *Della 'Laudatio . . .'* (See note 12 below), p. 8.

² Bruni, *Ep. VIII 4*, 1440, ed. L. Mehus (see note 4 to Chap. 10), vol. II, p. 111.

³ The references to the *Laudatio* in Bruni's correspondence soon after the appearance of the work are discussed in *Humanistic and Political Literature*, Chap. IV, pp. 72ff.

⁴ The *Laudatio* is composed of the following main parts which may be entitled by key-words occurring in the text, as follows: Introduction and survey of contents: *L* fol. 133v-134r; ed. Klette, pp. 84-86. "Qualis urbs ipsa est": *L* fol. 134r-141v; ed. Klette, pp. 86-90. "Quibus parentibus populus Florentinus ortus est": *L* fol. 141v-144v; ed. Klette, pp. 90-94. "Quibus artibus Florentia de principatu in Italia certavit. De virtute urbis qualis foris fuit": *L* fol. 144v-152r; ed. Klette, pp. 94-98. "Quare Florentia disciplina institutisque domesticis admirabilis est": *L* fol. 152r-156r; ed. Klette, pp. 98-105. For *L* and Klette, and for the textual basis of our quotations, see note 1 to Chap. 3.

⁵ That Aelius Aristides was used as a model is stated by Bruni himself in his *Ep. VIII 4*. For the rhetorical topics treated in classical city eulogies, cf. Th. C. Burgess in *Studies in Classical Philology* (Chicago), vol. III (1902), pp. 107ff., 153f.

⁶ *Laudatio*, *L* fol. 145v-148v; ed. Klette, pp. 94-96.

⁷ So especially F. Novati when, in 1898, he edited Bonvesino della Riva's *De Magnalibus Urbis Mediolani* (1288) and, in his preface, for the first time surveyed and appraised the surviving specimens of this literary genre (*Bullettino dell' Istituto Storico Italiano*, no. 20 [Rome, 1898], 7-50). After giving high praise to the medieval *Laudes*, Novati characterized Bruni's humanistic *Laudatio*

as a work "which is ready and glad to sacrifice the substance of things to eloquence and distinction of style, and endeavours not so much to set forth good reasons, as to give tenuous and subtle arguments" (p. 12). In a similar vein, E. Verga, republishing Bonvesino's work in an Italian translation in 1921, called Bruni's presentation "full of grace . . . , but poor in content" (*Bonvesino della Riva. Le Meraviglie di Milano*, trans. & comm. E. Verga [Milan, 1921], p. xlix).

[8] For Bonvesino's *De Magnalibus*, ed. by F. Novati, see the preceding note.

[9] Throughout Chap. 3, "A New View of Roman History and of the Florentine Past."

[10] See pp. 73 ff. above.

[11] *Laudatio*, L fol. 139v-141r; cf. Klette's reference, p. 90.

[12] See G. Kirner in the pamphlet *Della 'Laudatio urbis florentinae' di Leonardo Bruni: notizia* (Livorno, 1889), p. 13.

[13] "Sedet enim media inter Tyrenum et Adriaticum mare quasi regina quedam Italie" (*Laudatio*, L fol. 141r).

[14] See Klette's introduction, pp. 32f.; Kirner, p. 13.

[15a] L fol. 136v-139r; a few passages in Klette, pp. 89f.

[15b] L fol. 136v-137r.

[16] *Laudatio*, L fol. 139r. See the Latin text, as well as that of the following quotations from the *Laudatio*, in *Crisis: Appendices*, pp. 517 ff.

[17] See pp. 177f. and 180 above.

[18] For the bibliography on and investigation of the 1470/80 engraving cf. *Crisis: Appendices*, p. 518.

[19] *Laudatio*, L fol. 137v-138r.

[20a] *Laudatio*, L fol. 138r.

[20b] For this date, cf. H. W. Janson, *The Sculpture of Donatello*, vol. II (Princeton, 1957), pp. 26f.

[20c] The possible impact of Florence's struggle-for-independence on Florentine art has now been traced in some suggestive detail by Frederick Hartt, "Art and Freedom in Quattrocento Florence," *Essays in Memory of Karl Lehmann* (New York, 1965), pp. 114 ff. On Donatello's St. George, *ibid.*, pp. 125f.

[21] *Laudatio*, L fol. 152v; ed. Klette, p. 98.

[22] *Loc. cit.*

[23] Pp. 418 ff. below.

[24] The *Breve Memoria*, dated 1339. Cf. *Crisis: Appendices*, p. 519.

[25a] "Quemadmodum enim in cordis convenientia est, ad quam cum intense fuerint una ex diversis tonis fit armonia, . . . eodem modo hec prudentissima civitas ita omnes sui partes moderata est ut inde summa quedam rei publice sibi ipsi consentanea resultet . . .

Nichil est in ea preposterum, nichil inconveniens, nichil absurdum, nichil vagum; suum queque locum tenent, non modo certum, sed etiam congruentcm" (*Laudatio, L* fol. 152r).

²⁵ᵇ "Preterea non satis [? ᴍs: vis] est sitne aliquid in re publica maiorum auctoritate constitutum; sed quam ob rem id constitutum, intelligere oportet atque exponere. Causa enim rei scientiam facit." Cf. the edition of Bruni's constitutional analysis in *Humanistic and Political Literature,* Chap. vɪɪɪ, "An Epistolary Description by Bruni of the Florentine Constitution in 1413."

²⁶ Giannotti, *Opere Politiche e Letterarie,* vol. ɪɪ (ed. Polidori, Florence, 1850), p. 28.

²⁷ *Ibid.,* vol. ɪ, p. 70.

²⁸ See note 431 to Chap. 3 above.

²⁹ Enea Silvio Piccolomini's work had been unknown until 1905. Its dependence on Bruni's *Laudatio* was recently discovered by Berthe Widmer, "Enea Silvios Lob der Stadt Basel und seine Vorlagen," *Basler Zeitschrift,* ʟvɪɪɪ-ʟɪx (1959), 111ff.

³⁰ Cf. E. F. Jacob in his "Introduction" to *Italian Renaissance Studies: a Tribute to the late Cecilia M. Ady* (London, 1960), pp. 40-43.

³¹ Pier Candido Decembrio, *De Laudibus Mediolanensium Urbis Panegyricus* (see note 431 to Chap. 3 above), pp. 37f.

³² *Ibid.,* pp. 31f.

³³ *Ibid.,* pp. 32f.

³⁴ Enea Silvio Piccolomini (Pope Pius II), *Descriptio Altera Urbis Basileae* (1438), ed. in *Concilium Basiliense: Studien und Quellen zur Geschichte des Concils von Basel,* vol. vɪɪɪ (Basel, 1936), p. 202.

³⁵ *Ibid.,* p. 203.

CHAPTER 10

¹ See pp. 204f. above.

² This is the result at which we arrived by analyzing the political situation around 1400 and by revising the chronology of the political literature written under the impress of the war; see p. 36 above.

³ That is, of his development as a translator from the Greek; see p. 88 above.

⁴ An even remotely satisfactory chronology of Bruni's writings is wanting, partly because the chronology of Bruni's literary works depends largely on the information furnished by Bruni's letters, and Bruni's *Epistolario*—the best edition is still *Leonardi Bruni Arretini Epistolarum Libri VIII* (ed. L. Mehus, 2 volumes, Florence, 1741)—has fared exceptionally ill in modern research. When, some fifty years ago, F. P. Luiso, with the help of important manuscripts,

prepared his *L'Epistolario di L. Bruni*, a chronological rearrangement of Bruni's letters, the work was never published, even though it had been set up in print, and merely a summary checklist indicating Luiso's revised chronology and referring to the more important of his textual changes and additions is available in an appendix of this writer's *Leonardo Bruni Aretino, Humanistisch-Philosophische Schriften* (Leipzig, 1928), pp. 189-228. As to Bruni's literary writings, *Humanistisch-Philosophische Schriften*, pp. 159-189, contains, in another appendix, the first comprehensive chronological survey which, based *inter alia* on Luiso's epistolary findings, collects and integrates the widely scattered results that Bruni scholars had achieved by the mid-1920's. The only substantial supplement, published in 1932 by L. Bertalot in *Archivum Romanicum*, xv (1931), 298-301, is, unfortunately, couched in the language of an invective and is full of inaccuracies and distortions of fact; it should be consulted together with the rectifications given in *Archiv für Kulturgeschichte*, xxii (1932), esp. pp. 368-371. During the many years that have passed since the publication of *Humanistisch-Philosophische Schriften*, the writer has gradually come to recognize the inadequacy of many of the chronological assumptions accepted in the 1920's by Bruni scholars, and the corrections, beginning with the removal of the mystery that has always surrounded the genesis of the *Laudatio* and the *Dialogi*, have been used in many of the chapters of the present volume. This revised chronology of some of Bruni's works can easily be put together by consulting the index under "Bruni."

[5] See *Humanistic and Political Literature*, pp. 72ff.

[6] ". . . tandem etiam Bononiam occuparat." See *Crisis: Appendices*, p. 524, note 24.

[7] *Dialogi*, ed. Klette, pp. 67-69; ed. Garin, pp. 76-78. (For Klette's and Garin's editions see note 1 to Chap. 3.) The fact that the *Laudatio* is discussed in the *Dialogi* has been mentioned on pp. 54f. and 192 above.

[8] These are the conclusions reached in *Humanistic and Political Literature*, pp. 154ff., "The Date of *Dialogus I*."

[9] See *Humanistic and Political Literature*, pp. 69ff., "Two Versions of the *Laudatio*? A Blind Alley."

[10] In the only finished part of his Bruni studies, "Commento a una lettera di L. Bruni e cronologia di alcune sue opere," in *Raccolta di studii critici dedicata ad Alessandro D'Ancona* (Florence, 1901), pp. 85-95.

[11] R. Sabbadini, *Storia e critica di testi latini* (1914), p. 80. Similarly, G. Petraglione, *Archivio Storico Lombardo*, ser. iv, vol. viii (1907), 6.

[12] See note 6 above.

[13] Such is the gist of Luiso's argument, *Commento a Bruni*, pp. 91-92. The passage of Bruni's *Historiae* is in Santini's edition on p. 276. For objections to this daring reinterpretation cf. also *Humanistic and Political Literature*, p. 86.

[14] Bruni, *Ep. VIII 4*. Bruni, an admirer of Polybius, had undoubtedly taken his inspiration from Polybius x 21.8, where a quite similar distinction is made between ἐγκώμιον (encomium) and ἱστορία (history).

[15] Luiso was not ignorant of this character of Bruni's eulogy (*Commento a Bruni*, p. 92), but failed to consider the practical implications of Bruni's procedure.

[16] See the quotation in note 25 below.

[17] For the Latin text cf. *Crisis: Appendices*, pp. 524f., note 24.

[18] Salutati in his *Invectiva* avails himself of precisely the method that we are attributing to Bruni. See *Humanistic and Political Literature*, pp. 105f.

[19] See our analysis of the political development, pp. 31ff. above.

[20] See De Mesquita, *Giangaleazzo*, pp. 255-258.

[21] See p. 36 above.

[22] Pp. 378f. below.

[23] For the Latin texts of these quotations and those which follow, see the edition in *Crisis: Appendices*, pp. 524ff.

[24] Account of Florence's wars with Giangaleazzo in the chapter of the *Laudatio* on the "res foris gestae": "An quisquam tam absurdus ingenio aut tam a vero devius reperiri poterit qui non fateatur, universam Italiam in potestatem Ligustini hostis perventuram fuisse nisi hec una urbs suis viribus suoque consilio contra illius potentiam restitisset?" (*Laudatio, L* fol. 150v-152r; the entire part is omitted by Klette, p. 98).

[25] Excursus on Florence's wars with Giangaleazzo in the chapter of the *Laudatio* on Florence's scenic beauty: ". . . Nuperrime vero adversus potentissimum et opulentissimum hostem ita summa vi per multos annos contendit ut omnium mentes in admirationem converteret. Eum enim ducem, cuius opes atque potentiam et transalpine gentes et reliqua omnis formidabat Italia, spe elatum, victoriis exultantem omniaque miro successu quasi tempestatem quandam occupantem hec una civitas inventa (reperta *L, om. O*) est que non solum invadentem reprimeret cursumque victoriarum retardaret, verum etiam post longum bellum affligeret. . . ." (*Laudatio, L* fol. 137v-138r; omitted by Klette, p. 90).

[26] For further support of this reconstruction of the genesis of the *Laudatio* cf. *Humanistic and Political Literature*, pp. 93ff., "A Recent Abortive Approach to the Problems of the *Laudatio*"; "Salu-

tati's *Invectiva* as a Source of Bruni's *Laudatio*," *ibid.*, pp. 104ff.; and the discussion of "The Date of Bruni's *Ep. I 8*," *ibid.*, pp. 114ff.

CHAPTER 11

[1a] See the next paragraph.

[1b] See p. 41 above.

[1c] Bruni, *Humanistisch-Philosophische Schriften*, p. 161.

[1d] This has been shown in *Humanistic and Political Literature*, "The Date of the *Laudatio:* Summer 1403 or Summer 1404," pp. 99f., 102f.

[1e] *Ibid.*, esp. notes 6-11.

[1f] The history of Bruni's scholarly advance after 1402, based on the sources that become available once we are no longer hampered by an erroneous date of the *Laudatio*, has been told in *Humanistic and Political Literature*, pp. 114ff., "Bruni's Development as a Translator from the Greek (1400-1403/04): The Date of His *Epistola I 8*."

[2] Cf. pp. 214f. above and *Humanistic and Political Literature*, pp. 154ff., "The Date of *Dialogus I*."

[3] For full details cf. the first edition of *Crisis*, pp. 191-199.

[4] *Humanistic and Political Literature*, pp. 129ff., "One-Dialogue Manuscripts of the *Dialogi*."

[5] Cf. note 2 above.

[6] See p. 214 above.

[7] Cf. *Humanistic and Political Literature*, pp. 145ff., "The Title of the *Dialogi*."

[8] *Ibid.*, and first edition of *Crisis*, p. 193.

[9] Cf. the evidence in the first edition of *Crisis*, pp. 195f.

[10] *Dialogi*, ed. Klette, p. 41; ed. Garin, p. 44. A strong confirmation comes from the one apparent exception to the reliability of Bruni's statements. In his dedication-preface to his commentary and translation of the *two-book* Pseudo-Aristotelian *Economics*, Bruni, oddly, speaks of the "*libellus*" sent with this dedication to Cosimo de' Medici, just as he speaks about the "*disputationem illam in hoc libro tibi descriptam*" in his preface to the two dialogues. Even if there were no additional evidence, it could be presumed on the basis of the singular, "*libellus*," that Cosimo at that time received the *first* book of the *Economics* only. After this inference had been made in *Humanistic and Political Literature*, pp. 166ff., Josef Soudek, who used the proposition as a working hypothesis, succeeded in establishing that there exist in fact a considerable number of manuscripts which contain merely the dedication-preface and the first book of Bruni's *Economics* translation—an illuminating counterpart

to the situation in the case of the two dialogues where one-dialogue manuscripts are rare, and clear evidence that we may rely on the singular-form in the preface as a lead. Cf. J. Soudek, "The Genesis and Tradition of Leonardo Bruni's Annotated Latin Version of the (Pseudo-) Aristotelian *Economics*," *Scriptorium*, XII (1958), 260-268.

[11] ". . . cum est apud Colucium disputatum" (*Dialogi*, ed. Klette, p. 40; ed. Garin, p. 44).

[12] For details, see the first edition of *Crisis*, pp. 196f.

[13] *Ibid.*, pp. 197f.

[14] With one new participant, Pietro di ser Mino, "added" without explanation or recognizable cause.

[15] Cf. the first edition of *Crisis*, pp. 198f.

[16] Ed. Klette, p. 41; ed. Garin, pp. 44f.

[17] "Nolite enim putare meas esse criminationes istas; sed cum ab aliis quibusdam audivissem, ad vos heri, qua tandem de causa scitis, retuli" (ed. Klette, p. 81; ed. Garin, p. 94).

[18] The evidence is quoted in *Crisis: Appendices*, pp. 528f.

[19] The similarity between the *Dialogi* and Cicero's *De oratore* was already noticed by R. Sabbadini, *Giornale Storico della Letteratura Italiana*, LXXXXVI (1930), 131f.; but he used this discovery merely to establish Bruni's imitation of certain Ciceronian words and phrases. He made no attempt to ascertain whether the two dialogues show differences in their relationship to the classical model.

[20] Cicero, *De orat.* ii 15ff. Some essential preparations for the Ciceronian scene are already in i 99.

[21] ". . . sed cum ab aliis quibusdam audivissem, ad vos heri, qua tandem de causa scitis, retuli." See note 17 above. The "causa" had been explained by Niccoli at the beginning of his recantation: "Illud tamen ante omnia certissimum habetote, me non alia de causa heri impugnasse, nisi ut Colucium ad illorum [Dante, Petrarch, Boccaccio] laudes excitarem." "Haec ego ea de causa dico, . . . ut Colucium prae indignatione ad eorum laudes impellerem" (ed. Klette, p. 72f.; ed. Garin, p. 82f.).

[22] ". . . neque sane quid ipse sentiret, sed quid ab aliis diceretur, ostendit" (*De orat.* ii 41).

[23] ". . . hoc mihi proposueram, ut, si te refellissem, hos a te discipulos abducerem; nunc . . . videor debere non tam pugnare tecum quam quid ipse sentiam dicere" (*De orat.* ii 40).

[24] "Nox ista te, Nicolae, . . . nobis reddidit: nam eiusmodi a te heri dicebantur, quae a nostro coetu planissime abhorrebant" (ed. Klette, p. 83; ed. Garin, p. 96).

[25] "Nox te, nobis, Antoni, expolivit hominemque reddidit, nam hesterno sermone . . . nobis oratorem descripseras . . . inurbanum" (*De orat.* ii 40).

[26] Though the text of the second book of *De oratore*, as available about 1400, was fragmentary, Bruni may be expected to have known it from ii 19, and possibly from ii 13, on. See Sabbadini, *Le scoperte*, vol. I, pp. 100, 218; *Storia e critica* (1914), pp. 101ff.

[27] For some consequences for our appraisal of earlier interpretations of the *Dialogi* cf. *Crisis: Appendices*, pp. 530f.

[28a] For the historiographical basis of the observations that follow, see "Interpretations of Leonardo Bruni's *Dialogi ad Petrum Paulum Histrum*," *Crisis: Appendices*, pp. 394ff.

[28b] See the detailed discussion of the available evidence in *Humanistic and Political Literature*, Chap. VI, pp. 129ff., "One-Dialogue Manuscripts of the *Dialogi*."

[29] In the editions of Klette, Kirner, and Wotke (Greifswald, Leghorn, and Vienna, all three in 1889).

[30] Cf. "Interpretations of Bruni's *Dialogi*," *Crisis: Appendices*, pp. 395ff.

[31] First in "Dante nel Trecento e nel Quattrocento," published in 1921 (revised and complemented in Rossi's *Scritti di critica letteraria*, vol. I, [1930], pp. 293-332), and later in the third edition of his standard work, *Il Quattrocento* (1933), pp. 105-107.

[32] See *Crisis: Appendices*, p. 531, note 32.

[33] Including other theories derived from him; cf. *ibid.*, note 33.

[34] *Dialogi*, ed. Klette, p. 83; ed. Garin, p. 96.

[35] "Itaque ego istam defensionem aliud in tempus magis commodum differam" (*ibid.*, ed. Klette, p. 65f.; ed. Garin, p. 74).

[36] *Ibid.*, ed. Klette, p. 70; ed. Garin, p. 80.

[37] Kirner, in the introduction to his edition of the *Dialogi*, p. xxii.

[38] ". . . non magis Nicolai causam quam meam hoc sermone agi" (*Dialogi*, ed. Klette, p. 56; ed. Garin, p. 62).

[39] "Qui enim universam urbem laudarit, eundem hos quoque homines laudare par est" (*ibid.*, ed. Klette, p. 71; ed. Garin, pp. 80f.).

[40] Cf. *Crisis: Appendices*, p. 532, note 40.

[41] For this date, see pp. 253f. and 268f. below.

[42] Cf. *Crisis: Appendices*, p. 532, note 42. Salutati, *Ep. XIV 20* (to Bernardo da Moglio), January 8, 1406 (*Epistolario*, vol. IV, p. 146): Bruni was "anime plus quam dimidium mee, imo penitus idem ego." (Cf. also *Ep. XIV 21* [to Bruni], January 9, 1406 [*ibid.*, p. 157]: "si tu alter es ego, sicut arbitror teneoque. . . .") Salutati, *Ep. XIV 22*, March 26, 1406 (ibid., p. 160): Niccoli was Poggio's "alter ego."

[43] *Crisis: Appendices*, p. 533, note 43, and pp. 255f. below.

[44] See pp. 54 and 214 above.

[45] "Si tamen filii mei ad virtutem hortandi forent, vel a Deo id petendum, potius equidem optarem, ut M. Marcello aut L. Camillo similes essent, quam C. Caesari . . ." (ed. Klette, p. 69; ed. Garin, p. 78).

[46] Ed. Klette, p. 70; ed. Garin, p. 80.

[47] How greatly the verdict on the later course of Quattrocento Humanism depends on the correctness of this understanding of the *Dialogi*, may be seen from the important chapter in Rossi's *Il Quattrocento* (3rd edn., pp. 104-115) in which Bruni's *Dialogi* provide the framework for the subsequent appraisal of the Quattrocento attitude toward Dante and the Volgare. Throughout the Quattrocento (thus Rossi explains the relationship), we see "arising a vacillating state of mind, of which Bruni's little work is the very image" ("uno stato d'animo titubante, di cui è imagine l'operetta del Bruni," pp. 109f.). In light of our discovery that the two dialogues reveal an evolution from radical classicism to civic Humanism, the later history of the reputation of Dante and the Volgare can to some extent be rewritten. See the sketches on pp. 287ff. and 336ff. below and "Bruni's Alleged Classicism in the Controversy on the Origin of the Volgare," *Crisis: Appendices*, pp. 422ff.

Postscript for the Revised, One-volume Edition: During the decade which has passed since the above interpretation of Bruni's dialogues was proposed, their meaning has continued to intrigue students of Quattrocento culture with the effect that still another, basically different, approach has come to the fore; it might be called the *rhetorical hypothesis*. At its root lies the suspicion that the dialogues may yet be nothing else but a rhetorical exercise, in view of the fact that the work is introduced by Salutati's appeal to his younger friends to exercise themselves in *"disputationes"* and that later in the work we find two speeches of Niccoli, undeniably following rhetorical prescripts, "against" and "for" the three great Florentines of the Trecento. Eugenio Garin, who has been the chief promoter of this "rhetorical hypothesis," has proved that routine exercises in the art of speaking in favor and against (*sic et non*) a given subject were, indeed, employed in at least one Florentine school in contact with Salutati's circle: Cino de' Guidetti's "scuola di Santa Maria in Campo," of which Roberto de' Rossi was a member. Also, Salutati seems once to have tried his hand at such purely rhetorical exercises by composing two competing *"orationes,"* the one extolling the merits of hereditary monarchy, the other those of elective monarchy (in a mere draft by his hand, but never circulated; see Garin, *Rivista Critica di Storia della Filosofia*, xv [1960], 75f., and Ullman, *Humanism of Salutati*, p. 34). Against this background Garin argues: "It may be that Bruni's second dialogue was composed a few years after the first, as Hans Baron suggests; but this does not necessarily reflect a change of Bruni's position." "One ought not to exclude too quickly the idea that differences between the two books of the work may reflect not so much the successive composition demonstrated by Baron, as a *sic et non* [debate] on one and the same theme: a dialectical discussion, that is." (*La Rassegna della Letteratura Italiana*, XLIV [1960], 192).

Given the recent increase in our knowledge of the role played by rhetoric in late-Trecento culture, Garin's doubt is very much to the point, but the answer to his question must be negative. The fact that the *Dialogi* orations originated at a distance of several years makes the possibility of their having been planned together slim. We might at best venture upon the hypothesis that a few years after writing the first dialogue the author, under the impact of contemporary rhetoric, decided that it would be a desirable rhetorical feat to have the oration attributed to Niccoli followed by one taking the opposite side of the argument.

There is, moreover, despite Salutati's call for "exercise" in "*disputationes*" not the slightest hint of a *sic et non* design in the introductory discussion. Nothing of it is found in Salutati's preliminary definition: "*Exercitatio*, however, is co-ordination of our studies, careful search and elaboration of a subject basic to our studies: in one word, what I call a *disputation*" ("Est autem exercitatio studiorum nostrorum collocatio, perquisitio agitatioque earum rerum quae in studiis nostris versantur: quam ego uno verbo disputationem appello"; *Dialogi*, ed. Garin, p. 66). Nor does the Niccoli presented in the *Dialogi* suggest with his praise of the "philosophia . . . a Cicerone . . . aureo illo eloquentiae flumine irrigata" anything else than that Cicero taught us to add eloquence to philosophy, so that the student "learned not only to define his own position, but also to refute that of others" ("discebat non solum sua tueri, sed etiam aliena refellere"; *ibid.*, p. 54)—certainly the opposite of a program of rhetoric for its own sake. Furthermore, Salutati's championship of "*disputationes*" is in the course of the conversation said to have been shared by Luigi Marsili, the least probable protagonist of purely rhetorical exercises (*ibid.*, p. 50). As for Roberto de' Rossi's role in Cino de' Guidetti's school, his contribution to that circle had been an *attack* on rhetoric "on the ground that rhetoric was corrupting because of its double reasonings" ("perché corrutrice attraverso i duplici discorsi"), in the words of Garin (*Rivista Critica*, XV [1960], 76).

Summing up, neither within nor outside the *Dialogi* can anything new be found that would affect its interpretation. Our appraisal must still start from the proven fact that the two dialogues differ in their literary structure, because the first dialogue purports to be and actually is a faithful rendering of reactions of the members of Salutati's circle, whereas the second dialogue imitates a conversation depicted in Cicero's *De oratore* and thereby proves itself untrue to the promises given in the *Preface*. And just as this proof of the structural difference of the two dialogues still stands, so does the demonstration that all major details of Niccoli's speech in *Dialogus II* coincide with ideas also found in *later* works of Bruni, whereas the speeches attributed to Salutati and Niccoli in *Dialogus I* accord with what we know about these two men from other sources —strong confirmation of the inference that through the Niccoli of *Dialogus II* the author speaks his own mind. When weighed together with the proof that *Dialogus II* followed *Dialogus I* after the lapse of several years, the only possible interpretation of the two dialogues continues to be that Bruni, when writing *Dialogus I*, had still been a more or less undecided observer of Salutati's and Niccoli's divergent views, but that he had come into his own by the time *Dialogus II* was written.

As long as these observations retain validity, the two orations of Niccoli cannot be suspected of possibly being mere specimens of oratorical exercises. The mere fact that, in some formal features, they reflect the art of Ciceronian oratory and the practice of rhetorical schools does not subtract anything from the demonstrable genuineness of the ideas presented in this guise.

CHAPTER 12

[1] See p. 225 above.

[2] Cf. pp. 268f. below.

[3] Born February 16, 1331.

[4] See below, note. 7.

[5a] According to Poggio's *Oratio Funebris* on Bruni, ed. Mehus, p. cxix.

[5b] On the appearance of Bruni's name among the Florentine cathedral canons, cf. L. Martines, *The Social World* (note 54b to Chap. 14 below), p. 167.

[5c] Though little is known about Bruni's marriage, we have a description of his wedding in his *Ep. III 17*, of March 18, 1412.

[6] *Dialogi*, ed. Klette, p. 39f.; ed. Garin, p. 44.

[7] See *Laudatio*, L fol. 149v; ed. Klette, p. 97: To write a history of Florence would be an ambitious task, very different from referring to a few historical examples, as in the *Laudatio*, but a task "quod nos ut spero aliquando aggrediemur, et quo pacto singula ab hoc populo gesta sunt litteris memorieque mandabimus."

[8] "Omnes cives tibi habere gratias, Leonarde, debent" (*Dialogi*, ed. Klette, p. 68; ed. Garin, p. 76). Salutati did, indeed, express the same opinion on the value of the *Laudatio* in 1405; see *Crisis: Appendices*, p. 535.

[9] *Dialogi*, ed. Klette, pp. 70, 80; ed. Garin, pp. 80, 94.

[10] In the letter of September 13; see next note. On Bruni's correspondence during his stay at Viterbo see also pp. 240f. above and 252f., 293f. below.

[11] *Archivum Romanicum*, xv (1931), 322.

[12] On the composition of the *Laudatio in Funere Othonis Adulescentuli* at Viterbo in 1405 cf. *Crisis: Appendices*, pp. 535f.

[13a] "Quare . . . genus atque patria attendenda sunt, sine cuius splendore nec Themistocles quidem ille Atheniensis summae virtutis et industriae vir claritatem se unquam adepturum putavit" (*Laudatio in Funere Othonis*, ed. Santini in *Bruni e i "Hist. Flor. Pop.,"* p. 143).

[13b] "Duplicem . . . Seriphio iurgatori ignobilitatem inussit, patrie scilicet et persone, totamque nobilitatem suam a patria recognovit. Hec docta philosophi responsio; hec civis de patria benemerentis humilitas atque confessio."

[13c] ". . . cum videamus meliori virtute homines ex agro atque infimo loco natos illustres evadere."

[13d] Salutati's and Vergerio's letters were first published by Novati in *Epistolario di Salutati*, vol. iv, pp. 83f. and 366ff.; they have been reprinted with corrected dates (1402 or 1403) by L. Smith in *Epistolario di Vergerio*, pp. 253-262 (the quoted passages on pp. 255 and 259).

We do not know whether Salutati or Bruni, or both, were confirmed in their preference for the version of the anecdote in Plato's *Republic* (accessible through Chrysoloras) by any discovery that other ancient authors had followed Plato. Salutati might conceivably have seen the paraphrase of Plato's account in Origen's *Contra Celsum*, i, 29-30, for other works of Origen are found in extant manuscripts from Salutati's library (cf. Ullman, *Humanism of Salutati*, pp. 139f.). Bruni might have encountered the story with Plato's inferences in Plutarch's *Vita Themistoclis*, c. 18, since, by 1405, he already owned the Plutarchian biographies (cf. R. Sabbadini, *Le Scoperte dei Codici Latini e Greci* . . . [Florence, 1905], p. 52) and had started translating the *Vita M. Antonii*, soon to be followed by those of Pyrrhus and Cato. But whether or not either Salutati or Bruni had had this encouragement, they both overcame the medieval misunderstanding of the anecdote because they were guided in their interpretation by the Florentine conception of a true citizen's attitude, as the cited controversies and differences of judgment prove.

[14] See *Crisis: Appendices*, p. 537.

[15] *Ep. II 4*, ed. Mehus, vol. i, p. 35.

[16] *Ibid.*, p. 36. Cf. also *Crisis: Appendices*, pp. 537f.

[17] As has already been mentioned briefly on p. 241 above.

[18] See *Crisis: Appendices*, p. 538, note 18 for this date.

[19] *Ibid.*, note 19.

[20] *Ibid.*, note 20.

[21] Somewhat scornful and overbearing: for Salutati said in October with regard to Poggio's letter that he would answer in such a way "quod discat parcius male dicere; nec voluntatem reputet rationem discatque iuvenis parcere seni" (Salutati, *Ep. XIV 14, Epistolario*, vol. IV, p. 105).

[22] The two letters by Salutati are his *Ep. XIV 19* and *Ep. XIV 22*. For the evaluation of the Salutati-Poggio controversy by earlier scholars see *Crisis: Appendices*, pp. 538f.

[23] See Walser, *Poggius*, p. 32, n. 2.

[24] For Poggio's stay at Viterbo see Walser, *ibid.*, p. 22.

[25] See note 21 above.

[26] See pp. 240f. above.

[27] *Dialogi*, ed. Klette, pp. 63f.; ed. Garin, p. 72.

[28] Salutati, *Ep. IX 9*, August 1, 1395, *Epistolario*, vol. III, p. 84.

[29] Salutati, *Ep. XIV 19, Epistolario*, vol. IV, p. 135.

[30] *Ibid.*, pp. 134f., 144.

[31] As can be gathered from Salutati's subsequent letter to Poggio, of March 26, 1406. See the passages in question in Walser, *Poggius*, p. 36, n. 3.

[32] See the references in *Crisis: Appendices*, pp. 539f.

[33] *Epistolario*, vol. I, pp. 181ff., 342.

[34] *Ibid.*, vol. IV, pp. 143f., 166f.

[35] Bruni, in his *Vita di Petrarca:* "Ebbe il Petrarca nelli studi suoi una dote singolare, che fu attissimo a prosa ed a verso. . . . E questa grazia . . . è stata in pochi o in nullo fuor di lui. . . . Onde addiviene che Virgilio, nel verso eccellentissimo, niente in prosa valse o scrisse, e Tullio, sommo maestro nel dire in prosa, niente valse in versi," and so with all other poets and orators. "Il Petrarca è solo quello che per dota singolare nell' uno e nell' altro stile fu eccellente . . ." (*Bruni, Schriften*, pp. 66-67). Manetti, in his *Vita Francisci Petrarcae*, recast the very same ideas in full-sounding Latin phrases, adding Homer and Demosthenes to Virgil and Cicero (*Le Vite di Dante, Petrarca e Boccaccio*, ed. Solerti, [Milan, 1904], pp. 306-307).

[36] *Dialogi*, ed. Klette, p. 80; ed. Garin, p. 94.

[37] "Nec audebimus illum suis meritis ornare, praesertim cum hic vir studia humanitatis, quae iam extincta erant, repararit et nobis, quemadmodum discere possemus, viam aperuerit?" (*loc. cit.*).

[38] Thus Fra Guido da Pisa. Cf. *Crisis: Appendices*, p. 540, note 38.

[39] "E perciò, avendo egli [that is, Giotto] quella arte ritornata in luce che molti secoli sotto gli errori d'alcuni, che più a dilettar gli occhi degli ignoranti che a compiacere allo 'ntelletto de' savj di-

pignendo, era stata sepulta, meritamente una delle luci della fiorentina gloria dir si puote" (Boccaccio, *Decamerone*, Giornata vi, novella v). The passage in Boccaccio's *Trattatello in laude di Dante* runs: "Questi fu quel Dante, il quale primo doveva al ritorno delle Muse, sbandite d'Italia, aprir la via. . . . Per costui la morta poesi meritamente si può dire suscitata" (ed. Solerti, *op. cit.*, p. 13). For the elaboration of Boccaccio's views by Filippo Villani see *Crisis: Appendices*, p. 541.

[40] ". . . amotis vepribus arbustisque quibus mortalium negligentia obsitum comperit, restauratisque aggere firmo proluviis semesis rupibus, *sibi et post eum ascendere volentibus viam aperuit*" (Boccaccio, *Opere latine minori*, ed. A. F. Massèra [Bari, 1928], p. 195).

[41a] Boccaccio, *ibid.*, p. 196. On Jacopo Pizzinga's position and title, cf. now A. de Stefano in *Bollettino del Centro di Studi Filologici e Linguistici Siciliani*, v (1957), 183-187.

[41b] Cf. *Crisis: Appendices*, p. 542.

[42] For the date 1397 cf. Smith in *Archivio Veneto*, ser. v, vol. iv (1928), 99f.

[43] ". . . atque (ut vere dixerim) unicus fuit, qui per tot saecula exulantem, et iam pene incognitam dicendi facultatem in nostra tempora revocaret" (ed. Solerti, *op. cit.*, p. 299). The gradual abandonment of the identification of Petrarch's work with a revival of ancient poetry can also be illustrated by the history of Salutati's verdicts on Petrarch. Whereas in none of his later utterances did Salutati (see p. 258 above) find the focus of Petrarch's activities in poetry, he had made this identification in one of his earliest letters, an appraisal of Petrarch written before 1360 (in a letter to Nelli, ed. in Novati's *Epistolario*, vol. iv, p. 244).

[44] "Existimavique omnes, qui his nostris studiis delectantur, ei quamplurimum debere; quippe qui primus suo labore, industria, vigilantia haec studia *pene ad internicionem redacta* nobis *in lucem erexerit* et aliis sequi volentibus *viam patefecerit*" (Salutati, *Ep. XIV 22, Epistolario*, vol. iv, p. 161).

[45] ". . . studia humanitatis, quae *iam extincta* erant, *repararit* et nobis quemadmodum discere possemus, *viam aperuerit*" (*Dialogi*, ed. Klette, p. 80; ed. Garin, p. 94). See note 37 above.

[46] Boccaccio had said of Petrarch that by having himself crowned as a poet on the Capitol he had revived traditions forgotten for more than a thousand years, and thus "he opened a path for himself and those eager to ascend after him" ("sibi et post eum ascendere volentibus viam aperuit"). When we now find Poggio in his characterization of Petrarch employing the phrase that "he opened the path to those others who were eager to follow" ("aliis sequi volentibus viam patefecerit"), we cannot doubt that Boccaccio's words "eager to

ascend after him" ("ascendere volentibus") are reflected in Poggio's "eager to follow" ("sequi volentibus"). And since this significant term is not adopted by Bruni in his *Dialogus II*—the only words Bruni literally repeats from Boccaccio are "viam aperuit"—Poggio also must have known Boccaccio's letter.

[47] Boccaccio, therefore, does not exactly say, as Bruni and Poggio were to say, that Petrarch had opened a path for his "followers" or "for us"; but that he had "opened a path for himself as well as for those who wished to ascend after him" (*sibi et post eum ascendere volentibus viam aperuit*). And the expression "viam aperuit" is explained, immediately afterwards, as the rediscovery and restoration of the forgotten ascent to the "summit": "Inde helyconico fonte limo iuncoque palustri purgato, . . . in extremos usque vertices Parnasi conscendit. . . . Spem fere deperditam in generosos suscitavit animos ostenditque quod minime credebatur a pluribus, pervium scilicet esse Parnasum et eius accessibile culmen: nec dubito quin multos animaverit ad ascensum" (Boccaccio, *op. cit.*, pp. 195-196).

[48] Poggio, *Ep. II 16*, ed. Tonelli, vol. I, pp. 129f.

[49] ". . . cum primo libro viros praestantissimos doctissimosque Dantem, Franciscum Petrarcham, Johan. Boccacium, eorumque doctrinam, eloquentiam, opera impugnasset; secundo in superioris excusationem ipsorum est virtus laudata est (Poggio, *Oratio Funebris*, ed. Mehus in his introduction to Bruni's *Epistolae*, vol. I, p. cxxii f.).

[50] For *Dialogus II* and Poggio, see the quotations on pp. 260 and 265 above.

[51] "Posto che in lui perfetto non fusse, pur da sè vide e aperse la via a questa perfezione . . . ; e per certo fece assai, solo a dimostrare la via a quelli che dopo lui avevano a seguire."

[52] *Le Vite di Dante* . . . , ed. Solerti, p. 290. For the correct phrasing of this passage cf. *Crisis: Appendices*, pp. 544f.

[53] See p. 249 above.

[54] There is, indeed, a great deal of evidence that seems to favor the assumption that *Dialogus II* originated during Bruni's stay at Viterbo. Cf. the first edition of *Crisis*, pp. 241-245, and the Excursus "Indications that *Dialogus II* Was Written After Bruni Had Left Florence," in *Humanistic and Political Literature*, pp. 159ff.

CHAPTER 13

[1] See pp. 81f., 88 above.

[2] See B. Croce in *La Critica*, XXVII (1927), 426f., on Wesselofsky's place in these historiographical trends; Croce, *Storia della Storiografia Italiana nel Secolo Decimonono*, vol. I (Bari, 1921), pp. 118ff., 217, on "the low esteem for the age of the Renaissance,

as the period which marked the national ruin"; and G. Gentile, *G .Capponi e la Cultura in Toscana nel Secolo Decimonono* (Firenze, 1922), chapters v-viii, on the "nuovi Piagnoni," with the inclusion of P. Villari.

[3] Wesselofsky (see note 1 to Chap. 4 above), i, pp. 47-49, esp. p. 49.

[4] *Ibid.*, p. 49.

[5] Wesselofsky, ii, pp. 6f., 20.

For the long survival of these prejudices of mid-nineteenth-century scholars—identification of Humanism with the culture of the Tyrant courts, and the assertion that in the Quattrocento there existed everywhere a cleavage between the humanistic outlook and the inherited civic traditions—cf. the examples listed in *Crisis: Appendices*, pp. 546f., note 5.

[6] See Wesselofsky, grouping together Giovanni da Prato, Cino Rinuccini, and Domenico da Prato as representatives of the "scuola volgare," ii, pp. 48, 52-54.

[7] Pp. 76f. and 94ff. above. Cino's *Invettiva* is published in Wesselofsky, ii, pp. 303-316.

[8] See p. 383 below.

[9] See Wesselofsky, ii, pp. 322, 326.

[10] Published in Wesselofsky, ii, pp. 321-330. The basic studies on Domenico da Prato are by Wesselofsky, ii, pp. 54-67, and M. Casella in *Rivista delle Biblioteche e degli Archivi*, xxvii (1916), 1-40. Rossi, *Il Quattrocento*, pp. 231f., emphasizes the dry pedantry of Domenico's erudite poetizing.

[11] See Wesselofsky's opinion in note 46 to Chap. 14.

[12] He noted on p. 55 that Domenico was "aged" ("vecchio") when writing his preface-invective, and that he lived beyond the year 1425.

[13] A. Della Torre, *Storia dell' Accademia Platonica di Firenze* (1902), p. 221.

[14] Wesselofsky, ii, p. 325.

[15] That all the known facts of Domenico's life and literary activity combine to support the attribution of his invective to the time around 1420, is shown in *Crisis: Appendices*, pp. 548ff.

[16] "Per loro falso giudicio dannano Dante, messer Francesco Petrarca, messer Johanni Boccaci, messer Coluccio et altri."

[17] Doubts were already expressed by Casella, *op. cit.*, pp. 15-17. But we cannot hope to get beyond conjectures unless we determine for each of Domenico's arguments separately whether it can have been aimed at Niccoli or at Bruni.

As for the reference to Bruni's vindication of Boccaccio, which follows in the text, the last chapter of Bruni's *Vite di Dante e di Petrarca* includes a brief "Notizia del Boccaccio."

[18] Wesselofsky, II, p. 323.

[19] *Ibid.*, pp. 322f.

[20] *Ibid.*, p. 323.

[21] "Or non confondono questi dannosissimi uomini li animi non ancora fermi delli adolescenti e ricenti uditori, quando dicono, . . . non potersi alcuna cosa fare o dire sì bene, che meglio non sia stata detta o fatta per li antichi passati. . . . O depopulatori et usurpatori de quel bene che dare non possono! . . . Et se tutto è stato detto a bastanza secondo che dicono, a che favellano?" (*ibid.*, p. 324).

[22] Nothing but a desiderata list for investigators of manuscripts has come down to us from his pen; see note 3 to Chap. 4. To his biographers, Poggio, Manetti, Enea Silvio and Vespasiano da Bisticci, it appeared that he did not write because he had formed an ideal of the perfect classical style that was beyond his own reach. Cf. Voigt, *Die Wiederbelebung*, I, pp. 302f.

[23a] For a comparison of Domenico's text with Bruni's *Prologus in Vita Quinti Sertorii ex Plutarcho traducta* cf. *Crisis: Appendices*, p. 551, note 23.

[23b] Bruni, *Ep. II 1*, Lucca, 1408, ed. Mehus, vol. I, p. 28.

[23c] On Bruni's development to this position of great confidence in Florence, cf. H. Baron, "The *Querelle* of the Ancients and the Moderns as a Problem for Renaissance Scholarship," *Journal of the History of Ideas*, xx (1959), 17f.

[24] Books III and IV of the *Historiae Florentini Populi* were written in 1420 and 1421; see note 14 to Chap. 17.

[25] *Bruni, Schriften*, pp. 176f.

[26] Bruni's *Isagogicon Moralis Disciplinae* was written during the summer, 1423; see *Crisis: Appendices*, p. 613, note. 22. For the dates of Bruni's poetical works, see *Crisis: Appendices*, pp. 580f.

[27] Wesselofsky, II, pp. 325f.

[28] *Bruni, Schriften*, pp. 102f. and 161.

[29] Wesselofsky, II, pp. 328f.

[30] *Bruni, Schriften*, pp. 103f. and 78. For Domenico's familiarity with Bruni's translation of the *Nicomachean Ethics* see p. 279 above.

[31] Wesselofsky, II, p. 328.

[32a] This date has now been finally established by L. Martines in *Archivio Storico Italiano*, cxix (1961), 77, 83f. (Wesselofsky and, relying on him, the first edition of *Crisis* had assumed 1407).

[32b] The *Invective Against Certain Slanderers of Dante and Messer Francesco Petrarca and of Messer Giovanni Boccaccio, whose names are passed over in silence for the sake of decency—written by the learned and conscientious Cino di Messer Francesco Rinuccini, Florentine citizen, and rendered from the Latin into the Volgare* ("Invettiva contro a cierti caluniatori di Dante e di messer Francesco

Petrarca e di messer Giovanni Boccaci, i nomi de' quali per onestà si tacciono, composta pello iscientifico e ciercuspetto uomo Cino di messer Francesco Rinuccini cittadino fiorentino, ridotta di gramatica in vulgare") is published in Wesselofsky, II, pp. 303-316. For an evaluation of more recent studies of Rinuccini's *Invettiva*, especially by G. Gentile, see *Crisis: Appendices*, p. 552.

[33] "E de' libri del coronato poeta messer Francesco Petrarca si beffano, diciendo che quel *De viris illustribus* è un zibaldone da quaresima. Non dicono quanto e' fu gienerale in versificare così in latino come in vulgare. . . . Poi, per mostrarsi litteratissimi, dicono che lo egregio e onore de' poeti Dante Alighieri essere suto poeta da calzolai; non dicono che 'l parlar poetico è quello che sopra agli altri come aquila vola. . . . Lo inlustre ed esimio poeta Dante . . . gli umani fatti dipigne in vulgare più tosto per fare più utile a' suo' cittadini che non farebbe in gramatica. Nè tonando deridano e mali dicienti, però che 'l fonte della eloquenca, Dante, con maravigliosa brevità e legiadria mette due o tre comparazioni in uno rittimo vulgare che Vergilio non mette in venti versi esametri. . . . Il perchè tengo che 'l vulgare rimare sia molto più malagevole e maestrevole che 'l versificare litterale" (Wesselofsky, II, pp. 309-311).

[34] "Hunc igitur ego virum . . . a litteratorum collegio ideo heri disiunxi, ut non cum illis, sed supra illos sit" (*Dialogi*, ed. Klette, p. 75; ed. Garin, p. 86).

[35] "Sola enim hec in tota Italia civitas purissimo atque nitidissimo sermone uti existimatur. Itaque omnes qui bene atque emendate loqui volunt ex hac una urbe sumunt exemplum. Habet enim hec civitas homines qui in hoc populari atque communi genere dicendi ceteros omnes infantes ostenderint" (*Laudatio*, L fol. 155v; ed. Klette, p. 104). For the importance of this praise of Florentine attainments in the field of the Volgare see also p. 337 below.

[36] Wesselofsky, II, p. 309.

[37] *Ibid.*, p. 313.

[38] See Bruni in his "Prologus in Phaedonem Platonis," *Bruni, Schriften*, p. 4.

CHAPTER 14

[1a] See *Crisis: Appendices*, p. 555, note 1a.

[1b] ". . . che nel mio tempo la mia città crescendo in essa una brigata di giovani di maravigliosa indole, ex . . . . . (sic!) che sarebbe idonea nella città litter[at]issima d'Atene, e che di sua iscienzia, e mirabilità d'ingegno mi diletta, e alta isperanza nell' animo mi ripone" (*Responsiva*, ed. Moreni, pp. 246-247).

[2] See note 4 below.

[3] See pp. 287f. above.

[4] ". . . le vane e scioche disputazioni d'una brigata di garulli" (Wesselofsky, II, p. 306).

[5] *Ibid.*

[6] Bruni, letter to Salutati on the "cetus factus apud Colucium," September 13, 1405, published in *Archivum Romanicum*, xv (1931), 321 ff. Cf. *Crisis: Appendices*, p. 545, notes 54-55.

[7] "Della filosofia divina dicono che Varrone iscrisse molti libri dell' osservazione degli idei de' gientili con istilo alegantissimo, e molto eciessivamente il lodano, prepognendo in segreto ai dottori della nostra cattolica fede; e ardiscono a dire che quegli idei erano più veri che questo, nè si ricordano de' miracoli de' nostri santi" (Wesselofsky, II, p. 315).

[8] Already G. Gentile, in his *La Filosofia* (published in the series *Storia dei generi letterarii Italiani*, 1904-15; incomplete, but spanning the early Quattrocento), maintained at the beginning of the chapter on classicism and its relation to paganism that we should not rashly spurn Cino's contribution. Its actual background will emerge, with the help of new sources, from the discussion which follows.

[9] *Dialogi*, ed. Klette, p. 54; ed. Garin, p. 60.

[10] Salutati's *On the Labors of Hercules*, the first of the sources upon which we are going to draw, has been edited by B. L. Ullman (*De Laboribus Herculis*, Thesaurus Mundi, Zurich, 1951). Attention was first drawn to the guiding ideas of Salutati's treatise by A. v. Martin in some incisive paragraphs of his *Mittelalterliche Welt- und Lebensanschauung im Spiegel der Schriften Coluccio Salutatis* (Munich, 1913), pp. 142-149, and his *Coluccio Salutati und das humanistische Lebensideal* (Leipzig, 1916), pp. 63-66. The comprehensive work by J. Seznec, *La Survivance des Dieux Antiques. Essai sur le Rôle de la Tradition Mythologique dans l'Humanisme et dans l'Art de la Renaissance* (London: Warburg Institute, 1940), is chiefly concerned with iconographical themes and hardly mentions the problem of the "monotheism" of the ancient poets; it does not touch upon the fact that around 1400 there was a new phase of this train of thought. More recently, E. Garin's paper "Le favole antiche" (first published in 1953, reprinted in Garin's *Medioevo e Rinascimento*, Bari, 1954) has taken issue with the obliteration by Seznec and other authors of the differences between medieval and Renaissance attitudes toward ancient mythology. Garin points out some of the elements that distinguish, on the one hand, Petrarch and Boccaccio from the medieval writers, and, on the other, Salutati's ideas from Boccaccio's position. Further observations in the same direction have been added by F. Gaeta, "Aventura di Ercole," *Rinascimento*, v (1954), 252ff. Since Garin and Gaeta are little concerned with the development of a notion of secret

"monotheism" among the ancient poets, their studies and the chapter which follows complement each other. They arrive at some similar major results.

[11] That the Hercules treatise was meant to supplement Boccaccio's *Genealogiae* is stated by Salutati himself; ed. Ullman, pp. 456f. From the wording of the title, *De Laboribus Herculis,* this broad purpose may not be readily divined; but that wording stems from an early stage of Salutati's labors. During the last years of his life, Salutati elaborated and enlarged his work to such an extent that, when summarizing its contents in 1405, he used the earlier name of "Labores Herculis" for only one of the four books of the ultimate version, while giving the title of the entire work as "De sensibus allegoricis fabularum Herculis" (Salutati, *Ep. XIV 10, Epistolario,* vol. IV, pp. 76-77). The first chapter of the First Book is superscribed "De poesi contra detractores compendiosa defensio."

[12] Cf. the collection of examples in *Crisis: Appendices,* pp. 557f.

[13] *Ibid.,* pp. 558f.

[14] Cf. the quotations and references in *Crisis: Appendices,* p. 559, note 14.

[15a] Cf. *Crisis: Appendices,* p. 559, note 15.

[15b] *Ep. IV 15,* and *IV 18, Epistolario,* vol. I, pp. 298-307, 321-329; an English translation in E. Emerton, *Humanism and Tyranny,* pp. 290-308.

[16a] Published by B. L. Ullman in the appendix to his edition of *De Laboribus Herculis* as "Prima Editio" of the treatise. That the first version of Filippo Villani's *De Origine Civitatis Florentie* referred to *De Laboribus Herculis* as early as 1381/82 does not mean that the "prima editio" of Salutati's treatise was finished by that time. Being in personal contact with Salutati, Filippo could report on work in which Salutati was at the moment engaged. Cf. Ullman, *The Humanism of Coluccio Salutati,* p. 22, n. 3.

[16b] Ed. Ullman, p. 623, lines 16f., 25f.

[16c] Cf. *Ep. X 16,* April 23, 1398, to Pellegrino Zambeccari, *Epistolario,* vol. III, esp. pp. 292f.

[16d] *Epistolario,* vol. IV, pp. 170ff.; partial English translation in Emerton's *Humanism and Tyranny,* pp. 309-41, 346-77; a helpful summary in Taù, "Il *Contra* . . . (see note 19a below), p. 261.

[16e] Cf. *Epistolario,* vol. IV, pp. 197ff.

[16f] Von Martin, *Salutati und hum. Lebensideal,* p. 240, n. 1.

[17] Cf. the quotations collected in A. v. Martin, *Salutati und hum. Lebensideal,* pp. 64-65.

[18] See the examples in *Crisis: Appendices,* p. 562, note 18.

[19a] On the facts of Francesco da Fiano's life which follow see "Francesco da Fiano, Roman Humanist, and the Date of His In-

vective," *Crisis: Appendices*, pp. 401ff., as well as the important complements by Don Igino Taù, "Il *Contra Oblocutores et Detractores Poetarum di Francesco da Fiano*. Con appendice di documenti biografici," *Archivio Italiano per la Storia della Pietà*, IV (1964), 255ff., 333ff. A more detailed monograph on Francesco da Fiano's life and works has been prepared by the same author, and its publication is promised soon. Cf. also the introduction to "Un opuscolo inedito di Francesco da Fiano in difesa della poesia, a cura di Maria Luisa Plaisant," *Rinascimento*, Ser. II, vol. I (1961), 119ff.

[19b] This date has been established by Don Taù, *op. cit.*, 334.

[19c] For this date see *Crisis: Appendices*, pp. 405-408, as well as Don Taù, who, *op. cit.*, 266f., establishes 1399 as *terminus post quem*.

[19d] On this episode and the (not yet identified) personality of the orator, see G. Radetti, "Le origini dell'Umanesimo civile fiorentino nel Quattrocento," *Giornale Critico della Filosofia Italiana*, XXXVIII (1959), 115, n. 2, and Don Taù, *op. cit.*, 262, 276. Cf. also Maria Luisa Plaisant, *op. cit.*, 122.

[19e] The *Contra Ridiculos Oblocutores et Fellitos Detractores Poetarum* (*Against the Ridiculous Contradictors and Detractors, Steeped in Gall, of the Poets*), quoted extensively in the first edition of *Crisis* (vol. II, pp. 562-565) from the autograph in Cod. Ottobon. Lat. 1438, has become available in two critical editions in the cited studies by Maria Luisa Plaisant, *op. cit.*, 124-162, and Don Igino Taù, *op. cit.*, 295-331. Both editors confirm in detail and conclusively that most of the notes and corrections of the Ottobon. MS. stem from Francesco's own hand; see Maria Luisa Plaisant, 123, and Don Taù, 269ff. Don Igino Taù's edition is based on stricter paleographical principles, identifies many more of the authors used by Francesco, and is prefaced by a valuable discussion of the literary motifs, legends and medieval lore encountered in the treatise. Since this edition is not easily accessible, it will be quoted in the notes with the addition of page references to Maria Luisa Plaisant's less elaborate, but also reliable, presentation of the text. As for the historical significance of Francesco da Fiano's work, cf. also G. Radetti's study quoted in the preceding note, pp. 114ff.

[19f] For Boccaccio cf. his *Genealogiae Deorum*, XV 7, and passim, and his letter to Jacopo Pizzinga (1372)—see pp. 262f. above— esp. ed. Massèra, pp. 192, 194.

[20] Petrarch and Zanobi da Strada in their orations on the occasions of their coronations with the laurel as poets, in 1341 and 1355. For these orations cf. *Crisis: Appendices*, p. 562, note 20.

[21] "Quippe sive ipse Deus, sive natura, ipsius, qui cun[c]ta potest, docilis et erudita ministra, causa sit, non sine quadam cupiditate

laudis humane nascimur omnes. . . . Homines quidem sumus et
non marmorei, nec etiam adamantinum cor habemus. . . . Siquidem
Ieronimus, Augustinus, Ambrosius et Gregorius et, ut reliquos
sileam, Orizenes, licet sancti fuerint, homines tamen fuerunt. Et,
. . . quia omnes in cupiditatem glorie, quodam, ut sic dixerim, humanitatis unco pertrahimur, credo quandoque ardenti laudis et
humani preconii desiderio caluisse. Illos, preter uberem fructum vere
credulitatis nostre ex devotissimarum scripturarum suarum sacris
manantem eloquiis, nisi sperate et optate fame compositorum
voluminum ignitus mulxisset amor, profecto non tanta in eis floridi
et culti sermonis cura, non tante in eis studiorum et scribendi
vigilie crebruissent" (*Contra Detractores*, ed. Taù, cap. xxxvii). Cf.
Plaisant, pp. 158f.

[22] *Ibid.*, fol. 135r f.

[23] *Contra Detractores, loc. cit.*

[24] "Non solum apud cunctos populos, quos sacre religio christ-
tianitatis includit, sed apud quoscunque alios certum est Deum
omnia creasse rerumque cunctarum opificem extitisse . . ." (*ibid.*,
ed. Taù, cap. xxi). Cf. Plaisant, p. 139f.

[25] *Ibid.*, ed. Taù, cap. xxiii. Cf. Plaisant, p. 143.

[26] *Ibid.*, ed. Taù, cap. xxviii. Cf. Plaisant, pp. 148f.

[27] *Ibid.*, ed. Taù, cap. xxv. Cf. Plaisant, p. 145.

[28] *Ibid., loc. cit.* This passage and some of the citations from
Contra Detractores that follow are literally quoted in *Crisis: Appendices*, pp. 563ff.

[29] "Cur non ita prohibent Aristotilem et Platonem esse legendos?
Quibus nedum Christum venturum cognoscere, sed illum somniare
ab alto negatum est. Sed in hoc velim michi respondeat Augustinus,
respondeat etiam Orizenes. Si Homerus, Hesyodus, Pindarus,
Menander, si Cecilius, Plautus, Ter[r]entius et Lucillius complures-
que alii poete eloquio utriusque lingue preclari, fuerunt ante adven-
tum Christi per tam longa tempora, quomodo in eo credere potuerunt,
cum postea per annos innumerabiles natus est? Quomodo in eorum
mentibus ante tantam futurorum temporum longitudinem lux illa
veritatis, que illuminat omnem hominem, potuit illuxisse, siquidem
futura prescire non humanum sed divinum est? . . . Igitur, si
precedens tantorum futurorum temporum longitudo Christi cog-
nitionem abstulit poetis antiquis, an sit equitas, cum apud leges et
canones nulla statuatur de futuro delicto punitio, an iniquitas, illos
propter futurum peccatum in profundum baratrum opinione sua
mersisse, Augustini et Orizenis aliorumque catholicorum exquisitiori
juditio et maturiori equitati relinquo" (*ibid.*, ed. Taù, cap. xxv).
Cf. Plaisant, pp. 145f.

[30] See the first passage of the preceding note.

[31] Francesco, after exculpating the poets of pre-Christian times

in the manner cited above in note 29, makes this difference still clearer by continuing as follows: In an entirely different position were those poets "who shone in the time of Christ or later, and whom either the report of the marvelous works of the Son of God, . . . or the evidence they had seen with their own eyes, could and should have turned into professing Christians." Those among them who nonetheless failed to accept the truth were deserving of the most severe punishment, in contrast to the pre-Christian poets. At least Virgil, however, foresaw and foretold Christ; and Statius and Claudianus became Christians (*ibid.*, ed. Taù, cap. xxv-xxvi). Cf. Plaisant, pp. 146f.

[32] "Profanum dici non debet quicquid pium est. . . . Et fortasse latius se fundit spiritus Christi quam nos interpretamur. Et multi sunt in consortio sanctorum qui non sunt apud nos in catalogo" (Erasmus, *Convivium Religiosum; Opera Omnia*, ed. Clericus, vol. 1 [1703], pp. 681ff.).

[33] For these early sixteenth-century developments, and for the general perspective from which the attitude of Quattrocento humanists toward the doctrine of damnation of the pagans must be appraised, see the writer's article "Erasmus-Probleme. II. Der Humanismus und die thomistische Lehre von den 'gentiles salvati,' " *Archiv für Reformationsgeschichte*, XLIII (1952), 256-263.

[34] "Ubi nunc agat anima Ciceronis, fortasse non est humani iudicii pronuntiare" (Erasmus in the preface to his edition of Cicero's *Tusculanae Disputationes; Opus Epistolarum*, ed. P. S. Allen, vol. v [1924], p. 339).

[35] *Contra Detractores*, ed. Taù, cap. xxi-xxii. Cf. Plaisant, pp. 139-142.

[36] "Cur isti antiquos accusant poetas, deos quam plu[ri]mos in eorum poematibus nominantes? Equidem, si rem ac vim effectumque rei et non exteriorem verborum sonitum velimus inspicere, fides nostra suos etiam habet deos. Nam illi deos, nos vero sanctos vocamus . . ." (*ibid.*, ed. Taù, cap. xxiv). Cf. Plaisant, p. 144.

[37] *Ibid.*, fol. 139r.

[38] Ibid., fol. 142r.

[39] See pp. 124f. and 148ff. above.

[40] According to a local Roman legend, Peter was leaving Rome when, near the spot on the *Via Appia* where the church called *Domine Quo Vadis* now stands, he encountered the figure of his Master. To his question: "Domine quo vadis?" Peter received the answer "Venio iterum crucifigi." Thereupon the apostle, filled with shame at his weakness, returned to Rome to die the death of a martyr.—The passage in *De Fato et Fortuna*, lib. II cap. IX, to which we have referred, runs: "O virum dignissimum, qui in Christi tempora pervenisset, ut non fame gloriam ex suis illis virtutibus pro-

cedentem admiratus, sed veram beatitudinem agnoscens, pro certa germanaque iustitia proque veritate moriens, princeps nostrorum martyrorum haberetur." Then, on Socrates' thoughts in prison: "Hec secum similiaque versantem in illa gentilitatis cecitate maximoque errore doctrine et ignorantia summi boni Socratem, si sibi vere iustitie lumen et gratia christiani dogmatis illuxisset, sique Christum predicantem audisset, pendentem aspexisset in cruce, tandemque trihumphata morte iuxta sue prenuntiationis monita resurrexisse vidisset, putasne, si tamen astitisset divina gratia, metu mortis ab urbe Roma fugiturum fuisse, Christi confessionem et eterne ac incommutabilis veritatis causam deserturum?" (quoted by v. Martin, *Salutati und hum. Lebensideal*, pp. 64f.). The second book of *De Fato* was composed in 1396 according to W. Rüegg's findings, *Rinascimento*, v (1954), 150.

⁴¹ For Francesco's relations with Salutati compare the references in Novati's *La giovinezza di Coluccio Salutati*, passim. Novati calls Francesco "vecchio amico" of Salutati in *Epistolario di Salutati*, vol. IV, p. 171.

⁴² See *Crisis: Appendices*, pp. 403f.

⁴³ᵃ "Credo eos [the Bishops of Rome] secutos nebulonis cuiusdam sententiam, qui cum diffideret virtute sibi nomen comparare posse, Ephesi Diane templum cremavit. Ita hi nostre religionis antistites, cum urbis excellentiam pulchritudinemque parum admirari, consequi nullo modo possent, huiusmodi ruinam atque perniciem moliti sunt. Itaque tam inhumanam tamque efferam stultitiam maledictis insectemur" (ed. L. Bertalot in "Cincius Romanus und seine Briefe," *Quellen und Forschungen aus italienischen Archiven*, XXI [1929-30], 224f.).

⁴³ᵇ According to the English translation in L. Pastor's *History of the Popes*, vol. VIII (2nd edn.: St. Louis, Mo., 1923), pp. 245f.

⁴⁴ A *Responsio* of Francesco's to an "*Interrogatio ad . . . Franciscum de Fiano per . . . Leonardum Aretinum Transmissa*, videlicet quo tempore fuerit Ovidius, causam propter quam Ovidius fuerit in exilium relegatus, et si revocatus ab exilio fuerit ad patriam remissus, scire cupientem." See *Bruni, Schriften*, p. 179, and L. Bertalot in *Historische Vierteljahrsschrift*, XXIX (1934), 393.

⁴⁵ For the Latin text and the manuscript in which it has been preserved, see *Crisis: Appendices*, pp. 566f.

⁴⁶ Wesselofsky (II, p. 50): "During the last years of the Trecento, the elements of the future Medicean civilization are in a state of ferment ('gli elementi della futura civiltà medicea sono in fermento') among those men who, in their desire to shake off the yoke of the medieval tradition, are seen to bow their heads openly under the yoke of the principate which promised to free them of that tradition."

[47] "Della familiare iconomica nulla sentono, ma isprezato il santo matrimonio vivono mattamente sanza ordine, sanza curare che sia l'onor paterno, il beneficio de' figliuoli, che sarebono degni del giudicio di Cammillo e di Postumio ciensori di Roma, i quali l'avere di due uomini, ch'erano casti insino alla vecchiaia vivuti, comandarono che fusse confiscato in comune; ancora affermandogli degni di punizione, se in niuno modo di sì giusto ordine fussino arditi di ramaricarsi. Della politica non sanno qual regimento si sia migliore, o quello d'uno o quel di più, o quel di molti o quello di pochi eletti; fugono la fatica affermando che chi serve a comune serve a niuno, nè colla guarnaca consigliano la repubblica nè con l'armi la difendono. Nè si ricordano che quanto il bene è più comune, tanto à più del divino" (Wesselofsky, II, pp. 314-315).

[48] On the failure of some other attempts to include Bruni among the classicists accused by Rinuccini, cf. *Crisis: Appendices*, pp. 567f.

[49] For this aspect of Florentine Humanism in the Trecento see H. Baron in *History*, n.s, XXII (1938), 323f., *La Rinascita*, I (1938), 64f., and *Speculum*, XIII (1938), 15ff.

[50] In a letter written in his old age; cf. Wesselofsky, II, pp. 104, 382

[51a] Ed. Galletti (Florence, 1847), p. 40. The Volgare and Latin texts are reprinted in *Crisis: Appendices*, p. 569.

[51b] For this role of Filippo Villani's Dante chapter, cf. the illuminating remarks in Carlo Alberto Madrignani's "Di alcune biografie . . ." (cited in note 82 below).

[52] ". . . quod soleant recessus remotissimi bona alere studia" (ed. Galletti, p. 3).

[53] ". . . utilem ad detestationem negotiosae vitae, qua bonis temporalibus implicamur" (*ibid.*, p. 19). See also pp. 106f. above.

[54a] For more references to Filippo Villani's personality traits here emphasized, cf. *Crisis: Appendices*, p. 570, note 54.

[54b] After the appearance of the first edition of *Crisis*, the actual participation in public office of all these citizen-humanists has been systematically examined from the archival documents in Lauro Martines' fundamental work on *The Social World of the Florentine Humanists, 1390-1460* (Princeton, 1963), pp. 145ff., esp. 154-165 and 319f. Martines demonstrates that their engagement was quantitatively increasing rather than declining about and after 1400. This was largely enforced by the isolation encountered by families which were insufficiently represented in the higher offices and on powerful boards. This is a picture of practical continuance of active citizenship which remarkably conforms with our observation of a simultaneous growing commitment of the Florentine citizen-humanists to their republic. Martines, however, seems to me too much inclined to infer from his facts that the impact of humanist classicism

cannot have been very significant in alienating citizens from public action in a patrician society constantly driven to ambitious competition for crucial posts by the crude need of self-protection. This argument, to be sure, has a large degree of validity and should warn us not to overrate the potential long-term danger inherent in the humanistic classicism around 1400. But this must not blind us to the testimonies of contemporaries who definitely speak of the alienation of a number of humanist-citizens from their public responsibilities. In each individual case, our literary sources must be carefully weighed along with the documentary evidence, as will be attempted in the following pages.

[55a] See Vespasiano da Bisticci, *Vite di Uomini Illustri del Secolo XV*, ed. Frati, vol. III, p. 37. Manetti's appraisal of Rossi is from his unpublished *Adversus Judaeos et Gentes*. The Latin text of the cited passage and a discussion of the date of the treatise is found in *Crisis: Appendices*, pp. 570f.

[55b] We owe the entire archival evidence to the recent findings of L. Martines, *op. cit.*, pp. 156-159. These findings must, of course, be interpreted in the light of the fact that Rossi's name completely disappears from among the holders of elective office after 1393.

[56] Vespasiano da Bisticci, *op. cit.*, vol. II, p. 230.

[57] This emerges from the letter in which Guarino in 1418 thought it necessary to justify his marriage before Corbinelli and to refute Corbinelli's assertion, "mulieres magno philosophantibus impedimento esse." See Guarino, *Ep. 125*, *Epistolario di Guarino*, ed. R. Sabbadini, vol. I (Venice, 1915), pp. 213-215.

[58] See R. Blum, *La Biblioteca della Badia Fiorentina e i Codici di Antonio Corbinelli* ("Studi e Testi," vol. 155 [Città del Vaticano, 1951]), p. 42. Corbinelli's natural son may be presumed to have been born before Rinuccini's writing, because in 1410 he was named to be Corbinelli's sole heir, and it is improbable that Corbinelli would have made this important decision unless the bastard son had reached the age where his character and personality were recognizable.

[59a] All the archival information used in the discussion which follows is owed to L. Martines' researches, *op. cit.*, pp. 155, 319f., and his "Addenda to the Life of Antonio Corbinelli," *Rinascimento*, VIII (1957), esp. pp. 9-17. These findings have superseded the incomplete information available to Blum. In combination with what we know about Rossi and Niccoli, however, it will sometimes be necessary to interpret them differently from Martines' immediate conclusions.

[59b] I am not counting Corbinelli's repeated service, from 1403 onward, on the two—only approving or rejecting—city councils, because attendance in these assemblies was a matter of course for

a young patrician from one of the leading families like the Corbinelli. Cf. on this distinction Martines' pertinent remarks, *Rinascimento*, p. 10.

⁶⁰ᵃ From the biography of Niccoli in Manetti's *De Illustribus Longaevis*. The Latin text, reconstructed from the manuscripts, is in *Crisis: Appendices*, pp. 571f.

⁶⁰ᵇ Poggio, *Opera* (Basel, 1538), pp. 271, 275.

⁶¹ Niccoli's quarrels with his five brothers, at any rate, which cast a cloud upon his life, and in the 1420's caused a public scandal when the brothers insulted his concubine on the street (see Voigt, *Die Wiederbelebung*, I, p. 304), had according to Manetti's account already started by 1400. For Manetti blames these troubles for the well-known fact that Niccoli did not advance very far in his Greek studies under Chrysoloras (see *Crisis: Appendices*, pp. 572f.). It is, therefore, very possible—although it cannot be proven by direct documentary evidence—that Niccoli's conduct, not in harmony with the citizen's way of life, was resented and criticized at that early time, just as citizen-humanists like Bruni criticized Niccoli and sided against him after the incident with his mistress in the 1420's.

⁶² See pp. 110f. above.

⁶³ See pp. 149ff. and 163f. above.

⁶⁴ For the fragments of Rossi's work that have been preserved see *Crisis: Appendices*, p. 573.

⁶⁵ Rossi's original text is in *Crisis: Appendices*, pp. 573f.

⁶⁶ *Ibid*.

⁶⁷ᵃ *Ibid*. The Latin poem is published in *Crisis: Appendices*, p. 574.

⁶⁷ᵇ Quoted by L. Martines from the minutes of the *Consulte e Pratiche, op. cit.*, p. 257.

⁶⁷ᶜ Poggio, *Opera* (Basel, 1538), p. 271; cf. *Crisis: Appendices*, p. 573, for the Latin text. Giannozzo Manetti, in his *De Illustribus Longaevis*, also emphasizes Marsili's influence on the formation of Niccoli's mind.

⁶⁸ We owe our knowledge of Niccoli's political attitude, and of virtually all the following facts, to the *Oratio* by Lorenzo di Marco de' Benvenuti (*Oratio in Niccolaum Nicholum*, ed. G. Zippel, *Giornale Storico della Letteratura Italiana*, xxiv [1894], 168-179) written about 1420. For the character and trustworthiness of this source, see "An Informant on Niccolò Niccoli: Lorenzo di Marco de' Benvenuti," *Crisis: Appendices*, pp. 409ff.

⁶⁹ "Meministine igitur, cum mediolanensium ducis potentia premeremur, quibus verbis acerbissimis lacerares senatum atque omnes huius florentissime urbis magistratus ac rempublicam universam, partem civium ignavos ac dementes, partem ob nimiam

potentiam tyrannos ac predones appellans, tantam ex hoc patrie maximo periculo letitiam pre te ferens, quantam bonus civis in victoria percepisset?" (*Oratio, op. cit.,* p. 177).

[70] See pp. 405f. below.

[71] The Latin text of this passage and of the passages to which we will presently refer are found in *Crisis: Appendices,* p. 575.

[72a] *Ibid.*

[72b] This is the question asked, but not answered to his own full satisfaction, by L. Martines, *The Social World,* p. 164. All the following information on the archival evidence on Niccolò Niccoli and his family is owed to Martines, pp. 160-165.

[72c] Cf. note 59a above.

[73] *Crisis: Appendices,* p. 575.

[74] *Ibid.*

[75] *Ibid.*

[76] *Ibid.*

[77] See pp. 139f. above.

[78] See p. 95 above.

[79] On the date and authenticity of the poem *De Adventu Imperatoris* cf. *Crisis: Appendices,* pp. 575f.

[80] The Latin text is published *ibid.*

[81] On the civic-humanistic elements in Palmieri's *Della Vita Civile* cf. H. Baron, "La Rinascita dell' Etica Statale Romana nell' Umanesimo Fiorentino del Quattrocento," *Civiltà Moderna,* VII (1935), 11ff., and "Franciscan Poverty and Civic Wealth," *Speculum,* XIII (1938), 23f, the list of recent studies in *Crisis: Appendices,* p. 577, and A. Buck on Palmieri "als Repräsentant des Florentiner Bürgerhumanismus," *Archiv für Kulturgeschichte,* XLVII (1965), 77ff

[82] Bruni's estimate of Dante as a citizen who discharged his obligations toward his community by serving in public office and as *paterfamilias,* is contained in Bruni's *Vita di Dante.* This estimate is a feature of Bruni's vindication of Dante which emerged in the mature years of his Humanism, and must be added to the vindication of Dante the poet and historical thinker that had occupied Bruni since he had begun to emancipate himself from Niccoli's contempt of the *tre corone fiorentine.* For this civic aspect of Bruni's final appraisal of Dante see H. Baron, *History,* n.s., XXII (1938), 324ff. and *Bulletin of the John Rylands Library,* XXII (1938), 95ff.; also E. Garin, *La Rinascita,* IV (1941), 409ff. To prevent misconceptions, it should, however, be added that the admiration of Dante the citizen did not hinder Bruni, in his undogmatic, humanistic way, from also recognizing the values of the *vita contemplativa* when he was confronted with them in composing the companion *Vita di Petrarca.* Petrarch, he said, was the "wiser" of the two men

in not burdening himself with the active-political life, and in a sense it seemed more difficult and, as it were, more praiseworthy to remain true to oneself in the comforts of contemplation than in the hardships of the active life, in so far as it is more difficult for human nature to resist the temptations of good fortune than the challenges of adverse fortune. In a concluding comparison, therefore, Bruni allows for some "excellence" and "superiority" for Petrarch as well as Dante, each in his own way. But this eventual reconciliation does not change the fact that, in the *Vita di Dante*, Dante's engagement in the responsibilities of the active life had been powerfully presented as the only conduct which is in harmony with the social nature of man and may serve as a lasting model. Bruni's civic picture of Dante, therefore, exerted a deep impression throughout the Renaissance, and its traces are found even among Renaissance biographers of Dante outside Florence.

Of the delicate balance between Bruni's acknowledgments of antagonistic values in the two *Vite* of Dante and Petrarch, we now have a perceptive study by Carlo Alberto Madrignani, "Di alcune biografie umanistiche di Dante e Petrarca," *Belfagor*, XVIII (1963), esp. pp. 34ff. As for the impact of Bruni's Dante *Vita* on later Florentine writers—for details, cf. *Crisis: Appendices*, pp. 577f.—Madrignani's analysis of Giannozzo Manetti's Latin *Vitae* of Dante and Petrarch (*op. cit.*, pp. 42ff.) shows well that some aspects of Bruni's faith in the values of the civic life had by the 1450's been replaced by new ideals of studious withdrawal.

CHAPTER 15

[1] V. Rossi, *Il Quattrocento* (3rd edn., 1933), p. 228. For Giovanni da Prato's relations to Cino Rinuccini cf. also *Humanistic and Political Literature*, Chap. I, last pages of section I.

[2] Cf. above, pp. 89f., 275f., 317, and, for more details, *Humanistic and Political Literature*, pp. 31ff.

[3a] See the Excursus "The Date of the *Paradiso*," in *Humanistic and Political Literature*, pp. 34ff.

[3b] See "The *Paradiso degli Alberti* and the First Book of Bruni's *Historiae*: The Dissolution of the Florentine Legends of Totila and Attila," *Crisis: Appendices*, pp. 417ff.

[4] End of 1428, or early in 1429. See *Crisis: Appendices*, pp. 618f.

[5] This *Canzona morale di patria e di libertate* is published by Wesselofsky, II, pp. 435-440. For the date cf. *Crisis: Appendices*, p. 579, note 5.

[6] *Paradiso*, I, p. 2.

[7] *Ibid.*, pp. 47f., 52-54.

[8] A survey of the paragraphs of the *Paradiso* dealing with political and historical themes is in *Humanistic and Political Literature*, pp. 17ff.

[9] *Paradiso*, I, p. 2.

[10] "... che l'edioma fiorentino è si rilimato e copioso che ogni astratta e profonda mater[i]a si puote chiarissimamente con esso dire, ragionarne e disputarne" (*Paradiso*, II, p. 84). These words are attributed in the novel to the Paduan philosopher, Marsilio di Santa Sofia, and not to Luigi Marsili as E. Santini asserted in *Giornale Storico della Letteratura Italiana*, LX (1912), 290f. The passage is an acknowledgment of the national Florentine attainment, put into the mouth of a distinguished scholastic scholar from abroad who is forced to admit not having been sufficiently familiar with the Volgare in the past, but promises to do better in the future (*ibid.*, pp. 84f.). This scene in the novel undoubtedly reflects the patriotic aspect of Giovanni's own love of the Florentine Volgare.

[11] See note 35 to Chap. 13.

[12] For the dates of Bruni's *Canzone Morale*, *Canzone a Laude di Venere*, and *Novella: Storia di Seleuco*, all written during the 1420's and 1430's, cf. *Crisis: Appendices*, pp. 580f.

[13] "Ciascuna lingua ha sua perfezione e suo suono e suo parlare limato e scientifico" (*Bruni, Schriften*, p. 61).

[14] Until recently there has been little protest against the inveterate opinion (for which, as we have seen, Wesselofsky was greatly responsible) that during the greater part of the Quattrocento the effect of Humanism on Volgare literature was mainly of a negative nature: obliteration of Trecento Volgare to the benefit of humanistic Latin; and opposition, not help, to the Volgare when it again came to the fore in the second half of the Quattrocento. One of the props of this thesis, it is true, has long been tacitly abandoned; students realized the active part taken by some Florentine humanists in the vindication of the Volgare from the second third of the century onward, and especially the significant role played in this vindication by L. B. Alberti and Cristoforo Landino. But these observations did not bring about a re-examination of the opinion that Humanism—not merely in some groups and schools, but by its very nature—was the mortal enemy of the Volgare and did for a time succeed in deflecting the growth of Florentine and Italian literature. Writers like Alberti and Landino were looked upon as exceptions—as liberators from a prejudice that is thought to have dominated Florentine Humanism previously. This was the tenor of the basic monographic study in the field, V. Cian's "Contro il Volgare" (*Studi Letterari e Linguistici dedicati a Pio Rajna* [Milan, 1911], pp. 251-297)—a presentation of the subject which, in spite of the increased attention it paid to Alberti and Landino, has helped to

perpetuate the old view by its very title and by the repeated reference to the alleged common "pregiudizio umanistico" in matters of the Volgare. The situation is about the same in the still generally used introduction to the subject, the chapter "L'Umanesimo e il Volgare" in V. Rossi's *Il Quattrocento* (3rd edn.: 1933, pp. 104-115), where, side by side with an excellent analysis of many facts that should be a warning against rash generalizations, a genuine diatribe is found against the supposed shortsightedness of the early Renaissance humanists and their obnoxious influence on everything affecting the vernacular. The chapter, "The Fight for the Vernacular [in] Italy," in Vernon Hall Jr.'s *Renaissance Literary Criticism* (New York, 1945, esp. pp. 19-26) by and large follows this view of the early Quattrocento, giving it fresh currency within the framework of a comparative study of Italian, French, and English theories. Yet, some of the facts that should cause us to reconsider the accustomed perspective even for the early Renaissance have been known since E. Santini's study "La produzione volgare di Bruni" (*Giornale Storico della Letteratura Italiana*, LX [1912], 289-332). Perhaps the implications of Santini's view of Bruni could not be fully understood as long as it had not been incorporated in a more coherent interpretation of the phenomenon of Florentine civic Humanism. Although the thumb-nail sketch which we shall draw will leave room for qualifications and supplements, it will show conclusively that a coherent evolution of the linguistic and literary views of the Florentine citizen-humanists was already underway when Alberti and Landino produced their more conspicuous Volgare writings and language-theories.

Since the first publication of this chapter, the literary aspects of the Volgare controversy have been further traced in previously little-known detail by three useful studies: Hans Wilhelm Klein, *Latein und Volgare in Italien* (Munich, 1957); Riccardo Fubini, "La coscienza del latino negli umanisti: An latina lingua Romanorum esset peculiare idioma," *Studi Medievali*, ser. 3, vol. II, 2 (1961), 505-550; and Cecil Grayson's perceptive inaugural lecture, *A Renaissance Controversy: Latin or Italian?* (Oxford, 1960). It seems to me that the more politico-historical approach to the same problems, attempted in the present chapter, continues to be a necessary complement and can remain essentially unchanged.

[15] "Con tutto che queste sono cose, che mal si possono dire in vulgare idioma, pur m'ingegnerò di darle ad intendere . . ." (*Bruni, Schriften*, p. 60). To see in this frank and revealing statement merely the expression of a "pregiudizio umanistico," as Cian does in his study (p. 260), means overlooking the actual problem encountered by early Quattrocento humanists.

[16] *Della Vita Civile*, ed. F. Battaglia in "Scrittori Politici Itali-

ani," vol. XIV (1944), pp. 125f. For the date between 1432 and
1436 and the autograph of Palmieri's work see *Crisis: Appendices*,
pp. 583f., and a recent description of the autograph by L. Rainaldi
in *Rinascimento*, V (1954), 133ff.

[17a] Biondo, in the crucial paragraph of his *De Verbis Romanae
Locutionis* (in his *Scritti Inediti e Rari*, ed. B. Nogara in "Studi e
Testi," vol. 48 [Rome, 1927], p. 129), had begun by asserting
that even before the Germanic invasions any deviation, both inside
and outside Rome, from the norm of the literary language was
nothing but deterioration and barbaric infection: "In the period
preceding Cicero one sees those who lived outside of Rome or preserved in their domestic life in Rome some traces of barbarism ('aut
Romae domesticam habuerunt aliquam barbariem') remaining somewhat behind the gracefulness of Roman speech and tarnished by
that barbarity." After this disparaging introduction Biondo proceeds
to denounce the effects of the barbarian migrations quoted above:
"Postea vero quam urbs a Gothis et Vandalis capta inhabitarique
coepta est, . . . omnes sermone barbaro inquinati ac penitus sordi-
dati fuerunt; sensimque factum est, ut pro Romana latinitate adul-
terinam hanc barbarica mixtam loquelam habeamus vulgarem."

[17b] Cf. for what follows: "Quin etiam publicae administrationis
et privatim vivendi instituta accuratissime ab eisdem sunt mutata et
eo usque ipsius gentis processit insania ut romanorum caractere litterarum penitus postposito novas ipsi et sua ineptia gentis barbariem
indicantes cifras pro litteris adinvenirent [*print* adinvenerunt]. E
contra vero Ostrogothi aeque ac cives romani latinis delectati litteris
nullam in illis barbariem effuderunt" (*Italia Illustrata*, at the beginning of the section "Nona Regio: Marchia Tarvisina" [ed.
Verona, 1482, fol. H III verso-H IIII recto]).

[17c] Cf. the sketch of this continuing trend in Klein, *op. cit.*, pp.
57-59.

[18] "Atque latina lingua a vulgari in multis differt, plurimum
tamen terminatione, inflexione, significatione, constructione, et ac-
centu." "Haec ne quaeso mulierculae et nutrices et vulgus illit-
teratum dicent, quae nos litterati vix dicere valemus? Quid si probo
per ea tempora vulgarem sermonem distinctum a literato fuisse?"
(Bruni, *Ep. VI 10*, ed. Mehus, vol. II, pp. 66f.).

[19a] "Denique etiam hodie mulieres Romanae judicio meo ele-
gantissime loquuntur, et purius certe quam viri. Et quanquam non
litteratus sit earum sermo, potest tamen figura ipsa dicendi nitorque
verborum eloquentiam adjuvare." Bruni had listened to a certain
Roman matron. "Haec illa puro nativoque Romano proferebat sermone, ita ut admodum sim equidem delectatus, cum et verba nitorem
gravitatemque sententiae et pronunciatio ipsa vernaculam quandam
habere[n]t suavitatem. Hoc ego modo filiis matres, et nutrices alum-

nis profuisse ad elegantiam puto. Non quod casus inflecterent aut verba variarent ac terminarent litterate, sed quod purum et nitidum ac minime barbarum sermonem infunderent. Nam et habet vulgaris sermo commendationem suam, ut apud Dantem poetam et alios quosdam emendate loquentes apparet" (*ibid.*, p. 68).

[19b] See preceding note.

[19c] See pp. 349f. below.

[19d] For more details on the problems of criticism and interpretation raised by our reconstruction of Bruni's attitude toward the Volgare, see "Bruni's alleged Classicism in the Controversy on the Origin of the Volgare," *Crisis: Appendices*, pp. 422ff.

[20a] "Lo scrivere in istile litterato o vulgare non ha a fare al fatto, nè altra differenza è, se non come scrivere in greco od in latino. Ciascuna lingua ha sua perfezione e suo suono e suo parlare limato e scientifico" (in *Le Vite di Dante, Petrarca e Boccaccio*, ed. Solerti, p. 106; in *Bruni, Schriften,* p. 61).

[20b] Cf. H. W. Klein, *op. cit.*, pp. 23-28.

[20c] "Lo latino molte cose manifesta concepute nella mente, che il volgare fare non può . . . ; più è la virtù sua, che quella del volgare" (Dante, *Convivio*, I, v).

[20d] "La quale [la volgare] . . . egli primo non altramenti fra noi italici esaltò e recò in pregio, che la sua Omero tra' greci o Virgilio tra' latini" (Boccaccio, *Vita di Dante*, c. XIV; ed. D. Guerri in Boccaccio's *Comento alla Divina Commedia e gli Altri Scritti intorno a Dante*, vol. I [Bari, 1918], pp. 24f.).

[20e] "Molto più d'arte e di gravità ha nel parlare latino che nel materno" (Boccaccio, *Comento*, Prooemio Lezione I [ed. Guerri, p. 115]).

[20f] See note 10 above.

[21] "Uno strano sapore di modernità" (V. Rossi in his *Scritti di critica letteraria*, vol. I [1930], p. 328).

[22] For this date cf. *Crisis: Appendices*, pp. 585f.

[23] This sums up the contents of Manetti's preface, ed. in Solerti, *Vite di Dante, Petrarca e Boccaccio*, pp. 109-112.

[24] "Hanc suam materni sermonis poeticam hic noster poeta primus apud Italos perpaucis ante annis adinventam . . . non secus nobilitavit, quam aut Homerus graece apud Graecos aut Virgilius latine apud Latinos quondam suam quisque apud suos illustraverit" (*ibid.*, p. 138). The same idea had already been expressed in Boccaccio's *Vita di Dante* (see the quotation in note 20d above), and, no doubt, Manetti was drawing from this source. In spite of his plagiarism, however, the fact that he was ready to follow Boccaccio's opinion is remarkable. Two generations of humanistic classicists between Boccaccio and Manetti had refused to place the work of a Volgare poet on an equal level with its Greek and Latin counterparts, as several

examples on the pages that follow will illustrate. On the other hand, during the generation following that of Bruni and Manetti reference to the equality of the lifeworks of Homer, Virgil, and Dante became commonplace among Florentine writers.

[25] Benedetto Accolti, *Dialogus De Praestantia Virorum Sui Aevi;* published by G. C. Galletti (see above note 33 to Chap. 3), pp. 101-128. Composed between 1459 and 1464; cf. A. Gaspary, *Geschichte der italienischen Literatur,* II (1888), 179.

[26] ". . . a multis dubitatum scio, duplexne an unus loquendi modus esset" (Accolti, *op. cit.,* p. 122).

[27] For Salutati see Rossi, *Il Quattrocento,* p. 109, p. 119 n. 53, and v. Martin, *Salutati und hum. Lebensideal,* p. 220, n. 3. In Bruni's *Dialogus I,* Salutati is made to express precisely the same idea ("Dantem vero, si alio genere scribendi usus esset, non eo contentus forem, ut illum cum antiquis nostris compararem, sed et ipsis et Graecis etiam anteponerem," ed. Klette, p. 60; ed. Garin, p. 68). For Poggio see Rossi, *Il Quattrocento,* p. 110, p. 119 n. 55. The same reserve is apparent in Palmieri's praise that Dante, "fuori della lingua, poco si truova drieto a' sommi poeti latini" (*Della Vita Civile,* ed. Battaglia, p. 4). These utterances suggest the half-sympathetic attitude which must have been the starting-point for Bruni in his youth. By comparing that earlier estimate with the recognition of the Volgare as a language in its own right in Bruni's *Vita di Dante,* we can grasp the extent of the transformation which occurred during his life.

[28a] "Nec multifacio qua quisque lingua, materna scilicet, an Latina proloquatur; modo graviter, ornate, copioseque pronuntiet" (Accolti, *op. cit.,* pp. 121-122).

[28b] Cf. H. Baron, "The *Querelle* of the Ancients and the Moderns . . . ," *Journal of the History of Ideas,* XX (1959), 19.

[28c] On the history of the composition of the *Della Famiglia,* cf. Cecil Grayson's edition of Alberti's *Opere Volgari* (Bari: Laterza), vol. I (1960), pp. 379-380. The relationship of the work to civic Humanism (largely negative, since Alberti drafted it before having come in contact with Florence in 1434) has been excellently appraised by Grayson in "The Humanism of Alberti," *Italian Studies,* XII (1957), esp. 48f.

[29] ". . . quelli strani e avventizii uomini el simile se consuefaceano alla nostra, credo con molti barbarismi e corruttela del proferire. Onde per questa mistura di dì in dì insalvatichì et viziossi la nostra prima cultissima ed emendatissima lingua" (*Della Famiglia,* ed. Grayson, p. 154).

[30] "Ben confesso quella antiqua latina lingua essere copiosa molto e ornatissima, ma non però veggo in che sia la nostra oggi toscana tanto d'averla in odio. . . . E sento io questo: chi fusse più di me

dotto, o tale quale molti vogliono essere riputati, costui in questa oggi commune troverrebbe non meno ornamenti che in quella. . . . E sia quanto dicono quella antica apresso di tutte le genti piena d'autorità, solo perché in essa molti dotti scrissero, ·simile certo sarà la nostra s' e' dotti la vorranno molto con suo studio e vigilie essere elimata et polita" (*Della Famiglia*, pp. 155f.).

[31] In the "Proemio" of Alberti's *Teogenio*, probably written about 1440 (according to G. Ponte's recent propositions in *Convivium*, 1955) and published about 1442, we also read "che molti m'ascrivono a biasimo, e dicono ch'io offesi la maestà letteraria non scrivendo materia sì eloquente in lingua piuttosto latina."

[32] For the *Regole della Lingua Fiorentina*, also called *Grammatichetta Vaticana* (because it has been preserved in Cod. Vat. Reg. Lat. 1370), see Cecil Grayson's edition, *Leon Battista Alberti: La Prima Grammatica della Lingua Volgare*, "Collezione di Opere Inedite o Rare," vol. 125 (Bologna, 1964). Grayson's introduction makes attribution to Alberti himself as good as certain and, on the other hand, refutes the arguments on whose strength Bembo's direct knowledge of the *Regole* had been wrongly considered to be proven. Cf. Grayson, *op. cit.*, esp. pp. xivff., xlviii.

[33] Lorenzo de' Medici, *Comento sopra alcuni de' suoi Sonetti* (in *Opere*, ed. Simioni, vol. 1 [1913], pp. 18-22). For a fully rounded analysis, cf. now C. Grayson in *Italian Renaissance Studies: A Tribute to Cecilia M. Ady* (London, 1960), pp. 417-420.

[34] "E questo si può più presto chiamare felicità e prosperità che vera laude della lingua [latina] . . . ; perchè la propagazione dell' imperio romano non l'ha fatto solamente comune per tutto il mondo, ma quasi necessaria" (*op. cit.*, pp. 19-20).

[35] Which is the most adequate rendering of "lingue materni e naturali."

[36] *Op. cit.*, pp. 21-22.

[37] Landino (in his "Vita e Costumi di Dante" quoted in the following note): Dante "primo dimostrò quanto fosse idoneo il Fiorentino idioma, non solo ad exprimere, ma ad amplificare ed exornare tutte le cose che caggiono in disputazione." Dante "fu el primo che la lingua nostra patria . . . molto nobilitò e fecela culta et ornata. Trovò Omero la lingua greca molto già abondante e exculta da Orfeo e da Museo e da altri poeti più vetusti di lui. Trovò la latina Virgilio già elimata et exornata e da Ennio e da Lucrezio, da Plauto e da Terenzio et altri poeti vetusti amplificata. Ma innanzi a Dante in lingua toscana nessuno avea trovato alcuna leggiadria . . ." (pp. 191f.).

[38] See Landino's *Orazione quando cominciò a leggere in Studio i sonetti di M. Francesco Petrarca* (1460), edited in Fr. Corazzini's volume *Miscellanea di Cose Inedite o Rare* (Florence, 1853), pp.

125-134; and Landino's introduction ("Vita e Costumi di Dante") to his commentary upon the *Divina Commedia*, first published 1481, reprinted in Solerti, *op. cit.*, esp. pp. 191-193. Both sources have now been analyzed by M. Santoro, *Giornale Storico della Letteratura Italiana*, CXXXI (1954), 504-521, with many more particulars that complement our above examples.

[39] For some critical comments on Bruni's place in this galaxy cf. *Crisis: Appendices*, p. 589, note 39.

[40] *Vita e Costumi*, ed. Solerti (see note 35 to Chap. 12), pp. 192-193.

[41] "Ma non sia alcuno che creda non solamente essere eloquente ma pure tollerabile dicitore, se prima non harà vera et perfecta cognizione delle latine lettere" (*ibid.*, p. 192). An almost identical statement can already be found in the *Orazione*, ed. Corazzini, pp. 129f.

[42] ". . . è necessario essere Latino chi vuole essere buono Toscano" (Corazzini, *op. cit.*, p. 131). For an estimate of Dante and comparison with Homer and Virgil, by Landino's contemporary, Ugolino Verino, see *Crisis: Appendices*, p. 621.

[43] For a broader historical perspective on this result it should be noted that Vernon Hall, in his cited discussion on the history of Renaissance literary criticism in Italy, France, and England (see note 14 above), concludes that the Italian ideas that are comparable to those subsequently found outside Italy are encountered specifically in Florence, but, he thinks, not until the sixteenth century. At that time, he observes, "the fight for the vernacular" was different in Florence from that in the rest of Italy; "it was in Florence . . . that there was a love for the native soil transferred to the native tongue that finds an echo in French and English writings. . . . Characterized as they were by a strong feeling of local pride, the writings of the Florentines offer the closest parallels to the English and French writings on the subject of the vernacular" (pp. 35f.). What we believe our study has proved is that the roots of these characteristics lay as far back as the first decades of the Quattrocento. For further observations on this relationship from the perspective of the sixteenth century, cf. H. Baron, "The *Querelle* of the Ancients and the Moderns . . ." (see note 1 to Chap. 1 above).

After the completion of the manuscript for the first edition of *Crisis*, a picture of the relations between fifteenth-century Italian Humanism and Volgare literature that closely resembles our own view appeared in August Buck's *Italienische Dichtungslehren vom Mittelalter bis zum Ausgang der Renaissance* (Tübingen, 1952). In the chapter "Humanismus und volkssprachliche Dichtung" (cf. esp. pp. 97-112), Buck arrives at the same rejection proposed here of the opinion that the growth of Italian literature and the interest in the Volgare were merely held back by the Latin humanists. When in the second half of the Quattrocento the point is reached, says Buck, where a great school of Italian poetry reemerged, "the re-emergence does not occur . . . in opposition to Humanism, but as an evolution from the humanistic viewpoint" (pp. 100f.; for more details concerning the relationship of our results to Buck's conclusions cf. *Crisis: Appendices*, pp. 590f.). It is also important that with respect to the growth of Volgare prose, Paul O. Kristeller, in a fundamental paper on "The Origin and Development of the Language of Italian Prose" (first published 1946, reprinted in Kristeller's *Studies in Renaissance Thought and Letters* [Rome, 1956]) has arrived at quite similar conclusions. Kristeller points out that, although the first half of the Quattrocento cannot boast of any great Italian poet, "the development of literary Italian seems to have been quite different as far as prose is concerned." "More important than the theory is the actual practice of the humanists and their contemporaries. . . . The fifteenth century, including its earlier phases, shows no interruption or decline in the development of vernacular prose literature, but rather an advance and expansion, and the humanists took an active part in this literature" (pp. 477, 483f.). Our observations have shown that the growth of Florentine ideas concerning the nature and value of the Volgare is in perfect agreement with Kristeller's findings on the actual development of prose-writing in the vernacular.

Among Italian scholars, too, there have been signs since the early 1950's that a turning-point has been reached in the appraisal of the humanistic attitude toward the Volgare. In an exhaustive study of "Cristoforo Landino e il Volgare" (*Giornale Storico della Letteratura Italiana*, CXXXI [1954], 501-547), M. Santoro concluded that the Volgare in early Quattrocento Florence, "far from being suppressed by the Latin and suffering delay and decadence, as was often said not long ago, rather continued to develop," until the time of Lorenzo when Landino set forth the conclusive theory of the necessary "*trasferimento* to the Volgare of attainments made in Latin" —a "trasferimento" from one language to another which Humanism had learned from the attitude of ancient Rome toward Greek (pp. 501, 544ff.). For other recent acknowledgments that Quattrocento Humanism had to its credit accomplishments in Latin that were needed for the subsequent growth of the Volgare, one may refer to E. Garin's introduction to *Prosatori Latini del Quattrocento* (1952), pp. xviiff. (reprinted in Garin's *Medioevo e Rinascimento* [1954], pp. 119ff.) as well as to comments by M. Fubini in the *Giornale Storico*, CXXXI (1954), 579ff.

The linguistic facts behind this re-interpretation were presented in detail as early as 1941 by R. Spongano's *La prosa letteraria del*

Quattrocento (reprinted 1946 as an introduction to Alberti's *Della Famiglia*, and again in Spongano's *Due Saggi sull' Umanesimo* [Florence, 1964]). In this study, the transfer of numerous characteristics of humanistic Latin to the Volgare is described with the commentary that the Latin of the Florentine Trecento and Quattrocento, far from faithfully imitating the language of a past age, was itself a product of the period in which the Volgare developed and, therefore, "un idioma diverso dal volgare, [ma] una lingua—ossia un atteggiamento del pensiero—non diversa dal volgare" in all aspects which distinguish modern attitudes from those of antiquity (*Due Saggi*, pp. 52, 57ff.). One may add that even in this respect Leonardo Bruni, whose name is missing in Spongano's investigations, was among the early-Quattrocento humanists closest to the world of the Volgare; cf. this writer's tentative estimate of Bruni's Latin in his "Einleitung" to *Bruni, Schriften*, pp. xxivf., and also the appraisal of Bruni as a translator from the Latin into the Volgare (of Cicero's *Pro Marcello*) made by G. Folena in *La Rassegna*, LVII (1953), 160: "Nel lessico [Bruni] riesce a un equilibrio quasi perfetto fra la sfera di azione classica e quella volgare."

CHAPTER 16

[1a] For the relationship of the following analysis, which takes up and expands the theme of chapter 2, to earlier studies of Quattrocento politics, the reader is once more referred to "Interpretations of the Political Background of the Early Renaissance," *Crisis: Appendices*, pp. 379ff.

[1b] For this role of Pisa in the time of Giangaleazzo see pp. 27, 30, 33 above. For other details illustrating Florence's vital dependence, during the Giangaleazzo wars, on free passage through the Pisan ports, see *Humanistic and Political Literature*, pp. 42ff., "Pitfalls in the Dating of Loschi's *Invectiva*."

[2] The most satisfactory picture of the period of Ladislaus of Naples is still that contained in F. Gregorovius' *Geschichte der Stadt Rom im Mittelalter*, vol. VI (5th edn. 1908), pp. 577-616. A. Cutolo, *Re Ladislao d'Angiò-Durazzo* (2 volumes, Milan, 1936), is the best guide to the diplomatic events, but hardly speaks the last word on the historical significance of Ladislaus' conquest of Italy. See below, note 8.

[3] On the Florentine-Sienese league of 1409, see Scipione Ammirato, *Istorie Fiorentine*, end of lib. XVII (in the edition Florence, 1647, vol. II, pp. 949f.). Cf. Cutolo, *op. cit.*, vol. I, pp. 171-174, for documentary details on the final establishment of the league, especially concerning Siena. On the stanch cooperation of Florence and Siena in defending Tuscany against Ladislaus, cf. T. Terzani,

Bullettino Senese di Storia Patria, Ser. III, vol. XIX (1960), pp. 44f., 48f., 66.

⁴ See pp. 22f. above.

⁵ᵃ Nicolai Rubinstein, "Political Ideas in Sienese Art: The Frescoes by . . . Taddeo di Bartolo in the Palazzo Pubblico," *Journal of the Warburg Institute*, XXI (1958), 194-207, esp. 196ff., 205, 207. Rubinstein, p. 204, points out the probability that the Sienese citizen principally in charge of the project, the jurist Pietro de' Pecci, met directly with Bruni in 1413.

⁵ᵇ See the letters revealing dangerous insolvencies in Florence in 1406 in consequence of the huge enforced loans during the war, quoted by R. Piattoli (from the *Archivio Datini*) in *Giornale stor. e lett. della Liguria*, n.s. VI (1930), 228.

⁵ᶜ Gregorio Dati, *L'istoria di Firenze* . . . , ed. Pratesi, pp. 43, 136ff.

⁶ Leonardo Bruni, *Rerum Suo Temp. Gest. Comm.*, pp. 441, 443. On the indignation of such old leaders of the Giangaleazzo period as Gino Capponi (he imputed "treachery" to those ready to come to terms with Ladislaus) we have documentary evidence from the year 1414; see p. 368 below.

⁷ See pp. 326 and 328 above and 405 below; also *Crisis: Appendices*, pp. 412f.

⁸ Especially by A. Cutolo, who (*op. cit.*, passim, and in particular pp. 433f.) vigorously denied any "imperialismo napoletano" with the somewhat astounding comment that Ladislaus "took the offensive, occupied entire regions, and threatened the Papacy, Florence, and eventually the German King, only to defend himself."

⁹ "In tutto avea diretto l'animo a occupare la nostra libertà." "Desiderava lo Imperio . . ." (Domenico Buoninsegni, *Storia della Città di Firenze dall'anno 1410 al 1460* [Florence, 1637], p. 7; Giovanni di Paolo Morelli, *Ricordi*, ed. Branca, p. 520). Morelli, too, reports that Ladislaus "si gridò: 'A Firenze, a Firenze!'."

¹⁰ Ladislaus "libertati totius Italie inimicus semper extiterat"; "quem nichil aliud quam totius Italie servitutem machinantem vidimus." Lorenzo di Marco de' Benvenuti (see note 68 to Chap. 14), pp. 177-178.

¹¹ On Loschi's hope that Ladislaus, as monarch, would unite Italy, see G. da Schio, *Sulla vita e sugli scritti di A. Loschi vicentino* (Padua, 1858), pp. 171f. On Saviozzo's praise for Ladislaus on the same score, see N. Sapegno, *Il Trecento* (Milan, 1934), p. 473. If Cutolo had considered these facts from the history of contemporaneous publicism, he might have modified his verdict.

¹² Uzzano's opinion, given in a meeting of June 4, 1414, is reproduced in *Archivio Storico Italiano*, ser. VII, vol. XVII (1932), 82. The speeches of the members of the peace party and the rejoinders

by Corsini and Capponi, all in a meeting on May 17, are published in *Commissioni di Rinaldo degli Albizzi*, vol. i, pp. 235-237. C. S. Gutkind, *Cosimo de' Medici* (Oxford, 1938), p. 52, ascribes Capponi's exclamation "melius esset sub Ciompis esse . . ." to an alleged deathbed speech of Capponi, but this speech seems to have sprung from the author's fancy.

[13] *Commissioni*, vol. i, pp. 235f.

[14] These facts are assured by a simultaneous entry in the trustworthy *Diario Fiorentino di Bartolommeo di Michele del Corazza, 1405-1438*, published in *Archivio Storico Italiano*, ser. v, tom. xiv (1894), p. 253.

[15] *Commissioni*, vol. i, p. 239 (*Consulta* of June 26th).

Since the most likely place where a present-day student may become familiar with these events is the biography of Agnolo Pandolfini in Vespasiano da Bisticci's *Vite di Uomini Illustri del Secolo XV*, and since Vespasiano attributes to Pandolfini as one of his undying merits that he was courageous enough to win for Florence a safe and lucrative peace which had been senselessly obstructed by the bellicose oligarchy of Pandolfini's day, it should be said that Vespasiano's story, written about 1490, is a fantastic novel in this as in other respects. How thoroughly the real historical situation is distorted can be gathered from the fact that Vespasiano sees the lasting attainment of Pandolfini's diplomacy in the acquisition of Cortona for Florence by a deal (ed. Frati, vol. iii, pp. 120f.). But by that time Cortona had actually been Florentine for several years, as Guasti already noted in *Commissioni*, vol. i, p. 235. Also, Capponi's fears and opposition to a pact have, in Vespasiano's description, turned into the naive and sentimental story that the ruling optimates had been planning to execute Pandolfini after his return —a plan secretly communicated to Pandolfini by a peasant; only the general rejoicing, and the gratitude of large groups of the citizenry to the man who had done so much to promote peace, forced the optimates to abandon their evil design. (Vespasiano da Bisticci, *op. cit.*, pp. 123f.). Examples like this fable are a reminder of the extent to which the political face of early Renaissance Florence is bound to be distorted as long as we see it through the eyes of the artistically alluring authors of the late Renaissance, who wrote in a changed political atmosphere long after the events.

[16] Bruni, *Rerum Suo Temp. Gest. Comm.*, pp. 441, 443.

[17] ". . . nostra aetate potentia immodice adauctus, et cum potentissimo Mediolanensium duce et cum Ladislao bellicosissimo rege ita contendit, ut ab Alpibus in Apuliam, quantum Italiae longitudo protenditur, cuncta armorum strepitu quateret, ac transalpinos insuper reges magnosque exercitus ex Gallia et Germania commoveret. Accedunt ad haec Pisae captae; quam ego urbem . . . alteram Car-

thaginem . . . appellarim. . . . Haec mihi perdigna litteris et memoria videbantur" (Bruni, *Historiae*, p. 3).

[18] See the *Capitula Pacis cum Duce Mediolani* in *Commissioni*, vol. II (Florence, 1869), pp. 232ff., and the supplementary material in F. T. Perrens, *Histoire de Florence*, vol. VI (Paris, 1883), p. 272, n. 5.

[19] "Seems to have foretold," because these arguments are attributed to Capponi by Scipione Ammirato, *Istorie Fiorentine* (lib. XVIII, ao. 1420), who had access to archival documents since lost, but may have reshaped Capponi's speech in the light of subsequent events. The official minutes of the meetings held in 1420 have not been preserved.

[20] We know no more than this bare fact. A recent reconstruction of Uzzano's speech from notes made by Francesco Guicciardini a hundred years later remains unconvincing. See *Crisis: Appendices*, pp. 596f.

[21] For the events connected with the annexation of Genoa, cf. the still useful introductory note (pp. 20ff.) to the *Diario di Palla di Noferi Strozzi* (see note 39 below).

[22] Pandolfini in the *Pratica* of October 5, 1423, *Commissioni*, vol. I, p. 518. ("Et si Forlivium occupavit, non nobis abstulit. . . .")

[23] See the resolutions made "con somma unità," p. 375 below.

[24] Machiavelli, *Discorsi*, II 25.

[25] Rinaldo degli Albizzi, May 28, 1423; see *Commissioni*, vol. I, p. 442.

[26] Niccolò da Uzzano, May 19, 1423; *ibid.*, p. 413. The original text of the documents used here and in the notes which follow is printed in *Crisis: Appendices*, pp. 597ff.

[27] Words used in the message of the Florentine *Signoria* to Rinaldo degli Albizzi published in *Archivio Storico Italiano*, ser. IV, tom. XI (1883), p. 23.

[28] *Provvisione* of appointment of the *Dieci*, May 25, 1423, *ibid.*, p. 24.

[29] He attempts "non solum florentinam libertatem sed italicam occupare," says the document. *Provvisione* of appointment of the *Dieci*, Oct. 22, 1423, *op. cit.*, p. 300.

[30] Instruction for envoys to Milan, August 4, 1423, in *Archivio Storico Italiano*, ser. IV, tom. XI (1883), 47. Instruction for envoys to Pope Martin V, July 11, 1425, in *Commissioni*, vol. II, pp. 330, 332.

[31] Rinaldo degli Albizzi to Viero di Guadagni, October 12, 1423, in *Commissioni*, vol. I, p. 523.

[32] *Commissioni*, vol. II, p. 6.

[33] *Riformagione* (resembling a declaration of war) of March 6, 1424, in *Commissioni*, vol. II, pp. 47-49.

[34] "Dulce pacis elogium preferens . . ."; "a Florentino populo, suapte natura pacifico et tranquillo."

[35] *Ibid.*

[36] Matteo Villani, *Cronica*, esp. in the "Prologo" to lib. XI; Salutati, *Invectiva*, ed. Moreni, p. 182. The original text of these passages is printed in *Crisis: Appendices*, pp. 598f.

[37] Gregorio Dati, *Istoria*, ed. Pratesi, pp. 41, 55.

[38] *Ibid.*, p. 96.

[39] As is noted (pp. 32f.) in the *Diario di Palla (di Noferi) Strozzi*, in *Archivio Storico Italiano*, ser. IV, tom. XI (1883), which has been the basis for many of the preceding observations on the Florentine conduct in the summer of 1423. Palla Strozzi was on the board of the *Dieci* and, consequently, a first-hand witness. His central place in the political and cultural life of his time has attracted increasing attention; cf. Martines, *op. cit.*, pp. 316ff., W. H. J. Kennedy in *Studies in the Renaissance*, VII (1960), 67ff., and *Giovanni Rucellai ed il Suo Zibaldone*, a cura di A. Perosa, vol. I (London, 1960), pp. 63, 158. On Nanni degli Strozzi's personality see our last chapter, especially p. 412.

[40] ". . . che dopo la morte . . . del suo illustre padre, avendo il nostro Commune ridotta la casa de Visconti a termine, . . . si ritrasse. Dipoi più volte crescendo la potentia di questo illustre signore, essendo richiesti dovere etc., perchè desideravano vivere in pace; già mai si prestò gli orecchi, non a Cremona, non a Crema, non a Brescia, non a Parma nè a chi queste possedeano; a' quali se pur avessimo dimostrato voler dar favore, non sarebbono venute dove venute sono. . . . Nondimanco, perchè nostra natura s'inchina alla pace, fumo contentissimi. . . ." From Niccolò da Uzzano's answer to the Milanese envoys, Nov. 9, 1423, in Palla degli Strozzi's *Diario, op. cit.*, pp. 306f. The conformity of this answer with Nanni degli Strozzi's propositions is obvious and helps to explain Bruni's appreciation of Strozzi as one of the leading spirits in the struggle with Milan—the backbone of Bruni's Funeral Speech on Strozzi, as will be seen in our last chapter.

[41] See the instruction for Florentine envoys to Pope Martin V, July 11, 1425, in *Commissioni*, vol. II, pp. 328-333.

[42] See Chap. 18 and *Crisis: Appendices*, pp. 430ff.

[43] Giovanni Cavalcanti, *Istorie Fiorentine*, lib. II, cap. XXI.

[44] See Machiavelli, *Storie Fiorentine*, IV 7, a chapter which recapitulates the scene from Cavalcanti, *Istorie Fiorentine*, II 21, and Machiavelli's general judgment on the period in IV I and IV 14; in Perrens, *Histoire de Florence*, vol. VI, pp. 282-288.

[45] "Rimolatino per lo quale conforta Firenze dopo la rotta di Zagonara" by messer Antonio di Matteo di Meglio (called Antonio di Palagio), published in *Commissioni*, vol. II, pp. 75-80; and the

"Risposta" by "Ser Domenico al prefato Messer Antonio, in vice della Città di Firenze," published *ibid.*, pp. 80-85.

[46] *Op. cit.*, pp. 75f.

[47] P. 76.

[48] "Noi siam pur Fiorentini,/ Liber Toscani,/ in Tàlia specchio e lume./ Resurga il giusto sdegno per costume/ Avuto sempre a tempo,/ Nè più s'aspetti tempo;/ Perchè nel più tardar tutto è il periglio/ . . . Perchè nulla varrebbe il penter tardo" (pp. 78, 80).

[49] "Facciam danar, che bene aremo onori" (p. 81).

[50] P. 82.

[51] According to the figures of a statistical document preserved in Sanudo the younger's *Vite dei Dogi*, the revenues of Florence and Bologna were halved and that of Venice diminished by one-third during the thirty years from the early 1420's to the early 1450's. The document has been reedited in *Bilanci Generali della Repubblica di Venezia*, vol. I, tom. I (Venice, 1912; ed. L. Luzzatti), pp. 98f. Cf. the comments by Luzzatti, *ibid.*, and by C. Barbagallo in his *Storia Universale*, vol. III, 2 (Turin, 1935), pp. 1103f.

[52] In the form of the *Pratica*, an advisory meeting of *richiesti*— a type to which some of the other gatherings discussed in this chapter belonged—debating had a somewhat larger scope. But even the *Pratica* did not admit voting of any kind and is essentially characterized by what has been said about the *Consulta*. An excellent technical analysis of the proceedings in both types of advisory councils—basic agencies of Florentine constitutional life—has been given by F. C. Pellegrini in the article "Intorno ad alcune istituzioni della Repubblica Fiorentina," *Rassegna Nazionale*, XLIV (1889), 405-411. On the significance of the *Consulta* records, cf. also Felix Gilbert, *Journal of the Warburg and Courtauld Institutes*, XX (1957), 192-194, and Gene A. Brucker, *Florentine Politics and Society*, p. ix.

[53] See the extracts from the minutes of the *Consulta* on August 3, 1424, in *Commissioni*, vol. II, pp. 145-149. The passages which follow are found in their full original text in *Crisis: Appendices*, p. 602.

[54] These are reliable passages from the minutes. The fuller and rhetorically more impressive text as given by Cavalcanti, *Istorie Fiorentine*, lib. II cap. XXIII, must not be used since Cavalcanti evidently phrased the speech as he thought fit to serve *in maiorem gloriam* of Gianfigliazzi.

[55] "In adversis homines, qui liberi vivere volunt, demonstrari debentur, quoniam in prosperis unusquisque se gerit." "Virtus in adversitate perficitur; pro auro omni libertas non venditur."

[56] "Quantum maius est periculum, tanto provisio maior. Et ex-

timanda libertas ultra vitam est . . . Animus vinci non potest, nisi voluntarie."

[57] "Libertatem habere magnificat civitates et cives, ut notum est: et que sub thirannide sunt, civium sunt deserte, cum thiranni virtutes bonorum timent et omnino eos exterminant."

[58] "Quod inter cetera magna et laudabilia, que de Populo Romano scribuntur, duo memorantur: quod de adversis animum non minuerunt, et ex prosperis non sunt elati; et magnanimes fuerunt magis in adversis, quam prosperis. Lignum habere spem; et si incisus fuit, rursus frondescit et facit comam."

[59] "Tu ne cede malis sed contra audentior ito, quam tua te Fortuna sinet" (*Aen.* VI, 95f.).

[60a] "Animus reassumendus est, et viriliter incedere: et nos a Romanis originem habemus. Et sic tempore patris huius Ducis actum est, dum Bononiam occupavit. . . ."

[60b] See the description of this policy in Roberto Cessi's *Storia della Repubblica di Venezia*, vol. I (Milan, 1944), pp. 338-343.

[61] The second and third of the three speeches attributed to Tommaso Mocenigo in Sanudo's *Vite dei Dogi* (in Muratori, *Rerum Italicarum Scriptores*, tom. XXII, cols. 949-958 and 958-960). Mocenigo's alleged three speeches are usually assumed to have been delivered in January 1421, July 1421, and early in 1423. But the first speech is a forgery in its entirety (probably produced between September 1433 and August 1434), the second in its genuine parts can safely be placed in the second half of 1422, and the third falls into March/April 1423, since it was made by Mocenigo on his deathbed. These are the results reached in *Humanistic and Political Literature*, Chap. IX, "The Anti-Florentine Discourses of the Doge Tommaso Mocenigo (1422-23)." The passages to which we shall refer are from authentic sections of the second and third speech.

[62] Mocenigo, *op. cit.*, cols. 952-955 and 959.

[63] J. Burckhardt, *Die Kultur der Renaissance in Italien*, Neudruck der Urausgabe, ed. W. Goetz (Stuttgart, 1922), pp. 53f.

[64] Cf. pp. 151ff. above and the further references there given.

[65] Mocenigo, *op. cit.*, col. 952.

[66] "Ser Francesco Foscari . . . ha detto . . . ch'egli è buono lo soccorrere a' Fiorentini, a cagione che il loro bene è il nostro, e per conseguente il loro male è il nostro." Mocenigo, *loc. cit.* A furiously unrestrained, public speech traditionally supposed to have been delivered by Foscari at this time must not be used as a source, because it can be shown to be anachronistic; cf. *Crisis: Appendices*, pp. 603f.

[67] See Barbagallo's summary of these views, in his *Storia Universale*, vol. III, part 2 (Turin, 1935), pp. 1093f. Even more re-

cently, some Italian scholars have begun to reverse this trend by acknowledging the decisive role of political motives in the Venetian turnabout. Cf. the appropriate characterization in Cessi's *Storia della Repubblica di Venezia* (vol. I, pp. 363, 370f.), published in 1944, which reached conclusions (still unknown to this writer when the present chapter was written) that are in full harmony with the present analysis. Mocenigo's words, Cessi explains, were the "ultimate melancholy thought" of a period drawing to its close, when Venice, in spite of the establishment of her *terra-ferma* state, "had not yet given up the traditional prejudice of a policy of isolation." The younger generation, on the other hand, "embraced the principle of liberty and peace in Italy, which emerged . . . from . . . political equilibrium. . . . In 1397, the equilibrium had been maintained, for Venetian ends, by preserving the territorial integrity of the existing *signories* in the Venetian region; in 1425, . . . the tensions among small *signories* were replaced by the conflict among three great states: Florence, Milan, and Venice. . . . The stimulus of expansion . . . filled the Viscontean spirit with arrogance, . . . and this spirit, making defense an imperative necessity, called into life the coalition of the two great republics. . . . The liberty of Italy, which was invoked by both parties, prompted the establishment of the so-called equilibrium which was endangered by the expansion of the Visconti. . . . A higher necessity for equilibrium, and not a preconceived thirst for adventure, as Mocenigo had insinuated, drove the Venetian government into the Italian conflicts. . . ." For a consonant evaluation of Venice's intervention see N. Valeri, *L'Italia nell' Età dei Principati* (1950), pp. 425f. and 436ff.

[68] ". . . hanno et aranno quello pensiero alla conservazione del vostro stato . . . , che al loro proprio." Ridolfi to the *Decem balie*, August 14, 1425; *Commissioni*, vol. II, pp. 375f.

[69] See Ridolfi's letter of September 19, *Commissioni*, vol. II, pp. 402f. In fact, the Venetian government wrote to Filippo Maria that it looked upon the Florentines as "cari frategli," and that the intention of the new alliance with Florence was "di mantenere queste due Comunità in dolcezza di libertà" (*Commissioni*, vol. II, pp. 524f.). In a communication to the Emperor, the league with Florence was said to have been concluded "pro defensione et conservatione statuum nostrorum ac libertatis et pacificis [sic] status totius Italiae" (1426, Febr. 19; in *Rivista Storica Italiana*, v [1888], 460).

[70] See the text of the pact in *Commissioni*, vol. II, pp. 541-551.

[71] Andrea Biglia, *Historia Mediolanensis*, in Muratori, tom. XIX, cols. 78-85. For Biglia and the time of his writing cf. *Crisis: Appendices*, p. 605, note 71.

[72] Sabellico, *Rerum Venetarum Decades*, Dec. II lib. 9 (in the edition in the series "Degl' Istorici delle Cose Veneziane," tom. I, 1718, pp. 474ff.). On Sabellico and the lasting effects of the early-Quattrocento ideas on later Renaissance historiography see *Crisis: Appendices*, pp. 605f.

[73] The concept of *libertas Italiae* as the gist of Barbaro's thought and politics is described by N. Carotti (in *Rivista Storica Italiana*, ser. v, vol. 2 [1937], esp. pp. 20ff.) who refutes earlier attempts to find modern ideals of national unification in Barbaro's writings.

[74] The league had been concluded "libertatis Italiae et salutis populi Florentini, et dignitatis nostrae causa." This will compel "hunc hominem, qui nimia principandi cupiditate subigere Italiam imperio suo conatur, pacem accipere." Consequently, the common aim now is "ut Italia cum Patria tua salva sit." *Francisci Barbari et aliorum ad ipsum epistolae 1425-53*, ed. Card. A. M. Quirini (Brescia, 1743), letter no. 2, pp. 8f.; for the date, 1426, Febr. 12, see R. Sabbadini, *Centotrenta lettere inedite di Francesco Barbaro* . . . (Salerno, 1884), p. 17. On a later occasion Barbaro said: "Quia in Galliae [i.e. northern Italy's] libertate Etruriae . . . et universae Italiae quoque libertas est constituta." Ed. Quirini, *op. cit.*, no. 37, p. 52; 1437, Nov. 1 according to Sabbadini, *op. cit.*, p. 27.

[75] ". . . tamquam coacti pro conservatione status nostri ac libertatis . . . Florentie ac nostra et totius Italie, non potuimus aliter facere quod [*correctly* quam?] venire ad guerram cum prefato duce Mediolani." From a memorandum of Giuliano's on diplomatic transactions in northern Italy, in the *Secreta Senatus*, April 1426, in the Venetian Archives; quoted by S. Troilo, *Andrea Giuliano, Politico e letterato* . . . (Firenze, 1932), p. 50, n. 1.

[76a] Barbaro's letter (in Card. A. M. Quirini, *Diatriba praeliminaris . . . ad Francisci Barbari . . . epistolas* [Brescia, 1741], p. ccccxliv; the date, January 4, 1441, according to Sabbadini, *op. cit.*, p. 35) was addressed to Flavio Biondo, who was going to commemorate Barbaro's defense of Brescia in an historical narrative. He was hoping, Barbaro said, that, together with his *patria*, the *"liberi populi"* of Italy and the *"Romana Ecclesia"* would be grateful to him, "sicut pro communi libertate tam diu constantissime pugnavimus."

[76b] The impact of the restoration of Genoa's independence upon the political climate has been analyzed by G. G. Musso, "Politica e cultura in Genova alla metà del Quattrocento," *Miscellanea di Storia Ligure in onore di Giorgio Falco* (Milan, 1962), esp. 331-354; for Barbaro's letter, cf. 347-348.

[76c] *Ibid.*, p. 333.

[76d] *Ibid.*, pp. 333-334 (I read tentatively "exultabit" instead of the senseless "redundatur").

[76e] *Ibid.*, p. 334.

[77] Barbaro, *Epistolae*, ed. Quirini, no. 20, p. 33; Dec. 13, 1437, according to Sabbadini, *op. cit.*, p. 27. For Pietro del Monte's statement, and for Barbaro's, Giuliano's, and del Monte's connection with the republican approach of the Florentine humanists to history, see *Crisis: Appendices*, pp. 393f.

[78] In 1436, Manetti's *Laudatio Ianuensium ad clarissimos Ianue legatos Florentie commorantes* was dedicated by him to Genoese envoys who, after the successful Genoese revolt against Filippo Maria, came to Florence to negotiate an alliance. Eight years later, when Manetti was sent to Genoa as a Florentine envoy—the date, 1444, has been established by G. G. Musso, *op. cit.*, p. 350—Manetti transformed his sketch with the help of Genoese chronicles which he could then consult, into a larger composition approaching a concise history of Genoa, the *Laudatio Ianuensium ad illustrissimum principem dominum Thomam de Campo Fregoso Ianue ducem.* This history culminates in the political request that the supreme task of the Genoese Doge should be "defensio libertatis" in the widest sense; it could best be achieved "if you never abandon the alliance with Venice and Florence, concluded under happy auspices at the beginning of your reign." The two works are unpublished and little known. G. G. Musso, who has dealt with them (*op. cit.*, pp. 349-353) is preparing a critical edition.

[79a] See pp. 67ff. above and *Crisis: Appendices*, pp. 391ff.

[79b] Benedetto Accolti, *Dialogus De Praestantia Virorum Sui Aevi* (see note 25 to Chap. 15 above), pp. 116-120.

[80] Romanin, *Storia Documentata di Venezia*, vol. IV, pp. 213f.

[81a] Addressed to Federico Contarini. See R. Sabbadini, *Centotrenta lettere inedite . . .*, no. 129.

[81b] "Mediolanenses quoque in libertatem vocavimus et gloriosum hunc titulum praetendimus, non ut omnia subiecta nostro imperio sint, sed ut nos liberi etiam aliorum libertatis causam ageremus."

[81c] The "summa conclusionis" was "ut pacem diuturnam quam victoriam non diu duraturam, et communis libertatis gloriam quam praesens domesticorum et externorum bellorum periculum malimus et ita moderate cum sociis, cum hostibus, cum omnibus denique vivamus, ut diu principes libertatis Italiae, potius quam brevi tempore cupidi rerum novarum, auctores bellorum ac violenti domini esse haberi gloriemur."

[81d] On Cosimo de' Medici's policy in 1450-51, cf. more recently Vincent Ilardi, "The Italian League, Francesco Sforza, and Charles VII (1454-61)," *Studies in the Renaissance*, VI (1959), 129-166,

esp. 132. Ilardi's article makes a strong case for the thesis that, after Cosimo had thus laid the foundation for an equilibrium-system among the Italian states, he quickly found able followers in Pius II and especially Francesco Sforza, who between them can take chief credit for the preservation of the Italian power-balance during the latter part of the 1450's and around 1460 when the traditional pro-French policies of Florence, including those of Cosimo, were in danger of opening the door for an early French invasion into the Peninsula.

[82] For this role played by Cosimo, attested by the day-by-day reports of the Milanese envoy, Nicodemo da Pontremoli, see Perrens, *Histoire de Florence depuis la domination des Médicis,* vol. 1 (1888), pp. 120ff., 130ff.

[83] For evidence of Manetti's intercession for preservation of the Venetian alliance see *Crisis: Appendices,* p. 608, note 83.

[84] See the instructions for the Florentine envoys to the Pope, June, 1451, in Angelo Fabroni, *Magni Cosmi Medicei Vita,* vol. II (Pisa, 1788), pp. 199f.; to Charles VII, Sept. 10, 1451, in *Négotiations diplomatiques de la France avec la Toscane,* ed. Abel Desjardins, vol. 1 (Paris, 1859), pp. 62ff. ("essendo l'animo de' Veneziani di occupare Lombardia, e, col tempo, lo imperio d'Italia; e veggendo in gran parte a tal proposito la nostra Città potere ovviare . . ."); to Charles VII, Sept. 28, 1452, in Fabroni, pp. 200ff. The last quotation in the text is from Accolti (*Dialogus,* p. 119), who as an eye-witness judges that "solus Cosma" was the architect of the alliance with Francesco Sforza against Venice, whereas "magna pars Florentini populi" opposed it.

[85a] The anti-Venetian pamphlet of the 1470's is the *Lettera mandata a Vinitiani* by Benedetto Dei discussed in *Crisis: Appendices,* pp. 608f. and republished in *Archivio Storico Italiano,* cx (1952), 99ff. See *Crisis: Appendices, loc. cit.,* for Guicciardini's statements.

[85b] Simonde de' Sismondi, *Histoire des républiques italiennes du moyen âge,* vol. IX (Paris, 1815), pp. 270f.

[85c] Like Cessi in the first volume of his *Storia della Repubblica di Venezia* (see note 67 above). To Cessi it is "the evil genius of Sforza" in combination with "the expansionist Florentine policy" and Cosimo de' Medici's "diabolical astuteness" which destroyed "the noble and bold Venetian plan" of establishing peace and unification for Italy by associating the republics of Venice, Florence, and Milan (pp. 383-385). It should be noted that this latter conclusion could only be reached by omitting from the account the facts of Venice's association with Lodi and Piacenza and with Francesco Sforza—that is, the crucial events that caused the re-

orientation of Florentine politics. On Francesco Sforza's Italian policy, cf. the important rectifications by V. Ilardi in the article cited in note 81d.

CHAPTER 17

[1] See pp. 386f. above.

[2] See pp. 382f. above.

[3] See pp. 89f. and 335 above.

[4] For the colophon of the Gellius translation, October 1, 1425, see *Crisis: Appendices*, p. 610, note 4; for that of the Eusebius translation, May 11, 1426, cf. B. L. Ullman, *The Origin and Development of Humanistic Script* (Rome, 1960), p. 100.

[5] See pp. 326f. above.

[6] See Benvenuti's accusations in *Crisis: Appendices*, p. 610, note 6. Whether or not Benvenuti's interpretation of Niccoli's motives is correct, the fact that Niccoli did withdraw during the general rejoicing suggests that he had greatly exposed himself. Concerning Benvenuti's reliability cf. *Crisis: Appendices*, pp. 411ff.

[7a] See p. 258 above; according to Salutati's *Epistola XIV 19*, *Epistolario*, vol. IV, pp. 134ff. We are using the same letter in the discussion which follows.

[7b] ". . . videbis atque letabere quod hec nostra dua secula, quibus incidimus, non mediocriter emerserunt. . . . To vero et alter ille adeo vos duos malignos modernitatis estimatores exhibetis, quod non hominem homini, sed etatem etati, velut horum illorumque iudices, preferatis" (*ibid.*, pp. 132f.).

[7c] See the letters of 1425 quoted by Walser, *Poggius Florentinus*, p. 136, n. 2.

[8] "Solemus exsecrari tyrannos nos, qui nati sumus in liberis civitatibus, et profitemur nos hoc bellum suscepisse pro tuenda Italiae libertate" (*Epistolae*, ed. T. Tonelli, vol. I [1832], pp. 205f.).

[9] See p. 67 above.

[10] "Non enim unus aut alter imperat, non optimatum aut nobilium fastus regnat, sed populus aequo iure accitus ad munia civitatis. Quo fit, ut summi, infimi, nobiles, ignobiles, divites, egeni communi studio conspirent in causam libertatis."

[11] "Haec omnia accepta referimus a sola libertate, cuius diutina possessio ingenia nostra ad virtutis cultum erexit atque excitavit" (Poggio, *Opera* [Basel, 1538], p. 337). For the situation in which the letter was written, see Walser, *op. cit.*, pp. 184f.

[12] On the position of Poggio as a middleman between the particular outlook of the Florentine humanists and the more general tendencies of Quattrocento Humanism see H. Baron in *Speculum*, XIII (1938), 31ff.

[13] The following outline of Bruni's literary production from his return to Florence in 1415 to the end of the 1420's rests on a revision of the chronology of some of Bruni's works that was published in *Crisis: Appendices*, pp. 611-616. We will confine ourselves to brief references to those investigations.

[14] Cf. *Crisis: Appendices*, p. 611, note 14. For the dates of books v and vi see note 4 to Chap. 18.

[15] *Ep. X 25;* May 27, 1418. See pp. 281f. above.

[16] Composed in 1418, or possibly in the first half of 1419. Cf. *Crisis: Appendices*, p. 611, note 16.

[17] December 1421. See *Bruni, Schriften*, pp. 166f. The attribution to 1422 by the editor of *De Militia*, C. C. Bayley, with no indication of the reasons for his dating (*War and Society in Florence* [Toronto, 1961], pp. 3 and 362), has no basis. Bayley himself adds a further manuscript (in the Basel University Library) which gives the earlier date. S. Bertelli correctly points out the situation in 1420-21 which occasioned the composition in December 1421 (*Rivista Storica Italiana*, LXXVI [1964], 834-836).

[18] It had been prepared by a commission whose members "could rely for this preparation on the work and aid of Leonardo Aretino, who had been selected by the commission for this purpose." Different from the *Prologo* of the preceding Statute of 1335, the *Prooemium* of the Statute approved in 1420 gives a definition of "Guelfi" that conforms to the new politico-historical ideas of Florentine Humanism. This redefinition of the historical role of Guelphism, and probably the entire *Prooemium*, may therefore be considered as Bruni's intellectual property. (As such the *Prooemium* has been used on p. 21 above.) Edited in *Commissioni*, vol. III, pp. 621f.

[19] 1416-17; see *Bruni, Schriften*, p. 164. But note that the *Praefatio* to Pope Martin V and the *Praemissio* explaining Bruni's translation method were not prefixed until March 1419 or not much earlier. This follows from a letter of Bruni's to Sicco Polentone of March 31, 1419, published by L. Bertalot in *Archivum Romanicum*, XV (1931), 323. Cf. also E. Francheschini in *Medioevo e Rinascimento. Studi in onore di Bruno Nardi*, vol. I (Florence, 1955), 299.

[20] Between February 1420 and March 1421. The information given in *Bruni, Schriften*, pp. 164f., must be implemented and corrected according to the conclusions reached in *Humanistic and Political Literature*, pp. 166ff., "The Genesis of Bruni's Annotated Latin Version of the (Pseudo-) Aristotelian *Economics* (1420-21)."

[21] Probably in March 1417. See the discussion in *Crisis: Appendices*, p. 613, note 21.

[22] Summer 1423. *Ibid.*, note 22.

[23] Between the middle of 1423, and April 1426. Comparison with Bruni's other literary occupations during the same period allows the dating of *De Studiis et Litteris* in "1422/1429" (*Bruni, Schriften*, pp. 169ff.) to be reduced to this briefer span of time.

[24] Bruni's translations of Plutarch's *Vita Sertorii* and *Vita Pyrrhi* and Plato's *Epistolae*, which according to former assumptions might have been written as late as this period, can be shown to have originated as early as about 1410 according to the discussion in *Crisis: Appendices*, pp. 614f.

[25] Written between the middle of 1424 and the middle of 1426. See *Crisis: Appendices*, pp. 615f.

[26] 1402 to the spring of 1406. See the section "Florentine Sentiment in Bruni's Early Curial Period," pp. 245ff. above.

[27] 1415 to about 1421. See pp. 370 and 409f. above.

[28] On Bruni as chancellor, and on the nature of his public activities, we have the competent analysis in D. Marzi, *La Cancelleria Fiorentina* (Rome, 1910), pp. 188-198, now complemented by E. Garin's suggestive, interpretative chapter, "I Cancellieri Umanisti della Repubblica Fiorentina da Coluccio Salutati a Bartolomeo Scala," forming part of Garin's *La Cultura Filosofica del Rinascimento Italiano* (Florence, 1961). On the whole, Garin is inclined to attribute the most complete fusion of political and literary activities to Salutati, whereas in Bruni's life he sees an already incipient narrowing toward the merely scholarly pursuits of *literati*. In view of what we have observed—especially in Chapters 5 and 7—regarding Salutati's vacillations and inconsistencies, it would appear that the accents should rather be reversed.

CHAPTER 18

[1a] See pp. 378f. and 380 above.

[1b] For the background and the genesis of the panegyric of 1428, see "The '*Oratio Funebris*' on Nanni degli Strozzi': Its Date and Place in the Development of Bruni's Humanism," *Crisis: Appendices*, pp. 430ff.

[2] The parallelism of the two works is emphasized by their titles, since the oration on the Strozzi, in most early manuscripts and in Bruni's obituaries by Manetti and the Anonymous (see note 49 to Chapter 3), is called a "Laudatio"—*Laudatio Johannis Strozzae Equitis Florentini*. In spite of the conformity of this usage by contemporaries with Bruni's own usage in the Strozzi oration ("Laudationem vero illius merito congruentem . . . parare . . . conemur"), it is, however, for practical purposes preferable not to duplicate the essential word for reference, but to distinguish Bruni's *Laudatio* from his *Funeral Speech* (*Oratio Funebris*) on Nanni degli

Strozzi. As early as the end of the Quattrocento, Vespasiano da Bisticci, in composing a list of Bruni's works for his biography of Bruni, gave the title as *Orazione nella morte di messer Giovanni Strozzi* (ed. Frati, vol. II, p. 32), and the editors of the only printed edition of the speech—E. Baluze in his *Miscellaneorum . . . Hoc est, collectio veterum monumentorum,* vol. III (Paris, 1681), pp. 226ff., and G. D. Mansi in his *Stephani Baluzii Tutelensis Miscellanea novo ordine digesta . . . ,* vol. IV (Lucca, 1764), pp. 2ff.— by fusing the titles of the two manuscripts they followed, adopted the form *Oratio in funere Nannis Strozae Equitis Florentini.* It seems desirable that Bruni's work should continue to be cited in this familiar fashion because the speech is, and is meant to be, a Florentine counterpart to Thucydides' *Funeral Oration* of Pericles, and will be most adequately appraised when known under the same historic title as Bruni's *Funeral Oration.* For more accurate information on the manuscripts and the phrasing of the title cf. *Crisis: Appendices,* pp. 617f.

³ On this letter (already mentioned in notes 46 and 48 to Chap. 6), written by Bartolomeo della Capra, Archbishop of Milan, see R. Sabbadini, *Il Metodo degli Umanisti* (Florence, 1920), pp. 83f., and *Crisis: Appendices,* p. 432.

⁴ The completion of lib. v and VI, and the publication of lib. I-VI of the *Historiae Florentini Populi* must both fall between autumn, 1426, when Bruni returned from his diplomatic mission to Pope Martin V, and the first weeks of the year 1429. See the detailed discussion in *Crisis: Appendices,* pp. 618f.

⁵ "Florentini nuper in scriptis sua gesta redigi fecerunt sex libris distincta; Veneti etiam sua scripta componunt . . . , qui quidem quanto sua facta extollent, tanto et veteres et novas actiones nostras obscurare conabuntur. Leonardus Aretinus habuit pridem funebrem orationem pro Johanne Stroza equite florentino, quo quantum Principi quantumque patrie nostre detrahat non ignorant qui legerunt" (from the letter cited in note 3 above).

⁶ Thucydides, *The History of the Peloponnesian War,* II, 37 and 41. "The school of Greek culture" for τῆς Ἑλλάδος παίδευσις is G. Highet's rendering in his English translation of W. Jaeger's *Paideia,* vol. I (New York, 1939), p. 408.

⁷ Contemporary objections to Bruni's *Laudatio* are found in Pier Candido Decembrio's *De Laudibus Mediolanensis Urbis Panegyricus;* cf. *Archivio Storico Lombardo,* XXXIV (1907), 38f. For the growth of Bruni's historical thought from the *Laudatio* to the *Historiae* see pp. 64f. and 73f. above.

⁸ Ed. Baluzius, p. 3.

⁹ *Ibid.*

¹⁰ Pp. 139ff. above.

[11] "In omni principe populo" (*Laudatio*, L fol. 155v; ed. Klette, p. 104).

[12] "Denique studia ipsa humanitatis, praestantissima quidem atque optima, generis humani maxime propria, privatim et publice ad vitam necessaria, ornata litterarum eruditione ingenua, a civitate nostra profecta per Italiam coaluerunt" (ed. Baluzius, p. 4).

[13] The originality of Bruni's interpretation of Florence's cultural mission emerges from comparisons with the ancient city eulogies which Bruni may have remembered. Cf. the Greek praises of "Athens the schoolmaster of Greece" in Th. E. Burgess' study (see note 5 to Chap. 9), p. 152.

[14] As such it should be added to the sources collected in W. K. Ferguson's *The Renaissance in Historical Thought* (1948).

[15] Ricuperata di poi la libertà de' popoli italici per la cacciata de' Longobardi . . . , le città di Toscana e altre cominciarono a riaversi ed a dare opera agli studi ed alquanto limare il grosso stile. E così a poco a poco vennero ripigliando vigore," until Petrarch "rivocò in luce l'antica leggiadria dello stile perduto e spento" (*Bruni, Schriften*, p. 64f.; ed. Solerti, *op. cit.*, p. 289f.).

[16] For Florentine late-Quattrocento theories of the dependence of the flowering of literature and art on political freedom see *Crisis: Appendices*, pp. 621f.

[17] "Forma rei publicae gubernandae utimur ad libertatem paritatemque civium maxime omnium directa, quae, quia aequalissima in omnibus est, popularis nuncupatur" (*Oratio in Funere Nannis Strozae*, ed. Baluzius, p. 3).

[18] ". . . libertas, sine qua nunquam hic populus vivendum sibi existimavit" (*Laudatio*, L fol. 152v; ed. Klette, p. 98).

[19] "Sed ne ipsi legum vindices in summa potestate constituti arbitrari possint non custodiam civium sed tyrannidem ad se esse delatam, et sic, dum alios cohercent, aliquid de summa libertate minuatur, multis cautionibus provisum est. Principio enim supremus magistratus, qui quandam vim regie potestatis habere videbatur, ea cautela temperatus est ut non ad unum sed ad novem simul, nec ad annum sed ad bimestre tempus, deferatur" (*Laudatio*, L fol. 152v; ed. Klette, p. 99).

[20] *Laudatio*, L fol. 154v-155r; ed. Klette, p. 103.

[21] "Aequa omnibus libertas . . . ; spes vero honoris adipiscendi ac se attollendi omnibus par, modo industria adsit, modo ingenium et vivendi ratio quaedam probata et gravis. Virtutem enim probitatemque in cive suo civitas nostra requirit. Cuicunque haec adsit, eum satis generosum putat ad rem publicam gubernandam. . . . Haec est vera libertas, haec aequitas civitatis: nullius vim, nullius iniuriam vereri, paritatem esse iuris inter se civibus, paritatem rei publicae adeundae. . . . Atque haec honorum adipiscendorum

facultas potestasque libero populo haec assequendi proposita mirabile quantum valet ad ingenia civium excitanda. Ostensa enim honoris spe, erigunt sese homines atque attollunt; praeclusa vero, inertes desidunt; ut in civitate nostra cum sit ea spes facultasque proposita, minime sit admirandum et ingenia et industriam plurimum eminere" (ed. Baluzius, p. 3f.).

[22] Buonaccorso da Montemagno of Pistoia was a man about twenty years younger than Bruni and like him a newcomer from the Florentine territory to the intellectual middle-class of Florence. Again like Bruni he became a Florentine in spirit by his own choosing; he taught jurisprudence at the Florentine University and was employed in Florentine diplomatic missions abroad—activities which he preferred to the high offices in his native Pistoia to which he had been elected. His premature death in 1429 prevented him in the end from legally becoming a Florentine citizen. Since Buonaccorso was only 37 or 38 years old when he died, his *Disputatio* can hardly have been written very long before the 1420's; and since comparable Florentine literary documents that impugn mere privilege of birth, or insist upon the right of social ascent, do not fall before the late 1420's or early 1430's, it is most probable that the *Disputatio* was not written until shortly before Buonaccorso's death. That this work may be considered a product of the school of Bruni's civic Humanism is not only indicated by its tenor and line of thought, but also suggested by the somewhat embarrassing fact that in an unusual number of the manuscripts the work is ascribed to Bruni. For varied interpretations of the ascription of the work to Bruni cf. *Crisis: Appendices*, pp. 623f. There also exists an early fifteenth-century translation into the Volgare. The second half of the work—the plea of the plebeian—has been edited in E. Garin's *Prosatori Latini del Quattrocento*, in both the Latin and the Volgare versions, based chiefly on Casotti's still indispensable edition of 1718, but substantially corrected according to a few good Florentine manuscripts.

[23] This dependence does not seem to have been mentioned by any student, but the similarities between Buonaccorso's plebeian and Sallust's picture of Marius are so unmistakable there can be no doubt that Sallust served Buonaccorso as a model.

[24] "Sic itaque mortalium animus est: purus quidem ac liber ad suscipiendam nobilitatem ignobilitatemque dispositus. Nemo in hoc optimo et praestantissimo munere, humanitatis naturae largitionem accusare potest" (ed. Garin, p. 144). "Qui non sit clarus, se ipsum accuset; inique de fortuna queritur [preferable to Garin's reading, "quaeritur"]" (ed. Garin, p. 162). "Etenim cum intelligerem

praeclariora tum [so in numerous MSS; preferable to "tantum" in the printed editions] fore mortalium ingenia cum ad rempublicam accommodantur, totum me meac patriae concessi" (ed. Garin, p. 156).

[25] For bibliographical references concerning the vicissitudes of Buonaccorso's work, see *Crisis: Appendices*, pp. 625 ff. A more recent study of Tiptoft's translation and Medwall's play, by Rosemond J. Mitchell ("Italian *Nobilità* and the English Idea of the Gentleman in the XV Century," *English Miscellany*, IX [1958], esp. 32-37) confirms the judgment that in view of Medwall's performance "it would seem that English society was not yet ready to adopt Renaissance culture in its entirety." On the relationship of Tiptoft's translation to Mielot and the Latin original, cf. *ibid.*, 31 f.

The most important and comprehensive presentation of the gradually developing parallels to Italian "civic Humanism" in Renaissance England is now Arthur B. Ferguson, *The Articulate Citizen and the English Renaissance* (Duke Univ. Press, 1965); it points to Buonaccorso's role on pp. 36 f.

[26] Thucydides II, 37. Translation is that by B. Jowett.

[27] See p. 207 above and *Humanistic and Political Literature*, Chap. VIII, "An Epistolary Description by Bruni of the Florentine Constitution in 1413," where the letter is published.

[28] "Leges igitur nostre omnes ad hoc unum tendunt ut paritas sit et equalitas inter se civibus; in quo est mera ac vera libertas."

[29] "Nituntur enim leges nostre supereminentiam singulorum civium quantum fieri potest deprimere et ad paritatem mediocritatemque reducere."

[30] "Est enim hoc mortalibus natura insitum, ut via ad amplitudinem honoresque exposita, facilius se attollant; praeclusa vero, inertes desideant. Tunc igitur imperio ad Romanos traducto, cum neque honores capessere neque maioribus in rebus versari liceret, Etrusca virtus omnino consenuit longe plus inerti otio quam hostili ferro depressa" (*Historiae*, ed. Santini, p. 13).

[31] Cf. note 21 above.

[32] That Bruni's estimate of the role of liberty in the Florentine constitution was the product of political experience deserves emphasis for an understanding of his originality, in view of the fact that praise of "liberty" and of the institutions of the eulogized city was in itself nothing new, but had been a common topic of ancient city eulogies, especially in commendations of Athens. Cf. Th. C. Burgess (see note 5 to Chap. 9), p. 153.

[33] The date of Uberto Decembrio's *De Re Publica* is 1420, or not much later, according to M. Borsa, *Giornale Ligustico di archeologia, storia e letteratura*, XX (1893), 101 f. Borsa, *ibid.*, gives the

only available survey of the contents of the work, which seems to have been preserved merely in the manuscript Bibl. Ambrosiana B 123 sup. The following quotations are from two sections dealing with the selection of "custodes" by the prince, fol. 90r and 94r-95r; cf. *Crisis: Appendices*, p. 628. A few introductory paragraphs of the work have been recently published by E. Garin (*Medioevo e Rinascimento. Studi in onore di Bruno Nardi*, vol. 1 [Florence, 1955], pp. 345-347), passages which, says Garin, show that it was the gist of Decembrio's efforts to put in place of the medieval Plato, who had been "un teorico del sistema del mondo," a "Platone costruttore di uno stato razionale ed educatore del genere umano." This characterization tallies well with the observations that follow.

[34] "Repugnare etenim nature nemo feliciter potest. Quinymo more Gigantum pugnare cum diis asseritur" (fol. 90r). "Agat tamen unusquisque quod sibi proprium natura indulserit; . . . ut unusquisque proprium suum agat nec ad impropria se divertat, si forent etiam meliora. Grave est enim, ut sepe dixi, nature repugnare, et contra aquarum, ut aiunt, impetum enatare, cum secundo fluxu longe felicius vehi queat" (fol. 94r-94v). If the Prince, in his selection of the "custodes" of the state, allows himself to be guided by this knowledge, he will achieve "ut status sue rei p. utili stabilique regula gubernetur. Isto etenim ordine naturam suam singuli conservabunt" (fol. 95r).

[35] "Nam si nobile electumque ingenium vili ministerio nutrietur, non in proficuum, sed in malignum et reprobum effectum potius commutabitur. Ut enim in electis generosisque seminibus accidit, si in alienum et difforme eisdem solum transferuntur, a priori natura degenerant, deterioraque nascuntur, sic talium ingenia preter naturam translata nonnumquam proditiones accutissimas, coniurationes pestiferas et alia exquisita scelera meditantur, ad que natura rudiores aspirare nequirent. Rude etenim ingenium, ut ad bonum tardum inspicitur, sic ad perniciem obtussum redditur et ignavum" (fol. 94v).

[36] For the Latin text cf. *Crisis: Appendices*, pp. 629f.

[37] For the date of Bruni's Greek description of the "Politeia" of the Florentines (Περὶ τῆς πολιτείας τῶν Φλωρεντίνων) see *Crisis: Appendices*, p. 630. A Latin translation is in *Filippi Villani Liber* (see note 33 to Chap. 3), pp. 94-96.

[38] "Antiquitus siquidem populus cum armis in bellum exire . . . solebat. . . . Civitatis potentia maxime in multitudine erat, eamque ob causam populus primas obtinebat, adeo ut nobiles ferme omnes e Republica submoveret. Procedente vero tempore bellicae res conducto milite magis geri coeperunt. Tunc vero urbis potentia non in

multitudine, sed in optimatibus et divitibus consistere visa est, quo pecuniam in Rempublicam conferrent et consilio magis quam armis uterentur. Hoc pacto attrita sensim populi potentia in hanc quam obtinet formam Respublica deducta est" (*ibid.*, p. 96).

[39] "Florentinorum igitur Respublica neque optimatium tota est neque popularis, sed ex utraque forma commixta. . . . Extrema declinans haec Civitas mediae sortis homines recipit. Attamen ad optimates potius, et ditiores, non tamen ultra modum potentes, inclinat" (*ibid.*, p. 94). "Cum vero mixta Respublica sit, non a ratione abhorret, quaedam habere quae in popularem statum, quaedam vero quae in paucorum potentiam magis vergant. Popularia quidem illa. . . . Rursus ad optimatium statum tendunt multa. De omnibus quippe antea consulere, neque aliquid ad populum referre quod prius probatum non fuerit, et haec ipsa immutare populo non licere, sed opus esse probare simpliciter vel reiicere, maxime ad optimatium potentiam conferre mihi videtur" (*ibid.*, p. 96).

[40] *Arte della Guerra*, historical excursus at the end of lib. II.

[41] Giannotti, *Della Repubblica Fiorentina*, lib. III c. 5, lib. IV c. 7. "All active citizens," under the conditions of the Renaissance city-state, of course means those who possess "lo stato," i.e. the full citizen-rights—a group which excludes some of the lesser guilds and the laborers in the Florentine industries.

[42] It is to be noted that the first six books of the *Historiae* are not at all concerned with the Visconti; therefore, the fear of the Milanese must have been directed against Bruni's philosophy of history and his reading of the Italian past, as they emerge from the *Historiae*.

[43] *Oratio in Funere*, ed. Baluzius, p. 3.

[44] A history of these early Renaissance ideas and ideals of citizen-soldiership has never been attempted. Historians begin to pay attention to this aspect of Florentine thought only when they reach the time of Savonarola, or even not until they have to deal with the immediate background of Machiavelli. The consequence is one of the customary misconceptions concerning the civic attitude in the early Quattrocento. The evidence discussed on the following pages (it could be enlarged by moving the focus of attention outside of Bruni's circle and the humanistic school) should be sufficient to prove that here again is a chapter that can and must be added to a history of Florentine thought during the period of the Viscontean menace.

Postscript for the Revised, One-volume Edition: A history of the Florentine "militia tradition" and its ideas from Bruni to Machiavelli has now been supplied in C. C. Bayley's *War and Society in Renaissance Florence: The "De Militia" of Leonardo*

Bruni (Toronto, 1961). But Bayley's study places Bruni and the subsequent developments somewhat out of focus. It uses as a starting-point Bruni's *De Militia*, a treatise on the origin and nature of knighthood, which only indirectly (by its analysis of ancient military conditions) throws any light on Bruni's "militia" ideas. Bayley does not mention two appropriate sources, the *Preface* to the translation of Plutarch's *Sertorius* which expresses Bruni's criticism of the *condottieri* most forcefully, and the *Funeral Oration on Nanni degli Strozzi*, Bruni's apotheosis of a citizen-soldier. Nor does Bayley sufficiently point out the influence on Bruni and Palmieri of their views of ancient and Florentine history or make any effort to ascertain whether the non-Florentine late-Quattrocento writers, whose writings he analyzes in reconstructing the development of ideas from Bruni to Machiavelli, were in any contact with the Florentine environment. Also, though helpful through the material he assembles, Bayley's account is often not abreast of present knowledge. To mention only two instances, he erroneously contends, referring to a then unknown part of the *Annales*, that Salutati was guided by ideas of Tacitus (pp. 198, 202), and he knows Bruni merely as the author of one *Dialogus*, not of two *Dialogi* (see also note 17 to Chap. 17 above). Under these circumstances, the pages that follow (now somewhat enlarged) should remain useful in rounding out the picture of the consequences of the early-Quattrocento crisis.

[45] "Noi, o superbo, le nostre mura defenderemo, e se fia bisogno, per la nostra libertà ruineremo nel ferro" (Cino Rinuccini, *Risponsiva* [see above note 8 to Chap. 4], p. 216). For the relationship of this threat to the actual situation in 1397, cf. *Humanistic and Political Literature*, pp. 48f.

[46] ". . . ipso populo Florentino exeunte atque armis fruente" (*Laudatio, L* fol. 149v; ed. Klette, p. 97).

[47] "Dispeream, nisi haec nostra ad illorum comparationem veluti puerilia quaedam ludicra existimare compellor, expertia ordinis, expertia disciplinae, expertia scientiae rei militaris, nunquam collatis signis dimicare ausa, sed levibus certaminibus fugisque et insectationibus instar puerorum contenta" (*Bruni, Schriften*, p. 124. On the date, see note 24 to Chap. 17).

A middleman between Bruni and Machiavelli may have been Benedetto Accolti. He talks in his *De Praestantia Virorum Sui Aevi* at length about contemporary humanists (i.e. during the 1460's) who can find nothing good in the modern "*res militaris*" compared with that of antiquity, and who accuse the *condottieri* and their mercenaries of lack of discipline and readiness to expose themselves to danger. As these critics say, "raro ab eis aliquid egregium perpetratur facinus, et nedum urbes, sed nec etiam exigua oppida seu parva castella, nisi vix atque anxie, perraro expugnantur. Nullus in eorum castris ordo, nulla prorsus vigit disciplina. . . . Unde accidit quod in magnis praeliis . . . vix decem ferro pereant [*rather* pereunt?], gravia etiam si quando imminent pericula ignavissime fugiunt . . ." (*Filippi Villani Liber* [see note 33 to Chap. 3], pp. 107f.). Another possible middleman is Enea Silvio Piccolomini, later Pope Pius II, who, during the 1450's, in his *Commentaria* on Antonio Beccadelli's (called Panormita) widely read *De Dictis et Factis Alphonsi Regis Aragonum* remarked that the alleged military prowess of *condottieri* like Piccinino ought to be measured against the fact that they lived in Italy "inter homines, qui vel fugere vel capi, quam mori malunt." "At milites Italici mercatores videntur, ut equos et arma dederint ut liberi evadant, nimirum mercatorum stipendia merentur" (*Eneae Sylvii Piccolomini Opera Omnia* [Basel, 1571], p. 475).

[48] *Ethic. ad Nic.* III. 8. 1116b.

[49] "Hic quantum inter externi militis ac civis amorem intersit, perfacile apparuit. Ceteri enim, nihil magis quam salutem propriam aestimantes, e vestigio cesserunt; hic [Strozzi] autem caritatem patriae saluti propriae anteferens obtulit sese statim pugnae, corporeque suo viam claudere hostibus perrexit, compellans commilitones atque adhortans, hostique manu et pectore resistens, impetum omnium aliquandiu sustinuit" (*Oratio in Funere,* ed. Baluzius, p. 6).

[50] *Bruni, Schriften,* pp. 52f.

[51] "Hoc profecto nil aliud fuit quam propriam domesticamque multitudinem imbellem efficere, ut alios suarum fortunarum inspiciat defensores, ipsa vero nec defendere sese, nec pugnare pro patria sciat" (*Historiae,* ed. Santini, p. 186).

[52] "L'effecto è che in tutti i passati secoli non si truova alcuna città essere divenuta degnissima, se non con la virtù et colle proprie mani de' suoi cittadini. I cittadini sono quegli che desiderono l'onore, la gloria, la riputatione et habondante imperio della città. I cittadini appetiscono la conservatione, la salute, lo stato et mantenimento d'ogni loro bene, et, quando che sia, cercano la pacie, tranquillità et riposo di loro, de' loro figluoli et di tutte loro cose. I soldati condotti contro l'honore proprio antepongono, et sopra ogni cosa il prezo amano. . . . Rade volti l'antiche potentie conducevano soldati, se non necessitati da gravi danni ricevuti et da timore di pericolo gravissimo; et colle proprie persone feciono aquisti grandissimi, come si vede de' Romani, Cartaginesi, Ateniesi et molti altri. Et similemente nella nostra città quasi tutto quello si possiede, fu colle proprie mani de' nostri antichi padri conquistato" (*Della Vita Civile,* Bibl. Naz. II, IV, 81, fol. 92r-92v; cf. ed. Battaglia, p. 156).

[53] ". . . quali exerciti sieno migliori, o di soldati mercennarii et per prezo condotti, o veramente di proprii cittadini ragunati" (*Della Vita Civile*, MS. Florence Bibl. Naz. II, IV, 81, fol. 92r; cf. ed. Battaglia, p. 156).

[54] Stefano Porcari, *Orazione IV*. Ascribed to Buonaccorso da Montemagno in *Prose del Giovane Buonaccorso da Montemagno*, ed. Giuliari, "Scelta di Curiosità Letterarie," dispensa 141 (Bologna, 1874), pp. 55f.

[55] *Ibid.*, pp. 57f. and pp. 56f.

[56] ". . . i quali sempre colle proprie arme principalmente combattevano, reputandosi quasi a vergogna, che delle vittorie romane fosse cagione altri che i propri cittadini" (*ibid.*).

[57] For Porcari's discussion, in his orations, of many themes that at that time were uniquely characteristic of Florentine civic literature, see H. Baron, *La Rinascita*, I (1938), 62-64, and *Speculum*, XIII (1938), 22.

[58] Cristoforo Landino, *Carmina Omnia*, ed. A. Perosa (Florence, 1939), pp. 98f. Referred to by Bayley, *War and Society*, p. 226.

[59] Benedetto Accolti, *De Praestantia*, pp. 107f.; see note 47 above.

[60] Accolti, *op. cit.*, pp. 115f.

[61] *Ibid.*, pp. 112-114.

[62] Cf. F. Battaglia, *Enea Silvio Piccolomini e Francesco Patrizi: Due Politici Senesi del Quattrocento* (Florence, 1936), esp. pp. 89f., 101f.

[63] Francesco Patrizi to Nicodemo Tranchedini, "Ex Pistorio III° Kal. octobris 1457," relating from Pistoja "ut complures Florentini cives quotidie huc accedant, pestilentemque urbem relinquant." Subsequently a description of Patrizi's exchanges with these citizens. (Biblioteca Riccardiana, Florence, cod. 834, fol. 28.) Patrizi to Tranchedini, "Rome, die XXIII. Martii 1460": hopes that his appointment to the bishopric of Gaeta will not for long separate him "a consuetudine plurimorum Florentinorum civium, quos mihi amicos feci." "Magnifico Cosmo [de' Medici] hec ut communices, oro, et filiis suis excellentissimis, quos quidem tanti facio quanti parentes meos observantissimos" (*ibid.*, fol. 30b-31a).

[64] A. Luzio and R. Renier in the *Giornale Storico della Letteratura Italiana*, XIII (1889), pp. 431ff.

[65] This may be gathered from the fact that, in *De Optimo Cive*, Cosimo de' Medici is made to recommend to young Lorenzo that he use these two men as friends and councilors: "Habes Donatum Acciolum, habes Alemannum Renocinum, aliosque complures, quorum doctrina et peritia publicis privatisque in rebus uti pro arbitratu tuo poteris" (*De Optimo Cive*, ed. F. Battaglia, "Scrittori Politici Italiani," vol. 14 [Bologna, 1944], p. 199).

[66] This includes that Platina continued to defend the preeminence of the *vita activa* over the *vita contemplativa*. Cf. Platina's dedication of *De Optimo Cive* to Lorenzo de' Medici, ed. Battaglia, pp. 179f., and Battaglia's comment in his introduction, p. lxii.

[67] Pasquale Villari, *La Storia di Girolamo Savonarola*, vol. 1 (Florence, 1882), pp. 405ff.; Oreste Tommasini, *Niccolò Machiavelli*, vol. 1 (1883), pp. 343ff.

INDEX

(Numbers in parentheses refer to notes. Modern authors are listed for important references or in case of controversy.)

Acciaiuoli: Angelo degli, Cardinal, 249; Donato degli, 437

Accolti, Benedetto, 347, 396, 401, 435-437, 537(25), 550(79b), 551(84), 561-562(47)

Adige valley, 36

Alberti: family, 82; Leon Battista, 335, 343, 348-350, 352, 533 (14), 537(28c), 538(31); see also Regole della Lingua Fiorentina

Albertini, R. von, 465(1)

Albizzi: Maso degli, 43; Rinaldo degli, 374, 375-376, 544(27)

Albornoz, Cardinal, 17

Alfonso, King of Naples, 363

Alighieri, Dante, see Dante

Alps, 22, 36, 181, 203, 388

Ammirato, Scipione, 544(19)

Ancona, March of, 13

Anjou: House of, 96, 98; Charles, 97

antiquity in humanistic imitation and evaluation, 3-4, 175-176, 192-196, 229-232, 249-250, 329-331, 412-413, 420-426, 430-435; see also Classicism; Athens; Rome, ancient

Antonio di Mario, 405

Apennines, 15, 16, 22, 27, 31, 33, 37, 39, 174, 195, 219, 365, 367, 371, 373, 378, 388

Aquinas, Saint Thomas, 55, 199, 306

Arbia, see Montaperti, Battle of

Aretino, Leonardo (Bruni), see Bruni, Leonardo (Aretino)

Arezzo, 22, 248, 252, 360

Aristides, Aelius, 192-195, 283, 413, 504(5)

Aristotle, 148, 252, 289, 304; in Niccoli's critique of Scholasticism, 48, 234-235; *Analytica Posteriora* trans. by Rossi, 324; *"Economics"* trans. and annotated by Bruni, 410, 509-510(10), 553(20); *Nicomachean Ethics* trans. by Bruni, 279, 284, 410, 431-432, 553(19)

Armagnac, Jean, Count of, 177

Arno and Arno valley, 30, 182, 195, 203, 359

art of the Renaissance: analogies in humanistic literature and Renaissance art, 103-104, 156-157, 200-205, 209, 499 (27), 505(20c); late Trecento and early Quattrocento art, 3-4, 103-104, 156, 205; Quattrocento art, 156-157

Assisi, 34, 218, 360

Athens: ancient, 193-195, 250-251, 292, 352, 396, 412, 414, 415, 416, 418, 427; Duke of ("signore" of Florence), 21-22, 41, 95

Attila, see Totila

Augustine, Aurelius, Saint, 112, 113-118, 119, 126, 147, 156, 289, 296, 302, 303, 305, 306, 307, 308

Augustus, Emperor (Octavian), 55, 60, 67, 70, 76, 77, 129, 143, 144, 150, 154, 408, 477(31)

Avignon, 5, 16-18, 360

balance-of-power in the Quattrocento, see equilibrium and states-system

Balbus (in Cicero's *De Nat. Deor.*), 308

Bandini (d'Arezzo), Domenico, 59

Barbaro, Francesco, 85, 134, 394-395, 397-399, 407, 549(73)

Barnabas, Apostle, 198

Baron, H., 465-466(1, 2), 468 (9), 472-473(50), 474(7b), 478(38), 484-487, 492(45), 492-493(1), 499(27), 512-514(47), 507(4), 526(33), 528(49), 531-532(82), 541 (43), 552(12)

Bartolo da Sassoferrato, 161, 499 (32a, 33)

Basel, city, 209-211

Bath, city, 209

Bavaria, Duke of (Stephen III), 30, 177

Bayguera, Bartolomeo, 300

Bayley, C. C., 553(17), 560-561 (44)

Beccadelli (Panormita), Antonio, 414

Becker, M., 467(4b, 4g), 469 (12b)

Beda, the Venerable, 314

Bembo, Pietro, 350

Bentivoglio, Giovanni, 137

Benvenuti, Lorenzo de', 326, 328, 366, 542(10), 552(6);—Oratio in Niccolaum Nicholum, 405-406, 530(68)

Benvenuto (Rambaldi) da Imola, 477(34); and Petrarch, 499 (19, 22);—Comentum on Dante: historical ideas and historical criticism, 59, 62, 63, 99, 153-155, 475(19); date, 62, 477(34)

Bertalot, L., 507(4), 553(19)

Bertelli, S., 553(17)

Biglia, Andrea, 393, 471(29), 548(71)

Billanovich, G., 475(21)

Biondo, Flavio, 549(76a); on foundation and destruction of Florence, 72; on Volgare, 340-344, 349, 350, 535(17)

Bisticci, Vespasiano da, 72, 320, 321, 322, 529(55a, 56), 555 (2); limitations of his Vite as a source for the early Quattrocento, 543(15)

"Black Death" of 1348: 104

Boccaccio, Giovanni, aloofness from family life, 317; attitude to Dante and Giotto, 261, 317, 319, 516-517(39), 536(20d, 20e); attitude to Petrarch, 5, 261-262, 265, 266; historical place of Decamerone society, 82, 88, 275; and Tacitus, 58-59, 475(21);—on "gloria," 302; on Guelphism, 98; on monotheism of ancient poets, 297, 299, 522(10); on Volgare, 344-345;—as seen by Bruni, 293, 519(17); by Conversino, 141; by Domenico da Prato, 280; by Landino, 352; by Salutati, 255, 258;—Boccaccio's Genealogiae and Rinuccini, 291; and Salutati, 295, 523(11)

Bologna, 13, 16-17, 22, 26, 27, 29, 33, 35, 85, 94, 137, 360, 367, 368, 369, 371, 378, 400, 546(51); occupation by Giangaleazzo 1402: 39, 42-44, 186, 214, 216-218, 374, 471 (30)

Bologna, League of, 29-34, 178

Bonvesino della Riva, 196-198, 504(7)

Borghini, Vincenzo, 73

Bouwsma, W., 466(2)

Brescia, 36, 67, 300, 371, 372, 379, 394

Breve Memoria . . . di Firenze nell' anno . . . 1339 (anonymous), 206, 505(24)

Brucker, G., 467(4b, 4h), 468 (10a, 11a), 546(52)

Brunelleschi, Filippo, 3, 201, 202, 203, 334, 348

BRUNI, LEONARDO (Aretino), 3, 47, 330-331, 409, 448-449, 554(28)

Biographical, 85, 126, 245-247, 249-253, 300, 487(11), 514 (5b), 554(28); "civic Humanism" in Laudatio and

Dialogus II, 213, 242, 244-249, 290, 330; "civic Humanism" in the controversy on Themistocles' "nobilitas," 249-251; development of, 78, 243-254, 274, 280, 282-283, 286, 289-290, 291-294, 315, 320, 329-331, 370, 409-411, 412, 450, 454, 520 (23c), 531(82), 537(27); development as translator from the Greek, 87-88, 214, 226, 284; and the Volgare, 277, 283-284, 288, 333, 335, 337-348, 352, 539(39); as a Volgare writer, 541(43)

Historiography and historical methods, 6, 97-98, 142, 157, 167, 170, 172, 183, 207, 217-218, 282, 284, 362, 370, 414-418, 465(1), 475(20), 478(38), 508(14); Etruscan city-states and medieval communes *vs.* "Imperium Romanum," 65, 73-74, 98, 267-268, 417-418, 424-425, 428-429; on Roman Republic and the founding of Florence, 54-55, 58-64, 70-71, 74-75, 97-98, 195

Influence, 53-54, 66-73, 164, 268, 330, 346, 409, 512(47), 532(82), 539(39), 542 (5a); *see also* Machiavelli and Bruni

Political ideas, 427-433; on the Florentine constitution, 146, 205-209, 418-425, 427-430; on Giangaleazzo, 41, 471-472(41); on Guelphism, 20, 54, 66

and Aelius Aristides, *see* Aristides, Aelius; and Biondo, 72; on Boccaccio, 292-293; and Buonaccorso, 557(22); and Cicero, *see* Cicero, humanistic controversy on Cicero and Caesar; on Dante as a citizen, 531-532(82); *vs.* Dante's verdict on Caesar

and his assassins, 49-51, 147, 158, 281; and Dati, 168, 170-172, 205-206, 274, 278, 501(8); and Domenico da Prato, 277, 279-285, 520 (23a, 30); and Francesco da Fiano, 313; and Giovanni da Prato, 334-335; and Niccoli, 229, 233, 238-241, 244, 280-281, 286, 530(61); and Pericles' *Funeral Oration,* see Pericles' *Funeral Oration;* on Petrarch, 259-260, 262, 264-268, 280, 518(52); in Petrarch controversy of 1405-06, 254-258, 265-268; and Plato, 226, 289, 521 (38); and Polybius, 508 (14); and Poggio, 241, 246, 255, 256, 265-269; and Rinuccini, 278, 286-290, 292-293, 316, 528(48); and Salutati, 104, 147, 159, 165, 238-242, 244, 248, 250-251, 255, 269, 293, 500(39); and Tacitus, 58-60; and Vergerio, 126, 132; and Filippo Villani, 319-320

Chronology of Bruni's works and letters, 212-216, 506-507(4), 553(13), 559(37)

Carmen De Adventu Imperatoris (1397/98): 329-330, 531(79); date and manuscript, 531(79)

Dialogi (*Dial. I:* mid-1401; *Dial. II:* late 1403/early 1406, or—more probable—Aug./Oct. 1405), 47, 73, 75, 88, 228-233, 243-245, 268-269, 274, 449-450, 513-514(47); earlier interpretations, 232-234, 243, 511 (31), 512-514(47); references: to *Laudatio,* 54, 74, 192, 227; to Varro, 295; to Cicero's *De Oratore,* 229-232; earlier datings, 83, 87, 213, 214; date and composition, 226-228, 243-245, 247-

BRUNI, LEONARDO (cont.)
248, 253, 266-269, 518(54);
manuscripts and title, 227;
editions, 473(1), 511(29)
Laudatio (summer/autumn,
1403 or summer/autumn
1404), 69, 73, 75, 88, 90,
132, 172, 191-212, 239-240,
274, 283, 409, 449; earlier
interpretations, 504-505(7);
cited in *Dialogi*, 54, 74, 192;
Aristides as a model, 192-
195, 283, 413; and medieval
"Laudes," 196-198, 504-505
(7); historiographical ideas,
54-55, 58, 60-61, 63-66, 71,
74, 76, 414-415, 431; on
Volgare and "artes liberales,"
337, 416-417; on Florentine
constitution, 206-207, 418-
419, 424; civic sentiment, 48,
252-253; date, 83, 84, 87,
88, 213-225, 245, 508-509
(26); edition and manu-
scripts, 473(1), 504(4); influence, 66, 69-70, 209-211,
454, 479(41), 514(8); and
Salutati's *Invectiva*, 225
Trans. of Plato's *Phaedon*
(Sept. 1403/04-Dec. 1404/
March 1405), 87-88, 225-
226, 289, 521(38); date,
190
Trans. of Plutarch's *Vita M.
Antonii* (1404/05), 284
Laudatio in Funere Othonis
(1405, later than Aug. 8),
249-251; date, 515(12)
Trans. of Plutarch's *Vita Sertorii* (Oct. 1408/Jan. 1409),
282, 431, 435; date, 554(24)
Trans. of Plutarch's *Vita Pyrrhi* (autumn 1408/March
1412), date, 554(24)
Trans. of Plato's *Epistolae*
(Dec. 29, 1410/April 4,
1411), date, 554(24)
*Interrogatio ad Franciscum de
Fiano* (1412/25), 313-314;

date and manuscript, 527
(44)
*Epistolary description of the
Florentine Constitution in
1413*, 207, 424, 506(25b),
558(27-29)
*Historiae Florentini Populi,
Procemium and Lib. I-VI*
(1415-early 1429), 73-74,
191, 429; on ancient Rome
and Florence's origin, 60, 64,
65, 71; background and
Procemium, 172, 283, 324-
325, 370, 410-411, 415;
dates: *lib. I* (1415), 171;
lib. II (1418/19, probably
second half of 1419), *see
Crisis: Appendices*, p. 611 n.
14; *lib. III* (1420), 520
(24), 553(14); *lib. IV*
(1421), 409, 520(24), 553
(14); *lib. V-VI* (autumn
1426-early 1429), 414, 555
(4); publication of *I-VI*
early 1429, 283, 335, 555(4)
Trans. of Aristotle's *Nicomachean Ethics* (1416-17; *Praefatio* and *Praemissio* by early
1419), 279, 284, 410, 431-
439; date, 553(19)
Oratio in Hypocritas (March
1417), 410; date, 553(21)
De Primo Bello Punico (adaptation of Polybius; 1418 or
first half of 1419), 410;
date, 553(16)
*Procemium to Statute of the
"Parte Guelfa"* (1419/early
1420), 20, 410, 468(8),
553(18); date, 410, 553
(18)
Annotated trans. of the
(Pseudo-) Aristotelian *Economics* (*lib. I*: March 1420;
lib. II: Apr. 1420/March
1421), 410, 509-510(10);
date, 553(20)
De Militia (Dec. 1421), 343,
410, 432, 553(17)

Isagogicon Moralis Disciplinae (summer 1423), 410; date, 520(26), 553(22)

De Studiis et Litteris (mid-1423/Apr. 1426), 410; date, 554(23)

In Nebulonem Maledicum (i.e. Niccoli; about 1424), see *Crisis: Appendices*, pp. 411, 415, 528 n. 18

De Interpretatione Recta (mid-1424/mid-1426), 411; date, 554(25)

Oratio Funebris on Nanni degli Strozzi (autumn 1427-March/May 1428): 380, 412-424, 429-432, 455, 545 (40); date, 412; edition, 555(2); title, 554-555(2)

Canzone Morale (latter part of 1420's?), 337; date, 533 (12)

Canzone a Laude di Venere (Oct./Dec. 1429), 337; date, 533(12)

Le Vite di Dante e di Petrarca (May 1436): civic ideas, 347, 433, 531-532(82) and Volgare, 337, 338, 344-346, 404; historical appraisal of Petrarch, 267, 417, 518(52); and *Dialogi*, 233

Novella (Jan. 15, 1437), 337; date, 533(12)

Historiae Florentini Populi, Lib. IX-XII (1437/38-early 1444), 168, 171-172, 182, 274, 471(41); dates: *lib. IX* (1437/38), 172, 433; *lib. X-XII* (mid-1441-early 1444), 172, 502(10)

On the "Politeia" of the Florentines (1438/39), 427-428; date and editions, 559(37)

Commentarium Rerum Graecarum (adaptation of Xenophon's *Hellenica*; 1439), see *Crisis: Appendices*, p. 195

Rerum Suo Tempore Gestarum Commentarius (mid-1440/mid-1441), 366, 369-370; date, 502(10)

De Bello Italico (adaptation of Procopius; second half of 1441), see *Crisis: Appendices*, pp. 195, 630 n. 37

Epistola I 8 (Sept. 5, 1403, or Sept. 5, 1404), 226; date, 215, 225, 509(26)

Letter of Sept. 13, 1405, 249, 293-294

Ep. X 25 (May 27, 1418), 279, 281, 410, 553(15)

Ep. VI 10 (May 7, 1435), 305, 341-343

Brutus (Decimus Junius), 492 (42)

Brutus (Lucius Junius), the Elder, 56, 114-119, 130, 362

Brutus (Marcus Junius) and Cassius (Longinus, Gaius), 49-53, 64, 118, 119, 121, 125, 128-129, 156, 362, 474(10), 475(19), 480(43b)

Buck, A., 465(1), 531(81), 539-540(43)

Budapest, 130

Bueno de Mesquita, D. M., see De Mesquita

Buggiano, Comune of, 114

Buonaccorso da Montemagno, 420, 455, 557(22);—*Disputatio De Nobilitate:* 420-423, 557(22); and Bruni, 557(22); date and editions, 557(22); influence outside Italy, 421-423

Buoninsegni, Domenico, 469 (12b), 542(9)

Burckhardt, J., 152, 389-390, 489(11)

Burgundy, Court of, 421

Caesar, controversy on Caesar, "Respublica Romana," and "Imperium": in Middle Ages and Trecento, 57, 152-155, 475(19), 477(31); in Petrarch, 55-57, 119-120, 121,

123, 152; among Florentine humanists, 49-54, 76-77, 100, 118, 123-125, 147-150, 156-163, 243; Poggio, the Florentine, *vs.* Guarino and P. C. Decembrio, humanists at tyrant-courts, 66-70, 396, 407-408, 478-479(41), 479 (42); Caesar as seen in Siena, 362; as seen by Venetian humanists, 53, 67-69, 396; by Vergerio, 128, 133; among Visconti publicists, 37; earlier interpretations of the controversy, 475(19), 480 (43b);—debate on Caesar, or Sulla, as founder of Florence, 61-63, 71, 76, 99

Calò, G., 487(11), 494(20)

Camillus, Marcus Furius, 114, 243

Campaldino, Battle of, 433, 435

Capponi, Gino, 368-371, 542(6), 543(12, 15)

Capponi, G., 501(8)

Capo d'Istria, 126

Capra, Bartolomeo della, Archbishop of Milan, 413-414, 496(46, 48), 555(3)

Carotti, N., 549(73)

Carrara, Lords of Padua, 25, 29, 33, 37, 131-133, 136, 173, 388; *see also* Padua; Francesco II, the Elder ("il Vecchio"), 120, 127, 132, 137-138; Francesco III ("Novello"), 29, 129, 135; Jacopo, 139

Carthage, 370; *see also* Hannibal

Casalecchio, Battle of, 42

Cassius, *see* Brutus and Cassius

Castiglionchio, Lapo da, 18

Castiglione, Baldassare, 313

"Castato," Florentine, 384

Catilina, 62-63

Cato, the Younger, 77, 118, 119, 123, 125, 163, 362

Cavalcanti: Bartolommeo, 364; Giovanni, 364, 381, 384, 465(1), 545(44), 546(54)

Caxton, William, 421-422

Cecchi, Domenico, 438

Cellini, Benvenuto, 183

Cerretani, Bartolomeo, 170

Cessi, R., 547(60b), 548(67), 551(85c)

Chabod, F., 466(2)

Charlemagne, 97, 98, 154, 477 (31)

Charles IV, German Emperor, 23, 102, 120, 471(28), 492(44)

Charles VIII, French King, 97

Chaundler, Thomas, 209

Chiusi, town, 34

Chrysoloras, Manuel, 87, 126, 131, 226, 246, 320, 321, 530(61)

Chrysostomus, Johannes, 314

Church, *see* Papacy

Cian, V., 533(14), 534(15)

Cicero (Marcus Tullius), 70, 130, 263, 284, 302, 314, 341, 352; humanistic controversy on Cicero and Caesar, 67, 115, 118, 121-125, 127-129, 133, 145-151, 154, 157, 362, 466 (2), 492-493(1); quoted on decay of Rome in time of Caesar, 66, 478(41); compared by humanists with Petrarch, 258, 516(35); Erasmus on, 306-307;—his works among early humanists: *De Natura Deorum*, 307, 308; *De Officiis*, 426, 478(41); *De Oratore*, 229-231, 510 (19), 511(26), 514(47); *De Senectute*, 250; *Epistolae*, 121, 123-124, 493(6); *In Catilinam*, 64; *Orator*, 411

Cicero, Quintus, 63

"Ciompi" of 1378: 8, 109, 368

citizen-army and "condottieri," 276, 375, 378, 380, 385, 427-428, 430-439, 560-561 (44)

city-state republic in Renaissance Italy, 12-14, 24, 29, 41-42, 45-46, 68-69, 135, 138-140, 188, 276, 361, 395-396, 408,

415-419; *see also* Florence, political ideas *and* Humanism, Civic

Civic Humanism, *see* Humanism, Civic

Classicism, xxv f., 352-353; *see also* Humanism, Humanistic Classicism *and* art of the Renaissance

Claudianus, Claudius, 526(31)

Cola di Rienzo, 5, 102, 104, 119, 120, 261

Comines, Philippe de, 97, 489(11)

commune, medieval Italian, 8-9, 12, 27, 267, 276, 418

"condottieri," *see* citizen-army

Constance, Council of, 130, 312

Constantine, Emperor, 147, 154

constitutional life, humanistic interpretations of, *see* historiography, Quattrocento interpretations of constitutional life

"consulta" and "pratica" in Florence, 26, 384, 469(15a), 546(52)

Contarini, Federico, 550(81a)

Conversino (da Ravenna), Giovanni, 134-135, 144, 148, 152, 456, 494(30); attitude toward Giangaleazzo, Venice, and Florence, 68, 136, 137, 139, 140, 328, 416, 471(28), 495(40); Conversino and Salutati, 141, 148, 447, 495 (45);—*Dragmalogia*: 134-145; date, 135-136, 495 (32); manuscripts, 495(30); title, 494(30)

Corbinelli, Antonio, 321-323, 529-530(58-59b)

Corsini, Filippo, 43, 368

Cortona, city, 34, 360, 365, 543 (15)

Crema, city, 379

Cremona, city, 379

Cutulo, A., 541(2), 542(8, 11)

Croce, B., 518-519(2)

damnation of pagans, doctrine of, 304-308, 526(33)

Dante, 4, 125; political views, 24, 57, 60; on Volgare, 344, 536 (20c);—Interpretations by 14th-, 15th-, and 16th-century writers, 75, 261, 314, 317, 342, 346-347, 352, 536-537(24); in particular: Dante in Bruni's *Dialogi*, 48-50, 147, 158, 229, 234, 236, 242-243, 280, 288, 293, 512(47); Bruni's *Vita di Dante*, 331, 433, 531-532 (82); Domenico da Prato's invective, 280-281, 285; Trifone Gabriele's *Annotazioni*, 53; Giannotti's *Dialoghi*, 52-55; Landino's *Commento*, 50-51; Machiavelli's *Dialogo*, 51-52, 474(7b); Benvenuto Rambaldi's *Comentum*, 153-155; Rinuccini's *Invettiva*, 287-288; Salutati's *De Tyranno*, 100-102, 118, 147, 158; Filippo Villani's *De Origine*, 319-320

Dati, Gregorio, 157, 167, 448, 501(5); historical outlook and method, 77-78, 176-179, 201, 207, 483(65); and Bruni, 168, 170-172, 205-206, 274, 278, 501(7, 8); concept of "Fortuna," 171, 502(9); political ideas, 172-177, 179-188, 220, 358, 377-378, 469(14); on Florence after Giangaleazzo's death, 364-365;—*Istoria*: 158, 168-171, 175-176, 205-206, 213, 274, 324, 331, 472(42); earlier interpretations, 501-502(8); date, 167, 171, 500(1); editions, 500(2)

Decembrio, Pier Candido, 60, 408, 456; *De Laudibus Mediolanensium Urbis*, 69-70, 72, 209-210, 483(43l), 555(7)

Decembrio, Uberto, 38, 425, 456; —*De Re Publica*, 425-427, 558-559(33); date and manuscript, *ibid.*

Dei, Benedetto, 401, 551(85a)
Del Corazza, Bartolommeo, 543 (14)
Della Scala, *see* Scaligeri
Della Torre, A., 279, 519(13)
De Mesquita, D. M. Bueno, 469 (13)
Demosthenes, 352, 516(35)
Dido of Carthage, 49
Dominici, Giovanni, 299
Donatello, 3, 201, 205, 348, 505(20c)

Eberhard of Württemberg, Count, 422
economic conditions and attitude toward trade: in Florence, 8, 42, 44, 95, 104, 168, 177, 185, 328-329, 364-365, 377, 380, 381-384, 458, 470(19), 472(47), 488(6), 542(5b), 546(51); in Milan, 42, 44, 183-184, 186-187; in Venice, 139, 387-392, 546(51)
Einhard, *Vita Caroli Magni*, 194
Emerton, E., 497(1), 500(38)
Emilia, *see* Romagna-Emilia
Empire, medieval, 9, 16, 20-21, 36, 197; medieval idea of Universal Monarchy, 24, 48, 51, 57-58, 60-61, 65, 76, 102-103, 119, 129, 152-156, 492(44), 498(14), 445
England, 10, 67, 421-423
Ennius, 323
Ephialtes, 117
equilibrium and states-system: beginnings in the early Quattrocento, xxvi, 9-10, 13, 25-26, 29, 35, 41, 45, 173-177, 180-181, 185-186, 201, 276, 358-359, 368, 370, 374, 381-382, 390; stage reached by mid-Quattrocento, 398-403, 454, 550-551(81d); earlier interpretations, 547-548 (67); *see also* "Libertas Italiae" *and* political conditions and changes
Erasmus, 306, 307, 311

Ercole, F., 475(19), 497(1), 498(13a, 14)
"estates" in Italian states, 10, 466 (3)
Este, Marquises of Ferrara, 29, 33, 378, 408; *see also* Ferrara; Niccolò II, 137-139
Etruria, *see* historiography, city-state independence, Etruscan and medieval
Euganean Hills, 138
Euripides, 133
Eusebius' *Chronicon*, 405

Faenza, 27
Ferguson, A. B., 558(25)
Ferguson, W. K., 465(1), 478 (38), 556(14)
Ferrara, 29; *see also* Este; Humanism in Ferrara, 66
feudalism in Italy, 8-9, 10, 12; *see also* "estates"
Fiano, Francesco da, 300-303, 311-314;—*Contra Detractores Poetarum*, 301-309; date, 301, 524(19b-19d); manuscript, 524(19e);—*Responsio* to Bruni on Ovid, 313-314, 527(45); date and manuscript, 313, 404, 527 (44, 45)
Fiesole, town, 62-63
Florence: wars for independence, and policy of "libertas Italiae," xxvi, 10-13, 17-19, Chap. 2 *passim*, 90-91, 99, 173-188, 216-223, 329, Chap. 16 *passim*; policy of "libertas" of city-states in Tuscany, 22-23, 26-27, 361-364, 396, 468(10a, 11a, 11b), 469(15b, 15c), 470 (24b); constitution, 384, 546(52); for constitution, *see also* historiography, Quattrocento interpretations of constitutional life; economic conditions: *see* economic conditions, Florence; Florentine

historiography: see historiography, passim; Florentine Volgare: see Volgare and Volgare culture in the Florentine Quattrocento; literary and artistic portraiture of the city of Florence, 199-204, 505(18)

city-state society and Humanism: 4-7, 95-96, 140-142, 273-274, 417-421, 466(2); civic Humanism and political experience: xxvi, 10, 40, 45, 75-76, 78, 81-84, 87-89, 91-94, 96, 99, 105, 157, 166, 172, 204-205, 212-213, 245, 315-331, 336, 370, 387-389, 403, 404-405, 407-409, 411, 422, 425, 466(2); Florence's cultural leadership in the early Quattrocento, 6, 127, 132, 141, 190-191, 209-211, 421-423, 459, 495-496(46); phases of 15th-century Florentine culture, 350-353, 400-403, 428, 430-431, 438-439; see also: Humanism, Civic and "Vita activa" and "vita contemplativa"

political ideas: from Trecento to Quattrocento, 20-21, 24, 28, 162, 166, 315-316, 323-326; changing outlook from mid-Quattrocento, 401-402, 427-429; freedom and independence, 21-24, 41, 61, 77-78, 92-95, 184-188, 336, 361-364, 368-370, 374-387, 407-409, 414, 418-425, 468 (11a); see also: citizen-army; city-state republic; equilibrium; Guelphism and Guelphs; "libertas Italiae"; "ragione" in politics

Folena, G., 541(43)
Forlì, town, 373, 374, 376, 380
"Fortuna," conception of, 171, 502(9)

Foscari: Francesco, Doge of Venice, 391-392, 396-402, 547 (66); Marco, 97, 489(12)
France, and King of France, 10, 29, 31, 33, 96-99, 353, 359, 489(10); see also Charlemagne
Francesco da Fiano, see Fiano, Francesco da
Frascino, S., 500(38)
freedom, civic, see city-state republic
Friuli, March of, 388
(Pseudo-) Frontinus, Liber Coloniarum, 72, 482(54)
Fubini, R., 534(14)
Fueter, E., 478(38)
Fustel de Coulanges, 75

Gabriele, Trifone, 53
Gaeta, F., 522(10)
Galilei, Galileo, magister, 386
Garin, E., 466(2), 470(19), 473(1), 484(8), 489(25), 512-514(47), 522-523(10), 531(82), 554(28), 557 (22), 559(33)
Gellius, Aulus, 125, 405
Genoa, 26, 186, 371, 372-373, 376, 394-396, 471(30), 544 (21), 549(76b), 550(78)
Gentile, G., 519(2), 521(32b), 529(8)
"geometric spirit" in the Quattrocento, 197, 202
German kings, see Rupert; Sigismund; Wenceslaus
Gherardi, Giovanni, see Prato, Giovanni (Gherardi) da
Ghibellines, 9, 16, 20, 24, 36, 54, 77, 97, 468(8)
Gianfigliazzi, Rinaldo de', 385, 546(54)
Giannotti, Donato, 7, 364, 438; on Dante's verdict on Caesar and his assassins, 52-53; on Florentine constitution, 208, 429
Gilbert, F., 546(52)

Giotto, 104, 156, 261, 516-517 (39)

Giuliano, Andrea, 394, 395

Giustiniani, Leonardo, 134

"gloriae cupiditas," 114-119, 125-126, 302-303, 492(41d), 524(20)

Goldbrunner, M., 470(24b)

Gonzaga, Lords (later, Marquises) of Mantua, 29, 33, 408, 437; *see also* Mantua

Gordon, D. F., 474(10)

Gottolengo, *see* Ottolengo

Grayson, C., 534(14), 537(28c), 538(32, 33)

Greek studies, 126, 131, 284-285, 320, 321, 324, 416-417; *see also* historiography, parallel evolutions of Greek, Latin, and Volgare

Gregory the Great, 51, 53, 314

Gregory XII, Pope, 252, 360

Grosseto, town, 34

Guarini, Giovanni Battista, 71

Guarino da Verona, 3, 85, 134, 421; on Caesar and Roman Republic, 66-67, 408, 478-479(41-42)

Guelphism, Guelphs, 9, 16-24, 31, 36, 83, 96-98, 159, 165, 177, 220, 329, 444, 448, 467(4b, 4h), 468(8, 9), 471(28), 489(11); *see also* historiography, Guelphism and Roman Republicanism;—earlier interpretations, 467(4b), 468(9)

Guicciardini, Francesco: political and historical ideas, 7, 73, 208, 402, 551(85a); from early Quattrocento to Guicciardini, 151-152, 170, 438; an early-Quattrocento speech garbled by Guicciardini, 544(20)

Guidetti, Cino de', 512-513(47)

Guido da Pisa, 261, 516(38)

Guinigi, Francesco, 114

Gundolf, F., 480(43b)

Gutkind, C. S., 543(12)

Hall, V., Jr., 534(14), 539(43)

Hannibal, 55, 102, 176, 309, 329, 377

Hartt, F., 505(20c)

Hay, D., 466(2)

Hebrew language, 351

Highet, G., 555(6)

historiography and historical outlook: views for and against Dante's condemnation of Caesar's assassins, 49-54, 64, 75, 100, 118, 149, 154, 243, 475(19); "Respublica Romana" and "Imperium Romanum," 55-61, 64, 66-71, 74-78, 82, 86, 89, 102-103, 113-129, 132, 134, 140, 143-145, 148-154, 155, 160-162, 199, 242-243, 336, 361-362, 404, 408, 475(19), 478-479 (42, 43a), 483(65), 493 (1); medieval historical legends and their dissolution, 61-64, 97, 99, 153, 281-282, 446, 477(31), 478(37b); *see also* Caesar

character of Florentine historiography, 6, 46, 68, 142, 157-158, 350-351, 413-414, 496 (47), 560(42); Quattrocento historiography, 169-172, 175-179, 191, 203, 207, 288-289, 393, 447-448; from Quattrocento to late Renaissance, 465-466(1), 543(15), 549(72); *see also:* equilibrium and states-system; "Fortuna," conception of; "ragione" as standard in politics; "realism," politico-historical

city-state independence, Etruscan and medieval, *vs.* the predominance of Rome, 65, 74-75, 98, 267-268, 415, 424-425, 428-429, 556(16); Florence's foundation by republican Rome, 61-64, 71-73, 75, 76, 82, 87, 89, 99, 159, 195, 199, 415, 481-482(54),

483(65); Guelphism and Roman republicanism, 54, 66, 77, 242, *see also* Guelphism, Guelphs; liberty in Florentine history, 94-95, 99, 184-188, 221-224, 386-387, 404, 408-409

Quattrocento interpretations of constitutional life, 196-198, 205-211, 408, 418-425, 427-429, 506(25b); of the interdependence of culture with the political development, 67, 95-96, 261, 267, 273, 416-418, 556(16); of the origin and the historical right of the Volgare, 339-344, 349-350; of parallel evolutions of Greek, Latin and Volgare, 346-353, 438-439, 536-537 (24); *see also* "laudes" of cities; Petrarch, influence and Petrarchian tradition; "studia humanitatis"; Volgare and Volgare culture

Hitler, 40
Hohenstaufen, 16, 17, 21, 96, 97, 198, 360
Homer, 200, 347, 352, 516(35), 536-537(24)
Horace, 67, 143
Humanism: Humanistic Classicism, 3-4, 10-11, 47, 75, 234-235, 277, 290, 292-294, 302, 306-320, 329-330, 347, 352-353, 405-407, 451; earlier interpretations, 278;—Civic Humanism, xxvii f., 4-7, 48, 67-69, 104-105, 112-118, 127, 140-145, 242-244, 278, 328-331, 333, 337-339, 406-411, 416-423, 432-433, 451-452, 459-462, 466(2), 500(39), 531-532(82), 560(44); earlier interpretations, 275-277, 466(2), 519(5);—Humanism at tyrant-courts, 68-69, 71, 131-134, 136-145, 425-427; earlier interpretations, 276-277, 519(5), 527(46);

—during Trecento: *see* Trecento, mind of the; during Quattrocento: *see* Quattrocento, mind of the
Hungary, 130

Ilardi, V., 550-551(81d), 552 (85c)
Imola, town, 27, 376, 379, 380
Innocent VII, Pope, 225, 300, 302
Isocrates, 194
Italy, *see* political conditions; "estates" in Italian states; equilibrium and states-system: "libertas Italiae"; unification of the Italian Peninsula; national Italian sentiment; Florence; Venice; Milan; Naples; Papacy

Jacob, E. F., 506(30)
Janson, H. W., 505(20b)
Jerome, Saint, 111, 490(29, 31)
Joachimsen, P., 465(1), 478(38)
Josephus, Flavius, 154
Judas Iscariot, 49, 50
Justinian, Emperor, 118, 128

Kirner, G., 504(1), 511(37)
Klein, H. W., 534(14)
Klette, Th., 473(1)
Kristeller, P. O., 540(43)

Labienus, 123
Ladislaus, King of Naples, 325, 326, 328, 359-370, 373, 401, 405-406, 409, 410, 541(2), 542(6-12)
Lana, Arte di, in Florence, 93, 327
Landino, Cristoforo: on Dante, 50-53; the descent of Florence from republican Rome, 72, 481(49); Florentine merchants, 95; Volgare, 348, 352-353, 533(14); citizen-army, 435
Lanzoni, F., 478(37b)
Latin language, Quattrocento appraisals of, 284-285, 338-351 *passim*

Laudatio Leonardi Historici et Oratoris (anonymous), 71-72, 481(49), 554(2)

"laudes" of cities, ancient, medieval, Renaissance, 54, 58, 69-70, 74-75, 191-200, 206-207, 413, 504-505(5, 7), 556(13), 558(32)

Leghorn (Livorno), 359, 372

Leo X, Pope, 313

Lewis the Great, King of Hungary, 137

Liber Coloniarum: see Frontinus

"libertas Italiae," 30, 68-69, 390-403, 407-408, 428, 453-454, 547-548(67), 548(69), 549(73); *see also* equilibrium and states-system

Livy, 67, 70, 288-289

Lodi, town, 398

Lodi, peace of, 363

Lombardy: *see* Milan *and* Visconti, Lords of Milan

Loschi, Antonio, 37, 156, 300, 367, 471(32), 495(46), 542(11);—*Invectiva in Florentinos,* 76, 99, 100, 273, 377, 485-486; date, 90, 92; editions and manuscripts, 484(8)

Louis XIV, 353

Lucanus, 77, 125, 151, 154

Lucca, 15, 21-23, 34, 114, 218, 363, 395, 400

Lucretia, Roman matron, 115

Luiso, F. P., 215-217, 223, 506-507(4), 508(15)

Machiavelli: family, 385; Francesco, 386; Girolamo, 385

Machiavelli, Niccolò, 7, 438-439; family traditions, 385-386; —and Bruni, 70, 191, 208, 428-429, 431, 465-466(1), 481(47a), 561-562(47);— political analysis, 132-133, 151-159, 208;—views on Dante, 51-52, 474(7b); on early Quattrocento, 374, 381, 545(44); on "Fortuna,"

171; on freedom spirit in Tuscany, 303, 363-364; on history, 70, 73, 98, 170, 191

Madrignani, C. A., 528(51b), 532(82)

Malatesta, Carlo, 298

Manetti, Giannozzo: on the founding of Florence, 72; on Niccoli, 322-323, 530(60a, 61, 67c); political attitude, 395-396, 400, 551(83); on Rossi, 320, 529(55a);— *Adversus Judaeos et Gentes,* date, 529(55a);—*De Illustribus Longaevis,* date and manuscripts, 530(60a);— *Laudatio Ianuensium ad Legatos* and *Laud. Ian. ad Thomam de Campo Fregoso,* 395-396, 550(78);—Obituary on Bruni, 554(2);— *Vita Dantis,* 346-347, 352, 481(51), 532(82), 536(23, 24);—*Vita Petrarcae,* 269, 516(35); date, 536(22)

Manni, G., 500(2)

Mansion, Collard, 421

Mantua, 29, 32, 222, 281; *see also* Gonzaga

"Mantuan War," 31, 179-180, 201, 216, 218

Marcellus, Marcus Claudius, 243

Marius, Gaius, 163, 420, 557(23)

Marsepia, Queen, 143

Marsili, Luigi, 82, 96, 215, 260, 325, 488(9), 513, 530(67c), 533(10)

Marsilio di Santa Sofia, 533(10)

Martellotti, G., 492(45)

Martin, A. von, 299, 489(25), 491(38a), 497(1), 498(13a, 14), 522(10), 523(16f, 17)

Martines, L., 487(1), 514(5b), 520(32a), 528-529(54b), 529-530(55b, 59a, 59b), 531(72b)

Masaccio, 3, 348

Massa Marittima, town, 34

Mattingly, G., 473(50)

Medici: family and Medicean Principate, 163, 277, 384, 428, 438-439; Cosimo de', 4, 172, 320, 399-403, 427, 428, 551(82, 84), 550-551(81d), 563(63, 65); Giovanni de', 373; Lorenzo (brother of Cosimo) de', 394; Lorenzo ("il Magnifico") de', 53, 72, 73, 202, 203, 348, 350-352, 363, 436-438, 564(66)

medievalism, Middle Ages, 4, 8-9, 48, 61-62, 103-105, 149, 152-153, 203, 258

Medwall, Henry, 422-423, 558 (25)

Meglio, Antonio di, 382-383, 545 (45)

Mehus, L., 506(4)

Meiss, M., 104

Michelangelo Buonarrotti, 52, 474(10)

Mielot, Jean, 421, 558(25)

Milan: policy of expansion and unification of northern Italy, Chapters 2, 8, 16 *passim*; *see also* Visconti, Lords of Milan *and* Sforza, Francesco;—Milan in Bonvesino's description, 196-198, 504 (7); in P. C. Decembrio's description, 209-210;—economic conditions: *see* economic conditions, Milan;— "Respublica Ambrosiana," 396-399, 402-403;—Humanism and politico-historical literature in Milan, 5, 37, 38, 69-70, 140, 393, 408, 413-414, 425-427, 471(31-32); *see also:* Decembrio, Pier Candido; Decembrio, Uberto; Loschi, Antonio

Mitchell, R. J., 558(25)

Mocenigo, Tommaso, Doge of Venice, 389-392, 547-548 (66, 67); his speeches, 389; their dates, 547(61)

monarchy, universal, *see* empire, medieval

monotheism of ancient poets, *see* religion of ancient poets

Montaperti on Arbia, Battle of, 21

Monte, Pietro del, 67-69, 395-396, 480(43c)

Montemagno, Buonaccorso da, *see* Buonaccorso da Montemagno

Montecassino, 58-59, 475(21)

Morelli, Giovanni di Paolo, 465 (1), 472(42), 542(9)

Moreni, D., 484(8)

Mussato, Albertino, 5, 126

Mussi, Giovanni de', 38

Musso, G. G., 549(76b), 550 (78)

Naples, Kingdom of, 12, 186, 359-361, 364, 400-401

Napoleon, 40

national Italian sentiment, 36, 57, 140, 470(22), 471(28); *see also* unification of the Italian Peninsula

Neo-Platonism, Florentine, 112

Nero, Emperor, 77

Niccoli, family, 327

Niccoli, Niccolò: leader of Classicism, and the new philology, 3, 4, 59, 85, 263, 520(22); man of letters, withdrawn from civic responsibilities, 322-323, 326-329, 366, 405-406, 530(61, 68), 552(6); —on Dante and Petrarch, 229, 280-281, 292-293; on Roman Republic and Caesar, 479(43a); as portrayed in Bruni's *Dialogi*, 48-50, 228-240 *passim*, 255-269 *passim*, 277, 290, 512-513(47); relations to contemporaries: Bruni, 58, 229, 240-241, 280-281, 283, 286, 530(61); Domenico da Prato, 277-281; Marsili, 325; Poggio, 256, 406-407; Rinuccini, 277, 286-288; Salutati, 238-241, 268-269;—his guide (desiderata list) for searchers for manuscripts, 484(3), 520(22)

Nicodemo da Pontremoli, 551 (82)

Ninus, King of Niniveh, 288

Novati, F., 198, 504-505(7)

"Novi cives" in 14th-century Florence, 19

Origen, 305, 307, 314, 515(13d)

Orléans, Duke of (Louis of Valois), 31

Orosius, 491(37)

Orsini, family, 114

Ottolengo (or, Gottolengo), Battle of, 380, 412

Ovid, 143, 313-314, 527(44)

Oxford, 209

Padua, 19, 25, 27-29, 37, 85, 126, 129-131, 185, 222, 388; see also Carrara;—Paduan Humanism, 5, 68, 126-127, 129-134, 139-145, 147, 259, 361

"paganism" about 1400, 294-295, 522(8); see also religion of ancient poets

Palmieri, Matteo: attitude to Volgare, 335, 337-339, 347, 348, 352, 404; on citizen-army, 433-434, 561(44);— Della Vita Civile: 106, 330, 531(81); date, 433, 534-535(16); manuscript, 535 (16)

Pandolfini, Agnolo, 368-369, 373, 376, 543(15)

Papacy: Papal Church, 9, 15-21, 96, 128, 177, 360, 379; Papal Curia and Papal State, 12-13, 17-18, 23-24, 31, 42-44, 186, 360-361, 368, 380, 400, 469(12b); Humanism at the Curia, 85, 130, 241, 246-252, 282, 300-302, 309, 311-312, 339-340, 350, 407; see also Rome

Parma, 372, 379

Patrizi, Francesco, 437, 563(63)

Paulinus Venetus, 475(21)

Pavia, 40

Pavia, Truce of, 33, 35, 44, 91, 179, 181, 213

Pecci, Pietro de', 542(5a)

Pellegrini, F. C., 546(52)

Pericles' Funeral Oration (in Thucydides' History of the Peloponnesian War), 412-414, 416, 418, 423-424, 430

Perugia, 13, 22, 26, 34, 39, 44, 268, 360, 366, 367, 470 (24b)

Peter, Saint, the Apostle, 311, 526(40)

Petraglione, G., 507(11)

Petrarch, 5, 15, 86, 127, 138; on religion of ancient poets, 297, 299, 522(10); on Roman Republic, Cicero, and Caesar, 55-57, 60, 102, 119-124, 127-128, 148, 152, 160, 361, 498-499(19, 22);— early history of the appraisal of Petrarch, 254-268, 346, 352, 516(35), 517(43); influence, and Petrarchian tradition, in Trecento and Quattrocento, 3, 4, 113, 316-317, 347, 498-499(19, 22); in particular: in Bruni's Dialogi, 229, 235, 256-260, 262, 264, 265, 268, 280, 288, 293; in Bruni's Vita di Petrarca, 267, 417; in Domenico da Prato's invective, 280-281, 285; in Francesco da Fiano, 300; in the Petrarch controversy 1405-06, 241, 254-256, 264-268; in Rinuccini's Invettica, 287-288; in Salutati's writings, 105-106, 113, 116, 146, 151, 160, 257-259, 499(33)

Africa, 55-57, 102, 119, 134; Coronation Oration, and on "glory," 116, 302, 524(20); De Gestis Cesaris, 57, 60, 119, 152, 153, 499(19, 22);

"Mirror for Princes," 120, 132, 492(45)

Petrucci, Pandolfo, 363

Pharsalus, Battle of, 67

Philippi, Battle of, 156

Piacenza, 38, 398-399

"Piagnoni, Nuovi" ("Savonaroliani, Nuovi"), 276, 278, 518 (2)

Piattoli, R., 472(47)

Piccolomini, Enea Silvio (Pius II), 209-211, 506(29), 551 (81d), 562(47)

Pietro di ser Mino (di Lorenzo Sermini) da Montevarchi, 231

Pisa, 21-23, 27, 30, 33, 39, 178-180, 218, 328, 361, 364-365, 368, 541(1b); conquest and incorporation in the Florentine region-state, 253, 324-326, 359, 368, 370

Pistoia, 22, 557(22)

Pitti: Buonaccorso, 182-183, 465 (1); Jacopo, 170

Pizzinga, Jacopo, 261-262, 517 (41a)

Plaisant, M. L., 524(19a, 19e)

Platina, Bartolomeo, 437, 564 (66)

Plato, 155, 198, 258, 288, 289, 304; *Phaedon* trans. by Bruni, 87-88, 225-226, 289, 521(38); *Epistolae* trans. by Bruni, 554(24); trans. and influence of Plato's *Republic* in Milan and Florence, 210, 250-251, 425, 515(13d)

Pliny the Elder, 63

Plutarch, 282, 284, 431, 515 (13d), 520(23a), 554(24)

Po and Po valley, 14, 21, 25, 27, 30, 32, 180, 373

poets, ancient, 262-264, 314, 517 (43); *see also* religion of ancient poets

Poggio Bracciolini: historical place, and phases of his development, 3, 85, 130, 246, 300, 406-409, 454-455, 469

(12b), 552(11, 12); on Caesar and Roman Republic, 60, 66-67, 72, 396, 407-408, 478-480 (41, 42, 43a); attitude to Volgare, 341, 347; —and Bruni, 246, 247, 266-269, 409; and Niccoli, 240, 241, 323, 406-407; in the Petrarch controversy 1405-06, 254-256, 265-269; and Pietro del Monte, 68; and Salutati, 117, 215, 241, 406-407

Polentone, Sicco, 132, 134, 553 (19)

political conditions and changes in Italy, 8-11, 15-16, Chap. 2 *passim*, 357-359, 370, 387, 390, Chap. 16 *passim*, 444-445, 453, 472-473(50), 543 (15); *see also:* equilibrium and states-system; "ragione" as standard in politics; "libertas Italiae"

Poliziano, Angelo, 72, 351, 482 (54)

Polybius, 410, 508(14)

polytheism of the ancients, 298-299, 304, 307-308; *see also* religion of ancient poets

Pompey, 56, 129, 150, 156, 163, 362

Porcari, Stefano, 434-435, 563 (54, 57)

Por San Maria, Arte di, in Florence, 167

power politics and Machiavellianism in the Quattrocento, *see* "realism," politico-historical

Pratesi, L., 500(2)

"pratica" in Florence, *see* "consulta"

Prato, city, 471(30)

Prato, Domenico da, 279-285, 519(10), 519(15); and Bruni, 281-284, 520(23a, 30); —invective against Niccoli and Bruni: 277-280; date, 279-280, 519(15); edition, 519(10); —political poem in 1424, 382-383, 546 (45)

Prato, Giovanni (Gherardi) da, 317, 332-337, 532(1); vindication of Volgare, 333, 336-338, 345, 352, 533(10); —*Paradiso degli Alberti*, 81-82, 88, 275, 332, 335, 404; and Bruni's *Historiae*, 334-335; date, 82, 87, 88-90, 92, 333-334, 336-337; edition, 483(1);—*Canzone Morale di Patria*, 336

Ptolemy of Lucca, 55, 57, 474 (13)

Pyrrhus, King of Epirus, 330, 377

Pythagorean doctrines, 208

Quattrocento, mind of the, 3, 47, 201-202, 234-235, 263, 447-448, 533-534(14); *see also:* Trecento, mind of the, transition to Quattrocento; "geometric spirit"; "Fortuna," conception of; "realism"; "ragione"; historiography, Quattrocento historiography; art of the Renaissance

"querelle des anciens et des modernes," beginning in the Quattrocento, xxvii, 282-283, 346-348, 350-353, 396, 406-409, 435-436

Radetti, G., 466(2), 524(19d, 19e)

Raffael Santi, 313

"ragione" as standard in politics, 179-181, 184, 448

Rambaldi, Benvenuto, *see* Benvenuto (Rambaldi) da Imola

Ravenna, 27, 30, 198

"realism," politico-historical, and the ideals of the Quattrocento, 98, 144-145, 151-158, 198, 390-391; 499(27)

Redig de Campos, D., 474(8)

"Regnum Adriae," project of a, 31

Regole della Lingua Fiorentina (probably by Alberti), 350, 538(32)

religion of ancient poets, 112, 295-309, 522-523(10)

Ridolfi, Lorenzo de', 392

Rienzo, Cola di, *see* Cola di Rienzo

Rinuccini: family, 488(1); Alamanno, 437

Rinuccini, Cino, 93, 94, 96, 105, 142, 157, 273, 291-293, 332, 448, 487(11), 487(1), 519 (7);—political and historical outlook, 76-77, 90, 94-96, 98-99, 159, 167, 288-289, 315-317, 328, 431, 520 (32a); views on Dante and Petrarch, 287; on Volgare, 287, 333, 339, 352;—and Bruni, 286-290, 292-293, 316, 528(48);—*Invettiva:* 277-278, 285-295, 298, 307, 309, 315-316, 321-324, 330; earlier interpretations, 277; date, 286, 289-290, 485; edition, 520(32b);—*Responsiva:* 94-95, 99, 166, 273, 291, 328; date, 76, 83, 84, 87, 91, 92, 212, 485(9); edition, 484(8), 488(2)

Riva, Bonvesino della, *see* Bonvesino della Riva

Robert, King of Naples, 139

Romagna-Emilia, 13, 15, 22, 23, 33, 360, 371, 373, 376, 377, 378, 379, 384

Rome: political conditions, 13, 23, 329, 366, 367; *see also* Papacy *and* Cola di Rienzo; ruins of ancient Rome, 3, 312-313, 527(43);—ancient Rome in Quattrocento thought, 175-176, 341-344, 376-377, 386, 393, 396, 404, 420; *see also* historiography *passim*

Rossi, Roberto de', 320-321, 324-325, 512-513(47), 530(64); in Bruni's *Dialogi*, 227, 230-231, 236

Rossi, V., 233-234, 243, 501(8), 511(31-33), 512(47), 534 (14), 536(21)

Rubinstein, N., 468(10a), 477 (31), 482(54), 542(5a)

Rüegg, W., 527(40)

Rupert, German king, 36, 140, 213, 220

Rustici, Cencio de', 312-313

Sabbadini, R., 215, 494(30), 496 (47), 507(11), 510(19)

Sabellico (Coccio), Marcantonio, 393, 549(72)

Sallust, 64, 420, 557(23)

Salutati, Coluccio, 5, 85, 100-118, 146-166, 447, 487(11), 489 (24), 490(25); attitude to Petrarch's Humanism, 105-106, 111, 113, 151, 160, 254, 258, 260-261, 490(30), 499(33), 517(43), in the Petrarch controversy of 1405-06, 254-256; civic Humanism and "vita activa," 106-118, 500(39); earlier interpretations of Salutati, 107, 113, 489-490(25), 554 (28)

in the debates on Cicero as a Roman citizen, 123-125, 145-151, 157; on Plato and Aristotle, see Crisis: Appendices, p. 554; on the preeminence of law over medicine, 111-112, 490-491(33, 34); on the religion of the ancient poets, 112, 295-299, 309-311; on Socrates, 310-311; on Themistocles' "nobilitas," 250-251, 515(13a-13d)

historical ideas and historical criticism: Florence's foundation by Sulla's veterans, 63-64, 76, 87, 89, 99-100, 159; the Roman Republic, Cicero, Caesar, and Dante, 60, 100, 113-118, 123-125, 145-152, 156, 160, 167, 310, 324, 347; —political outlook: continua-

tion of the traditional Guelph idea, 96-99, 159; the Emperor's supremacy legally recognized, 499(32a), see also Salutati, De Tyranno; Florence as protagonist of liberty, 22-23, 28, 93, 124, 160, 468 (11a, 11b); pacific policy of a commercial city, 28-29, 377, 488(6)

relations to contemporaries: Bartolo, 499(32a, 33), Benvenuto Rambaldi, 153; Bruni, 104, 159, 164-165, 214, 238-242, 246, 255, 269, 280, 430, 500(39), 514(8), in Bruni's Dialogi, 47-48, 88, 227-229, 236-243, 248, 268-269, 512-514(47); Giovanni Conversino, 141, 495(45); Francesco da Fiano, 312; Giovanni da Prato and his Paradiso, 82; Niccoli, 238-241, 268-269, 280; Poggio, 117, 254-256, 268-269, 406-407; Vergerio, 127, 146; Filippo Villani, 106-107, 319, 324, 523(16a)

Declamatio, 115;—De Fato, 156, 310-311, 527(40);—De Laboribus Herculis, 118, 295-299, 302, 310; phases of composition, and title, 523 (11), 523(16a);—De Seculo, 106-109;—De Tyranno, 60, 100-103, 120, 146-152, 155-166, 274, 292, 324, 430, 499(32a); date and editions, 101, 489(22), 497(1); earlier interpretations, 498(13a, 14), 500(38), De Tyranno in Bruni's Dialogi, 147, 242; —Epigrams in the Palazzo della Signoria, 147;—Invectiva, 76, 96-101, 159, 161, 274, 377, 489(10), 508 (18); date, 83-91, 99, 101, 212, 225, 484-487(9); editions, 484(8); Invectiva and

Salutati, Coluccio (cont.)
  Bruni's *Laudatio*, 227;—Two
    Orationes, 512(47)
Salvemini, G., 465(1), 478(38)
San Miniato, Giovanni da, 111,
  299
Santini, E., 465(1), 478(38), 501
  (8), 533(10), 534(14)
"Santissima Lega" of 1454-55,
  363, 400
Santoro, M., 539(38), 540(43)
Sanudo, Marin, 546(51), 547
  (61)
Sarzana, town, 489(11)
Sasso, G., 466(1)
Saviozzo da Siena, 37, 367, 542
  (11)
Savonarola: Girolamo, 8, 97, 276,
  438-439; Michele, 132
Scaligeri (Della Scala), Lords of
  Verona, 15, 21, 25, 37, 173;
  see also Verona; Mastino, 94
Schedel, Hartmann, 203
Schevill, F., 467(1)
scholasticism in eyes of humanists,
  48, 234
Scipio Africanus Maior, 55, 57,
  102, 176, 309, 408
Secchia (river), 27
Semiramis, Queen, 143
Seneca, Lucius, "the Elder," the
  rhetorician (not yet distin-
  guished from Lucius Annaeus
  Seneca, the philosopher), 66-
  67, 259, 298, 478-479(41)
Seriphos, island, 250-251
Sermini, Pietro, *see* Pietro di ser
  Mino da Montevarchi
Seznec, J., 522(10)
Sforza, Francesco, 399-402, 551
  (81d), 552(85c)
Siena, 22, 26-27, 30, 34, 39, 174,
  178-180, 360-364, 366, 369,
  395, 396, 400, 437, 469
  (15c), 542(5)
Sigismund, Emperor, 130, 207,
  424
signory, *see* tyranny of the Renaissance
Sismondi, Simonde de, 402

Smith, L., 493(12), 494(19, 20)
Socrates, 306, 310, 323, 526-527
  (40)
Solon, 125
Soudek, J., 509-510(10)
Spain, 438
Sparta, ancient, 396, 427
Spini, G., 474(10)
Spoleto, 34
Spongano, R., 466(2), 540-541
  (43)
Stackelberg, J. von, 60
states-system of the Quattrocento,
  see equilibrium and states-
  system
Statius, 526(31)
stoicism and early humanists, 7,
  121, 123, 125, 127, 148,
  258, 296-297, 307
Strada, Zanobi da, 302, 475(21),
  524(20)
Strozzi: family, 378, 385; Nanni
  degli, 378, 380, 412-414,
  430, 432, 545(40); Palla
  (di Noferi) degli, 379, 544
  (21), 545(39)
"studia humanitatis," 195, 248,
  260, 263, 266, 408, 417
Suetonius, 194
Sulla, Lucius Cornelius, 63, 71-
  73, 76, 82, 87, 89, 149, 150,
  159, 163 482(54)

Tacitus, 58-61, 66, 70, 170, 475-
  476(20-25a), 478-479(41),
  561(44)
Tarquinius Superbus, King, 115
Taù, Don Igino, 524(19a-19c,
  19e)
Terence, 341
Thameris, Queen, 143
Themistocles, 249-251, 515(13)
Theodosius, Emperor, 154
Thucydides, 194; *see also* Pericles'
  Funeral Oration
Tiptoft, John, 421, 558(25)
Torquatus, Manlius, 114, 115
Totila (often confused with At-
  tila), 97-98
Trajan, Emperor, 51, 53, 154

Tranchedini, Nicodemo, 563(63)

Traversari, Ambrogio, 85

Trecento, mind of the, 4-5, 15-16, 18, 57-58, 102-104, 113, 118-120, 125, 133, 144, 151-156, 160, 164, 169, 196-198, 203, 206-207, 263, 316-317, 446-447, 492(44), 528(49); transition to Quattrocento, xxv, 3, 7-8, 103, 104, 107-108, 112, 157, 192, 198, 263, 297, 311, 314, 330-331, 443-446, 457; *see also* art of the Renaissance, late Trecento *and* "realism," politico-historical

Treviso, 25, 29

Trexler, R. C., 469(12b)

Turchi, Pietro, 485-486

Tuscany, 10, 15, 23, 33-34, 111, 173-177, 179-180, 185, 195, 213, 220-222, 360, 361, 364, 365, 366, 368, 371, 418, 468(11a); *see also* historiography; city-state independence, Etruscan and medieval; —interrelations of Tuscan city-republics, 21-24, 26-28, 30, 34, 361, 468(10a, 10b), 469(15b)

tyranny of the Renaissance, 10, 11-15, 120, 131, 133, 135-136, 276-277, 361, 416, 425, 427, 470(19); *see also* Humanism at tyrant-courts

Ullman, B. L., 478(38), 484-487, 490(28c), 491(38a), 523 (16a)

Umbria, 13, 15, 22, 23, 34, 213, 360, 367

unification of the Italian Peninsula, 10, 15-16, 24, 34, 36-41, 136, 276, 360, 366-367; earlier interpretations, 549 (73); *see also* political conditions *and* equilibrium and states-system

Uzzano, Niccolò da, 368, 372, 374, 379, 385, 544(20, 26)

Valdilamone, Battle of, 380

Valeri, N., 472-473(50), 548(67)

Valerius Maximus, 289

Valla, Lorenzo, 72, 481(52)

Vannozzo, Francesco di, 37

Varchi, Benedetto, 73, 482(54)

Varese, C., 465(1), 502(8)

Varro, Marcus Terentius, 294, 295, 296, 299, 307, 308

Vasoli, C., 465(1)

Vaucluse, 122

Vellutello, Alessandro, 53

Venice: equilibrium policy and expansion, 12-13, 25-27, 29, 32-33, 35, 42-44, 130, 173, 179-180, 185-186, 359, 366, 387-403, 547(67); economic conditions: *see* economic conditions, Venice;—Venetian Republic and Humanism, 67-69, 126, 135, 138, 139, 350, 394-395, 403; *see also:* Humanism, Civic; Barbaro, Francesco; Monte, Pietro del

Venice, Peace of, 35, 44, 216-217, 219

Vercelli, Cathedral Library of, 493(6)

Verga, E., 505(7)

Vergerio, Pier Paolo, 3, 85, 126, 300; Vergerio and the Padua of the Carrara, 126, 129-134, 494(20); phases of his development, 129-130, 494 (25, 29);—on Cicero, Roman Republic, and Roman Empire, 127-129, 132, 145; on Themistocles' "nobilitas," 251; appraisal of Petrarch, 263-264;—and Bruni, 126, 130, 132, 226, 227; and Bruni's *Dialogi*, 226, 227, 228; and Salutati, 127, 132, 134, 146, 215, 447, 515 (13d);—fictive letter to Petrarch in the name of Cicero, 127, 493(14), 497(2a);— *De Monarchia*, 133-134; date, 494(25);—*De Ingenuis Moribus*, date, 494(20)

Verino, Ugolino, 73, 482(55), 539(42)

Verona, 5, 15, 25, 28, 39, 185, 388, 437; Cathedral Library, 121; *see also* Scaligeri

Vespasiano da Bisticci, *see* Bisticci

Vicenza, 5, 25, 37, 39, 388

Villani: family, 203, 207; Giovanni, 62, 197, 318; Matteo, 20-21, 169-170, 177, 318, 377, 467-468(4a, 5-7), 476 (28)

Villani, Filippo, 5, 528(54a); Classicism and "vita civilis," 317-320; views on Caesar, Roman Republic, and Florentine history, 62, 72, 89, 477 (33); on Dante, 517(39), 528(51b);—Filippo and Salutati, 106-107, 324, 523 (16);—*De Origine Civitatis*, 5, 62, 95, 318-319; revisions and editions, 477(33)

Villari, P., 276, 519(2)

Vinci, Leonardo da, 47

Virgil, 49, 67, 70, 116, 117, 143, 259, 261, 263, 281, 297, 314, 347, 352, 386, 516 (35), 526(31), 536-537 (24); statue at Mantua, 298

Visconti, Lords (later, Dukes) of Milan, 15-16, 20, 22, 41, 177, 359, 377-378, 397;—the State of the Visconti, *see* Milan;—Bernabò, 95, 471 (3);—Giangaleazzo: 25-42, 129, 163, 245, 326, 329, 357, 359, 364, 371, 390, 431; in contemporary opinion, 28, 37-38, 68, 70, 73, 94-96, 105, 136-140, 167, 173-188, 191, 195, 204, 210, 213-224, 326, 336, 367, 370, 374, 386-387, 401; earlier interpretations, 469(13), 471 (29);—Giovanni, Archbishop, 15, 16, 95, 137, 471 (28), 488(3);—Filippo Maria: 69, 220, 278, 334, 336, 363, 370-387, 395, 396, 407-409, 411; in contemporary opinion, 394, 405, 414, 425, 432-433

"Vita activa" and "vita contemplativa," 7, 106-113, 121-125, 128-130, 135, 157, 316-331, 459, 528-529(54b), 529(57); *see also* Humanism, Civic

Viterbo, 241, 249, 253, 255, 268, 269, 293

Vittorino da Feltre, 134

Voigt, G., 214

Volgare and Volgare culture in the Florentine Quattrocento, 6, 285; earlier interpretations, xxvii, 214, 275-278, 519(5, 6), 533-534(14), 539-541(43);—phases of the relationship of Florentine Humanism to the Volgare, 195, 288, 333, 335-353, 404, 416, 452, 533 (10);—*see also* historiography, origin and historical rights of the Volgare *and* historiography, parallel evolutions of Greek, Latin, and Volgare

Volterra, 16

Walser, E., 480(43d)

"War of the Eight Saints," 23-24, 114, 360, 469(12b)

Wells, town, 209

Wenceslaus, German king, 31, 36, 329

Wesselofsky, A., 214, 275-278, 286, 315, 483(1), 519(5, 6), 527(46)

Wotke, K., 511(29)

Wyle, Niclas von, 422

Zagonara, Battle of, 380, 381, 382, 384, 407

Zambeccari, Pellegrino, 125, 523 (16c)

Ziliotto, B., 493(14)

Zonarini, Giuliano, 297